A CONTEST OF CIVILIZATIONS

THE LITTLEFIELD HISTORY OF THE CIVIL WAR ERA

Gary W. Gallagher and T. Michael Parrish, editors

This book was supported by the Littlefield Fund for
Southern History, University of Texas Libraries

This landmark sixteen-volume series, featuring books
by some of today's most respected Civil War historians, surveys
the conflict from the earliest rumblings of disunion through the
Reconstruction era. A joint project of UNC Press and the
Littlefield Fund for Southern History, University of Texas Libraries,
the series offers an unparalleled comprehensive narrative
of this defining era in U.S. history.

A Contest of Civilizations

EXPOSING THE CRISIS OF AMERICAN EXCEPTIONALISM IN THE CIVIL WAR ERA

Andrew F. Lang

THE UNIVERSITY OF NORTH CAROLINA PRESS

CHAPEL HILL

Designed by Richard Hendel
Set in Miller, Modern No. 20, and Antique No. 6 by Tseng Information Systems, Inc.
Manufactured in the United States of America

The University of North Carolina Press has been a
member of the Green Press Initiative since 2003.

Jacket illustration: *The Outbreak of the Rebellion in the United States 1861*, ca. 1865, by
Christopher Kimmel. Justice scowls at Jefferson Davis, Alexander H. Stephens, and other
Confederates who had recently shattered the United States through secession and civil war.
Liberty stands confidently behind President Abraham Lincoln, who rallies loyal citizens to
the cause of Union. In the foreground, a hapless James Buchanan dozes while the nation
cracks and burns. The sun rises in the distance, symbolizing an enduring nineteenth-century
American faith in the United States' exceptional standing in the world. (Library of Congress)

Library of Congress Cataloging-in-Publication Data
Names: Lang, Andrew F., 1982– author.
Title: A contest of civilizations : exposing the crisis of American
exceptionalism in the Civil War era / Andrew F. Lang.
Other titles: Littlefield history of the Civil War era.
Description: Chapel Hill : The University of North Carolina Press, 2021. | Series: Littlefield
history of the Civil War era | Includes bibliographical references and index.
Identifiers: LCCN 2020032946 | ISBN 9781469660073 (cloth ; alk. paper) |
ISBN 9781469660080 (ebook)
Subjects: LCSH: Exceptionalism—United States. | National characteristics,
American. | Group identity—United States. | United States—History—
Civil War, 1861–1865—Influence. | United States—Civilization.
Classification: LCC E468.9 .L365 2021 | DDC 973.7/1—dc23
LC record available at https://lccn.loc.gov/2020032946

MIX
Paper from
responsible sources
FSC
www.fsc.org FSC® C008955

For Margaret (2017)
and Jamie (2019),
my children born during
the writing of this book

CONTENTS

FIGURES

A CONTEST OF CIVILIZATIONS

Prologue
THE YOUNG MEN'S LYCEUM, 1838

★ ★ ★

Abraham Lincoln, congressman-elect from Illinois, ca. 1846, the first known daguerreotype of Lincoln, likely captured by Nicholas Shepherd. The thirty-seven-year-old Lincoln sat for this image on the eve of assuming his only term in Congress, eight years after delivering the Lyceum Address and fifteen years before assuming the presidency. (Library of Congress)

He was tall and lanky, had a chirpy voice, boasted an awkward countenance. He was hardly extraordinary: an obscure state legislator, a common man living a competent life. Few people outside his small prairie village had ever heard of him. Yet few people outside that same village could explain the world the way he did. He was not haughty, but he possessed an uncanny ability to untangle complexities and to give practical voice to an innermost conviction. A self-educated man living in an age of democratic self-determination, his unusual mastery of language made him seem a simpleton, but it also made him a poet, if not a prophet. Though not yet thirty years old, this trifling country lawyer understood the American gospel. He grasped his republic's purpose. He prized the delicate national fabric on which he and his fellow citizens trod. And when he spoke, people listened, for his words conveyed a fluent message.

His name was Abraham Lincoln, and in 1838 he stood before the Young Men's Lyceum, a group of aspiring citizens who gathered in Springfield, Illinois, to receive lectures and debate ideas. Speaking on a cold January evening, the young orator delivered a rousing but subtle speech titled "The Perpetuation of Our Political Institutions." Such was hardly a unique topic in early nineteenth-century America. It was an age of great revolutions in democracy, technology, communication, and markets. It was an age of zealous liberalism, in which free, independent, ambitious individuals could ascend to the pinnacle of society. It was an age of tribute to the American Revolution, which had unleashed a white middle class obsessed with swelling economic opportunities. There was much to commemorate in those decades after 1776. The republic had expanded rapidly, its citizens enjoyed a degree of liberty unimaginable in nearly every corner of the globe, and the march of progress seemed unimpeded. But rather than recounting the glorious achievements of the past and lauding the present, the young Lincoln instead issued a warning, rooted no doubt in his own anxieties about the future. What if, he asked, the very attributes of the American founding—constitutional liberty, popular democracy, economic progress—had also planted the poisonous seeds of national decline? The arresting question compelled any honest observer to examine a paradox of the American character.[1]

To be sure, Lincoln remained faithful to what he considered the United States' unique global mission. "We find ourselves in the peaceful possession, of the fairest portion of the earth, as regards extent of territory, fertility of soil, and salubrity of climate," he said of the mystic bounties of North America. "We find ourselves under the government of a system of political institutions, conducing more essentially to the ends of civil and religious liberty, than any of which the history of former times tells us." The founding generation had birthed an exceptional "political edifice of liberty" never before seen by the nations of the world. Theirs was a republican Union timeless in its purpose and enduring in its commitment to safeguarding the natural rights of life, liberty, and the pursuit of happiness. To convey "gratitude to our fathers, justice to ourselves, duty to posterity," subsequent generations of Americans had to reaffirm their loyalty to the "legacy bequeathed us, by a *once* hardy, brave, and patriotic, but *now* lamented and departed race of ancestors." The founders' sacred claim that government derived its legitimacy from the just consent of a free people would never perish from the earth so long as the people themselves gave their full measures of devotion to sustaining its life.[2]

Americans thus lived in a peculiar moment. Given that the nation, in Lincoln's telling, was formed unlike any other in world history, its potential decline and fall would result from equally unique, perhaps unprecedented circumstances. "Shall we expect some transatlantic military giant, to step the Ocean, and crush us at a blow? Never!" Lincoln proclaimed. "All the armies of Europe, Asia and Africa combined, with all the treasure of the earth ... with a Buonaparte for a commander, could not by force, take a drink from the Ohio, or make a track on the Blue Ridge, in a trial of a thousand years." The American republic confronted an enemy far more pernicious than even the most lethal foreign legion. The "approach of danger" could only "spring up amongst us. It cannot come from abroad. If destruction be our lot, we must ourselves be its author and finisher. As a nation of freemen, we must live through all time, or die by suicide."[3]

Lincoln implied that the United States resided in but was not of the world. As far as he was concerned, the republic was not regulated by the same history, the same currents, the same inevitability that sealed the fates of other nations. In America, shared belief in the rule of law, equality under the law, and the popular consent of law theoretically forged among the people a sober, moderate political consensus. Yet Lincoln reflected on troubling reports of vigilante justice supplanting the law as the foundation of civil society. "The growing disposition to substitute the wild and furious passions, in lieu of the sober judgment" imposed uncommon strains upon a republic founded on deliberative reason. Scenes of mob violence dotted the national landscape, in which "gamblers to negroes, from negroes to white citizens, and from these to strangers; till, dead men were seen literally dangling from the boughs of trees upon every road side." A mob in St. Louis even kidnapped "a mulatto man" whom they dragged through the streets, chained to a tree, and burned to death. "Such are the effects of mob law; and such are the scenes, becoming more and more frequent in this land so lately famed for love of law and order."[4]

When free citizens exchanged the rule of law and democratic pluralism—the very attributes that *sustained* liberty—for faction and mob justice, they threatened a republic that moderated the sordid passions of human nature. Republics ordered liberty through representative institutions and a virtuous citizenry. But unrestrained vigilantism attacked the republican body like an unyielding pandemic. "By the operation of this mobocratic spirit ... the strongest bulwark of any Government, and particularly of those constituted like ours, may effectually be broken down and destroyed—I mean the *attach-*

ment of the People." Mobocracies fomented great anxieties among a free people who would inevitably cry out for a strongman to deliver order from the chaos. As demonstrated by the histories of other nations, such demagoguery typically morphed into dictatorship, the law lost all purpose, and liberty itself soon dissolved into unbending repression. To reject the rule of law and the moderation of democratic institutions was to radicalize and endanger the republic from within.[5]

Oppressed peoples across the world understood this dark formula all too well. "At such a time and under such circumstances, men of sufficient talent and ambition will not be wanting to seize the opportunity, strike the blow, and overturn that fair fabric [of Union], which for the last half century, has been the fondest hope, of the lovers of freedom, throughout the world." Radicalism and revolution, reaction and suppression: this apparently was the inevitable cycle of human existence elsewhere around the globe. "New reapers will arise, and *they*, too, will seek a field. It is to deny, what the history of the world tells us is true, to suppose that men of ambition and talents will not continue to spring up amongst us. And, when they do, they will as naturally seek the gratification of their ruling passion, as others have so done before them." If Americans surrendered to "the caprice of a mob, the alienation of their affections from the Government is the natural consequence."[6]

If the people could instigate national dissolution, only they could maintain national health. It was not enough for Americans to live merely in their present, infatuated with individual commercial enterprise. As a free people they possessed a duty, if not a burden, to preserve for future generations the same political moderation that made their republic of liberty the envy of the world. "Danger to our political institutions" arose from foolish claims that oppression, rejection of the popular will, or eternal bondage could never occur in the United States. "We hope all dangers may be overcome; but to conclude that no danger may ever arise, would itself be extremely dangerous." Americans had to remain conservative, guarded against antirepublican elements in their midst, skeptical of vicious mobs and cunning demagogues. Only then would the republic endure, moderating the excesses of popular passion, balancing the freedom of self-interest with the common good. "Let every American, every lover of liberty, every well wisher to his posterity, swear by the blood of the Revolution, never to violate in the least particular, the laws of the country; and never to tolerate their violation by others," Lincoln reminded his audience. "Let every man remember that to violate the law, is to trample on the blood of his father, and to tear the character of his own, and his children's liberty." In short, let the American founding ideal "become the *political religion* of the nation."[7]

Challenges abounded even in this simple solution. By the 1830s, Americans could no longer connect to a piece of *"living history"* from the Revolution. Though once "a fortress of strength," *"those* histories are gone," buried by "the silent artillery of time." The further Americans traveled from the founding era, the more they grew divorced from the foundational ideas of Union itself. Such forgetfulness encouraged dangerous temptations toward populist passion and demagogic seduction, leading the people toward beliefs that humans were *not* all created equal, that governments did *not* derive their legitimacy from popular will, that constitutions were *not* sources of stability but, rather, annoying impediments to societal progress. The ailments of the present mandated a return to the self-evident truths of the past, a reforging of the bonds between future generations and the founding era.[8]

The founders' "temple of liberty" would stand only insofar as the people revered its transcendent construction. "Their ambition aspired to display before an admiring world, a practical demonstration of the truth of a proposition, which had hitherto been considered, at best no better, than problematical; namely, *the capability of a people to govern themselves*." But popular zeal alone was no longer enough to preserve the founding ideal. "Passion has helped us; but can do so no more. It will in future be our enemy." Americans had to show restraint because the fate of liberty demanded that they do so. The right of representative government mandated sober adherence to the law, political moderation through compromise, and tolerance for collective civil liberties. Therefore, only "reason, cold, calculating, unimpassioned reason, must furnish all the materials for our future support and defence. Let those [materials] be moulded into *general intelligence*, [*sound*] *morality*, and in particular, *a reverence for the constitution and laws*." Only then would the American Union continue to stand as the world's last, best hope.[9]

Twenty-three years after he delivered his impassioned address before the Springfield Young Men's Lyceum, Abraham Lincoln assumed the American presidency and confronted the very specter of lawless chaos that he once anticipated as a prescient frontier orator. By 1861, the crisis of national dissolution and an impending civil war confronted Americans with the impossible realization that somehow they had fomented their own national death, as reason had been traded for passion and the Union traded for mob rule. As Lincoln outlined in his first inaugural address, "Plainly, the central idea of secession, is the essence of anarchy," which shattered all "restraint by constitutional checks," once "the only true sovereign of a free people." Though they had long claimed superiority to the world's corrupted nations, Americans were now consumed by an overwhelming anxiety that their own fellow citizens had forever destroyed an exceptional if not sacred republic of, by, and for the people.[10]

Introduction

THE CIVIL WAR ERA AND THE PROBLEM
OF AMERICAN EXCEPTIONALISM

As a young orator, Abraham Lincoln described a powerful concept of American life with which countless of his fellow citizens identified. Though neither he nor his contemporaries would have employed the phrase "American exceptionalism" to explain the relation of their Union to the world, nearly all nineteenth-century Americans recognized its influential assumptions. Americans of diverse persuasions heralded an incomparable republic that they believed stood apart from the nations of the world. Viewing themselves as distinct not only from other human societies but also from the course of history itself, nineteenth-century Americans considered their nation an unprecedented beacon of liberty within a world of oppression and decay. They cherished their democratic heritage and constitutional stability. They prided themselves on being educated, religious, temperate, and ever ready to aid their fellow citizens. They imagined themselves peopling an energetic capitalist society that fired a vibrant, entrepreneurial, independent, white middle class. They prized the ideals of political moderation and compromise, the alleged counterpoints to global radicalism, hierarchy, and aggression. Only in the United States, so went the thought, could free people pursue independence liberated from the notorious power of government coercion. In this contemporary reading of national life, the American Union charted a progressive course that transcended global decline, imbued with "a special and unique destiny to lead the rest of the world to freedom and democracy."[1]

The concept of American exceptionalism has long undergone scholarly scrutiny. The end of the Cold War and the rise of globalization influenced a generation of scholars seeking to pull American history out of its protective exceptionalist shell, which had celebrated an inimitable founding, an egalitarian democratic political culture, and an economic system that mitigated class tensions. Histories that focused solely on the nation-state, this new literature countered, ignored the powerful global influences on the historical evolution of the United States. Moreover, critics have indicted the nation's failure to realize its own values and fully conquer its original sins. Chief among these failings were slavery and intractable racism; gender inequities; selfish individualism, avaricious materialism, and economic inequality; and the violent, domineering colonization of North America, the Western Hemisphere, the Pacific, and the world itself. A new era of American historiography thus dis-

7

The Triumph, *ca. 1861, by Morris H. Traubel, features Liberty's loyal legions conquering the demons of slavery. The promise of the founding generation survives the republic's foremost threat and lives in heavenly eternity. (Library of Congress)*

couraged what appeared to be a tired national provincialism in favor of seeing the United States as "a nation among nations," one whose unbridled vices
exceeded its empty virtues. Comparative approaches, transnational histories,
and Atlantic studies now place the United States as part of the wider world,
offering a counterpoint to a once isolated and triumphalist historical narrative.[2]

However, as prominent historian Michael Kammen once noted, the project
of qualifying national histories sometimes "fail[s] to recognize that American
exceptionalism is as old as the nation itself and, equally important, has played
an integral part in the society's sense of its own identity." Although scholarly
consensus no longer commemorates an exceptional national past, those who
lived the American past overwhelmingly regarded their country as separate
and distinct from the rest of the world. As early as the nation's founding,
American contemporaries claimed the United States as the sole protectorate of long-contested global theories on the role of government. As the pro-
pagandistic pulse of early exceptionalist rhetoric, Thomas Paine proclaimed
in his immensely popular *Common Sense* (1776) that the United States was
"an asylum for mankind," a nation in "which more freedom is enjoyed, and
a more happy state of society is preserved, and a more general prosperity is
promoted, than under any other system of government now existing in the
world." Predicated on "self-evident truths" that had reverberated across the
Enlightenment-era Atlantic world—that humans are endowed equally with
rights that come from nature and not from the state—the federal Union
seemingly had conquered the inevitability of global history to stand as an
inimitable, stable republic of liberty. Whereas other nation-states had been
established on ethnic or religious lines, the American citizenry heralded their
founders' vision of an ideal democratic experiment unshackled from a divine-
right monarchy and ruling class. "Citizens, being thus collected from various nations," a Pennsylvanian reflected as early as 1794 on the essence of the
United States, "formed a character peculiar to themselves, and in some respects distinct from that of other nations."[3]

The mass of citizens measured their democratic republic against what they
imagined as an antidemocratic world dominated by imperial oligarchs; privileged aristocrats; and noble kings, queens, and lords. Americans took pride
in their democratic republic and hoped that the nations of the world would
emulate their liberal example. But the citizenry also imagined large swaths
of the global community either incapable or averse to performing moderate,
progressive, democratic governance. In the American mind, the nineteenth-
century world churned with extreme revolutions and violent counterrevolutions. This dismal progression was exemplified by the French Revolution's
"reign of terror," Napoleon's subsequent military dictatorship, and the ultimate restoration of the Bourbon monarchy. Viewed alongside the Haitian
Revolution and other enslaved revolts, many white Americans grew increas-

ingly certain that the nations of Europe, Latin America, and the Caribbean could never rise above incessant political, class, and racial conflict. Nations appeared to swing from one extreme to the other, lurching into gory revolutions that were ultimately beaten back by brutal, illiberal reactionaries. Americans of varied political affiliations anticipated that recently sovereign Latin American republics (1791–1830), followed by the 1848 democratic revolutions that swept Europe, would proliferate republicanism across the world. However, with the Old and New Worlds seemingly vulnerable to the destructive sway of grassroots radicalism and monarchical reaction, most of those fledgling republican experiments failed, contributing to a powerful exceptionalist conviction that the United States remained a lone democratic nation surrounded by dangerous and radical influences.[4]

Subsequent generations considered the Union, in contrast to the rest of the world, a matchless republic sustained by a limited government that promoted political equality and served the common liberties of the people. This manifest sense of national purpose, this manifest destiny seemingly ordained by divine Providence, was especially pronounced during the nineteenth century, in which diverse constituencies—northerners and southerners, African Americans and whites, women and men, scores of foreign observers, and waves of immigrants—claimed the American nation to be ordained and extraordinary. When President Abraham Lincoln designated the United States as the world's "last best, hope" in which representative "government of the people, by the people, for the people, shall not perish from the earth," he echoed exceptionalist beliefs that dated to the nation's founding. At a time when popular democracy, economic mobility, and political liberty had faltered throughout much of the world, the American nation ostensibly triumphed among modern human political endeavors. Lincoln's framing of national purpose resounded with white northerners and African Americans, both enslaved and free. In a terrible paradox, white southerners, who enslaved millions of humans, translated similar exceptionalist convictions to argue that only in the United States could liberty, democracy, and slavery coexist.[5]

Engaging mid-nineteenth-century American exceptionalism compels modern audiences to take seriously the concept as historical contemporaries understood and deployed it and not as a validation or refutation of exceptionalism's legitimacy. Large segments of the citizenry defined the United States as the political manifestation of "civilization," the organizing principle of nineteenth-century American exceptionalism. As a discourse, concept, and practice, "civilization" infused the national vernacular to describe the United States' commanding place in the modern world. To reach a state of civilization, explained Ralph Waldo Emerson in a widely regarded 1862 essay, was to "progress from the rudest state in which man is found," evolving into "a highly organized [society], brought to supreme delicacy of sentiment, as in practical power, religion, liberty, sense of honor, and taste." As Lincoln had once urged in his 1838 Lyceum Address, to be civilized was to be restrained, moderate in sentiment and deed, unemotive of passion, devoted to constitutional reform, dedicated to individual and societal advancement, and willing to permit free, popular institutions to restrain and channel the destructive tendencies of human nature. Above all, Emerson concluded, "civilization depends on morality," the act of transcending base and regressive human instincts to achieve the "highest civility" for the common good.[6]

As an overwhelming preponderance of the nineteenth-century national population, white Americans defined their republican Union as the pinnacle of civilized Western nations. Republics facilitated for enlightened citizens political and social equality, industry and independence, energy and growth, mobility and improvement. A civilized nation allegedly conquered the barbaric state of nature to obviate retrograde, deteriorating savagery. To guard against cultural decay, Emerson explained, civilization depended on "the absolute illumination we call Reason." Civilization organized sovereign individuals who "learn[ed] the secret of cumulative power, of advancing one's self. It implies a facility of association, power to compare, the ceasing from fixed ideas" as the only means of ordering liberty. An antagonist to barbarism, civilization was at once an active process and a chosen state of being. As such, "the term imports a mysterious progress," drawing distinct currency from notions of race, culture, and ethnicity. "In the brutes is [no civilization]; and in mankind, the savage tribes do not advance. The Indians of this country have not learned the white man's work; and in Africa, the Negro of today is the Negro of Herodotus." According to myriad white Americans, much of the non-Anglo world had been consumed by "Africanization"—an alleged barbaric state of primitivity conditioned by blackness—"Indianization"—a so-called savage tribalism averse to progress, property rights, individualism, and the rule of law—or "Mexicanization"—the seeming inability of Latin American nations to practice effective, restrained, and legitimate democracy.[7]

As a self-proclaimed civilized republic, the American Union guarded against the ostensible forces of internationalist regression. The exceptionalist concept of Union was thus punctuated by profound paradox. The nation that announced as its sacred mission the protection of personal liberty and human equality was the very nation that disqualified myriad women, most African Americans, and many Indigenous people from formal political inclusion. The enduring puzzle of Union was that the republic was founded of and for the people but not represented by *all* of the people. The rule of law, market capitalism, and universal white-male suffrage had indeed created the largest democracy anywhere in the nineteenth-century world. But those same national attributes also barred millions of Americans from political participation, facilitated the United States' growth into the world's foremost slaveholding nation, and dismantled "uncivilized" Native sovereignties that seemingly obstructed the white republic's manifest continental destiny. A contingent outgrowth of nineteenth-century American political culture held that white citizens would control the Union. The presence of Indigenous nations and communities of color performed striking cultural work in forming Anglo notions of a civilized, exceptional Union. Many white Americans assumed that these groups were in but not of the republic, that their yet fully developed stations on the spectrum of civilization barred them from equal inclusion and participation in a democratic nation.[8]

It is difficult for us in the modern era to understand why the exceptionalist faith in Union so consumed the American disposition, especially when the concept seems so flawed and inconsistent. But few attributes of American life were more influential in shaping a powerful national consciousness that above all else privileged the preservation of the founding generation's birth of a republic predicated on sovereign individual liberty. "To appreciate the unexampled advantages bestowed by the Omnipotent upon this favored Republic, this youngest child of civilization," reflected the overt exceptionalist, historian, and diplomat John Lothrop Motley in 1868, "is rather to oppress the thoughtful mind with an overwhelming sense of responsibility." Motley voiced a prevailing nineteenth-century attitude in which the United States reached across time and beyond generations to stand as "the world's great hope." In his telling, Americans had been charged with directing the course of nations, subordinated only to the power of nature's law. That "law is Progress," Motley concluded, "the result Democracy." Motley echoed the convictions of countless free citizens who embraced an abiding obligation to uphold the democratic republic and its ideals of liberty and equality, opportunity, and advancement. Otherwise, the radical forces of international "isms"—oligarchism, monarchism, atheism, communism, socialism, fanaticism, and abolitionism, at least according to whites skeptical of racial egalitarianism—would transform the United States into a nation among corrupted nations.[9]

An overwhelming majority of white Americans privileged a conservative political culture to preserve their republic from "internationalism." Though exceptionalist rhetoric often painted the United States as a divinely chosen entity divorced from the regular course of human affairs, the citizenry lived in fear of their democratic republic declining and collapsing into revolution. As a state of mind and a set of practices, nineteenth-century conservatism fueled a "positive nationalism" that sought to preserve a moderate republic within a seemingly radical, antidemocratic world. "Conservatism, taken in its more tangible aspects, is simply the law of habit applied to the institutions and arrangements of society as now existing," explained the influential *Harper's Weekly* in 1859. "It is the principle by which we value things in their political and social connections for what they have demonstrated themselves to be." As Lincoln warned at the Young Men's Lyceum, if Americans spurned their republic's sources of democratic stability—the rule of law, representative institutions, political compromise, due process, and constitutional checks—the world's seeming penchant for social upheaval, sweeping revolution, lawless anarchy, and centralized reaction would inevitably deteriorate the Union from within. A conservative republic featured modern, progressive popular sovereignty even willing to countenance radical—but not revolutionary—measures in specific and moderating ways to *conserve* a stable political center. To abandon processes of political moderation was to reject the Constitution's timeless charge for all generations to strive toward "a more perfect Union," one based on justice, domestic tranquility, and the general welfare. Conservatism bound together the past, present, and future in a common cause to "secure the Blessings of Liberty to ourselves and our Posterity."[10]

A Contest of Civilizations engages the paradoxical questions raised by nineteenth-century exceptionalist conviction, civilizationist discourse, and conservative practice. How could an inimitable republic, conceived in liberty and devoted to propositions of equality, stand by midcentury as the largest slaveholding nation in the modern world? How could a people who claimed to chart an unprecedented, stable course in human affairs experience a hostile national collapse and welcome a violent civil war? How could the people who waged that war believe in a restrained and civilized contest while sanctioning fundamental transformations and even radical actions to serve their respective national causes? How and why could the world's largest enslaved population in less than a decade emerge as fully emancipated citizens of the very republic that once licensed their bondage? How could a conservative white population who valued constitutional stability and who looked askance at racial egalitarianism accept such alterations to the Constitution in the name of greater biracial equality?

Answers to these questions resided in the powerful and ultimately irreconcilable problem of mid-nineteenth-century American exceptionalism: competing and often discordant conceptions of civilization inhabiting the same republic, derived from the centrality of slavery in a land of freedom. Though the United States "could not contain two nations," acknowledges a pair of leading scholars on the concept of civilization, "two nations developed because of slavery. One defined itself as civilized because slavery gave it a prosperous economy, a genteel ruling elite, and a secure place in the liberal world. The other defined itself as civilized because commercial and industrial prowess secured its place in that same world." The powerful hold of slavery within a constitutional republic fostered divergent and even hostile understandings of the nation's founding. Abraham Lincoln understood this tension when he averred in 1858 that the Union "cannot endure, permanently half *slave* and half *free*." Slaveholding adherents and nonslaveholding advocates by midcentury had come to believe that their antagonists had contaminated the American political system, the Declaration of Independence, the Constitution, and civilization itself with radical internationalism that betrayed the Union's exceptional global standing. These contested interpretations of American civilization, measured against perceptions of international extremism and global revolution, informed the coming of the Civil War, modeled the formation of the Confederate States of America, gave meaning to the Union cause, shaped the war's conduct, influenced the process of emancipation, and posed significant implications for national restoration and hemispheric reorganization.[11]

The Civil War era showcased concerted attempts by diverse groups of Americans to purge what they perceived to be the malignant forces of antidemocratic internationalization within American politics and culture. Only a categorical war could place the United States and the Confederacy in positions of strength on the international stage, with each nation prepared to "Americanize" the globe. And yet, did not a violent and transformative war itself transgress the exceptionalism that Americans advertised to a seemingly pugnacious international order? The era exhibited profound irony in the ways in which Americans accepted civil war, its destructive capacity, and its radical changes as means to *preserve* and *safeguard* their self-defined but contested attributes of American civilization: Union, democracy, and, for African Americans and some whites, racial egalitarianism, on the one hand, and slaveholding liberty and white supremacy, on the other. Lincoln recognized this striking paradox in his second inaugural address. Though all Americans in 1861 "deprecated war" and "all [parties] sought to avert it," because the fate of American civilization was at stake, "one of them would *make* war rather than let the nation survive; and the other would *accept* war rather than let it perish. And the war came." Waging war in the name of civilization was itself seen as a welcome, enlightening act that did not violate but, rather, confirmed the superiority of American institutions and popular democracy.[12]

Belligerent Americans held fast to the ideal of conservative moderation to navigate the tumults of sectionalism, disunion, the war's immense scale of death and widespread destruction, the end of slavery, and the trials of Reconstruction. To be sure, conservatism did not mean rigid, static aversion to modern progress, democratic reform, and national change. Rather, it meant approaching the uncertainties of the present with reasoned caution, using the rule of law and the proven, limiting principles of constitutional democracy to make necessary, periodic, and often fundamental alterations to *conserve* a nation's exceptional attributes. "Conservatism does not reject new ideas and oppose all reforms," instructed *Harper's Weekly*. "But it resists change unless change is demanded by urgent and imperative reasons." Reform, not revolution, remained the ideal. Most midcentury Americans, regardless—or, rather, *because*—of their national affiliations in the United States or Confederacy, justified sweeping, previously unthinkable changes to *preserve* what they considered exceptional about their respective free-labor and slaveholding civilizations. A conservative reacted against perceived threats from revolutionary extremism, fanatical excesses, or uncivilized militancy to prevent infections to prevailing political institutions and social norms. Moderation, appeals to the law, and entreaties to the common good from one party were used to counteract the unjustified extremes of the other. Conservative reform aimed to cleanse ostensible revolutions from further poisoning civilization. "American conservatism is a common-sense estimate of political society as organized in our institutions," *Harper's* concluded. "It merely reasons that the present vindicates the order of affairs as working among us, and hence that patriotism and philanthropy may afford to be satisfied."[13]

Conservatism produced within the Confederacy and the United States affirming nationalisms that aimed to safeguard more than they destroyed. Founding a new slaveholding republic or preserving the United States *as* a republic mandated that democratic institutions and the rule of law direct the transformations occasioned by modern war. Citizens of both nations professed explicit aversions to reactionary "fanaticism." According to Confederates, threats to a stable slaveholding order sanctioned secession and authorized the building of an independent constitutional republic sustained by a strong but flexible government, white popular sovereignty, and African American bondage. In turn, to uphold the Union, loyal American citizens relied on law and democratic consent to justify an increasingly broad, hard war *against* the Confederacy, implementing emancipation and later the Fourteenth and Fifteenth Amendments as tools of national preservation. That both sides remained inherently conservative—meaning, they applied their conceptions of American democracy to conducting the Civil War and its aftermath—established at the conflict's outset the conditions for a violent, metamorphic contest. The era's transformations thus possessed once inconceivable implications. Indeed, the slaveholders' war of secession *against* the United States led to universal emancipation and ultimately constitutional biracial citizenship and male suffrage *within* the United States.[14]

A Contest of Civilizations surveys the ways in which nineteenth-century Americans understood their nation, the sectional crisis, the Civil War, and the processes of reunion within the context of global events, Atlantic ideologies, and domestic fears of international influence. The book does not interrogate how the international community regarded the United States' midcentury crisis of national sovereignty. Beyond the links that Americans themselves drew to give meaning to their own national predicament, the book also does not compare the "ordeal of the Union" with the many contemporary civil conflicts that riddled the nineteenth-century globe. Ultimately, in this book, nineteenth-century Americans speak for themselves to outline their diverse concepts of nationhood during an era of immense, uncertain turmoil. When possible, the narrative abstains from modern-day criticism, instead locating rhetoric and action within their contemporary contexts. The nineteenth-century world was far different from the twenty-first, and it does little good to impose current standards onto those historical values that are otherwise repugnant.[15]

The book unfolds in three parts to explore how contested visions of civilization and Union, joined by rituals of conservative moderation, shaped the foremost epoch in U.S. history. Each part derives its title from a line in the Gettysburg Address, among the foremost orations in the American exceptionalist tradition. Part I, "Conceived in Liberty," surveys how the galvanizing concept of Union informed nineteenth-century American identity. Born from the New World's first antimonarchical revolution, the Union stood as a constitutional republic committed to safeguarding universal natural rights and limiting the coercive power of government. An avowed empire of liberty, the Union abolished traditional global barriers to social or political equality, including feudal orders, entrenched aristocracies, established state churches, or divine-right monarchies. By midcentury, the American Union boasted the world's largest white popular democracy and a burgeoning middle class, attributes that oppressed peoples across the Atlantic rim—particularly in Latin America, the Caribbean, and Europe—had sought but failed to procure. Because of their nation's self-proclaimed ideals, virtually all white Americans—and even many African Americans—recognized the Union and its founding principles as the democratic exceptions to international tyranny and political repression.[16]

The Union nonetheless exhibited the very political and social exclusions and even tyrannies that white Americans professed to oppose. Over the past half century, historians have rightly devoted a great deal of ink to the pervasive racism, white supremacy, and patriarchal culture that shaped the lives of nineteenth-century Americans. Women, enslaved African Americans, and free people of color lived daily with the repercussions of these national attitudes. But the remarkable extent to which these groups also *embraced* exceptionalist discourse to resist oppression and advocate for social equality and political liberty reveals a great deal about the period's historical implications. Enslaved African Americans particularly resisted the unjust constraints of human bondage. Some pursued liberation by rebelling against the overwhelming power of a white supremacist slaveholding society. Free people of color even deployed the concept of Union and engaged the institutions of civic democracy as cudgels against their exclusion from the nation's founding and their excision from formal politics. They rejected the ways in which many white Americans designated grotesque images of blackness to justify slaveholding in the name of white liberty. They scorned white proposals to colonize black people in the Caribbean or Africa. They proliferated a vibrant popular press that preached a message of eternal deliverance *within* the Union. They mobilized and petitioned for constitutional reform, equal political rights, universal suffrage, and formal citizenship in the very nation that had consigned generations of their people to second-class status and even lifetimes of bondage. Some even utilized the legal system to sue for civil liberties and freedom from slavery. As a distinct racial minority in an overwhelmingly white republic, they sought the protections and guarantees afforded by the same rule of law that sanctioned racial discrimination and human enslavement. As exceptionalists themselves, African Americans demanded that the United States live up to its founding ideals. Their message was clear: to secure a more perfect Union, white Americans would have to honor their own self-proclaimed yet unfulfilled commitments to life, liberty, justice, and equality for all.[17]

Slavery created the greatest conflict within the national consensus. Though in 1776 each state of the newly proclaimed republic sanctioned slavery, the ideals of the Declaration of Independence, religious conviction, and economic necessity encouraged local antislavery movements. Beginning with the sovereign Vermont in 1777, northern legislatures unfolded statutory processes of creating free states. From 1780 to 1804, states north of the Mason-Dixon Line initiated methods of gradual emancipation, in some cases extending limited civil and suffrage rights to freedpeople. The Northwest Ordinance of 1787 forbade slavery's expansion into the northwestern territories, portending the admission of future nonslaveholding states north of the Ohio River. That same year, the Constitutional Convention banned American participation in the transatlantic slave trade beginning in 1808. And though slaveholders desired that the entire enslaved population count toward congressional representation, the Constitution limited slaveholding representation through the Three-Fifths Clause. While delegates compromised with slavery to forge the Union, "The plain unmistakable spirit of that age, towards slavery, was hostility to the PRINCIPLE, and toleration, ONLY BY NECESSITY," Abraham Lincoln later assumed in 1854 when outlining his political theory of Union. The Constitution's system of federalism and the Bill of Rights' protection of free speech, press, and petition—which African American and white abolitionists exercised to solicit state and federal governments—sheltered antislavery reform efforts. In prioritizing democratic consent and constitutional prerogatives, federalism protected antislavery movements that challenged the assumption that the United States would be a uniform slaveholding republic. "Had there been no anti-slavery agitation at the North," remarked Frederick Douglass, "there would have been no active anti-slavery anywhere to resist the demands of the slave-power at the South." The Declaration, the Constitution, and the Bill of Rights guarded nascent abolitionism during an era in which influential slaveholders claimed those same documents legitimized a powerful empire of slavery.[18]

In the antislavery imagination, slaveholders acted as grassroots revolutionaries who constantly threatened to sever the Union while simultaneously appearing as unaccountable oligarchs who aimed to consolidate slaveholding power *within* the Union. The Republican Party ultimately charged slaveholding southerners and sympathetic northern Democrats of conniving an internationalist "Slave Power conspiracy." Republicans alleged that the "Slave Power" intended to eradicate the Constitution and subvert the democratic process, transforming the United States into a militaristic oligarchy. This nefarious scheme threatened to overturn the antislavery precedents of the

American Revolution by hijacking the federal government, expanding slavery across the vast continent, and even infiltrating nonslaveholding northern states with human bondage. In this scenario, common citizens, unable to compete with armies of enslaved laborers, would never be able to pursue economic mobility and achieve personal independence, themselves beholden to the stifling commands of slaveholding aristocrats. Ultimately, the enfeebled, desecrated republic would be laid bare to domination by European despots and other tyrannical powers. Enslaved and free people of color themselves also saw within the American "Slave Power" a relic of Old World barbarism. Only through active resistance could African Americans demand the Union's promise of birthright liberty and the republic's founding ideals expressed in the Declaration of Independence and Constitution. Replacing human bondage with universal freedom would finally confirm the United States' exceptional standing in the world.[19]

Southern slaveholders likewise perceived revolutionary intrigue at the heart of efforts by white and black antislavery activists who threatened to restrict the spread of slavery. They feared the global influences of abolitionism, European socialism, and restive racial barbarism infecting American political and social institutions. If radical Republicans barred enslaved human property from proliferating across the continent and even the hemisphere, then enslaved people would explode in a Caribbean-style racial revolution and sunder the very white liberty allegedly guaranteed by the Union, Constitution, and slavery itself. To maintain their peculiar society, slaveholders wielded a powerful central state to silence antislavery critics. They secured laws that limited African American mobility and freedom. And they deployed the U.S. military to conquer and expand slaveholding territories. Slaveholders worked throughout the nineteenth century to rewrite the American Revolutionary heritage, attempting to excise the enduring ideal of universal human equality proclaimed in the Declaration of Independence. By exploiting the Constitution's protection of property and its Three-Fifths Clause, they consolidated a disproportionate share of political representation to exert slaveholding authority.[20]

Part II, "Now We Are Engaged in a Great Civil War," demonstrates how contested visions of Union contributed to disunion and a war between two modern mid-nineteenth-century nations. Slaveholders had long enjoyed political prestige in the U.S. government. They expected that the institution of slavery would spread unfettered across the republic, blanket the continent, and ultimately ensconce the hemisphere. For mid-nineteenth-century American slaveholders, slavery fashioned the cornerstone of modern life. The institution ensured social stability and white political equality by organizing "civilized" and "barbaric" races in their allegedly natural conditions of freedom and servitude. Any interference against this arrangement, any interruption to a slaveholding Union ordered by law and seeming democratic consent, might have to be met with an unprecedented response. When Abraham Lincoln assumed the presidency and the Republican Party took control of the federal apparatus in 1861 on pledges to restrict the continental spread of slavery, slaveholders sensed a radical and irrevocable transformation of the Union's standing in the world. They feared that Republicans would abrogate the constitutional protections afforded to enslaved property, engage in redistributive socialism of slaveholding assets, and incite bondpeople into bloody racial insurrections. The often threatened but always implausible path of secession now greeted slaveholders as a rational option to *preserve* their exceptional dimensions of American civilization. Disunion and the formation of the Confederate States of America as a new slaveholding republic occurred at a rapid pace to withstand an onslaught of supposed racial egalitarianism.[21]

As American exceptionalists, Confederates framed their nation-building effort as a peaceful exercise in democratic self-determination. In the spirit of 1776, Confederates rebelled against the ostensible excesses of government tyranny. In the spirit of 1861, they also rebelled against the perceived excesses of racial tyranny. The Union was expendable. But the slaveholding *ideas* of Union were borderless. Newly appointed president Jefferson Davis explained the scope of Confederate purpose. A stalwart American nationalist who believed that the United States' exceptional standing in the world hinged on the preservation of slavery and white liberty, Davis condemned Republican abolitionists for corrupting and radicalizing the old republic. To oppose the "continuous series of measures . . . devised and prosecuted for the purpose of rendering insecure the tenure of property in slaves," and to resist the "fanatical organizations" that "were assiduously engaged in exciting amongst the slaves a spirit of discontent and revolt," Confederates sundered the United States to build a new nation that *conserved* their self-defined ingredients of American exceptionalism: slaveholding, the rule of law, and a limited democracy sustained by white supremacy. Confederate constitutionalism did not tolerate antislavery dissent, marshaling a powerful central state against any democratic coalition hostile to slavery. Slaveholding independence intended to repel the kind of enslaved insurrections and radical abolitionism that had toppled New World slave societies, including the United States. "We are upholding the great principles which our fathers bequeathed us," South Carolina Presbyterian minister James Henley Thornwell declared of the seeming moderation of secession and nation-building. Confederates claimed the natural right to pursue an unprecedented experiment in white slaveholding nationalism. "We are not revolutionists," Thornwell concluded. "We are resisting revolution. We are upholding the true doctrines of the Federal Constitution. We are conservative."[22]

As the preeminent voice of the United States' antislavery coalition, Abraham Lincoln indicted slaveholding threats, disunion, and the Confederacy's war against the republic as unjust violations of American democracy. On the eve of the election of 1860, Lincoln asked of southern slaveholders and their Democratic allies, "You say you are conservative—eminently conservative—while we are revolutionary, destructive, or something of the sort. What is conservatism? Is it not adherence to the old and tried, against the new and untried? We stick to, contend for, the identical old policy on the point in controversy which was adopted by our fathers who framed the Government under which we live; while you ... insist upon substituting something new." The "something new" sought by slaveholders was the unobstructed, unlawful aggrandizement of a powerful institution that Lincoln scorned as antithetical to the nation's founding. A stalwart adherent to the rule of law, Lincoln grudgingly recognized the legal protection of slavery within the federal system. But he also believed in the constitutional restrictions on slavery's expansion across the Union's vast western territories. The Declaration and Constitution favored common citizens pursuing personal independence and economic mobility liberated from unfair competition against slaveholding oligarchs who used their crony, privileged association with government to subvert the law and grab the best lands to spread their institution. In the wake of his presidential victory, to maintain the loyalty of volatile slaveholders and to preserve the Union, Lincoln supported a Republican-proposed constitutional amendment that would legalize the permanent protection of slavery in the states where it existed. But slaveholders still sought an unrestricted slaveholding Union. "To strengthen, perpetuate, and extend this interest was the object for which the insurgents would rend the Union, even by war, while the government claimed no right to do more than to restrict the territorial enlargement of it," Lincoln recalled in his second inaugural address.[23]

For Lincoln, slaveholding secessionists and Confederates had rejected the moderation of law and the stability of popular democracy in pursuit of an internationalist transformation of the Union's exceptional global standing. Though he and the loyal American citizenry had once been "devoted altogether to *saving* the Union without war," they *welcomed* war in the service of national preservation. The cause of Union remained the loyal citizenry's foremost and unwavering wartime purpose. To countenance an exceptional republic's death through secessionist balkanization would be to acknowledge before the world the failure of popular government of, by, and for the people. That the struggle, according to Lincoln, "is not altogether for today—it is for a vast future also" mandated that a free people conduct a war for Union to uphold the enduring antislavery vision of the founding generation. The radicalism of disunion and the contingencies of war waged against a powerful slaveholding nation imposed radical and once unthinkable demands. "As our case is new, so we must think anew, and act anew," Lincoln instructed Congress in December 1862. Though the Republican Party had long pledged to protect slavery where it existed, an unprecedented slaveholders' war *against* the Union fundamentally altered how the loyal citizenry understood their republic, its democratic purpose, and its international standing. "We must disenthrall our selves," Lincoln explained, and recognize that "the dogmas of the quiet past, are inadequate to the stormy present." Widespread and precipitous emancipation, once an impossible affront to national stability, the rule of law, and a white-dominated society, had emerged by 1862 as a critical and even radical means of national preservation against future slaveholding obstructions and wars of secession.[24]

According to the mass of loyal white citizens, emancipation complemented and even purified, but never transcended, the cause of Union. The measure "is recommended as a means, not in exclusion of, but additional to, all others for restoring and preserving the national authority throughout the Union," Lincoln counseled the Congress in December 1862. To restore a republic with the slaveholding cancer that had shattered national accord and sparked a devastating war would invite a future of endless strife and perpetual chaos. Doing so would also suggest that somehow slavery could continue to coexist in a republic committed to individual liberty, spreading indelible stains upon the sacred national fabric. As Lincoln reflected in his October 1863 Thanksgiving Proclamation, loyal citizens waged war against the Slave Power and welcomed emancipation "to heal the wounds of the nation and to restore it as soon as may be consistent with the Divine purposes to the full enjoyment of peace, harmony, tranquility and Union." Emancipation thus challenged white Americans to honor the nation's founding ideals outlined in the Declaration of Independence. "We say we are for the Union," Lincoln reminded the American public. The passionate trial of civil war allowed the United States finally to liberate itself from oligarchic slaveholding tyranny in the same way that war occasioned liberation for individual enslaved people. "In *giving* freedom to the *slave*, we *assure* freedom to the *free*," Lincoln concluded, "honorable alike in what we give, and what we preserve." The options were self-evident: "We shall nobly save, or meanly lose, the last best, hope of earth."[25]

Civil War produced rapid changes to the national disposition to *save* a democratic republic. An unequivocal emancipation—once an unlikely and even undesirable prospect for most white citizens prior to the conflict—within *four years* dismantled a dangerous antidemocratic oligarchy from again challenging the nation's constitutional sovereignty. "It is extraordinary how completely the idea of *gradual* emancipation has been dissipated from the public mind everywhere, by the progress of events," the *New York Times* announced in 1864. "Before the rebellion, it was accounted the very extreme of Antislavery fanaticism to believe in the possibility of immediate emancipation without social ruin." Apart from the Haitian Revolution, New World emancipations had occurred slowly over time to accommodate the great alterations away from unfree labor. "The change of opinion on this subject is a remarkable illustration of the practical aptitude of the American mind," the *Times* concluded in recognizing the elasticity of conservative action. "With hardly an effort, theories and prejudices, that had apparently rooted themselves in it so deeply as to become a part of it, are discarded, and new ideas, in keeping with a new condition of affairs, are conceived, and conformed to, almost by universal consent."[26]

African Americans likewise welcomed the Civil War as their long-awaited moment of deliverance. By 1860 the United States had grown into one of the world's few remaining and imposing slaveholding powers. When dreaming of and pursuing their own liberation, black Americans had long identified with the stirring accounts of enslaved revolts in the Caribbean and triumphal New World emancipations. By 1861, with the advent of war, myriad African Americans finally considered emancipation in the United States a distinct reality. Though barred from citizenship in the nation's body politic, they petitioned the Lincoln administration to serve as volunteer soldiers in Union armies. They advocated that the cause of Union also embrace the cause of universal human freedom. They demanded full assimilation into the very nation that had long marginalized and enslaved generations of their people. Above all, they mobilized in support of a war effort that they expected would finally re-form the old slaveholding Union into a multiracial, egalitarian republic committed to human dignity and equality before the law. "This country BELONGS TO US; and ... we assert the right to live and labor here," prominent New York intellectual J. W. C. Pennington declared in 1863. "In this struggle we know nothing but God, Manhood, and American nationality, full and unimpaired." War occasions fundamental change, and African Americans embraced the moment—perhaps their *only* moment—to strike for an enduring reformation of the nation's sacred ideals.[27]

To secure their nations' respective wartime purposes, Unionists and Confederates pledged to wage a restrained and civilized war. Both sides subscribed to the Enlightenment-era theory of "just war," which guided belligerent conduct through reasoned limitation, adherence to the international laws of war, and respect for civilian noncombatants. As described by Francis Lieber, one of the Union's and the nineteenth-century Atlantic world's foremost authorities on military law, "Men who take up arms against one another in public war do not cease on this account to be moral beings, responsible only to one another and to God." Both the United States and the Confederacy conducted war with state-sanctioned armies, retained democratic civilian control of the armed forces, derived military policy from national and international rules, and vindicated conduct according to "military necessity," a contemporary justification for escalating martial conduct as long as it conformed legally to the national purpose. As Lieber explained, a distinct irony underwrote the character of modern war: "The more vigorously wars are pursued the better it is for humanity. Sharp wars are brief." Peace was the ultimate end of war. Thus, a civilized war at once imposed careful restraints and invited profound devastation to occasion a swift but decisive verdict. The elasticity of military necessity inflamed the Civil War's violence and enhanced its rapid transformations. But each national people advertised themselves to the world as civilized belligerents who remained beholden to the laws of war and state-sanctioned conduct. Exceeding the self-defined justifications for conducting war and discarding the laws of war would endanger the Union and Confederate causes before the world, summoning violent belligerent reprisals and provoking international censure.[28]

Emancipation informed each nation's concept of military necessity. To delegitimize the Confederacy's international standing and to shatter the organizing principle of the slaveholding republic, Union military policy turned slavery *against* the Confederate war effort. Through congressional statute, executive proclamation, and military doctrine—indeed, through the rule of law—the United States recognized the freedom of enslaved people who flocked to Union armies, divesting southern plantations and Confederate armies of critical, coerced labor. And to inflate Federal ranks, the United States invited formerly enslaved men to enlist in Union armies. Donning blue uniforms and wielding remarkable military power, African American Union soldiers ruptured the Confederate nation's slaveholding foundation and earned the gratitude of the loyal republic that had once authorized human bondage. The revolutionary implications of African American soldiering conveyed a signal moment "in universal history," remarked prominent nineteenth-century historian George Bancroft. Emancipation "decided the result of the war," he averred. "It took from the public enemy one or two millions of bondmen, and placed between one and two hundred thousand brave and gallant troops in arms on the side of the Union."[29]

Confederates in turn regarded emancipation as an unjust violation of civilized warfare. They condemned African American troops as unlawful insurrectionists who defiled the laws of nature and nation. To combat what they considered the United States' unwarranted escalation of racial barbarism, Confederates authorized the reenslavement and execution of black Union soldiers—and their white officers—who "revolted" against the Confederate state and who rebelled against an ostensibly natural racial order. But in extraordinary demonstrations of martial restraint, African American soldiers largely refused gratuitous reprisals against such Confederate policies. Their civic participation in United States armies—rather than as illicit insurgents—underscored the moral authority of emancipation and marginalized the Confederacy on the world stage as a nation of aberrant slaveholders.[30]

Part III, "Shall Not Perish from the Earth," explores the purposes and contested meanings of Reconstruction. In the wake of Appomattox, dismantling the Confederate nation and its armies mandated a limited peace in which the United States did not pursue excessive reprisals against former rebels. The death of the American Slave Power convinced an overwhelming preponderance of white loyal citizens that former Confederates would return to the Union, accept the demise of secession and slavery as verdicts of a just war, and again enjoy the fruits of democratic citizenship in a chosen nation. Republicans nevertheless debated the pragmatism of such a lenient restoration. So-called radicals like Frederick Douglass and Thaddeus Stevens argued that the fanaticism of the Confederacy's war for slaveholding sovereignty had to be countered with equally radical measures to *preserve* the Union from ever again collapsing into future conflagrations sparked by the enemies of human liberty. Emancipation itself required definition. Uncompromising Republicans joined freedpeople to call for immediate enfranchisement and citizenship of the formerly enslaved; they advocated limiting the political rights of former Confederates; they advanced confiscation and redistribution of slaveholders' land; and they called for a coercive military occupation to dismantle the sovereignty of former Confederate states. That which appeared impossible in the American tradition prior to 1861 had emerged for some Republicans, by 1865, as rational antidotes to centuries of slavery, antidemocratic aristocracy, and disunion. But for most Republicans, preserving the Union as a moderate republic required maintaining the careful balance between white southern democratic self-determination and a consensus of national loyalty. Additional work, they believed, particularly in the idealistic realm of black civil rights, did not spring forth from the verdicts secured at Appomattox.[31]

The political moderation of local self-restoration soon revealed its inherent, devastating flaws. The contested visions of American exceptionalism that had once sundered the Union remained just as vibrant in the wake of civil war. Former Confederates transformed the South into a Caribbean-style postemancipation hierarchy of white freedom bolstered by black pseudo-slavery. Their swift efforts, however, did not reveal the postbellum moment to be a continuation of the Civil War, nor even a war by other means. White southerners did not again rebel against the United States in order to build a new slaveholding republic. Former Confederates aimed to *reform* the nation from within—through racial violence and political chaos—into a white nationalist state that defied liberal equality, the rule of law, and the verdicts of Union and emancipation.[32]

Reconstruction was principally a limited effort to restore the republic and ensure an enduring national peace. The era served ultimately as a referendum on the meaning of Union itself. White southerners asked whether the United States would defy the alleged barbarism of emancipation and stand as the world's foremost white supremacist republic. African Americans asked whether the United States would at last fulfill its claims to universal equality and liberty set forth in the Declaration of Independence and the Constitution. The white loyal citizenry and Republicans asked whether the United States would finally be liberated from the powerful antidemocratic obstructions long imposed by slaveholding aristocrats. As they always had, Americans probed the meaning of national exceptionalism. To preserve the concept of Union, Republicans pursued an unprecedented program of political transformation aimed at neutering the political power of resurgent southern oligarchs. They adopted nearly every proposal once deemed too radical in order to *conserve* democratic republicanism and uphold common civil rights. A military occupation of the former Confederacy reformed state governments into committed biracial, free labor, egalitarian domains. The enfranchisement of freedmen, joined by the guarantees of formal citizenship and equal protection of the law, expanded a vast biracial democracy that mobilized against the old slaveholding order. Just as emancipation had once been a means toward the ends of Union, so too were the Reconstruction Acts of 1867, the Fourteenth Amendment of 1868, and the Fifteenth Amendment of 1870 methods—radical, unprecedented methods—of *preserving* the republic. Most white southerners, however, regarded the amendments and Reconstruction as the nineteenth-century world's most devastating revolution.[33]

Reconstruction featured extraordinary national changes. African Americans desired, and for a time secured, that which had long existed in the American tradition but which had been deprived by centuries of slavery: political equality, personal sovereignty, and economic mobility. Placing their faith in American creeds and institutions, freedpeople endorsed democratic republicanism as the source of their liberty and equality. Men participated in state constitutional conventions, voted in overwhelming numbers, and held political office on the local, state, and federal levels. Women also played dynamic roles. From testifying before Congress on the brutalities of racial and sexual violence that engulfed the postemancipation South, to securing legal recognition of their marriages, and even suing for reparations from former slaveholders, women employed the civic institutions of democratic life to secure a sturdy foundation of liberty. Above all, myriad African Americans used Reconstruction as a platform to declare to the world that they were indeed *American*, that they were both *in* and *of* the Union. "It is certainly known by southern as well as northern men that the colored people of this country are thoroughly American; born and raised upon American soil and under the influence of American institutions," declared Mississippi congressman John Roy Lynch, among the scores of black officeholders for whom formerly enslaved people cast their votes in the late 1860s and early 1870s. Born enslaved in 1847 on a Louisiana cotton plantation, Lynch's life reflected the remarkable transformations occasioned by war and emancipation. Though he entered the world segregated from liberty, by the early 1870s he stood free as a member of the very legislative body that once sanctioned his enslavement.[34]

The vast reach of Reconstruction reflected an enduring paradox of American exceptionalism: how to preserve the Union with something so self-evident as liberty alongside something so unnatural in the nineteenth-century experience as biracial equality. Republicans assumed that constitutional reform and African American citizenship and suffrage would safeguard the republic from again fracturing into civil war. But the attributes that aimed to stabilize, liberalize, and modernize the Union inspired an anarchical insurgency from white southerners who refused to countenance the death of their race-based civilization. The very purpose of Reconstruction—dismantling the slaveholding aristocracy and preserving the Union from antidemocratic obstacles—facilitated its striking success and fueled its devastating shortcomings. To combat an insurgency that hijacked the democratic process, undermined the rule of law, and terrorized black citizens to secure political power and white supremacy required unprecedented centralization and force. In their effort to preserve the Union, white Republicans sought two incompatible ends that reflected competing dimensions of exceptionalist conviction: an authentic, antislavery, biracial democracy that lived within a decentralized and demilitarized republic. Only federal force could ensure the lasting ideal of racial equality, yet a preponderance of nineteenth-century white Americans privileged an antimilitaristic constitutional Union that stood apart from the world's political absolutisms. Republicans ultimately traded the enforcement of racial equality for the enduring stability of Union, a calculation that underscored the era's continuity. Though conquered on the battlefield in 1865, ex-Confederates and former slaveholders took advantage of Republican moderation to assemble the edifice of Jim Crow segregation, which dominated southern life for the next century.[35]

Yet because Reconstruction had been enshrined into the U.S. Constitution, its promise was and continues to be entrenched for all time. Indeed, the wellspring of American exceptionalism waters an enduring faith in the ideals of Union. That natural rights are enduring means that they will always invite unlimited claims for their unlimited protection. To strive for a more perfect Union conceived in liberty and dedicated to equality was—and is—the essential charge of Americanism. Abraham Lincoln proclaimed in 1838 at the Young Men's Lyceum that only Americans could author their own national destiny. It was a destiny conditioned by bold claims, entrenched anxieties, and human limitations in securing the United States within the global order. Above all, it was a destiny contingent on maintaining within the world a democratic republic predicated on notions of political liberty and civil equality, an effort as palpable, timeless, and contested in Lincoln's day as it is in our own.

PART I
Conceived in
Liberty

★ ★ ★

The situation of the Americans is therefore entirely exceptional, and it is to be believed that no [other] democratic people will ever be placed in it.

ALEXIS DE TOCQUEVILLE,
Democracy in America

1
Union

★ ★ ★

In 1861, in the wake of his electoral triumph to the presidency, Abraham Lincoln reflected on what he considered the "philosophical" attributes of American nationhood. In many ways, the United States resembled the nations of the world. The citizenry claimed a common language and heritage. The country boasted vast agrarian domains dotted by burgeoning metropolitan centers. And the national governing charter outlined modern processes of administration and oversight. Though a young republic within a world of ancient nations, the United States had stabilized from the tentative days of its infancy to enjoy an abounding adolescence. As a physical space, the republic could grow with seeming indeterminacy. The law safeguarded the individual acquisition and proliferation of property, forging an independent middling class. In short, the American Union had emerged as a nation among the prosperous community of Western nations.[1]

For Lincoln, however, the United States also transcended the meaning of nationhood itself. The Union's prosperity, its security, its vast expanse were "not the result of accident." Even the bold act of rebelling against colonial oppression and establishing a new nation "are not the primary cause of our great prosperity. There is something back of these, entwining itself more closely about the human heart," Lincoln imagined, as he reflected on the republic's founding. The Union was unique among the nations of the world because it was *not* merely a nation. The Declaration of Independence proclaimed an unprecedented national "principle of 'Liberty to all'—the principle that clears the *path* for all—gives *hope* to all—and, by consequence, *enterprize*, and *industry* to all." The first nation ever to center individual human dignity at the apex of national purpose, the Union pledged as its signal obligation the protection and propagation of individual rights to life, liberty, and happiness. This lofty ideal held that ordinary people were not consigned as helpless wards of the state, their coerced labor enriching the coffers of favored elites. The nation's citizenry, Lincoln alleged, claimed the liberty to chart sovereign lives freed from arbitrary state-sanctioned oppression. The Union's founding principles fostered a timeless "promise of something better" for all its citizens, a sacred commitment that Lincoln believed had "secured our free government, and consequent prosperity."[2]

Lincoln underscored the centrality of Union as the foundational pillar of early nineteenth-century American life. Union evoked pledges of national ac-

America Guided by Wisdom: An Allegorical Representation
of the United States Depicting Their Independence and Prosperity, *1815*,
by John J. Barralett and engraved by Benjamin Tanner, depicts symbolic aspects
of nineteenth-century American exceptionalism. Under the watchful eye of
George Washington, the young republic is blessed by the confident rays of Divine
Providence, the future is boundless and bountiful, and the nation is secure from the
contaminations of the world. Gender assumes a critical role in the formation of the
republic: men are seen expanding the nation while women provide virtue at home.
(Library of Congress)

cord, embodied a special test of popular government, and aroused egalitarian appeals. According to the Anglo-American citizenry, the Union stood apart from a global order of monarchies, aristocracies, and oligarchies in which noble patricians ruled with subjective fiat. As a free people who claimed the rational capacity to self-government, white Americans defended a constitutional Union that guaranteed their civil liberties, political equality, and economic opportunity as the essential national purpose. In an elegant analogy, Lincoln explored how these *"principle[s]"* of nationhood have "proved an 'apple of gold' to us. The *Union*, and the *Constitution*"—indeed, the physical nation and the rule of law—"are the *picture* of *silver*" that encase, boast, and enhance the apple of liberty displayed in the Declaration of Independence. "The picture was made, not to *conceal*, or *destroy* the apple; but to *adorn*, and *preserve* it. The *picture* was made *for* the apple—*not* the apple for the picture."

In Lincoln's reading of national life, the Constitution, as the governing charter of Union, limited the government from encroaching on or redefining the Declaration's natural right to liberty. The national purpose was thus open for all to gaze at, to imagine, to claim as their own. Americans possessed a universal charge to conserve the picture and reinforce the frame so that the apple would live forever.[3]

The Union's unique national purpose nevertheless yielded an inconsistent application of its ideals. Though the United States was premised on the notion that no human should bow to domineering tyrants, not all Americans ate equally from the Union's apple of liberty. Some had been forever deprived of its sustenance altogether. Mid-nineteenth-century America boasted the greatest white popular democracy anywhere in the world. But the very attributes that sustained that republic—the rule of law, a vast and seemingly uncluttered continent, and even notions of liberty and civilization—displaced sovereign Indigenous nations, marginalized free people of color, created the world's largest slaveholding empire, and excluded women from representative democracy. For instance, slaveholders ordered their liberty by asserting a natural and lawful right to owning human property even as enslaved people claimed that the same rights of nature sanctioned their emancipation. Indeed, the very timeless and universal attributes that underwrote the national purpose privileged free white citizens foremost. Marginalized groups thus levied powerful critiques against the soaring rhetoric of white liberty to contest the Union's shortcomings and to demand that the republic polish its sacred apple as the universal fruit for all of humanity.

Even those segregated or enslaved within the nation looked to the Union as their foremost tool for liberation. As Lincoln explained, because the Union was as much an enduring ideal as it was a nation, the republic invited unlimited claims for inclusion and equal protection, even if white Americans routinely rejected those petitions. Nineteenth-century women and African Americans voiced what Lincoln called the "most happy, and fortunate" principles articulated in the Declaration of Independence to dispute their second-class positions in the republic. In practicing an informal but dynamic politics, they challenged the idea that "American" denoted only elite, free, white men. John Adams anticipated as early as 1776 how the powerful concept of Union would forever inspire such quests for liberty and equality. "We have been told that our Struggle has loosened the bands of Government every where. That Children and Apprentices were disobedient—that schools and Colledges were grown turbulent—that Indians slighted their Guardians and Negroes grew insolent to their Masters," the conservative and no doubt apprehensive Adams outlined on the eve of declaring independence. As Lincoln later believed, the republic's founders had not conducted a typical exercise in nation-state formation. They had unleashed a universal revolution in human affairs. "There will be no End of it," Adams predicted. "New Claims will arise. Women will demand a Vote. Lads from 12 to 21 will think their Rights not enough attended to, and every Man, who has not a Farthing, will demand an equal Voice with any other in all Acts of State. It tends to confound and destroy all Distinctions, and prostrate all Ranks, to one common Levell."[4]

The contemporary sense that the Union enjoyed a special international mission was punctuated by the failure of democracy throughout the nineteenth-century world. Across the Atlantic rim, common people demanded liberation from oppressive regimes only to be met with violent, state-sponsored repression. The collapse of democracy in Europe and Latin America fostered an acute domestic impression that only the United States promoted the kind of popular government that humans had long sought, but failed, to procure. Though republics dated to antiquity and dotted the nineteenth-century globe, Americans regarded their Union as the world's foremost beacon of freedom. Although the promise of universal liberty coexisted in a democratic nation that limited access to that liberty, oppressed Americans also believed that few places on earth held the *ideal* of liberty like the United States.

Discourses of Union

For white nineteenth-century Americans, the idea of Union informed a national purpose distinct from all other human societies. The republic supplanted "a corrupt Old World monarchy with a pure New World republic," fastening the principles of "liberty and equality" to the nation's bedrock. "The whole of Europe was originally divided into small warlike clans, and the combination of these clans form its present great divisions," *Niles' Weekly Register*, a foremost voice of American civilization, explained of European tribalism. Conversely, "the fruits of union"—consent, liberty, reason, and egalitarianism—were "the origin of the American republic." In changing their form of government through revolution, early Americans transformed the functioning assumptions of society. Discarding what John Quincy Adams called "a race of kings, whose title to sovereignty had originally been founded on conquest," republicanism replaced monarchism, egalitarianism replaced hierarchy, sovereignty replaced dependence. "Our political revolution of '76," noted Abraham Lincoln in 1842, "has given us a degree of political freedom, far exceeding that of any other of the nations of the earth. In it the world has found a solution of that long mooted problem, as to the capability of man to govern himself." A decade later, the *New York Daily Tribune* echoed a widespread conviction "that American nationality ... is a thing of ideas solely, and not a thing of races. It is neither English nor Irish, nor Dutch, nor French.... Our nationality is our self-government, our system of popular liberty and equal law.... Aside from the identity of our national principles we have no national identity, nor shall we for centuries."[5]

On his grand tour of the United States in 1831, the young French aristocrat Alexis de Tocqueville explored these many claims of American uniqueness. In a celebrated but often misappropriated passage Tocqueville declared, "The situation of the Americans is therefore entirely exceptional, and it is to be believed that no [other] democratic people will ever be placed in it." He did not concede the superiority of the United States more than he acknowledged the oddities of the American character. Isolated by a "proximity from Europe," Americans exhibited a fierce "social egalitarianism" underwritten at once by "meritocratic tendencies" and a hatred of centralized authority. Tocqueville observed that Americans peopled a nation unlike any other in the world, unbound from a feudal past, absolved from noble ruling classes, and uncorrupted by an established state church. The citizenry's social standing and economic destiny depended not on the static happenstance of birth but instead on "purely material things. Their passions, needs, education, circumstances—all in fact seem to cooperate in making the inhabitant of the United States incline toward the earth." Americans did not have time for "science, literature, and the arts"; they paraded "uniquely commercial habits" in the quest for mobile independence. "The free institutions that the inhabitants of the United States possess and the political rights of which they make so much use recall to each citizen constantly . . . that he lives in society," Tocqueville concluded.[6]

Tocqueville regarded the Union as a unique experiment in democratic republicanism. Republics organized free citizens along a consensus of political and social equality, safeguarding individual liberty from government coercion and economic immobility. "I am *affectionately* attached to the Republican theory," testified Alexander Hamilton. "I desire *above all things* to see the *equality* of political rights, exclusive of all *hereditary* distinction, firmly established by a practical demonstration of its being consistent with the order and happiness of society." Republics drew profound meaning from what they were not: aristocracies, nobilities, and monarchies. The founding generation stripped from the new American republic inherited titles, laws of primogeniture, and landed ranks, marginalizing institutional aristocracies from procuring exploitative, undue privileges from government. Reflecting a widespread sense of what Tocqueville later observed as the "equality of conditions," common citizens were not born into fixed or predetermined stations. A republican citizenry could chart lives of mobility in their pursuit of personal independence. "In North America there were no 'feudal' structures that had to be smashed," fostering a civic consciousness deeply suspicious of concentrated power and divine license. "Republics are created by the virtue, public spirit, and intelligence of the citizens," remarked Supreme Court Justice Joseph Story in 1840. "They fall, when the wise are banished from the public councils, because they dare to be honest, and the profligate are rewarded, because they flatter the people, in order to betray them."[7]

As Story well understood, republics since antiquity typically surrendered the civic virtue necessary to sustain an equitable society. Foreign powers did not have to invade and conquer a republic; republicans possessed their own capacity for self-destructive faction. Early Americans nevertheless exuded a boastful confidence that their Union transcended the immoveable, inevitable, decaying tides of history. "We have it in our power to begin the world over again," announced Thomas Paine on the eve of American independence. The United States offered an unprecedented "asylum for mankind," a refuge against a "world [which] is overrun with oppression." *This* new republic ostensibly broke from the traditions and assumptions of the Old World, challenging the interminable idea that some were born to rule and others were born to be ruled. In America, so went the thought, aristocratic privilege, divine right, class stagnation, and republican decline were *not* humanity's natural and inexorable fates. "Those who would like to imitate us," a Bostonian informed Alexis de Tocqueville, "should remember that there are no precedents for our history." A South Carolina orator voiced a common refrain in 1848 when he reminded his audience how "the American revolution, regarded merely as the division of one country from another[,] was ... an ordinary occurrence among European nations, but considered as establishing the dogma that governments were to be the work of the popular will, it formed an era in the history of the world."[8]

The Union at once closed the long march of human history and inaugurated a new epoch altogether. History taught that republics inevitably deteriorated because they could not withstand "the modern civilization and refinement Europe called progress." Proponents of the American republic upheld theirs as the product of human reason and agency, designed to *embrace* and *direct* modern progress. Herman Melville expressed this boundless optimism when he averred in 1850, "The past is dead, and has no resurrection; but the Future is endowed with such a life, that it lives to us even in anticipation. The past is, in many things, the foe of mankind; the Future is, in all things, our friend." Though the world had seemingly failed to secure universal natural rights did not mean that American posterity would suffer similar misfortunes. "We Americans are driven to a rejection of the maxims of the Past," concluded Melville, "seeing that, ere long, the van of nations must, of right, belong to ourselves." Absolution from the rigid forces of national tradition and divine-right governance permitted Americans to chart a new birth of global freedom. "We are so young a people that we feel the want of nationality, and delight in whatever asserts our national 'American' existence," prominent diarist George Templeton Strong acknowledged in 1854. "We have no, like England and France, centuries of achievements and calamities to look back on; we have no *record* of Americanism."[9]

Americans therefore welcomed a mission to model their Union for the world. "Trusted with the destinies of this solitary republic," explained Thomas Jefferson in 1809, the Union would illustrate the ideal of self-government "to be lighted up in other regions, of the earth." Only a rational and liberated people, observed Alexander Hamilton in the first entry of *The Federalist*, could "decide the important question, whether societies of men are really capable or not of establishing good government from reflection and choice, or whether they are forever destined to depend for their political constitutions on accident and force." If Americans extinguished what George Washington termed "the sacred fire of liberty," the inescapable rot of history would suffocate the republic. "Our beloved country is set up by Providence, as a great exemplar to the world, from which the most enlightened and best governed of the ancient nations have much to learn," believed Boston orator Edward Everett. When he announced in 1835 that "our country is eminently characterized as the depository of liberty," Kentucky Presbyterian minister John Breckinridge likewise believed that governments the world over had rejected representative self-government. "What do the rights of man mean, at Vienna, or St. Petersburg? What does sovereign mean in America? What does good government mean at Madrid? What does freedom, or liberty of the press, or Christianity mean at Rome at this day? Our freedom is our peculiarity, as it is our glory; our institutions make our country."[10]

Presenting an exceptional republic to the world informed a vibrant civil religion that gave spiritual meaning to Union. A cultural synthesis of "evangelical Protestant religion, republican political ideology, and commonsense moral reasoning" provided an "ethical framework, a moral compass, and a vocabulary of suasion for much of the nation's public life." Baptist preacher Richard Furman thus urged his congregation in 1802 to "look forward, with pleasing hopes, to a day when America will be the praise of the whole earth; and shall participate, largely, in the fulfillment of those sacred prophecies which have foretold the glory of Messiah's kingdom." Recognizing that human depravity inevitably morphed into tyranny, a synthetic civil religion stoked a fiery faith that God predestined Americans to convert the world through their democratic example. Humans could hardly create something as sacrosanct as liberty. But a chosen people could *shelter* liberty within the confines of an elected nation. "We Americans are the peculiar, chosen people—the Israel of our time; we bear the ark of the liberties of the world," Melville explained. "God has given to us, a future inheritance, the broad domains of the political pagans." Americans invited their own eternal destruction if the sanctified errand in republican governance strayed from God's plan for civilization. "I do not know if all Americans have faith in their religion," Tocqueville confessed, "but I am sure that they believe it necessary to the maintenance of republican institutions." Such a widespread conviction "does not belong only to one class of citizens or to one party, but to the entire nation; one finds it in all ranks."[11]

Faith in the republic's providential calling fostered widespread fears of disunion. The United States provided to its citizens immense political, economic, and spiritual bounties. "The importance of [these] benefit[s] is easy to be understood, by considering the sure and tremendous miseries which would follow disunion," the inevitable feature of a "bloody and mournful ... human history," observed Unitarian minister William Ellery Channing. If Americans succumbed to internal discord, if quarrelsome parties consolidated and plotted their own power, the United States would emerge as a nation among fallen nations. Visions of the Union's collapse held Americans hostage to the global if not eternal consequences of national balkanization. Hamilton warned that disunion signaled "a state of perpetual vibration between the extremes of tyranny and anarchy," measured against its antonyms outlined in the federal Constitution: justice, domestic tranquility, the common defense, the general welfare, and the blessings of liberty. Disunion erased the organizing principles of the republic, terminating its exception to global tyranny. "Prophecies of disunion," explains a leading scholar on the subject, "were meant to alert the people that they had betrayed the promise that they would erect a shining 'City on a Hill' as a moral beacon for the world, and had betrayed the constitutional covenant on which the security of the nation rested." [12]

The citizenry believed that disunion entailed a principal cause: irreconcilable factions radicalized by antirepublican internationalism. By their very nature, explained James Madison, factions defied the moderation of national consensus, rooted in "instability, injustice, and confusion ... the mortal diseases under which popular governments have everywhere perished." A republic spread over a vast continent, organized by diverse communities, and surrounded by Old World colonial influences lent itself to schisms. George Washington thus cautioned in his 1796 farewell address against "designing men [who] may endeavor to excite a belief that there is a real difference of local interests and views" superior to the consensus of Union. European nobles who hungered for control of North America were incentivized to sew discord among the American public, exploiting regional interests for their hemispheric agendas. "Dangerous ambition more often lurks behind the specious mask of zeal for the rights of the people," Hamilton warned. "History will teach us that the former has been found a much more certain road to the introduction of despotism ... overturn[ing] the liberties of republics." If Americans welcomed internationalized factions into the republic, disunion would materialize either from one cabal seeking to consolidate existing power or from oppressed parties seeking refuge from foreign coercion. In either event, disunion portended the endless, fractious wars of Europe severing a once-united North American republic.[13]

The specter of disunion foreshadowed civil war. Few images characterized Old World barbarism more than the rupture of nations "into a group of independent military powers, wasted by eternal border wars, feeding the ambition of petty sovereigns on the lifeblood of wasted principalities," averred famed orator Edward Everett. For statesman Daniel Webster, the anarchical threat of civil war anticipated "the broken and dishonored fragments of a once glorious Union; on States dissevered, discordant, belligerent; on a land rent with civil feuds, or drenched ... in fraternal blood." Republics rarely survived what Hamilton labeled the "desultory and predatory" ruin of civil conflicts that descended into "plunder and devastation," stripping morality, virtue, and restraint from its combatants. Limitless in conduct and revolutionary in implication, civil wars supplanted a republican government with a despotic military tyrant whose violent and coercive reign consolidated warring factions. And Americans little doubted that monarchical powers would intervene in a continental civil war to facilitate the Union's violent balkanization, Europeanizing the smoldering regions into repressive colonial outposts. Pennsylvania senator George M. Dallas thus declared in the 1830s that any faction that provoked disunion condemned American posterity to eternal damnation, "recklessly involv[ing] the American people in the horrors, uncertainties, and fatal consequences of civil war," a trial from which it would be impossible "to rebuild the edifice of our great, and glorious" Union.[14]

The radical bloodlust of the French Revolution organized American concerns of disunion, civil war, social violence, and the overall health of the republican Union. When French revolutionaries overturned their monarchy in 1789, Americans celebrated what they considered the global flowering of their own revolution. Liberty had traveled across the Atlantic to plant a republican future on the European continent. But French antimonarchism soon rejected republican moderation, embracing a radical democratic egalitarianism that devolved into anarchical mob violence and political massacres. Upheavals in France stoked domestic American fears that international revolutions gone awry would poison the Union. The nation's first political parties were especially shaped by the French aura. Federalists and their conservative ideological progeny were deeply skeptical of Jacobin mobs destabilizing domestic civil society, inviting militant despots to seize power and regulate social anarchy. The Republican Party and its egalitarian descendants countered that, although admittedly violent, the French Revolution served an essential antimonarchical crusade. Both positions underscored a collective American conviction that revolutionary violence and bloodshed, followed by coercive counterrevolutionary measures, reflected the Old World's passion for chaos and coercion. "Reigns of terror," either from democratic mobs or imperial monarchs, stunted the progressive march of democratic civilization. Any republic riddled with violence and subverted by absolutism could never order liberty.[15]

The French Revolution inspired the American citizenry to divorce itself from the international order. George Washington encouraged the United States in 1796 to have "as little political connection as possible" with Europe, "engaged in frequent controversies, the causes of which are essentially foreign to our concerns." Why align "our destiny with that of any part of Europe, entangle our peace and prosperity in the toils of European ambition, rivalship, interest, humor or caprice?" Praising what he deemed the United

States' unique place in global history, John Adams answered Washington's inquiries two years later. "Our Country remains untainted with the Principles and manners, which are now producing desolation in so many Parts of the World," he remarked about the terror in France. But Adams offered a clear warning: "Should the people of America, once become capable of that deep ... simulation towards one another and towards foreign nations, which assumes the Language of Justice and moderation while it is practicing Iniquity and Extravagance [and] rioting in rapine and Insolence[,] this Country will be the most miserable Habitation in the World." For the uncommonly pessimistic Adams, the United States could well emulate France, submitting to the inevitable forces of history and human nature. Only a dedicated anti-internationalism, the rule of law, and moral virtue could secure "the local destination assigned Us by Providence." A single bulwark guarded the Union from international decay: "Our Constitution[,] made only for a moral and religious People. It is wholly inadequate to the government of any other."[16]

The French Revolution's radical mobocracy and subsequent military dictatorship under Napoleon Bonaparte underscored prevailing American beliefs that only diffused governing power and restrained constitutionalism could guard against disunion and civil war. As Adams indicated, the U.S. Constitution established rules and boundaries to guard civil society from deteriorating into state-sponsored anarchy or tyranny, despotism or coups. Constitutionalism channeled faction to order liberty across a vast and diverse republic, checking democratic excesses, fostering pluralism, and limiting centralized authority. Americans could never permit a native Cromwell, Hanover, or Robespierre to despoil Providence's blessed continent that grew far from Europe's corrupted shores. A system of stable political moderation, explained the Constitution's author James Madison, "must first enable the government to control the governed; and in the next place oblige it to control itself." The Constitution redistributed governing authority away from divine monarchs to free citizens, codifying the natural rights outlined in the Declaration of Independence. Dispensing power horizontally across jealous and competing branches of government and vertically between federal and state governments limited natural tendencies toward unbridled authority, coercion, and violence. For Americans wary of the Old World's seeming passion for monarchy, aristocracy, and dictatorship, only constitutional republicanism could restrain the ambition, power, and greed necessary to chart a unique global order.[17]

The Constitution fueled what Madison called the "extended republic." Republics throughout history failed, he averred, because their small, self-contained homogeneity spawned incompatible factions competing for unchecked power. In his foundational *Federalist No. 10* Madison envisioned a sprawling and ever-expanding American republic imposing virtue to "reduce the possibility that any faction would become dominant and hence be in a position to oppress the rest." A republic that promoted rather than stifled diverse interests forced political moderation and compromise, "mak[ing] it less probable that a majority of the whole will have a common motive to invade the rights of other citizens." The extended republic would not either collapse into mob rule or succumb to the seductions of populist demagogues. Instead, popular liberty would flourish at the local level, distinguishing the sundry interests that arranged the American landscape. Madison aimed to harness human nature against itself. When any one faction inevitably sought unlimited, universal power, "it will be more difficult for all who feel it to discover their own strength, and to act in unison with each other." A continental republic bonded a diverse people who otherwise possessed few ideological and cultural adhesives. "We differ about forms and modes in politics, but this difference begins to submit to the restraints of moral and social obligation," Philadelphia intellectual Benjamin Rush wrote in 1790 when advertising the advantages of Union to a European correspondent. "Order and tranquility appear to be the natural consequence of a well-balanced republic, for where men can remove the evils of their governments by frequent elections, they will seldom appeal to the less certain remedies of mobs or arms."[18]

By the time of his national tour in the 1830s, Tocqueville observed how Madison's conception of local liberty powered a vibrant but restrained nationalism. "The public spirit of the Union itself is in a way only a summation of provincial patriotism.... In defending the Union, he defends the growing prosperity of his district, his right to direct affairs within it, and the hope of making plans of improvement prevail that will enrich him," recorded the young Frenchman. "The Union is a great republic in extent; but one could in a way liken it to a small republic because the objects with which its government is occupied are few. Its actions are important, but they are rare. As the sovereignty of the Union is hindered and incomplete, the use of that sovereignty is not dangerous for freedom. Neither does it excite those immoderate desires for power and attention that are so fatal to great republics. As everything does not necessarily converge at a common center, neither does one see vast metropolises, or immense wealth, or great misery, or sudden revolutions." Indeed, continental republicanism aimed to moderate and guard the nation against the despotism of disunion and civil war. Madison's vision appeared fully realized when William Henry Seward observed in 1844, "The institutions we enjoy have a tendency to strengthen their own deep foundation in the elements of national character and popular affection. The anxiety to save these institutions from serious danger or overthrow is the predominating motive of every citizen on every occasion of public action. He holds his own share of sovereignty by the same tenure which limits their existence, and he derives that sovereignty from the equality which they secure."[19]

Little in human nature naturally produces compromise between factions. There certainly was nothing inherent in the American character that foretold a consensus of political moderation. But compromise and restraint became self-proclaimed mainstays of American political culture because the white citizenry subscribed to upholding a stable Union that protected their civil liberties. Surrendering to the temptations of absolutism or mob rule would strip *all* liberty from the body politic. Despite the rancorous and often dangerous politics of the 1790s, Washington, Adams, and Jefferson established fundamental traditions of political moderation: elected representatives surrendering power to the will of popular elections, consenting to peaceful transfers of power, and disavowing retributive violence against political opponents. Maintaining a republic for "the admiration and anxiety of the wise and virtuous of all nations," explained John Adams in 1796, demanded "prudence, justice, temperance, and fortitude." When his bitter rival Jefferson succeeded Adams four years later, the new president added, "Every difference of opinion is not a difference of principle," the foremost being the Union itself. Convictions of providential destiny and a sense of national superiority forged a moderate political culture that contemporaries believed would forestall the revolutionary devastation of their republic. "I am among those who are most anxious for the preservation of the Union of the States, and for the success of the Constitutional experiment of which it is the basis," avowed Madison in 1836. "We owe it to ourselves, and to the world, to watch, to cherish, and as far as possible, to perfect a new modification of the powers of Government, which aims at the better security against external danger and internal disorder, a better provision for national strength and individual rights, than had been exemplified under any previous form."[20]

Though the early national republic endured persistent risks of disunion and fringe rebellions against federal authority, moderate political coalitions marginalized hostile factions to the Union. Discontented political minorities typically threatened disunion to secure more equitable positions *within* the republic, recognizing the striking degree to which the citizenry was willing to compromise to preserve the nation. A collective national memory, a common religion, and the powerful bonds of democratic republicanism routinely confronted the specter of disunion. "The great good of the Union," explained William Ellery Channing, "preserves us from wasting and destroying one another. It preserves relations of peace among communities, which if broken into separate nations, would be arrayed against one another in perpetual, merciless, and ruinous war. It indeed contributes to our defense against foreign states, but still more it defends us from one another. This we apprehend to be the chief boon of the Union." Mississippi senator Jefferson Davis, at once an ardent defender of state rights and an overt American nationalist, likewise cherished the "fundamental principles" of Union, which, he declared in 1850, "has illustrated the blessings of liberty. As a nation, it is, though yet in the freshness of youth, among the first Powers of the globe, and casts the shadow of its protection over its citizens, on whatever sea or shore ... they may wander." For Davis, disunion summoned a foolish trek into civil war, anarchy, and despotism.[21]

A moderate constitutional republic produced one of the nineteenth-century world's largest popular democracies. By the early 1830s, the republic had liberalized civic participation and eliminated property-based suffrage requirements for white males. If republicanism taught that sovereign rationality ordered society, then democracy emphasized that only the broadest base of citizens could be trusted with the sacred reins of political power. American heads of state now shared political authority with commoners, challenging European notions that only propertied elites could manage a republic. By 1830 most states boasted an 80 percent participation rate among its voters (all of course white and male); no European nation could claim a comparable achievement. By modern standards the nineteenth-century United States appears terribly undemocratic, depriving citizenship and political equality to African Americans, women, Indigenous peoples, and non-European migrants. But by any objective measure of its time, the United States was among the world's most liberal societies, bestowing nearly universal democratic privileges and equitable economic opportunity on common white men.[22]

American democracy encouraged an antiaristocratic political economy. The Union promoted ordered liberty and advertised upward mobility as critical bulwarks against Old World oppression, privilege, and hierarchy. White Americans heaped scorn upon any institution or faction deemed antagonistic to the republic's common good and individual improvement. "Democratic peoples have a natural taste for freedom," observed Tocqueville. "But for equality they have an ardent, insatiable, eternal invincible passion. . . . They will tolerate poverty, enslavement, barbarism, but they will not tolerate aristocracy." If a virtuous people rallied behind a demagogue who promised that only he could deliver earthly riches, the republic would fast transform into an aristocratic oligarchy in which government stripped collective liberty to dispense special largesse to the ruling class's favored constituents. Once-free citizens would then labor for the pleasure of noble elites who centralized state power to concentrate their personal wealth. Elected representatives had to protect the citizenry's right to claim the fruit of their labor. Tocqueville's "equality of conditions" spoke to citizens' equitable access to the market and the impartial legal protections to acquire property. According to one prominent scholar, the theory of free labor held that "when all laborers in a society received the full fruits of their labors, then the wealth distribution was a just and natural distribution. The nations of the world exhibited not equitable distributions of wealth but enormously lopsided ones." Indeed, a democratic republic guarded against the "maldistribution of wealth" endemic to European class stagnation, poverty, dependence, and servitude.[23]

The white citizenry demanded that government not impede the pursuit of individual autonomy, a prospect that "mitigated class consciousness and conflict in the United States." The Scottish Enlightenment philosopher Adam Smith averred in his influential *Wealth of Nations* (1776) that a republic possessed "only three duties" necessary to ensure economic liberty: preventing the devastations of invasion or war; "protecting, as far as possible, every member of the society from the injustice of oppression"; and "erecting and maintaining certain public works and certain public institutions" to encourage the acquisition and proliferation of property. Though a market economy created an unequal distribution of wealth, white citizens opposed government dispensing arbitrary social or economic privileges to favored constituents. In 1844, Ralph Waldo Emerson considered the "new and anti-feudal power of Commerce the political fact of most significance to the American." Nineteenth-century capitalism complemented the era of political democratization, feeding the citizenry's obsession with upward mobility and personal independence. Despite the very real anxieties and uncertain fluctuations wrought by capitalism, Americans engaged with the market economy to produce goods and services to meet local, national, and international demands. The early republic did not entirely endure the jarring arrival of a "market revolution" that disrupted a tranquil, premodern subsistence culture. Market economies had existed long before American independence, tying mercantile colonies to European metropoles. What occurred during the early nineteenth century was little more than the expansion and consolidation of prevailing markets, ones now fueled by democratic republicanism rather than colonial dependence.[24]

The two-party system promoted an antiaristocratic political culture. By the late 1820s, both the Democratic and Whig Parties worked within Madison's idea of the extended republic to marginalize zealous revolutionaries and forge moderate political coalitions. The parties could not speak only on behalf of political favorites or regional factions. They had to appeal instead to the broadest and shared national ideal. In this way, "both party axes wished to avoid legislative favoritism to individuals and establishment of monopolies; all parties operated within the boundaries set by the American concept of the distribution of wealth." Democrats and Whigs maintained electoral legitimacy by boasting themselves the guardians of—and casting their opponents as the adversaries of—economic independence, upward mobility, and individual liberty. The rancor of American democracy thus acted as a check on itself. Neither party could appear as a domestic host to rapacious internationalists who salivated to hijack the Union. "So long as the two powerful national parties flourished, they served to buffer conflicting interests and ideologies," writes an authoritative political historian, "and also helped to eliminate extremists and ideologues."[25]

Members of the Democratic Party, the descendants of Thomas Jefferson's egalitarian republicanism, vowed to protect common white citizens against unaccountable institutions and privileged elites. The party looked askance at powerful economic establishments that promoted an artificial, unaccountable, monied aristocracy. Advancing a populist message of white equal opportunity, Democrats advocated a level economic arena to mitigate extremes of wealth and poverty. As the party's principal messenger throughout the 1820s and 1830s, Andrew Jackson lambasted "monopoly and all exclusive privileges ... granted at the expense of the public." Jackson especially loathed the Bank of the United States, which he condemned as a symbol of aristocratic internationalism. "It is to be regretted that the rich and powerful too often bend the acts of government to their selfish purposes" in the vein of European oligarchs, he declared in his 1832 presidential veto of the bank's recharter bill. "Equality of talents, of education, or of wealth can not be produced by human institutions," but instead must be *protected* by government to permit individuals the unfettered ability to rise as equal citizens regardless of station or ability. The Union's "true strength consists in leaving individuals and States as much as possible to themselves," Jackson concluded, "in making itself felt, not in its power, but in its beneficence; not in its control, but in its protection."[26]

Whigs countered that individual liberty *depended* on active government intervention to forestall the rise of an American aristocracy or oligarchy created by demagogic politicians. If the federal government promoted a national economy, conditions would be ripe for any individual's moral and economic improvement. The Whig economic theory turned on what Kentucky senator Henry Clay labeled the "American System." A combination of the Bank of the United States, federal tariffs, and internal improvements guarded the American economy from dependence on the rest of the world. "We must naturalize the arts in our country; and we must naturalize them by the only means which the wisdom of nations has yet discovered to be effectual; by adequate protection, against the otherwise overwhelming influence of foreigners," Clay announced in 1824. The American System created a national market in which domestic merchants, farmers, manufacturers, and laborers could compete on the world stage. Though a national economy transcended localism, citizens could unleash their commercial energies to secure individual independence on a continental infrastructure nurtured by government. Only then could the Union withstand the pervasive economic "disorders and violence" of Europe. "The best security against the demoralization of society," Clay concluded, "is the constant and profitable employment of its members. The greatest danger to public liberty is from idleness and vice."[27]

Merchants, shopkeepers, clerks, and farmers populated a prosperous white American middle class. A favorable political culture, the rule of law, capitalist innovation, the virtue of private property, and effective combinations of free trade and protectionism gave "the United States the world's highest standard of living and the second-highest industrial output," surpassed only by Great Britain. Compared to Europeans, Americans enjoyed higher birth rates and lower death rates, facilitated in part by waves of immigration and territorial expansion. An upwardly mobile society likewise depended on public education to maintain the republican experiment. American education endorsed industry, independence, and virtue, essential attributes for sustaining a vibrant and stable republic. Even "a moderate education," averred a young Abraham Lincoln in 1832, permitted citizens "to read the histories of [their] own and other countries, by which [they] may duly appreciate the value of our free institutions." Notable educational reformer Horace Mann later explained Lincoln's rationale: "If we do not prepare children to become good citizens — if we do not develop their capacities, . . . enrich their minds with knowledge, imbue their hearts with love of truth and duty, and a reverence for all things sacred and holy, then our republic must go down to destruction, . . . and mankind must sweep through another vast cycle of sin and suffering, before the dawn of a better era can arise upon the world." Exceeded only by Sweden and Denmark, the United States in 1850 boasted an 89 percent literacy rate among free white citizens, thanks to a national mail service and a highly democratized proliferation of newspapers, pamphlets, and libraries.[28]

Upward mobility, self-sufficiency, and moral and material improvement would be impossible, so the thought went, without unfettered access to territorial abundance. White citizens thus regarded North America as the wellspring of nineteenth-century democratic liberty. Imagined as a vast, endless space freed from despotic coercion, unburdened from cultural decay, and untainted by feudal decadence, the continent resonated as a refuge for free white people. Jefferson considered North America an egalitarian "empire for liberty," unfolding "a rising nation, spread over a wide and fruitful land, traversing all the seas with the rich productions of their industry." Marching as "pioneers of the advance of civilisation," Anglo-Americans were called to republicanize the continent, radiating their liberty to the world. Only an unspoiled and seemingly uninhabited land could eliminate colonial oppression and sustain a vast republic to stand as "a vast and splendid monument, not of oppression and terror, but of Wisdom, of Peace, and of Liberty, upon which the world may gaze for ever," added Massachusetts statesman Daniel Webster. "We live in what may be called the early age of this great continent," Webster deduced. "The *principle* of free government adheres to the American soil. It is bedded in it, immovable in its mountains." The republic would never decline and fall to self-interested factions because the republic *was* the continent, each an unsullied tapestry on which its citizens could chart a consensual, unobstructed future.[29]

White Americans embraced a "manifest destiny to overspread the continent allotted by Providence for the free development of our yearly multiplying millions," John O'Sullivan, editor of the popular *Democratic Review*, remarked in 1845. "No country has been so much favored, or should acknowledge with deeper reverence the manifestations of the divine protection," pronounced Democratic president James K. Polk, whose election in 1844 embodied the expansionist ethos. "An all-wise Creator directed and guarded us in our infant struggle for freedom and has constantly watched over our surprising progress," the sanguine executive observed, "until we have become one of the great nations of the earth." Polk's secretary of the treasury, Robert J. Walker, confirmed "that a higher than earthly power still guards and directs our destiny, impels us onward, and has selected our great and happy country as a model and ultimate centre of attraction for all the nations of the world." Whigs agreed that the United States had secured its place within the global community. "The whole Continent of North-America appears to be destined by Divine Providence to be peopled by one *Nation*—speaking one language— professing one general System of religious and political principles and accustomed to one general tenor of social usages and customs," declared John Quincy Adams. "The land is the appointed remedy for whatever is false and fantastic in our culture. The great continent we inhabit is to be physic and food for our mind," opined Ralph Waldo Emerson in 1844. "The bountiful continent is ours, state on state, and territory on territory, to the waves of the Pacific sea."[30]

Few nations during the nineteenth century expanded as rapidly across a continent as the United States, which surpassed similar settler movements in South Africa, Australia, and Alaska. "There are two great peoples on earth today," Tocqueville believed; "these are the Russians and the Anglo-Americans. ... All other peoples appear to have nearly reached almost the limits that nature has drawn and to have nothing more to do than preserve themselves." Only the United States and Russia "march ahead at an easy and rapid pace on a course whose bounds the eye cannot yet perceive." Between 1820 and 1860, the American population quadrupled in size, with between 80 to 90 percent living in rural areas. The ability to claim cheap, rich, and abundant land fueled Madison's extended republic and Jefferson's "empire for liberty." The American West diffused a rapidly expanding population and advertised white mobility and independence. "The faculties of a citizen of the United States operate on a scale of which the common people of Europe, crimped and cribbed as they are in one unvaried circle of monotonous, unrewarded labor, can form no conception whatever," opined a popular essay in the *United States Review*, among the foremost champions of Manifest Destiny. The "cheapness of land, the vast space for expansion," reported the article's main character, Brother Jonathan, "is the key to that irresistible progress which has alarmed the statesmen of Europe, astonished the world, and paved the way to that rapid, almost incomprehensible ascent towards the summit of national dignity and power."[31]

Continental expansion powered violent and contested ideas about national inclusion. Few people endured the devastations of Manifest Destiny more than sovereign Indigenous nations. If the Union ensured the ostensible progress of civilization, bolstered by the rule of law, civil liberties, private property, free-market capitalism, and popular democratic consent, an abundance of white Americans regarded Native people as barbaric impediments to a dynamic and progressive Anglo republic. Myriad white citizens believed that communal land use, aversions to technological and industrial innovation, ignorance of law, and unfamiliarity with individual autonomy had apparently stagnated Natives against modernization. According to diplomat John Lothrop Motley, North America had languished under centuries of Indigenous primitivity. "It was but yesterday ... that the Mohawk and the Mohican were tomahawking and scalping each other." But with the proliferation of Anglo democratic institutions, "to-day, grandeur, luxury, wealth, power" blanketed the continent. Civilization "imports a mysterious progress," explained Ralph Waldo Emerson, "and in mankind, the savage tribes do not advance. The Indians of this country have not learned the white man's work." In the Anglo mind, Natives occupied stateless and apathic positions on an otherwise thriving and progressive American landscape. Nothing could halt what feminist and Minnesota settler Jane Grey Swisshelm called "the westward march of civilization," the inevitable progress of white democracy and ordered liberty.[32]

A sovereign Anglo republic depended on dismantling Indigenous nations, which were seemingly antithetical to a civilized Union. "What good man would prefer a country covered with forests and ranged by a few thousand savages to our extensive Republic, studded with cities, towns, and prosperous farms embellished with all the improvements which art can devise or industry execute," asked President Andrew Jackson, who endorsed the detribalization of Native sovereignties in 1830. If Indians remained "unwilling to submit to the laws of the States and mingle with their population," they would be transported to reservations and supervised by republican missionaries. There they would be cleansed of "apathy, barbarism, and heathenism," explained an Indian affairs agent in 1848, prepared for new lives of "energy, civilization, and christianity." Between 1831 and 1841, federal forces removed tens of thousands of Cherokee, Choctaw, Chickasaw, Seminole, and Creek Natives to reservations in present-day Oklahoma, opening the American Southeast to independent and voracious white settlers. Scores of whites rationalized the removal of Native peoples as part of the unavoidable Americanization of the continent. "The Americans are a homogenous people" who "swell in one great and unbroken flood," William H. Seward explained in 1844 of the racialized dimensions of American nationalism. "Without speculating on the ultimate destiny of ... those unfortunate classes [of Indians], we may assume that the feeble resistance they offer to the aggrandizement of the Caucasian family is becoming less and less continually, and will finally altogether disappear." Jackson likewise resolved that history had never prepared Native Americans to incorporate into the United States, a white republic destined to improve the continent amid a stagnant world. "Is it supposed," he concluded, "that the wandering savage has a stronger attachment to his home than the settled, civilized Christian?"[33]

Native removals underscored prevailing Anglo beliefs that Indigenous people could never fully assimilate as civilized participants of American democracy and free-labor capitalism. Cherokee Elias Boudinot protested this gross reality of nineteenth-century American life. He proclaimed, "The Cherokees have advanced so far and so rapidly in civilization," even to the point of "forsak[ing] their ancient employment." Indigenous people did not suffer from the inability to "civilize," though Boudinot regarded the very premise as an unjust Anglo demand. The "powerful obstacles" of white "prejudices" imposed impossible demands upon Native peoples. It mattered little that the Cherokee had adopted American public education, spoke English, and exercised local democracy. And it was immaterial, according to Boudinot, that the Cherokee desired a multiethnic Union of "one continuous abode of enlightened, free, and happy people." Only "two alternatives" confronted Native sovereignties: "They must either become civilized and happy," defined by the unachievable standards of white Americans, "or[,] sharing in the fate of many kindred nations, become extinct." Wannuaucon Quinney, a Mohican displaced to Wisconsin, explained the predictable implications. He pondered how he could ever commemorate the Fourth of July, the celebratory day for "a people, who occupy by conquest, or have usurped the possession of the territories of my fathers, and have laid and carefully preserved, a train of terrible miseries, to end when my race shall have ceased to exist."[34]

Boudinot and Wannuaucon censured Anglo-Americans for reserving the Union only for those whom whites defined as civilized, enlightened, restrained. At once consistent with and contradictory to its self-appointed mission, the Union ostracized forces of racial internationalization hostile to white democracy. German émigré and American law professor Francis Lieber averred in 1853 that republicanism was exclusively an Anglo-American trait. Even the most downtrodden white citizen could experience the promise of equal sovereignty and formal political participation within the federal Union. "Thousands of men without property who have quite as great a stake in the public welfare as those who may possess a house or enjoy a certain amount of revenue" sustained a white democracy that in turn protected their natural rights. "We have only to repeat that an extensive basis of representation is doubtless a characteristic of Anglo liberty," Lieber concluded. Though a republic of and by the people, the Union limited the self-evident proposition of human equality as a fundamental national principle. Native Americans joined African Americans, Mexicans, Chinese, and even Mormons—adherents of a uniquely American faith condemned by evangelical Protestants as a false and barbaric religion—as unwelcome groups relegated to the margins of national life.[35]

If the removal of Native Americans contradicted the United States' founding principles, the vast presence of black slavery in a land of white liberty imposed the greatest strain on the discourse of Union. The institution of slavery assumed a powerful role in shaping and contesting the Union's place in the nineteenth-century world. No other institution presented greater conflicts within the national consensus. Though eventually localized to the American South in the wake of the Revolution, slavery was very much a national and even global institution, connecting disparate regions of the republic to the world. Slavery depended on and influenced nearly every contemporary claim of American civilization, from declarations of human equality to the protections of constitutional liberty, from democratic republicanism to national expansion, from continental hegemony to hemispheric authority. In modern New World slave societies, particularly Brazil, Cuba, and the United States, slavery did not operate on the incidental margins of contemporary life. Within the Union's slaveholding states, the institution was a key determinant of political power, market economics, racial hierarchy, and cultural evolution. Global proponents regarded slaveholding as a rational and efficient means of organizing labor and securing white independence. The institution ultimately assured the progress of nations by regulating the boundaries between civilization and so-called racial barbarism.[36]

American slavery both mirrored and stood apart from its New World counterparts. Like any market system, the institution produced agricultural commodities—specifically, large-scale cash crops—to meet insatiable global demands. And hemispheric slavery depended on strict legal codes to sustain dynamic economic growth and global trade. Regional, national, and international laws sanctioned the right of slaveholding while greatly suspending the mobility of the enslaved. Among the key attributes of a slave society, slaveholders enjoyed nearly universal control of and access to bondpeople's lives. A vast impermeable gulf segregated the disparate worlds of freedom and slavery, public concepts defined entirely by white ruling classes. Race assumed *the* central role in distinguishing New World slavery, an institution "exclusively identified with people of African descent." Between the early sixteenth century and 1808, forced migrations shuttled millions of kidnapped Africans from their ancestral continent to burgeoning European colonies in the Caribbean, Brazil, and North America. Though slavery dated to antiquity, its New World iteration thrived on racial subornation. Enslavers exercised toxic notions of racial science, civilization, and barbarism to justify holding Africans in life-long captivity to labor-hungry Europeans and Anglo-Americans. By the dawn of the nineteenth century, slavery had eclipsed transnational boundaries to become a truly hemispheric organization of diverse but antagonistic races.[37]

The proliferation of New World slavery depended on the institution's active mobility. Slaveholders in the United States joined their hemispheric peers in moving and inflating the institution across vast spaces. Jefferson's idealistic vision of an independent white western "empire for liberty" also permitted slaveholders to populate the Mississippi and Red River valleys with vast cotton and sugar plantations manned by armies of enslaved people. "The political economy of slavery and the territorial limit of the United States ran along the same line," explains a prominent scholar. Federal policies, government agents, rapacious speculators, and voracious citizens displaced Native peoples and European competitors, redistributing the institution from the Atlantic seaboard into the heart of the continent. At the same moment in which early nineteenth-century American expansionists displaced Indigenous nations, imperial slaveholders extended the institution throughout the interiors of Jamaica, Brazil, Cuba, parts of the British West Indies, and the American South. The rapid mobility of hemispheric bondage thus remained contingent on sympathetic governments and modern economic productivity. Slavery could never stall or stagnate, lest it might wither and die upon exhausted soils. From the cotton gin in the United States to industrial sugar mills in Cuba, technological innovation and entrepreneurship enhanced agricultural output, thereby enhancing the institution's efficiency and profitability. But it was the evil conceit of slavery itself that permitted swift mobility: the inflexible authority of one individual to own another's labor and body, all sanctioned by powerful, approving governments. Indeed, "the assignment of workers to tasks and geographic settings they would not voluntarily have chosen ... was enduring and explains why slavery was crucial to the rise of the Atlantic economy."[38]

While the United States reflected the mobile dynamism of hemispheric slavery, factors derived from the concept of Union distinguished slaveholding in the American republic. The sanctity of private property and the rule of the law were essential to slavery's national consolidation. In *Federalist No. 10*, James Madison regarded the protection of individual property as "the first object of government." The acquisition and proliferation of property fueled personal sovereignty, which in turn fueled individual virtue. Though a slaveholder himself, Madison considered enslaved people as innately human, "regarded by the law as a member of the society" and thus "a moral person," he continued in *Federalist No. 54*. But the law also affixed enslaved people with a dual persona "when it views them in the mixed character of persons *and* property." Since state laws defined and sanctioned slavery, and the Constitution upheld the right of citizens to obtain property, generate capital, and reclaim fugitive slaves, slaveholders defined bondpeople according to the chattel principle. As the nation's porous borders expanded across the continent, slaveholders regarded the legal movement of human property as their essential, natural, and legal privilege.[39]

The constitutional protection of American slavery facilitated the institution's domestic growth. Between the sixteenth and nineteenth centuries, more than 16 million African captives arrived in the New World; nearly 70 percent landed in Brazil and the Caribbean, while a mere 6 percent arrived in British North America, and subsequently the United States. But by 1860, nearly two-thirds of all unfree laborers in the Western Hemisphere resided in the American South. Although the United States in 1808 joined Great Britain in ceasing formal participation in the international slave trade, the American enslaved population more than doubled between 1800 (894,000) and 1830 (2 million), and then doubled again between 1830 and 1860 (4 million). After 1808, enslaved Americans of African descent were truly homegrown, populating a uniquely domestic but also transnational institution. Unlike the New World's major slave societies in Brazil, Cuba, and Haiti (before independence), "in purely material terms slavery in the South was *less* oppressive," at least in relative terms. Better health, relatively favorable climates, and comparatively mild labor conditions fostered longer life spans, higher birth rates, and lower death rates in the United States. An equal sex ratio—men far outnumbered women in most hemispheric slave colonies—ensured the natural self-reproduction of American slavery. And the geographic ability to expand and diffuse the institution, a process guaranteed by federal policy, protected by the rule of law, and governed by the demand for unfree labor, meant that slavery would take root across vast continental spaces.[40]

The conditions of American slavery made the institution powerful, profitable, mobile, significant to national development, and unlikely ever to occasion gradual widespread emancipations. Among the most consequential distinctions between American and New World slaveries was the pervasive absenteeism of slaveholding planters in Brazil, Cuba, and Jamaica. Though labor on Caribbean and South American plantations was often deadly, enslaved people there possessed relative autonomy to farm their own plots of land or move about with comparative ease. Absentee planters often resided in Europe and thus did not experience the daily rhythms of slavery and mastery. Conversely, because American slaveholders retained a "resident mentality," identifying the plantation as *the* source of personal independence, hemispheric distinctions between slavery and freedom rarely permeated the American South. American planters lived intimately among their enslaved property; assumed an active role in buying, trading, and selling human commodities; and managed a plantation's productive capacity. Prominent slaveholder James Henry Hammond called his South Carolina plantation his "little kingdom," in which only he exerted "despotic sway." Slaveholding assured Hammond's personal sovereignty in a white democracy; liberty and mastery thus fused to erect an impenetrable barrier between white and black. "The planters here are essentially what the nobility are in other countries," profiting from the stable "independence" guaranteed by an endless supply of bound, unfree, and immobile labor.[41]

The personal power of mastery underwrote an insidiously unique feature of American slavery: the internal slave trade. At once a booming commercial enterprise and the avenue by which to expand the burgeoning institution, the domestic American slave trade was "one of the largest forced migrations in world history, [as] more than a half-million African-American men, women, and children were transported from the Upper South to the Lower South." Reliant on the rule of law, the space in which to move, and the comparative stability, health, and growth of the enslaved population, the trade in human commodities wove the institution into the national fabric. Slavery's geographic diffusion closed most routes to enslaved resistance, reminding those in bondage that their earthly fate was to labor for the glory of white planters. Families were routinely separated and distributed across the vast continent, while federal laws—particularly the Fugitive Slave Law of 1850—thwarted encroachments against human trafficking. Though most northern states authorized emancipation in the wake of the American Revolution, in part to uphold the republic's founding principles and also because enslaved labor was not profitable in nontropical climates, "the extension of slavery into the Mississippi Valley gave an institution that was in decline at the end of the eighteenth century new life in the nineteenth." Meanwhile, by the 1830s and 1840s, convicted by abolitionist critiques, the declining value of agriculture, and mounting unrest among enslaved people, the British, Dutch, and French began abolishing slavery in their New World colonies. At the same moment at which the hemisphere moved toward emancipation, "the Deep South of the United States became the new center of gravity of the [world's] plantation economy": by 1860, six of the ten wealthiest counties per capita in the nation were in southern slaveholding states.[42]

American slavery rapidly evolved into a powerful institution, enshrining the republic among the world's foremost agricultural producers. Like any modern economic system, slavery depended on national and global market economies. The planting, growing, picking, marketing, indemnifying, selling, and shipping of southern agriculture connected New Orleans slave markets, Mississippi plantations, New York merchant houses and insurance brokers, New England woolen manufacturers and shipbuilders, London financiers, and Liverpool textile factories. Slavery fit seamlessly "in a nation that equated growth with progress," uniting diverse sectors of American capitalism and promoting national economic growth. "The question of slavery concerns the peace and safety of our political family," explained prominent South Carolinian Robert Hayne. "With nothing connected with slavery can we consent to treat with other nations." Likewise, "our country is the most favored of lands, in its peculiar fitness for the production of Cotton, Corn, Wheat, Rice, Tobacco, Sugar," added a leading agriculturalist in 1853. "Our Cotton is the most wonderful talisman of the world. By its power we are transmuting into whatever we want. It is adding to the industry, trade and commerce of the world, as nothing else does, or ever did before." By 1860, enslaved American laborers produced three-quarters of the world's most coveted agricultural product:

cotton. In fact, American cotton yields "doubled each decade after 1800," and as early as 1830, "cotton shipments accounted for more than half the value of all exports from the United States." The republic's economic sovereignty and international prestige depended in great measure on harnessing unfree labor to proliferate capital. Slavery was thus an overwhelming engine of national economic life. Enslaved people in 1860 constituted a financial worth of $3 billion, an asset that transcended *collective* national investments in manufacturing, railroads, and banks. Only the Union's vast continental lands exceeded the worth of bondpeople, whose individual market value "rose by 122 percent between 1845 and 1860." At the height of slavery's dominance of American economic life, a healthy, young, male field laborer typically sold in the New Orleans slave markets for $1,800, a figure which translated in 2019 to approximately $55,000.[43]

While slavery operated as a central feature of national life, white southerners developed devastating justifications to rationalize holding humans in bondage. From the earliest days of the republic, slaveholders both regarded the enslaved as aliens populating a distinct black nation *within* a white Union and, at the same time, believed that the institution established the bedrock of civilization. These visions were made even more problematic because American slaveholders lived in an age of global liberationist revolutions. Framed within the American Revolution's claim that governments were instituted to promote individual liberty and the French Revolution's radical celebration of human rights, slavery endured profound challenges from Enlightenment philosophy. Declarations of independence and equality reverberated across the Atlantic to shake colonial slave societies. As the northern United States conferred abolition in the wake of the republic's birth, enslaved people on the French Caribbean island of St. Domingue rose in bloody rebellion against their subjugation. Beginning in 1791, bands of poorly equipped Dominican rebels, wielding the era's passionate entreaties of liberty and equality, slayed their seemingly unconquerable masters, repelled Napoleon's formidable legions, and secured their own national independence. Founded in 1804, the free black nation of Haiti joined the United States as to that point the New World's only independent anticolonial republics. But in the white imagination, Haiti demonstrated the debilitating implications of black revolution. A fledging nation born seemingly of bloodshed and massacre, Haiti thereafter deteriorated into the alleged antithesis of republican virtue. Political instability, military coups, and rigid labor orders sequestered the Caribbean state from the world's "civilized" nations. Unlike with subsequent democratic revolutions in the Atlantic world, the United States refused official recognition to the new island nation.[44]

The Haitian Revolution exposed the paradox of New World slavery. Existing as an archetype of colonial oppression, St. Domingue had been joined in an ironic way to the very source of its own liberation. Stirred by chords of liberty emanating in revolutionary France, the Caribbean island bubbled with instability as the deleterious grip of human bondage clashed with the trans-atlantic rhetoric of freedom. Haitian rebels claimed self-evident, universal principles to justify their independence. While Haiti established a precedent for New World emancipations, terrified whites across the Atlantic world questioned the legitimacy of a nation born of enslaved insurrection. If one of the world's foremost slave societies could fall so suddenly, if whites could be massacred by black insurrectionists, if the entire transatlantic balance could be so radically altered, would not every international slaveholding empire follow the fate of this small Caribbean outpost?[45]

Perhaps more than any white American contemporary of his day, Thomas Jefferson interrogated these questions as a slaveholding egalitarian. Condemning the institution as a "moral depravity" and a "hideous blot," Jefferson confronted the gross conceit of bondage: that slavery rejected human equality, degraded all who encountered it, and promoted the very despotism that the American republic professed to oppose. Enslaved people had not freely chosen to live in the New World, yet their captivity underwrote the independence of white enslavers. Jefferson thus imagined slavery functioning as an incessant civil war waged between a "captive nation" of enslaved people and a free white republic that sanctioned their enslavement. The nature of slave-holding exposed profound implications to a Union founded on self-evident notions of individual liberty. No nation could long stand as the world's providential beacon of freedom while tolerating and expanding human bondage. "Indeed I tremble for my country when I reflect that God is just," he wrote a decade before the Haitian Revolution in his *Notes on the State of Virginia*, "that his justice cannot sleep forever." Though he regarded slavery as a temporary impediment on the progressive path of human liberation, Jefferson also anticipated a bloody racial revolution sundering the United States. "Deep rooted prejudices entertained by the whites; ten thousand recollections, by the blacks, of the injuries they have sustained; new provocations; the real distinctions which nature has made; and many other circumstances, will divide us into parties, and produce convulsions which will probably never end but in the extermination of the one or the other race."[46]

For Jefferson, emancipation did not present a simple alternative to slavery's combustible belligerency. He regarded the institution at once as a stabilizing agent against racial annihilation, the source of his personal independence, and a waystation for people of African descent who occupied a seeming middle ground between barbarism and civilization. Though endowed with inherent natural rights, enslaved peoples' allegedly antiquated origins abroad, joined by the inhibiting effects of slavery at home, stunted their moral and intellectual growth. "The blacks, whether originally a distinct race, or made distinct by time and circumstances, are inferior to the whites in the endowments both of body and mind," Jefferson opined. Anglo and African Americans thus could never forge equal political and social bonds in a republic predicated on personal sovereignty and independent reason. To obviate what he considered the impossible integration of the races, Jefferson proposed that enslaved people should be released from bondage and then "colonized to such place as the circumstances of the time should render most proper." The United States was further obligated "to declare them a free and independant people, and extend to them our alliance and protection." Jefferson acknowledged the impossibility of a biracial American nation. Whites refused to internationalize the Union with a seemingly degraded African race; enslaved and free people of color had yet seemingly to demonstrate fitness for inclusion in a progressive, modern, democratic republic. People of African descent, so explained white colonizationists like Jefferson, could live only abroad, striving toward civilization at their own pace, blessed by an Anglo-American nation eager to rid itself of racial contamination.[47]

Jefferson echoed a widespread contemporary belief that held African Americans as in but not of the nation, unqualified for equal inclusion in the Union, distinctly American but somehow also foreign. Scores of like-minded slaveholders, and even some white abolitionists in the early republic, shared Jefferson's vision of a hostile black "captive nation." During the early nineteenth century, as the American enslaved population ballooned and trembled with instability, colonizationists promoted black emigration as a conservative solution to the radical implications of emancipation and enslaved insurrection. White reformers also used colonization to evade the thorny issue of biracial political and social equality. Yet the movement for gradual emancipation and colonization never fully materialized. Jefferson's death in 1826 coincided with the meteoric expansion and democratization of the republic in which slavery became inextricably linked to national power and conceptions of white citizenship. Slaveholders demanded a strong national government that guaranteed the stability of an institution predicated on black subordination. On his national tour during the early 1830s, Tocqueville observed slavery's overwhelming role in defining notions of white liberty. While the United States was hardly unique in maintaining a thriving slaveholding society, "the Americans are, of all modern peoples, those who have pushed equality and inequality furthest among men. They have combined universal suffrage and servitude." Egalitarian white democracy was most effectively consolidated when integrated alongside its stark contrast in human bondage. "It is claimed that the Americans," concluded Tocqueville, "by establishing universal suffrage and the dogma of sovereignty, have made clear to the world the advantages of equality. As for me, I think that they have above all proved this by establishing servitude, and I find that they establish the advantages of equality much less by democracy than by slavery."[48]

White southerners by the 1830s came to regard slavery as the organizing principle of Union. The institution was not a marginal exception to democratic life. It fulfilled myriad social and political purposes, from the role of government to claims of white liberty and notions of citizenship. Prominent Kentucky slaveholder Henry Clay parroted Jefferson when he acknowledged in 1839, "I prefer the liberty of my own country to that of any other people; and the liberty of my own race to that of any other race. The liberty of the descendants of Africa in the United States is incompatible with the safety and liberty of European descendants. Their slavery forms an exception—an exception resulting from a stern and inexorable necessity—to the general liberty of the United States." Slavery functioned in the Union unlike anywhere else. If the Union hosted God's earthly designs, the ubiquity of bound labor fueled the advancement of Anglo civilization and stabilized the republic against racial revolutions. "The wonderful development of this western continent, effected only through and by the means of slavery," averred noted South Carolina intellectual Louisa McCord, "her immense produce scattered over our globe, carrying food and clothing to the hungry and the destitute; her cotton and her sugar sustaining not only herself but the might of Europe's most powerful nations; her ever increasing expanse of new land, opening an asylum for Europe's starving millions, and staving off menaced revolutions—what are these but the glorious results of American negro slavery?"[49]

For McCord, slavery thrived because it arose from the state of nature, arranging the races in seamless, organic ways. Only whites were "made for liberty," she explained, hardly obfuscating the Union's social, political, and racial design. "The question of race is, then, most important in the consideration of negro slavery." She even queried whether "the civilized world be convinced that all the races do not have the same abilities, enjoy the same powers, or show the same natural dispositions, and are not, therefore, entitled to the same position in human society." Even if one professed skepticism of slavery, McCord argued, no one could contest how "well is the negro fitted for his position." Humans simply could not tamper with a preordained institution of civilization. A captain in the U.S. Army named Robert E. Lee indicted slavery as a "moral and political evil in any country." But in echoing McCord's disquieting racialist logic, Lee endorsed the institution as a force of white liberty and a civilizing custom for people of African descent. The "blacks are immeasurably better off here than in Africa, morally, socially & physically," he opined in 1856. To be sure, Lee was not offering a tacit antislavery critique of the institution. In fact, he regarded slavery as a critical process in the evolution of human affairs. "The painful discipline they are undergoing, is necessary for their instruction as a race, & I hope will prepare & lead them to better things. How long their subjugation may be necessary is Known & ordered by a wise & merciful Providence." Lee believed that any attempt to disrupt providential institutions, especially from white agitators and black revolutionaries, would invite "the storms & tempests of fiery Controversy." For slaveholders like Lee, a stable and enduring Union of white liberty and black bondage fueled the essence of American exceptionalism. "In this country alone does perfect equality of civil and social privilege exist among the white population, and it exists solely because we have black slaves," echoed a Virginia newspaper also in 1856. "Freedom is not possible without slavery."[50]

The intimate relationship of slavery to national growth, technological innovation, continental expansion, and global connectedness inspired widespread efforts to reform the institution if not decenter it from American life. Though vibrant abolitionist coalitions worked to end slavery throughout the Atlantic world, slaveholders and antislavery activists in the United States operated in the same body politic. Cuba, Brazil, and the British and French West Indies all experienced abolitionist critiques emanating from distant overseas metropoles. But because the American Union comprised both slaveholding and nonslaveholding states within the same federal orbit, proponents of each persuasion competed within the democratic system to perpetuate their distinct interests. Deploying the discourse of Union, antislavery proponents contended that the inefficient, hackneyed institution thwarted market diversification, stunted capitalist ingenuity, and wasted natural resources. Some argued that slaveholding could never coexist in a republic dedicated to human equality. Others likewise disparaged the foul injustice of enslaving one individual to enable the liberty of another. Ultimately, antislavery critics challenged the assumption that the United States had been founded on the principles of human bondage. A Fourth of July oration as early as the 1790s exemplified the antislavery contention that the institution was incompatible with American exceptionalism. "Deceitful" and "inconsistent" to its national ideals, "while America boasts of being a land of freedom, and an asylum for the oppressed of Europe, she should at the same time foster an abominable nursery for slaves to check the shoots of her glorious liberty."[51]

Americans of African descent voiced the republic's most vocal critiques against slavery and widespread racial discrimination. Excised from the nation's founding, their destinies seemingly contingent on notions of Anglo progress, African Americans lived largely as wards of a white republic. Enslaved people were coerced to perpetuate and grow the Union, but they were deprived political representation in the very system that their unfree labor sustained. Human bondage thus fueled an aristocracy of privileged white landowners who enriched their independence on the toil of a subjugated race. The institution at once stigmatized blackness as a label of social inferiority and political exclusion and conferred universal liberty upon whiteness. The Union even deprived from free people of color the full privileges of citizenship, limiting mobility and expunging African Americans from the nation's formal body politic. William Wells Brown, who was born enslaved in Kentucky and ran away to freedom in Ohio, emerged by the 1850s as a leading opponent of these impossible national dynamics. He excoriated the empty celebrations of white Americans who upheld an exclusionary republic of liberty, an unequivocal slaveholding nation. "Slavery had no legal existence till the [Constitutional] convention of 1787 gave it legal existence, protection. Here our fathers had failed to carry out the principles of the great Declaration." Brown condemned the devastating contamination of the founding era: the Declaration of Independence had come to apply only to white men, while the Constitution inflated the political representation of slaveholders who commanded an active, robust federal government that spread racial slavery across a rapidly expanding nation.[52]

Only direct and active resistance against state-sanctioned inequality could occasion political and social freedom. The Haitian Revolution thus joined the American Revolution in informing nineteenth-century African American identity. Haiti's example "of black self-liberation and independence" stood as powerful reminders that even the world's most oppressed people could secure liberty. Myriad African Americans understood themselves as connected to a revolutionary nineteenth-century world in which they as much as any other subjugated community pursued the era's promise of liberation. When in 1810 a gathering of black Bostonians saluted their ancestral African home as "the land of our forefathers," they also commended the "Government of the U. States" and endorsed the "Liberty to our African brethren in *St. Domingo*." As the world's first independent black republic, Haiti even motivated stalwart African American abolitionist Martin Delany to call for all black Americans to emigrate out of their "captive nation" and return to "the civilization and enlightenment of Africa." For Delany, slavery erased from the United States any claims to international exceptionalism. "There have in all ages," he remarked in striking echoes of Jefferson, "in almost every nation, existed a nation within a nation—a people who although forming a part and parcel of the population" were deprived of any political or social equality. Like the Haitian revolutionaries before them, only African Americans could shape their liberated future, populating a new republic far removed from the decayed corruptions of the Anglo Atlantic world.[53]

While several thousand black emigrants settled independently in the Caribbean, Liberia, and Canada, the nineteenth-century black emigration movement never fully materialized or overwhelmed the "hope of winning citizenship and equality within the United States." William Wells Brown questioned the premise of emigration because "it degraded [our] people in the eyes of the white public" by signaling gross notions of black inferiority. As the foremost African American abolitionist of his generation, Frederick Douglass likewise questioned the efficacy of colonization. Born enslaved, Douglass too absconded from bondage, secured his freedom, and became an international symbol of human agency. He expected that the world, and the United States in particular, would eventually be cleansed of slaveholding. But "we are of the opinion that the *free* colored people generally mean to live in America," he declared in 1849 in his prominent newspaper, the *North Star*. "While our brethren are in bondage on these shores, it is idle to think of inducing any considerable number of the free colored people to quit this for a foreign land." For more than two centuries the enslaved "colored man toiled over the soil of America, under a burning sun and a driver's lash" to establish the earthen foundation of American civilization. All African Americans thus possessed the right and prerogative to make a more perfect Union of global liberty. "We live here," he concluded, "have lived here—have a right to live here, and mean to live here."[54]

Douglass nevertheless excoriated the Union for sanctioning the shameful, degrading barbarism of slaveholding. In hundreds of writings and public speeches, Douglass turned the rhetoric of American exceptionalism against itself to show whites that slavery was not a southern problem but, rather, a *national* problem in which quiet ambivalence toward the institution translated into active complicity in tarnishing the Union's founding principles. In 1852, delivering a much-anticipated Fourth of July address to a largely white abolitionist audience in Rochester, New York, Douglass praised the United States' imitable birth, extolling the founders for inaugurating a series of global revolutions against tyranny. He celebrated the American Revolution as humanity's crowning victory, one in which natural rights to life and liberty unshackled the perverted chains of oppression. "The 4th of July is the first great fact in your nation's history—the very ring-bolt in the chain of your yet undeveloped destiny," he pronounced in the American exceptionalist tradition. "Stand by those principles" embedded in the Declaration of Independence; "be true to them on all occasions, in all places, against all foes, and at whatever cost."[55]

And then Douglass silenced his audience with piercing questions. "What have I, or those I represent, to do with your national independence? Are the great principles of political freedom and of natural justice, embodied in that Declaration of Independence, extended to us?" The queries were especially deafening considering Douglass's international reputation as a man who had thrown off the chains of enslavement to emerge free, educated, and cosmopolitan. But the impossible menace of race had segregated Douglass from partaking in the Union's bountiful abundance. As Jefferson once acknowledged, men like Douglass were in but not of the republic, present as a form of labor but absent as democratic citizens. Blasting "the rich inheritance of justice, liberty, prosperity and independence," which "is shared by you, not by me," he condemned the United States' unique national experiment, which privileged some at the expense of others. "The Fourth of July is *yours*, not *mine*," he proclaimed. "*You* may rejoice, *I* must mourn." And in words that shook the national spirit, Douglass asked, "What, to the American slave, is your 4th of July?"[56]

Douglass heralded the imposing power of American civilization, but slavery had foisted deeply flawed, contradictory, and even dangerous implications upon a republic of liberty. Looking at the United States' founding "from the slave's point of view," he saw a nation that "seems equally hideous and revolting. America is false to the past, false to the present, and solemnly binds herself to be false to the future." So long as slaveholding remained a central feature of national life, the American ideal could never extend natural rights to all of humanity. "Go where you may, search where you will, roam through all the monarchies and despotisms of the old world," Douglass challenged his listeners with exceptionalist rhetoric that any white nineteenth-century American no doubt understood, "travel through South America, search out every abuse, and when you have found the last, lay your facts by the side of the everyday practices of this nation, and you will say with me, that, for revolting barbarity and shameless hypocrisy, America reigns without a rival." For Douglass, the Union was indeed exceptional: only in the United States did liberty and slavery cohabit in an unholy alliance.[57]

If Douglass's central purpose was to expose American hypocrisy, his chosen method was to scorn the limited reach of the revolutionary heritage. Every outgrowth of the American Revolution—the Declaration of Independence, the Constitution, the rule of law, freedom of religion, freedom of speech, commercial capitalism, national expansion, and international relations—had been corrupted by slavery. "Americans! your republican politics, not less than your republican religion, are flagrantly inconsistent. You boast of your love of liberty, your superior civilization, and your pure Christianity, while the whole political power of the nation ... is solemnly pledged to support and perpetuate the enslavement of three millions of your countrymen." Struck by their inconsistencies, Douglass asked why white Americans condemned European monarchy when they tolerated the aristocratic "tyrants of Virginia and Carolina" ruling the Union with iron fists, leather whips, and martial force. Americans welcomed desperate refugees from Europe, "but the fugitives from your own land, you advertise, hunt, arrest, shoot and kill" in the doleful name of law, compromise, and Union. Slavery debased the entire American experiment, Douglass concluded, impeding progress, promoting vice, planting the violent seeds of national dissolution. "Oh! be warned!" he concluded. "A horrible reptile is coiled up in your nation's bosom; the venomous creature is nursing at the tender breast of your youthful republic," and if not terminated, would devour all in its terrible midst.[58]

Douglass denounced the impossible reality of nineteenth-century African American life: the limited access to liberty in a nation in which the rule of law restricted or altogether prohibited black freedom. This distressing condition was made even more daunting during the 1850s when the federal government consolidated slaveholding power and the Supreme Court criminalized African American citizenship in the infamous *Dred Scott* decision (1857). For Charles L. Remond, a free man of color and Massachusetts abolitionist, the Union, as a nation, as a set of principles, was dead. Remond adopted the discourse of American exceptionalism to demonstrate how the Union had transcended history by rejecting progress, by regressing toward barbarism, by ignoring modernity's emphasis on human rights. As "we search into the records of the past or look into the present, no man can fail to see that, as our country has grown in years," Remond announced in 1858 at a gathering of abolitionists in New York City, "American slavery has grown in numbers, in cruelty, in everything calculated to degrade its victims, and outrage humanity at large." The national spirit of liberty had failed to ensconce the entire continent, subsumed by an ever-expanding slaveholding republic. White supremacy drew sustenance at once from cruel, degraded enslavers, cultural ambivalence toward black humanity, and the democratic toleration of a government that practiced violent racial oppression. Remond thus called "for a dissolution of the Union," citing the "complete failures upon the great question of Republicanism, Democracy, and Liberty"—"our Union, and Government, and Constitution are failures."[59]

Nevertheless, scores of African American intellectuals appropriated the language of American civilization and the concept of Union to challenge inequality, critique the folly of human bondage, and contest the unjust racial exclusions hosted by a white democracy. A national community of writers, orators, and thinkers furnished much of the antislavery movement's philosophic vigor. They employed the same exceptionalist rhetoric to defy a slaveholding state as that which slavery's apologists used to justify their sprawling dominion. Through a proliferation of newspapers, pamphlets, public speeches, and political conventions, free African Americans and even enslaved people carved out important, active spaces in the national dialogue. They deemed constant the principles of the American Revolution, which they believed would, in a not-too-distant future, overwhelm slavery's grip on domestic life. The United States, one writer averred, existed as "the only reasonable republic on earth," due to the simple yet unassailable truths showcased in the Declaration of Independence. The affirmation of universal liberty sheltered in a destined nation, acknowledged Philadelphia intellectual James Forten as early as 1813, "embraces the Indian and the European, the savage and the Saint, the Peruvian and the Laplander, the white man and the African." Such notions were so self-evident, rooted so clearly in the immutable laws of nature, that divine providence never intended North America to rot from the debilitating evils of Anglo supremacy and black bondage. "This we fully believe to be the ultimate design of God," affirmed the editor of a black newspaper in 1859. "On this continent, which for so many centuries lay buried from the sight of civilization, God intends ... ultimately to bring men of every clime, and hue, and tongue, in one great harmony, to perfect the greater system of man's highest earthly government. Then shall be the reign of perfect peace."[60]

African American exceptionalists proclaimed that the Declaration of Independence and Constitution resonated a timeless universalism. If the national charge was to strive toward a more perfect Union, conceived in liberty, equal justice, and domestic tranquility, then slavery could live only as a temporary exception to American life. Black critics charged that white slaveholders had manipulated the nation's founding in catastrophic ways, but Frederick Douglass argued that the republic's founders never "intended" the Constitution to be "a slave-holding instrument." In the same Fourth of July address in which he lambasted white supremacy, Douglass also hailed "the Constitution [as] a glorious liberty document" in which "there is neither warrant, license, nor sanction of the hateful thing" of slavery. Douglass later imagined that a republic of multiracial equality—the only logical ideal of the nation's founding—"could not well have been designed at the same time to maintain and perpetuate a system of rapine and murder, like slavery; especially, as not one word can be found in the constitution to authorize such a belief." A black political gathering in Chicago thus resolved in 1853, "that in contending for our civil and political rights, we plant ourselves firmly upon the principles of the *Declaration of Independence* and the Preamble of the Constitution." And even in the wake of the *Dred Scott* decision, a "New England Convention of Colored Citizens" reaffirmed the United States "as 'native land,' clinging to and cherishing it with the same tenacity and affection, for which those of white complexion are characterized." The evils of white supremacy "will cease from the hearts when injustice and wrong shall depart from the practices of the American people toward the colored inhabitants of our country and the world."[61]

National change depended on black political action. "The elevation of our people in the land," announced the New England Convention, required free people of color to practice American democratic traditions, from exercising otherwise very limited voting rights, to forging systems of business and commerce, to pursuing education and social mobility. Though a white republic still regulated the lives even of free African Americans, each act of individual sovereignty contested the nearly impenetrable obstacles of white supremacy. Try as it might, the state could never erase the independence of mind and thought. When Harriet Jacobs acknowledged in 1861 "that liberty is more valuable than life," she voiced a prevalent ideal that centered individual dignity at the heart of human nature. As a formerly enslaved woman who escaped from bondage, Jacobs harbored great ambivalence toward a nation in which she experienced the sexual brutalities, the separation of families, and the horrific uncertainties wrought by slavery. But through her own unceasing quest for freedom and in her moving personal narrative of enslavement, she produced a kind of autonomy that confronted the power of slavery itself. If African Americans remained unable "to exchange slavery for such a hard kind of freedom," Jacobs concluded, human rights would continue to be defined and limited by white slaveholders.[62]

Harriet Tubman likewise announced in 1859, "The white people had got the Negroes here to do their drudgery, and now they were trying to root them out and ship them to Africa, but they can't do it. We're rooted here and they can't pull us up." For Tubman, freedom nourished the American landscape to produce an authentic national spirit that stood adamantly against slavery. But the conditions of a slaveholding republic mandated that African Americans pursue their own liberty and defy the white constructions of Union that restricted black liberation. Tubman thus directed widespread, clandestine, underground networks of enslaved and free people who joined white abolitionist allies in funneling bondpeople out of the South and into the North, sometimes even to Canada. Though they may not have shattered the institution of slavery, and though the act of escape often meant living as refugees, their acts demonstrated the exact purposes for which the Union had been established: individuals pursuing the natural human instinct for liberation against tyranny. While they may have lived within the largest slaveholding nation in the world, myriad African Americans honed their political instincts and prepared their "captive nation" for what they deemed the inevitable "day of jubilee."[63]

Harriet Jacobs and Harriet Tubman exhibited a dual political persona. As formerly enslaved people, their lived experiences of enslavement and freedom contributed to the public discourse about American exceptionalism. As women, they also spoke to a broader cultural critique about the limits and meaning of Union. Nineteenth-century American life viewed women and men as residing in distinct private and public spheres. Within the so-called cult of domesticity, men were considered public actors who engaged in commerce and high politics, while women occupied private spaces to impart virtue, refine the family, and stabilize the home against political-economic transformations in democracy and capitalism. White women were excluded from the formal body politic, deprived of voting privileges and, by extension, technical political representation. The tangible aspects of national exceptionalism—constitutionalism, individual mobility, egalitarianism—were indeed embedded in gendered and racialized notions of American democracy. "Woman has no political existence," the fervent abolitionist and feminist Sarah Grimke decried in 1837 regarding a white masculine republic. "She is a cipher of the nation; or, if not actually so in representative governments, she is only counted like the slaves of the South, to swell the number of lawmakers who form decrees for her government, with little reference to her benefit, except so far as her god may promote their own." As Grimke would have well understood, the ideology of democratic republicanism birthed from the American Revolution replaced monarchy "with a common brotherhood of sovereign men who now represented the public interest." Abolitionist Lydia Maria Child likewise linked women's subordination with slavery. "I was indignant for womankind made chattels personal from the beginning of time, perpetually insulted by literature and law and custom."[64]

And yet, like Grimke and Child themselves, white American women hailed among the nineteenth-century world's most literate populations. By 1860, women's literacy rates in New England alone hovered around 95 percent. For countless white middle-class women, a domestic life emphasized childhood and adolescent education. Thus, "in an apparent paradox, the concept of a woman's sphere *within* the family became a springboard for extension beyond the hearth." Women used the written and spoken word to forge influential political identities. Changes in national economic and social life, joined by revolutions in communication, fueled feminist reform movements that questioned the gendered assumptions of Union, particularly male suffrage, political representation, and property ownership. The Seneca Falls Convention in 1848 embodied white American women's contributions to the discourse of Union. The convention's principal organizers, Elizabeth Cady Stanton and Lucretia Mott, spearheaded a rewriting of the Declaration of Independence to condemn the "repeated injuries and usurpations on the part of man toward woman, having in direct object the establishment of an absolute tyranny over her." In this gendered reading of national purpose, the Seneca Falls Declaration proclaimed men *and* women as equal recipients of nature's sacred laws to life, liberty, and equality.[65]

Feminist reformers believed that women's equal participation in democracy—through voting, officeholding, and representation—would reform the Union into the world's foremost protectorate of human dignity. Stanton cited the United States at once as exceptional and commonplace. The republic remained the world's leading nation to proclaim universal equality, while mirroring the international order in denying political and social equality to women. "In every country and clime"—including the American Union—"does man assume the responsibility of marking out the path for her to treat,—in every country does he regard her as a being inferior to himself and one whom he is to guide and controul." Engaging the paradoxical threads of exceptionalist discourse, she concluded, "the great truth [is] that no government can be formed without the consent of the governed." Meanwhile, as the woman suffrage movement dawned in the United States, much of the Atlantic world in 1848 erupted in democratic revolution as oppressed peoples pursued the very liberties boasted by the American republic.[66]

The Union and the World

White nineteenth-century Americans regarded their revolution as a world-historical moment in which free people unchained the yoke of tyranny to chart a new course in human affairs. They expected their declarations of independence to inspire subsequent global revolutions against monarchy, aristocracy, and nobility. Holding their republic as superior to the world's autocratic tyrannies, they believed that only this nation derived from self-evident truths and ordered by constitutional liberty could pave the one true path toward global emancipation. Revolutions in France (1789), Haiti (1791), Central

America (1790s–1830s), Greece (1821), and Belgium (1830) and across mainland Europe in 1848 aimed to expand the very republican future birthed by the American model. "Our age has been marked above all others by the suddenness of its revolutions," remarked William Ellery Channing in 1829. "The events of centuries have been crowded into a single life. The history of the civilized world, since the bursting forth of the French Revolution, reminds us … the incidents of a reign are compressed into an hour. Overwhelming changes have rushed upon one another too rapidly to give us time to comprehend them, and have been so multiplied as to exhaust our capacity of admiration." However, most of the democratic revolutions across the early nineteenth-century world failed, accentuating American exceptionalist convictions.[67]

The Latin American revolutions illustrated the hope and ultimate despair in the United States about a global republican future. With much of Europe preoccupied by Napoleon's attempts to conquer the continent, New World liberation movements undermined Spanish, French, and Portuguese colonialism. Between 1810 and 1826, new republics replaced nearly all of Spain's western colonies, including an independent Mexico, which expanded the republican footprint on North America. Americans praised the emancipation of once oppressed peoples, seeing a special link between the revolution of 1776 and those of the early nineteenth century. The hemisphere's emerging "sister republics" joined the United States in erecting a sturdy partition between New World liberation and Old World subjugation. Endorsing the New World's deliverance from antirepublican imperialism, the United States was typically the first nation to recognize the new Latin American republics as legitimate, independent states. As a foremost champion of the revolutions, Henry Clay announced in 1821, "The people of the United States [take] deep interest which they feel for the success of the Spanish provinces of South America, which are struggling to establish their liberty and independence."[68]

Though favorable toward the new Central and South American republics, a deep anxiety permeated the white American mind. Testimony from Thomas Jefferson and John Quincy Adams exemplified conflicting appraisals of the revolutions. "And behold! another example of man rising in his might, and bursting the chains of his oppressor, and in the same hemisphere. Spanish America is all in revolt. [T]he insurgents are triumphant in many of the states," Jefferson proclaimed in 1811. But were Latin Americans truly imbued with the dispassionate virtue necessary to harness a republican future? Or were the chains of colonial statism and theocratic oppression too powerful to overcome? "There the danger is that the cruel arts of their oppressors have enchained their minds, have kept them in the ignorance of children, and as incapable of self-government as children. [I]f the obstacles of bigotry & priestcraft can be surmounted we may hope that Common sense will suffice to do everything else." Adams, another vocal advocate of Latin American independence, regarded diplomatic recognition as a "moral obligation of civilized and

Christian nations." Yet he too sensed repressive impulses embedded in the Spanish colonial character, which barred "free or liberal institutions" from flourishing. "Arbitrary Power, military and ecclesiastical," Adams added, "was stamped upon their education, upon their habits, and upon their institutions. Civil dissension was infused into all their seminal principles. War and mutual destruction was in every member of their organization, moral, political, and physical."[69]

The Latin American republics endured swift political and social destabilizations, promoting an acute sense of U.S. exceptionalism. "It need not surprise us, that, under circumstances less auspicious, political revolutions elsewhere, even when well intended, have terminated differently," averred Daniel Webster in 1825. "It is, indeed, a great achievement, it is the masterwork of the world, to establish a government entirely popular on lasting foundations; nor is it easy, indeed to introduce the popular principle at all into governments to which it has been altogether a stranger." The new nations suffered from persistent military coups and the rise of caudillos, demagogic authoritarians who commanded loyalty through fear and manipulation, co-opting weak governing institutions to bend to their populist will. Legislative bodies could not harness functional representative democracies, the citizenries beholden to powerful forces of state control. Governing establishments often failed to accommodate the ethnic diversity of the new states; the inability to expand populations led to stifling oligarchies controlling access to land. Civil strife, revolts from oppressed laborers, political and military subversions, and the inability to exert territorial control foundered the precariously weak nations. "By the 1860s," writes a leading scholar, "nearly all the Spanish American republics had plunged into civil wars that pitted liberal republicans and their peasant followings against conservative landed elites allied with military and church leaders."[70]

Mexico offered a disquieting example of weak New World republics. Clouded by racial, religious, and national chauvinism, white Americans eyed their continental neighbor as a nation unfit for the privileges of self-determination. Gross disparities of wealth, a seeming lack of industriousness, a penchant for demagogic seduction, and an ostensibly lawless culture all grew from an unholy marriage between military rule and state religion. Distinct overtones of white supremacy governed skeptical appraisals of Mexican republicanism. "The Spanish and Indian do not make a race of people with patriotism and candor enough to support a republic, much less to form, sustain and establish one out of the present deranged fabric called the Republic of Mexico," an incredulous observer noted in 1846. "At the present time," echoed a Pennsylvanian, "much [as] we would deplore such a retrograde movement, there is no doubt but that a monarchical government would be best suited for this country. A sovereign at the head of the army and the throne supported by the clergy would without difficulty suppress all of the internal dissensions." Democracy seemingly could not be replicated outside of a civilized Anglo republic. By 1860, Mexico had endured fifty transformations of government, ruptured by persistent instability and political upheaval.[71]

White Americans feared that the unrelenting weakness of Central America would invite European despots to descend on the Western Hemisphere and reclaim their lost colonies. Once instigated, the devious project of Old World imperialism would never cease, warned Secretary of State John Quincy Adams. "Russia might take California, Peru, Chile; France, Mexico—where we know she has been intriguing to get a monarchy under a Prince of the House of Bourbon, as well as at Buenos Ayres. And Great Britain, as her last resort, if she could not resist this course of things, would take at least the island of Cuba for her share of the scramble. Then what would be our situation—England holding Cuba, France Mexico?" Monarchical puppet governments throughout the Caribbean and the Americas might isolate the United States among rapacious tyrants hungry to infiltrate the region's lone standing republic. To ensure national security against potential European incursions, the Union might well have to surveil citizens suspected of harboring internationalist sympathies and even impose heavy taxation to support a standing army, militarizing the republic for perpetual war. Only authoritarianism could combat hostile foreign influence, thereby radicalizing a moderate republic. President James Monroe thus announced in 1823 that "the American continents, by the free and independent condition which they have assumed and maintain, are henceforth not to be considered as subjects for future colonization by any European powers." The Monroe Doctrine declared to the world that only the United States would direct hemispheric progress, resisting the militant, unstable, internecine forces of Europeanization.[72]

The United States' swift continental expansion had as much to do with chauvinistic notions of Manifest Destiny as it did security against internationalism. Expansionist-minded Americans disregarded hemispheric borders and existing sovereignties as arbitrary markers of Old World contamination. God's mandate to populate North America with democratic institutions and republican equality seemingly cleansed toxic internationalization from an otherwise egalitarian continent. The continent had long endured Europeanization, famed Bostonian Edward Everett explained in 1829; this Anglo-American idealism had been "subjected to foreign rule, and left unshielded, to receive every impression that could be stamped on it by foreign ascendancy." Strokes of good fortune, violent aggression, and swift diplomacy sparked territorial upheaval across the North America and consolidated national sovereignty. The Treaty of Paris (1783), which ended the American Revolution by surrendering British holdings to the United States; Napoleon's ceding of Louisiana (1803); the Monroe Doctrine closing the Western Hemisphere to European incursions (1823); and the subsequent white settlement of the Mississippi River valley coincided with the hemispheric collapse of the British, French, and Spanish empires. Meanwhile, the expansionist spirit at once sparked an international war with Mexico (1846) and diplomatic crises with British Canada. The United States claimed from each conflict the vast Southwest and the northwestern Pacific territories.[73]

While democratic republicanism failed to expand throughout much of the New World, a new round of revolutions in the Old World portended an egalitarian reformation of Europe. Beginning in 1848, liberals across the continent rebelled against entrenched monarchies, established churches, and aristocratic ruling classes. Royal nobilities fell in France and Italy; Austria, Prussia, and Hungary established republics and launched constitutional reforms; Irish republicans sought to overthrow British colonial rule; and Pope Pius IX took flight from Rome. From Paris to Berlin, Vienna to Prague, and Rome to Budapest, common citizens demanded political suffrage and economic equality. Europe seemed finally to shed the relics of monarchical privilege to enter a new era of republican civilization. Americans overflowed with nearly universal praise, seeing the democratic revolutions as a glorious validation of the Union's global example. "We are responsible not only to ourselves but to others," South Carolina orator Nelson A. Mitchell declared at a Fourth of July celebration. "The course of events among other nations ... will satisfy us what a large influence we have exercised over their fortunes." The stagnating forces of history were yielding to the inevitable march of liberty; "there needed no elaborate argument to convince the people of the old world of the stability of free institutions, when, turning their eyes ... across the broad expanse of the Atlantic, they might contemplate the sublime spectacle of a" true republic. The revolutions not only emulated the American example but also portended national, economic, hemispheric, and ideological security. Monarchies likely would not be planted in the New World now that they had begun to wither in the old.[74]

Despite their democratic promise, the European revolutions seemed to morph into unchecked mob rule. "French Revolution No. 3. Democratic influenza running through Europe," New York diarist George Templeton Strong scoffed in his diary. "French provisional government—absurdity, sentimentality, and melodramatic monkeyism of every kind; decrees that 'everybody shall have everything, and secondly everything else is hereby abolished.'" Some conservative Americans looked with distress at what they saw as labor radicalism destabilizing Europe. Demanding fundamental economic and political transformations, agitated French workers obstructed the streets of Paris during the turbulent "June Days," assaulting private property in the name of socialist reform. An American correspondent for the *New York Courier and Enquirer* recoiled at the ensuing clashes between protestors and the French National Guard. Though he initially sympathized with the people's entreaties for property rights and stable wages, the writer castigated the rioters whose "violence is equaled by their cruelty; in defiance of all civil usage, they have murdered their prisoners either behead[ing] them … or hanging them to their window bars. Such is the action of the advocates, of what they call a Social Republic!" Disgusted by reports of civilians butchering French soldiers in the open public, he concluded, "The European masses lacked an education which would teach them the uses of liberty." They had been seduced by a poisonous continental ideology: "Socialism … that shameless doctrine which instructs us that all the systems of Public Liberty now current throughout the civilized world are spurious … is the doctrine which has set on the workmen of Paris to their revolt."[75]

If Paris was any indication, nearly each democratic revolution failed to secure republican liberty, succumbing either to mob rule or violent state-sponsored reprisals. National military forces quickly repressed democratic insurgents in France, Hungary, and Italy to reestablish monarchical authority and papal legitimacy, while popular movements elsewhere ultimately dissolved. Americans looked aghast as powerful monarchs and cunning nobles by 1850 consolidated power through reactionary, antidemocratic centralization. According to some American critics who traveled the continent, nations discarded their claims to liberty when either an unbending, authoritative central state or an unbending, radical populace competed for absolute authority. Charles Edward Lester, an American diplomat who served in Italy for much of the 1840s, spoke for myriad of his fellow citizens when he reproved the use of mercenary soldiers, professional militaries engaging restive civilians, and the widespread execution of prisoners. Monarchical reprisals suggested to Lester that republicanism could never take hold in Europe. "The ultimate cause of the failure of European nations, in the establishment and maintenance of liberal institutions, during and after the Revolution of 1848, was *the political incapacity of the people*. We do not believe that Europe is qualified for Republican institutions, nor that she could enjoy or perpetuate them, even if they were conceded by those who sway the power." Lester harbored little "faith myself in the capacity of any great people in the world, either to establish or to maintain Republican institutions, except the people of the United States." Harking to the white racial consensus in the wake of the Latin American revolutions, Lester even denounced "the capacity of any *race*" to practice "free Constitutional Governments, except the Anglo Saxon."[76]

With the establishment of Greek and Belgian independence earlier in the century, Americans could point only to a handful of successful revolutionary movements, a stark reminder of Europe's alleged incapacity for self-government. Viewing other nations as unable or unwilling to practice effective democracy, Americans imagined their republic standing alone amid an antirepublican world. "Behold," declared Samuel Scott, a schoolteacher in Philadelphia, "France possessor [of] a liberty unsuited to its wants; Italy again subjected to the cruel yoke; and … Hungary trodden down upon by the Austrian conqueror." Hopeful that republicanism would still save the international community, "let our Union's example be an inducement to others to show the same fraternal affection," Scott advocated with no uncertain trepidation, "and let liberty arise triumphant as the sun." While Scott yearned for a hopeful future, disenchanted New England writer George Ticknor surmised that republics "cannot grow on the soil of Europe; at least, not republics in the sense we give to that word. There is no nourishment for them in the present condition or past history of the nations there." While the nations of the world attempted but often failed to democratize and liberalize, the American republic remained "replete with instruction and furnishing abundant grounds for hopeful confidence," concluded President Franklin Pierce in 1853. Prevailing as a beacon of global liberation, the Union symbolized for the world the "potent appeal for freedom"; "the power of our advocacy reposes in our example."[77]

The wake of 1848 sparked one of the largest migration movements in all American history. Displaced by economic depression, political oppression, or widespread famine, 3 million émigrés from Germany, Ireland, France, Hungary, and Italy arrived in the United States between 1845 and 1855. Known as the "Forty-Eighters," famed liberal revolutionaries landed on American shores to a hero's welcome. Few expatriates enjoyed more widespread acclaim than the Hungarian freedom fighter Louis Kossuth. Heralded as a sympathetic survivor of monarchical oppression, Kossuth toured the United States as a republican celebrity, delivering rousing speeches to throngs of captivated Americans. To liberate Europe's subjugated masses, Kossuth implored American political support and military intervention to topple the continent's suffocating monarchies. An urbane politico, Kossuth "arouse[d] us to a consciousness of the majesty of our national position and to the responsibilities it involves; to show us that we cannot safely sleep while despots are forging chains for the yet unfettered nations," explained New York editor Horace Greeley. "And if we have no regard for others' rights, we must assume an attitude of resistance to the expanding dominion of the autocrat if only to secure our own."[78]

Kossuth's appeals received great national fanfare. The Democratic and Whig Parties each contributed financial aid to his cause. And political activists known as the Young Americans, drawn from a new generation that did not descend directly from the American Revolution, advocated breaking with George Washington's hallowed warning against foreign entanglements to assist and even shape the world's march toward a progressive, republican future. The Young America Movement, however, occupied a minority position on the American landscape. In January 1852, Abraham Lincoln articulated mainstream national thought in a series of resolutions on "the arrival of Kossuth in our country." Americans sympathized with "the right of any people ... to throw off, to revolutionize, their existing form of government, and to establish such other in its stead." Though "non-intervention" remained "a sacred principle" of American foreign policy, the United States could offer something far greater than tangible aid. Forging enduring ideological alliances with "the people of every nation struggling to be free" isolated reactionary despots who trampled on "the more sacred principles of the laws of nature and of nations—principles held dear by the friends of freedom everywhere, and more especially by the people of these United States." Faithful "to the principles of our free institutions," the American republic welcomed anyone seeking "the cause of civil and religious liberty" to populate its abundant land and stand as the singular bastion of freedom in a world of despotism.[79]

Lincoln's supportive but no doubt cautious approach to the 1848 revolutions underscored a collective unease with European demagoguery even when charismatic democrats like Kossuth preached a sympathetic message. Devoid of moderation and seduced by passion, opined Tennessee senator John Bell, Europeans retained "wild and visionary schemes and theories of society and government of liberty and universal equality [which] have brought obloquy upon the very name of republicanism throughout Europe." The year 1848 unleashed sweeping social movements across the Atlantic and spawned an upsurge in radical political activism in the United States, including the women's rights crusade, the emergence of Spiritualism, and a committed program of labor rights. Conservative Americans thus grew wary of the rapid influx of European migrants, imagining continental fanaticism descending upon the republic. By the early 1850s, a reactionary anti-immigrant and anti-Catholic nativist movement gripped the nation. Nativism warned that migrants would corrupt the Union with Old World radicalism, blind obsession with authority, and stagnant economic dependence. At once devious revolutionaries and destitute ne'er-do-wells, non-Anglo immigrants would internationalize a liberal republic into a decaying European vassalage. To channel nativist passions, the Know-Nothing Party—also known as the American Party—pledged the power of government to form a Protestant ethnic state through the "repeal of all Naturalization Laws" and the expulsion of "all foreign paupers." The party thus promised to uphold "American Constitutions & American sentiments," support "none but Americans for office," and ensure "death to all foreign influences, whether in high places or low!"[80]

The Know-Nothings suffered poor electoral returns throughout the late 1840s and 1850s; nativism was faltering as a viable political program. "The nativist movement had relatively little impact" because "there was always a certain air of futility" about its legitimacy. Some Americans impervious to nativist sentiment valued a collective national identity that transcended ethnic distinctions. Congregationalist minister Henry Ward Beecher condemned "that most un-Americanism Native Americanism" to argue that the concept of Union *depended* on immigrants who valued liberty. "We take them as a tribute from every nation under the sun—the young, the earnest, the best blood, the motive power of the nation. Such blood, mingled with ours, if educated and Christianized, will give stamina, variety, genius and all the elements of national power and progress such as were never before brought together." Abraham Lincoln likewise in 1858 framed the American republic as an idea that traversed ethnic boundaries. When white native-born Americans gathered each July to commemorate national independence, "we find a race of men living in [1776] whom we claim as our fathers and grandfathers." Memories of the revolutionary dead pulsated in the national soul, joining the past to the present. "We are historically connected with" the dawn of American life; "we feel more attached the one to the other, and more firmly bound to the country we inhabit."[81]

Lincoln rejected the idea that nationhood was reserved only for those who traced their roots to the founding generation. "There is something else connected with it. We have besides these men," he explained, "half our people who are not descendants" of the Revolution. Those "who have come from Europe—German, Irish, French, and Scandinavian" consider "themselves our equals in all things." United by the transcendent creeds of 1776, "they have a right to claim [the American idea] as though they were blood of the blood, and flesh of the flesh of the men who wrote that Declaration, and so they are." National assimilation formed an "electric cord" that "links the hearts of patriotic and liberty-loving men together." Nativism reeked too much of European nationalism, in which race, ethnicity, blood, or religion determined national inclusion. The Union derived its legitimacy neither from divine nobility nor from aristocratic lineages but, rather, from an enduring proposition that all humans enjoyed equal rights to life, liberty, and happiness. As a nation of popular consent, the United States would endure "as long as the love of freedom exists in the minds of men throughout the world."[82]

While Lincoln regarded the Union as the world's foremost egalitarian republic, he also confronted the terrible paradox of American life. The widespread presence of slaveholding in a land of liberty exposed how Lincoln's fellow citizens had willfully implanted the exclusionary habits of European governance on United States' soil. Enslaving one human to serve another confirmed "all the arguments in favor of king-craft" long endemic to the Old World. In much the same way that European nobles and elite aristocrats organized national inclusion through ethnic ancestry, American slaveholders had adopted "the arguments that kings have made for enslaving the people in all ages of the world." The notion that some were born to rule and others were born to be ruled permitted "men of one race . . . enslaving the men of another race." For Lincoln, slaveholding affronted the nation's founding principles, threatening to undo the egalitarian civilization to which an oppressed world turned as its last hope. "If we cannot give freedom to every creature, let us do nothing that will impose slavery upon any other creature," he announced, no doubt worried about the fate of international liberty. Otherwise, Americans consented "to make this one universal slave nation," forever imperiling the Union's universal appeal.[83]

The commanding place of slavery in the American republic unsettled Lincoln. The Union pledged to preserve "the spirit which prizes liberty as the heritage of all men, in all lands, every where." But slavery threatened to erase the United States' *love of liberty* which God has planted in our bosoms." The institution embodied every element of hostile internationalism the Union claimed to oppose: aristocracy, antidemocratic politics, and a hierarchical society ordered along immovable class, social, and racial distinctions. "As I would not be a *slave*, so I would not be a *master*. This expresses my idea of democracy. Whatever differs from this," Lincoln outlined in 1858, "is no democracy." Slaveholding transformed an egalitarian republic into the kind of despotic, exclusionary nation that oppressed peoples across the world sought to flee. Therefore, the republic could neither reject the appeals of European immigrants nor accept the enslavement of African Americans. Though the former did not descend from the American Revolution, and the latter had been excised altogether from the nation's founding, white Americans obliterated the spirit of liberty through their willful toleration of nativism *and* slavery. "You have planted the seeds of despotism around your own door," Lincoln warned his fellow citizens who "succeeded in dehumanizing the negro" by ignoring the basic human right to live free from tyranny. "The logic of history" foretold the future of the Union if Americans refused to confront their appalling national contradiction. "Familiarize yourselves with the chains of bondage, and you are preparing your own limbs to wear them," Lincoln concluded. "Accustomed to trample on the rights of those around you, you have lost the genius of your own independence," an independence rooted in the founding principles of human equality and individual consent. Should Americans reject these essential democratic prerogatives, they "become the fit subjects of the first cunning tyrant who rises."[84]

For a people wary of disunion, civil war, and revolutionary upheaval, slavery imposed impossible strains on a republic predicated on universal liberty and the social and political exclusion of an entire race of people. Though he implored a renewed commitment to the notion "that all men are created equal," Lincoln lived in a nation that had emerged by the 1850s as the world's most liberal democracy *and* its largest slaveholding country. It was truly an exceptional republic, one underwritten by universal truths and splintered by hypocritical deeds.[85]

2

Causes

★ ★ ★

As the third year of civil war enveloped the United States, Abraham Lincoln rose in April 1864 to address the Baltimore Sanitary Fair. Long burdened by the need to explain the higher purposes of the war's gruesome weight on American life, the president again rationalized what seemed to be an ever-lasting national trial. "When the war began," Lincoln offered, "neither party, nor any man, expected it would last till now. Each looked for the end, in some way, long ere to-day." Such simple prophecies had been shattered by the im-measurable deaths of young men, wrecked by once idyllic landscapes trans-formed into gory killing fields, and undercut by the rapid transition of an en-slaved people now embarking on a new birth of freedom. The war had already occasioned such unprecedented consequences, yet the relentless conflagra-tion continued. What possibly could have caused such a remorseless struggle? Why had the mystic chords of American memory failed to stanch the national bloodletting? And how could a Union of and by the people forsake its better angels of humanity?[1]

Lincoln implored his audience to consider how the war would settle the organizing principles of Union. In Lincoln's mind, the United States stood as the lone outpost of freedom in a world of oppression. "The world has never had a good definition of the word liberty," observed the president, "and the American people, just now, are much in want of one." Americans had long en-joyed an exceptional global position because "we all declare for liberty." But the Civil War exposed that "in using the same *word* we do not all mean the same *thing*." Such an inconspicuous acknowledgment might have reminded Lincoln's spectators why the war had come in the first place. "With some the word liberty may mean for each man to do as he pleases with himself, and the product of his labor; while with others the same word may mean for some men to do as they please with other men, and the product of other men's labor. Here are two, not only different, but incompatable things, called by the same name—liberty. And it follows that each of the things is, by the re-spective parties, called by two different and incompatable names—liberty and tyranny."[2]

Lincoln's wartime remarks reflected a long-standing national anxiety.[3] White Americans had forever regarded liberty as the right of free people to live unburdened from the coercive forces of autocratic governments or an-archical factions. But somewhere in the national past, American civilization

Practical Illustration of the Fugitive Slave Law, *1851, by E. C. Del. A satirical condemnation of the notorious Fugitive Slave Law in which abolitionist William Lloyd Garrison and a free man of color protect an enslaved woman from a devious federal agent, who, riding an ineffectual Daniel Webster, symbolizes the powerful violence of legalized slave catching enhanced by the Compromise of 1850. The image reproves the chaos of a Union increasingly committed to elite slaveholding interests. (Library of Congress)*

had shattered into discordant strains of liberty. How could the United States serve as a model to the world when its citizens no longer consented on the nation's fundamental ideal? Though Americans adhered to the idea of Union, they failed during the early national era to agree on how these basic concepts should be presented to the world.[4]

Nineteenth-century Americans feared above all else the destabilization of national sovereignty. A dissonant, balkanized republic that trembled on the verge of collapse invited disunion, civil war, and international conquest, turning a once exceptional republic into a decided failure. Hoping to stem radical threats to the Union, the American citizenry between 1787 and 1850 remained faithful to moderation and compromise. But the spiritual bond of Union was severed when white Americans claimed as their manifest destiny the right to populate the continent. The explosive place of slavery in the American future,

CONCEIVED IN LIBERTY

a long contested but compromised feature of national life, exposed the irreconcilable ideas of Union about which Lincoln later spoke. The failure of democracy in Europe in the wake of the 1848 revolutions coincided with the United States' annexation of Texas, the acquisition of vast western lands from Mexico, the tortured attempts to organize the seemingly open continent, and the seductions of spreading slavery into the West and the Caribbean. Riddled with the anxiety of serving as a singular bastion of democracy, Americans debated how their rapidly expanding nation should present democratic liberty to an autocratic world. Unable to compromise over the future of slavery in the western territories as a result of the 1854 Kansas-Nebraska Act, a political system once championed by moderation now bowed to competing and sometimes irreconcilable strains of liberty.[5]

Disunion possessed nuanced but evident origins, rooted in uncompromising ideas of American exceptionalism. The inability to produce stable republics in Europe, the Caribbean, and Central America convinced mid-nineteenth-century Americans of the United States' precarious status as the world's foremost representative democracy. A sense of paranoid isolation gripped the national imagination as an extremist, radical world seemed to impinge upon the Union. Distinct conceptions of national exceptionalism thus competed for control of a federal government that would either perpetuate the world's largest slaveholding republic or restrict the expansion of an institution considered antithetical to economic freedom and individual mobility. American slaveholders had long regarded the Union, the rule of law, and the bountiful continent as essential protections for their sacrosanct institution of human bondage. They argued that the ostensible white liberty to hold property in humans and proliferate slavery across the hemisphere forestalled revolts by enslaved people and stabilized a natural order of white supremacy and black servitude. In their telling, the American republic stood as the noble exception to global emancipations gone horribly awry. Enslaved people, free African Americans, and white antislavery critics countered in often divergent ways that the Union's powerful slaveholding class used the power of government to thwart personal liberty. For those who opposed an American empire of slavery, slaveholders had built a rigid oligarchy that subverted the Constitution and manipulated the federal state to serve their elite interests at the expense of democracy and individual freedom.[6]

The ultimate failure of political compromise signaled a dangerous vulnerability to a republic fallen seemingly under the sway of internationalism. With the rise of the Republican Party, an organization that promised to neuter slaveholding political power and envisioned a national antislavery future, white southerners, and even some northern Democrats, claimed that the federal government might well renege on its time-honored pledge to sustain a powerful slaveholding Union. Proslavery advocates had long contended that American civilization had been dedicated to marginalizing radical abolitionism, which they claimed had led to bloody Caribbean enslaved rebellions and hemispheric emancipations. Republicans, and Abraham Lincoln specifically, countered that slaveholders had corrupted the federal government under the auspices of an international "Slave Power conspiracy," which sought to restrict the inevitable march of universal liberty. The seeds of civil war were planted firmly in a domestic landscape, nurtured by global conditions, and watered by fears of internationalization.[7]

Toward a Slaveholders' Union

For slaveholders across the Atlantic world, the early nineteenth century dawned with an overwhelming dilemma: any nation built on slavery could collapse into racial strife and reorder the entire globe. The same antimonarchical impulses that fed the war for American independence later inspired the French (1789) and Haitian Revolutions (1791). Without the United States and Haiti, the slaveholding evolution of the Western Hemisphere would have been entirely different. In 1819, when the Missouri territory applied for statehood, perceptions of slavery's national existence had already been shaped by the three Atlantic revolutions in America, France, and Haiti. Keenly aware of their unstable global community and their entrenched dread of disunion, Americans who weighed Missouri's admission as a slave state shaped their arguments according to violent events in Europe and the antislavery precedents that emanated from the Caribbean and the American Revolution. Slaveholding proponents and antislavery activists each sought a settlement divorced from what they perceived as revolutionary extremism. Although it sometimes appears as a sudden and unanticipated sectional quarrel about the national expansion of slavery, the origins of debate over Missouri's admission to the Union had been firmly established during the late eighteenth century and cultivated by subsequent global conditions.[8]

Antislavery reformers between 1790 and 1815 associated slaveholding, both in the United States and in the Caribbean, as the rawest source of Jacobinism, the powerful symbol of violence from the French Revolution's "Reign of Terror." American anti-Jacobins accused slave owners of perpetuating a brutal institution that imperiled the progress of civilization. Desperate to avoid the bloody fate of France, one abolitionist advised in 1796 that "if we seriously regret those horrid scenes of violence which have been perpetrated by [the Reign of Terror which] have desolated France: If we mourn at the tragic tale, of those multitudes of innocent lives, who have bled under the awful blade of the guillotine ... [we] hope that the revolutions of America and France are but introductory movements towards a general emancipation of human nature." Seeking to abolish violent tendencies from American life, early antislavery advocates decried slavery's terror, its uncivilizing nature, and its propensity to corrupt an otherwise virtuous republic through the quest for unbridled racial mastery. Humanitarian impulses thus helped fuel the abolition of slavery in northern states during and after the American Revolution. Early antislavery vigor also set an important precedent in which Congress prohibited the institution from spreading into the old Northwest Territory. Slavery occupied a foreign place in the national future: "Its discordancy with the principles of the revolution," acknowledged John Jay in 1819, and "its being repugnant to the [human rights outlined] in the Declaration of Independence."[9]

More than two decades of anti-Jacobin critiques of human bondage prepared antislavery politicians to negotiate the problem of Missouri. Exposed to charges that slavery bred violence, subjected to claims that Caribbean slave rebellions (especially Haiti in 1791 and Barbados in 1816) confirmed slavery's immorality, and moved by arguments that slavery damaged the United States' exceptional democracy, New York congressman James Tallmadge's proposed ban on slavery in Missouri underscored the power of Atlantic antislavery activism. "On this subject," Tallmadge advised his colleagues about expanding slavery, "the eyes of Europe are turned upon you." Reminding Americans that the world had long sought the dissolution of the young republic, Tallmadge warned, "The enemies of your Government, and the legitimates of Europe, point to your inconsistencies." Influenced by a rising tide of transatlantic abolitionism that dated to the American Revolution, Tallmadge explained that slavery violated the United States' founding principles while also feeding European critiques of American hypocrisy. Secretary of State John Quincy Adams thus offered, "If the dissolution of the Union must come, let it come from no other cause but this. If slavery be the destined sword in the hand of the destroying angel which is to sever the ties of this Union, the same sword will cut in sunder the bonds of slavery itself. A dissolution of the Union for the cause of slavery would be followed by a servile war in the slave-holding States, combined with a war between the two severed portions of the Union." For Adams, only a single alternative could obviate the horrors of civil war: "the extirpation of slavery from this whole continent."[10]

Southern advocates for Missouri's admission as a slave state also wielded the rhetoric of Jacobin violence to buttress their position. Slaveholders loathed the radical overtures of French egalitarianism. They indicted French appeals to fraternal equality as the central causes of the Haitian Revolution, which collapsed the hierarchical and racial stability critical to the maintenance of all slave societies. Failure to expand slavery into Missouri, leaving enslaved populations to concentrate and rankle in the East, inspired bitter fears of the institution bursting into brutal enslaved massacres. Exposure to British proslavery apologist Bryan Edwards's thesis that abolitionism inspired slave insurrections, combined with memories of Haiti and the recent slave uprising in Barbados, American slaveholders dreaded that slavery had become too precarious, had been subjected to inflated abolitionist rhetoric, and had been corrupted by the restive enslaved themselves. Slavery *had* to move westward, diffusing a growing population to avert "the lessons of St. Domingue." As one proslavery observer declared, "Our negroes are truly the Jacobins of the country; that they are the anarchists and the domestic enemy; the common enemy of civilized society and the barbarians who would, IF THEY COULD, become the DESTROYERS OF OUR RACE."[11]

While both sides of the Missouri debate accused opponents of stoking violence and fomenting disunion, compromise efforts marginalized political extremes. Moderates consented to admitting Missouri to the Union as a slave state and Maine as a free state, while also establishing a boundary line at parallel 36°30′ to dampen sectional embers. Indeed, the 36°30′ line aimed to uphold the national precedent of limiting slavery's territorial expansion by reserving western lands for free white laborers. Debates over the future of slavery revealed profound fears of internationalization, which might throw the United States into the same violent chaos that had fractured other parts of the world. The crisis of 1819–20 also exposed the marked racialization of American political rhetoric. Both antislavery and proslavery proponents warned that the institution might well collapse the republic in the same way that France had fallen to the forces of radicalism and Haiti had plunged into the dreaded depths of racial insurrection. Tallmadge indeed warned that enslaved people, sullen by the chains of bondage, would necessarily rebel to secure a freedom already bestowed by nature's God. "Envious [of the] contrast between your liberty and their slavery, must constantly prompt them to accomplish your destruction," he cautioned slaveholders. But the opposing fears of rebellion also influenced proslavery southerners who were desperate to maintain a stable social order, a supposedly natural hierarchy of racial subordination. The modern world had revealed the sobering fate of societies torn asunder by political strife and social violence.[12]

Focused critiques of slavery, like the one James Tallmadge struck against Missouri's admission as a slave state, echoed prevailing condemnations of human bondage. Strong and vibrant, the early antislavery movement succeeded in tempering proslavery features of the U.S. Constitution, banned national participation in the transatlantic slave trade after 1808, and connected like-minded reformers in America and Great Britain. Abolitionist societies, civic organizations, and newspapers dotted the northeastern landscape as white and black antislavery activists petitioned global allies. The United States' unique commitment to democratic liberty augmented the world's crusade against human bondage. "Aside from slavery," the confident Boston abolitionist William Lloyd Garrison informed English onlookers, "I regard America as a brilliant example to the world. Only wash from her escutcheon the bloody stain of slavery, and she will stand forth as a noble example for others to follow." Others looked to Haiti to spur domestic opposition to enslavement. Haitian refugees who arrived in the United States during the early 1790s spread news of the revolution and bonded with African Americans and white abolitionists. The image of Toussaint Louverture and the fantasy of black independence thereafter inspired scores of black activists and enslaved peoples who linked the fate of American slavery to its late Caribbean counterpart. "The immolations and martyrdoms on the plains of St. Domingo, in opposition to cruel and aristocratic oppression," African American abolitionist Charles B. Ray noted in classic exceptionalist rhetoric, "should be as 'balms to our souls, and incense to our worship.' They are sureties to us, that as a race, *we cannot be crushed.*"[13]

As abolitionism morphed into a steadfast crusade, slaveholders across the Atlantic world moved quickly to vanquish the movement. Though a distinct political minority, American slaveholders attempted to guard the early republic against the extremes of radical abolitionism and enslaved insurrection. And they had good reason to fear. Whites in Charleston, South Carolina, alleged that Denmark Vesey—a free black laborer who lived in the city— planned in 1822 to incite a rebellion that would seemingly collapse the Low Country's tenuous hold on its black majority. Accusing Vesey of harboring sympathies with Haitian rebels and unsettled by the antislavery critiques of Missouri, white authorities forced "confessions" from Vesey and his conspirators, leading to the execution of thirty-five individuals. White Charlestonians screamed that such plots stemmed from the agitation of antislavery propaganda that traveled freely across the Atlantic, inspiring the enslaved with hopes of eternal deliverance. "The despots of Europe know," one South Carolinian declared, "that if judiciously encouraged, a disruption of our Union may reward their labors." Convinced that the rising tide of British antislavery activism had filled James Tallmadge with delusions of grandeur, and paranoid about the French Revolution's adverse influence on the enslaved in St. Domingue, rabid Carolinians warned that the Union would collapse if radical abolitionists and haughty slaves were allowed to breed disruptive chaos.[14]

The late 1820s and early 1830s seemed to confirm slaveholding suspicions about the reach of international abolition. Few published tracts testified to Haiti's antislavery allure more than David Walker's *Appeal to the Coloured Citizens of the World* (1829). Walker, a free man of color born in North Carolina, lived his formative years encircled by slavery. Struck by the institution's racial peculiarities and disillusioned with the empty rhetoric of liberty that churned in the early American soul, Walker absconded to Boston, where he exploited his fierce antislavery convictions. Firing the white and black imaginations, the *Appeal* summoned enslaved people across the Western Hemisphere to throw off their shackles and claim a just liberty. Walker declared that the enslaved could not wait for small bands of white liberators to declare black freedom. Only the most victimized causalities of Atlantic slavery could cleanse the New World of its debilitating ills. The nexus of the struggle would take place—indeed it could *only* take place—in the United States, "in this *Republican Land of Liberty.*" Slavery had infected the world's great empires, seducing England, France, Spain, and Portugal into lustful imperial quests. All Europeans shared in the destructive advent of New World slavery, but Walker condemned Americans as exceptionally guilty. Only in the United States did whites have the gall to declare fealty to universal freedom while depriving natural rights from an allegedly inferior race. A nation conceived as the province of God's careful design, only to violate so blatantly providence's most basic commands, invited inevitable devastation.[15]

And Walker beckoned the impending crisis. Distracted by the riches spawned from the breaking backs and torn bodies of those they exploited, slaveholders would scarcely see the day when God would "appear fully in behalf of the oppressed, and arrest the progress of the avaricious oppressors." The entire nation would someday yield to God's inflexible hand, from which all white Americans would "rise up one against another, to be split and divided, and to oppress each other, and sometimes to open hostilities with sword in hand." But Walker anticipated divine intervention only when the enslaved called upon God, mobilized through their own active and united resistance. "The person whom God shall give you"—like Moses to the Israelites, Toussaint to the Haitians, and Jesus to all humanity—"give him your support, and let him go his length, and behold in him, the salvation of your God."[16]

The Haitian Revolution underscored "the glory of the blacks and terror of tyrants," inspiring similar plots in British Demerara and in Denmark Vesey's South Carolina. Yet Walker understood the tenuous capacity of even the most focused resistance. Unity could occasion deliverance. But even an independent Haiti had ultimately collapsed into a fledgling black republic isolated among rapacious white empires. "Let our enemies go on with their butcheries, and at once fill up their cup. Never make an attempt to gain our freedom of *natural right*, from under our cruel oppressors and murderers, until you see your way clear," he cautioned. "When that hour arrives and you move, be not afraid or dismayed," for providential guidance would ultimately harvest freedom's fruit. Walker thus counseled against rash violence, inviting his brethren to be of one mind and one spirit, stoking the flames of resistance, defying the pull of apathy, and preparing for the day of battle, that glorious moment on which the blow for interminable freedom could be struck.[17]

The *Appeal* reads on occasion as a wartime manifesto, a call to destroy the nation from within. Walker was profoundly disillusioned with the United States as a *place*, a land corrupted by the evils of slavery. "Is this not the most tyrannical, unmerciful, and cruel government under Heaven[?]" he questioned. In striking exceptionalist rhetoric, he asked his audience "to search the pages of [history]" to find "a set of human beings, [who mistreated] as the white Christians of America do us, the blacks, or Africans." However, almost in spite of itself, the *Appeal* turned the call to violent resistance on its head. As much as he lambasted Thomas Jefferson's unashamed hypocrisy—a powerful slaveholder pronouncing the equality of all men—Walker embraced the central truths embedded in the Declaration of Independence and remaining wedded to the United States as an *idea*. While he steadfastly believed that only a war could erase slavery, Walker did not seek a fundamental cleansing of the nation's exceptionalist ideology, nor did he countenance the founding of an independent black republic. He blasted weak colonization schemes—efforts by moderate whites to settle African Americans outside the United States in hopes of alleviating racial strife and violence—and avowed that America "is as much ours as it is the whites." And he scoffed at the notion that abolition would unleash bloodthirsty freedpeople in fits of blind revenge against their former masters. Such allegations are "at variance with our feeling or design, for we ask ... for nothing but the rights of man." Slaveholding bred fear, danger, violence, and resentment. It was an unnatural condition at odds with liberty. "Set us free, and treat us like men, and there will be no danger, for we will love and respect ... and protect our country," he promised.[18]

For David Walker, only African Americans could showcase for the world the United States as an exceptional civilization underwritten by universal liberty. He thus called on his black readers to "prove to the Americans and the world, that we are MEN, and not *brutes*, as we have been represented, and by millions treated." The nation could realize its earthly mission only when the enslaved united, pursued a liberation of their own making, secured political equality, and lived as dispassionate, virtuous citizens. Black activists long deliberated whether the United States should be transformed into an independent black republic, whether deliverance could be achieved only by emigrating to the Caribbean and Africa, or whether the nation itself could be perfected internally. Walker's *Appeal* sought to unite freed and enslaved peoples in a common cause, stimulating an already active political awareness in the African American community.[19]

For American slaveholders, Walker's *Appeal* underscored critical problems about slavery's place in a white republic. Southern whites feared that the pamphlet's incendiary message would politicize enslaved people, forging dangerous bonds with international abolitionists and unleashing insurrections throughout the region. Their fears seemed to materialize when enslaved Virginian Nat Turner led a revolt in 1831 that killed more than fifty whites in Southampton County. That same year, William Lloyd Garrison inaugurated *The Liberator*, an abolitionist newspaper that called for immediate and universal emancipations. A Virginia attorney condemned Turner's heinous act as "the damnable spirit of fanaticism engendered by Northern publications," no doubt eyeing Walker and Garrison's periodicals. The Virginia General Assembly subsequently criminalized literature like the *Appeal*, prohibiting its appearance anywhere in the Commonwealth. Individuals suspected of concealing and distributing pamphlets that promoted insurrections among the enslaved would be sentenced to death. Walker's writings, the limits of black resistance, and the terror of white southerners thus seemed to confirm Thomas Jefferson's long-held suspicion: that American slavery operated as a constant state of war between displaced Africans who lived as captives within the boundaries of a white republic. He warned in 1814 that peace could dawn only "whether brought on by the generous energy of our own minds; or by the bloody process of St Domingo." The American South appeared to be hurtling toward cataclysmic destruction.[20]

Then, in 1833, Jamaica erupted in a massive slave revolt, which, perhaps more than any other event, galvanized British antislavery forces. Proslavery apologists had long warned that concentrated enslaved populations, mixed with antislavery agitation, inevitably produced such violent massacres. Interpreting the Jamaican revolt as a sure sign of enslaved people's humanity and their thirst for freedom, Parliament began abolishing slavery in the British West Indies in 1834. American slaveholders looked at British abolition with grave concern. Linking the failure of British slavery with the disaster of the Haitian Revolution, Hugh S. Legare feared that the Atlantic basin's displaced freedpeople would flood the American mainland. Caribbean emancipations would produce, "at the mouth of the Mississippi, a black population of some 2,000,000 free from all restraint and ready for any mischief." South Carolina's William C. Preston warned that American abolitionists would replicate the British model. Although a small "neglected, despised" faction, Preston cautioned that the dedicated efforts of British abolitionists Thomas Clarkson and William Wilberforce occasioned a successful campaign to garner the public's support and to exploit planters' indifference. If American abolitionists appealed to the seduction of liberty just as David Walker had done, "it is evident that this succession of dangerous excitements will never end but by the removal of its cause." American slavery now seemed to be balanced precariously within a world rife with instability and insanity.[21]

American slaveholders sensed ominous warnings embedded in the Haitian Revolution, Denmark Vesey's conspiracy, David Walker's *Appeal*, Nat Turner's revolt, and British emancipation. Each event testified to the Atlantic world's creeping flirtation with abolition, a movement stirred by bold public remonstrations and the violent torrents of black insurrection. They were the same warnings that Thomas Jefferson cited during the volatile 1790s. Jefferson believed that empires of slavery would collapse in the same destructive manner as St. Domingue. Remembering "how all the whites were driven from all the other islands, may prepare our minds for a peaceable accommodation between justice, policy & necessity," he proposed in 1797. Only a gradual "mode of emancipation" and recolonization of African-descended people would alleviate the terrible fate awaiting white slaveholders. Though he condemned slavery as unjust, Jefferson also regarded African Americans as violent creatures capable of collapsing the very racial civilization that underwrote his personal liberty. "If something is not done, & not soon done," he counseled, "we shall be the murderers of our own children." For Jefferson, the national future could not countenance the tranquil integration of white and black Americans. "From the present state of things in Europe & America," he agonized about the revolutionary turmoil gripping the Atlantic world, "the day which begins our combustion must be near at hand; and only a single spark is wanting to make that day to-morrow." A peaceable abolition and the unequivocal expulsion of people of color could kill the cancer of slavery before enslaved people killed the Union.[22]

In a marked transformation, American slaveholders between the 1820s and 1850s rejected Thomas Jefferson's counsel. To contest abolitionism, they redefined his construct of slavery as a perpetual condition of war, claiming instead that the institution unveiled a peaceful, unparalleled path toward modernity and equality for all white men. They no longer posed as idle sponsors of an institution that they, like Mr. Jefferson, once claimed to be necessary but evil. Now, amid the conditions of race war and international emancipations, they had to stake out a new life for their institution. They had to defy fellow white southerners—especially those of the Upper South and even Jefferson himself—who owned enslaved people but who also considered gradual emancipation and colonization safe alternatives to the sudden deluge of enslaved rage. And they had to venture where few in the modern Atlantic world had heretofore seen only in their dreams: they had to prove that slavery fashioned the cornerstone of American civilization, standing as the bold face of democracy, guaranteeing an unambiguous white liberty. The discursive spirit of American exceptionalism was now straddling the backs of bound laborers whose toil plowed white people's glorious, liberating, and purifying futures.[23]

In one of the many quintessential defenses of American slavery to emerge after the 1820s, William Harper, a cosmopolitan born in the British Caribbean who came of age in Charleston, South Carolina, averred in 1838, "Every society which has attained civilization, has advanced to it through" slavery. Situating the enslaved and free in safe, immovable, providential stations, slavery guaranteed to the white ruling class "higher virtues, and more liberal attainments." Masters and slaves enjoyed a natural, mutually beneficial relationship, the latter emerging from barbaric African roots into Christian enlightenment, while "the tendency of Slavery is to elevate the character of" enslavers. Not peculiar but, rather, inherently natural, bondage cradled the future. "The uncontradicted experience of the world is, that in Southern States where good government and predial and domestic slavery are found, there are prosperity and greatness." Yet "where either of these conditions is wanting," evident throughout the abolitionist world, "degeneracy and barbarism" oppress emancipated nations. For Harper, slavery regulated the turbulence of modern life, slowed artificial societal evolution, fostered security, and ensured tranquility. He thus condemned abolition as foolish and ruinous. "Can any sane mind contemplate such a result without terror," he asked of emancipation's devastating effects on agricultural production and social order. "Does not *self defence* then demand of us, steadily to resist the abrogation of that which is productive of so much good?"[24]

Echoing Harper's theme of slavery as just, modern, and natural, young South Carolina congressman James Henry Hammond appealed in 1836 to white fears of black insurrection to justify American slavery's eternal life. Entrenched within a paranoid white mind, the specter of Haiti crossed party lines, flouted sectional frontiers, and arrested even the most ambivalent white nonslaveholders. Hammond warned that forces of radical internationalism threatened "to subvert the institutions of the South" and sever the entire republic. Rejecting Jefferson's argument that slavery's presence fed continuous racial strife, Hammond claimed that its existence, if protected and secured, forestalled race war. If slavery's bonds loosened, international and domestic abolitionists would "desolate the fairest portion of America, and dissolve in blood the bonds of this Confederacy." American antislavery societies, drawing inspiration from similar European organizations, had fomented a national contagion that "spread with unparalleled rapidity." Hammond even alleged that a sympathetic New York colleague had seen the inherent danger in international abolitionists aligning with American reformers and enslaved people to devastate the South. "I endeavor to convince my neighbors that [antislavery literature] are false," Hammond's correspondent pleaded, "and that if they join the cry of abolition, they must partake of the enormous sin of bringing on a civil war, of destroying our Union, and of causing the renewal of the horrors of St. Domingo."[25]

Hammond maintained that only a strong, committed, antiabolition federal state could thwart such violent "fanaticism." So foreign a concept to the American disposition, abolition had to be extinguished from the national soul. As the essence of civilization, slavery had to be secured; it had to expand across the American landscape to ensure national security. Although a natural institution, Hammond reminded his audience that slavery could indeed end, just as the world had proven, "through the medium of the slaveholder—or the Government—or the slaves themselves." If not vigilant, the Union could become corrupted—evil could infect God's earthly kingdom, sparking an inferno of racial bloodlust. Hammond did not have to convince his fellow slaveholders of the horrors of insurrection. He instead asked if, in the wake of emancipation, *northerners* would be willing to admit African Americans as citizens, "and place their political power on an equality with their own?" Were white Americans prepared to see their nation sullied by blackness, tarnishing the "perfect equality with the white representatives of an Anglo-Saxon race," or even "to see [the formerly enslaved] placed at the heads of your Departments; or to see perhaps some Toussaint, or Boyer, grasp the Presidential wreath and wield the destinies of this great Republic?" Peaceful coexistence between the races defied the stability of *Herrenvolk* democracy, Hammond charged, as the example of British emancipation proved. Almost recalling David Walker's appeal to armed conflict, Hammond warned that abolition would produce "civil war between the whites and blacks," creating "horrors such as history has not recorded."[26]

Slaveholders in the Atlantic world's three largest slave societies—Brazil, Cuba, and the American South—used Harper and Hammond's ideas to challenge the dangers of abolitionism. Yet "only in the United States did slaveholders have to share power with men whose economic interests did not depend on slavery." Democracy placed abolitionists and slaveholders in the same political sphere, both influencing the delicate balance of American politics. Each could shape popular opinions, and each competed in a political culture predicated on majority rule. And each depended on the actions of enslaved people—either in resisting their bondage or in dwelling in eternal servitude—to bolster their positions. Cuba and Brazil did not possess such social and political conditions; instead they were governed by colonial elites who easily dismembered any threat to their slave-based civilizations. "Slaveholders everywhere governed through undemocratic means," writes a prominent scholar, "but only in the United States did these undemocratic means coexist uncomfortably with a democratic society." Indeed, British Caribbean planters, an ineffectual minority in Parliament, lost their sprawling New World empire when an antislavery majority, moved at once by slavery's appalling inhumanity and colonial unprofitability, canvassed the English public. The same devastating sway of democracy would not—*could* not—overwhelm American slaveholders, who claimed to live on the frontier of modernity and progress.[27]

Wealthy planters in the United States possessed a distinct advantage not enjoyed by American abolitionists or West Indian slaveholders: direct access to and democratic control of political power. Slaveholders dominated the national government, influencing policy, diplomacy, law, and military institutions. They enjoyed disproportionate control of the federal bureaucracy, shaped executive appointments, and used their wealth and power to command support of moderate northerners and nonslaveholding southern whites. In the long trail of slavery's disappearance in the North following the American Revolution and its demise in the British Caribbean, American slaveholding presidents guided the reins of federal power to expand the United States into a "slaveholding republic." Jefferson acquired Louisiana; Monroe claimed Florida and closed the Western Hemisphere to European interference; Jackson rid the Southeast of pesky Indians, opening the world's richest cotton fields to white settlement; Tyler and Calhoun annexed Texas; and Polk justified a war with Mexico to extend United States territory to the Pacific Ocean. The future of American slaveholding depended on rapid continental expansion and territorial aggrandizement. For each new slaveholding state added to the Union, slaveholders inflated their representation in the Senate, while the Constitution's Three-Fifths Clause allotted slaveholding representation in the House according to a state's enslaved population. More slaveholding states meant more slaves, and more slaves guaranteed the democratic political influence of slaveholders, who derived much of their power and wealth from the very people whom they oppressed and who did not have a voice or a vote in their own congressional representation.[28]

Contrary to the image of American slaveholders as a small, isolated band who looked to states' rights as their only refuge against a rising tide of Atlantic antislavery agitation, the slaveholding class of the 1830s and 1840s enjoyed immense national prestige and used federal power to protect and consolidate their Union. Control of the national institutions and acquisitions of rich planting lands allowed slavery to explode across the burgeoning continent, defying the consistent march of emancipation in the Caribbean, Central American republics, and Mexico. "Without the aid and countenance of the whole United States, we could not have kept slavery," James Chesnut Sr. acknowledged, especially when it seemed "that the world was against us." When Memucan Hunt admitted in 1836 that the acquisition of Texas would protect American slavery, he disparaged "the fanaticism of the world [which] is daily increasing upon the subject of domestic slavery." Yet celebrating what he considered America's distinguishing characteristics, Hunt cited the slaveholding Union as "the purest system of government which the wisdom of man has been enabled to devise."[29]

When American military arms conquered the Deep South and renovated Jefferson's "empire of liberty" into an inescapable "cotton kingdom," Andrew Jackson celebrated the gifts bestowed to all white Americans. "The wealth and strength of a country are its population," he declared in the wake of Indian removal, "and the best part of the population are cultivators of the soil. Independent farmers are everywhere the basis of society, and the true friends of liberty." Although cunning planters and avaricious creditors transformed the land into exorbitant cotton outfits, consolidating the tiny ruling class's powerful influence, Jackson's appeal to white equality framed how American slaveholders vindicated the swift movement of their institution. The slaveholding republic thus thrived on a promise that *all* white men lived equally in a slave society. No other nation could boast the kind of liberty that flourished in the American Union. When South Carolinian Edward Brown claimed, "Slavery has ever been the step-ladder by which civilized countries have passed from barbarism to civilization," he argued that enslaved labor had allowed the United States to emerge as an international bastion of productivity and efficiency. "Hence," he averred, "it results, that slavery must either have existed in America, or the world must have foregone the chief advantages of its discovery." Slavery assured universal white independence because "the great object of man, and the ruling principle of his soul, is to obtain happiness." Halting the growth of a civilizing institution would be as futile as defying the immutable laws of nature. "So strong is the aversion to the human race to any violent or sudden alteration in the modes of life, that any attempt at introducing such," Brown concluded, would "confirm a people in their original barbarity and misery."[30]

For influential slaveholders, any impediment to slavery's rapid continental aggrandizement affronted the Union's organizing principles and stunted national progress. Slaveholding politicians thus used government power to silence, or "gag," antislavery critics in Congress, barred the postal service from distributing abolitionist propaganda—notably David Walker's *Appeal*—and even refused to recognize Haiti as a legitimate republic. When Congress received in 1838–39 more than two hundred appeals to accept the fledging Caribbean nation, one "moderate" white southerner responded that such petitions "are treason." "I pronounce the authors of such things traitors—traitors not to their country only, but to the whole human race." Between 1820 and 1844, both the Democratic and Whig Parties, desperate for southern support in each election cycle, understood that slaveholding power governed national politics. Neither party countenanced abolitionism, relegating the movement to the fringes of American political life. Slaveholding politicians took advantage of such hesitancy, propagating fears of racial unrest if abolitionists entered the political mainstream. Referencing the Caribbean context, James Henry Hammond in 1836 blamed abolitionists and their allies in Congress for "excit[ing] a servile insurrection [through] their meetings, publications, lectures, and missions," the very reasons for which the notorious "gag rule" had been instituted.[31]

One had to look no further than Texas to see how the power of a slaveholding Union safeguarded the interests of a planter class that marginalized abolitionist protests. After securing independence from Mexico in 1836, Anglo-Americans who populated that cotton-rich territory sought immediate annexation to the United States. Texas at once became a symbol of how the slaveholding republic functioned and how the expansion of slavery continued to inspire fears of internationalization, representing the dramatic, unintended consequences of British abolition. Unable to compete with their free-labor holdings in the Caribbean and wholly dependent on cotton from the American South, British imperialists craved Texas's rich economic production. Perhaps Texas could become a British protectorate, a direct free-labor source of cotton that mitigated the monopolistic power of American slavery. And thus Texas became even for the most moderate white Americans a pragmatic question of national security. If Great Britain established a foothold in Texas, influencing Mexico, Latin America, and the Caribbean, the United States would almost certainly be compelled to place a permanent military presence in the Southwest. But control of Texas's cotton and thus control of international markets, Arkansas senator Ambrose Sevier remarked, "tend more successfully to insure our peace and security than a standing army."[32]

Proponents of the slaveholding Union professed a more immediate concern about the very real possibility that the British might colonize and abolish slavery in Texas, thereby undermining the institution's hemispheric stability. With the British directing the worldwide ship of abolition, an emancipated Texas would alienate the South and legitimize domestic abolitionist critiques. Duff Green, one of the loudest proponents of Texas's annexation, spoke for many slaveholders when he explained that Britain was attempting to compensate for the disastrous mistake of West Indian abolition. "The effect of abolition of slavery in the British West India colonies has been to ruin the planter, to hand over his property to the emancipated slave and to convert those islands into black colonies of England." The sarcoma of abolition, John C. Calhoun averred, would spread unchecked from Texas to the South, a region hemmed in by an increasingly abolitionist world. England's "grand scheme of commercial monopoly" would provoke a brutal racial conflict "of the most deadly and desolating character; to be terminated in a large portion in the ascendency of the lowest and most savage of the races and a return to barbarism."[33]

What might happen if the slaveholding Union, the vanguard of civilization in Calhoun's estimation, collapsed due to international agitation? The scenario sounded eerily reminiscent of the French Revolution's declarations of universal liberty spiraling horribly out of control and upending an otherwise stable slaveholding society in St. Domingue. As Calhoun explained in 1844, British intervention and emancipation in Texas "would be followed by unforgiving hate between the two races, and end in a bloody and deadly struggle between them for the superiority. One or the other would have to be subjugated, extirpated, or expelled; and desolation would overspread their territories, as in Santo Domingo, from which it would take centuries to recover." In Calhoun's ironic and twisted calculation, annexation and the spread of slavery necessarily stabilized and preserved long-standing social orders and ensured that the United States would not crumble in the same needless manner as so many previous slaveholding nations.[34]

John Quincy Adams, a stalwart antislavery Whig congressman from Massachusetts, fiercely opposed Texas's annexation. Adams condemned aggressive slaveholders and their Democratic allies in conspiring to transform the American republic into a sprawling empire of slavery. "The annexation of Texas to this Union is the first step to the conquest of all Mexico, of the West India Islands, of a maritime, colonizing, slave-tainted monarchy, and of extinguished freedom," he opined in June 1844. "The whole people of the United States" harbor "a deep, deep, deep, interest in the matter." But most Americans, Adams was convinced, "dearly as they loved the Union, would prefer its total dissolution to the act of annexation of Texas." Though disunion inspired great fear, so did "a military monarchy" enslaving free citizens into bound subjects of an imperial slaveocracy bent on continental domination. Texas would undo the United States' republican foundation, catering to a band of elite, oligarchic slaveholders who used democratic platforms to play on people's racial fears. To preserve the Union as founded, Adams acknowledged, "the freedom of this country and all of mankind depend upon the direct, formal, open and avowed interference of Great Britain to accomplish the abolition of slavery in Texas."[35]

Adams attacked aggressive territorial aggrandizement with a dire warning to American slaveholders. If rapid continental acquisitions sparked war with Great Britain or Mexico, or even stoked a widespread enslaved insurrection, the president possessed constitutional powers enhanced by international law to declare military emancipation as a just measure to wage war. "When your country is actually in war, whether it be a war of invasion or a war of insurrection," Adams warned his slaveholding colleagues in 1842, "by the laws of war an invaded country has all its laws and municipal institutions swept by the board, and martial law takes the place of them." Foreign belligerents also could claim emancipation as legal military necessity to hinder the enemy's ability to make war and even could demand permanent abolition as a condition of peace. Continental expansion caused international wars, and war shattered slavery, thereby authoring slaveholders' own destruction. Adams detested their hubris. Though he dreamed of slavery's destruction, he held the Union's preservation above all else. "Our liberties," he concluded, "will stand as little chance" if reckless slaveholders waged a hemispheric war purely to expand their repugnant institution.[36]

Adams's defense of Union confronted the era's infatuation with Manifest Destiny. Texas represented, in the words of fellow critic Ralph Waldo Emerson, "one of those events which retard or retrograde the civilization of ages." Looking to the future as a confirmation of national uniqueness, Henry Clay agreed that Americans "have ... far higher duties ... to perform toward our country, toward posterity, and toward the world." Clay vowed that the United States should continue to perfect itself from within, protecting the personal liberties of *all* Americans, expanding the base of economic opportunity, and presenting itself to the world as a beacon of egalitarianism. Texas, however, unleashed dangerous slaveholding imperialism through rapid, militaristic expansion. "Once begin it, and *where* will it end?" one Whig questioned. "Shall we *ever* have territory enough for ambition, though we have enough for our wants?" As one popular magazine declared, republics survived on moderation and choked on greed. "The true vocation of this great republic," it explained, "is not aggrandizement but national growth." The distinction was subtle but clear: the Union should expand as an idea, not as a militant territory that had lost all sense of itself as a nation set apart from world history.[37]

Yet as Democratic slaveholding expansionists made clear, the Union's political moderation was best preserved when a white republic blanketed the continent. Unfolding the promise of white American liberty, thwarting the imperial designs of Great Britain, ensuring the supremacy of American markets, and dampening the threat of any social and racial unrest seduced many into supporting the annexation of Texas, which Congress approved in 1845.

As one Democratic supporter of annexation declared, westward growth "produces that life and that energy which animates the American mind, and which literally makes us so extraordinary a race of people." The problem of slavery, however, drove a wedge between Democratic expansionists and Whig restrictionists. The history of the early republic and the Atlantic world taught that slavery was hardly a local issue. The institution manipulated the nation and the world simultaneously. Despite the political rancor and fearmongering, Americans managed to compromise and moderate on issues that had long plagued the rest of the world. But if Texas was any indication, the future expansion of slavery might well strain the coalescing bonds of American civilization.[38]

Democracy, Compromise, and the Meaning of Union

Despite fierce disputes between slaveholders and abolitionists, mid-nineteenth-century white Americans almost uniformly presented themselves to the world as inheritors of a unique democratic experiment, peopling a land of abundant opportunity, progress, and modernity. Crossing party lines and defying sectional boundaries, gales of national fortune stirred the American spirit. "America is the country of the Future," Ralph Waldo Emerson observed in 1844. "It is a country of beginnings, of projects, of vast designs and expectations. It has no past: all has an onward and prospective look." Americans no doubt would have sensed the optimism and apprehension that riddled Emerson's assessment. His future of "vast designs" was just that: a future foretold, but somehow still unknown. Although American civilization boasted great national abundance, citizens feared that the future itself might well collapse their unique destiny. That they presented themselves to the world as exceptional meant only one thing: that the world and its sameness, its corruption, and its strife, could infect the Union both from within and from without. Perhaps more than anything else, Americans feared that their politics and culture would internationalize and unhinge their special democracy. There would always be a United States. But would the subversive whims of foreign design undermine the American mission?[39]

That question became paramount in the wake of Texas's annexation. An international crisis of sovereignty erupted with neighboring Mexico when each nation disputed precisely where the border divided both republics. The diplomatic quarrel produced a war waged between 1846 and 1848 to determine the Western Hemisphere's premier republican nation-state. The U.S.-Mexico War signaled the zenith of a mid-nineteenth-century American nationalism predicated on racial, cultural, and political exceptionalism. The Union boasted a militant prerogative to consolidate North America's porous borders in accordance with its providential and democratic mandate. Only American arms, argued proponents of the war, could rinse Mexico of its tainted republicanism, its Catholic idolatry, and its uncivilized barbarism. Rabid advocates of war condemned Mexicans as "reptiles in the path of progressive democracy" who "must either crawl or be crushed." The boundless West beckoned; the far reaches of the Pacific called; and new gateways extending far from the Gulf summoned. The United States' path to international greatness was blocked only by the corrupted lands of the Montezumas. "Let our arms now be carried with a spirit which shall teach the world that, while we are not forward for a quarrel," Walt Whitman declared, "America knows how to crush, as well as how to expand!"[40]

Whigs protested what they deemed an unjust war of imperialistic aggression. Dreams of continental expansion had long stoked the American imagination, but calculated martial aggrandizement smacked of profligate excess. Invading and conquering sovereign nations, averred Georgia representative Alexander H. Stephens, undermined the uniqueness of American republicanism, propelling the United States toward a *"downward progress*. It is a progress of party—of excitement—of lust for power—a spirit of war—aggression—violence and licentiousness. It is a progress which, if indulged in, would soon sweep over all law, all order, and the Constitution itself. It is the progress of the French Revolution." Americans had long presented their Union as a beacon of antimilitaristic and anticolonial moderation. Gross jingoism eliminated reason and militarized an otherwise virtuous citizenry into bloodthirsty madness. For Whigs, territorial expansion could transpire only through peaceful deliberation. Stephens imagined a time "when the whole continent will be ours, when our institutions shall be diffused and cherished, and republican government felt and enjoyed throughout ... from the far south to the extreme north, and from ocean to ocean." Americanization of the hemisphere unfolded "not by the sword, but by voluntary association," the essential quality of an empire of liberty.[41]

The United States nevertheless emerged triumphant in 1848, claiming from Mexico the vast western territories that stretched from Texas to the Pacific Ocean. The unique republican experiment had never before been so vindicated. Yet the grand conquest revealed a troubling problem about the United States' place in the world. As the renowned historian David M. Potter once so hauntingly acknowledged, the war and its stunning territorial bounties signaled "an ironic triumph for 'Manifest Destiny,' an ominous fulfillment for the impulses of American nationalism." Manifest Destiny was a uniquely American derivative of events transpiring across the mid-nineteenth-century world: central states projecting power through nationalistic expression even while those very nations felt the limits of their own control. Not merely Providence's sanction to expand across the continent, Manifest Destiny was also an anxious attempt to explain to the international community, seemingly torn asunder by political and social strife, that the United States could somehow project continental power and elude internal dissolution. The declarations of national authority and the boundaries of central state power reflected a lingering problem from the Age of Revolutions as nations attempted to balance stability against the obstinate challenges to their legitimacy.[42]

By 1848 the nineteenth-century nation-state indeed found itself in a precarious position. Although charged with upholding stability, governments across the world came under increasing scrutiny as common peoples demanded that the state serve as the central source and protectorate of liberty. At the same moment the United States fulfilled its continental destiny, Europe erupted in a series of democratic revolutions to safeguard the rights of workers, limit aristocratic largesse, and topple oppressive monarchies. The rising tide of midcentury liberal nationalism gave voice to a transatlantic dialogue that spoke of the enduring promise of self-determination. "The progress of nationalism, constitutional governments, and new freedoms," explains one leading scholar, "defined the era." Anything that conflicted with liberty, claimed American proponents of Manifest Destiny and European liberals, conflicted with the goals, purposes, and direction of the nation-state. But how would that liberty be distinguished, and who would determine its scope? "Americans are evidently preoccupied with one great fear," Alexis de Tocqueville had earlier observed. "They perceive that among most peoples of the world, the exercise of rights of sovereignty tends to be concentrated in few hands, and they are frightened at the idea that it in the end it will be so with them." Would the new continental acquisitions reflect a consensual understanding of American civilization? Ralph Waldo Emerson forecasted these questions at the outset of the U.S.-Mexico War. "The United States will conquer Mexico," he surmised, "but it will be as the man swallows the arsenic, which brings him down in turn. Mexico will poison us."[43]

As Emerson predicted, tying national expansion to the fate of liberty at once unmasked limits of state power and exposed the republic's political instability. The United States experienced a profound crisis of liberal consensus when David Wilmot, an obscure Democratic congressman from Pennsylvania, proposed in 1846 that slavery would be barred from *any* lands acquired from the war with Mexico. The nation-state's sanction to define liberty had come under unprecedented scrutiny. Hardly an abolitionist, Wilmot imagined the vast West as an endless region in which white settlers could establish lives independent from the corrupting tendencies of the East, freed from the unfair influence of powerful slaveholders, and shielded from the presence of African Americans. "The negro race already occupy enough of this fair continent; let us keep what remains for ourselves, and our children," he underscored, "for the free white laborer, who shall desire to hew him out a home of happiness and peace." Picturing a life "without the disgrace which association with negro slavery brings upon free labor," Wilmot indicted slaveholders for stoking an international war to spread their sullied institution. "The treasure and blood of the North will not be poured out in waging a war for the propagation of slavery over the North American continent," the congressman concluded.[44]

Wilmot's opposition to slaveholding expansion sparked a great debate on the essential place of liberty in the American Union. Henry Clay, a moderate who championed compromise at the expense of sectional tribalism, also opposed the U.S.-Mexico War as a gross attempt to transform the United States. "War unhinges society, disturbs its peaceful and regular industry, and scatters poisonous seeds of disease and immorality," advised the Kentucky senator, echoing his prior opposition to Texas's annexation. Although a prominent slaveholder, Clay feared the rapid, dangerous speed with which war would drape human bondage across a free republic. Long a proponent of gradual emancipation and colonization, Clay, like Wilmot, envisioned a white American future free from racial discord. He thus saw nefarious slaveholding designs in the war with Mexico. He beseeched his fellow citizens in late 1847 "to disavow, in the most positive manner, any desire, on our part, to acquire any foreign territory whatever, for the purpose of introducing slavery into it." Conquering Mexico would spread slavery into new states in which teeming black majorities would overwhelm their white overlords, yielding "collisions and conflicts" and "shocking scenes of rapine and carnage." To maintain "moderation and magnanimity, as with the view of avoiding discord and discontent at home," Clay opposed "conquest ... for the purpose of propagating or extending Slavery." For Henry Clay, militant expansion consolidated the Union into a slaveholding kingdom, an imposing obstacle to national security and international greatness.[45]

For prominent African American abolitionist Frederick Douglass, the U.S.-Mexico War exposed the hopeless corruption of the two-party political system. Though Whigs had claimed to oppose the conflict, they continued to fund the war effort and encouraged the triumph of American arms. And in the vein of Stephens and Clay, too many Whigs callously imagined a national future that excised black Americans from the bountiful liberties found in the vast West. But the Democrats, according to Douglass, exuded plain evil. "They are the accustomed panderers to slaveholders: nothing is either too mean, too dirty, or infamous for them, when commanded by the merciless man stealers of our country." They had stoked an unjust war of international conquest "to perpetuate the enslavement of the colored people of this country." The major political parties had weaponized the Union against any kind of sovereign black mobility. Whigs scoffed at the idea of biracial equality; Democrats were obsessed with their "slaveholding crusade." The republic was aimless, devoid of any purpose other than consolidating political power to maintain white supremacy. "Grasping ambition, tyrannic usurpation, atrocious aggression, cruel and haughty pride, spread, and pervade the land," Douglass bellowed. "The civilization of the age, the voice of the world, the sacredness of human life," once embodied in the American Union, had now shattered under "the mad spirit of proud ambition, blood, and carnage, let loose in the land."[46]

Slaveholders who had long depended on the federal government's consent to maintain and spread the world's largest slave society saw in Wilmot's Proviso, Henry Clay's warnings, and Frederick Douglass's activism violent thwarts to their own liberty. Senator John C. Calhoun condemned his wayward congressional colleagues for reneging on their long-standing commitment to expand slavery. If antislavery restrictionists continued to fill the halls of Congress, Calhoun averred, slaveholders "are to be entirely excluded from the territories which we already possess." Such an unthinkable prospect defied national precedent and enclosed the southern states within a hostile republic ruled by a radical antislavery political class. The Union would thereafter teeter on an unsustainable hierarchy of despotism and racial unrest. Guaranteeing slavery's unobstructed future would instead "uphold this glorious Union of ours" and moderate the turbulence of national growth. "I would rather meet any extremity upon earth than give up one inch of our equality—one inch of what belongs to us as members of this great republic!" The restriction of slavery stunted the nation's unique experiment in republicanism, creating distinct classes of political privilege and subservience. Should slaveholders "not claim our share of the 'unpeopled' territory' in the West," averred Mississippi senator Jefferson Davis, white southerners would fail "to preserve that equality which will enable us to check interference in our domestic affairs." Such a scenario would "sink [the South] in the United States Congress to the helpless condition which Ireland occupies in the British parliament," fomenting revolutionary resentment that might well spark disunion.[47]

Restricting slavery defied everything that Calhoun and Davis considered just about American civilization. Antislavery radicals allegedly preached the immorality of human bondage in defiance of the laws of nature. They condemned slaveholders for their perfidious corruption of American life. And they blocked the diffusion of slavery across the hemisphere, undermining the critical safeguard against enslaved rage. Above all, Calhoun charged, antislavery restrictionists invited bondpeople to rise in insurrection and deluge the South in blood. "The day that the balance between the two sections of the country . . . is destroyed, is a day that will not be far removed from political revolution, anarchy, civil war, and wide-spread disaster," he warned. If Wilmot and his ilk succeeded, the Union would be transformed into a foreign state always hovering on the edge of racial inferno. "I think I see the future. If we do not stand up as we ought," Calhoun concluded, looking with dread at an emancipated globe, "the condition of Ireland is prosperous and happy—the condition of Hindostan is prosperous and happy—the condition of Jamaica is prosperous and happy, to what the condition of the Southern States will be if now they should not stand up manfully in defence of their rights." Slavery had to spread for American civilization to live.[48]

Slavery's place in the American future assumed even greater significance when the 1848 European revolutions, particularly in France, transformed into radical socialist reform movements that demanded equal and universal rights for laborers. A string of emancipations then blanketed both the European continent and colonial outposts, as the inchoate French republic abolished West Indian slavery, Prussia liberated its serfs, and Hungary eradicated involuntary servitude. "France is not prepared to become a Republic," beset by the anarchy of popular passion, Calhoun asserted. French revolutionaries and American antislavery radicals were each enslaved to "erroneous opinions now entertained both in Europe and this country by the movement, or popular party, as to in wh[at] liberty consists, and by what means, it can be obtained and secured." Revolutions produced profound social and political instability, explained fellow South Carolina intellectual William F. Huston. "The history of the last seventy years has been a series of startling changes," he catalogued in 1848, "of precocious and hot house growth." Torn by war and sundered by faction, "Europe ... has been a battle field; revolution has followed revolution so fast, that steam presses can hardly chronicle the shifting lines of states." The modern world seemed to bubble with anarchy. "What is the advantage we possess over the past?" he asked. "Are the mass better fed?—better clothed?—happier? more contented?—even freer?" The specter of revolution was not far from fracturing the slaveholding Union, Calhoun concluded: "The example about to be presented by Europe will be eventually pernicious to the United States, which are always imitating where they should set the example, and following where they ought to lead."[49]

In the deleterious wake of the European revolutions, Americans viewed theirs as the only functional democracy in the world, stoking profound unease about the nation's destiny. Painfully aware of antidemocratic internationalization, Americans in their ensuing domestic struggle to organize the lands acquired from Mexico debated how best to safeguard liberty and thwart global suppression. But they did not realize, David Potter explains, that "the forces which opposed nationalism in Europe were entirely unlike those which opposed it in America." Fearing oligarchy, dreading military coups, and shunning statism, Americans placed absolute faith in democracy to stem the forces of extremism. But it was democracy itself that most threatened the United States' internal stability. American democracy, Tocqueville noted, created an aggressive adherence to "equality in freedom." And in the midcentury age of liberal nationalism Americans viewed the state as the foremost guardian of liberty, the antithesis of arbitrary privilege and centralized coercion. Tocqueville indeed recognized that Americans "have an ardent, insatiable, eternal invincible passion" from which "they will not tolerate aristocracy," which invited illegitimate rule by international forces and "alleged encroachments of the central power."[50]

Tocqueville observed the impossible paradox of American democracy's antiaristocratic tenor: an equal obsession with democratic majority rule. "In the United States, political questions cannot be posed in a manner so general and so absolute, and all the parties are ready to recognize the rights of the majority because they all hope to be able to exercise them to their profit one day." A popular majority demanded universal consent from which "no obstacles" may "even delay its advance, and allow it time to hear the complaints of those it crushes as it passes." Though Tocqueville recognized American democracy's broad egalitarianism, he remained apprehensive about a democratic majority's tendency to undermine liberty. "What I most reproach in democratic government, as it has been organized in the United States, is not, as many people in Europe claim, its weakness," the Frenchman outlined, "but on the contrary, its irresistible force. And what I find most repugnant to me in America is not the extreme freedom that reigns there, it is the lack of a guarantee against tyranny." Democratic majority rule was imbued with tyrannical impulses to quash any hostile menace that threatened its life. But to oppose a democratic majority was to oppose popular government and the national consensus, thus imperiling the nation's security. Who would define David Wilmot's white egalitarian democracy? Who would determine the boundaries of John C. Calhoun's slaveholding liberty? Who would adhere to Henry Clay's progressive moderation? And would anyone recognize David Walker's basic appeal to universal freedom and Frederick Douglass's condemnation of a political system corrupted by and beholden to slaveholding interests?[51]

The ensuing territorial crisis of 1850 bore out Tocqueville's concerns. The shape and design of Wilmot's Proviso, joined with the failure of European democracy and the flowering global emancipations, transformed what was once a political dispute over slavery's expansion into a vehement referendum on the scope of democratic majority rule. The decade following the U.S.-Mexico War featured violent contests for the majority political domination of the federal government. As a leading historian notes, "The goal was to claim and wield, not limit, state power" in the effort to forge a binding relationship between the nation-state and liberty. Slaveholders and nonslaveholders competed for jurisdiction of the federal apparatus, locating the nation's future, its expanding borders, and its claim to liberty within their distinct notions of civilization. Thus, the power of ever-changing majorities inspired accusations from opponents who claimed that despotic international antagonisms had seized opposing political coalitions and the reins of government purposely to annihilate the liberty of the minority.[52]

Confronted with the nearly impossible task of admitting new states carved out of the vast western lands acquired from Mexico, American political culture in 1850 encountered the profound shock of internationalization. Would the new states resemble the egalitarian ideal of the 1848 revolutions and the free-labor society of the North, or would they embody the plantation South's reflection of white racial privilege and the stability of European aristocracy?

This question prompted paranoid expressions that volatile international radicalism had crept into the domestic political system. The West represented the infinite unknown in which two versions of American civilization—freedom and slavery—collided in a bout for eternal supremacy. The contest would decide not only the fate of a sparsely populated western territory. It would also determine how the United States presented itself as the last best hope of liberty for a world desperately in need of ideological guidance.[53]

The territorial crisis of 1850 embodied a long-standing dispute over the shape and disposition of American exceptionalism. As a direct source of republican liberty, the use, widespread ownership, and imagined implications of land fomented the fierce political quarrels that came in the wake of the war against Mexico. Southern slaveholders had long fancied themselves as part of an international gentry, an exclusive class of white men whose mastery of the land and people created absolute power and unlimited liberty, at least for themselves. Although sensitive to charges of aristocracy, slaveholders nonetheless fashioned a hierarchical society predicated on racial inequality and dependence so that their own white democracy could flourish. Dominance of vast acreage yielded lives of leisure, inspired intellectual pursuits, and maintained a stable society constructed on "natural" racial orders. For white southerners, claimed a Democrat from Alabama, slavery and plantation agriculture served "a vital reality, an essential principle of their very organism, and indissolubly interwoven into the very framework of their being." Any questioning of this system, any alternative vision, any unusual substitution for slavery-based liberty was met with stern reprisal.[54]

Responding to the Wilmot Proviso and critiques from the emergent Free Soil Party, a political organization born in 1848 and dedicated to restricting slavery in the West, slaveholders shaped their arguments in 1850 with one eye toward Europe and the other toward the Caribbean. The turbulent revolutions in France, which rose with democratic promise but deteriorated into a socialist demise, convinced some southerners that the same "fanaticism" infected northern critiques of slavery's expansion. After all, the new French republic had abolished slavery in the West Indies in a supposed commitment to egalitarianism. Reacting seemingly to Wilmot, French abolitionism, the rise of European socialism, and the arrival of German refugees who allegedly spread revolutionary labor propaganda throughout the South, one congressman decried the fate of southern liberty: "The power to dictate what sort of property the State may allow a citizen to own and work—whether oxen, horses, or Negroes," he declared, "is tyrannical." Mississippi senator Jefferson Davis likewise blasted northern politicians for aligning with European revolutionaries who together internationalized the Union's constitutional safeguards. "The European Socialists, who, in wild radicalism ... are the correspondents of the American Abolitionists, maintain the same doctrine as to all property, that the abolitionists do as to slave property. He who has property, they argue, is the robber of him who has not," explained Davis. "And the same precise theories of attack at the North on the slave property of the South . . . , if carried out to their legitimate and necessary logical consequences," would "superinduce attacks on all property, North and South."[55]

Few white southerners better articulated the principle of slaveholding civilization better than Davis. Wealthy, temperate, and influential, he embodied the promise of a slaveholding Union in his relentless assault on antislavery restriction. Like his idol John C. Calhoun, Davis indicted "abolitionism" as a foreign cancer, a wicked disease that infected the American soul, balkanizing a moderate and stable Union into warring factions. Wilmot's Proviso and pretentious Free Soilers, Davis charged in a defiant speech delivered in 1850, exuded "the clamor of a noisy fanaticism" in their "declar[ation] of war against the institution of slavery." Human bondage brought stability to the Union. But international abolitionists intended "that very Government is to be arrayed in hostility against an institution so interwoven with its interests, its domestic peace, and all its social relations." Davis even asked whether antislavery restrictionists' defiance of ordered liberty and their radical incursion upon national security were "just cause[s] for war." Extolling his fellow senators to see the cataclysms wrought by global emancipations, Davis pointed to "the history of St. Domingo and . . . the present condition of Jamaica" as signs of "the greatest catastrophe" awaiting the Union. Slavery forestalled war; its abolition, and even its restriction, invited revolutionary bloodshed.[56]

For Davis, war arrived when foreign agents threatened to halt the Union's peaceful, progressive march toward modernity. Abolitionism—and to Jefferson Davis, David Wilmot was just as much an abolitionist as Frederick Douglass and William Lloyd Garrison—affronted the basic laws of nature, sullying the Union's providential charge. "Was this Constitution," Davis asked of the charter of American civilization, "formed for the purpose of emancipation?" He did not even deign to answer such a preposterous question. Slavery's presence, its growth, its bountiful future, he instead argued, charted a wholly distinct path from the world's fanciful delusion with egalitarian liberalism. Bondage civilized all whom it touched, bringing the enslaved African especially "into a Christian land. It brought him from a benighted region, and placed him in one where civilization would elevate and dignify his nature." And it cultivated the world's richest planting soils, on which "in certain climates only the African race are adapted to work in the sun." Slavery thus occasioned balance, effected stability, defied natural obstacles and climatological barriers, and ensured prosperity. Emancipation had transformed Haiti, Mexico, and Jamaica "from being among the most productive and profitable colonies" into wastelands of "decay, [which] are relapsing into desert and barbarism." Why, then, should American slaveholders submit to radical territorial restrictions, especially when "the disunion of these States . . . will be a sad commentary upon the justice and wisdom of our people"?[57]

Free Soilers responded that the power of southern slavery might well transform the United States, by way of the West and the still-thriving Caribbean and South American slave societies, into aristocratic slaveholding lands pledged to economic inequality and social immobility. The Free Soil Party enjoyed the influence and support of radical migrants who fled Europe as refugees of the 1848 revolutions. They condemned aristocratic slaveholders' unjust domination of land as the pernicious twin of despotic European autocrats who coerced laborers into procuring exorbitant profits for their overlords. "As a contest between truth and falsehood, between the principle of Liberty and the rile of slavery," Charles Francis Adams announced at the party's 1848 convention, "the question now before us is one, which involves the proposition whether we shall deduce government from the consent of the governed." The northern component of the agrarian republic had evolved a culture in which small, self-sufficient family farms eschewed dependence and privilege and instead celebrated independent competency. For moderate antislavery northerners and European migrants, free control of the land afforded lives of autonomy and economic mobility, qualities which, after 1848, seemed exclusive to the United States. A Wisconsin journal spoke for many American advocates of free labor shortly after the European revolutions faded into anarchy. "Millions of Germans, Irishmen, Englishmen, and Frenchmen," it averred, "are perishing for want and necessities of life. By Land Monopoly, they are precluded from being their own employers, and although able and willing to work, they are denied employment."[58]

If land was kept free—that is, if slaveholding oligarchs did not enjoy the state-sanctioned privilege to acquire vast territories through the exclusion of small-time farmers—equitable numbers of free white men could pursue lives of economic independence. Indeed, the Free Soil Party drew its initial strength from the 1848 European democrats who, in their quest to overthrow the existing ruling class, provided a model for antislavery activists in the United States. The ultimate consolidation of monarchism and aristocracy convinced some Free Soilers that the fate of liberty rested only in the American Union, in which the vast West safeguarded a liberal future. "Can you not, all of you, buckle on your armor, and rousing the people by an eloquence suited to the crisis," pleaded Salmon P. Chase, an Ohio senator dedicated to free laborism, "achieve a victory for Freedom, which will prove that the world is not wholly given over to reaction—that it will compensate, in some measure, for our defeats in [Europe]?" If slavery expanded its reach across the vast continent, Chase implied, the United States might as well consider itself the second coming of the British aristocracy. Montgomery Blair, who hardly boasted progressive views on race, believed that the South had wielded "all political power and social consideration . . . in the hands of the slaveholders, who are occupied, like the English aristocracy, almost exclusively with political affairs and amusements." If slavery spread to the West, the worst and most destructive European traditions—the very ones against which the revolutionary fathers fought so passionately—would yet again turn the United States into a sad colonial reflection of the Old World.[59]

Few free laborers spoke more directly about the egalitarian dimensions of American liberty better than New York senator William Henry Seward. A stalwart opponent of human bondage, Seward condemned his slaveholding Union, which mocked its founding national charters. An affront to the natural state of humanity, "slavery is only a temporary, accidental, partial, and incongruous" condition. "Freedom, on the contrary, is a perpetual, organic, universal one, in harmony with the Constitution of the United States." Seward was deeply anxious about his republic's place in the modern world: "The most alarming evidence of our degeneracy ... is found in the fact that we even debate such a question" as slavery's relation to liberty. Because "Britain, France, and Mexico have abolished slavery, and all other European States are preparing to abolish it as speedily as they can," Seward demanded that the Union immediately halt the spread of human bondage. While constitutional constraints and security considerations barred immediate abolition, restricting expansion demonstrated slavery's "incompatibil[ity]" with "natural rights, the diffusion of knowledge, and the freedom of industry." Ultimately, the institution "subverts the principle of democracy, and converts the State into an aristocracy of a despotism."[60]

Seward framed slaveholding as the perverted tool of international tyrants. "It was introduced on this continent as an engine of conquest, and for the establishment of monarchical power, by the Portuguese and the Spaniards, and was rapidly extended by them all over South America, Central America, Louisiana, and Mexico." But as the nineteenth-century world moved increasingly toward free labor, the fruits of enlightened reason, independence, and the leveling of "all classes of men" cooled the violent tensions once imposed by European monarchs. Seward warned of the United States' precarious status as the world's only nation to harbor *both* slavery and free labor, an unsustainable and disastrous combination. Sober political compromise would not tolerate future arbitrations between American slaveholders and egalitarians. "It is an irrepressible conflict between opposing and enduring forces, and it means that the United States must and will, sooner or later, become either entirely a slaveholding nation, or entirely a free-labor nation." Seward knew that "the slaveholding class" would stop at nothing to emerge victorious. Through "threats of disunion" and a rapacious diplomatic corps to "annex foreign slaveholding States," the Slave Power, emulating Old World monarchs, would "carry slavery into all the territories of the United States" and erect a sprawling "aristocracy of slaveholders." Seward nevertheless promised that "the people of the United States have been no less steadily and perseveringly gathering together the forces ... to confound and overthrow, by one decisive blow, the betrayers of the constitution and freedom forever."[61]

Faced with apparent threats to their slaveholding republic, white southerners convened in 1850 at Nashville, Tennessee, to ponder the future of Union. There, William Gilmore Simms imagined a dangerous radicalism arising from an abolitionist West. "We have been harrassed and insulted, by those who ought to have been our brethren, in their constant agitation of a subject vital to us and the peace of our families. We have been outraged by the gross misrepresentations of our moral and social habits, and by the manner in which they have denounced us before the world." Simms declared that if antislavery fanatics defined the terms of American civilization and continued to regard slaveholders as estranged enemies of the national community, he would advocate breaking the bonds of Union. Perhaps slavery—the essence of white liberty, in his estimation—would best be protected *outside* the United States, allowed to spread freely across a world in desperate need of the South's agricultural bounty. Accepting the potential necessity of secession, another white southerner declared, "We desire disunion," not because white southerners had developed a wholly new national identity, but instead to ensure "that we might be freed from the dominion of a majority, whose political creed is their interest, and whose religion is fanaticism. We consent to our own degradation, when we remain in common bonds with those who regard us as their moral and religious inferiors, and who use the common halls of our government, to give constant expression to that feeling."[62]

As it always had, threats of disunion mobilized political moderates who feared the collapse of the American republic. In the wake of democracy's failure in Europe, moderates had even more reason to stem the tide of secession, which they saw as a fanatical response to a political dispute. A Philadelphia newspaper cautioned that disunion would "*Europeanise* this continent," instigating "national subdivision, wars, standing armies, aristocracy, dynasties, poverty, ignorance, degradation, incessant fraud of upper classes to retain exclusive privileges, and occasional and bloody struggles of lower classes for rights which they would not know how to recover, enjoy or maintain." Pleading for "both sections" not to succumb to radical passions, the newspaper branded disunion "the greatest evil which could befall this continent and the world." Maryland Whig Reverdy Johnson likewise shuddered at the "inconceivable evils" of civil war shattering "a Union which dispenses to all everything that any contrivance of human society can dispense." Dissolving the nation posed an indelible threat to the future of global liberty. "This glorious and mighty republic, now the pride and admiration of the world, will be broken into withered and scattered fragments; and all by suicidal hands."[63]

Whatever else they may have thought about free labor and slavery, the mass of white northerners and southerners feared even more the implications of revolution, strife, coups, and reactionary uprisings. Still smoldering under the ashes of those very calamities, Europe, Central America, and the Caribbean unveiled what would happen in the United States if disunion occurred. Even some committed slaveholders used the European example to dissociate secession as a practical recourse against political oppression. "Revolutions ought not to be made too easily," the Southern Rights Association of South Carolina explained, lest they inevitably collapse into authoritarianism and tyranny, thus imperiling slavery to eternal destruction. "Witness France, where revolutions have become the bloody toy of the multitude; who fight for they know not what; spurning today the idol of yesterday, and calling for revolution as they would a parade." Jefferson Davis supported the Nashville Convention to *avert* the radicalism of disunion. "To check aggression, to preserve the union, peaceably to secure our rights requires prompt action," propelling rational minds to *subvert* "the energy of revolution" in favor of "the preservation of the Constitution." Terrific visions of ruinous upheaval thus inspired moderates from both sides to secure a compromise, which did not completely mollify slaveholding and free-labor interests, but which seemingly preserved the United States from sliding into the same morass of destruction that had befallen Europe and the New World.[64]

A leading voice of moderation, Massachusetts senator Daniel Webster framed the essence of compromise. Addressing his rigid colleagues on both sides of the debate, Webster renounced the radicalism of disunion. "There can be no such thing as a peaceable secession," which shattered all that made the Union pure, unique, and whole. "Shame upon us! if we, of this generation, should dishonor these ensigns of the power of the Government, and the harmony of the Union, which is every day felt among us," he remonstrated. Aghast at the utter madness of national divorce, Webster imagined that Providence's bountiful harvest, bestowed upon a chosen and exceptional people, would forever disappear within the bitter tangle of fratricidal conflict. "This Republic now extends, with a vast breadth, across the whole continent," sustained by "youthful veins [which] are full of enterprise, courage, and honorable love of glory and renown." Unbound from a "monarchical throne" and liberated from the "iron chain of despotic power," the Union stood apart from a corrupted world, "founded upon principles of equality" whose "daily respiration is liberty." Disunion would join the devastated American state to its pathetic international counterparts. "To break up this great Government! to dismember this great country! to astonish Europe with an act of folly, such as Europe for two centuries has never beheld in any government," Webster concluded, would extinguish the world's lone flame of liberty.[65]

In the same vein that he forged the Missouri Compromise of 1820 and tempered South Carolina nullification in 1833, the nationalist Whig Henry Clay joined with Webster to promote compromise measures. Balancing slaveholding and free-labor interests, Clay endorsed California's admission to the Union as a free state; called for a stronger fugitive slave law; recommended that the slave trade in Washington, DC, be abolished; sponsored a reduction of Texas's western boundaries; and advocated deferring the question of slavery's place in the newly formed New Mexico and Utah territories. These proposals did not meet the absolute demands of either slaveholding expansionists or antislavery restrictionists. Nevertheless, Clay stoked the discursive spirits of moderation and exceptionalism to advance his compromise. "Every member of this body is desirous of restoring once more peace, harmony, and fraternal affection to this distracted people," Clay explained to the Senate. "Compromise is peculiarly appropriate among the members of a republic, as of one common family," he instructed on the enduring power of Union. To abjure conciliation would toss the world's foremost experiment in sober republicanism into the fury of civil war. Clay thus encouraged all to "pause at the edge of the precipice, before the fearful and disastrous leap is taken into the yawning abyss below." Equally fearful of the Union's collapse, Illinois Democrat Stephen Douglas allied with Clay in a bipartisan effort to work tirelessly in uniting extremists from both sides with moderates who favored national balance. With swift, unflagging vigor, Douglas convinced enough sectional partisans that their respective interests would best be preserved *within* the Union. And the compromise came. The Union was preserved.[66]

The Compromise of American Exceptionalism

In the wake of the Compromise of 1850, moderate Whig president Millard Fillmore praised Congress's restraint in the face of national collapse. The "final settlement" to the vexing issue of slavery's future had secured "the peace and welfare of the country." The Union's political moderation endorsed "the spirit of conciliation" to jettison "doubts and uncertainties in the minds of thousands of good men concerning the durability of our popular institutions." Rather than acting as a subversive agent, democracy proved "that our liberty and our Union may subsist together for the benefit of this and all succeeding generations." Privately, Fillmore confided his hatred for slavery, "an existing evil" that nearly sounded the republic's untimely death. The compromise indeed dealt severe blows to the American Slave Power by admitting California as a free state—thereby enlarging the Senate's antislavery coalition—and liberating the nation's capital from the traffic in human labor. However, to maintain the Union "we must endure [the institution]" and "give it such protection as is guaranteed by the Constitution." Fillmore understood slavery's lethal allure, and he prayed that "we can get rid of it without destroying the last hope of free government in the world." Only compromise, even with the most toxic customs of national life, could preserve American civilization.[67]

Yet Fillmore asked for the impossible. Seeking a future that at once compromised with slavery and imagined its eternal demise posed irreconcilable demands. The mutual concessions forged in 1850 indeed demonstrated the ability to quell the dangers of disunion and even limit the Slave Power's expansion. But at what cost? And what, precisely, had Americans negotiated? The Compromise of 1850 preserved the Union while also compromising the basic meaning of Union itself. Compromise assured a perpetual nation, while conceding the scope of American liberty to slaveholders. To compromise with slavery meant entrenching the institution within the republic, compelling Americans to legitimate its active place in national life. Insofar as it signaled the endurance of moderation, the marginalization of slaveholding secessionists, and even the restriction of slavery's westward expansion, the Compromise of 1850 guaranteed the Union as a slaveholding domain. To stand as exceptions to global turmoil, national disintegration, and sectional upheaval, Americans had to live in lasting union with human bondage.[68]

No plank in the compromise spoke to Fillmore's dilemma more than the Fugitive Slave Act of 1850. Because all the fiery sermons involved slavery's *western* future, few nonslaveholding white Americans initially considered absconded enslaved people a problem of the *national* future. Few who lived outside the South's large plantation districts had ever encountered slavery, much less African Americans. But the revitalized fugitive slave law weaponized the federal government into an enforcement agency to regulate enslaved movement and to compel universal white obedience. The law forced local, state, and federal governments to act in unified pursuit of runaway slaves, criminalizing any shelter and aid given to fugitives, incentivizing federal slavecatchers to align with local magistrates to track slaveholders' restive and mobile property, and bringing antislavery communities under the centralized purview of national regulation. In a devastating blow to federalism, the law disregarded the popular democratic will of northern states that had abolished slavery in the decades after the American Revolution. Aiming to temper the imbalance brought by California's admission as a free state, Henry Clay and Stephen Douglas assumed that a rigorous and active fugitive slave law would mollify slaveholding obsessions with sectional equilibrium and national power. And they were right. "The continued existence of the United States as one nation," the *Southern Literary Messenger* explained on behalf of all slaveholders, "depends upon the full and faithful execution of the Fugitive Slave Bill."[69]

Perhaps more than ever before, the Union was now synonymous with slaveholding. If the Compromise of 1850 limited slavery's westward growth, the new fugitive slave law expanded slavery's northern boundaries. Even the most ambivalent opponents of slavery could not ignore their direct collusion in safeguarding the institution's aggressive life. Helpless onlookers witnessed the ugly, heart-wrenching episodes of fugitives stolen from freedom, families ripped apart, their victims shipped to hungry plantations, and federal agents breaching the safe confines of autonomous local communities. While myriad northerners—including Presidents Fillmore, a Whig, and Franklin Pierce, a Democrat—pledged to uphold the sanctity of compromise, others damned their legal complicity on behalf of slaveholding interests. Ralph Waldo Emerson spoke for countless opponents of compromise when he condemned his fellow statesman from Massachusetts, Daniel Webster, for promoting the unholy decree in the name of Union. "The most detestable law that was ever enacted by a civilized state," Emerson charged, transformed "the fairest and most triumphant national escutcheon the sun ever shone upon, the free, the expanding, the hospitable, the irresistible America"—indeed, "the blessing of the world"—"into a jail or barracoon for the slaves of a few thousand Southern planters, and all the citizens of this hemisphere into kidnappers and drivers for the same."[70]

African Americans joined with white northerners to denounce the Union as the world's unrivaled slaveholding nation. Confined in slavery and trapped in freedom, black critics alleged that they lived as subversive foreigners in the United States. "There is not even a single spot in this broad land, where [African American] rights can be protected," prominent abolitionist and free woman of color Charlotte Forten protested from Massachusetts. Forten derided northern whites for routinely heralding individual liberties as symbols "of their vaunted *independence*. Strange that they cannot feel their own degradation—the weight of the chains which they have imposed upon themselves" by acquiescing to and compromising with slaveholding oligarchs. Regulated by the power of a militarized state that barred their people structurally, politically, and institutionally, while sanctioning the enslavement of millions, convinced many black Americans that they subsisted at the margins of national life. "We are politically, not of them, but aliens to the laws and political privileges of the country," pronounced Martin Delany, one of the most passionate voices of African American resistance. "Our descent, by the laws of the country, stamps us with inferiority." As David Walker once implied, the United States had failed to abide its sacred mission, leaving many black Americans disillusioned with life in a slaveholding police state. H. Ford Douglas, a prominent black intellectual who considered the Union a tragic emblem of liberty, in 1850 cautioned that any society that "fails to protect the rights of man ... ought to be erased from the category of nations, and be numbered with the sleeping despotisms that have long sunk beneath the proud and majestic march of advancing civilization."[71]

Only focused resistance and unified purpose could stem the overwhelming tide of oppression collapsing on free and enslaved communities. "IT IS YOUR SOLEMN AND IMPERATIVE DUTY TO USE EVERY MEANS, BOTH MORAL, INTELLECTUAL, AND PHYSICAL THAT PROMISE SUCCESS," Henry Highland Garnet announced in his personal publication of David Walker's *Appeal* in 1848. "Let your motto be RESISTANCE! RESISTANCE! RESISTANCE! No oppressed people have ever secured their liberty without resistance," he wrote, referring to enslaved uprisings in Haiti, Demerara, South Carolina, and Jamaica. A meeting of free New Englanders of African descent located the Fugitive Slave Act among the Atlantic world's worst despotisms. The measure defied the egalitarian purpose of Union and reflected the stifling racial and monarchial hierarchies that held oppressed peoples in eternal abeyance.

If free African American communities in the North aligned with clandestine networks of enslaved people, each exhibiting "noble disregard of the unconstitutional" law, perhaps they could demonstrate the power of common people "finally triumphing over the Government," a prospect "humiliating to the Slave Power."[72]

The example of Haiti loomed large in this kind of resistance. "The Haytiens are the only people who achieved their independence by the sword, unaided by other nations," resolved another African American political meeting, and "they have maintained it to the present hour." Their unyielding desire for liberty, "which have been progressive steps towards Republicanism, is full confirmation of their capacity for self-government." Yet despite calls for insurrection, a remarkable number of black intellectuals pledged devotion to the American *idea* as the underpinning of civilized resistance. "We profess to be republicans, not jacobins nor agrarians," one writer acknowledged, suggesting that radical means of change had to be softened by moderate ends. The United States could be reformed according to its true commitment to universal liberty, a speaker at a black convention in Boston reminded his audience, because the republic endured as "a great principle, *the fraternal unity of man*."[73]

The formation of local black militias functioned as a bellicose yet restrained bulwark against the slaveholding Union. African Americans in the North had long commemorated West India Day, when, on August 1, 1834, Parliament abolished slavery in the British Caribbean. Gathered in great public celebrations featuring prominent speakers and civic meetings, West India Day offered political solidarity with hemispheric liberation movements. Parades boasted streamers emblazoned with the popular slogans "No Union with Slaveholders" and "America! With All Her Faults We Love Her Still." When the Compromise of 1850 strengthened the Fugitive Slave Law, African American militias sprang up throughout the free states to defy the gross abuse of federal power. These militias enjoyed a prominent place during West India Day celebrations, standing as militant barriers to slavery's collapsing boundaries. Functioning as miniature armies, militias encouraged fugitives to seek refuge behind their protective lines. African Americans sheltered their liberty by whittling militarized spaces out of a white culture deeply skeptical of black belligerence. The Haitian tradition of free peoples aligning with the enslaved, coupled with the American tradition of virtuous civic engagement, formed strong corporate bonds within black communities. "One of the most beautiful exhibitions of honor, associated with national patriotism," extolled J. W. Lewis, a free black intellectual, "is the conduct of Tousaint Laoverture, the African chieftain, and Washington of Hayti."[74]

The act of forming militias conformed to long-standing American citizenship rituals in which bearing arms and providing for local defense functioned as careful restraints against centralized tyranny. African American militiamen did not see themselves as pugnacious rebels pursuing a revolu-

tionary racial coup. Fostering a remarkable sense of autonomy, militia formation defied existing racial hierarchies and demonstrated black men's fitness
to practice civic norms. Recognizing the fruitless, bloody endeavor of outright insurrection, African American leaders counseled that subtle forms of
resistance would be imperative to contest slaveholders' commanding reach.
Henry Highland Garnet considered slave revolt "inexpedient," a suicidal mission against an entrenched militarized state. The hemisphere's most successful insurrections—Haiti, Demerara, and Jamaica—did not originate in outright revolt; instead they were products of enduring but restrained "strikes."
As David Walker once advised, neither the enslaved nor their free allies had to
instigate an authentic, full-scale rebellion to chip away at the edges of oppression. Engaging public opinion through speeches, pamphlets, and newspapers;
encouraging and harboring runaways; and forging alliances with European
abolitionists abroad and white activists at home all forged important spokes
in the democratic wheel of resistance. From community mobilization to institutional development, African Americans pursued social and legal emancipation through slow, deliberate means. As the history of the British West
Indies had demonstrated in the 1830s, networks, organization, and movement ultimately unfolded liberation. If they remained mobilized and committed to Atlantic revolutionary ideals, while disavowing radicalism, the day
of jubilee would arrive.[75]

Slaveholders emerged from the Compromise of 1850 both confident and
cautious. Although they saw that moderate interests remained willing to compromise with slavery in order to preserve the Union, many interpreted biracial antislavery activism as a lingering symptom of European and hemispheric radicalism. The twin catastrophes of 1848—the domestic antislavery
crusade and the consolidation of international extremism—convinced Georgia judge Joseph Henry Lumpkin that "the violent assaults of these fiends
have compelled us in self defense to investigate this momentous subject in all
of its bearings." Slaveholders thus used the Union itself to boast their region,
their institutions, and their civilization as vindication of the world's most exceptional slave society. "We possess all the elements of greatness and power,"
a North Carolina periodical noted. "Peace smiles upon us from all quarters
of the globe; a material prosperity, unparalleled in the annals of the world,
surrounds us; our territory embraces almost the entire continent; we enjoy
wide-spread intelligence and universal plenty; we are happy, WE ARE FREE."
Though American slaveholders made up only 1 percent of the national population, they possessed 90 percent of all southern wealth and enslaved most of
the region's bound people of color. They transposed their exorbitant affluence
and social clout into a nearly impenetrable control of the Democratic Party,
which they used to advance and consolidate their elite, political interests.[76]

Southern slaveholders fashioned a powerful independence at home and
abroad. Promoting free trade, experimenting with technological innovation,

employing the central state to maintain and expand their institutions, mastering domestic and global exchange markets, deploying federal power to regulate enslaved fugitives, aligning with fellow hemispheric slave societies, and articulating a defense of human bondage based on allegedly modern racial science instilled in slaveholders a cocky faith that the world's future rested in the American South. "We defend the system of African slavery as existing among us, not upon the ground of *temporary expediency*," South Carolina social commentator Louisa McCord explained, "but as a *fixed and permanent necessity* from the nature of things and the nature of men." As prominent proslavery theorist George Fitzhugh averred, the northern United States had joined France in organizing societies based on fallacious notions of "universal liberty and equality," which he regarded as "destructive to the morals, [and] to the happiness of society." Rather than promoting social mobility and economic independence, these radical declarations of human rights had instead yielded debilitating societal regressions occasioned by modern capitalism. The market economy, Fitzhugh alleged, fostered social resentment among and between classes as industrial workers competed for tenuous employment and employers hired "the laborer who will work for the least wages." This dangerous volatility produced strikes, riots, and even revolutions. Conversely, in the conservative, moderating, and reputable practice of slavery, "there is no rivalry, no competition to get employment among slaves." The system furnished a steady stream of bound, unfree labor, which produced a "lofty and independent" status to and "elevat[ed] the character of the master." The enslaved, according to Fitzhugh, enjoyed the consistent fulfillment of their daily needs, sustenance, and shelter, regardless of their ability or aptitude. As "the beau ideal of Communism," plantation slavery prevented turbulent class, racial, and market conflicts. "A state of dependence is the only condition in which reciprocal affection can exist among human beings—the only situation in which the war of competition ceases, and peace, amity and good will arise." McCord thus concluded, "Were negro slavery really injurious to the world, abolitionists would be right." Slavery's efficiency, its productivity, and its stability allegedly protected the Union from oozing as "a running sore among the nations," giving "a new home to the homeless and a new world to progressive and aspiring man."[77]

Such remarks betrayed the anxious conceit with which slavery's apologists heralded theirs as among the remaining and thriving slaveholding societies in the world. They scoffed at the economic miscalculations made by the British in 1833 and the French in 1848 to liberate their West Indian slaves; they laughed at the seemingly unsophisticated and weak black republic in Haiti; and they sneered at the apparent worldwide obsession with free labor, which they claimed had proven a fool's game in the cutthroat arena of international capitalism. "The position which the Southern United States hold to the commercial and industrial world," remarked an author in *DeBow's Re-*

view, a widely circulated southern agricultural journal, "is one of the most remarkable phenomena of modern times." American exceptionalism was spun entirely out of cotton, "which has gradually enveloped the commercial world, and bound the fortunes of American slaves so firmly to human progress, that civilization itself may almost be said to depend upon the continual servitude of the blacks in America." The world's bold experiment in abolitionism had failed. Free labor in the Caribbean could not compete economically, could not produce nearly enough staple products, and could not integrate the black and white races. Slavery's permanent, cheap conditions, bolstered by abundant land, fierce mobility, government sanction, and international demand for cotton, had populated the South by 1860 with 4 million enslaved people, who comprised two-thirds of the Western Hemisphere's subjugated laborers. If it had been its own independent country, the American South would have "rank[ed] as the fourth most prosperous nation in the world in 1860." "No power on earth dares to make war upon" the American South, which "carr[ies] the whole civilized world," remarked James Henry Hammond.[78]

Foreshadowing the South's commanding global position, one commentator explained in 1852 that cotton and slavery were "destined to make a new era in the intercourse of nations, and to develop new sources of civilization." Yet "the great difficulty is among ourselves," rooted in American political culture and the uncertainties of democracy. "It is not over-production, or foreign competition, that we have to dread, but the denial of equal rights in the Union, that endangers us." Only connecting the slaveholding Union to the broader world of unfree labor would safeguard the republic amid abolitionist threats. The hemispheric assembly of slavery and antislavery societies fulfilled both "dreams and nightmares," in which Cuba and Brazil joined with the United States to lead the world toward a new slaveholding future, while Haiti and Jamaica embodied the deep-seated fears of a tortured abolitionist past. By acquiring "Cuba and St. Domingo," envisioned Mississippi congressman Albert Gallatin Brown, "we could control the productions of the tropics, and with them the commerce of the world." But Brown did not halt his imagined march in the Gulf. "I want Tamaulipas, Potosi, and one or two other Mexican states, and I want them all for the same reason—for the planting and spreading of slavery. And a foothold in Central America will powerfully aid us in acquiring those other States." Only the unchecked hemispheric expansion of the slaveholding Union could ensure slaveholding prosperity.[79]

To guard against encroaching international abolitionism, slaveholding nationalists employed the U.S. military to secure their institution and expand it across the hemisphere. In the decade following the war against Mexico, slaveholders populated the military establishment in overwhelming numbers. They commanded influence as the secretaries of war and navy while also chairing the powerful congressional Committee on Military and Naval Affairs.[80] As the martial institutions of state power and diplomatic force, the army and navy

shaped continental and hemispheric landscapes in the slaveholding interest. Secretary of War Jefferson Davis (from 1853 to 1857) reformed the military into a slaveholding ally by expanding the size of the army, promoting
increased military budgets, and concentrating federal forces throughout the
vast western territories. "We should not allow the Abolitionists to Colonise
Kansas [and New Mexico] by emigrant societies without making an effort to
counteract it by throwing in a Southern population," he averred in 1855. "The
country on the Pacific is in many respects adapted to slave labor, and many of
the citizens desire its introduction." Davis endorsed an imposing continental
military presence to secure western lands, displace Indigenous peoples, map
and survey territory, and prepare the region for railroad access. Then, "our
people with their servants, their horses and their cows would gradually pass
westward over fertile lands" and display "the advantage of their associated
labor." A united slaveholding republic, secured by a "border once established
from East to West," guaranteed "future acquisitions to the South" and satisfied
"the great purpose for which our Union was established."[81]

Slaveholding nationalists argued that expanding the institution through
continental and hemispheric annexations marginalized global abolitionists
and thwarted enslaved rebellions. "We claim the right of expansion," Mississippi governor John Quitman declared in his support of private filibustering
expeditions to conquer Cuba, "as essential to our future security and prosperity.... [We] require more elbow room, to guard against the possibility that
a system of labor now so beneficent and productive might, from a redundant
slave population confined to narrow limits, become an ultimate evil." For like-
minded champions of slavery's global expansion, the American South had
no true borders. Slaveholders imagined their institution's fluidity extending
throughout the Caribbean, bleeding throughout the West, and floating freely
beyond the oceans. "The United States constitution, recognizing property in
slaves," explained Jefferson Davis, protected the institution as it progressed
across the hemisphere, "in vessels or in territories, on the high seas, or on the
Pacific slope. Wherever our flag floats as the emblem of sovereignty, the citizen of the United States has a right to claim from the general government, the
shield of the constitution, and the enforcement of its guarantees." This was
the slaveholding Union in action. It was part of and carefully separated from
the world. And it wielded weapons to stem internal and external dissidence.
Emancipation through nightmarish revolution (as in Haiti) or through legislative reform (as in the British and French West Indies) would never occur in
the United States.[82]

Davis framed a broader white southern worldview that anticipated future
attempts to restrict the spread of slavery. The United States was exceptional,
explained Georgia's Thomas R. R. Cobb, because it had thwarted the dreadful strife that had so needlessly infected the slaveholding world. "Remove the

restraining and controlling power of the master," he argued, "and the negro becomes, at once, the slave of his lust, and the victim of his indolence, relapsing, with wonderful rapidity, into his pristine barbarism." Haiti and Jamaica "are living witness to this truth." Committed slaveholders would not permit another James Tallmadge or David Wilmot to manipulate the American political system in the ways that William Wilberforce and French radicals had corrupted European and Caribbean institutions. So when Democratic Illinois senator Stephen A. Douglas proposed in 1854 that "popular sovereignty"—direct, majority-rule democracy—should organize and populate the remaining lands of the old Louisiana Purchase, slaveholders listened with cautious optimism that democracy could be manipulated to fulfill their—and, they argued, the world's—interests. What could confirm the veracity of American exceptionalism more, Douglas asked, than the power of the people's voice to settle the contentious future of slavery? Douglas averred that democracy was "the principle in defense of which the battles of the revolution were fought. It is the principle to which all our free institutions owe their existence, and upon which our entire republican system rests."[83]

Slaveholders welcomed Douglas's proposal to shatter the 36°30' line, long considered a holy doctrine of political compromise. Since 1820, 36°30' had protected western territories for free, energetic, and industrious white citizens. Under Douglas's proposal, the federal government would no longer uphold its venerable commitment to protect the West as an antislavery bastion of free labor. Now slaveholders could claim the legitimacy of "popular sovereignty" to commandeer the vast frontier, suppress powerless nonslaveholding whites, and implant their elite institution across the continent. Though he intended Kansas-Nebraska to fulfill northern fantasies of a transcontinental railroad, Douglas's measure instead consolidated the Democratic Party as the Union's foremost organization committed to advancing the interests of a distinct, privileged, slaveholding class. When the Kansas-Nebraska Act barely passed a divided Congress, slaveholding advocates flooded the new territories to "vote" on the American future. Undiluted democracy, however, morphed into abject violence. Elections were manipulated, voters were threatened, office seekers were attacked, and local and state governments bowed to pathetic corruption. Was this the "manifest destiny" that God had ordained for the United States? Or had Tocqueville's ominous concerns about American democracy finally been realized? After all the decades spent posturing to achieve some type of moderated settlement to curtail slaveholding radicalism from overwhelming American civilization, the national character stood trial on the bloody plains of Kansas—and it was found severely wanting. Antislavery moderates who had long and grudgingly compromised with slavery in order to preserve the Union looked with disgust at the chaos and violence perpetrated by slaveholders. It was one thing to argue vehemently in favor of slavery, even to the point of screaming threats of disunion. But it was another thing altogether to kill in slavery's name. European social and political violence had finally arrived in the United States.[84]

The antislavery movement, long marginalized politically and fractured internally among radical and moderate elements, crystallized into a boisterous opposition to "Bleeding Kansas." Antislavery critics had often charged that the institution spread the violence of the French "reign of terror," but until now the accusation seemed to be more a hyperbolic expression of frustration than a genuine critique. Kansas changed that. Razing printing shops, disrupting elections, and murdering Free Soilers undercut the sanctity of law and social order. The mob violence propagated by slaveholding allies grew from a long tradition of antiabolitionist and antiblack hostility sometimes even conducted by white northerners and westerners opposed to African American political equality and economic mobility. Former Whig George Melville Weston claimed that "a reign of terror which has muzzled the press and silenced free speech" were the only ways that slaveholders could secure power. They had transformed into American Jacobins, consolidating power through undiluted bloodshed. At the same time, Weston painted violent slaveholders as conservative European reactionaries who desired not to "leave the Union but to rule it." Violence in the name of slaveholding seemed to transpose the sobriety of American republicanism with European revolutionaries who ruptured society at once from the grassroots and from the top down. "If the Slave Power succeeds in its attempts," remarked one concerned observer, "farewell to the republic—farewell to liberty—and hail instead, glory, conquest, military [ideas], a military dictator, and finally a monarchy." For moderate antislavery proponents, Kansas obliterated a political culture once built on democratic moderation.[85]

Slaveholding violence committed in the wake of the Kansas-Nebraska Act signaled to Charles Sumner, a vehement critic of slavery in the U.S. Senate, that American exceptionalism had undergone a dangerous transformation. In a blistering speech, the Massachusetts abolitionist cited the radical collapse of moderation to be the principal "crime against Kansas." "Speaking in an age of light, and in a land of constitutional liberty, where the safeguards of elections are justly placed among the highest triumphs of civilization," Sumner declared in customary rhetoric, "the very shrines of popular institutions ... have been desecrated." Slaveholders' "tyrannical usurpation" of democracy and their "rape of a virgin territory" in the shameful quest for power hijacked the purity of American political temperance. The violent aggrandizement of slavery subverted the process of democratic republicanism, the only check against anarchy. "Hirelings, picked from the drunken spew and vomit of an uneasy civilization," conducted ferocious "border incursions" brought from "barbarous ages or barbarous lands" to "American soil." The Union now stood on an exposed precipice of internationalization, "attended by the subversion of all Security," riddled "with the plunder of the ballot-box, and the pollution of the electoral franchise." If Kansas displayed "the best Government," Sumner asked in sober reflection, "then must our Government forfeit all claim to any such eminence"?[86]

Opponents to Kansas-Nebraska indicted popular sovereignty for the decadent collapse of political moderation. When Douglas catered to an elite band of slaveholders and shattered the political restraint ensured by the old 36°30′ line, even the most moderate observers sensed that the Union had been seized by radical fanatics. Although a slaveholding Democrat, Texas senator Sam Houston confronted Douglas's program and begged for moderation to check political violence. "We are not acting alone for our-selves," he warned, "but are trustees for the benefit of posterity." Powerful slaveholding oligarchs had already unleashed their rabid minions to exploit American political institutions through extra-constitutional violence. Houston cautioned that stripping the balance of compromise from national life would further instigate "anarchy, discord, and civil broil" at the expense "of peace, of harmony, and prosperity." Labeling the Louisiana Purchase, the acquisition of Florida and Texas, and the U.S.-Mexico War as "great violations of the compact between the States, and consequent increase of the Slavery power," Henry Wadsworth Longfellow likewise rebuked his fellow northerners for falling prey to the seduction of continental aggrandizement, which compelled their obedience to slaveholding demands. Dedicated Whig Amos Lawrence could thus no longer countenance a tainted political culture that catered to duplicitous slaveholders. "We went to bed one night, old-fashioned, conservative, compromise, Union Whigs," he noted with disgust at the injustice of the fugitive slave law and Kansas-Nebraska, "and waked up stark mad Abolitionists."[87]

Liberty in the name of slavery, the violent quest to dominate free land, and the radicalism injected into a once moderate political system now seemed to expunge any exceptional worth from the national soul. The Whig Party thus collapsed, unable to maintain a consensus between its northern and southern delegations. Its demise opened a political vacuum into which flooded disaffected Free Soilers and anti-Douglas Democrats who yearned to reclaim the mantle of liberty from a democracy seized by fanatical slaveholders. The newly emergent Republican Party, an organization committed to halting slavery's dangerous expansion, asserted that a slaveholding Union typified the worst tendencies of the British nobility and wielded the same weapons of war as French revolutionaries. "The Republican Party is sounding throughout all our borders a deep-toned alarum for the safety of the Constitution, of union, and of liberty," explained a concerned William H. Seward. "The Republican party declares that, by means of recent treacherous measures adopted by Congress and the President ... the constitutional safeguards of citizens, identical with the rights of human nature itself, hitherto a fortress of republicanism, will pass into the hands of an insidious aristocracy, and its batteries be turned against the cause which it was reared to defend." A slaveholding Union, its brutal passions and its lust for power, betrayed the basic foundations of constitutional democracy. A nation dedicated to universal liberty no longer could compromise with and mollify an elite oligarchy that sought the permanent consolidation of its imperial ambitions.[88]

Republicans maintained that a phantom "Slave Power" conspiracy had co-opted American government and life. A British economist defined the "Slave Power" as "that system of interests, industrial social and political springing from slavery which ... seeks admission as an equal member into the community of civilized nations." Americans likewise outlined the Slave Power as an antidemocratic process of "control in and over government which is exercised by a comparatively small number of persons ... bound together in a common interest, by being owners of slaves." This aggressive, internationalist band of oligarchs had seized government—and particularly the Democratic Party—in purposeful subversion of the popular will to fulfill their authoritarian visions. A manifestation of the long, frustrating reality of living in a Union dominated by slaveholders, the theory organized American fears of centralization, arbitrary privilege, self-interested corruption, and crony political manipulation. Republicans thus condemned slaveholders as "alien" to the American tradition, foreign imposters who threatened to surrender the United States to corrupt global interests. Slavery "retards the development of the material resources of the country," alleged a Michigan Republican, "checks the onward march of civilization ... and with fearful rapidity, [is] undermining the very foundations of our government." Devious slaveholders would stop at nothing to blanket the continent with slavery, that "relic of barbarism" that affronted the progress of nations.[89]

Slavery had to be confined, or else powerful slaveholders would form what a Cincinnati newspaper decried as "one great homogenous slaveholding community." Ohio senator Benjamin Wade charged that slaveholders functioned as part of an international conspiracy "which reigns and domineers over four fifths of the people of the South; which rules them with a rod of iron; which gags the press; which restrains the liberty of speech." The Supreme Court's infamous decision in the *Dred Scott* case (1857) confirmed Wade's suspicions. Ruling at once that slavery must be protected in its undiluted expansion across all states and territories, and that by virtue of race African Americans were excluded from the nation as citizens, the Court blessed the most righteous sacraments in slaveholders' secular political religion. A congressman from Connecticut thus claimed that the South had nearly achieved "the complete overthrow of democratic institutions, and the establishment of an aristocratic or even monarchical government." Control of the nation's diplomatic corps, power of all branches of government, hegemony of the Democratic Party, domination of land policy, and unyielding mastery of enslaved labor all informed the Slave Power's impossible grip on national life. As international conspirators, radical slaveholding elites had achieved the "complete subversion of the natural rights of millions," blasted Massachusetts senator Henry Wilson. They "constituted a system antagonistic to the doctrines of reason and the monitions of conscience, and developed and gratified the most intense spirit of personal pride, a love of class distinctions, and the lust of dominion."[90]

Republicans equated southern plantations to aristocratic British landed estates, which manipulated vast acreage and tied landless laborers into eternal dependence. Viewing open land as the central source of virtue, Republicans championed the small family farm, an institution that stimulated independent mobility and furnished free individuals with a direct stake in politics and society. The unchecked spread of plantation slavery instead created a hierarchical class structure that replicated Europe's social immobility. If slaveholders claimed the best lands and slavery overwhelmed the capitalist market, common citizens could never accumulate capital, acquire private property, enjoy democratic influence, or advance toward economic independence. "Whatever advantages large plantations have," Frederick Law Olmsted observed during a grand tour of the 1850s American South, "they accrue only to their owners and to the buyers of cotton; the mass of the white inhabitants are dispersed over a greater surface, discouraged and driven toward barbarism," while the enslaved "rapidly degenerate[e] from all that is redeeming in savage-life." Slavery's aristocratic trappings curtailed national progress, added Charles Sumner, and "degrades our country, and prevents its example from being all-conquering." Carl Schurz, a refugee from the European upheavals, pleaded for slaveholders to recognize that they paddled uselessly against the tide of civilization. "Are you really in earnest when you speak of perpetuating slavery?" he asked, undoubtedly aware of the suffocating power of oligarchy and aristocracy. "Stop and consider where you are and in what day you live. ... This is the world of the nineteenth century.... You stand against a hopeful world, alone against a great century, fighting your hopeless fight."[91]

To guard against slavery's aristocratic influence and oligarchic control, Republicans asserted an inflexible doctrine that portended a startling future for the slaveholding Union. "FREEDOM IS NATIONAL AND SLAVERY SECTIONAL," declared a resolution from one of the party's first organizational meetings. No issue ranked higher in the Republican pantheon than restricting slaveholders' stubborn stranglehold on American democracy. A preponderance of the new party, pledged to the limits of constitutional restraint, understood that slavery could not be federally abolished in states where it currently thrived. But making freedom national and slavery sectional meant fundamentally transforming the federal government's long-standing alliance with slaveholding interests. Republicans vowed no longer to compromise with slavery's sprawling expansion; they renounced federal submission to the fugitive slave law's national aggression; and they pledged to reignite the long-silenced egalitarianism of American democracy. If slavery could be reduced to an antiquated relic, if it could be surrounded by a "cordon of freedom," the institution would wither and perish, sparking an equitable distribution of continental liberty for free citizens. "All federal enactments in behalf of slavery will be repealed," announced Republican Indiana senator George W. Julian, "the vast power and patronage of the National Government will be rescued from the active and zealous service of the slave interest, and dedicated as actively and zealously to the service of freedom." The Union had long suffered from the corruptions of slaveholding. But "the peculiar institution shorn of its 'nationality,' and staggering under its own weight," Julian predicted, "will inevitably dwindle and die."[92]

Long before the birth of the Republican Party, African American abolitionist Frederick Douglass anticipated the "cordon of freedom" as the only international buffer against slaveholding belligerence, given that his nation had willfully expanded slavery while most Atlantic societies abolished the institution. "I want the slave holder surrounded, as by a wall of antislavery fire," Douglass announced to a British audience in 1846, "so that he may see condemnation of himself and his system glaring down in letters of light." American slaveholders had to be isolated, they had to be marginalized, and they had to have the entire world—including their own nation—turned against their unholy crusades. "I want him to feel that he has no sympathy in England, Scotland, or Ireland; that he has none in Canada, none in Mexico, none among the poor wild Indians," declared Douglass. Only a concentrated international sequestration could humiliate American slaveholders into relinquishing their iron grip on national life. Douglass pled for a global alliance of abolitionists to lambast the American slaveholder, who, "stunned and overwhelmed with shame and confusion, [would be] compelled to let go the grasp he holds upon the persons of his victims, and restore them to their long-standing rights."[93]

Douglass imagined an emancipated biracial American republic smothering the hemisphere's lingering slave societies. As head in 1859 of the African Civilization Society, a group dedicated to liberating black Americans from the oppressions of national life, Henry Highland Garnet explained that African Americans assumed principal responsibility for "civilizing" the world's African-descended nations. He imagined the American South as the "grand centre of negro nationality, from which shall flow the streams of commercial, intellectual, and political power which shall make colored people respected everywhere." Rather than absconding from the United States, Garnet called for African Americans to radiate American civilization across the Atlantic world. "In Jamaica," he noted, "there are forty colored men to one white; Hayti is ours; Cuba will be ours soon, and we shall have every island in the Caribbean Sea." Imagining a Western Hemisphere populated by free, thriving Americans of color—in much the same way that slaveholders imagined a transcontinental empire of slavery and Republicans advocated the "cordon of freedom"—Garnet's vision underscored the United States as "the great example of all nations aspiring to become free." By the mid-1850s, black abolitionist critiques of slaveholding seemed to integrate within the new Republican Party, a mainstream political organization dedicated to slavery's permanent marginalization.[94]

Few white Republicans expressed the antislavery vision of American exceptionalism better than Abraham Lincoln. Linking a world governed by tyranny to a Union long occupied by an unscrupulous Slave Power, Lincoln explained that "the real issue in this controversy—the one pressing upon every mind—is the sentiment on the part of one class that looks upon the institution of slavery *as a wrong*, and of another class that *does not* look upon it as a wrong." The American people confronted an unequivocal moral dilemma. "It is the eternal struggle between these two principles—right and wrong—throughout the world." Despite the United States' impossible paradox—slaveholding in a land of freedom—Lincoln maintained that the republic continued to enjoy a unique international mission, which grew from the nation's founding in 1776. Blessed with timeless and interminable doctrines, the Union lit a "torch . . . [for] a benighted world—pointing the way to their rights, their liberties, and their happiness." Yet the global brethren of tyrants—aristocrats, oligarchs, monarchs, and slaveholders—continued to infect the United States and blunt its providential destiny. In a most practical formulation, the West had to be kept free in order to secure a stable future for *all* Americans. Where else in the world, Lincoln asked, did a region so unsullied by human corruption present such fertile opportunities for cultural enrichment, political equality, and economic mobility? Where else offered such an obvious contrast to the slaveholding South, a mirror itself of an inequitable world?[95]

Lincoln envisioned the United States and its boundless territories as a liberal symbol for disfranchised peoples. "The sympathies of this country, and the benefits of its position, should be exerted in favor of the people of every nation struggling to be free." But the promise of free labor hung in a precarious balance in a Union so acquiescent to slaveholding. "One of the reasons why I am opposed to Slavery is just here," Lincoln reflected publicly. "I want every man to have the chance—and I believe a black man is entitled to it—in which he *can* better his condition." Slaveholding depended on arbitrary and unfair privileges dispensed by unaccountable governments, obstructing the natural free will of *all* who encountered the institution. "I take it that it is best for all to leave each man free to acquire property as fast as he can." Only then would "the humblest man [have] an equal chance to get rich with everybody else." When debating Stephen A. Douglas for Illinois's Senate seat in 1858, Lincoln imagined a Union still blessed by a kind Providence "who had shielded America against unfriendly designs from abroad." Yet the Slave Power proliferated stifling hierarchies throughout the republic. Lincoln thus blasted Douglas's popular sovereignty as an amoral accommodation to white southern visions of a vast slaveholding empire. When they "grab for the territory of poor Mexico, an invasion of the rich lands of South America, then the adjoining islands will follow, each one of which promises additional slave fields." Rather than greet the world at the water's edge, Americans had to resist its seductive intrusions and chart an alternate course of liberal opportunity.[96]

The institution's rapid continental aggrandizement showed no sign of abating. If slaveholders continued their destructive march, the Union would degenerate into a rigid aristocracy in which privileged elites, who scorned the virtue of individual free labor, extracted wealth from powerless slaves, hapless whites, and a federal state that catered only to its oligarchic overlords. Indeed, slaveholders manipulated the laws and shaped government policy to promote their elite interests at the expense of the common good. The Union stood on a dangerous precipice. Lincoln wondered what it even now meant to be an American, to live in a nation roiled by the impossible slaveholding barriers of undue privilege and undemocratic political power. "Our progress in degeneracy appears to me to be pretty rapid," he worried. "As a nation, we began by declaring that *'all men are created equal.'*" But the sacred Declaration had been perverted through internationalization: "We now practically read it 'all men are created equal, except negroes.' When the Know-Nothings [an anti-immigrant and anti-Papist political party] get control, it will read 'all men are created equal, except negroes, *and foreigners, and catholics.'* When it comes to this I should prefer emigrating to some country where they make no pretense of loving liberty," he remarked with disgust, "to Russia, for instance, where despotism can be taken pure, and without the base alloy of hypocracy."[97]

For Lincoln, unchecked slaveholding "deprives our republican example of its just influence in the world." Echoing the global antislavery refrain, he denounced the institution as a "monstrous injustice," "'the one retrograde institution in America ... undermining the principles of progress, and fatally violating the noblest political system the world ever saw.'" The Slave Power created an antidemocratic ruling class that tarnished a constitutional republic's guarantee of political and social equality, regardless of race. "The enemies of free institutions," Lincoln affirmed, "taunt us as hypocrites," which "causes the real friends of freedom to doubt our sincerity." Such charges seemed entirely justified. Lincoln condemned the Democratic Party—and even the entire American political system—for its perverse acquiescence in the continental spread of slavery. "The difference between the Republican and the Democratic parties," he announced in 1858, "is, that the former consider slavery a moral, social and political wrong, while the latter *do not* consider it either." In their shameful quest for political power and influence, Democrats exhibited an "utter indifference whether slavery or freedom shall outrun in the race of empire." Their disgraceful vacillation legitimated the *Dred Scott* decision, which shattered the Constitution's assurance of government "to secure the blessings of freedom." The arguments that favored a slaveholding Union defied rationality and credulity, particularly because the Constitution itself possessed "no mention of the word 'negro' or of slavery." The republic had not been founded on ethnic distinctions or the slaveholding principle. The nation's roots clung to the enduring propositions of human equality and the popular consent of the governed. But slaveholders and their Democratic accomplices had rewritten "the great charter of liberty suggesting that such a thing as negro slavery had ever existed among us." Their willful conspiracy ignored the Constitution's otherwise purposeful "covert language," which signaled "that the fathers of the Government expected and intended the institution of slavery to come to an end." For Lincoln, the Declaration, the Constitution, and the Union had always worked in tandem to place slavery on "the course of ultimate extinction." The institution was fundamentally at odds with the American character.[98]

Compromise and political moderation now seemed impossible because constitutional liberty no longer enjoyed national consensus. "Our republican robe is soiled, and trailed in the dust," a dangerous implication that placed all Americans "into an open war with the very fundamental principles of civil liberty." In his famous 1858 retort to popular sovereignty, Lincoln claimed that slavery's corruption of American democracy "will not cease, until a crisis shall have been reached," because "'a house divided against itself cannot stand.'" The Union "cannot endure" peacefully balanced between slaveholding and egalitarian civilizations. Nor could the republic long endure the shameful political ambivalence on the slavery question. "I do not expect the Union to be dissolved—I do not expect the house to fall—but I do expect it will cease to be divided." The United States would always exist among the community of nations. But it was fast nearing an absolute consolidation in much the same way the Atlantic world fell sway to anarchy and despotism. One solution remained available. "Let us re-adopt the Declaration of Independence, and with it, the practices, and policy, which harmonize with it. Let north and south— let all Americans—let all lovers of liberty everywhere—join in the great and good work." On that day, he said, "we shall not only have saved the Union; but we shall have so saved it ... for millions of free happy people, the world over." Once a preponderance of Americans recognized that the great "Charter of Freedom applies to the slave as well as to ourselves, that class of arguments put forward to batter down that idea" would no longer "break down the very idea of a free government" and would preserve "the very foundations of free society."[99]

In 1856, Republicans nominated for the presidency John C. Frémont, the romantic "path-finder" of the American West and an outspoken abolitionist. The party platform reaffirmed Republican commitments to halt slavery's westward expansion and to uphold the constitutional protections of slavery where it already existed. Republicans also denounced the mob rule that had descended upon Kansas. The "barbarism" of slaveholding had infected the territories, sustained by an unjust "military power" that had imposed "tyrannical and unconstitutional laws." Above all, Republicans accused the American Slave Power of tarnishing "the spirit of our institutions as well as the Constitution of our country, [which] guarantees liberty of conscience and equality of rights among citizens." Only by condemning slavery as "a huge crime, a system of lawless violence," Frederick Douglass explained in his endorsement of Frémont, would the American people support overt efforts to collapse the institution. For Douglass, Frémont's candidacy portended world-historical implications. Republican victory "will prevent the establishment of Slavery in Kansas, overthrow Slave Rule in the Republic, protect Liberty of Speech and of the Press, give ascendency to Northern civilization over the bludgeon and blood-hound civilization of the South, and mark of national condemnation on Slavery ... [to] inaugurate a higher and purer standard of Politics and Government." Though Frémont lost to moderate northern Democrat James Buchanan, he carried eleven nonslaveholding states to Buchanan's five, while Republicans made significant gains in the House of Representatives. Perhaps Douglass was right: the Republicanization of the Union might someday signal the death knell of the American Slave Power.[100]

Slaveholders responded to the rise of the Republican Party with predictable distress. The "cordon of freedom," Lincoln's egalitarianism, and Douglass's radicalism seemed to echo the world's mania with abolition. One commentator worried that Republicans intended to isolate the slaveholding South among a hemispheric free-soil utopia, "a general system of hybrid-peonage" in which Mexico, Central America, and the Caribbean joined the United States in a "Black Republican" realm. Slaveholders—and even some moderate free-state Democrats who were deeply concerned about racial amalgamation and unrest—imagined clandestine radicals slinking into the political system to corrupt stable institutions and hatch revolutionary schemes. Condemning Republicans as agents of social upheaval and progenitors of racial chaos, slaveholders and their Democratic allies claimed that a mainstream political segment of the Union had become actively opposed to tranquil stability. One of the only parties in the world to encourage and draw political capital from enslaved people escaping their plantations, Republicans acted in open defiance of the Fugitive Slave Act. They cultivated a troubling alliance with slaves, who themselves wielded a peculiar political influence unseen in Cuba or Brazil, the Western Hemisphere's other slave societies. "Republicans are treacherous," one prominent slaveholder asserted, "deeply imbued with infidelity, socialism, and most horrid of all isms—abolitionism, the sum of all villainies." "I look upon the abolitionists as our worst enemies on earth." Slavery was needed now more than ever to order liberty and to strengthen white democracy. If not, suggested a South Carolinian, the South would be "reduced to a state of colonial vassalage, stripped of power in the Federal Government, confined to the strictly tropical regions."[101]

Proslavery writers maintained that Republican politics, the free-labor ideal, and global abolitionism encouraged domestic enslaved insurrections. Tapping long-standing fears of foreign agitation, they recalled British abolitionists who allegedly justified and stoked Caribbean rebellions as the necessary requisites of emancipation. And they remembered abolitionists at home who, in their early and persistent agitations, accused slaveholders of marshaling an oppressive American "reign of terror." Shocked by Republican senator William H. Seward's declaration in 1858 that the United States fast spiraled toward an "irrepressible conflict" between progressive free labor and degenerative slavery, John C. Calhoun's son, Andrew, cursed Republicans who stood poised "to plunge the dagger into the heart of those they call fellow-citizens if they do not deliver up their property, as a holocaust to their scheming and unholy ambition." Such rhetoric, slaveholders claimed, would mobilize bondpeople, organize Republican ranks, and reorient the nation toward abolition, only to spark "a war of races." "This result is inevitable," wrote a critic of abolitionism as early as 1850. "The history of the French and British West Indies is proof of this."[102]

To guard against the rabid onslaught of an abolitionist war, some powerful slaveholders aimed to turn their dream of hemispheric empire into reality. Only an equally imposing "cordon of slavery" could contest the Republicans' "cordon of freedom." The American South thus *was* the North American continent; it *was* the Western Hemisphere; it *was* the Atlantic world. "Shall the great Mississippi," Senator Andrew Butler asked, "after impelling onward along its majestic course productions of all kinds, wealth, commerce, and population, so many signs of the mighty approach of a new, great, and enterprising civilization ... announce to the democracy of the world that the advantages and the glory of American institutions will not pass forward"? Slavery was so natural, so malleable, and so civilizing that arbitrary national boundaries could not contain its discursive embrace. "We have almost found our western limit," an Alabama periodical reminded readers. "The shores of the Pacific and the great central desert of North America already bound our development westward, and it must turn southward, where decaying nations and races invite our coming." For the remainder of the 1850s, powerful slaveholders and their Democratic cronies attempted to annex Cuba and parts of northern Mexico; funded private filibustering expeditions to conquer Nicaragua; labored to reinstate the transnational African slave trade; and used federal power to consolidate and protect slaveholding interests. Only through such measures could slaveholders ensure peaceful tranquility, provide the world with material abundance, and shield themselves from the extraordinary dangers of international abolitionism now seemingly embedded in the Republican Party.[103]

Haiti in Virginia

In 1855, William Wells Brown, a strident African American abolitionist and formerly enslaved man who escaped his bondage, drew from the prophecies of David Walker to predict slavery's demise.[104] As the American Union stood as the world's largest slaveholding domain, Brown echoed Walker's sweeping call to defy the international Slave Power. In a unique marriage of the Haitian and American revolutionary traditions, Brown announced that the unavoidable clash between the enslaved and their white masters would soon arrive. He envisioned that "a Toussaint, a Christophe, a Rigaud, a Clervaux, and a Dessaline, may some day appear in the Southern States of this Union." Although uncertain when this moment would dawn, Brown believed that "the day is not far distant when the revolution of St. Domingo will be re-enacted." And he warned that "the God of Justice will be on the side of the oppressed blacks." Providence had no other choice, Brown explained, in an uncompromising comparison of Toussaint Louverature and George Washington. While both patriots led subjugated peoples toward victory against all odds, and "each succeeded in founding a government in the New World," only "Toussaint's government made liberty its watchword." Conversely, "Washington's government incorporated slavery ... an institution that will one day rend asunder the UNION that he helped form."[105]

As a former bondman himself, Brown remained disillusioned with the American republic for balancing white liberty on enslaved backs. Yet he could not ignore what would happen when freedom's army finally marched. Groaning under the weight of slavery, linked in suffering to the tortured spirit of Haiti, "the slave in his chains, in the rice swamps of Carolina and the cotton fields of Mississippi, burns for revenge." Indeed, "the indignation of the slaves of the south would kindle a fire so hot that it would melt their chains, drop by drop, until not a single link would remain; and the revolution that was commenced in 1776 would then be finished, and the glorious sentiments of the Declaration of Independence ... would be realized." A black insurrection, the likes of which the world had never seen, might finally place American civilization in its superior perch among the community of nations.[106]

Such aspirations nearly became reality in October 1859, when the long-anticipated moment of enslaved deliverance finally befell the slaveholding Union. The dreams of David Walker and William Wells Brown seemed to manifest when white New England abolitionist John Brown, who earned both infamy and adulation for his categorical response to "Bleeding Kansas," stoked an insurrection against slavery in Virginia. Brown sought to capture the federal arsenal at Harpers Ferry, arm local slaves, and stoke a revolution that would kill slavery everywhere from the Chesapeake Bay to Georgia. With plantations in smoldering ruins and slaveholders consumed with terror, the formerly enslaved would build the Republicans' "cordon of freedom," secure Henry Highland Garnet's "grand centre of negro nationality," and complete the Atlantic world's long march of emancipation. Perhaps the blood of slave-holders would finally cleanse the United States, occasioning a lasting, biracial peace, aligning a tardy Union with its exceptional destiny.[107]

Although his plan ultimately failed, few Americans could escape the over-whelming symbolism, hopeful prospects, and ominous future of John Brown's exploits. William Lloyd Garrison, the fiery Boston abolitionist who believed in the divine sanction to strike against slavery, considered Brown's raid "an indi-cation of progress, and a positive moral growth." Framing the Harpers Ferry invasion as the dawn of a new American epoch, Garrison could not "but wish success to all slave insurrections." He saw in John Brown the essence of purity, just as he saw in the enslaved the essence of gross victimization. Both were thereafter joined in common cause and suffering, compelling all antislavery Americans to see the immediacy of direct biracial action lodged against human bondage. "I see in every slave on the Southern plantation *a living John Brown*," he declared in words that undoubtedly chilled all slaveholders. "I see *four millions of living John Browns* needing our thoughts, our sympa-thies, our prayers, our noblest exertions to strike off their fetters." Rooted in the self-evident claim to universal liberty, Brown's actions would "disarm, in the name of God, every slaveholder and tyrant in the world." Thus, "we have a natural right," as God gave Brown himself the right, Garrison concluded, "to seek the abolition of slavery throughout the globe."[108]

Abolitionists hailed Brown as a martyr pledged to cleansing the United States of its sins. Dedicating themselves to the promise of insurrection, sup-porters connected Brown's raid to the international setting in which it so obvi-ously belonged. "It is only the body of Toussaint L'Ouverture which sleeps in the tomb," Brown's son declared, linking his father's martyrdom to the Hai-tian Revolution, "his soul visits the cabins of the slaves of the South when night is spread over the face of nature. The ears of our American slaves hear his voice [throughout the region], proclaiming that the despots of America shall yet know the strength of the toiler's arm, and that he who would be free must strike the first blow." The insurrectionist spirit now seemed to grip the national soul. Each slaveholder was now a target; each plantation was now a battlefield on which to wage a climatic war; and the modern antislavery world was now trained against American South. African American abolition-ist James Redpath praised Brown, vowing that all opponents of slavery "must carry the war into the south." Only then could the United States undergo a true transformation in which the "immediate eradication of slavery" would lead to biracial "national equality and power," and "tropical confederacies" populated by the formerly enslaved would surround, harass, and assault a dying American South.[109]

Slaveholders saw Brown's raid in precisely the same manner. South Caro-lina fire-eater Robert Barnwell Rhett concluded that a white radical north-erner aligning so effortlessly with the enslaved to incite a fanatical insurrection proved the inevitable and "total annihilation of all self-government or liberty in the South." With the rise of the Republican Party and the volatile unrest among the enslaved, future John Browns, just as Garrison predicted, would co-opt "an ignorant, semi-barbarous race, urged to madness by the licentious teaching of our northern brethren" and plunge the nation into unending racial hostilities. Although a U.S. Marine detachment led by Virginia slaveholders Robert E. Lee and J. E. B. Stuart thwarted Brown's designs, the radicalism of international abolition appeared fully mobilized on American soil. Slaveholders saw just how tenuous their grip on American life had become. "There is an indissoluble connection between the principles of the Republican party," proclaimed Laurence M. Keitt, Rhett's fellow South Carolina radical, "and their ultimate consummation in blood and rapine on the soil of Virginia." Brown's apparent alliance with Republicans and their mutual dependence on enslaved people convinced Keitt that "our Negroes are being enlisted in politics." The specter of whites mobilizing black slaves "alarms me," he admitted, "more even, than every thing in the past." If slaveholders were not vigilant, "Northern men [will] get access to our Negroes to advise poison and the torch."[110]

After decades of thwarting abolitionism in the United States, it now appeared to American slaveholders that the world's penchant for revolutionary emancipations had radicalized an otherwise moderate white republic. The world had long ago embraced abolition, but the United States had remained seemingly immune to such revolutionary enterprises. Yet with the advent of the Republican Party, the terrifying specter of John Brown, the swelling alliances between white northerners and enslaved people, and the overwhelming menace of racial barbarism, the Union seemed on the verge of transforming into another nation among corrupted nations. "The Harper's Ferry invasion has advanced the cause of Disunion, more than any other event that has happened since the formation of the Government," noted a troubled *Richmond Enquirer*. "Let disunion come" if "the horrors of servile war [are] forced upon us." Charles Eliot Norton, a renowned antislavery Boston author, sensed the same sentiment in the wake of Brown's raid and execution. Few events had "done more to confirm the opposition to Slavery at the North, and to open the eyes of the South to the danger of taking a stand upon this matter opposed to the moral convictions of the civilized world." American civilization now boasted two unique designs: a Union conceived in the time-tested promises of slavery, and a Union dedicated to egalitarian liberty. "The question of Slavery is *the* question, the all absorbing topic of the day," declared Abraham Lincoln on the eve of his nomination to the presidency. "The whole American people, here and elsewhere—all of us wish this question settled." The citizenry would indeed settle the question as they prepared for the election of 1860.[111]

PART II
Now We Are Engaged in a Great Civil War

If republican principles are to perish in America, they will succumb only after a long social travail, frequently interrupted, often resumed; they will seem to be reborn several times, and they will disappear without return only when an entirely new people has taken the place of the one that exists in our day.

ALEXIS DE TOCQUEVILLE,
Democracy in America

3

Purposes

★ ★ ★

A year after John Brown's raid on Harpers Ferry, Abraham Lincoln won the presidential election of 1860. Fearing that the Republican ascendency posed a clear danger to one of the world's few remaining slaveholding societies, delegates to South Carolina's secession convention voted unanimously, on December 20, 1860, to break from the Union. After years of threatening secession, the Palmetto State had finally "resumed her position among the nations of the world, as a separate and independent State." By March 1861, six additional states of the Deep South had followed suit and formed a new nation: the Confederate States of America. Alexander H. Stephens, the recently appointed vice president and a moderate who had long opposed disunion, encouraged the remaining slaveholding states to embark with the Confederacy on a new peaceful life free from the agitations of international abolitionists. Stephens's address announced both to uncommitted white southerners and to the world the new Confederate nation's unprecedented purpose. Confederates aimed to establish a nation that upheld the rule of law, protected the citizenry's liberty, and honored the limited nature of American democracy, all rooted in the stability of slaveholding and white supremacy. The Confederacy, Stephens explained, pledged to restore the blessings of a more perfect Union that the United States had failed to secure.[1]

Preserving a society predicated on slavery and racial subordination formed the "cornerstone" of Stephens's new republic. The old Union had seemingly countenanced the dangerous rise of antislavery radicals who pledged bloody insurrections to transform the United States into another nation fallen to the forces of racial and social revolution. Republican "fanatics" sullied the sacred destiny of white liberty by preaching a blasphemous gospel of racial egalitarianism ostensibly proclaimed in the Declaration of Independence. In rejecting the ideals of the American founding, "Our new government," Stephens clarified, "is founded upon exactly the opposite ideas; its foundations are laid, its cornerstone rests, upon the great truth that the negro is not equal to the white man; that slavery, subordination to the superior race, is his natural and moral condition." He thus announced to the international community the Confederacy's manifest purpose: "This, our new Government, is the first, in the history of the world, based upon this great physical, philosophical, and moral truth." The nineteenth century's drive toward global emancipation placed the Confederacy on an exceptional course, one that defied history and paved a glori-

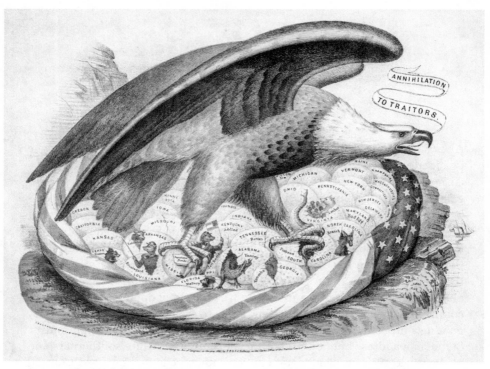

The Eagle's Nest. The Union! It Must and Shall Be Preserved, *1861,*
by E. B. & E. C. Kellogg. An eagle sits atop a nest made of the American flag,
holding eggs that symbolize all the states of the Union. From the cracking eggs of
the southern states emerge foul and pestilent creatures populating the Confederate
States of America, the principal threat to the Union's nest of perpetual nationhood.
(Library of Congress)

ous future. To restore "the proper status of the negro in our form of civilization," Stephens outlined, "was the immediate cause of the late rupture and
present revolution." Disunion, once an unthinkable, radical prospect in the
American tradition, now provided a cogent recourse against unchecked racial
fanaticism. Stephens could therefore embrace that which he once opposed
as a moderate Whig: the collapse of the United States. But he defined his as
a conservative revolution to *circumvent* revolution. Any people who pledged
themselves to the self-evident veracity of nature's law—slavery's comfortable
assurance of white democracy—would assume an enviable perch atop the
community of nations.[2]

More than a year later, in December 1862, President Abraham Lincoln explained to the U.S. Congress the purpose of waging war against Stephens's
Confederacy. "*We* cannot escape history," announced the president, well aware
of "the fiery trial through which we pass." Affirming that "we know how to

save the Union," and recognizing that the world watched closely, Lincoln engaged Stephens's declaration that slavery had both caused the great conflict and defined the Confederacy's international standing. The president acknowledged that the war for Union—preservation of the world's foremost democratic republic—had occasioned by late 1862 an additional wartime purpose: emancipation. In the years prior to disunion and war, Lincoln's emancipation had once been as unthinkable as Stephens's secession. But "in *giving* freedom to the *slave*," the president now explained about the necessities of national change to facilitate national preservation, "we *assure* freedom to the *free*— honorable alike in what we give, and what we preserve."[3]

For Stephens, emancipation at once confirmed white southerners' long-held fears about the Republican Party and validated the Confederacy's status as the world's lone slaveholding republic. But for Lincoln, emancipation did not alter the loyal citizenry's effort to preserve the Union from the dangerous machinations of aristocratic slaveholding secessionists. It instead gave legitimacy to his claim that the United States, as a universal beacon of freedom, was worth restoring in the first place. A nation that boasted of itself as "the last best, hope of earth," the symbol of liberty in a world governed by tyranny, could not preserve democracy in a Union dominated by the Slave Power. Coming to terms with the nineteenth century's contradictory strands of freedom compelled the Union to acknowledge that nature's laws applied to *all* people—not merely white Americans. "The way is plain, peaceful, generous, just," Lincoln advised his audience, "a way which, if followed, the world will forever applaud." International egalitarians had long sought to secure liberty's place within the protected confines of a nation-state. What better place and in what better scenario could humanity's elusive search for liberty forever be settled than within a "people's contest" to define the exceptional promise of Union?[4]

Both Alexander H. Stephens and Abraham Lincoln articulated the broad purposes for which the Confederacy and the United States waged war. Each belligerent sought to define the object of the democratic nation-state and the contested ways in which liberty aligned with nationalism. Western peoples across the nineteenth-century world had long struggled to organize these disputed ideals, only to be met with failure and state-sponsored retribution. France had promised a republican revolution, yet devolved twice into monarchical centralization; Central America and the Caribbean had proven perpetually unstable; and the capacity of European democracy failed to withstand state reprisal in the wake of 1848. The American Civil War occurred during an international moment in which the United States appeared to be emulating the global tradition of national collapse. For Lincoln, disunion and civil war unfolded as crises of national anarchy unleashed by aristocratic elites who, like the world's monarchs, oligarchs, and nobles before them, aimed to shatter the majority will of a free people. For Stephens, secession in the name of slaveholding embodied white democratic self-determination, the unalienable right to discard the yoke of corrupted and tyrannical governments.[5]

The Union and Confederate citizenries ultimately saw in their respective national purposes the occasion to preserve the fragility of international democracy. Both sides considered it their destiny to model the democratic essence of American civilization to a world that had forsaken liberty. Confederates would finally prove that a slaveholding republic, a bugbear long targeted by international radicals, could thrive by preserving democracy for white men. Confederates warned that the age of emancipation had spawned the dangerous notion that democracy could exist on egalitarian terms unwedded to its self-evident and stabilizing counterpart, slavery. The new nation would hence demonstrate how human bondage provided social and political order, tempered the excesses of democracy, protected the natural rights of God's chosen few, and paved the road to modernity through agriculture and free trade. Unionists countered that the war would at last show the world that self-government, long the object of aristocratic ridicule, could endure any violent threat. A democratic people, acting within the hallowed spirit of 1776, would prove that the American experiment would continue to lead the world toward new births of freedom, despite petty and dangerous intimidations posed by radical slaveholders. In their contested efforts to preserve democracy, Unionists and Confederates sought to eliminate the dangers of radical internationalization, which both republics deemed antithetical to American exceptionalism. Only a war could preserve what slaveholders and opponents to human bondage had failed to conserve in peace.[6]

Disunion

Abraham Lincoln's election in 1860 flung slaveholders into a panicked frenzy. After decades of searching for ways to protect slavery within the Union, secessionists preached that the institution could live and thrive only outside the United States now that Republicans controlled the levers of federal power. The Union, they argued, now embodied the world's radical antislavery tendencies, which had transformed once great slave societies into decaying outposts of racial amalgamation and economic stagnation. So-called fanatics bent on bringing the destructive project of New World emancipation to the American South had hijacked the Union to which slaveholders had long looked as the Western Hemisphere's divinely sanctioned protectorate of human bondage. Secessionists felt trapped, isolated among teeming John Browns and Toussaint Louvertures, and governed arbitrarily by free-labor abolitionists. Only the peaceful separation from a Union now stripped of its protective slaveholding republicanism could guard against the damaging tide of global history. Mississippi attorney Thomas J. Wharton spoke for many when he claimed that "slavery, of all property in the world, most needs the protection of a friendly government." And by 1860, few governments existed anywhere—except for

Brazil and Cuba—friendly to the institution so central to slaveholding life. The secessionist impulse thus emerged not out of a sense of separate southern identity or even an idealistic campaign for political equality. Rather, it materialized to maintain security and to preserve the slaveholding design of American democracy against foreign contamination, all guided by the unbending control of centralized governing power.[7]

In a quintessential justification of disunion, prominent Alabama legalist Jabez L. M. Curry argued that only a peaceful secession could safeguard the essential foundation of American civilization. The election of Abraham Lincoln embedded global radicalism within a vulnerable Union, sanctioned by a despoiled national political system. This "unprecedented" corruption left slaveholders "overwhelmed with the intelligence of Abolition success." The Republican Party's rapid ascendency imposed revolutionary changes on the federal government, transforming the nation's founding principles and the Union's international standing. The American founders had "indulged in no such sickly sentimentality or false philosophy as Lincoln," because "they never dreamed that the Declaration of Independence included negroes," whom "they made no pretence of emancipating." The entire constitutional system long guarded against extremism and protected "against invasion or domestic violence." Now that "abolitionism has triumphed," Curry averred, "Lincoln's administration will still have the mastery, and require obedience, and compel the support of northern interests, the development of northern ideas, the security of northern power, and the destruction of African slavery. The institution of slavery is put under ban, proscribed, and outlawed."[8]

For Curry, the "triumph of abolitionism" consolidated the federal government into a weaponized central state. In histories of the Atlantic world, American slaveholders had long read of military dictators who waged coercive wars against their citizenries and their institutions. The Republican Party thus paralleled European despots who crushed the democratic revolutions of 1848, imposing tyranny against peaceful self-determination. Republicans furthermore capitalized on a protracted war waged by antislavery fanatics "sent in our midst to excite insurrection," embodied "by John Brown and his murderous confreres." With troubled memories of Lincoln's promise of placing slavery "'*in the course of ultimate extinction*,'" and of William H. Seward's warning of an "'irrepressible conflict,'" Curry alleged that "the animating principle of the party is hostility to slavery." Now that the Republicans rejected political compromise and scoffed at democratic moderation, the entire antislavery coalition issued "a declaration of war against our property and the supremacy of the white race." With control of the military, ambassadorships, the federal treasury, and national territories, the new administration could unleash unfettered hostilities against slavery's present and its future, waging "an unceasing crusade against our civilization."[9]

The United States, Curry concluded, had morphed into a foreign nation, one governed by an alien, revolutionary cabal. The Union had never before been stripped of its slaveholding promise, never before been divested of its constitutional checks, and never before bowed to anti-American radicals. "The possession of the Government by a hostile, sectional party, places our destinies under the control of another and distinct people," Curry offered. "To the slaveholding States, it is a *foreign government*, which understands not our condition, defers not to our opinions, consults not our interests, and has no sympathy with our peculiar civilization." For Curry, slaveholders had not changed. They did not live in a romantic past divorced from the progress of modernity. No, they *were* the modern world, justified by their once exceptional Union, the only nation on earth pledged to the timeless prosperity, essential security, and prudent stability of slavery. Antithetical to the American character, Republicans now promoted "oppressive taxation, foreign rule, emancipation of negroes and equality with them." The old Union had *withstood* these unnatural conditions "to prevent the domination of a foreign people." In this extraordinary moment of crisis, "provisional, temporary, and irregular governments must be established to prevent anarchy and social disorder." The United States was thus expendable: "Of all fantasies that ever disturbed an excited brain, the most ridiculous is the idea, that Liberty is dependent upon the continuance of this Government." Slaveholding civilization now had to traverse borders and relocate in a new and favorable nation.[10]

The Mississippi legislature justified disunion in January 1861 on the same grounds outlined by Jabez Curry. "Our position is thoroughly identified with the institution of slavery," the state's declaration of secession announced, "the greatest material interest in the world." National separation circumvented two dangerous crises: the peril of depriving the world of the South's unparalleled agricultural bounty, and the threat of killing human bondage, the vital element of modernity. Despite the Atlantic world's emancipationist impulse, slavery "supplies the product"—cotton—"which constitutes by far the largest and most important portions of the commerce of the earth." Endangering slavery defied "an impervious law of nature," which mandated that "none but the black race" could harvest the "necessities of the world." Therefore, "a blow at slavery is a blow at commerce and civilization," one an earthly obligation, the other a providential summon. Because the antislavery faction blocked hemispheric expansion, ignored the Fugitive Slave Act, "advocates negro equality, socially and politically, promotes insurrection and incendiarism in our midst," and "recently obtained control of the government," secession offered the only check against "the mandates of abolition." Otherwise, "utter subjugation awaits us in the Union." Rerouting the lifeblood of American civilization toward a new, certain, and safe future would ensure humanity's everlasting survival.[11]

Not all slaveholders so willfully embraced secession. Though no doubt fearful of Republican intentions and opposed to emancipation and racial equality, some white southerners viewed disunion as destructive and revolutionary. A rash separation, North Carolinian Jonathan Worth explained, would forever tarnish the nation's exceptional disposition. "I still believe that no respectable and stable government can ever be established in America, except on the plan of a Union," he opined. No matter how radical the Republicans might be, secession "wickedly and foolishly" shattered the delicate balance of democracy, turning the United States into a volatile host of warring factions. "Even on the plan of a peaceful separation, North America will soon become Mexicanized," generating civil wars, military coups, and rival claims to governing legitimacy. If the slaveholding states founded a new nation, argued Virginian William C. Rives, "a separate Confederacy, sprung from secession, must soon fall to pieces under the operation of the same disintegrating principle." Disunion would initiate "endless feuds and strifes," consuming all Americans "in the throes and convulsions of revolutionary France, or in the anarchy and turbulence of our Mexican and South American neighbors." The community of nations, whether through unthinking passion or racial inferiority, had proven incapable of democratic republicanism. "This model republic," declared Alexander H. Stephens, was "the best which the history of the world gives any account of." If one compared the Union to "France, Spain, Mexico, the South American republics, Germany, Ireland ... Prussia; or if you travel further east, to Turkey or China," no American would "find a government that better protects the liberties of its people."[12]

Slaveholding skeptics of disunion argued that secession would produce unprecedented social and political revolutions from which the American South would never recover. "If the Union be dissolved now," asked Texas senator Sam Houston, "will we have additional security for slavery?" Houston understood what all slaveholders instinctively knew: that war, especially civil strife, would bring a swift, decisive death to slavery. The instability of armed conflict, imaged in the history of St. Domingue, ruptured slavery's secure foundations, loosening the chains of bondage and bringing the enslaved into deadly conflict with their white masters. The federal government, warned Jonathan Worth in his indignant treatise against secession, would use the occasion of civil war to "beget the most diabolical purposes." All white southerners would incur the swift sword of abolitionist radicalism in all its terrible fury when Republicans "proclaim freedom to the slaves and arm them against us." Marylander John Pendleton Kennedy thus urged secessionists to abandon their fantasies of conquering the hemisphere. Slavery's lasting destruction would result from "such impracticable conceits as these," breaking the Union, the world's foremost protectorate of human bondage, "into discordant fragments whose jars may illustrate the saddest moral of blighted hopes the world has ever known!"[13]

Secession ultimately triumphed because its proponents argued that the Union was already corrupted, that the revolution against American life had already occurred, and that the fate of civilization depended on a new birth of slavery outside the United States. Secession and even war *against* Republicans seemed safer alternatives to national degradation and enslaved insurrection *imposed* by Republicans. Firebrand South Carolina secessionist Robert Barnwell Rhett outlined the pure rationality of disunion: "The Government of the United States is no longer the Government of Confederated Republics, but of a consolidated democracy. It is no longer a free Government, but a despotism." Like-minded advocates agreed that secession stemmed the turbulent revolutions of the Atlantic world. "No despotism is more absolute than that of an unprincipled democracy," Presbyterian minister Benjamin Morgan Palmer reminded white southerners, "and no tyranny more galling than that exercised through constitutional formulas." Thus, "this Union of our forefathers is already gone." Palmer saw in the ascendant Republican Party the specters of Haitian rebels, French radicals, and British monarchs conspiring against slaveholders. Rebuke secession, Palmer warned, and "the institutions of your soil will be overthrown; and within five and twenty years the history of St. Domingo will be [our] record." Abolitionists, speaking "from Jacobin conventicles and pulpits" and infiltrating government, had poisoned the spring of national life. "But now the voice comes from the throne," and just as the monarchs of 1848 had silenced the sacred hope of democracy, "the decree has gone forth that the institution of Southern slavery shall be constrained within assigned limits."[14]

Palmer framed two major arguments used to validate disunion: first, that Republicans would obliterate constitutional government, emancipate enslaved people, and promote black insurrections throughout the South; and second, that secession embodied the hallowed right to self-determination. "A spirit of ultra fanaticism," opined Jefferson Davis, "organized" the Republican Party "for the purpose of obtaining the administration in Government" to use "its power for the total exclusion of the slave States from all participation in the benefits of the public domain." International abolitionists could now weaponize the federal government and raise illicit armies of black men to stoke insurrections throughout the South. Lincoln's election signaled a dramatic transformation in constitutional governance. A strong, stable federal state had long secured slavery from dangerous external forces, carefully expanding the institution's boundaries, imposing dynamic laws to assure order, and using diplomatic and military tools to shelter bondage at home and abroad. Republicans now seemed poised to turn the entire federal apparatus against slaveholders. "To-day our government stands *totally revolutionized* in its main features," Mississippian William L. Harris announced. Long-standing pledges and compromises to maintain the stability of a slaveholding Union were now extinct. In its place, contended Alabama's Stephen F. Hale, were "the inauguration of new principles and a new theory of government." Abolitionism replaced slaveholding republicanism as the chief purpose of American governance. "The triumph of this new theory of government destroys the property of the South, lays waste her fields, and inaugurates all the horrors of a San Domingo servile insurrection," Hale alleged, and "the light of our civilization goes down in blood."[15]

Republican victory legitimized the deadly insurrections once waged by Toussaint Louverture, Denmark Vesey, Nat Turner, and John Brown. Never before in American life had the Union faced such grave conditions. When "the antislavery sentiment was merely speculative," when it could be controlled and marginalized, "we had not right to complain," reasoned Virginia secessionist George Wythe Randolph. "But now that it has become an efficient agent in the government, it is no longer safe for a slave State to remain under that government." The Republican triumph signaled the culmination of a destructive international radicalism that began with the French Revolution, inspired the Haitian slave revolt, corrupted the sensibilities of British antislavery activists, traveled the Atlantic to the Americas, and moved John Brown to wage war on his fellow citizens. "The history of abolitionized Governments," Randolph concluded, "is a history of abolitionized people. Look at England, France, Denmark, and at their magnificent Colonies; the pearls of the Antilles, sacrificed without remorse." Abolitionism and its insurrectionist hosts now infected the American government. Republicans "will use the sword for our subjection," predicted the fiery *Charleston Mercury*. "The ruin of the South, by the emancipation of her slaves, is not like the ruin of any other people." A federal state that directed enslaved revolts would produce "suffering and horror, unsurpassed in the history of nations," producing "the loss of liberty, property, home, country—everything that makes life worth having."[16]

Enslaved insurrections would result in heaps of decayed cotton, degenerated plantations, and dead white people. "Slavery," one writer noted, "makes the South a blooming Eden. Its abolition ... would make it a Jamaica,—or even worse a St. Domingo." Should Republicans restrict the spread of slavery, the "Africanization of the South" would feature ineffectual freedpeople roaming uninhibited. "Imagine the misery, the crime, the poverty, the barbarism, the desolation of the country," the writer cautioned. Slave insurrections carried consequences well beyond the terrifying rape and murder of white southerners. Rebellions, as the slaveholding world had long witnessed, also yielded social revolutions that shattered the most fundamental of nature's laws. "To adopt any policy by which slavery would be hemmed in, within its present limits," Virginian James Holcombe warned, "provid[es] for a renewal upon our own soil of the scenes of St. Domingo." Such "destruction of slavery" would force white laborers to produce cotton and rice, a prospect that "does not admit of debate," because "the existence of African slavery becomes a question of civilization." Destroying bondage through race war inevitably undermined "the guardianship of an inferior race" and forced slaveholders "in a debasing school of political degradation for civil and social equality with their emancipated slaves."[17]

While slaveholders argued that secession protected their institution from international emancipation, they also maintained that disunion and the pursuit of a separate nationality preserved the basic ideals of republican self-determination. Slaveholders seceded to circumvent the radical transformations brought to an otherwise democratic political system and stable social order. Telling the world that their movement epitomized the democratic promises of 1776 and 1848, secessionists argued that disunion protected private property, upheld self-government, and sustained ethnic nationalism, all of which preserved global republicanism. Secession sustained the glory of the American Revolution and fulfilled the failed nineteenth-century European independence movements. The "age of nationalism" preached that freedom and sovereignty were best protected within independent nations willing to shelter the liberties of their people. Yet the old Union, in the same despotic manner as the nations of Europe, willfully flouted the people's will and even sought to coerce citizens from embarking on a new peaceful destiny. Jefferson Davis voiced this conservative justification of secession. "Our present condition, achieved in a manner unprecedented in the history of nations, illustrates the American idea that governments rest upon the consent of the governed," he explained, "and that it is the right of the people to alter or abolish governments whenever they become destructive of the ends for which they were established." Thus, "we have changed the constituent parts, but not the system of our Government."[18]

Free people, secessionists argued, *could* pursue life, liberty, and happiness unburdened from the oppression of central governments bent on limiting (white) men's natural rights. Disunion provided a necessary and rational response to the United States' betrayal of republican government. "The right of the people to self-government in its fullest and broadest extent," announced Louisiana senator Judah P. Benjamin just before he resigned his seat to follow his state out of the Union, "has been a cardinal principle of American liberty." William Meade, an Episcopal bishop in Virginia, thus pledged that a peaceful secession would "show the world that a republic is not a failure; that it may divide, yet live and prosper." Only secession could protect the liberties outlined in the Declaration and the Constitution, sacred texts which once made the United States the envy of the world. As Presbyterian minister and prominent southern theologian James Henley Thornwell petitioned, the North and South should divorce amicably, which "would be something altogether unexampled in the history of the world. It would be the wonder and astonishment of the nations."[19]

The loyal citizenry of the Union could not countenance a peaceful farewell to wayward Americans. The United States comprised a perpetual nation, one that resisted separation whenever disgruntled minorities opposed the peaceful returns of electoral democracy. The revered consent of a free people must be upheld lest revolution transform a nation that celebrated the capacity of self-government. "Why should there not be a patient confidence in the ultimate justice of the people?" Abraham Lincoln asked during his first inaugural address. "Is there any better or equal hope in the world?" The president reaffirmed this basic democratic creed when he charged, "The central idea of secession, is the essence of anarchy." The American tradition did not approve such a radical flouting of the rule of law, the absence of which unleashed national disorder. "A majority, held in restraint by constitutional checks, and limitations, and always changing easily, with deliberate changes of popular opinions and sentiments, is the only true sovereign of a free people." Secession portended radical but also impossible transformation for an otherwise conservative Union. "The States have their status in the Union, and they have no other legal status. If they break from this they can only do so against law and by revolution." The Union had preceded and thus created the states. Only a republic composed principally of *the people* could check the advent of tyranny, repression, and autocracy. "Whoever rejects it," the president countered, will "fly to anarchy or to despotism."[20]

Unionists linked secession with hemispheric and international political destabilizations. The act harked back to the recent Central American, Caribbean, and European pasts, in which weak governments frequently collapsed under the weight of political and military turmoil, inviting despots to grasp and wield tyrannical power. "If there be disunion," predicted New York diarist George Templeton Strong, "a strong government will come into being somehow" and shatter the republican experiment. Centralization, coercion, and revolution were the only logical outcomes, because "democracy and equality and various other phantasms will be dispersed and dissipated and will disappear forever." Understanding that revolutions rarely ended in their stated, peaceful purposes, and convinced that disunion would produce subsequent political ruptures from both within and without the United States, one Republican predicted that the flight of southern states would balkanize North America and "'Mexicanize' our government." The federal Union, long the bulwark of political stability in the Western Hemisphere, now stood on the same precipice of collapse that had befallen the region's hapless republics. "Shall the disgraceful history of Mexico be reproduced on our soil?" asked Martin B. Anderson, president of the University of Rochester. As demonstrated in the violent history of the Latin American republics, secession would kill "the root of all civilization and [halt the] progress of all political blessing." Only a united nation furnished "protection for peace or virtue, freedom, religion, or the arts of life."[21]

Loyal citizens cautioned that secession would fulfill southern fantasies of a slaveholding empire that blanketed the Western Hemisphere. As the antithesis of Old World aristocratic privilege, free-labor egalitarianism might well be cordoned within a hemisphere once again ruled by oligarchic slaveholders who commandeered rich planting lands to consolidate their officious power. Republicans opposed any last-minute sectional compromise that permitted the continental expansion of slavery. Any political settlement to stem disunion would surely accommodate slaveholders' desires to expand into the Caribbean and Central America. In this scenario the Union would be preserved, but at what cost? The very elements that inspired secession—slaveholding mandates to ensure slavery's expansion—would then embark on an ineluctable path toward North *and* South American empires of slavery. And future slaveholding demands on the federal government, in which disunion would be wielded as an ever-present threat, would no longer encompass merely the status of slavery in the United States and its territories. "A year will not pass," Lincoln predicted in January 1861, "till we shall have to take Cuba as a condition upon which they will stay in the Union," and that will "put us again on the high-road to a slave empire." Compromise had long ago revealed itself to be a perverse tool wielded by slaveholders to consolidate their sectional interests. The secession crisis now exposed the international implications of this obsolete political tactic.[22]

The Lincoln administration's pledge to halt the continental expansion of slavery confronted the long-standing alliance between the Democratic Party and southern slaveholders. This corrupting political association, Lincoln explained, gave slaveholders constitutional protections and "acts of Congress of their own framing, with no prospect of their being changed." Republicans were justified in asking the southern states for "a prohibition against acquiring any more territory" in exchange for guaranteeing slavery's limited domestic existence. But as late as December 1860, mere weeks after Lincoln's electoral triumph, President James Buchanan inquired, "How easy would it be for the American people to settle the slavery question forever and to restore peace and harmony to this distracted country!" Sectional rancor could be soothed only if slaveholders were "let alone and permitted to manage their domestic institutions in their own way." As a moderate northern Democrat and one of the slaveholding South's foremost allies, Buchanan reasoned that "as sovereign States, they, and they alone, are responsible before God and the world for the slavery existing among them." Indeed, "the people of the North are not more responsible and have no more right to interfere than with similar institutions in Russia or in Brazil." But when slaveholders tied their hemispheric ambitions to the fate of Union, loyal citizens had little choice but to oppose what they considered political extortion. To accommodate secession, to compromise with slaveholding demands, to expand slavery's continental boundaries would yield, as one writer claimed, "quarrelling and warring ... amongst little petty powers which would result in anarchy."[23]

Disunion seemed to confirm the scathing criticisms of European intellectuals who scoffed at the madness of democracy. They condemned the fallacious notion that politics and government rested on the consent of common people. Secession exposed the inherent flaws of popular sovereignty. In 1861, a British earl gazed upon "the trial of Democracy and its failure," noting with glee "that the dissolution of the Union is inevitable, and that men before me will live to see an aristocracy established in America." A French royal official likewise scoffed to an American in Paris, "No republic ever stood so long, and never will. Self-government is a Utopia, Sir; you must have a strong Government as the only condition of a long existence." The Union's loyal citizenry knew all too well of democracy's storied failures in Europe. They, like Abraham Lincoln, believed that the collapse of democratic republicanism in the United States would smother the hopes of representative government and economic independence throughout the world. "This is the age of nationalities," a Boston newspaper declared in May 1861, referring to European efforts in the 1840s to fashion equitable democracies. "Fired by our example, the oppressed of the world would have aspired to the dignity of nationalities. Shall the first to set the example, and the grandest in the procession of the nations, suffer its nationality to depart, at the bidding not of a foreign foe, but of rebel traitors of the soil?" Disunion was not merely a political question. It was a referendum on the meaning of the nation-state itself, one rooted in either aristocratic privilege or democratic inclusion, hierarchy or egalitarianism, human freedom or human bondage.[24]

The Union's nationalistic response to secession appeared to be somewhat contradictory. Was not the entire basis of American civilization—outlined in the Declaration of Independence and drawn from the notion that all humans enjoyed equal, natural rights—founded on the self-evident prerogative of oppressed peoples discarding tyrannical and corrupted governments? Had not Americans cheered beleaguered European and Latin American revolutionaries when they too revolted against domineering oppressors? Loyal citizens had to explain to the world how their opposition to secession derived not from a hostility to self-determination but instead from a conviction that a people's republic remained inviolate and unalterable. "The right of revolution is not denied," acknowledged the *New York Times* in April. Democratic republicanism welcomed sober constitutional changes, especially when "contemplated with calmness." However, "that Treason should be claimed as a right—that anarchy should rule—it is this which thrills with indignant amazement." The nation *was* the people, Lincoln explained, a fact that distinguished the United States from the rest of the world. Disunion was impossible because, as the Constitution proclaimed, "We the People" had joined together "to create a more perfect Union," one that could not be discarded at the whim of political dissenters who lost a fair and just election.[25]

Harper's Weekly, a popular journal of mainstream political and cultural sensibilities, sketched the historical context of secession's illegitimacy. In an essay proclaiming that "the history of all nations is the same," the writer argued in April 1861 that European nationalism had long unfolded as a series of upheavals, consolidations, revolts, and ethnic alliances. In fact, secession was "one of the oldest doctrines of barbarous nations," a pathetic practice that invited tribalism and internal collapse. "Nationality and freedom" coexisted only when "the civilized man is to bow to constituted authority for the sake of its advantages." The torturous history of Europe revealed the striking absence of liberty because nations rarely maintained peaceful cohesion. "In one word," the author concluded, "civilization centralizes. Barbarism divides." So when Cassius M. Clay, the American minister to Russia, declared a month later, "We the people of the United States of America ... are fighting to maintain our *nationality*," he voiced a loyal consensus that framed secession as the irrevocable split between a free people and their nation. Petty European squabbles, which had long divided that continent into chaotic confederacies, had proven the inherent weakness of nations not founded on law, order, and liberty.[26]

No event better captured the radicalism of secession than the firing on Fort Sumter, a U.S. Army installation that anchored the harbor at Charleston, South Carolina. In the rapid wake of disunion, slaveholding delegates had met in Montgomery, Alabama, to forge a new nation, the Confederate States of America. On April 12, 1861, seeing the defiant Union fort as an illegitimate violation of the Confederacy's new national sovereignty, rebel artillery assailed the garrison, compelling U.S. forces to surrender it. The loyal northern citizenry erupted that slaveholders had finally occasioned that which they had always threatened: undermining American democracy through militant violence in a manner consistent with European nobles who crushed their own citizens' popular appeals. The "Slave Power" had now committed its most despicable act, exposing its violent lust for supremacy and its complete disregard for political moderation. "In truth, this Southern rebellion has betrayed all the elements of a Southern reign of terror. The seceded states," the *New York Herald* thundered a week after Fort Sumter, "have fallen under the fearful despotism of a set of Jacobins, with a mob at their heels, as stupid and remorseless as the Jacobins and their mob of the first French Revolution." Such pugnacious reactionaries, Lincoln echoed, embodied the Old World's aversion to democracy. "It is now for [us] to demonstrate to the world," he told Congress on July 4, 1861, "that those who can fairly carry an election, can also suppress a rebellion—that ballots are the rightful, and peaceful, successors of bullets."[27]

The subsequent war between the United States and the Confederacy was a conflict rooted in the irreconcilable ideals of American democracy and Union. Since 1776, the modern world had witnessed the rise and fall of republics, liberation movements, and democratic insurgencies, most of which had deteriorated into coups, military dictatorships, or monarchical consolidations. That the rest of the world had failed to secure the blessings of liberty convinced Unionists and Confederates that their war served as the ultimate trial to settle the fate of global democracy. Only one side could emerge victorious, standing as the "true" representative of Americanism, the sole nation to mid-wife the founding generation's birth of freedom. Proponents of each national cause appointed their understanding of American exceptionalism to justify to the world their national purposes. The conflict hinged on defining two republics pledged to popular sovereignty, natural rights, modernity, progress, and political moderation. Despite their notable differences, despite the rampant political dissension that roiled the antebellum era, and despite the obvious contradictions between enslaved and free societies, both nations saw the war as the final contest to determine the unique and supremely exceptional meaning of American civilization.[28]

The Slaveholding Republic

On January 21, 1861, Jefferson Davis announced his resignation from the U.S. Senate. In a sober reflection on the late national rupture, Davis urged white southerners to divorce the Union peacefully, acting on their natural right of self-determination. "It has been a conviction of pressing necessity, it has been a belief that we are to be deprived in the Union of the rights which our fathers bequeathed to us," Davis instructed. His fellow citizens had long heard the disquieting "theory that all men are created free and equal" and that "the sacred Declaration of Independence has been invoked to maintain the position of the equality of the races." Now that the federal government seemed no longer committed to protecting slavery and "stir[s] up insurrection among our slaves," endangered white southerners were compelled to seek refuge outside a radicalized nation. "When you deny us the right to withdraw from a Government which thus perverted threatens to be destructive of our rights," he warned, "we but tread in the path of our fathers when we proclaim our independence, and take the hazard." Secession "is not done in hostility to others, not to injure any section of the country," but stems "from the high and solemn motive of defending and protecting the rights we inherited, and which it is our sacred duty to transmit unshorn to our children."[29]

States of the Deep South followed Davis's counsel and founded a new nation, the Confederate States of America, the world's largest slaveholding republic. It was a unique nation, pledged to white democracy *and* the unbending security of black bondage. Delegates to the Montgomery convention appointed Davis—a symbol of moderation, unity, and slaveholding preeminence—president of the new republic. In his two February inaugural addresses delivered in 1861 and 1862, Davis justified a peaceful secession and asserted that the old Union had despoiled American republicanism. Careful to disavow a radical revolution, Davis condemned abolitionist Republicans for repudiating the founders' vision of a sovereign union of sovereign states, threatening to exercise the levers of federal power against their slaveholding citizens, and proclaiming universal racial equality. The "declared purpose of the compact of Union," he responded to counter Abraham Lincoln's belief in a perpetual nation, "had been perverted from the purposes for which it was ordained, and had ceased to answer the ends for which it was established." The Confederate project intended to stabilize a popular sovereignty in which a limited government upheld "the rights of person and property." The Union was expendable; the doctrines that it was charged to maintain were interminable. As Confederates, "we hope to perpetuate the principles of our revolutionary fathers. The day, the memory, and the purpose seem fitly associated."[30]

Davis lauded the Confederacy as the world's foremost republic pledged to the defense of white liberty. Rebelling against centralized tyranny and racial egalitarianism, the new Confederacy would "save ourselves from revolution which in its silent but rapid progress, was about to place us under the despotism of numbers, and to preserve in spirit, as well as in form, a system of government we believed particularly fitted to our condition." Davis argued that American civilization was now protected safely outside the old Union, which had failed to sponsor the general welfare of its entire citizenry. To "promote the happiness of a confederacy, it is requisite that there should be so much of homogeneity that the welfare of every portion shall be the aim of the whole. Where this does not exist, antagonisms are engendered which must and should result in separation." A confederation of states, which shared the same interests and rejected the coercive excesses of government, promoted a national consensus of shared white equality. The Confederate experiment, "unprecedented in the history of nations," showcased a people rebelling to preserve the very republican form of government from which they fled. This new nation, "composed of States homogenous in interest, in policy, and in feeling," offered the "promise for mankind." The Confederacy thus emerged as "the last hope," Davis promised, "for the perpetuation of that system of government which our forefathers founded—the asylum of the oppressed and the home of true representative liberty." The world would finally witness a nation beholden to the consensual will of a people freed from the hostilities of radical political agitators.[31]

Confederates dreamed of proving democracy's lawful temperance to the United States and to a world seemingly hostile to self-determination. Declaring that they sought only a peaceful withdrawal from the old Union, Confederates imagined that their national destiny reinstated republican virtue to North America. The Union's radicalization, its rejection of Christianity, and its spurning of constitutional liberty convinced North Carolinian Clara Hoyt that only the Confederacy could shoulder the burden of American civilization. "May our Southern Constellation take [the] high place from which America has fallen," she announced, "and shine the brighter, to the oppressed of all nations, to guide them on to liberty." The United States had long stood as the global advocate of free will and liberation, once championing democratic revolutions in South America, Mexico, Greece, and throughout Europe. Waging war against southern self-determination exposed the Union as an illegitimate hypocrite opposed to "the inalienable right to change ... forms of government at will." Alexander Stephens asked, "Why this war on their part against the uniform principles and practices of their own government?" The answer was at once simple and horrific: "to exterminate our southern institutions"; "to put the African on an equality with the white man"; and "to conquer and subjugate independent and sovereign states." Following in the bloody tracks of international despots, the United States waged war "against right, against reason, against justice, against nature."[32]

The international community would undoubtedly sympathize with the Confederate movement because it embodied everything that oppressed peoples in the nineteenth-century world had long sought but failed to secure: an independent nation composed of a distinctive people who shared common interests, an ethnic identity, and a modest political culture. Subjugated populations across the globe would recognize the war launched by the United States as another violent, militaristic coercion against the popular will. The Union's war machine and its dictatorial president, observed a group of southern editors, were "bound to put down secession as a European government puts down rebellion—by force of Arms." How could Western civilization, Confederates asked, claim to be progressive and enlightened when its leading nations wielded autocratic weapons against its once fellow citizens? The Union had transformed into an "imperial power," noted another Confederate, one that joined Parisian and Roman monarchs notorious for crushing their own people's yearning for freedom in 1848. "The world never saw such a drama as is now being enacted here," Arkansan Albert Pike concluded. "We shall establish a new Republic, that shall outlast us and our children," and "shall still prove to the world that the great experiment has *not* failed, and that men *are* capable of governing themselves."[33]

Confederates defined theirs not as a radical separatist movement that defied enlightened nationalism. Theirs *was* a civilized nation, curtailed by law, bolstered by a formal military apparatus, and governed by a free people. Few places on earth had realized the true potential of self-government, Secretary of State Robert Toombs reminded his diplomatic envoys as they sailed for Europe in the spring of 1861. The new southern republic exhibited its own "independent government, perfect in all its branches, and endowed with every attribute of sovereignty and power necessary to entitle them to assume a place among the nations of the world." Confederates did not seek furious retribution through war even though so-called Republican abolitionists had aimed to "overthrow the constitutional barriers by which our property, our social system, and our right to control our own institutions were protected." Like all republics, the new nation desired an enduring peace and "admission into the family of independent nations." Because secession proved their democratic legitimacy, Confederates asked only for the "friendly recognition which are due to every people capable of self-government and possessed of the power to maintain their independence." Toombs concluded that Confederate liberation, the only source of "future happiness and tranquility," bolstered "the moral and physical strength to hold and cause [our] position to be respected."[34]

The Confederate nation boasted to the world a republican government derived from political moderation and racial privilege. No experiment in democratic self-determination could thus succeed without a legitimate constitution, the essence of political modernity, the safeguard against radicalism, and the epitome of civilized nationalism. The Confederate Constitution highlighted the new republic's commitment to a powerful central government and announced the nation as a cohesive civil entity guarded by the rule of law. Pledged to the separation of powers, skeptical of faction, and wary of decentralization, the new constitution resembled the United States' national charter. Yet the governing document ratified in 1861 announced the southern republic's unique purpose and its distinguishing characteristic: the eternal preservation of slavery within the nation-state. Confederate constitutionalism protected the new republic from any "law denying or impairing the right or property in negro slaves." Bold in its imagination and striking in its implications, the Constitution legitimized a continental empire of slavery, curing the damages imposed by fanatical Republicans in the old Union. Indeed, when the Confederacy expanded abroad "the institution of negro slavery, as it now exists in the Confederate States, shall be recognized and protected." The government pledged to guard against any fugitive belligerence, assist slaveholders in confiscating absconded property, and vow that "no slave" would ever "be discharged from such service or labor." The Confederacy would not easily tolerate a robust system of federalism, which protected dissenting social movements and political activism. Slaveholders could now populate the continent assured that their new government would maintain the institution wherever it traveled. Nationhood was now and forever underwritten by slavery.[35]

The Confederate Constitution healed the irrevocable scars in the old United States' charter. Antagonists to human bondage could no longer threaten slavery, the organizing principle of civilization. To protect white democratic liberty against hostile abolitionism, the new nation now marginalized even ambivalent critics of slavery. "For proof of the sincerity of our purpose to maintain our ancient institutions," Jefferson Davis reminded the citizenry, "we may point to the Constitution of the Confederacy and the laws enacted under it." Vice President Alexander H. Stephens made even more explicit the Constitution's indispensable function: "The new constitution has put at rest *forever* all the agitating question[s] relating to our peculiar institution — African slavery as it exists amongst us — the proper *status* of the negro in our form of civilization." The old Union's Constitution protected slavery but also breathed profane ideas of racial equality. "Our revolution thus far is distinguished from popular revolutions in the history of the world," Stephens spoke of the Confederacy's conservative foundations. The new republic organized an extraordinary marriage of statutory, constitutional, and natural laws. "Stand[ing] upon eternal principles of truth" guaranteed "the ultimate success of a full recognition of [the slaveholding] principle through the civilized and enlightened world."[36]

Few nations had ever joined popular sovereignty with the stability of slavery, "the cause of humanity and civilization." This unprecedented endeavor in statecraft dignified all who cherished self-determination because "our people partake of the true American character," explained editor James D. B. DeBow of this slaveholding exceptionalism. "They are not for breaking down all the forms of society and of religion, and of reconstructing them" in the same failed vein of the United States, Latin America, and the Caribbean, "but prefer law, order, and existing institutions, to the chaos which radicalism involves." The Confederate nation kept all white men "free from the dangerous heresies which not only marred the beautiful theory of Republican government, but were fast dissolving Republican liberty," explained Alabamian James Ferguson Dowdell. "Let distinction of color only, be distinction of class—keep all white men politically equal—the superior race—let the negro be the subordinate, and our Government will be strong and our liberties secure." Slaveholding nationalists had long argued that bondage "conduces to national strength," DeBow continued, offering a tangible counterpoint to unregulated liberty, guarding against volatile market economies, and erecting sturdy social barriers to protect white democracy. The Confederacy thus charted an unparalleled course in human affairs, "inaugurat[ing] a new civilization" in which "negro slavery will be its great controlling and distinctive element."[37]

Confederates imagined their slaveholding nation as a modern beacon that guided the world into a new dawn of racial solidarity, economic power, social conservatism, and material progress. When they placed slavery at the center of their national experiment, Confederates defied the Atlantic world's emancipationist trajectory. The mid-nineteenth-century nation-state increasingly experimented with varying extents of free labor. The British, French, and Dutch had eliminated slavery from their colonies, Russia had freed its serfs, and Central American republics had undergone antislavery transformations. And of course, the Union's northern states had emancipated enslaved people in the wake of the American Revolution. Conversely, "we do not place our cause upon its highest level," Confederate Episcopal bishop Stephen Elliott explained, "until we grasp the idea that God has made us the guardians and champions of a people whom he is preparing for his own purposes and against whom the whole world is banded." Divine providence gave slavery to the American South as a natural mode of security, a cradle of social stability, a source of racial solidarity. Elliott condemned the extraordinary folly of New World abolition, which stemmed from "the false philanthropy of Europe" when "God permitted a Christian nation [England] to try the experiment of emancipation on a small scale." The "wretched and ruinous result of idleness, of dissipation, of anarchy," he scoffed, "satisfied our people that it was the veriest mistake ever made by a wise nation."[38]

Only a slaveholding republic rowing against waves of international abolitionism could preserve white liberty. George Fitzhugh, one of the antebellum era's foremost proslavery apologists, indicted the "bombastic absurdities in our Declaration of Independence" for distorting the sacred pursuits of life, liberty, and property. "Those doctrines," he denounced, "exported from America to France ... blew up first the French monarchy, and soon thereafter all the monarchies of Western Europe," exceeded only by the "disruption and dislocation of all the ties of society." The Atlantic world's stable hierarchies then ruptured when the American, French, and Haitian Revolutions preached a common human freedom. Ultimately, nineteenth-century emancipations and the rise of the Republican Party signaled the dangerous collapse of modern life. Both were premised on the fanatical notions of unchecked democracy rooted in racial and class equality, inflicting impossible demands on limited governments. When Republican abolitionists radicalized the old Union, slaveholders had no choice but to withdraw and reclaim their misplaced liberty. Establishing the Confederate republic "was reactionary and conservative," Fitzhugh explained, "a rolling back of the excesses" of the American Revolution, "a solemn protest against the doctrines of natural liberty [and] human equality." Throughout "Europe and America," he concluded, "liberty was degenerating into licentiousness." Only the new Confederacy could conserve the kind of limited democracy rooted in human slavery that history had sanctioned and on which the international community had reneged.[39]

Confederates aimed to stem the destructive tide of global revolution. Failure of the new national experiment would complete the nineteenth century's devastating social transformations. Otherwise the entire continent would become Europeanized, averred Rev. James H. Thornwell of South Carolina; once bountiful slaveholding lands would be "converted into subject provinces," delivering a fate "worse than that of Poland and Hungary." Confederate nation-building thus attempted to derail the modern world's extreme train of abuses. "We are struggling for constitutional freedom," Thornwell explained, "we are upholding the great principles which our fathers bequeathed to us." Confederates did not seek to create something new; they merely strove to preserve that which was already self-evident. As "the dominant nation of this continent, we shall perpetuate and diffuse the very liberty" once secured by the Union. "We are not revolutionists," he affirmed, "we are resisting revolution." While the United States and the world had been hijacked by radicals who sought to transform nature itself, "we are conservative. Our success is the triumph of all that has been considered established in the past." Thornwell imagined the Confederacy charting a vast future in which the world realigned with truth, justice, moderation, and slavery. "The peace of the world is secured if our arms prevail," he concluded. "We are, therefore, fighting not for ourselves alone, but, when the struggle is rightly understood, for the salvation of this whole continent."[40]

As early as 1861, prominent South Carolina socialite Mary Chesnut foreshadowed Fitzhugh and Thornwell's subsequent perspectives. She too recognized that democracy in the United States had become too radical, too egalitarian, riddled with political chaos. "Republics," she imagined, "everybody jawing, everybody putting their mouths in, nothing sacred, all confusion of babble ... republics can't carry on war. Hurrah for [our new] strong one-man government." Chesnut celebrated how the Confederate framers had created a nation of remarkably transparent foundations. The Confederacy stemmed the excesses of democracy with a sturdy central government, a robust executive, and limited privileges of citizenship. "One begins to understand the power which the ability to vote gives the meanest citizen," she concluded. In curtailing democracy, the new slaveholding republic excluded more than half of its population from high politics, including Chesnut herself. In addition to the perpetual, legalized enslavement of an entire race, the new republic also omitted women from the formal body politic, signaling an unusually commonplace mode of nineteenth-century state formation. At the precise moment at which the United States' citizenry demanded a more egalitarian democracy liberated from the discriminating privileges granted by slaveholding, the Confederate nation restricted its politics along lines of race *and* gender. White male slaveholders would ostensibly command the destinies of a majority of "the people" who themselves were deprived of political representation.[41]

Confederate women nevertheless emerged as dynamic political players in the new national project. With approximately 80 percent of the white male military-age population serving in Confederate armies, white women assumed unprecedented public roles traditionally reserved for men. From participation in Ladies Aid Societies to service as nurses at the war front, from populating the government bureaucracy in Richmond to managing plantations and enslaved labor, women's industry at once sustained the quest for national independence and facilitated a level of gender parity never seen in the American South. Yet myriad women protested what they deemed an overwhelming wartime burden. They had to negotiate the increasing hardships of war as domestic leaders, public workers, and masters of slaves, all the while excluded from the Confederate body politic. Of concern particularly for poor women was food scarcity and skyrocketing inflation, wartime conditions that threatened basic survival. Women across the socioeconomic spectrum thus petitioned government, rioted against food shortages, and demanded that the Confederate state mitigate their suffering. But their public appeals, though often successful and no doubt political in nature, exhibited a peculiar character, one derived from the gendered and racialized assumptions of Confederate nation-building. When they petitioned government, women rarely referred to themselves as "citizens," the essential attribute of political inclusion in the democratic-republican ethos. Instead, as historian Stephanie McCurry demonstrates, they employed the term "soldiers' wives," a gendered label that linked women to the "official" members of the Confederate body politic, free white men. Women mobilized as a forceful wartime political entity that sought protections from the state. But when they also eschewed explicit notions of citizenship, concludes McCurry, they reflected the Confederacy's "deep investment in limiting democracy . . . to the exclusion of free women and enslaved men and women from political life."[42]

Viewing themselves as a stable, hierarchical nation of white masculine mastery, Confederates claimed that nowhere else than in their new republic was slavery more profitable, more secure, more innovative, and more dynamic. Bolstered by capitalist markets and organized by vast networks of technology, transportation, and commerce, the Confederacy fastened the pillars of modern life into the slaveholding cornerstone. Independent from abolitionist agitation, "the establishment of a Southern confederation," read an editorial in *DeBow's Review*, guaranteed "our rights and possessions would be secure, and the wealth being retained at home, to build up our towns and cities, to extend our railroads, and increase our shipping." Modern mid-nineteenth-century slavery could not function without urban centers, financial hubs, efficient transportation, scientific experimentation, and industrial processing—indeed, the safe, progressive assurances once provided by the old Union. To sustain slavery's life, the Confederacy now subsidized industry, promoted economic development, encouraged western expansion, and constructed railroads. Only by linking the modern nation-state to human bondage could Confederates "become the freest, the happiest, and the most prosperous and powerful nation upon earth." They had every reason to believe that their republic would be the envy of the modern world, and they invited the world to align with their exceptional endeavor.[43]

To bring essential security to slavery, Confederates distinguished the Western Hemisphere as a slaveholding domain, although only Brazil and Cuba—the former a Catholic monarchy, the latter a Spanish protectorate—joined the southern republic as the Western Hemisphere's remaining slave societies. Only a burgeoning republic of slaveholders, aligning with hemispheric champions of unfree labor, could command global prestige. "We will expand, as our growth and civilization shall demand—over Mexico—over the isles of the sea—over the far-off Southern tropics," imagined Robert Barnwell Rhett, "until we shall establish a great Confederation of Republics—the greatest, freest, and most useful the world has ever seen." To feed, clothe, and provide for the world necessitated *control* of the world's agricultural markets. With emancipation, once great slave societies had squandered their claims to independence and modernity. "We are to be embraced in the same moral category as Cuba and Brazil, and the North are to feel for us the same accountability," Jefferson Davis explained in 1861 about the necessity of hemispheric slaveholding alliances. The vast region that stretched beyond the Confederacy's Gulf shores offered "the West India Isles, which, under the old Union, were forbidden fruit to us, and there [are] the Northern parts of Mexico," Davis also noted. An avowed slaveholding nation, assured in its boundless growth, perfected in the art of free trade, stimulated by intellectual diversity, and anchored by social stability, could redeem the world.[44]

While slaveholders dreamed of expanding their institution across the globe, Confederate foreign policy restrained those ambitions toward forging international and continental proslavery coalitions. Moderate Confederates such as President Davis and the Confederacy's first secretary of state, Robert Toombs, pledged their slaveholding republic as a global ally of free trade and unfree labor. Confederate envoys encouraged Spain to consolidate slavery in Cuba and the Dominican Republic; they favored alliances with unfree labor in Mexico; and they pursued diplomatic networks with Brazil. "The institution of domestic slavery in one country and that of peonage in the other," Toombs explained to a Confederate diplomat in Mexico, would "establish between them such a similarity in the system of labor as to prevent any tendency on either side to disregard the feelings and interests of the other." Meanwhile, long desirous of unobstructed routes to the Pacific, Davis authorized military invasions to claim Arizona Territory for the Confederate nation, fulfilling slaveholding visions of a vast southwestern empire of slavery. Hemispheric partnerships would protect the institution by opening new markets and catering to global demands for southern agrarian products. "An agricultural people, whose chief interest is the export of a commodity required in every manufacturing country," Davis outlined, "our true policy is peace, and the freest trade which our necessities permit." The president prayed for "the fewest practicable restrictions upon the interchange of commodities" and desired "little rivalry between our and any manufacturing or navigating community."[45]

Confederates advertised their enviable cotton crop as the chief tool for forging diplomatic alliances. Slaveholders had long believed that the United States enjoyed international prestige because the modern world survived on southern agriculture. By 1860, Great Britain and France imported between 80 and 90 percent of their nations' cotton from the American South, and more than two-thirds of the world's cotton supply originated on southern plantations. An independent Confederacy now controlled the entire balance of international cotton trading: "This goodly land of ours is unequalled, or at least unsurpassed by any other part of the habitable globe in the character and variety of its natural products," hailed Vice President Alexander Stephens. Blocking the world's access to cotton, Davis assured his citizens, would "bring ruin upon all those interests of foreign countries which are dependent on that Staple." Confederate envoys thus traveled to Europe convinced that metropolitan elites would grant legitimacy to the slaveholding republic, seduced by free trade, sympathetic to the Confederacy's rigid social hierarchy, and desperate to feed their nations' textile mills. The new southern nation boasted far greater stability than the Union's radical free-labor democracy. "The cards are in our hands," vowed the *Charleston Mercury* in 1861, "and we intend to play them out to the bankruptcy of every [European] cotton factory."[46]

The mid-nineteenth century seemed the perfect moment to secure Confederate diplomatic ambitions. The American Civil War contributed to hemispheric destabilizations as nation-states and colonial territories underwent fundamental transformations of authority. By 1861, with the United States distracted by the dual crises of disunion and war, Spain reacquired the Dominican Republic, Mexico collapsed into civil war, France prepared to reassert a New World presence, and England aimed to capitalize on the deterioration in North America. Although the United States traditionally regulated European meddling in the Western Hemisphere, separatist movements and civil conflicts invited international powers to flood the region. "The Monroe Doctrine is very dead for all time to come," declared Virginia journalist George Bagby. Confederates welcomed European nations to participate in the American crisis, gambling that foreign incursions anywhere between the tip of South America and the upper reaches of Canada would establish critical buffers between the United States and Confederacy. George Fitzhugh even called on France to reconquer the "paradisiacal isle of Hayti," which "will be best for us." Claiming that healthy international rivalries sustained the balance of hemispheric power, "we of the South, strengthen ourselves by multiplying rival nations, and thus preventing the undue preponderance of any one of them." French recolonization of Haiti and the subsequent expansion of slavery throughout the Caribbean "would weaken and divide the North, and benefit us," while also eliminating an island nation born of enslaved insurrection.[47]

France did not occupy its former slaveholding colony. Emperor Napoleon III instead pursued a bold incursion into Mexico. The Mexican republic, long riddled by political, social, and religious volatility, experienced its own domestic rupture alongside the crisis of the American Union. Both conflicts featured the enduring struggles between nineteenth-century national sovereignty, liberal equality, and conservative reaction. While the United States collapsed under the impossible burden of slavery, Mexico buckled under the pressure of liberals, led by Benito Juarez, who pursued just reforms against the hierarchical Catholic Church and a powerful national military. Since national independence in 1821, both institutions contributed to domestic instability and both sought to thwart Juarez's crusading reforms. The Mexican liberals saw the United States as a sympathetic champion of liberty, a nation that espoused a shared commitment to republicanism. And they viewed the Confederacy as an imperial nation bent on expanding its continental footprint. Secession and political-religious consolidation thus weakened the United States and Mexico, creating attractive vacuums for hungry European nations, as well as the Confederacy, to impose hemispheric obstructions.[48]

Napoleon considered the Confederacy essential to his "Grand Design" of reestablishing France's North American empire. He saw in the slaveholding nation an antirepublican ally that shared the French monarchy's hierarchical conservatism, one that also provided a geographic buffer against the Union. "We are interested in seeing the United States powerful and prosperous, but we have no interest in seeing that republic acquire the whole of the Gulf of Mexico," he acknowledged, "and become the sole dispenser of the products of the New World." Confederate victory would weaken the United States' hemispheric influence and protect against antislavery agitations, which threatened the world's cotton production. French armies pushed with determination through Mexico until they reached the capital city in June 1863. Forcing Juarez's liberals to retreat, the French and their conservative Mexican allies took control of the national assembly and voted to bestow Maximilian, the archduke of Austria, as the new monarch of Mexico. Maximilian accepted the offer, stepping foot onto his new kingdom in May 1864. Napoleon had his puppet and also had a friendly nation nearby—the Confederate States of America—that pledged to support his schemes.[49]

With shrewd pragmatism, Confederates welcomed the French incursion, interpreting Napoleon's Mexican adventure as an opportune shift in international relations. Congenial European nations descending on the Western Hemisphere, they reasoned, would formally recognize the Confederacy and legitimize slaveholding independence. James Williams, a Confederate representative in Europe, considered the French presence in Mexico the logical result of democracy's failure across the continent. The North American crisis indicated "that there may exist as ruthless a despotism under the forms of democratic or republican freedom as could be developed under the absolute rule of a single despot." Confederates and the French-Austrian monarchy checked the radical excesses of American democracy and Mexican liberalism. "It cannot be denied that in almost every other part of the American continent the experiment of democratical institutions has ended in complete and hopeless failure," Williams observed. Egalitarian overtures had collapsed social orders everywhere from South America to the Caribbean to the American Union, fueling the wars that engulfed Mexico and the United States. "Mexicans may well hail the establishment of different political institutions, founded upon a properly organised monarchy, as the turning point in their destiny," Williams concluded, "the full stop in their downward careers, the harbinger of a great future for the nation." John Slidell, the Confederate minister in Paris, agreed that the "foreign occupation of [Mexico] would excite the most violent opposition at the North," and "we, far from sharing such a feeling, would be pleased to see a steady, respectable, responsible government established there soon."[50]

Napoleon's scheme offered the Confederacy imperative sources of national security and ideological legitimacy. "We should prefer France as our neighbor," George Fitzhugh considered, "not only because we do not wish to be hemmed in and surrounded by Yankees, but also because we wish, now, to see a balance of power established in America." A stable Mexican monarchy distracted a weakened United States and offered trade networks of war material, cotton, and agriculture cut off by the federal blockade and stunted by battlefield reverses. The nearby establishment of an Old World monarchy also shielded the Confederate States against liberal reform and radical abolitionism. "Cementing together all the Republics and States of South America, as he has cemented together the fragments of a United Italy," explained a Louisianan, Napoleon would launch "a power fully equal in magnitude to that of the United States." It only made sense for Confederates to embrace the French emperor because "our territory is too vast, our population yet too sparse, and our domestic institutions too precarious to allow us to stand alone before the world." Confederates believed that they had established the conditions for Napoleon's entrée into the New World. They had embraced a slaveholding nationalism that stood unique among nations, while also uniting with the forces of international conservatism, ordered stability, and regulated progress.[51]

A Liberal—and Conservative—Union

Few among the loyal citizenry of the Union explicated the United States' wartime purpose better than Abraham Lincoln. The president deemed the Confederacy the product of an illegitimate conspiracy hatched by an elite aristocratic minority. And he understood the Civil War both as a national event and as a universal trial that posed world-historical implications. For Lincoln, the conflict tested two enduring ideas: the sanctity of democratic liberty—the right of free people to chart unencumbered political destinies—and Union—preservation of a republic within a world burdened by undue privilege and political repression. The inimitable American nation organized free citizens along customs, shared experience, divine intervention, social equality, constitutional restraint, and "the mystic chords of memory." The republic was much more than a collection of states and people. As a physical nation, it was underwritten by common, timeless, and self-evident truths guaranteed by the rule of law. To upset such a delicate and unique balance would relegate the United States to a place among the world's undistinguished nations. Thus, as Lincoln explained privately, "the central idea pervading this struggle" was to "prov[e] that popular government is not an absurdity. We must settle this question now, whether in a free government the minority have the right to break up the government whenever they choose. If we fail it will go far to prove the incapability of the people to govern themselves."[52]

If the Union deteriorated into "the essence of anarchy," the delicate flame of international liberty would be rendered meaningless. Therefore, "this is essentially a People's contest," Lincoln informed Congress on July 4. "On the side of the Union, it is a struggle for maintaining in the world, that form, and substance of government, whose leading object is, to elevate the condition of men." The United States, in Lincoln's egalitarian view, had long served as a global beacon of liberty in which common people freed from authoritarian coercion enjoyed the independence to rise socially and improve economically. If the democracy that protected these ideals collapsed, all who cherished what Lincoln once termed the "promise of something better" would be deprived of "an unfettered start, and a fair chance, in the race of life." The Union comprised energetic citizens who forged autonomous lives through free and unencumbered labor. If elite slaveholders legitimated a new nation predicated on human bondage, they would forever undermine the natural right of all humans to claim the due fruit of their labor. If the Union could be broken so easily, if the rule of law no longer guarded rational, sovereign individuals, the American citizenry themselves could never be fully free.[53]

For Lincoln, the American war would either preserve or destroy the United States' distinctive international errand. The conflict "is not altogether for today—it is for a vast future also," he prophesied. The Founding Fathers' sacred work, the destiny of free peoples, and the fortune of nations hinged on what happened in the American crisis. "This issue embraces more than the fate of the United States. It presents the whole family of man, the question, whether a constitutional republic, or a democracy—a government of the people, by the same people—can, or cannot, maintain its territorial integrity." Lincoln conceived of the United States in spiritual and pragmatic terms. He understood the Union at once as an idea—that law and democracy ordered liberty to forge equal social and political relations—and as a physical space—an inviolable nation governed by a moderate constitutional consensus. He thus asked of the current crisis, "'Is there, in all republics, this inherent, and fatal weakness,'" in which injurious forces of discontent could undermine the will of a free citizenry? Did freedom inevitably sanction internal ruptures, legitimizing malcontents who sought separate destinies? "'Must a government, of necessity, be too strong for the liberties of its own people, or too weak to maintain its own existence?'"[54]

Abraham Lincoln spoke to the loyal citizenry's quest to preserve a democratic republic amid the world's political absolutisms, social hierarchies, and aristocratic indulgences. When he declared, "We shall nobly save, or meanly lose, the last best, hope of earth," he disclosed that the Union's moral ideals—liberty, economic independence, rationality, moderation, and individualism—depended on the triumph over tyrannical slaveholders. The nineteenth century featured myriad authoritarian, monarchical, and centralized consolidations against the popular will, and the Confederate war again threatened the liberty of common citizens. Merging the nineteenth century's prolific nationalism with the era's idealistic liberalism, Lincoln welcomed the war as a national cleansing, healing the chafing scars once applied by the Slave Power's political whip. The slaveholders' rebellion thus joined European autocracies and Central American dictatorships in defiance of political moderation, unmasking the Confederacy's unholy alliance with international despotism. "It is a war in favor of a privileged class; a war upon the working classes; a war against popular majorities; a war to establish in the New World the very principles which underlie every throne of Europe," echoed the *New York Times* in 1862. "The enemies of popular liberty beyond the sea can never be brought to look with approval and pleasure at the spectacle of successful democratic institutions, which this country, until two years ago, happily presented." The "Southern oligarchy," the *Times* concluded, intended "to prove, if possible, the democratic experiment a failure."[55]

Unionists sought to prove to the world that a nation conceived in liberty could triumph against radical separatist cabals who undermined the legitimate, peaceful, political process through secession and civil war. If American democracy collapsed under the weight of disunion, international nobles, monarchs, and tsars could finally label the United States a hypocritical and failed experiment in popular democracy. Global elites could then subjugate *their* people without the Union standing as the moral exception to international coercion and tyranny. The "contest in which we are engaged is not merely a struggle between secession and Union," declared *Harper's Weekly*, "but is really the final decisive contest between free popular government on the one side, and government by an oligarchy or a monarch on the other." Union defeat would confirm European critiques of democracy, validating the imperial consolidations in the wake of 1848. "Our war is being waged to determine whether or no[t] a democratic republican government can maintain itself against domestic insurrection," *Harper's* continued. However, if "the slave power of the South succeeds in establishing a separate national existence, based upon human slavery and military power," the writer warned, "the oligarchs of Europe will well say that republics are impracticable, and human self-government a delusive dream."[56]

Appealing to Union was not an abstract philosophical exercise. Confederate triumph would poison the American well of liberty with the international toxins of inequity, injustice, and intemperance. Eventually, predicted the stalwart antislavery activist Lydia Maria Child, an independent Confederacy, with its aristocratic lethargy, its violent aggression, and its shameless greed, would infect the United States. Waging a war for Union necessarily "decide[d] whether this is to be a free country, where working-men elect their own rulers, and where free schools give all an equal chance for education." Slavery decayed all that it touched, degenerating civilization and extinguishing moral improvement. Its continental coup would compel all Americans "to live under despotic institutions, which will divide society into two classes, rulers and servants, and ordain ignorance, as the convenient, nay even *necessary* condition of all." The United States would always exist, but a continental republic of slaveholders would forever stem American progress and halt the Union's once inevitable progressive march. A Union of common liberty and egalitarian opportunity had to vanquish the encroaching forces of international slaveholding radicalism. "Unless the rebels are conquered," Child warned, "they will assuredly invade *us*, and force their institutions upon the whole country."[57]

Child's vision framed a broader anxiety among the loyal citizenry that the Confederacy's rise would balkanize the North American continent. The crisis of national sovereignty exposed the dangers of confederated governance long espoused by European elites and American slaveholders. Confederated nations did not turn on the moderate, united political consensus of virtuous citizens. As loosely aligned states that consented to voluntary national association, they abided by the contractual consent of minority interests. When noble sovereigns who competed for civic and territorial power deemed their confederated body threatened by breaches of contract, they removed their state from the collective association. The Old World "of aristocracies, of monarchies, and of despotisms," explained a Presbyterian minister, resorted to "armed revolution" when confederations collapsed. Such dangerous systems infected the "new world of democratic ideas, and purely representative sovereignties, and universal suffrage." German émigré and American law professor Francis Lieber indicted confederations as the preferred form of government for European nobles. They produced "many little kingdoms," he explained, "or the breaking up of one country ... into jarring and unmeaning sovereignties, that have not the strength to be sovereign."[58]

Lieber opined that the Confederacy introduced a Europeanized governing structure to North America in defiance of "the normal type of modern government[,] the National Polity." The Union stood apart from the Old World, strengthened by a constitutional republicanism that limited coercion and channeled faction to uphold the popular will. "It is the political organism permeating an entire nation," Lieber advocated of a people's republic, "that answers the modern political necessities, and it alone can perform ... the high demands of our civilization." The Union thrived on the consent of the governed, "not a string of beads in mere juxtaposition on a slender thread, which may snap at any time and allow the beads to roll in all directions." When discordant beads of the polity broke and departed on errant paths, the nation contracted a dangerous cancer, withered, and died. So long as the Confederacy claimed independent nationhood, it legitimated a perilous form of government that defied popular democracy.[59]

With the miscarriage of free, fair, and open elections, confederacies often disintegrated into what Lincoln called "the essence of anarchy." The president echoed Lieber to argue that republics invited internal chaos when the people broke from constitutional consensus. "I hold that in contemplation of *universal law* and of the Constitution, the Union of these States is perpetual," the president outlined. "Perpetuity is implied, if not expressed, in the fundamental law of all national governments." While unity grew from natural law, disunity summoned unending division and turmoil. What might prevent future secession movements if the Confederate rebellion succeeded? The Union would lose all legitimacy if borders were constantly redrawn, if national traditions frequently collapsed, or if unfamiliar political cultures were frantically established. Americans would be consumed in endless wars, stalled in their mission to model ordered liberty for the world. Consensus of the federal majority—one that resisted tyrannical factions and protected the rights of the minority—functioned as the "only true sovereign of a free people." A system that permitted any other course, Lincoln counseled, would "fly to anarchy or to despotism." Only sober and judicious democratic institutions could nourish the liberty, fashion the stability, and uphold the legality that sustained a functioning republic.[60]

Nineteenth-century Americans long held their Union as the sole source of hemispheric stability amid disorderly and combative nations whose weak governments rose and fell with frightening speed. Secretary of State William H. Seward accused secessionists of hatching an illegitimate "revolution . . . to create a nation built upon the principle that African slavery is necessary, just, wise, and beneficent, and that it may be expanded over the central portion of the American continent and islands without check or resistance, at whatever cost and sacrifice to the welfare and happiness of the human race." Such an act was at once "absolutely unnecessary" and catastrophic. For Seward, the civil war that spawned from secessionist nation-building followed the hazardous patterns set by Central American revolutionaries who established rival confederacies absent any kind of unifying consensus. "Success of this revolution," Seward predicted, would occasion "a practical overthrow of the entire system of government" and would also establish "the first stage by each confederacy in the road to anarchy, such as so widely prevails in Spanish America." Failure to preserve the Union would yield two independent North American states that battled for permanent control of the continent, instigating unending military conflicts and political conspiracies. Chronic instability would rupture the Western Hemisphere for generations. "Division of this great and hitherto peaceful and happy country into two hostile and belligerent republics" might well produce years of "servile war, filling the whole country with desolation. The end would be military despotism, compelling peace where free government had proved an absolute and irretrievable future." A well-read student of international affairs, Seward later declared, "Revolutions are epidemical [and] threaten the stability of society throughout the world."[61]

Seward warned that secession and war threatened to displace peaceful hemispheric republicanism with imperial colonialism and monarchical absolutism. A once democratic but now severed and weakened Union would invite sympathetic European nobles to align with aristocratic slaveholding Confederates. "Our country, after having expelled all European powers from the continent," Seward anticipated, "would relapse into an aggravated form of its colonial experience, and, like Italy, Turkey, India, and China, become the theatre of intervention and rapacity." Collapse of the Union, "for whatever cause, would be destruction of the safety, happiness, and welfare of the whole American people," a prospect that guaranteed "any popular form of government impracticable in an age and in a region where no other than just such a form of government is known or could be tolerated." American democracy had long ensured hemispheric stability. But a slaveholding revolution portended that "the equilibrium of the nations, maintained by this republic, on the one side, against the European system on the other continent, would be lost, and struggles of nations in that system for dominion in this hemisphere and on the high seas ... would be renewed." The United States' unique and providential role in human affairs would forever cease, "the progress of freedom and civilization, now so happily inaugurated, would be arrested, and the hopes of humanity which this the present century has brought forth would be disappointed and indefinitely postponed."[62]

Some foreign audiences questioned the Union's limited and theoretical purpose of national preservation. Carl Schurz, a steadfast Republican, antislavery partisan, and a German veteran of the democratic revolutions of 1848, sensed, from his ministerial post in Spain, European ambivalence toward the maintenance of Union. Although liberalism yielded to coercion throughout much of Europe, "the sympathies of the liberal masses ... are not as unconditionally in our favor as might be desired," Schurz informed Secretary of State Seward. Was not the Union challenging Confederates' right to self-determination, the same liberal prerogative to which oppressed peoples appealed in their quest for freedom? "It is exceedingly difficult to make Europeans understand," Schurz explained, "not only why the free and prosperous North should fight merely for the privilege of being reassociated with the imperious and troublesome slave States," given the commonplace nature of national ruptures "in monarchical Europe." Schurz detected foreign distaste with the United States waging an allegedly empty and hypocritical war. Unionists could not assert the sanctity of self-government when denying that basic right to their once fellow countrymen. "To crush the independent spirit of eight millions of people, is with rapid strides approaching the lines which separates government from the attributes of arbitrary despotism," a condition that Schurz and much of Europe knew all too well.[63]

The crux of the matter hinged on the place of slavery in a war for national unity. European critics alleged that the United States could not claim the mantle of liberalism while millions remained enslaved. But many of the nation's leaders—beginning with the president himself—refused to crusade against slavery. "I have no purpose, directly or indirectly, to interfere with the institution of slavery in the States where it exists," Lincoln reiterated in his 1861 inaugural address. "I believe I have no lawful right to do so, and I have no inclination to do so." To defeat the rebellion through emancipation would be revolutionary. Indeed, for moderate white northerners, wartime abolition violated federal law; alienated the critical Border States, portending additional secessions; threatened the cause of reunion with the rebellious states; employed the army to initiate drastic social changes; unleashed enslaved people in revolt against their white masters; and disrupted job markets and white employment. The government waged war only for the limited purpose of restoring federal authority, not desperate, indiscriminate, and revolutionary social transformations.[64]

Schurz countered that Europeans expressed "a feeling of surprise and disappointment" that "the destruction of slavery [failed] to be the avowed object of the policy of the Government." The fate of international liberalism allegedly *depended* on the eradication of bondage. "The war would be in fact nothing else than a grand uprising of the popular conscience in favor of a great humanitarian principle." As a disillusioned refugee from 1848 who believed in liberal nationalism, Schurz understood the logic in both Lincoln and Europe's stance on the Union war. He believed in constitutional moderation—the antithesis of European coercion—but his instincts pressed him to see the war as a purification from the national stain of human bondage. "It is my profound conviction that, as soon as the war becomes distinctly one for and against slavery, public opinion will be so strongly, so overwhelmingly in our favor," aligning the Confederacy "upon the side of a universally condemned institution."[65]

Stalwart African American abolitionist Frederick Douglass joined the European critique of the Union war effort. Both an outspoken proponent of American exceptionalism and a scathing critic of the slaveholding Union, Douglass considered the war an unquestioned and unavoidable mandate to destroy slavery. The slaveholders' "war for the destruction of liberty must be met with war for the destruction of slavery," Douglass announced in 1861. Union and emancipation were not mutually exclusive. Bondage, he argued, infected free peoples, contaminated nations, and stunted progress, compelling national preservation to align with emancipation. How could the nation reunite with elite slaveholding oligarchs who willfully hijacked democracy, violently disparaged federal harmony, and grossly violated human dignity? "A long and tame war, waged without aim or spirit," admonished Douglass, "arrests the wheels of civilization" because the cancer within national life remained untreated. A war for Union *depended* on emancipation. "*To put an end to the savage and desolating war now waged by slaveholders, is to strike down slavery itself,* the primal cause of that war," he announced. A preserved Union could not fuse again with slavery, long the crushing impediment to national consensus. An emancipated Union, however, would harvest "law abiding Liberty" [and] "fill the whole land with peace, joy, and permanent safety."[66]

European mediation became a real possibility by the summer of 1862, with little indication among the loyal citizenry to expand the war's scope beyond national preservation. Great Britain and France particularly felt the war's adverse influence. The Union's blockade of southern ports dramatically reduced cotton shipments to European markets, which crippled British and French textile mills. Each nation—especially Napoleon III's France—also looked at the North American destabilization with insatiable desire. Europeans even declared the Civil War a humanitarian crisis, an impossible stalemate that consumed infinite lives. One British critic who considered the conflict devoid of purpose believed that "every principle of humanity demanded prompt intervention to stop so dreadful an effusion of blood and the mutual exhaustion of both parties." Governed by economic concerns (cotton), altruism (the anxieties of an escalating, futile, and bloody war), fear (the British sensed that an escalating conflict would stimulate slave rebellions and race wars in the South), and strategic designs (that a shattered Union and the formation of two American republics would decenter the balance of Atlantic power), European nations moved toward intervening and brokering a peace with the American belligerents.[67]

The diplomatic implications of emancipation linked to the purpose of Union itself. Slaveholders "have aimed a murderous blow at the heart of the country whose destiny they so long controlled," remarked John Lothrop Motley, the United States' ambassador to Austria. "By levying war, [Confederates] put it in our power, without any violation of law to repair the wrongs done." The old slaveholding Union died through secession, and "if we neglect this opportunity of doing justice, I feel that we shall perish as a nation." Given that Europe sensed this very circumstance, Motley pleaded, "a proclamation of emancipation ... would strike the sword from England's hands" and neuter Napoleon, who "is ready, & desirous of giving the slaveholders' confederacy a lift with a large auxiliary force by sea & land." A Christian delegation likewise petitioned President Lincoln that emancipation would dismantle the revolutionary internationalism long imposed by slavery. "The toleration of that aristocratic and despotic element among our free institutions was the inconsistency that had nearly wrought our ruin and the caused free government to appear a failure before the world, and therefore the people demand emancipation to preserve and perpetuate constitutional government." The measure thereby offered a cure to national balkanization. The Union could not battle "a rebellion for the destruction of the Government and the perpetuity of Slavery," remarked Harper's Weekly. "A true Conservatism aims first and always to preserve the vital principle of the Government." Emancipation would forever preserve the Union's liberal democracy from separatist factions, marginalize the Confederacy as a slaveholding relic, and bar Europe from recolonizing North America.[68]

The contingencies of war coalesced during the early summer of 1862 to move Abraham Lincoln toward embracing emancipation as a measure to enhance the purpose of Union. When the United States' Army of the Potomac failed to capture Richmond, Virginia, Gen. Robert E. Lee's aggressive counteroffensives extended the war indefinitely and sustained the slave-holding republic's international standing. Meanwhile, thousands of enslaved people had used the upheaval of war to flee their plantations and shatter the chains of bondage as they sought refuge behind Union army lines. And the mounting threats of European intervention joined an increasingly unstable military situation. To combat these challenges, in late July Lincoln presented to his cabinet a draft of a preliminary proclamation of emancipation. But his advisers warned that the potential radicalism of such an unprecedented mea-sure might alienate a northern public skeptical of a swift revolution in racial and social relations. Lincoln had to guide the public in seeing how emanci-pation aided the task of national preservation. With discerning prudence, he outlined his rationale in an August public letter published in the *New York Tribune*. Lincoln reiterated that his "paramount object in this struggle *is* to save the Union, and is *not* either to save or to destroy slavery. If I could save the Union without freeing *any* slave I would do it, and if I could save it by freeing *all* the slaves I would do it; and if I could save it by freeing some and leaving others alone I would also do that." The restoration of national authority re-mained paramount, Lincoln assured his fellow citizens, because "what I do about slavery, and the colored race, I do because I believe it helps to save the Union."[69]

Abraham Lincoln issued the Emancipation Proclamation in the wake of the Battle of Antietam, the September 1862 clash that thwarted Robert E. Lee's Confederate invasion of the United States. On January 1, 1863, the president's order declared, the Union would recognize the universal freedom of all enslaved people who resided in the rebellious states. Framed within the context of Union, Lincoln continued to justify emancipation on practi-cal grounds. "This plan is recommended," he vowed to the American people, "as a means for restoring and preserving the national authority throughout the Union." Governed by constitutional restraints, the measure grew from the president's war powers, assisted the federal war effort by depriving unfree labor to the Confederate war machine, and eliminated the malignant source of sectionalism and secession. Emancipation would not transcend the cause of Union, even if such calculations "would help us in Europe." The stakes far exceeded the delicate balance of international diplomacy and global opinion. "Slavery is at the root of the rebellion," Lincoln instructed, and "constitutional government is at stake. This is a fundamental idea, going down about as deep as any thing." While "the occasion is piled high with difficulty," he concluded to Congress, "this assurance would end the struggle now, and save the Union forever."[70]

Lincoln recognized the profundity of the moment, in which the exigencies of civil war shattered long-standing Republican pledges to safeguard slavery's national life. "The dogmas of the quiet past," he explained in a remarkable grasp of historical philosophy, "are inadequate to the stormy present." Lincoln understood that free people were not constrained by the unremitting force of historical inevitability. That people possessed the natural rights of reason and personal sovereignty meant they could shape their present to meet the unanticipated and contingent demands of the future. Emancipation was not predestined. It was a rational but once inconceivable response to national disintegration in the name of slaveholding. "As our case is new, so we must think anew, and act anew," Lincoln instructed. "We must disenthrall our selves, and then we shall save our country." Any fractured nation striving to conserve the ideal of democratic liberty could not restore itself in a tarnished slaveholding image. "Fellow-citizens, *we* cannot escape history," that powerful confluence of events that confronted the basic meaning of Union. Democracy, as the natural political expression of *all* humans, could no longer be reserved for a select few. That "we say we are for the Union" mandated that "in *giving* freedom to the *slave*, we *assure* freedom to the *free*." Otherwise, "we shall nobly save, or meanly lose, the last best, hope of earth."[71]

The loyal citizenry understood emancipation, once an unthinkable prospect, as a pragmatic means by which to crush the Slave Power and preserve the republic. Stalwart antislavery statesman Charles Edwards Lester contextualized the great change in the northern disposition. "We had attempted an impossibility," he reflected on the frustrations of the antebellum era. "*We had tried to make Liberty and Slavery live together in the same soil.*" The oligarchic slaveholders who had transformed the federal government into their personal fiefdom and then broke the Union would now have their arbitrary dominion shattered by the weapons of war. Those who enjoyed public prestige, who rolled in ill-gotten wealth, and who threatened the Union to safeguard their sullied power would no longer rise to independence on the backs of bound people's labor. Free Soilers had long opposed the Slave Power's haughty elitism, linking the southern regime to the same tyrants who opposed popular sovereignty throughout the Atlantic world. "We are fighting the battle of Democracy against Aristocracy," a writer for *Harper's Weekly* explained, "which has been fought out in most of the countries of Europe." The war would result either in the "overthrow of the Aristocracy as a privileged class, or," the author concluded, "the establishment of an oligarchy and the overthrow of Democratic institutions in the United States." Emancipation relieved the Union, once a slaveholding entity, from the discriminating advantages of social hierarchy and racial privilege. The nation would now favor the independence, ambition, and will of each citizen to rise unencumbered. "The Southern people once emancipated," Carl Schurz acknowledged, "will not let a broken-down aristocracy think for them, but they will think for themselves, like freemen; they will have the aspirations of freemen, centered in truly free institutions." No longer coerced by slaveholding muscle, the Union would now liberate "every human being [to] enjoy the fruits of his labor with dignity and independence."[72]

According to loyal proponents, emancipation modernized the Union and marginalized the Confederacy as a relic of Old World savagery. Abolition "recognizes and declares the real nature of the contest, and places the [Union] on the side of justice and civilization, and rebels on the side of robbery and barbarism," announced Frederick Douglass. Presbyterian minister William G. T. Shedd explained that emancipation cleansed God's chosen nation from a depraved institution that showered sin upon a providential populace. "The position which the American people and their Government have taken before God and the world, is that the system of human bondage is an unjust one," he preached to his New York City congregation shortly after Lincoln proclaimed emancipation. Slavery "has no foundation in the ordinance of God, or in the natural rights which he established." Only a baptized and justified Union could secure eternal liberty. When Ralph Waldo Emerson described emancipation as "a progressive policy," meeting the "demand of civilization," he argued that democratic institutions, unsullied by slaveholding coercion, guaranteed "morality [as] the object of government." The old slaveholders' Union, one that hijacked democracy and stole individual lives for personal enrichment, thwarted moral progress. Thus, as Douglass concluded, emancipation unburdened the Union "from the dreadful ravages of revolution and anarchy," perching America "as a queen among the nations of the earth."[73]

Condemnations of slaveholding as a primitive artifact translated into an antislavery renovation of North America. Republicans long recoiled that American exceptionalism sprang from the United States' stature as the largest slaveholding nation in the mid-nineteenth-century world. Unburdened from slaveholders' political obstructions, Lincoln's party used the upheaval of war to shape a new egalitarian republic that no longer genuflected to slavery. Emancipation crested a rising wave of transformative wartime legislation that liberalized the continent by shattering the old Union's marriage to bondage. As early as 1861, when enslaved people flooded Union army lines, the federal government refused to return absconded human property to slave owners. In codifying a degree of African American freedom, the Confiscation Acts undercut the old Fugitive Slave Law and established new liberal demands upon government. In 1862, the Republican Congress abolished slavery in the District of Columbia and recognized both Haitian and Liberian independence, legitimizing black republics across the Atlantic world. "Justice, civility, and self-interest," the New York Times declared in support of these recognitions, "will undoubtedly mark progress on our part." So long as slaveholders "ruled in our legislative halls, and dictated our National policy," the Union could never align with the world's free black nations. Prior to the war, "it was fated that the race which plays so tragic a part in our own history, should be everywhere wronged and despised by the American Republic." Now, with the dismantling of the slaveholding regime, "happily, that horrible incubus is lifted off the nation."[74]

Republicans then transformed the American West into a continental beacon of free-labor egalitarianism. Congress enacted laws throughout 1862 that promoted middle-class progress and capitalist economic stability. The Homestead Act granted millions of acres of public land to settlers who would travel west, populate the territories, and improve their property. The act granted access to continental abundance, individual independence, and upward economic mobility. Free labor, long stifled by slaveholding aristocrats, Lincoln explained in 1861, "is the just, and generous, and prosperous system, which opens the way to all—gives hope to all, and consequent energy, and progress, and improvement of condition to all." Securing the fruits of individual labor furnished a democratic check against aristocratic political manipulation. "Let [all citizens] beware of surrendering a political power which they already possess, and which, if surrendered, will surely be used to close the door of [economic] advancement," warned Lincoln. To promote broad-based educational opportunities, the Morrill Land Grant Act assigned public lands for the establishment of state universities that specialized in the mechanical and agricultural arts. Accessing practical education cultivated an informed, marketable, restrained, and autonomous citizenry in their pursuit of propertied independence. Finally, the Pacific Railroad Act linked the republic's continental and international economic ambitions. Authorized by the people's representative as consensual acts of democratic moderation, Congress's remarkable efforts dismantled slaveholding privilege, which had once limited common citizens from achieving individual self-sufficiency. "Commerce and civilization go hand in hand," noted one Republican, "civilization of that high type which shall spread the cultivated valley, the peaceful village, the church, the schoolhouse, and thronging cities."[75]

Reforming the national landscape from a rigid social hierarchy into an equitable middle-class standard preserved American moderation, equity, and justice. And it solved the revolutionary terror of disunion, guaranteeing that the Slave Power would never again threaten national harmony. "If the country is severed in twain," reflected *Harper's Weekly*, "the future which lies before us is plainly depicted in the history of Mexico and Central America: incessant wars, constant subdivisions, a cessation of honest industry and agriculture, a decay of trade, a disappearance of wealth and civilization, and in their stead chronic strife, rapine, bloodshed, and anarchy." Republicans had effectively marginalized the Confederacy as a distinct abnormality that defied modern nationhood. "I cannot imagine that any European power would dare to recognize and aid the Southern Confederacy if it became clear that the Confederacy stands for slavery and the Union for freedom," Lincoln predicted. Emancipation accommodated much of the international community's aversion to human bondage, demonstrating to enlightened nations the United States' moral arc while the Confederacy remained bound to an illegitimate and out-moded institution. Lincoln's proclamation "is creating an almost convulsive reaction in our favor all over this country," Henry Adams rejoiced from London. "A great popular movement" hostile to aristocracy "rests altogether on the spontaneous action of the laboring classes and has a pestilent squint at sympathy with republicanism."[76]

Emancipation placed the United States alongside the international community in eliminating slave societies from a world increasingly dedicated to some kind of human liberation. Slaveholders had become, according to a Philadelphia pamphleteer, "aliens and foreigners" because they conspired through war to establish "a great independent slave power on this continent." Rather than merely *declaring* itself the protectorate of hemispheric republicanism, the Union now *acted* on its commitment to a common liberty. Lincoln even suggested that wartime emancipation connected the United States to hemispheric republics that had proscribed the institution earlier in the nineteenth century. "During the last year there has not only been no change of our previous relations with the independent states of our own continent, but, more friendly sentiments than have heretofore existed, are believed to be entertained by these neighbors, whose safety and progress, are so intimately connected with our own," he informed Congress in December 1862. "This statement especially applies to Mexico, Nicaragua, Costa Rica, Honduras, Peru, and Chile." The emancipated republics of the New World now forged a liberal partition between themselves and the Confederacy's fanciful alliance with Old World autocracy.[77]

The United States now protected individual liberty, economic independence, and a popular sovereignty that reflected the will of free people. Lincoln outlined these sentiments in a letter to workingmen in Manchester, England, a group that endorsed the Union's free-labor agenda. "It has been often and studiously represented that the attempt to overthrow this government, which was built upon the foundation of human rights, and to substitute for it one which should rest exclusively on the basis of human slavery, was likely to obtain the favor of Europe," the president advised the Englishmen shortly after he signed the Emancipation Proclamation. But the nation could never perish, Lincoln later clarified. Only in the Union did "every man [have] a right to be equal with every other man." If an equitable republic collapsed through disunion, *all* individuals—white *and* black—surrendered "an open field and a fair chance for [their] industry, enterprise, and intelligence." Emancipation represented "the ultimate and universal triumph of justice, humanity, and freedom" because it secured free-labor egalitarianism, an essential democratic attribute under attack across much of the world. As Lincoln outlined to Congress in 1861, "Labor is prior to, and independent of, capital. Capital is only the fruit of labor, and could never have existed if labor had not first existed. Labor is the superior of capital, and deserves much the higher consideration." Aristocracies suffocated nations when "a few men own capital, and that few avoid labor themselves … by hir[ing] or buy[ing] another few to labor for them." In an antiaristocratic republic, "the free hired laborer [was] never fixed to that condition for life." The Union featured unbound individuals working for themselves, securing economic independence, and employing for compensated assistance "the prudent, penniless beginner in the world" who "toil[ed] up from poverty" to obtain personal sovereign liberty, facilitating a "system, which opens the way to all" and provides "improvement of condition to all."[78]

Emancipation was as much about liberating the Union from slaveholding oligarchs as it was about liberating the individual from oppressive coercion. Few people embraced the egalitarian promise of free labor more than African Americans. A free woman of color named Hannah Johnson petitioned President Lincoln on this score. She contested the premise of legally codified slavery because "the poor slave did not" make the laws that permitted white enslavers to unjustly steal and manipulate bondpeople's industry. "Robbing the colored people of their labor is but a small part of the robbery," Johnson advised Lincoln in July 1863. "Their souls are almost taken, they are made bruits of often." Johnson's candid, heartrending observation underscored the rapidity with which formerly enslaved people discarded what black abolitionist Harriet Jacobs called the "old habits of slavery" when they secured their freedom behind Union lines. But Jacobs did not frame the dawn of freedom as a triumphal end to lifetimes of bondage. In surveying the refugee camps within Union armies, she documented the "misery" of the "poor sufferers" who attempted to define the scope of liberation. From rampant disease, deplorable living conditions, and even abuse from some Union soldiers, freedom appeared to Jacobs an empty, uncertain condition.[79]

Yet Jacobs also observed how even in the trial of freedom African Americans exhibited the traits of republican citizenship. "Many have found employment, and are supporting themselves and their families," she recorded. "They are quick, intelligent, and full of the spirit of freedom." Freedpeople embarked on legitimating their marriages, pursuing education, forming voluntary associations, ensuring religious freedom, and earning wages as auxiliary personnel for Union armies. Charlotte Forten, a teacher and a free woman of color who came of age in abolitionist Massachusetts, relocated to the South Carolina Sea Islands to join the Union's "Port Royal Experiment," a haven for black free labor and education. In her extraordinary journals, Forten documented the swift transitions from slavery to freedom. "Talked to the children a little while to-day about the noble Toussaint L'Ouverture," the hero of the Haitian Revolution. "It is well that they sh'ld know what one of their own color c'ld do for his race. I long to inspire them with courage and ambition … and high purposes." In their quest to secure a degree of personal sovereignty and the human right to self-dignity, freedpeople exposed the profound folly of slavery.

Liberty was as much an enduring human condition as slavery was a gross, unnatural affront to civilization. In the wake of emancipation, they expected the United States to reform into a beacon of biracial egalitarianism.[80]

While emancipation fundamentally transformed African Americans' relations to the federal state, the war also occasioned unprecedented social and political changes for white Union women. As more than 2 million northern men volunteered to serve in Union armies, myriad women considered their wartime contributions as equivalent forms of disinterested national service, an essential prerogative of republican citizenship. Northern women fostered dynamic public roles by spearheading relief organizations, particularly the U.S. Sanitary Commission. The republic's largest and most vital wartime voluntary association, the Sanitary Commission reflected decades of northern reform movements organized by women. The commission aided Union armies through fundraisers, collections of medicine, and campaigns for food and clothing. Meanwhile, as women labored in government offices, in industrial munitions centers, and at the front as nurses, their public service performed similar political work as men who marched as soldiers and legislated as politicians. A collective war for Union loosened the strict separation between public and private gendered spheres. For white northern women, "the Civil War [w]as a moment when antebellum experiences of space collapsed," writes historian Judith Giesberg, "and women produced spaces where they ceased being the object of war and became its subject."[81]

White northern women negotiated the domestic home front and the public war front, which often coalesced into one broad front of women's politics. In much the same way that a war for national preservation confronted the place of slavery in a democracy, the contest also raised questions about the gendered assumptions of Union itself. "In this crisis of our country's destiny, it is the duty of every citizen to consider the peculiar blessings of a republican form of government, and decide what sacrifices of wealth and life are demanded for its defence and preservation," prominent feminists Elizabeth Cady Stanton and Susan B. Anthony declared in 1863 to rally northern women. "Woman is equally interested and responsible with man in the final settlement of this problem of self-government," each burdened with the duty of liberating the nation from slaveholding revolutionaries. Knitting clothing and socks, caring for wounded soldiers, and even sacrificing husbands and sons, Stanton and Anthony explained, made women essential wartime participants. But women possessed a commanding influence that extended well beyond tangible service to the republic. When Union women consented to and even encouraged their husbands to leave home and serve in the armies, they facilitated a powerful mode of gender politics that subordinated the private family to the public nation. Yet in a striking paradox, to preserve the Union ultimately was to preserve preexisting domestic gender relations—either when men returned home or when wives *demanded* that husbands return home—even as some women came "to see themselves as individuals who related to the nation-state, not indirectly through male family members, but on their own, independent, terms."[82]

Though an emancipated Union and a free-labor continent aimed to thwart European intrusions into the Western Hemisphere, the Confederacy's lure of free trade, cheap cotton, and efficient, unfree labor beckoned France to invade Mexico. "The traditional ambitions of Governments seldom die out, and the aggressive lust of despotism is as enduring as despotism itself," scoffed the *New York Times* regarding Europe's insatiable imperial desires. When French fleets descended on the hemisphere in the spring of 1862, the loyal citizenry worried that monarchical reaction would filter throughout Central America and find a friendly ally in the Confederate republic. Napoleon III's antics, warned the *Times*, would "establish this species of Monarchism on the ruins of the Democratic Government founded in the Western World," inaugurating "a grand struggle between the votaries of Republicanism and the votaries of Monarchy." The slaveholders' rebellion and the French colonization of Mexico posed dire national security implications. "If this nation were broken into fragments, and two or three republics were to rise upon its ruins, we should be a feeble people, incapable of self-defense," stalwart Republican Thaddeus Stevens acknowledged on the eve of Napoleon's arrival. "The Old World would shape our institutions, regulate our commerce, and control all our interests," imperiling the Union's continental vision. Unionists thus sensed European monarchs and Confederate oligarchs conspiring to undermine the United States' liberal, free-labor democracy. The "upholders of absolutism in Europe and the upholders of slavery in the United States," a northern reformer explained, maintained a "common cause [to] strike a blow against republican liberty on the American continent, in the hope of rendering arbitrary power more secure in both hemispheres."[83]

Remarkably, the French-Confederate coalition never materialized. From the United States and Great Britain both exerting powerful diplomatic and militant postures against the French, joined by battlefield verdicts that increasingly favored the Union, Napoleon gambled that recognizing the Confederacy might well harm his imperial ambitions. Although his hemispheric dreams depended on Confederate victory, Napoleon could ill afford a risky war with the British and Americans, especially as Secretary of State Seward continually promised "a collision between France and the United States and other American Republics." It was hardly an empty threat: six thousand Union troops arrived in November 1863 to occupy South Texas, impeding Confederate-Mexican trade webs and presenting an imposing military presence against any possible alliance between the monarchists and slaveholders. The Union's successful efforts eventually forced Napoleon away from the American conflict while also permanently marginalizing the Confederate republic on the world stage. Indeed, the incipient southern nation failed to achieve the international recognition that it so desperately needed to brandish its slaveholding legitimacy. Perhaps the forces of democracy and the popular will of a free people were strong enough after all to combat the nineteenth century's tyrannical legions of reactionary monarchism.[84]

In November 1863, the same month in which Maximilian assumed the throne of Mexico and U.S. armies occupied South Texas to exert American influence against French imperialists, Abraham Lincoln dedicated a national cemetery as the final resting place for Union soldiers killed at the July battle of Gettysburg. Compelled to justify the unimaginable human cost of war, Lincoln's address voiced the enduring purpose of American civilization. Though, as he surmised, "the world will little note nor long remember what we say here," Lincoln framed the Civil War as a referendum on the nation's founding. When the American "fathers brought forth on this continent a new nation, conceived in liberty and dedicated to the proposition that all men are created equal," their design sheltered individual natural rights within a constitutional republic. The United States now found itself "in a great civil war" that tested "whether that nation or any nation so conceived and so dedicated can long endure." The Union's war against the Confederacy embodied nineteenth-century struggles between liberty and despotism, democracy and aristocracy, progress and reaction, republicanism and monarchism. If slaveholding secessionists succeeded in severing an egalitarian republic in the name of human bondage, they would signal that the founders' work was *not* self-evident, that the rights they put forth in the Declaration and Constitution were *not* universal, that there could exist an alternate American nation, one rooted in oppression, slavery, and hierarchy.[85]

The founding "proposition" was thus at stake. American civilization now featured two warring societies, each devoted to clashing readings of 1776. Only one republic could sustain the founding idea that all humans possessed an equal right to liberty. The other nation rowed against the tide of history, darkening the continent with a fallacious conception and a decadent mission. The Union's gruesome triumph at Gettysburg symbolized humanity's quest to live free from tyranny, unbound from coercion, and relieved from unrequited toil. The nineteenth-century world had failed to nationalize liberty, according to Lincoln, and only the United States protected individual autonomy from authoritarian coercion. Sustaining the noble struggle to preserve democracy against aristocratic slaveholding despotism advanced "the unfinished work" of the thousands of young men who fell in the quest of national preservation. "These honored dead" bequeathed their "last full measure of devotion" to a moral cause that transcended time and generations. They "gave their lives" so that the Union "shall have a new birth of freedom," ensuring for common citizens the equality of opportunity and the right to unobstructed political liberty.

Their sacrifice assured "that government of the people, by the people, for the people shall not perish from the earth."[86]

The *preservation* of American democracy depended on the *process* of democracy. Few events better exemplified the quest to uphold the world's last best hope than the presidential election of 1864. If Unionists boasted themselves the international protectors of popular government, only a free and open election during the midst of civil war could legitimate their cause. Suspending the election to justify Abraham Lincoln's indefinite reign would reek of European centralization, substantiate global critics who denounced the weakness of democracy, and validate the Confederate rebellion. Republicans and their Democratic opponents each abided by the sanctity of constitutional restraint, consenting that the people's voice must govern national politics. Abraham Lincoln even acquiesced to a two-party electoral process that might well overturn his presidential mandate to suppress the rebellion and unite an emancipated republic. In a dramatic recognition of the efficacy of both liberalism and moderation, Lincoln agreed to change the Republican Party's name temporarily to the Union Party and to name Southern Democrat Andrew Johnson as the vice presidential candidate. "It will be my duty to so co-operate with the President elect, as to save the Union between the election and the inauguration," Lincoln informed his cabinet during the summer of 1864 when he predicted that the Republicans might lose the election on account of an enduring war and mounting bloodshed. George B. McClellan, the Democratic nominee and Lincoln's former commanding general, also approached the election with moderation, promising to "exhaust all the resources of civilized nations, and taught by the traditions of the American people, consistent with the honor and interests of the country, to secure such peace [and] reestablish the Union."[87]

Lincoln and McClellan each faithfully executed the free electoral process, the former yielding to the allure of democracy and the latter acting as a loyal opposition. Partisan Republicans nonetheless framed the election as a transformative contest between Union and radical balkanization. McClellan's pledge of peace, some alleged, portended the restoration of slaveholding oligarchs holding the nation hostage to their revolutionary demands. "To-day is to be decided whether this Nation *lives*, or *dies* at the hands of traitors!" announced a Republican campaign poster. "If the Union and government is not maintained, the nation is disgraced before the civilized world." Francis Lieber warned that the Democrats would reinstate the slaveholders' powerful hold on labor and economic mobility. "The dominion of Southern landholders," he announced to fellow German immigrants, would sustain "a land where the working man should be delivered over to a grinding tyranny far worse than any endured in the oppressed countries of Europe." A freeborn African American recognized that Democratic victory, the arrival of peace and reunion, and constitutional protections given to slavery would nullify emancipation. "Where is the man to be on this broad continent, who is more desirous of seeing the South achieve her independence with slavery for its cornerstone than George B. McClellan?"[88]

The election proved the viability of democratic institutions. Abraham Lincoln won the election of 1864 with 55 percent of the popular vote. McClellan carried only one free state—New Jersey—while Union soldiers in the field enjoyed the unprecedented opportunity to cast ballots as absentee citizens in overwhelming support of Lincoln. "It has long been a grave question whether any government, not *too* strong for the liberties of its people, can be strong *enough* to maintain its own existence, in great emergencies," Lincoln remarked several days after his electoral triumph. While "the present rebellion brought our republic to a severe test," he admitted, "the election was a necessity. We can not have free government without elections; and if the rebellion could force us to forego, or postpone a national election, it might fairly claim to have already conquered and ruined us." Popular sovereignty as the antidote to anarchy triumphed when McClellan conceded defeat, unlike slaveholding secessionists in 1860–61. He would not lead a military coup to defy his political adversaries, nor did he encourage Democrats to contest the election. He instead resigned from the army and suspended his political ambitions. "The people have decided with their eyes wide open," he declared, testifying to democracy's persistent strength. "I am therefore even now a private citizen, & shall direct myself to the active pursuits of civil life." The United States remained exceptional, Lincoln concluded, when "a people's government can sustain a national election, in the midst of a great civil war. Until now it has not been known to the world that this was a possibility." Republicans now held a stunning mandate to preserve a Union committed to the Slave Power's eternal destruction, to refuse an armistice with secessionists, and to pursue the outright dissolution of the Confederate nation. Those efforts depended above all else on the conduct of citizen-armies who waged a just war in search of a lasting peace.[89]

4

Conduct

★ ★ ★

A month before Confederates fired on Fort Sumter, Gen.-in-Chief Winfield Scott of the U.S. Army revealed his fearful visions of an impending civil war. Though Scott trusted that the Union would emerge victorious in any forthcoming military conflict, he sensed the nation following in the international tradition of revolutionary collapse. Forecasting "two or three years" to "conquer the seceded States by invading armies" numbering "three hundred thousand disciplined men," Scott flinched at the discomfiting image of an American civil war trailing in the bloody wake of nineteenth-century Atlantic civil conflicts. "The destruction of life and property," he prophesied, "would be frightful," compounded by the "enormous waste of" untested volunteers and civilians. He envision the nation sinking into endless financial debt with the South reduced to "fifteen devastated Provinces not to be brought into harmony with their conquerors." The United States might well be compelled to exact punishing retribution, erecting an unbending military leviathan to hold the former rebels "for generations by heavy garrisons ... followed by a Protector or an Emperor." The exorbitant price of reunion would transform a once exceptional United States into another nation fallen to the uncivilized devastations of civil war and central state militarism.[1]

Five days after his nascent republic compelled the Union to surrender Fort Sumter, John B. Jones, a clerk in the Confederate War Department, considered that no people had ever "engaged in a more just and holy effort for the maintenance of liberty and independence." From radical abolitionist agitations, to the election of a revolutionary Republican president, to the United States' mobilization of seventy-five thousand soldiers to crush southern democratic self-determination, the Union's "series of aggressions ... fully warranted the steps we [are] taking for resistance and eternal separation." Much like Winfield Scott, Jones imagined the United States fast mutating into a dangerous military state bent on destroying the essence of southern life. "The Government at Washington are going to wage war immediately" with "an army of 700,000" troops to invade and "subjugate the South, free the negroes," and execute the new republic's civil leaders. Jones thus petitioned a formal Confederate army, populated with "the ardor of volunteers," to "sweep the whole Abolition concern beyond the Susquehanna, and afterward easily keep them there." Only a just and decisive military victory could safeguard Confederate independence from the United States' "superior numbers" and fallacious

Sherman's March to the Sea, *ca. 1868, by Felix O. C. Darley. Union general William T. Sherman observes the scale of destruction wrought by his famous march from Atlanta to Savannah in late 1864. Sherman's army devastates every aspect of Confederate war-making ability, from tearing up railroads and telegraphs to shielding the escape routes of enslaved African Americans. Waging war in the name of national preservation justified the legalized application of what Sherman called the "hard hand of war," which included emancipation. (Library of Congress)*

"pretext of saving the Union and annihilating slavery." Salivating with radical militarism, "the Yankees would *dare* to enter upon such enterprises in the face of an enlightened world" whose people allegedly sympathized with the moderation of Jones's Confederacy.[2]

A year later in the early summer of 1862 following his demoralizing rebuff outside the gates of Richmond, Maj. Gen. George B. McClellan penned a cautionary letter to Abraham Lincoln. McClellan assured the president of his sincere dedication to the Union's preservation, a cause that "must never be abandoned; it is the cause of free institutions and self government." That the conflict against slaveholding rebels "assumed the character of a war," however, "it should be conducted upon the highest principles known to Christian Civilization." Echoing Scott's concerns of an escalating civil war, the Army of the Potomac's dashing commander denounced unfolding Union policies that now sanctioned the confiscation and destruction of property, the imprisonment and execution of unlawful irregular combatants, and the blanket destruction of slavery. Espousing "constitutional and conservative" wartime policies "pervaded by the influences of Christianity and freedom," McClellan reminded the president how an enlightened world scrutinized the American war. A contest restrained by dispassion and limited by moral reason "would receive the support of almost all truly loyal men, would deeply impress the rebel masses and all foreign nations, and it might be humbly hoped that it would commend itself to the favor of the Almighty."[3]

Lincoln soon justified the very military conduct that Jones predicted and that had so filled Scott and McClellan with angst. Seeking to mollify the skeptics of escalating wartime policies—the suspension of habeas corpus, the confiscation and destruction of belligerent property, and emancipation—Lincoln offered that "the constitution invests its commander-in-chief, with the law of war, in time of war." He outlined the principle of military necessity, a legal doctrine stating that "property, both of enemies and friends, may be taken when needed," depriving adversaries the use of crucial war material. "Armies, the world over, destroy enemies' property when they can not use it; and even destroy their own to keep it from the enemy," he explained. "Civilized belligerents do all in their power to help themselves, or hurt the enemy, except a few things regarded as barbarous or cruel. Among the exceptions are the massacre of vanquished foes, and non-combatants, male and female." In this context, Lincoln justified the Union's war-making methods, particularly the recently issued Emancipation Proclamation, which functioned as a military measure to help Union armies exercise a wider latitude in the quest of national preservation.[4]

It might well appear that Scott, Jones, McClellan, and Lincoln agreed on very little about the military scope of the Civil War. Yet they all expected that wartime conduct should be restrained in some way by an adherence to law and regulated by the moral reason of enlightened peoples. While they diverged on the specific latitude for wartime conduct, each participant concurred that conscious moderation informed how civilized nations waged modern war. In fact, Unionists and Confederates both drew from the same tradition of democratic restraint to underwrite mutual expectations of a limited war. Like Scott and McClellan, Jones bemoaned the destruction of property, the devastation brought to a once bucolic nation, and the menace of civil war growing to unprecedented, lethal scales. And as Lincoln declared of the United States, Jones suggested that the Confederacy could never claim legitimacy among the Western community of nations if it propagated an escalating, vicious war without moral, legal justification, or unrestrained by public institutions.[5]

Unionists and Confederates conceived of their nations as beacons of martial enlightenment for the rest of the world to emulate. Each citizenry organized their military cultures and practiced war in accordance with their democratic principles. They determined that their own civil war must be conducted in a civilized manner. Disapproving of international revolutions gone radically awry, the wartime generation vowed to wage armed conflict that obeyed the rules of war, maintained the sanctity of civilian control of the armed forces, and balanced careful distinctions between formal soldiers and civilians. Although Americans had long drawn on a European heritage to construct their own military tradition, they also aspired to transcend the seeming "internationalization" of armed conflict: arbitrary destruction, retributive state violence, and merciless reprisals against enemies who claimed a democratic heritage. Martial civilization demanded that armed conflict must be conducted in traditional and controlled ways to facilitate a peaceful reunion. War must be won or lost on the battlefield by soldiers in uniform led by professionally restrained officers. And it must not involve, much less be waged by, civilians on the home fronts or behind the lines, as was so typical in other civil wars.[6]

Modern critics may point to wartime episodes sullied by uncivilized, heartless atrocity, the very kinds of wartime cruelty condemned by Scott, Jones, McClellan, and Lincoln. From clandestine murders of civilians and soldiers, to the disgusting execution of U.S. Colored Troops by Confederate military forces, to the chaotic guerrilla war that debilitated the fringes of the wartime landscape, to the astounding number of battlefield casualties, the Civil War often appears to the modern eye as a brutal, limitless, and exceptionally violent war. The ostensible evolution from Scott and McClellan's restricted conflict, into Lincoln's fundamental transformation of the American South, into Jones's devastating carnage of the American landscape, led one prominent historian to label the American Civil War an unprecedented "'ideal type'" of "total war," a harbinger to the destructive and absolute conflicts of the twentieth century.[7]

Yet imagining the Civil War within the context of World Wars I and II, Vietnam, and especially the modern day's perplexing military conflicts overlooks a commanding nineteenth-century American culture that *disavowed* total war against "civilized belligerents." The democratic ideals of moderation and restraint—even if contemporaries often tested, expanded, or ignored the boundaries of that restraint—demanded distinctions between belligerent and noncombatant, conformed to the international laws and customs of war, and disavowed blanket extermination of public, legitimate enemies. The Civil War generation looked to their conceptions of "civilization," "barbarism," and an antimilitaristic ethic to frame how enlightened nations waged war. They understood wartime conduct to be part of a modern martial ethos that distinguished not between *levels* of violence but instead between *kinds* of violence. Whatever forms of warfare took place within this ethos—whether deploying massive armies of citizen-soldiers in search of decisive battlefield verdicts, disavowing guerrilla warfare, proclaiming emancipation as military necessity, or waging "hard" war against civilians—both sides claimed that they waged a civilized war that conformed to their respective national purposes. Seeing the Civil War as an unwarranted or unjust conflict betrays a desire to interpret the era as the "violent and remorseless revolutionary struggle" against which Abraham Lincoln so passionately warned.[8]

Framing a Just War

The nineteenth-century Atlantic world experienced an extraordinary reordering of imperialist, colonialist, and statist domains. Old World hierarchy and New World colonization ruptured through emancipationist movements that petitioned governments to shelter liberty and human rights within the nation-state. From the American colonies, to France, and to Haiti, later extending to Central and South America, rocking Caribbean slave societies, consolidating in the streets and countryside of Europe, and finally consuming the United States, common peoples rose in the name of liberation to discard the yoke of central-state authority. Nineteenth-century military conflicts thus materialized from rebellions, insurgencies, and independence movements that challenged centers of power; emerged from claims for liberal equality; and featured wars between nations to settle territorial disputes or questions of land and labor use. Wars were no longer fought as limited, distant contests between kings who exercised divine claim to regional sovereignty. The rise of nineteenth-century Atlantic nationalism meant that modern war sought to uphold or contest liberalism and define the limits of the nation-state in combating threats to its legitimacy.[9]

Between 1840 and 1880, 177 "war-like confrontations" riddled the globe, ranging from Indigenous rebellions to formal international wars waged by modern nation-states. The American Civil War transpired in the same mid-century as Europe's democratic revolutions; Mexico's civil war between liberals, nationalists, and imperialists; China's Taiping Rebellion, in which 23 million civilians died; Paraguay's gory war against the Triple Alliance of Argentina, Uruguay, and Brazil; the Crimean War, a religious and territorial conflict fought between Russia and an alliance of the Ottoman, French, and British empires; the wars of Italian and German Unification; the Paris Commune; and the devastating conclusion to the United States' three-hundred-year crusade against Indigenous North American nations. Because internal rebellions and external threats destabilized nation-states, governments often employed retributive means to maintain territorial integrity and retain powerful holds on recalcitrant populations. "The use of atrocities to quell domestic uprisings," writes one historian, "was commonly justified as being necessary for the preservation of order." The French Revolution's Reign of Terror "annihilated" 130,000 civilian foes of the new republic. In Central and South America, early nineteenth-century caudillos replaced imperial governors by wielding powerful, demagogic, and martial power against their revolutionary-minded citizens. And to contest the 1848 European liberation movements, Habsburg armies claimed national and military "necessity" to storm Vienna and Paris, executing or imprisoning more than ten thousand civilian demonstrators. Atlantic governments claimed "extraordinary measures to maintain order, even if this meant intentionally killing sometimes large numbers of civilians."[10]

Yet *because* liberalism permeated the nineteenth-century Atlantic world, modern warfare invited noteworthy limitations. Recognizing the powerful ways that war had changed since the late eighteenth century, the just war tradition aimed to rationalize the use of armed conflict while restricting military force through law and moral reason. Citizenries now claimed unlimited political ideals, and nations now wielded modern technology, which portended indefinite wars, foreshadowed shocking destruction, envisioned gross dislocation and refugee crises, and heralded the merciless targeting of civilians. Atlantic liberals thus consented that enlightened peoples could limit the overwhelming impact of war upon society. Deriving from Enlightenment thinkers Hugo Grotius, John Locke, and Emmerich de Vattel, the nineteenth-century just war tradition recognized—and aimed to limit—the human dimensions of modern war.[11]

In his widely regarded *The Law of Nations or the Principles of Natural Law* (1758), Vattel argued that civilized belligerents conducted war with state-sanctioned armies to pursue the national interest, in turn sustaining the humanity of civilians and soldiers. "At the present day war is carried on by regular armies," and civilians "have nothing to fear from the sword of the enemy," wrote the Swiss intellectual. "Such treatment is highly commendable and well worthy of Nations which boast of their civilization." Enlightened combatants thus subscribed to "the voluntary Law of Nations" to restrain "forbidding acts that are essentially unlawful and obnoxious," such as assassinations, massacres, and unwarranted destruction. Yet the voluntary principle also "tolerates every act which in its essential nature is adapted to attaining the end of the war." International law and the standards of Western enlightenment sanctioned the escalation of conduct if belligerents could demonstrate reasonable martial necessity. "The pillage and destruction of towns, the devastation of the open country by fire and sword, are acts no less to be abhorred and condemned on all occasions when they are committed without evident necessity or urgent reasons," Vattel concluded. Just war rested at once on human reason and moral conscience to limit excessive violence, while also permitting broad intensifications in belligerent conduct to secure the ends of war.[12]

Initiated in the wake of the American and French Revolutions, just war reflected notable changes in nineteenth-century warfare. Nations and peoples now went to war to procure, shelter, and resist the ideal of liberty. Citizens who emerged from the Age of Revolutions as dynamic political actors demanded that governments respond to and reflect their popular will. Rational and independent, citizens enlisted in large armies to wage war for the national interest, causes to which free peoples were intimately connected. International elites worried that the passionate mobilization of citizen-armies would instigate mass destruction and justify unthinkable conduct in unyielding nationalist furies. Republics, some critics alleged, did not possess a competent dispassion to wage civilized war. The bloody hunger for autonomy and a hatred of authority would inspire unlimited, inhuman combat. Yet civilized nations espoused the just war standard, expecting belligerents to define the *jus ad bellum*—the justification for waging war—and maintaining *jus in bello*—restraining wartime conduct in adherence to the legal and ethical customs of war. Nineteenth-century wars thus pitted nations-in-arms in pursuit of unlimited ideological objectives. But the ethos of just war limited a belligerent's military conduct in accordance with national legitimacy and the international laws of war.[13]

The foremost American theorists of the just war tradition, Henry W. Halleck—a West Point–trained officer in the U.S. Army—and German American law professor Francis Lieber, recognized the powerful changes in nineteenth-century Atlantic warfare. Inspired by European and Enlightenment philosophies, Halleck and Lieber during the late antebellum period paved an intellectual foundation of just war theory over which Civil War armies would later march. Both agreed that civilized nations resorted to armed conflict only after the exhaustion of all peaceable alternatives. "Wars have frequently been, in the hands of providence," explained Halleck, "the means of disseminating civilization, if carried on by a civilized people." And thus, as Lieber wrote in 1838, "we do not injure in war, in order to injure, but to obtain the object of war": a secure and lasting peace. "War does not rest on the contest of argument or reason; but it by no means absolves us from all obligation toward the enemy, on various grounds. They result in part from the object of war, in part from the fact, that the belligerents are human beings." After "an enemy is rendered harmless by wounds or captivity, he is no longer my enemy."[14]

Protection of civilians and the advent of peace functioned at the heart of Lieber and Halleck's conceptions of just war. Respecting private property and recognizing the humanity of passive populations "is so plain a maxim of justice and humanity that every nation, in the least degree civilized, acquiesces to it," Halleck offered. Yet while Lieber advocated restraint toward civilians, he also endorsed the broad use of military power to occasion a definitive end to war. "When nations are transgressed in their good rights, and threatened with the moral and physical calamities of conquest, they are bound to resort to all means of destruction, for they only want to repel. First, settle whether the war be just; if so, carry it out vigorously; nothing diminishes the number of wars so effectually." Democracies thrived best in peace. Wars were just only when defined and conducted with efficient, rational, and limited means to affect their own swift yet decisive ends. "I am not only allowed," he maintained, "but it is my duty to injure my enemy, as enemy, the most seriously I can, in order to obtain my end." But the very national ideals at stake also informed *how* wars were waged and *when* wars ceased. "The more actively this rule is followed out the better for humanity, because intense wars are of short duration."[15]

Lieber and Halleck understood war as a contest to preserve—not discard—modern civilization. Halleck endorsed the right of belligerent nations "to appropriate to our own use the property of the enemy," but he condemned the gratuitous "waste and useless destruction" of civic institutions, religious structures, and property divorced from the avenues of conflict. "There is a limit," Halleck offered, "beyond which we cannot go. It is necessity alone that justifies us in making war and taking human life, and there is no necessity for taking the life of an enemy who is disabled, or for inflicting upon him injuries which in no way contribute to the decision of the contest." Lieber adopted a more liberal condemnation, arguing against any act that "will cruelly afflict [a belligerent] after he has ceased to be an enemy." Both theorists ultimately recognized that wars waged by democracies could spiral out of control. The passions of free people, the unredeemable loss of sovereignty, the faith in national righteousness might well "justify" any act taken against an aggressor. But for nations to reestablish amiable relations with the civilized world, restraint and directed destruction had to be balanced so that the national ideal could remain intact during the dawn of peace. Otherwise the nation risked "being looked upon as savage barbarians," concluded Halleck. "The general rule by which we should regulate our conduct toward an enemy, is that of moderation."[16]

Civil War military conduct functioned within the tradition of just war outlined by Lieber and Halleck. Americans waged war to contest irreconcilable ideas of Union and the limits of national sovereignty. The United States sought the enduring restoration of a democratic republic absent the militancy of the international Slave Power. The Confederacy aimed to establish an independent slaveholding republic absent the dangers of international abolitionism. National and moral interests demanded that waging an uncompromising war served as the only means of shaping a lasting peace, either as a united republic or as two independent states sharing in the continent's providential bounty. Both nations sought democratic legitimacy within the Atlantic world. Wartime conduct thus had to conform to an imagined sense of American superiority while also demonstrating to the civilized world that republics could adhere to restrained and limited military practices. Drawing as much from the global as they did from the local, viewing the nations of the world as inherently belligerent, sensing common peoples routinely subjugated at the hands of coercive military states, and condemning destructive wars that seemed to swell with bloody passion, white Americans justified and distinguished their war from the world's pugnacious disposition.[17]

The United States went to war to preserve the republic and to uphold popular democracy. Secession, the formation of a belligerent Confederate state, and the attack on Fort Sumter posed a military threat to the sovereignty and security of the Union. Later, during his second inaugural address, Lincoln reminded the world of the United States' *jus ad bellum*, the rightful claim to wage war: "One [party] would *make* war rather than let the nation survive; and the other would *accept* war rather than let it perish." It was "a war upon the first principle of popular government—the rights of the people," he had explained at the war's outset during his 1861 message to Congress. To reject with armed force a free people's democratic will manifested "monarchy itself," demanding a just, unified response "against this approach of returning despotism." Lincoln's call for seventy-five thousand volunteers to quell the rebellion was thus a conservative response—sanctioned by the Constitution and ordered by the laws of war—to the militant radicalism of national disintegration. Because "the present condition of public affairs presents an extraordinary occasion," announced the president three days after Fort Sumter fell, "I appeal to all loyal citizens to favor, facilitate and aid this effort to maintain the honor, the integrity, and the existence of our National Union, and the perpetuity of popular government, and to redress wrongs already long enough endured." Lincoln authorized limited means—the display and execution of military force to topple radical secessionists—to achieve limited ends—the restoration of the recalcitrant states into the Union, a rationale that remained consistent through the duration of the conflict.[18]

Loyal citizens justified war as a rational process of reunification. As a New York City pastor reminded his congregation in November 1862, "The American Government is not waging an unjust war for foreign conquest, but a righteous war against domestic treason and rebellion." He further warned against "the demoralizing influence of national ambition" and "the lust of conquest." Thus, if Union armies waged war as European tyrants bent on annihilating Confederates, averred a Baltimore bishop, any "hope of peace" would be lost. To "'conquer'" rebels seemed "undesirable and injurious both to the North and to the South." The United States "looks only to the purpose of bringing back the Seceded States to their organic condition," not as subjugated colonies but as equal partners in the federal system. "We have known hitherto in this country so little of the actual realities of war on a grand scale" sparked by "the violent opposition to the government," wrote Philadelphia academic Charles Stillé about the nation's unique trial. "This is the experience of all nations," he continued, " and our Southern rebels do not differ in their capacity from the rest of mankind." While Confederates embodied international hostility to order, reason, and moderation, the United States could not emerge as a vanquishing imperialist. The loyal citizenry justified war only "to disarm the rebellion, and rid ourselves for ever of the pestilent tribe of domestic traitors" in service "to the great principles which underlie all modern civilization."[19]

A just war demanded that the Slave Power's revolutionary grip on American life surrender and perish. Ralph Waldo Emerson welcomed war because the United States had failed "to hold together two states of civilization: a higher state, where labor and the tenure of land and the right of suffrage are democratical; and a lower state, in which the old military tenure of prisoners or slaves, and of power and land in a few hands, makes an oligarchy." The militant internationalization of American life had "poisoned politics, public morals, and social intercourse in the Republic," sparking disunion and an unjust war. "To destroy the Union, and to establish in its stead a Confederacy based upon Human Slavery as its corner stone," agreed a pamphleteer, was "a crime against this Nineteenth Century." The aristocratic rebellion against American constitutionalism had to be suppressed by a trial of arms. "Civilization would retrograde" if slaveholding rebels expanded their republic across North America, forever holding the United States and the world hostage to its militant demands. "The Southern Government is a military oligarchy," explained a Union army officer. "The head of the oligarchy is in Richmond, and when the head falls a Union sentiment will be bound to burst forth in the South, which will soon entomb the body of this foul conspiracy."[20]

Confederates justified war to resist what they considered a militant obstruction to peaceful self-determination. As self-proclaimed democratic nation-builders, "our true policy is peace," Jefferson Davis announced to the world in his February 1861 inaugural address. "We have entered upon the career of independence, and it must be inflexibly pursued." Notwithstanding the decades of bitter sectionalism, "if a just perception of mutual interest shall permit us peaceably to pursue our separate political career, my most earnest desire will have been fulfilled." Though Davis prayed for an undisturbed separation from the old Union, "if this be denied to us, and the integrity of our territory and jurisdiction be assailed," he declared in anticipation of Union forces refusing to surrender Fort Sumter, "it will but remain for us, with firm resolve, to appeal to arms ... on a just cause." Davis later condemned the United States' military invasion of the Confederacy as a gross repudiation of "our right to self-government," leaving Confederates no recourse "but to prepare for war." The founding of a new constitutional government and the formation of a decorous military establishment aimed "to save ourselves from a revolution which, in its silent but rapid progress, was about to place us under the despotism of numbers." Only a successful contest of arms could "preserve in spirit, as well as in form, a system of government we believed to be peculiarly fitted to our condition."[21]

Davis appealed to the universal language of liberation with which oppressed peoples across the Atlantic world would empathize. In his telling, Confederates suffered as victims of a centralized, militant United States, which had refused a peaceful national separation. Theirs was thus a "just cause" in the "struggle for our inherent right to freedom, independence, and self-government." Davis pledged his incipient nation as a body of moderates who desired "only to be let alone." They waged war not for uncivilized "conquest" or unjust "aggrandizement." They instead battled against "those who never held power over us [who] shall not now attempt our subjugation by arms. This we will, this we must, resist to the direst extremity." That Confederates acted "in the exercise of a right so ancient, so well-established, and so necessary for self-preservation" only battle and bloodshed could uphold natural rights. If not for the Lincoln administration's allegedly excessive resort to arms, "the right of a people to self-government, peace, happiness, and prosperity would now smile on our land." Only when the unrighteous abolitionist "pretension is abandoned the sword will drop from our grasp." Otherwise, should Confederate armies fail upon the fields of battle, the flicker of democratic liberation for subjugated white peoples across the globe would be extinguished.[22]

Loyal Confederates waged war to secure the territorial integrity of their slaveholding republic. In the process, they condemned the United States as unlawful, barbaric aggressors who defiled civilized peace. The Confederate Congress praised the new nation's peaceful founding in the "struggle for the preservation both of liberty and civilization." Though "the utmost conservatism marked every proceeding and public act," the United States discarded enlightened restraint and brought a mindless, "wicked" war "against all our protests." How could Americans, who claimed a democratic heritage and a Christian faith, so willfully abandon moral restraint? "We all know that the enemy have nothing of that kind [of principle] to fight for," averred Confederate nurse Kate Cumming. "We have never wished to subjugate them or to take away their liberties, but have begged like supplicants, to be left to ourselves, with the sin of slavery on our own shoulders." Confederates thus claimed to wage war on behalf of reason, virtue, and liberty, exposing for the world the allegedly repugnant radicalism of the United States. "As far as I have been able to judge," confided Gen. Robert E. Lee to President Davis, "this war presents to the European world but two aspects. A contest in which one party is contending for abstract slavery & the other against it. The existence of vital rights involved does not seem to be understood or appreciated." National sovereignty "depends upon ourselves alone. If we can defeat or drive the armies of the enemy from the field, we shall have peace."[23]

The Union and Confederacy's *jus ad bellum* rested on a moral foundation of Christian Protestantism. Though such conflicts were seemingly hostile to the sacred commandment "Thou shall not kill," Americans justified holy campaigns of modern war against those who waged uncivilized, unjust crusades. The war was a test of divine Providence, a trial of arms to judge and cleanse a corrupted people. Sectionalism, political dissension, slavery, abolitionism, materialism, disunion—the selfish, impure contaminations of the collective American soul—had tarnished God's earthly kingdom. Imagining themselves as soldiers in Heaven's armies, Unionists and Confederates considered their nations unbreakably moral, each ordained to stand as tangible antidotes against global corruption. Evangelical millennialism—a belief that the actions of God's earthly agents prepared the world for Christ's return—framed each nation's causes as moral quests to be secured only on the fields of battle. Because the sins of internationalization had torn the republic and polluted the continent, the Civil War unfolded as an uncompromising trial against the enemies of God's exceptional designs.[24]

Citizens of both republics confronted the disquieting uncertainty of whether Providence truly justified their causes. How could it be, pondered Abraham Lincoln in his second inaugural address, that a just God could privilege one people over another when "both read the same Bible, and pray to the same God; and each invokes His aid against the other"? Because human bondage had corrupted the American character, "He gives to both North and South, this terrible war, as the woe due to those by whom the offence came." It was a righteous contest, the fateful verdict predetermined beyond humanity's ability to foresee. Loyal citizens of the Union could proceed merely "with firmness in the right, as God gives us to see the right." That "right" was the Union itself, announced Congregational minister William Orne White, and "our struggle [is] righteous in the sight of God." Only the United States and its democratic government sheltered humanity's divine liberties. "Might we not feel that God was better pleased with our course than with that of those persons who are leagued against our Government," Orne asked his flock. "For, what is the dark corner stone upon which they propose to build the fabric of their new edifice," he queried in a rhetorical allusion to Confederate vice president Alexander H. Stephen's definition of slaveholding nationalism. "They may wish to be independent ... but independent *of* what, and independence *for* what?"[25]

For evangelical Unionists, God mediated a destructive war to shape the nation in his holy image. Unitarian minister Henry Bellows considered the war a rebirth for "civil and spiritual powers," cleansing both the church and the state. "The contest before us," he proclaimed at the war's outset, "is one in which some long-rooted and deeply-bedded errors fatal to our peace, our national morals, our religion and our power and prosperity, are to be exterminated." Slavery and secession had "to be blotted from our political vocabulary," never again wielded against the republic. "The undivided sovereignty of the United States is to be finally vindicated, and the nation is not to lay down its arms while a single traitor to the flag remains," he summoned. The United States' torturous sectional trials had thus converted into a "holy war" waged by God's armies to uphold "American Nationality, the Constitution, the Union ... in the name of civilization, morality, and religion." Though blessed with abundant bounty and decades of stable peace, added Lincoln in his March 1863 National Day of Prayer, "we have forgotten God," the prime source of American exceptionalism. "We have vainly imagined, in the deceitfulness of our hearts, that all these blessings were produced by some superior wisdom and virtue of our own." Only a bitter war could occasion a lasting peace, a new national dawn in which *all* Americans, reunited in a firm reliance on God, would instill his blessings on earth in preparation for their heavenly lives.[26]

Killing and dying on behalf of God's chosen republic justified the horror of civil war. Though their deaths were devastating to family and friends, individual soldiers had to be sacrificed on the altar of the nation to ensure the nation's lasting salvation. Congregationalist Horace Bushnell hailed the "many names made sacred by the giving up of life for the Republic." Battlefields soaked with the blood of patriots cleansed the Union in the same way that Jesus's wrenching but selfless sacrifice washed away humanity's sins. But Americans, like all fallen peoples, did not deserve the eternal deliverance bestowed by Christ and his earthly soldiers. "It has been a wretched fault of our people that we have so nearly ignored the moral foundations of our government. Regarding it as a merely human creation, we have held it only by the tenure of convenience. Hence came the secession," Bushnell reflected on God's judgment. "In these rivers of blood we have now bathed our institutions, and they are henceforth to be hallowed in our sight. Government is now become Providential." War would bestow a new and just life to the Union, furnished "by our dead Americans," whose sacrifice unveiled "the right of this whole continent to be an American world, and to have its own Americans laws, and liberties, and institutions."[27]

Confederates responded with an equally ardent religious passion, condemning the United States for failing to uphold God's sacred mandates. "The tyranny of an unbridled majority, the most odious and least responsible form of despotism, has denied us both the right and the remedy," proclaimed Jefferson Davis in February 1862. "We are in arms to renew such sacrifices as our fathers made to the holy cause of constitutional liberty." Davis alluded to the Confederacy's divine calling, in which white southerners replanted the slaveholding seeds of God's earthly order in a new republic freed from abolitionist depravity. That free peoples established governments to protect rights and institutions ordained by God—the liberty ordered by slavery and the hallowed virtue of white self-determination—inspired a dogmatic martial fervor. God had chosen enlightened peoples of Anglo descent—and white southerners in particular—to order a chaotic world, to limit humanity's sinful excesses. Only human bondage could restrain, cultivate, stabilize, and civilize humankind's uncouth zeal. The United States had seemingly rejected God's most sacred institution, waging war against his divine creations. Confederates looked with anxiety at an increasingly secularized world in which sinful human passions corrupted institutions otherwise designed to withstand moral depravity. "The parties in this conflict are not merely abolitionists and slaveholders," announced Presbyterian theologian James Henley Thornwell, "they are atheists, socialists, communists, red republicans, jacobins on the one side, and the friends of order and regulated freedom on the other. In one word, the world is the battleground—Christianity and atheism the combatants; and the progress of humanity the stake."[28]

War occasioned the opportunity to cleanse the dangerous "isms" that had long infected the American character. As Thornwell declared, abolitionism, socialism, egalitarianism, and absolutism had to be expelled to procure an enduring peace. The United States' military invasion of a sovereign slaveholding republic portended nineteenth-century secular sins of armed coercion, emancipation, and insurrection, which shattered the fragile balance of God's earthly civilization. It was therefore just to wage war against those who defied Providence, those who conducted an uncivilized war in pursuit of an unrighteous cause. "If the affairs of the world are regulated at all by God," observed Episcopal pastor Stephen Elliott, "we cannot suppose that the destiny of a great Christian nation, such as these United States were, would be disregarded by him or unaffected by his control." The Union once stood as "a mighty power in the earth, a controlling element in the progress of the world." However, the old republic "coalesced rapidly with infidelity, and ended in a bold defiance of the word of God, and of the principles of his moral government." When northerners rejected God's will, seduced by the "heinous sin" of abolitionism, and "presumptuous [in their] interference with the will and ways of God," Americans invited "a punishment [which] is now scourging it from its one ocean to the other." The Confederacy stood athwart history's secular tide to uphold God's cherished institution, "slavery, which was the immediate cause of this revolution."[29]

Confederates aimed to rebuild God's earthly kingdom through the trial of war. "We are working out a great thought of God," Episcopalian James Warley Miles acknowledged, "namely the higher development of Humanity in its capacity for Constitutional Liberty." Grateful that the United States presented such a stark contrast to the Confederacy's moral virtue, Miles hailed the unprecedented opportunity of his new nation to boast the true essence of American civilization. "We have the glorious, but awfully responsible mission of exhibiting to the world that supremest effort of humanity—the foundation of a political organization, in which the freedom of every member is the result of law, is preserved by justice, is harmonized by the true relations of labor and capital, and is sanctified by the divine spirit of Christianity." Confederate armies bore a terrible but critical obligation: ensuring that a free republic would never again disregard slavery. "We have a great lesson to teach the world with respect to the relation of the races," Miles proclaimed about the Confederacy's self-evident foundations: "that certain races are permanently inferior in their capacities to others." Secured in the agrarian domains of the southern republic, enslaved people "contribute to the benefit of humanity in the position in which God has placed [them] among us. In developing and exchanging our peculiar agricultural resources we have a mission of peace and benefaction to the world."[30]

Waging a Just War

Despite crusading rhetoric that invited limitless devastation upon unholy enemies, a just war compelled the United States and Confederacy to outline the *jus in bello*, the legal restrictions in conducting war. Wartime actions that rejected enlightened morality and constitutional restraints undermined the legitimacy of both republics and forestalled a lasting peace. Unionists and Confederates professed an ethical obligation to practice war in a civilized manner. Because their respective foes were also somehow Christian and shared an Anglo-American heritage, citizens of both nations could not abandon their *own* moral restraint. To mitigate the transformative and destructive tendencies of nineteenth-century warfare, the Civil War generation brandished three tools of just war doctrine to conduct a civilized contest of arms: the United States treating the Confederacy as a public belligerent nation; each republic deploying antimilitaristic dual armies of citizen-volunteers and professional officers; and both nations subscribing to the laws of war, in which the ambiguous legal concept of "military necessity" sanctioned martial destruction while also restraining armies' ability to wage war. Each category placed democratic citizens—whether as soldiers, as ambitious officers at the head of armies, as residents on the home front, or as civil officials—at the center of wartime conduct, limiting their exposure to war, their participation in war, and the scale of destruction occasioned by war. Both nations utilized the very doctrines and institutions of democracy over which they battled to pursue a just and lasting peace.[31]

Civilized Belligerents

The American war was among the world's first armed contests in which the international laws of civil war regarded rebels as public belligerents. Though the United States never bestowed national or political legitimacy on the Confederacy, the Union's wartime actions abided Vattel's definitions of civil war, thereby holding the slaveholding republic as a functional wartime nation. "When a Republic is divided into two opposite factions, and both sides take up arms, there exists a *civil* war," wrote the eighteenth-century jurist. For Vattel, a civil war was distinct from a rebellion or insurrection. When the revolting party became "sufficiently strong to make a stand against" the existing nation, the original republic could only "make formal war." Vattel focused less on "the justice of the cause" for which rebelling parties fought; he was more concerned with limiting the inevitable atrocities so common in civil conflicts. "Civil war breaks the bonds of society and government" and "gives rise, within the Nation, to two independent parties, who regard each other as enemies and acknowledge no common judge. Of necessity, therefore, these two parties must be regarded as forming ... two separate bodies politic, two distinct Nations." Mutual regard for their enemies as members of belligerent nations imposed critical restraints among the combatants, binding each to international legal standards. Given that both parties claimed standing among civilized nation-states, "the belligerents should have recourse to the same means for preventing excesses of war and for re-establishing peace as are used in other wars." To legitimize their national purposes, "it is perfectly clear that the established laws of war, those principles of humanity, forbearance, truthfulness, and honor, which we have earlier laid down, should be observed on both sides."[32]

Although the American conflict unfolded as a rebellion against state authority, it was also waged by Confederates to create a sovereign republic out of an existing sovereign nation. The Confederacy did not direct an insurgent coup to topple, transform, or occupy the United States to secure equitable treatment within the existing national system. It instead claimed legitimate status as an independent member of the global community of nations. "The method of the rebels is war, and a war of desperation and vindictiveness. The Government must now," observed *Harper's Weekly* in August 1861, "also treat the suppression as a matter of war." The United States thus confronted a dilemma when the secessionist states organized a new constitutional government, established national military institutions, and, in the spring and summer of 1861, defeated Union forces at Fort Sumter and the first battle of Bull Run. The Union either could hold southern rebels as lawless, traitorous insurrectionists, or follow in the Atlantic legal tradition that treated the conflict as a formal, public war. Because the Union encountered a foreign adversary equipped with large, powerful armies, "from the beginning there was a persistent determination to treat the Rebels as alien belligerents,—as a hostile and distinct people,—to blockade, instead of closing, their ports," recorded Secretary of the Navy Gideon Welles. "Other governments had reason to claim that we had initiated them into the belief that the Federal Government and its opponents were two nations."[33]

Treating Confederates as legitimate belligerents who populated a nation-state and not as actual traitors limited the reprisal and carnage that would otherwise occur in a true rebellion. Combating a literal civil war would identify Confederates as outlaws subject to indefinite imprisonment, blanket executions, and wholesale annihilation. Military governments might thereafter strip power from civil authorities, holding the southern states as permanent colonies to a coercive United States. Though the loyal citizenry routinely indicted Confederates as "rebels" or "insurrectionists," such labels served as rhetorical devices to delegitimize the slaveholders' cause before the world. To preserve the Union and present democracy in its best international light, loyal citizens had to persuade the "rebels" again to become citizens of the republic. Lincoln "thought it proper to keep the integrity of the Union prominent as the primary object of the contest," thus limiting and restraining the ways in which *both* nations waged a civilized war. Indeed, the Union's shrewd treatment of Confederate "nationhood" mandated that Confederates themselves employ the moderating principles of contemporary statecraft in conducting a limited war against the United States. If federal armies eschewed "inhumanity, barbarism, and cruelty" when confronting Confederates, opined a loyal senator, "when war is over there may be mutual respect and confidence, that the ancient relations of commerce and trade may return unimpaired ... mak[ing] us once more one Government and one people with one destiny."[34]

Granting the Confederacy de facto national legitimacy never endorsed the slaveholding republic's national purpose or identity. But the tactic did sanction a formal blockade; prevented Union armies from arresting, trying, and executing uniformed enemies as rogue criminals; authorized nonretributive imprisonment of enemy soldiers who were subject to exchange and parole; conceded immunity to civilian enemies who did not impede the progress of war; limited the confiscation or destruction of property only to that which could be used in a military capacity by the enemy; and invited foreign nations to acknowledge Confederate belligerent rights. In late 1861, President Lincoln even ordered the release of two Confederate envoys—rather than trying each as unlawful traitors—captured by the Union navy as they traveled to Europe aboard the English HMS *Trent* to seek diplomatic recognition. Though Secretary of State William H. Seward impeached the Confederacy as "a Power existing in pronunciamento only," the U.S. Supreme Court outlined the avenue by which the federal government applied belligerent power status to the Confederacy. Ruling in the *Prize Cases* (1863), which upheld the constitutionality of the Union's blockade of southern ports, the Court unpacked the legal paradox of civil war. "When the party in rebellion occupy and hold in a hostile manner a certain portion of territory; have declared their independence; have cast off their allegiance; have organized armies; have commenced hostilities against their former sovereign, the world acknowledges them as belligerents, and the contest as a *war*." Writing in the vein of national jurisprudence and Vattel's legal theories, the Court "implied that what really made an internal conflict tantamount to an interstate war was not the goal for which the dissidents were struggling, but rather the material scale on which the hostilities were taking place."[35]

Treating the Confederacy with public belligerent status linked the United States' restrained martial conduct to its wartime purpose. "We are in arms to save the Union," the *New York Times* declared at the war's outset. "The South must be made to feel the full respect for the power and honor of the North: she must be humbled, but not debased by a forfeiture of self-respect, if we wish to retain our motto—*E pluribus unum*—and claim for the whole United States the respect of the world." As a pulse of mainstream loyal thought, *Harper's Weekly* routinely characterized the war as a contest between national belligerents. A May 1862 editorial announced that the cause of reunion would be meaningless if loyal citizens "sacrifice[ed] the fundamental principles of our political system." Otherwise, "the work of suppression will cost dear."

Harper's averred the following year, "So far as fighting and the course of war are concerned—the rebels have been a foreign power. If the war had been with English or French troops in possession of the Southern section, it would be conducted exactly as it is to-day." And despite the hundreds of thousands of soldiers who lay dead by 1864, *Harper's* reaffirmed the theme of moderation. "The war for the Union and the rights secured by the Constitution is a war for [the South's] social and political salvation, and our victory is their deliverance." Discarding the legal distinctions of civil war through an interminable annihilation of Confederates would shatter the moderate purpose of national restoration. "It is not against the people of those States, it is against the leaders and the system which have deprived them of their fair chances as American citizens, that this holy war is waged."[36]

Antimilitarism and the Dual-Army Tradition

The legal dimensions of civil war translated into shared military cultures projected by each nation. Citizenries of both the Union and Confederacy waged their wars with a dual army of professional officers leading amateur citizen-soldiers. Citizens of republics demanded absolution from coercive central states and, in turn, they enacted a disinterested civic virtue to ensure a nation's survival during times of military crisis. Only politically minded and ideological citizens devoted to the endurance of their republics could wage war on behalf of the national interest. Citizen-soldiers did not view themselves as ambivalent professionals, and they largely rejected the selfish seductions of mercenary service. The autonomy certified by democratic liberty and the dispassion harvested by republican virtue conditioned volunteer enlistments far more than arbitrary state compulsion. Uniformed volunteers in both armies thus presented themselves as altruistic public servants who yearned for victory and a return to the peaceful, unfettered pursuits of civilian life. Only voluntarism could preserve national fortunes, silencing the international critics of democracy who sneered at Americans' incapacity for self-government.[37]

Derived from one of the world's most politically active societies, Union and Confederate volunteers embodied a fierce democratic ethic, which they reinforced through military service. Citizen-soldiers rarely discarded their civic identities as free men who rejected the stifling conditions for soldiers serving in nineteenth-century state armies. They aspired to show the world that despite a terrible civil war, they came from peaceful societies that looked askance at centralized militant statism. They served in order to ensure that their republics transcended domestic and international tyranny. That they did not already comprise standing military forces—institutions traditionally composed of mercenaries or professionals—meant that citizen-volunteers best sheltered their nations' exceptional identities and causes. Fiercely democratic and deeply skeptical of the permanent, unbending conditions of military life, volunteers demanded equitable treatment, guarded the democratic right to elect and demote officers, and insisted on degrees of autonomy while in the ranks. The culture of citizen-voluntarism therefore absolved deep-seated fears that the uncertain conditions of modern war would undermine ordered liberty.[38]

Loyal citizens of the Union hailed their volunteers as conscious guardians of the republic whose civic virtue distinguished American democracy from international militarism. As he toured the Union army encampments spread throughout Washington, DC, the Boston intellectual and reformer James Freeman Clarke noted in December 1861 how the nation's capital resembled the great fortress cities of Europe, "but with a difference." Washington did not host "a mere standing army, to be wielded blindly in the interests of despotism, but an intelligent army of freemen, come to protect liberty and law." Thousands of individuals had willingly volunteered to soldier on behalf of the Union "to defend the Declaration of Independence, and the Constitution, laws, and traditions of the land." Conversely, "The great armies of the world — those of France, Russia, and Austria," *Harper's Weekly* averred in 1862, "are filled wholly by conscription. Volunteering is unknown in those countries." Abraham Lincoln thus praised American soldiers as "thinking bayonets," enlightened citizens who placed the national good over their personal self-interest. "With us every soldier is a man of character and must be treated with more consideration than is customary in Europe," the president explained to a French correspondent during the summer of 1862. Hardly drawn from an insensitive bellicosity, the citizen-soldier tradition disavowed permanent obligation to the state. "The armies of Europe are machines," alleged Ulysses S. Grant. They "have very little interest in the contest in which they are called upon to take part." Because the loyal citizenry waged war to preserve a people's republic of liberty, "our armies were composed of men who were able to read, men who knew what they were fighting for, and could not be induced to serve as soldiers, except in an emergency when the safety of the nation was involved."[39]

While enlistment motivations ranged from steadfast ideological devotion to self-interested pragmatism, few among the Union's 2 million citizen-soldiers would have disagreed that the republic's global mission depended on the triumph of national armies. "Their great work," Secretary of State William H. Seward acknowledged of the republic's soldiers in 1864, "is the preservation of the Union and in that, the saving of popular government for the world." That same year, George H. Hepworth, a chaplain for a Massachusetts regiment, praised Union volunteers as "the most disinterested men we have, [who] should be held in the warmest regard. The people have vindicated their right to republicanism. The thoughtful, honest, self-sacrificing are," he declared, "showing the world in how high estimation they hold our ... free government." Echoing Abraham Lincoln's statement of national purpose, an Ohio volunteer claimed that a fractured United States would halt "the onward march of Liberty in the Old World, [and] will be retarded at least a century,

[as] Monarchs, Kings, and Aristocrats will be more powerful against their subjects than ever." An Indiana soldier likewise imagined that defeat would forever erase the Union's standing as "the beacon light of liberty & freedom for the human race," expunging "all the hope and confidence of the world in the capacity of men for self-government." Lincoln thus acknowledged the dominant role of military events and institutions in securing the national purpose: "the progress of our arms, upon which all else chiefly depends, is as well known to the public as to myself."[40]

Incentivized to bear the hardships of war, the United States' volunteers linked the Union's preservation to the fate of international liberty. "I have no misgivings about, or lack of confidence in, the cause in which I am engaged," Rhode Island volunteer Sullivan Ballou confided to his wife. "I know how strongly American civilization now leans upon the triumph of [the] government, and how great a debt we owe to those who went before us through the blood and suffering of the Revolution," he explained in July 1861. "I am willing, perfectly willing to lay down all my joys in this life to help maintain this government." A week later, Ballou died at the first battle of Bull Run. The following year, despite the Union's December 1862 rout at Fredericksburg, John Wilson, who soldiered in the Forty-Third New York Volunteers, still could not "believe that such a great country as this, such a government, such a Nation, will be permitted to be torn asunder and totally disabled; to be wrecked, and thrown to the winds; to be made the object of mockery of the world." Only sustained, rigorous military service would "attain the grand object": "to crush the rebellion."[41]

Foreign-born immigrants who marched in Union armies understood particularly well the perilous balance of American democracy. Aspirants of economic improvement or refugees from despotic governments, many immigrants considered the American republic the world's last hope for economic opportunity and civil liberty, especially in the wake of Europe's failed 1848 democratic revolutions. For a substantial fraction of the foreign-born soldiers who populated 25 percent of Union armies, the American Civil War represented an extension of the Atlantic world's long, tired struggle for political rights and economic freedom. Indeed, the wartime Union's military and political leaders included Carl Schurz, Gustave Cluseret, Thomas Meagher, Franz Siegel, and Frederick Salomon, all veterans of 1848. "For them," writes a leading historian of European immigrants who served in Union armies, "the feeling of duty to their new home country was a major motivation to join the fight against what they saw as an unjustified rebellion of the southern states."[42]

For these émigrés, slaveholding oligarchs who waged war against a liberal republic personified the European despots of 1848. The United States thus *had* to be preserved from "this perfidious revolution against the best government in the world," wrote Adolph Frick, a German American who served in

Missouri. "I am satisfied with myself and am doing my duty as a citizen of this republic," echoed Magnus Brucker, a fellow German and revolutionary "Forty-Eighter" who escaped to the United States in 1849. He "despised *Sclavery*" because "it is incompatible with a free *Republic*" and "the progress of culture and civilization." Though he once feared civil war, by 1864, while serving as a surgeon in the Twenty-Third Indiana Volunteers, Brucker recognized that "there's nothing we can do except *destroy [Confederate] armies* and then dictate peace terms, prohibit *Sclavery* in all parts of the United States, in order to end the quarrel once and for all, and to open up this country for free labor and to keep it free for our children and our children's children."[43]

Brucker voiced a common refrain among foreign-born soldiers who feared that the collapse of Union would extinguish liberty throughout the world. Peter Welsh, a Canadian-born volunteer of Irish descent, soldiered in the Twenty-Eighth Massachusetts and considered that the sacred protections of citizenship compelled free people to uphold the government. "This country is very different," he declared in June 1863 from the Virginia front: only the United States valued distinct individuals as the lifeblood of a nation. "Here thousands of the sons and daughters of Irland have come to seek refuge from tyranny and persecution at home," aspiring to "raise themselves to positions of honor and emolument." Because the Union was not a blood-and-soil ethnic state, all free people were obligated to preserve "the best and most liberal government in the world." Each individual held "a vital interest in the preservation of our national existence the perpetuation of our institutions and the free [execution] of our laws." Edward Rolfe reminded his son that "we left our Native [England] to better our condition in life." Waging war "in an Enemys Country putting my life for My Country & ... for My Family & the rising Generation" mandated his service in the Twenty-Seventh Iowa Volunteers. And as George Cadman, another native Englishman who served in an Ohio regiment, assured his wife, "If I do get hurt I want you to remember that it will be ... for Liberty all over the World that I risked my life, for if Liberty should be crushed here, what hope would there be for the cause of Human Progress anywhere else?"[44]

Confederates likewise positioned volunteers at the center of their national war effort. Citizens of the new southern republic retained the essential attributes of a democratic people skeptical of compulsory military states. The *Richmond Enquirer* regarded volunteer soldiering "emphatically [as] an Americanism, and grows out of the fact that ours is a citizens' Government." Volunteering on behalf of the nation underwrote the Confederate republic's avowed moderation. "Here standing armies are not necessary, as in monarchical countries," because free men who served as temporary soldiers "are intelligent, and understand the issues of the war, and feel that it is *their* war." "My whole heart is in the cause of the Confederacy," a citizen-officer wrote from Tennessee in May 1862, "because I believe that the perpetuity of [r]epublican principles on this Continent depends upon our success." Only an enlightened populace could negotiate the sudden, wartime conversion of citizenship in one nation into citizens of a *new* nation. "Our Army is no hireling soldiery. It comes not from paupers, criminals, or emigrants. It was originally raised by the free, unconstrained, unpurchasable assent of the men," resolved the Confederate Congress. In the same vein as Abraham Lincoln's "thinking bayonets" description, the Congress concluded, "Our soldiers are not a consolidated mass, an unthinking machine, but an army of intelligent units."[45]

As many as 850,000 men served in Confederate armies, a nearly full mobilization of the new republic's white male military-age population. While they cited diverse reasons for volunteering—the idealism of defending one's home, family, and nation, the pragmatism of avoiding the 1862 military draft, or the necessity of financial restitution—uniformed Confederate soldiers no doubt marched on behalf of the world's largest slaveholding nation. Ordering a republic on the stability of racial hierarchy depended entirely on the triumph of Confederate armies. And countless soldiers knew it. For Reuben Pierson, who served in the Ninth Louisiana Volunteers, the Confederacy preserved "that rich legacy bequeathed" to *all* white southerners: "the enjoyment of our glorious institution," slavery. Through militant firmness "we will be acknowledged as one of the best governments that holds a place in the catalogue of the nations of the earth." Union armies might well "pour forth their fury and rage," but "we will defeat them or perish upon the soil of our loved and cherished southern republic." William C. Nelson, a volunteer officer from the Seventh Mississippi, which served in R. E. Lee's Army of Northern Virginia, thought "this war was ordered by Providence, as a means of settling definitely and conclusively the question of slavery: if slavery is a divine institute, I believe we will be successful, that our independence will be recognized and the Southern Confederacy will be established as a Government with slavery as its great distinctive feature."[46]

Born without a functioning military establishment, the Confederacy had to build a war machine on the virtuous energy of its white male citizens. "The maintenance of our cause rests on the sentiments of the people," Jefferson Davis noted in October 1861 as he praised the democratic spirit of Confederate military culture. Yet the very passions that fueled a war for national sovereignty spawned an independent guerrilla resistance against the enemies of Confederate nationhood. Steeped in romanticism, segments of the Confederate populace early on presented themselves as a national people in arms, idolizing the American "minute men" whose defiance against inequitable military invasions defended a free citizenry. To withstand "a long and bloody continental war," averred a Virginia editorialist, "the public heart is stirred": "Who can resist a whole people, thoroughly aroused, brave to rashness, fighting for their existence?" Designating themselves guardians of home and hearth, uniformed combatants disavowed the rigid constraints of the formal army, defending family and community from Yankee barbarism. "This revolution," promised a Tennessee writer, "is the spontaneous uprising and upheaving of the people." Only unbridled individualism could contest an unjust invasion. "They will never see their Southern brethren subjected to the horrors of war without the boldest and most efficient resistance."[47]

However, the very image of an insurgent "people's war," one unmoored from state regulation and consent, undermined Confederate claims of national legitimacy. Though embedded in an idealized American martial past, guerrilla warfare possessed few limitations, functioning on the volatile margins of democracy. If the Confederacy was to stand on the world stage as a stable, moderate nation, the new republic had to establish a functional government, raise state-sanctioned military forces, and place careful limits on the nationalist passions of modern war. Republics had to balance state power against individual liberty, at once avoiding centralized tyranny *and* unchecked mob rule. And perhaps most important, guerrilla conduct might well spark destructive retaliation from Union armies against the Confederate home front, imperiling slavery as the lifeblood of the new nation. The Confederate military establishment thus privileged professional West Point–trained officers to lead the national armies and not, counseled President Davis, "'path-finders' and holiday soldiers." Only "men of military education and experience in war" could channel a democracy's *rage militaire* into ordered, calculated violence. The West Point ethos considered irregular warfare fit only for barbarians, an uncivilized practice that would isolate the slaveholding republic from an enlightened global community. So when Davis spoke of "the position which we have assumed among the nations of the earth," he compelled Confederates to maintain a civilized martial disposition, informed by "a well-instructed and disciplined army." Only then could the Confederacy maintain national integrity, ensure the stability of slavery, and keep lawless insurrectionists from waging war independent of state authorization.[48]

In accordance with Davis's vision, Confederate civil and military leaders at the war's outset rejected guerrilla warfare. "Guerrilla companies are not recognized as part of the military organization of the Confederate states," responded Secretary of War Judah P. Benjamin to a citizen's 1861 request to raise a partisan unit. Citizens could volunteer for uniformed military service only in authorized state regiments and deployed to national armies. "The officers and men of all military organizations formed within the limits of the Confederate States, if they would have the countenance and protection of the Government, must conform strictly to the laws and usages of civilized nations," added a War Department memo. The Confederate nation could not surrender military oversight to an unchecked citizenry. All soldiers instead "must be commissioned and paid by the Government and subject to its orders, in complete subordination to its authority." Otherwise southern partisans should expect from Union armies "all the cruelties inflicted upon alleged outlaws or pirates," spawning a "departure of the enemy from the usages of warfare practiced by civilized nations." Given that in such cases "the [Confederate] Government would possess no right to interfere in your behalf," all white male volunteers should "be armed and tendered for war in the usual way."[49]

The Confederacy's disavowal of guerrilla warfare spoke to the moderate commitment of *both* nations to regulate their citizenries' martial passions. While the United States and the Confederacy favored the republican tradition to raise democratic citizen-armies, each nation tempered volunteerism alongside a professional officer corps. American notions of civilized warfare existed in a specialized ethos in which statesmen crafted policy, professional officers implemented the will of civilian authorities, and uniformed volunteers, restrained by the professional culture of discipline, enacted the state's will on the field of battle. Enhanced by dual-army antimilitarism, professional military leaders implemented limited military theories and strategies to disavow irregular or unauthorized combat. Anglo assumptions about enlightened warfare drew powerful contrasts against so-called uncivilized Native American combat. Derided as "savage" and "primitive," Indigenous warfare—much like guerrilla warfare—conjured images of invisible, craven, stateless insurgents stalking their unsuspecting human prey, whom Indians murdered with seemingly unjust ferocity. West Point's institutional emphasis on moderation, restraint, and hierarchy permeated the officer corps of both nations, ensuring an equitable martial balance between the American belligerents. As a leading scholar of the era's martial conduct notes, "The experience of the Civil War reveals that states matter. The most destructive nineteenth-century wars, like the Caste War of the Yucatan or the Taiping Civil War, involved actors who did not aspire to statehood or who rejected the Western laws of war." Anything beyond the prescription of state-sanctioned conduct was deemed illegitimate.[50]

West Pointers believed that improperly trained and undisciplined citizen-soldiers would transform into uncontrollable mobs, visit unjust devastation upon civilians and nonmilitary property, and imperil national legitimacy. In the wake of the Union's chaotic July 1861 retreat from the bloody fields near Bull Run, Virginia, Col. William T. Sherman condemned the "flying masses" of U.S. volunteers who abandoned all restraint when fleeing to Washington. "It was as disgraceful as words can portray," he described of the soldiers' destruction of dwellings and confiscation of crops. "Democracy has worked out one result," he scoffed at the collapse of order. "The difficulty is with the masses—our men are not good Soldiers" because "each private thinks for himself." Professional officers in both armies feared that callous volunteers would humiliate each nation before the world. "It is very important that the volunteer troops be organized & instructed as rapidly as possible," explained Maj. Gen. Robert E. Lee in May 1861. "Keeping the yet unsullied reputation of the army, and that the duties exacted of us by civilization and Christianity are not less obligatory in the country of the enemy than in our own," he reminded his subordinates on the eve of the 1863 Pennsylvania Campaign. "No greater disgrace could befall the army, and through it our whole people, than the perpetuation of the barbarous outrages upon the unarmed."[51]

Though skeptical of volunteer egalitarianism, effective officers nonetheless recognized that Civil War armies comprised free citizens who refused to discard their democratic character. Drawn from a liberal nineteenth-century American ethos, both volunteers and officers as peacetime citizens enjoyed social and political equality. While effective armies demanded rigid hierarchical order, democratic emphases on fairness, consent, and individualism infused Union and Confederate ranks. "An army is an aristocracy," averred volunteer Union officer Thomas Wentworth Higginson. "No mortal skill can make military power effective on democratic principles." Yet *only* a democratic people possessed the ideological will to sustain a long, bloody war, "because no other can so well comprehend the object, raise the means, or bear the sacrifices." That citizens fueled the lifeblood of a republic, possessed the capacity for reason, and waged war in the national interest demanded that they be treated not as soulless mercenaries but as virtuous individuals. "The white American soldier," Higginson continued, "doubtless, the most intelligent in the world, is more ready than any other to comply with a reasonable order, but he does it because it is reasonable, not because it is an order." Officers of citizen-soldiers thus could not dehumanize their men. They had to respect democratic sensibilities because "the discipline of our soldiers has been generally that of a town-meeting or of an engine-company, rather than that of an army." Effective but restrained discipline and leadership produced battlefield triumphs, at once the principal means of achieving the national objective and concluding a volunteer's military career.[52]

Union and Confederate military leaders drew from prominent European theorists to formulate strategy, execute battlefield maneuvers, and pursue decisive battlefield victories. To secure the national causes through martial conduct required both republics to retain "a reasonably effective monopoly on large-scale violence associated with the standing armies of nation-state Europe." Still, West Point emphasized the virtue of brief wars measured by identifiable objectives and organized concentrations against an enemy's vulnerable points. To avoid what they considered the shocking devastation of European conflict, West Pointers early on emphasized the concentration of armed force to compel the enemy's submission. Perhaps a single invasion or battle would end the conflict with minimal carnage. Gen. Winfield Scott proposed in May 1861 "to envelop the insurgent States and bring them to terms with less bloodshed than by any other plan." Though he was not a graduate of the U.S. Military Academy, Scott spoke to a spirit of professional restraint that disavowed unchecked militarism. Encircling the Confederacy with federal troops and strangling its coastlines with an imposing naval blockade would demonstrate to white southerners the futility of resistance, bringing the rebellion to a controlled close.[53]

But even Scott recognized the flaw in his own plan. "The great danger now pressing upon us," he confided, is "the impatience of our patriotic and loyal Union friends. They will urge instant and vigorous action, regardless, I fear, of consequences." Scott's vision of war contrasted with the democratic conditions of a "people's contest." When President Lincoln replaced Scott with the brash and promising George B. McClellan, the Union's new principal field commander linked the republic's ideological objective to its requisite military conduct. "The fate of the nation and the success of the cause in which we are engaged," McClellan declared in September 1861, "must be decided by the issue of the next battle." McClellan's philosophy derived from the writings of Antoine Henri Jomini, a Swiss military theorist who served in Napoleon's grand armies. Distraught by the overwhelming personal and material destruction of modern war, Jomini encouraged the concentration of superior force against "the point where the enemy was weakest." He believed that a single decisive battlefield victory would end a conflict, thus preserving life and facilitating postwar reconciliation. "To bring this war to a speedy close," explained McClellan, "it will be necessary that our Active Army shall be much superior to the enemy in numbers, so as to make it reasonably certain, that we shall win every battle."[54]

Yet Jomini's prescription for a swift battlefield resolution was the very attribute of nineteenth-century warfare that debilitated McClellan. While the Union's chief general executed Jominian philosophy to capture broad swaths of enemy territory and march on the belligerent capital, McClellan balked at the prospect of swift, concentrated, pitched battle. Though often mocked as a weak military practitioner, McClellan's martial worldview grew from profound Atlantic martial influences. Trained in the art of West Point moderation, McClellan was also molded by the carnage of the Crimean War (1853–56), which he observed as part of an American military delegation. "You see at a glance what a bloody & determined strife was there enacted, & are half surprised that you do not still see in heaps around you the dead bodies of the gallant French & brave English, & the thrice heroic Russians," he wrote in 1855 after a gruesome engagement at Sebastopol. "It was really an epoch in one's life to walk through the remains of that ruined city," McClellan concluded. "The impression it made upon me can never be erased."[55]

Hesitant to throw his 120,000 soldiers of the Army of the Potomac against Confederate foes, McClellan instead applied moderate lessons gleaned from Crimea to his Civil War military campaigns. Though a learned expert in administration, logistics, and siege warfare, professional military practices which nearly compelled the fall of Richmond, Virginia, in May 1862, McClellan could not countenance the scale of human suffering wrought by the decisive Napoleonic battle. Likely conditioned by his exposure to European warfare, McClellan moved with a cautious restraint, slow to engage the enemy, guarding against needless destruction. But when Robert E. Lee's Confederate Army of Northern Virginia repelled McClellan in a blistering, aggressive counteroffensive for seven consecutive days in late June, the horror of battle dazed the Union commander. "I am tired of the sickening sight of the battlefield, with its mangled corpses & poor suffering wounded! Victory has no charms for me when purchased at such cost." George B. McClellan would not transplant the Crimea to America. So he remained on the Virginia peninsula until President Lincoln relieved him of command. McClellan's was not so much a short-sighted outlook as it was a misplaced understanding of the kind of conduct necessary to wage a democratic civil war. Although he employed contemporary military philosophies to direct a civilized contest, McClellan's approach did not conform to the nationalist passions of nineteenth-century conflict.[56]

The United States' premier wartime general, Ulysses S. Grant, presented a stark contrast to McClellan and Winfield Scott. A proponent of "successive, simultaneous advances" across a vast military front, Grant's philosophy "ran afoul of mid-nineteenth-century principles of mass and concentration, which demanded one offensive at a time." As he acknowledged during a postwar interview, "If men make war in slavish observances of rules, they will fail. No rules will apply to conditions of war as different as those which exist in Europe and America." Refusing to be bound by rigid European theories, Grant rejected the Jominian idea of maneuver and exploitation against an enemy's vulnerable points, particularly cities and locales. He practiced war like Napoleon, who "made war in his own way, and not in imitation of others. War is progressive," explained Grant, "because all the instruments and elements of war are progressive." Both Grant and Napoleon understood that political and ideological wars required concentrated and coordinated force against an enemy's center of gravity: the army. Serving in the Union's western forces in 1862 exposed Brig. Gen. James A. Garfield to Grant's understanding of the unique conditions of America's civil conflict. "One thing is settled in my mind," averred the future president. "Direct blows at the rebel army, bloody fighting is all that can end the rebellion. In European wars, if you capture the chief city of a nation, you have substantially captured the nation. The army that holds London, Paris, Vienna, or Berlin, holds England, France, Austria, or Prussia. Not so in this war. The rebels have no city the capture of which will overthrow their power. . . . Hence our real objective point is not any place or district, but the rebel army," which "we must crush and pulverize."[57]

Confederate armies represented what Napoleon, Garfield, and Grant considered the "nation in arms." Massive citizen-armies buoyed by popular fervor embodied a nation's wartime purpose and moral legitimacy. Permanently disabling enemy military institutions collapsed the belligerent nation's capacity to wage further war. While such bloody methods yielded a shocking number of causalities, only aggressive, synchronized offensives against enemy armies could definitively end a people's war. "The art of war is simple enough," Grant explained: "Find where your enemy is, get at him as soon as you can, and strike him as hard as you can, and keep moving on." Hardly a callous butcher, Grant approached war with just and calculated reason. "I want to push on as rapidly as possible to save hard fighting," he explained in the wake of his 1862 triumphs at Forts Henry and Donelson. "These terrible battles are very good things to read about for persons who lose no friends but I am decidedly in favor of having as little of it as possible. The way to avoid it is to push forward as vigorously as possible." Grant implemented this philosophy to score striking triumphs in Tennessee, Mississippi, and Virginia, paving a triumphant road to Appomattox.[58]

The United States' principal Confederate adversary, Robert E. Lee, waged war in a similar manner. When Confederates early on discarded Jefferson Davis's prescribed cordon defense of their vast national territory, Lee recommended concentrating soldiers into large mobile field armies to husband limited resources and repel Union invasions. Campaigning in the Napoleonic and American traditions, Lee understood that aggressive actions produced pivotal battlefield triumphs, catering to the impatient demands of wartime democracies. "So strong is my conviction of the necessity of activity," he advised Davis, "that we cannot afford to keep our troops awaiting possible movements of the enemy." He thus advocated an offensive-defensive strategy, which conceded territory to occupying United States forces but also gave Confederate armies the flexibility to dictate the tempo of war. Lee envisioned Confederate forces inflicting defensive casualties on invading Union legions while searching for opportune moments to strike a decisive offensive blow. "It is impossible for [the enemy] to have a large operating army at every assailable point in our territory as it is for us to keep one to defend it. We must move our troops from point to point as required," he counseled. "Partial encroachments of the enemy we must expect, but they can always be recovered, and any defeat of their large army will reinstate everything."[59]

The offensive-defensive strategy served a distinctly political end. In the nationalist vein of George Washington and Napoleon, Lee's Army of Northern Virginia *was* the Confederate republic, the principal institution to repel the United States' invasion of seemingly sovereign territory. Appreciating his enemy's delicate democratic sensibilities, Lee waged war to shatter the resolve of loyal Union citizens. While his aggressive June 1862 counteroffensives preserved Richmond against McClellan's Union army, Lee was disheartened by the ultimate verdict of the Seven Days campaign. "Under ordinary circumstances the Federal Army should have been destroyed." Because it was not, the war would continue, expand in scope, and delay Confederate independence. "Our enemy has met with a heavy loss from which he must take some time to recover & then recommence his operations," he confided. "Our success has not been as great or complete as I could have desired." Either a Washington-style war of attrition or a decisive Napoleonic triumph in which Lee's army permanently disabled the Army of the Potomac would collapse northern morale and turn the Union home front against the Lincoln administration. Such was the rationale of his 1862 and 1863 invasions of the United States. Though "hazard[ous] in military movements," the Maryland and Pennsylvania campaigns portended direct paths to peace. Invading the United States and "giv[ing] all the encouragement we can ... to the rising peace party of the North" underscored his awareness of modern democracies at war. "It is plain to my understanding that everything that will tend to repress the war feeling in the Federal States will inure to our benefit," he announced just before clashing with the Union army at Gettysburg. "I do not know that we can do anything to promote the pacific feeling, but our course ought to be shaped as not to discourage it."[60]

Lee waged a remarkably consistent war. Inflicting staggering causalities in offensive actions at the Seven Days, Second Manassas, and Chancellorsville battles, a stalwart defensive stand at Fredericksburg, and his twin invasions of the United States, which culminated at Antietam and Gettysburg, Lee executed the offensive-defensive strategy to collapse Union purpose. A people's contest demanded that United States' military institutions had to be destroyed and that the loyal citizenry had to be forced to quit the war. Yet because the strategy was distinctly political, it was met with an equally powerful response. Lee's inability to secure the decisive Napoleonic victory meant that his strategy could be turned against him. When Ulysses S. Grant confronted Lee in Virginia during the 1864 Overland Campaign, the Union's overall field commander countered with *his* philosophy of sustained, aggressive offensives. Lee's stubborn defenses blunted Grant's unrelenting strikes, producing nearly sixty thousand Union causalities in six weeks, ending in stalemate, and portending Republican electoral defeat in the 1864 elections. "I had to attack and attack," acknowledged Grant, because "every blow I struck weakened him, and when at last he was forced into Richmond it was a far different army from that which ... invaded Maryland and Pennsylvania. It was no longer an invading army." Modern mid-nineteenth-century Atlantic conflict still privileged the Napoleonic era's demonstration of overwhelming force. Among the West Point–trained officers who waged the Civil War, Grant and Lee understood that a just war demanded aggressive, unremitting battlefield confrontations to dismantle the enemy's national will.[61]

The quest for a decisive battlefield victory joined with nineteenth-century innovations in technology and industry to produce a modern contest of arms. The American Civil War boasted the mass mobilization of civilian populations, national commerce, and economies to sustain armies campaigning across a vast continent; the use of innovative weaponry, particularly rifle muskets and cannon; swift modes of transportation and communication, specifically rail-roads, maritime craft, and telegraphs; and the exploitation of ideological pro-paganda to sustain the nations in arms. A pillar of scholarly literature has long held that nineteenth-century American obsessions with Napoleonic ag-gression, combined with the irrepressible conditions of modernity, made the Civil War exceptionally violent and hopelessly destructive. Conventional wis-dom holds that Old World military tactics—Napoleonic mass concentration and frontal assaults—united with the targeted power of advanced weaponry yielded "a level of carnage that foreshadowed the wars of the century to come." Civil War armies could never secure a decisive battlefield outcome, so goes this idea, because of the overwhelming power to kill and maim, thus forcing the belligerents by 1864 into defensive trenches fifty years *before* the Great War in Europe.[62]

Yet rather than foreshadowing twentieth-century mechanized warfare, the Civil War transpired among contemporary nineteenth-century conflicts that likewise featured modern technologies, ideologies, and tactics. For instance, Prussia outfitted national armies with the rifle musket in 1842, while French imperial campaigns in North Africa (1846), the Crimean War (1853–56), and the Second Italian War of Independence (1859) all commissioned the fash-ionable weapon. Although railroads and telegraphs were novel inventions by the 1850s, Prussian, British, and French armies had institutionalized the new technologies as wartime mainstays. Despite the American war featuring mass ideological armies bolstered with modern technology, Civil War armies were either similar in size or sometimes smaller than Napoleon's legions, suf-fering *fewer* percentages of casualties than early nineteenth-century Euro-pean clashes at Leipzig, Borodino, Auerstadt, Eylau, and Waterloo. Between the early eighteenth and mid-nineteenth centuries, wars fought even with smoothbore muskets typically occasioned similar or greater casualty rates than the American Civil War. As the foremost historian of the rifle musket writes, "Civil War combat did not produce more casualties than did other wars in different places and time periods." And because of the rifle musket's frus-trating unpredictability, the Americans were among the final Atlantic bellig-erents to employ the weapon. The Franco-Prussian War of 1870–71 featured fresh breechloading rifles, a far more revolutionary firearm than its rifled pre-decessor.[63]

The scarcity of the decisive Civil War battle had little to do with outmoded tactics and technological innovation. Instead, "the ground truth of Civil War armies' geographic positioning" helps explain the enormous but also re-stricted bloodletting. Civil War armies developed an "equilibrium of compe-tence" based on military traditions that emphasized cautious defensive opera-tions, commanded by professional officers with shared backgrounds, and outfitted with amateur volunteers. Inconsistent leadership directed armies of raw citizen-soldiers untrained in formal combat, battlefield discipline, and modern weapons technology, yielding an ineffective use of the rifle musket. Causalities and indecisive contests often stemmed from analogous military cultures that counterbalanced each nation's martial acumen. "The rapid, well sustained attack, which in many of the great European combats has led to important successes, *does not appear adapted to qualities of the Federal soldiery*," wrote Henry Charles Fletcher, a British officer who observed the war. "Neither side can be manoeuvred under fire, and this is about the secret of the whole present American War," noted fellow English soldier E. O. Hewett. "They are not good enough either in morale or field movements to advance, change position, or retire," and they often "get into confusion and break." Moreover, few battles offered unobstructed fields of fire, compelling massive armies to negotiate uneven and diverse terrains choked with materiel and clogged with the suffocating smoke of battle. "Europeans frequently criticised our war, because we did not always take full advantage of a victory," recalled William T. Sherman. "The true reason was, that habitually the woods served as a screen, and we often did not realize the fact that our enemy had retreated till he was already miles away and was again intrenched."[64]

"Equilibrium of competence" informed professional inclinations toward cautious restraint in the wake of battle. While commanders often searched for the pivotal battlefield victory, they "tended to miss many opportunities to make their battles more decisive." Despite myriad conclusive battlefield verdicts—First and Second Manassas, Shiloh, the Seven Days, Fredericksburg, Chancellorsville, Gettysburg, and Cold Harbor—sustained combat typically exhausted the armies, foiling commanders from capitalizing on their gains. Generals could ill afford to destroy their *own* armies—the principal vehicles of national purpose—in annihilating the enemy. Pragmatism often mandated the reorganization of armies, the husbanding of lives, and delays in campaigning, transforming the conflict into a war of attrition. And as a democratic people who professed innate Christian sensibilities, some commanders could hardly bear the scale of death brought upon their fellow citizens. "They call me a butcher," exclaimed Ulysses S. Grant, "but do you know I sometimes could hardly bring myself to give an order of battle? When I contemplated the death and misery that were sure to follow, I stood appalled." Recognizing that national sovereignties could be paved only upon the bodies of fallen soldiers, Robert E. Lee sighed, "What a cruel thing is war" after his victory at Fredericksburg. "To separate & destroy families & friends & mar the purest joys & happiness God has granted us in this world. To fill our hearts with hatred instead of love for our neighbors.... My heart bleeds at the death of every one of our gallant men."[65]

While an estimated 750,000 soldiers perished in the conflict, the American Civil War was not as deadly as it could have been; other civil conflicts of the time equaled or surpassed it in destruction. Professional officers often "found their most violent inclinations strongly checked by a potent mix of religious scruple and effective civil authority." Indeed, civilian control of the Union and Confederate military establishments limited the injurious potential of the conflict against both soldiers *and* civilians. Each nation fielded armies commanded by military professionals who consented to the democratic restraints of civil-military relations. A trial of constitutional governance mandated that each belligerent maintain the most cherished martial restraints in the republican tradition. Managing a wartime democracy compelled the people's elected representatives to determine the length, scope, and acceptable conduct necessary to pursue each nation's objectives. Military commanders on both sides thus answered ultimately to elected civilian leaders, an assumption that guarded against civilian atrocities or coups d'état. The Thirty Years' War, the English Civil War, the French Revolution, and the Napoleonic Wars, in which unchecked military dictators directed standing armies to topple governments, seize power, and wage total war against civil institutions *and* civilians, loomed large in the American imagination. If the United States and Confederacy had disavowed lawful restraint, uninhibited and ambitious military leaders might well have collapsed the moderate republics into a series of coups or political revolutions, replacing constitutional and democratic checks with martial rule. Autocratic leviathans might have thereafter employed monopolistic state violence to command loyalty through coercive militancy.[66]

The Civil War posed a substantial test of professional military submission to civilian authority. Largely conservative, West Point officers favored a comfortable, apolitical distance from raucous nineteenth-century American democracy. Once the war began, however, that very conservatism infused Union armies with distinct partisanship. Many officers identified privately with the Democratic Party, looking askance at the Republicans' committed antislavery activism and the Lincoln administration's close relationship to the congressional Joint Committee on the Conduct of the War. An overt partisan institution, the committee included so-called radicals who viewed the war as a crusade to reconstruct the South into an antislavery, free-labor, Republican stronghold. Professional officers questioned whether their military service would be exploited for distinctly political ends in which Republicans directed federal armies to transcend a limited war for sectional reunion.[67]

No less than Union general-in-chief George B. McClellan emerged as a leading wartime critic of the Lincoln administration. A prominent and outspoken Democrat, McClellan considered himself providentially appointed to preserve the republic from radical secessionists *and* inept Republicans, both of whom he blamed for instigating secession and war. From the outset he condemned the Lincoln administration for its apparent belligerence and its hopeless inexperience in military affairs. Antislavery fanaticism and martial incompetence, McClellan believed, would provoke a needless and escalating destruction of the South, endangering reunion and revolutionizing constitutional governance. "It is perfectly sickening to have to work with such people

& to see the fate of the nation in such hands," he confided to his wife. Only God could "free the nation from the imbeciles who curse it." The entire administration was clumsy at best and treasonous at worst. "It is terrible to stand by & see the cowardice of the Presdt, the vileness of Seward, & the rascality of [Secretary of War Simon] Cameron—[Secretary of the Navy Gideon] Welles is an old woman—[Attorney General Edward] Bates an old fool.... I am thwarted & deceived by these incapables at every turn."[68]

While at the head of Union armies, McClellan joined with Democratic leaders to voice his discontent with Republican policies, especially when emancipation emerged in 1862 as a central wartime event. And he routinely rebuffed the president, treating the commander in chief as a maddening subordinate. Yet Lincoln retained McClellan as his principal military commander, careful not to provoke skeptical Democrats or antagonize McClellan's fiercely loyal soldiers in the Army of the Potomac. The republic could ill afford a political or military coup led by a populist military commander who could summon unquestioned allegiance to himself and his army. Understanding that political considerations guided a wartime democracy, Lincoln opted for battlefield verdicts to determine McClellan's fate. The failed Peninsula Campaign, joined with "Little Mac's" refusal to pursue Lee in the wake of Antietam, forced Lincoln to remove the beloved yet beleaguered general.[69]

Lincoln was moved not only by military events. By the fall of 1862, with emancipation an official wartime policy, Lincoln became convinced that McClellan's cautious inaction stemmed from his opposition to Republicans' handling of the war. The president even wondered whether McClellan had transformed the Army of the Potomac from the republic's principal wartime institution to conquer Confederate rebels into a partisan tool of the Democratic Party. Reports then surfaced at the White House that elements within the army portended a "revolution in the North." Maj. John J. Key claimed that "the 'traitor' element near McClellan had constantly grown bolder," animated by "daily talk[s] of overthrowing the Government and making McClellan dictator." Usurping a war for Union in favor of an insurrectionary war of emancipation, Key claimed, justified "absolving the army from its allegiance: that a movement should be made upon Washington to restore the Constitution."[70]

Lincoln traveled to McClellan's headquarters in southern Maryland to "satisfy himself personally ... of the purposes intentions and fidelity of McClellan, his officers, and the army." Though content with the general's loyalty, Lincoln nonetheless relieved both Key and McClellan from command. The president acted principally out of military necessity, but he also removed perilous sources of instability from the army and the war effort. "I had been brought to fear that there was a class of officers in the army, not very inconsiderable in numbers, who were playing a game to not beat the enemy when they could, on some peculiar notion as to the proper way of saving the Union," Lincoln explained to Key. "When you were proved to me ... to have avowed yourself in favor of that 'game,' and did not attempt to controvert the proof, I dismissed you as an example and a warning to that supposed class." Still, McClellan's removal sparked widespread outrage and protest throughout the ranks, and some soldiers even threatened mutiny. "There were several European officers present, to whom the whole [affair] was utterly unintelligible," observed Union artillery officer Charles S. Wainwright. "They repeatedly said: 'I cannot understand you Americans; here we see a large army with officers and men devotedly attached to their commander, and yet they allow him to be taken from them without a remonstrance. Why don't the army march to Washington, and make the President reinstate him?' Doubtless that would have been the way were we French or Germans, but our people are naturally too law abiding."[71]

Despite the passions aroused by McClellan's departure, Wainwright's observation rang true. McClellan calmed the unruly soldiers, respecting Lincoln's prerogative of civilian oversight. The former commander declared, "Stand by General [Ambrose E.] Burnside," whom Lincoln appointed in November 1862 to lead the Army of the Potomac, "as you have stood by me, and all will be well." Though McClellan's Democratic political allegiance created rifts between the army and the president, he also rejected the radicalism of a coup. He recognized that his partisan animus against Republicans was far subordinate to the national purpose. Constitutional legitimacy trumped radical political expediency. A war for "the Constitution of our country & the nationality of our people," he announced in his farewell to the army, demanded dispassionate fealty to each lest the exceptional idea of Union dissolve in the process.[72]

Challenges to the Union's wartime civilian supremacy did not vanish with McClellan's departure. After Robert E. Lee humiliated Burnside in the December 1862 debacle at Fredericksburg, Lincoln replaced the discredited commander with Gen. Joseph Hooker, who boasted that only he could conquer the invincible Army of Northern Virginia. Hooker inherited a depressed Union army whose high command was riddled with political strife, which he exploited to consolidate authority. As a *New York Times* war correspondent claimed, Hooker "has talked very openly about the absurdity of the [Army of the Potomac's disastrous withdrawal from Fredericksburg], denounced the commanding general as incompetent, and the President and Government at Washington as imbecile and 'played out.'" A steadfast Republican, Hooker condemned the Lincoln administration at once for exerting *too much* restraint against Confederates and for meddling in the army's affairs. The *Times* reporter even conveyed Hooker's alleged belief that the Union would never salvage the war effort "until we had a dictator, and the sooner the better."[73]

Accustomed to his general officers' partisan tendencies, Lincoln warned Hooker to respect the constitutional boundary between civil authority and military leadership. "You are ambitious," wrote the president. But "you have taken counsel of your ambition, and thwarted [Burnside] as much as you could, in which you did a great wrong to the country." Moreover, "I have heard, in such way as to believe it, of your recently saying that both the Army and the Government needed a Dictator. Of course it was not *for* this, but in spite of it, that I have given you the command. Only those generals who gain successes, can set up dictators. What I now ask of you is military success, and I will risk the dictatorship." Like his dismissal of Key, Lincoln's rebuke of Hooker asserted the civilian commander in chief's unquestioned supremacy in the military hierarchy. Even triumphant military heroes would never supplant the people's democratic representatives. Lincoln afforded Hooker the leeway to prove himself in battle. But when Lee nearly destroyed the Army of the Potomac in May 1863 at Chancellorsville, Lincoln relieved the chastened Hooker. After George Gordon Meade assumed command of the army in June 1863, followed by Ulysses S. Grant's appointment the following year as general-in-chief of Union armies, the United States never again faced the acute challenges to civil-military relations once posed by McClellan and Hooker.[74]

The Confederacy also maintained the supremacy of civilian authority. The tense and often acrimonious relationship between President Jefferson Davis and Gens. P. G. T. Beauregard and Joseph E. Johnston imposed palpable stresses on the Confederate military apparatus. While the president at times reassigned or relocated his military subordinates, generals always acceded to Davis's orders even if they disputed his judgment. Beauregard acknowledged in early 1863, "I am the last fault-finding man ... in the service, when my personal interests alone are at stake; but when the comfort of my troops or the public good is in question, I only regret that I am not a Robespierre." But despite such seemingly dangerous and even radical sentiments, Beauregard knew better than to convey extremism into the political and military arenas, let alone try to commandeer power in the radical style of Robespierre. Although the Confederacy boasted fierce pockets of opposition to the Davis administration, no one overrode the president's constitutional authority as commander in chief. In fact, as wartime presidents Davis and Lincoln functioned within similar constitutional structures, each making military decisions within the popular national interest as they perceived it. Military officers executed the presidents' wishes even when these same commanders harbored doubts about the wisdom or efficacy of the chief executives' vision.[75]

As historian T. Michael Parrish acknowledges, "In our efforts to understand more fully what happened in the American Civil War, perhaps we should consider what did *not* happen. The Civil War was not dominated by political or military radicals either in the United States or Confederacy. As a result, the war did *not* explode into a revolutionary conflict in which personal vendettas, violent coups, high-level assassinations, conspiracies, or terrorism played a significant part. The Civil War was indeed a bloody struggle, but it was a struggle that was nearly always restrained and guided by fundamental democratic principles, one of the most prominent being the supremacy of civilian control over commanders of extremely powerful military forces." Although they detested each other, Davis, Beauregard, and Johnston, and, in turn, Lincoln, McClellan, and Hooker, all adhered to what they understood to be their obligation as democratic Americans: to uphold foundational constitutional prerogatives, particularly civilian authority over robust military establishments. Unlike the nineteenth century's Yucatan Caste War, the Chinese Taiping Rebellion, the Mexican War of the Reform, or the Paraguayan War of the Triple Alliance, the American Civil War was not resolved through revolutionary violence or by militaristic despots determined to seize undue power. Military leaders on both sides willingly restrained themselves and conducted their military affairs within the bounds of the rule of law, as executed by the citizenry's duly elected representatives.[76]

Military Necessity and the Laws of War

As the United States' principal civilian authority, Abraham Lincoln insisted that the Union's martial conduct adhere to the rule of law.[77] If the American Civil War epitomized a trial of constitutional governance, and if the anarchy of secession reeked of militant mob rule, the United States had to be bound by legal restraints in combating national balkanization. Waging war against Confederates in the same manner that secessionist oligarchs rejected constitutionalism would delegitimize the Union's international standing. Though disunion and civil war portended unimaginable constitutional crises, Lincoln maintained that the cause of Union meant little if the process disregarded the moderation of constitutional and international jurisprudence. "I therefore consider that, in view of the Constitution and the laws," he announced in his first inaugural address, "the Union is unbroken; and to the extent of my ability, I shall take care, as the Constitution itself expressly enjoins upon me, that the laws of the Union be faithfully executed in all the States." While the United States treated the Confederacy as a de facto national belligerent, Lincoln's steadfast belief in an inviolable Union also regarded the rebellious southern states as in temporary and unjust insurrection against the federal government. By never acknowledging the Confederacy's international political legitimacy, he thus employed the constitutional war powers delegated to the commander in chief to combat a domestic rebellion.[78]

An essential attribute of the just war tradition, military necessity sanctioned martial conduct permissible under the international laws of war—and, in the case of the United States, the Constitution—to secure a belligerent's wartime purpose. Military necessity restrained wartime nations from excessive conduct because belligerents had to justify *how* their martial conduct corresponded to the national objective. By its very nature, the concept allowed broad escalations in the scope of war, while also holding a belligerent to legal and ethical restraints. As Lincoln acknowledged, "Military measures [must] be strong enough to repel the invader and keep the peace, and not so strong as to unnecessarily harass and persecute the people." Claims of military necessity materialized because secessionists had rejected the Constitution's guarantee that each state maintain a republican form of government, thereby suspending any constitutional protections. "So that to prevent its going out, is an indispensable means, to the end, of maintaining the guaranty mentioned," Lincoln instructed, "when an end is lawful and obligatory, the indispensable means to it, are also lawful, and obligatory." The ends of preserving the Union thus necessitated the implementation of executive war powers. The president either "could perform this duty, or surrender the existence of the government," thereby assuring the death of the constitutional order and the Union itself.[79]

The president possessed an array of constitutional mechanisms to suppress internal rebellions, restore national stability, and return the republic to a condition of ordered liberty. "My purpose is to be, in my action, just and constitutional," he explained, "and yet practical, in performing the important duty with which I am charged, of maintaining the unity, and the free principles of our common country." From the outbreak of war, Lincoln used his legal authorization to call federal troops and enlarge the army; proclaim a blockade of southern ports; suspend the writ of habeas corpus; declare martial law throughout much of the Union; arrest private citizens, newspapermen, and politicians suspected of disloyalty; permit military courts to try dissidents due to the inefficiency of civil courts; suspend the publication of at least two newspapers; approve property confiscation; and ultimately proclaim emancipation in the rebellious states.[80]

The suspension of habeas corpus offers an instructive example of military necessity. A sacred entitlement of the Anglo-Atlantic legal tradition, habeas corpus protects individuals from coercive police states, prohibiting governments from arbitrarily arresting citizens without cause. The writ guards against clandestine and indefinite detainment. Defendants possess the right to be notified of charges brought against them, assuring a public showing before a judge or court, and advising offenders on legal methods of recourse. But the Constitution permits suspension of the writ when during "Cases of Rebellion or Invasion the public Safety may require it." And "ours is a case of Rebellion," Lincoln declared unequivocally, "a clear, flagrant, and gigantic case of Rebellion." The American Civil War, the president explained, was the culmination of a three-decade-long conspiracy in which the internationalist Slave Power colluded to sunder the Union. When "I was elected contrary to their liking," and "they had taken seven states out of the Union, had seized many of the United States Forts, and had fired upon the United States' Flag," insurgents commenced a rebellion that transformed "into the present civil war." Lincoln thus suspended the writ from Washington, DC, to Maine, ordering military authorities to arrest citizens suspected of harboring Confederate sympathies. Subversive dissidents found aiding the slaveholders' rebellion, who "are not adequately restrained by the ordinary process of law," would face trial by military courts. Lincoln justified military necessity on the suspicion that Confederate insurgents might topple additional loyal states, hinder restoration of the constitutional order, and expand an already massive war front.[81]

When he argued that suspending the writ preserved the public safety, Lincoln also maintained that "this authority has purposely been exercised but very sparingly." Indeed, the federal government arrested approximately fourteen thousand dissidents during the war, a miniscule percentage of the Union's 22 million loyal citizens. Such moderation was reflected in Lincoln's insistence that war powers were a temporary but necessary means of restoring the Union's normal constitutional functions. "I too am devotedly for them *after* civil war, and *before* civil war, and at times 'except when, in cases of Rebellion or Invasion, the public safety may require' their suspension," he noted. "If I be wrong on this question of constitutional power, my error lies in believing" that somehow the government could wield only the tools of civil peace to negotiate the unparalleled conditions of civil war. He appealed both to Attorney General Edward Bates and to Congress to judge the suspension. Bates opined, "In case of a great and dangerous rebellion ... the public safety requires the arrest and confinement of persons implicated in that rebellion," and thus "the President has lawful power to *suspend the privilege* of persons arrested under such circumstances." Congress agreed. As the supreme branch of popular government—the one that, according to Lincoln, possessed "constitutional competency" and "better judgment" to legislate the citizenry's democratic will—Congress passed the Habeas Corpus Act of 1863, authorizing additional executive wartime actions.[82]

Some of the Union's committed citizenry were nonetheless startled by the government's severe efforts at curtailing secessionist threats within the loyal states. Maryland particularly experienced the reach of federal power in the Lincoln administration's effort to retain the loyalty of the slaveholding Border State in close geographic proximity to Washington, DC. The U.S. Army enforced a widespread military occupation of the state, stationing federal troops in major cities to enforce the law and detain citizens whom the government suspected of plotting secessionist conspiracies. Lincoln argued that constitutional and international law vindicated the unprecedented occupation to combat the unprecedented exigencies of civil war. But some Unionists— particularly Democrats who distrusted the Lincoln administration—claimed that the swift measures violated the distinguishing characteristics of an antimilitaristic republic. "Our institutions have received such a blow, that men will apprehend a repetition of these revolutionary proceedings" until the Union resembles the "Countries of Europe where war seems to be the normal condition of the people," Baltimore doctor Samuel Harrison observed in the wake of federal soldiers occupying the city in May 1861. If the Union was inviolable, so too were the common civil liberties enjoyed by free citizens. If a national crisis could so swiftly abrogate constitutional restraints, irrevocable damage would befall a republic that once stood apart from the world's centralized autocracies and oppressive military states. "We can no longer talk about down trodden Hungary, England, Poland, the censorship of the press, and other fruits of despotism," Baltimore socialite and Unionist Hester Ann Wilkins Davis confided to her diary in June. "We once thought them choice exotics, which we did not care to transplant. Who ever dreamed of their springing up indigenous in our midst"?[83]

To avoid the perpetual wars and rampant balkanization so endemic to European life, Lincoln had to act in an extraordinary but temporary and lawful manner to erase the revolutionary threat of disunion. Only then could the republic retain its secure constitutional foundation. Loyal intellectuals conversant in international law endorsed the president's methods as rational anti-insurrectionist remedies. "In this national crisis, it is not argument that we want, but that rare courage which dares commit itself to a principle," averred Ralph Waldo Emerson. "Government must not be a parish clerk, a justice of the peace. It has, of necessity, in any crisis of the State, the absolute powers of a Dictator." Philadelphia historian Charles Stillé likewise explained, "No nation has ever gone to war without violating in some essential manner the well-settled rules which govern it in times of peace, and the dictatorship of the Romans, and the suspension of the writ of habeas corpus, are only different ways of recognizing the same great necessity." The *North American Review*, a literary periodical, judged that because "peace and war cannot exist in the same place at the same time ... let us be thankful that it is so seldom that this constitutional martial rule is over us." Though the order was "a private inconvenience," the president employed necessary war powers "to suppress insurrection," a "great public good to be obtained by the preservation of the constitutional government of the country."[84]

When U.S. armies penetrated the Confederacy in 1861 and early 1862, military commanders carried the Lincoln administration's assumption that most white southerners retained a powerful loyalty to the Union. A radical coterie of aristocratic secessionists, moderate Republicans believed, had unlawfully hijacked the South and stoked a rebellion that most civilians rejected. Federal military forces entered the region with caution, appealing to white southern allegiance rather than to unrestrained war. Brig. Gen. Ambrose E. Burnside's February 1862 proclamation to the citizens of North Carolina typifies the United States' early conciliatory overtures. Our "mission ... is not to invade any of your rights, but to assert the authority of the United States," while disbanding the "few bad men in your midst." Inflamed "by the worst passions of human nature," secessionists had duped white southerners about the United States' moderate intentions. Union armies had not arrived "to destroy your freedom, demolish your property, liberate your slaves, injure your women." The government desired only to reestablish national sovereignty and constitutional integrity in a united republic. Appealing to a shared Christian ethic and the "virtuous loyalty and civilization" of the American character, "the government asks only that its authority may be recognized"; it possessed no desire "to interfere with your laws" or "your institutions."[85]

Yet on entering the Border States and invading the Confederacy, Union field commanders encountered the same ambiguities of national balkanization and military necessity confronted by their president. Myriad white southern civilians at the war's outset at once rejected federal conciliation and the Confederate government's disavowal of guerrilla warfare, engaging Union legions as unlawful combatants. The West Point ethos had long regarded irregular warfare as fit only for crude barbarians whose shameful conduct rejected martial restraint and scoffed at human dignity. "The guerrilla system," declared Secretary of War William L. Marcy during the U.S.-Mexico War, "is hardly recognized as a legitimate mode of warfare, and should be met with the utmost allowable severity." In 1861, Henry W. Halleck likewise declared that guerrillas "are guilty of the highest crime known to the code of war," acting in the same perverted, uncivilized manner as "murderers, robbers, and thieves." Attacking United States columns with clandestine ferocity and impeding the restrained march toward reunion, white southern guerrillas disrupted Union operations, murdered individual soldiers, and convinced federal commanders that they faced a revolutionary enemy far more ubiquitous than a cabal of radical secessionists.[86]

Union military officers indicted guerrilla warfare as the unsullied practice of inferior nations and peoples. That irregular combatants refused quarter to Union soldiers, attacked supply trains, and assassinated guards on picket duty led an exasperated Gen. Benjamin F. Butler to demand, "Is this civilized or savage warfare? It reads precisely like the history of similar strategy by Toussaint l'Ouverture toward the French forces in San Domingo." When skulking, slivering, ghostly masses concealed their identities and repudiated honorable pitched battles, it "savors rather of Indian than of civilized warfare." William S. Rosecrans echoed Butler's racialized trope of white guerrillas when he led Union armies into western Virginia in August 1861. Confederates "have introduced a warfare only known among savages. In violation of the laws of nations and humanity," the slaughter of defenseless, unsuspecting Union soldiers reeked of antiquated racial barbarism. "Scalping their victims is all that is wanting to make [guerrilla] warfare like that which seventy or eighty years ago was waged by the Indians against the white race." Even the popular press distinguished guerrilla conduct through a racial lens. "When the history of this rebellion is written," explained *Frank Leslie's Illustrated Newspaper*, "it will be recorded that the 'Chivalrous South' was the first civilized nation which openly ignored the code of honorable warfare and resorted to all the odious devilries of the Chinese and other nations, whose sole refinement is in every cruel expedient—poisoning wells, hanging prisoners without distinction to age or sex, or assassinating unwary men."[87]

Guerrillas seemed to transgress enlightened (white) military conduct, soured by alleged racial and cultural decay. Decrying their perversion of modern war, Henry W. Halleck announced in 1861 that all civilian combatants "are by the laws of war in every civilized country liable to capital punishment" and immediate execution. Guerrillas surrendered their status as legal belligerents *and* "forfeited their civil rights as citizens by making war against the Government." Only the just "law of military retaliation" could combat an enemy so foreign to the American disposition. The unjust insurgency compelled Halleck to reflect on the United States' approach to a war for national preservation. "Peace and war cannot exist together," he outlined in an official general order. "We cannot at the same time extend to rebels the rights of peace and enforce against them the penalties of war. They have forfeited their civil rights as citizens by making war against the Government, and upon their own heads must fall the consequences." The implication was clear. Only "military power can now put down the rebellion," thus Union armies were compelled to wage unequivocal war against belligerent white southerners, their social institutions, and their political establishment.[88]

And so, to "repress the daily increasing crimes and outrages" that ravaged Missouri, free-soil abolitionist general John C. Frémont in August 1861 declared martial law, approved the execution of captured guerrillas, authorized blanket confiscation of Confederate property, and declared enslaved people's immediate emancipation. Sanctioned by military necessity as a just reprisal against uncivilized war, "the object of this declaration is to place in the hands of the military authorities the power to give instantaneous effect to existing laws." Early the following year, Maj. Gen. David Hunter, also a committed antislavery commander, declared that Florida, Georgia, and South Carolina, "having taken up arms against" the Union, forfeited all constitutional protections. An unjust insurrection waged by a hostile citizenry thereby necessitated martial law and the explicit emancipation of all enslaved people, whom Hunter "declared forever free."[89]

President Lincoln revoked both Frémont and Hunter's proclamations on the basis that military necessity possessed distinct purposes and imposed critical limitations. The unauthorized orders, Lincoln explained, were "*purely political*, and not within the range of *military* law or necessity." The laws of war permitted confiscation of property only when the enemy employed that property to sustain their war machine. "If the General needs them, he can seize them, and use them; but when the need is past, it is not for him to fix their permanent future condition." Frémont's orders suggested to Lincoln that a "farm shall no longer belong to the owner, or his heirs forever; and this as well when the farm is not needed for military purposes as when it is, is purely political, without the savor of military law about it." Only civilian authorities could therefore determine whether emancipation served "a necessity indispensable to the maintenance of the government," especially considering the legal permanence of abolition. "The proclamation in the point of question, is simply 'dictatorship,'" establishing a martial fiefdom in which "the general may do *anything* he pleases—confiscate the lands and free the slaves of *loyal* people, as well as disloyal ones." According to Lincoln, absent the democratic consent of civilian authorities, wartime emancipation levied an unwarranted response against rebellious white southerners.[90]

The seeming radicalism of Frémont's order framed the context in which Lincoln counseled in late 1861 against the war deteriorating into "a violent and remorseless revolutionary struggle." A conflict that repudiated legal boundaries might well inspire excessive Confederate reprisals, alienate both moderate northerners and loyal southerners, and spark future secession movements. And as was no doubt part of Lincoln's calculation, "civilized warfare," writes a leading authority on American legal history, "prohibited acts that might incite slaves into a war of servile insurrection and indiscriminate violence." Preserving the republic through transformative revolution, the president reminded loyal citizens, undermined "the integrity of the Union ... as the primary object of the contest." Frémont's sweeping actions tested the limits of civilized restraint in much the same way that guerrilla warfare strained the boundaries of Confederate state legitimacy. Loyal critics pointed to Frémont's popular reputation as an aristocratic sycophant whose "ignoran[ce] of our institutions" sprang from his haughty "European style." Indeed, Frémont populated his command with German "Forty-Eighters," radical émigrés who had fled to the United States after the 1848 European revolutions. They regarded the Union's war against secessionist slaveholders as an extension of European liberals' midcentury efforts to democratize and collapse entrenched cabals of wealthy, landed elites who had consolidated their power against the common, powerless underclasses. Moderate loyal citizens scorned Frémont's emancipation decree as the lawless internationalization of republicanism, the Europeanization of American democracy.[91]

While his actions may have been misplaced, Frémont had responded to hostile military contingencies that plagued Union armies of invasion. Guerrilla resistance waged by a violent citizenry obstructed federal authority, convincing enough Union commanders that they had entered a truly radicalized region mobilized entirely for war. U.S. forces then faced an additional burden as hundreds of enslaved African Americans flocked to Union lines, seeking refuge, aid, and freedom. An escalating humanitarian crisis joined a mounting realization that enslaved people's forced toil bolstered the Confederate home front, supported Confederate armies, and constructed imposing fortifications to impede Union military operations. The Confederacy in effect boasted *two* armies, one composed of white citizen-soldiers and one populated by bondpeople whose coerced, unfree labor sustained the slaveholding republic's national sovereignty.[92]

Gen. Benjamin F. Butler untangled these seemingly impossible strands in

May 1861 from his post at Fort Monroe, Virginia. In a remarkable compilation of legal reasoning and humanitarian logic, Butler established a foundational component of military necessity that echoed but moderated Frémont's rash dictum. When he confronted at nearby Hampton "a large number of negroes" who had absconded from their involuntary construction of Confederate batteries, Butler retained the men to work behind *Union* lines, while employing the women to wash clothes and prepare food for the republic's troops. Such acts prompted critical questions: "What is their state and condition," asked Butler. "Are they free?" Given that their "work in [Confederate] trenches as property" was "liable to be used in aid of rebellion," Butler regarded the African Americans as "contraband of war," an international legal standard that authorized confiscation by Union armies. He then engaged the premise of slaveholding property to undermine Confederate claims of national and moral legitimacy. If the "contraband" were truly property, "they have been left by their masters and owners, deserted, thrown away, abandoned," thereby erasing "all proprietary relation" as chattel. Statutes of the old slaveholding Union, particularly the Fugitive Slave Law, were no longer relevant. "In a state of rebellion I would confiscate that which was used to oppose my arms," Butler explained, "and take all that property which constituted the wealth of that state, and furnished the means by which the war is prosecuted, besides being the cause of the war."[93]

Congress codified Butler's logic in the First Confiscation Act, which President Lincoln approved in August 1861. Remarkably broad but purposeful in scope, the act declared that any property used to fuel the insurrection could be "seized, confiscated, and condemned." Because it was "too powerful to be suppressed by the ordinary course of judicial proceedings," the Confederate war against the Constitution divorced the rebellious states from legal protections for private property. Congress bestowed on Union armies the authority to judge all rebel assets "to be lawful subject[s] of prize and capture wherever found." And in the vein of Butler's "contraband order," the act stipulated that any person who coerced undo labor from civilians—specifically, from enslaved people—to facilitate war "against the Government and lawful authority of the United States" surrendered "his claim to such labor." A hallmark of military necessity, the First Confiscation Act employed legal reasoning to justify the demands of modern war. The statute permitted Union armies to appropriate enslaved southerners as prizes of war, depriving the Confederate war effort of critical labor. If federal force could divest the faux southern republic from its marriage to human property, the slaveholders' insurrection would wither and die.[94]

The Confiscation Act responded to the profound challenges of vanquishing a large-scale modern rebellion. The inability to defeat Confederate armies, joined with guerrilla harassment, convinced countless Union soldiers that they faced a nation in arms, an alien people hostile to moderation, antagonistic to reason, and averse to civilization. "The whole country is full of Guerilla bands numbering hundreds. All the People are armed," a disgusted William T. Sherman scoffed in 1862. "We have been learning our full share of the realities of this conflict rendered more terable in this section than any other from the savage and brutal mode in which it is waged by our enemies," acknowledged a Pennsylvania volunteer, "who carry on a war more barbarous than any waged by the savages who once inhabited the same country." Although triumphant at the April 1862 battle of Shiloh (among the bloodiest battles ever to befall the Western Hemisphere to that point in history), Ulysses S. Grant "gave up all idea of saving the Union except by complete conquest." But military commanders relied on the law to issue general orders outlining the broad scope *and* the careful limitations of confiscation. While the laws of war outlined "fixed and well-established rules," Halleck reminded his soldiers that international jurisprudence "allows no cruel or barbarous acts on our part in retaliation." Military law "permits any retaliatory measures within the prescribed limits of military usage," and the "laws of the United States confiscate the property of any master in a slave used for insurrectionary purposes." Any act that transcended this congressional limitation violated the spirit of the law. Soldiers "do not make laws but they should obey and enforce them when made."[95]

Despite restrictive general orders that forbade wanton destruction and pillaging, Union soldiers interpreted confiscation policies as a license to wage war against the Confederate home front. When they appropriated private property, seized civilian food sources, and dismantled fences for firewood, soldiers rarely considered the loyalty of the citizens whom they targeted, holding civilians and even entire communities accountable for unlawful warfare. Troops burned public buildings, and sometimes even entire towns, that they suspected of harboring civilian combatants. "As I go through this traitor country," harangued an Ohio volunteer marching through Missouri, "two impulses are struggling in my heart, one to lay waste as we go—like destroying angels, to kill & burn and make the way of the trangressors hard—the other is to wage a civilized warfare.... Our boys only wait for the word, to make the land desolate." For Iowan Charles O. Musser, reprisals against hostile civilians in Arkansas *were* civilized and just responses to unscrupulous warfare. After witnessing the murder of one comrade and another "poor fellow [shot] through both thighs," Musser vowed, "We are in for fighting to the last rather than give way to traitors and rebels. we will kill, 'burn,' and destroy every thing before us to gain our end." Benjamin C. Lincoln, a volunteer officer in the Thirty-Ninth Massachusetts, likewise reported that his men in Maryland "are all full of revengeful feelings and the inhabitants are certainly in danger of them." Lincoln documented his soldiers "carrying off boots, shoes, butter, tobacco, cigars ... and other stuff much of which was of no use to any of the soldiers." Though he believed "private property should be respected," Lincoln could do little to curtail his soldiers' outrage at violent civilians, especially given that "many of the inhabitants are disloyal," in which case "their goods [could be] legally confiscated."[96]

Gen.-in-Chief George B. McClellan expressed grave reservations about the swift escalation in Union military conduct. Though he acknowledged that destruction of property was "unavoidable from a state of war conducted according to the established usages of civilized nations," McClellan nevertheless wondered, "To what extent can the right of confiscation legally be carried?" At what point did the government sanction soldiers' "cupidity or revenge" in violating what Henry Halleck had once condemned in his legal treatise as "the promiscuous pillage of private property," the unjust reprisals "forbidden alike by the law of nature, and the rules of war"? McClellan anticipated the conflict spiraling into an irrepressible revolution, breaching the "highest principles known to Christian Civilization." An artillery officer in the Army of the Potomac captured how the evolving pressures of war marginalized McClellan from myriad other officers. "McClellan is doing his best to make our men behave themselves; his orders are very strict against everything like pillage, or any offence to the inhabitants. But he is not well supported in it by all his subordinate commanders, many of them allowing their feelings of hatred to the rebels to interfere with their obedience of orders, and some even condemning him for too great leniency towards them." Serving on the front lines exposed U.S. soldiers to an enemy that could not be conciliated or coaxed into returning to the Union. Only "complete conquest," as U. S. Grant had observed, would occasion the end of war.[97]

Confederates responded to an escalating war by altering their own military culture established in 1861. Though Confederate civil and military officials deemed guerrilla warfare an uncivilized martial practice, the Congress in April 1862 passed the Partisan Ranger Act, which authorized President Davis to raise regiments of irregular combatants as legitimate soldiers who marched under the Confederate flag and whose conduct would be sanctioned by the state. Drawn from a rich tradition of Atlantic warfare that tied "free-corps" units to nation-states, the act codified irregular conduct by stunting "the excesses of unrestricted guerrilla fighting." Responding to the slaveholding republic's incapacity to check the citizenry's democratic passions, the law restricted white southerners from engaging in illegitimate, independent operations while also channeling popular militancy in service to the state. Partisan units would act independent of formal armies, their use determined by district commanders to meet local contingencies. Some partisans would be deployed on raids across the contested borderlands between the Upper South, the lower North, and the middle West, while others would harass Union operations deep within the Confederacy.[98]

Despite its legal restraints, the Partisan Ranger Act backfired profoundly. Confederate officials found it nearly impossible to organize irregulars toward useful national ends. The law convinced myriad white southern men that they now had legal protection to act at their own discretion, either in the ranks as formal partisans or even as unauthorized guerrillas. "If supplied with arms we will pledge ourselves to take the field the greater part of every year during the war and kill or capture some of the enemy every two or three days," one petitioner wrote to the Confederate government in search of a partisan commission. Dissolving any limiting principles of conduct, the act *increased* the number of unauthorized guerrilla bands that prowled along the war's fringes. That the law assigned partisan units to serve at the pleasure of the Confederate government, which could assign enlisted guerrillas to strategic locales as officials deemed necessary, erased the essential independence of irregular warfare. Southern guerrillas now operated at once against Yankee invaders and an increasingly coercive and restrictive Confederate military establishment. The results were disastrous. Even when they entered Confederate service, partisans earned notorious reputations for poor discipline and disgraceful, uncontrollable violence toward home front civilians and federal armies. "The advantages anticipated from the allowance of corps of partisan rangers . . . have been very partially realized, while from their independent organization and the facilities and temptations thereby afforded to license and depredations grave mischiefs have resulted," admitted Secretary of War James A. Seddon. "They have . . . come to be regarded as more formidable and destructive to our own people than to the enemy."[99]

The codification of guerrilla warfare, an affront to the civilized ethos of West Point, secured the dual ire of Confederates and Unionists. "Experience has convinced me," Robert E. Lee lectured, "that it is almost impossible to prevent [Partisan Rangers] from becoming an injury instead of a benefit to the service." Lee scorned the law for threatening Confederate national legitimacy. "The system gives license to many deserters & marauders, who . . . commit depredations on friend and foe alike." Their demoralizing influence drained the formal armies of critical recruits who instead savored pointless, ill-gotten bounty. Union general Benjamin Butler excoriated partisans as "undisciplined and lawless men, brought from a neighboring state into a community where they have neither interest nor restraint." Being legally named as "'Partisan Rangers' . . . neither alters their conditions, their habits, their disposition, or acts" as guerrillas who violate "the rules of civilized warfare." Union legal theorist Francis Lieber admitted that historical precedent held partisans as lawful combatants, but the distinctions between legitimate partisan and illicit guerrilla remained vague. "The difficulty regarding free-corps and partisans arises from the fact that their discipline is often lax" because "they are often obliged to pillage or to extort money from the places they occupy." The United States regarded partisans as lawful but unjust additions to a civilized war between nations, permitting in-kind reprisals against the Confederacy. Unable to control irregular activity, joined by assurances of escalating retaliation from the Union, the Confederate government repealed the Partisan Ranger Act in early 1864, divorcing the nation from the unchecked radicalism of guerrilla warfare. It is worth remembering that approximately fifty-three thousand Confederate *and* Union guerrillas may have operated during the war, a minuscule number compared to the roughly eight hundred thousand soldiers who served in the regular Confederate army. To be sure, Confederate national legitimacy depended entirely on demonstrating to the world that the slaveholding republic practiced modern war with attendant restraint through legitimate, state-sanctioned — not irregular — institutions.[100]

Responding to accelerations of guerrilla violence and McClellan's failure to capture Richmond and defeat Robert E. Lee's army, the Lincoln administration in June 1862 authorized a second U.S. army to serve in Virginia. A war that had swelled in size and scope necessitated elastic means to combat militant challenges to national sovereignty. In contrast to McClellan's conservative Army of the Potomac, the new Army of Virginia boasted distinct Republican sensibilities. The army featured a political officer corps commanded by John Pope, an antislavery advocate who endorsed the destruction of Confederate infrastructure and even emancipation as a principal war aim. "War means desolation and death," Pope announced, "and it is neither humanity nor wisdom to carry it out upon any other theory. The more bitter it is made for the delinquents, the sooner it will end." Here was just war theory articulated in its raw essence. Civilized belligerents had to adapt to the mutable contingencies of war to secure the national purpose, even when such adjustments necessitated martial but legal escalation.[101]

Military necessity had as much to do with defeating an enemy as it did with legitimizing and codifying one's *own* prevailing conduct. The formation of a partisan Republican army reflected what was already happening on the ground, where individual Union soldiers had expanded the boundaries of military conduct. Pope issued a series of general orders in June and July 1862 that underscored the war's intensification. Orders No. 5 and 19 gave soldiers in the Army of Virginia acute power to "subsist upon the country in which their operations are carried on." The army sustained itself on the bountiful Virginia countryside, appropriating livestock, fence rails, and sundry goods. But the orders also imposed critical restraints against unlawful or unnecessary pillaging. "Neither officer nor soldier has any right ... to enter the house, molest the persons, or disturb the property of any citizen whatsoever," read Order No. 19. Soldiers could forage for food and procure private property "solely by the order of the commanding officer of the troops present." Enlisted men who violated the orders "will be severely punished," because "acts of pillage and outrage are disgraceful to the army." Troops could not secure unlimited or unnecessary bounty. "Vouchers will be given to the owner, stating on their face that they will be payable at the conclusion of the war," read Order No. 5. However, to receive compensation and to limit the temptation of engaging

Union soldiers as unlawful combatants, civilians had to produce "sufficient testimony being furnished that such owners have been loyal citizens of the United States since the date of the vouchers."[102]

Pope's orders labeled civilian insurgents as unlawful combatants. Disgusted by the frustrating first year of war, in which guerrillas debilitated Union armies and murdered innocent soldiers, Pope announced in Order No. 7 that "no privileges and immunities of warfare apply to lawless bands of individuals not forming part of the organized forces of the enemy nor wearing the garb of soldiers." Attacking federal troops, molesting railroads, cutting telegraph wires, and destroying bridges all constituted "outrages disgraceful to civilized people and revolting to humanity." Illegitimate belligerency expanded a gratuitous war and forestalled peace. It was therefore just to order civilians who violated martial law to "be shot, without awaiting civil process." Rather than granting his own armies unchecked discretion, Pope's orders placed the onus of wartime conduct—and by virtue of military necessity—entirely on white southern civilians. Confederates invited their own destruction if they transgressed the rule of law. Federal armies would respect the legal immunity of all noncombatants who "remain at their homes and pursue in good faith their accustomed avocations," and for those southerners "willing to take the oath of allegiance to the United States." But "those who refuse," concluded Order No. 11, "will be considered spies, and subjected to the extreme rigor of military law."[103]

Abraham Lincoln did not revoke Pope's orders like he had the previous year with John Frémont's emancipation decree. Forming the Army of Virginia and appointing Pope were purposeful acknowledgments that the intensifying scope of military necessity had shifted with the Union's inability to neuter Confederate resistance. The escalation in conduct reflected Republican wartime purpose. Lincoln reminded a fellow Unionist that the antidote for peace lay not "in rounding the rough angles of the war, but in removing the necessity for the war." The conflict would cease and "the Army will be withdrawn so soon as [loyal] State government[s] can dispense with its presence; and the people of the State can then upon the old Constitutional terms, govern themselves.... If they will not do this, if they prefer to hazard all for the sake of destroying the government, it is for them to consider whether it is probable I will surrender the government." Lincoln refused to "give up the contest, leaving any available means unapplied," and therefore vowed "not [to] do *more* than I can, and I shall do *all* I can to save the government." But "I shall do nothing in malice. What I deal with is too vast for malicious dealing."[104]

Lincoln's subtle statements framed a national conversation about the military necessity of emancipation. From the conflict's opening salvos, proponents of wartime emancipation argued that the cause of Union was contingent on and indistinguishable from abolition. Because the cancerous ideology of slavery had ruptured the republic, Confederates were not "erring brothers," averred Frederick Douglass; rather, they were foreign mercenaries who could not be reintegrated into the Union as slaveholders. They "are waging a barbarous war, of unparalleled ferocity, marshalling the savage Indian" to kill the world's only true democracy. A preponderance of white southerners clearly did not yearn for liberation from the international Slave Power. They *were* the Slave Power, waging "a war of ideas, not less than of armies," added Republican congressman George Julian in early 1862. Union armies had to dismantle the retrograde, uncivilized society that had flung "the great Model Republic of the world [into] the throes and spasms of death." As Douglass concluded, "He who to-day fights for Emancipation, fights for his country and free Institutions, and he who fights for slavery"—or tacitly countenanced a national reunion in which it was preserved—"fights against his country and in favor or a slaveholding oligarchy."[105]

Framed within the ethos of just war, advocates endorsed military emancipation as inflexible, rational, and antimilitaristic. "The rebels have placed in our hands," Julian declared, "the grand weapon" of emancipation when they justified national collapse and waged war to establish slaveholding sovereignty. "The policy of emancipation has been born of the circumstances of the rebellion," in which stalwart Confederate resistance, guerrilla warfare, and the problem of enslaved labor undercut a conciliatory national reunion. Ethical reason justified the United States to "use it as a matter of clear and unhesitating duty." International law further legitimated the wisdom of emancipation. "The law of nations applicable to a state of war takes from this rebel power every constitutional refuge it could claim in a time of peace," Julian outlined. "Putting down slavery as a 'military necessity'" was consistent with Vattel's international law, to which civilized belligerents subscribed. "'Since the object of a just war is to repress injustice and violence,'" Julian read from Vattel's treatise, "'we have a right to put in practice against the enemy every measure that is necessary in order to weaken him.'" Military emancipation was at once unyielding and judicious because "the common laws which govern a war between nations apply to the conduct of a civil war."[106]

Ralph Waldo Emerson outlined the rational basis for wartime emancipation. "As long as we fight without any affirmative step taken by the Government, any word intimating forfeiture in the rebel States of their old privileges under the law," explained the New England abolitionist, "they and we fight on the same side, for Slavery." Echoing Julian's logic, Emerson proposed that "Congress can, by edict, as a part of the military defense which it is the duty of Congress to provide, abolish slavery." Then, as rational humans who shaped their own destiny, "the slaves near our armies will come to us." While the enslaved had flocked to Union lines ever since the war began, federal recognition of their human dignity would incentivize countless more to amputate their unfree labor from the Confederate war machine, rupturing the slaveholding republic from within. Rather than setting the Confederacy ablaze, imprisoning or executing millions of white southerners, or colonizing the vast region, Union armies could steer the inherent contradictions of Confederate nationhood against the slaveholding republic itself. "Instantly, the armies that now confront you must run home to protect their estates, and must stay there, and your enemies will disappear." The United States would then have created a dual war front, stretching Confederate forces to the verge of collapse. Given that enslavement "cannot live but by injustice," Emerson asked, "why should not America be capable of a second stroke for the well-being of the human race"? Positioning the Union war effort alongside 4 million obvious allies "costs so little," and "rids the world, at one stroke, of this degrading nuisance, the cause of war, and ruin to nations."[107]

Military emancipation paved an antimilitaristic road toward an enduring peace. Secession and civil war unfolded as crises of national sovereignty unleashed by slaveholding militants who aimed to shatter a free people's popular will. Frederick Douglass warned early in 1862, "Restore slavery to its old status in the Union and the same elements of demoralization which have plunged this country into tremendous war will begin again to dig the grave of free Institutions." A republic that did not dismantle the slaveholding oligarchy would be forever "taxed to keep a standing army in the South to maintain respect for the Federal Government." From London in the same year, Henry Adams likewise argued, "There can be no peace on our continent so long as the Southern people exist. . . . I don't much care whether they are destroyed by emancipation," because "we must not let them as an independent state get the monopoly of cotton again." Preserving the Union with slaveholding intact would "compel us to support a standing army no less large than if we conquer them and hold them so, and with infinite means of wounding and scattering dissension among us." The "only means of a lasting peace," added George Julian, was to prevent the restoration of "slavery to its ancient rights under the Constitution, and allow it a new cycle of rebellion and crime." Only a democracy emancipated from the Slave Power—not the kind of rigid military state against which Douglass, Adams, and Julian warned—would thereafter shield the republic against aristocratic, oligarchic, slaveholding radicalism.[108]

Even if most Union soldiers did not enlist to destroy slavery, the experience of war exposed for federal volunteers the same wisdom, pragmatism, and antimilitarism presented by wartime emancipation. Soldiers had long grumbled about protecting loyal citizens' property, particularly enslaved people, whom the troops identified as unwilling accomplices to the Confederate war effort. And as military campaigns dragged on, as the inability to vanquish rebel armies tested Union resolve, blue-coated soldiers daily witnessed enslaved labor strengthening the very armies that defied federal authority. "The enemy must be weakened by every honorable means, and he has no right to whine about it," Maj. Gen. Samuel Curtis wrote from St. Louis. "The rebellion must be shaken to its foundation, which is slavery, and the idea of saving rebels from the inevitable consequences of their rebellion is no part of our business while they persist." Depriving Confederates of military labor undercut the insurrection in critical ways, especially if Union armies could appropriate that labor for themselves. "We jayhawk all we can and entice away all the negroes we can. I believe, and the government will find it out some day," wrote an officer in the Fifty-Fifth Ohio Volunteers, "that the only way to put down this rebellion is to hurt the instigators and the abettors of it. Slavery must be cleaned out." Hastening a definitive end to the war mandated equipping Union armies with all viable but legitimate weapons. "We are in for any measure that will put down this rebellion, *constitutional or not*," fellow Ohioan George Landrum wrote in support of emancipation. "'*Military necessity*,' that's the cry that suits me."[109]

For other Union soldiers, the necessity of emancipation transcended martial pragmatism. Extinguishing human bondage through the trial of civil war would stabilize the republic. Slavery had long revolutionized the American South, populating the region with aristocratic oligarchs hostile to democratic sovereignty. "It is not merely that this terrible war may be ended" when U.S. armies conquered the Confederacy, explained Vermont private Wilbur Fisk. "The great principles of a free government" had to be emancipated from the vile influence of slavery lest "the progress of civilization and freedom may not be rolled back for ages, or receive a blow from which they may never recover." Union armies had to ensure that "slavery must fall, and fall forever," relieving the nation from incessant belligerency. "Never in a war before did the rank and file feel a more resolute earnestness for a just cause," Fisk concluded. While marching with the Tenth Connecticut Volunteers, William Augustus Willoughby agreed that emancipation forestalled revolutionary rebellions from again severing the Union. The act "will Inaugurate a new System of Laws and customs among the people in abolishing old ideas and establishing new ones." Maine volunteer Nathan Webb concurred: "Now we've got the power and chance, I say take the opportunity to eradicate this evil from the nation."[110]

Legislative actions in the Republican Congress underscored the strident faith in efficient and just military campaigns against slavery. As Union armies struggled to suppress the rebellion during the spring and summer of 1862, Congress debated whether to broaden legal confiscation policies. In the wake of McClellan's failure to capture Richmond and destroy Lee's Army of Northern Virginia, Republicans responded to the crisis of a lengthy war by passing the Second Confiscation Act, which President Lincoln signed into law in July. Styled "an act to suppress Insurrection, to punish Treason and Rebellion, to seize and confiscate the Property of Rebels," the law certified wartime emancipation as military necessity. Because conventional battlefield engagements had failed to defeat secessionists, the United States had to target the Confederacy's inherent national purpose and claim to international legitimacy.

"If we are ever to put down the rebellion we cannot afford to refuse any of the means recognized by the usage of civilized warfare," explained Republican politico R. R. Enos. "The slave must be armed and sent against his master—our armies must find subsistence as far as possible at the expense of the enemy.... [Those] who would do for the best interests of their country without regard to slavery must be put at the head of our columns.... The people are ripe for extreme measures."[111]

The act portended massive, if not interminable, disruptions to the American Slave Power. The law fundamentally altered the federal government's long-standing connection to human bondage by shattering the antebellum fugitive slave statutes that had long sustained the old slaveholders' Union. Loyal citizens—many of whom marched in Federal armies—were now relieved from returning runaways to masters currently in rebellion against the republic. The U.S. Army transformed into an antislavery shelter, guaranteeing freedom for enslaved people who fled their plantations and the coercive labor regimes in Confederate armies. The law's breadth targeted the slaveholding foundation of southern civilization, declaring "forever free" all people enslaved to those "engaged in rebellion against the government of the United States," all people who broke from their masters and took "refuge within the lines of the army," and all people "being within any place occupied by rebel forces and afterwards occupied by the forces of the United States." Sanctioning multiple mechanisms "to insure the speedy termination of the rebellion," any person who engaged in unjust insurrection against the United States forfeited their property employed in the act of waging war. The president could then transfer the commandeered assets "for the support of the army of the United States." Finally, the law enhanced the president's constitutional war powers. From "employ[ing] as many persons of African descent as he may deem necessary and proper for the suppression of this rebellion," to colonizing the formerly enslaved outside the United States, to offering "pardon and amnesty" to rebellious Americans, Lincoln now possessed flexible executive authority to pursue a lasting peace.[112]

Republican proponents vindicated the Second Confiscation Act within the international laws of just war. "It is the undoubted right and the duty of every nation, when engaged in a righteous war," explained Iowa senator James W. Grimes, "to avail itself to every legitimate means known to civilized warfare to overcome its enemies." Legalist Grosvenor P. Lowery likewise located confiscation as a legal precedent embedded in antiquity, the Enlightenment, and the modern era. Though a nation could deploy continual, targeted violence "until it has repulsed the threatened danger and obtained security for the future," belligerents could not exceed "the end or object of the war. For it would be to no purpose to have a right to do a thing if we could not make use of the necessary means to bring it about." The law of nations therefore compelled a civilized belligerent to employ means not only "with respect to the cause of the war, but also with respect to such fresh causes as may arise." Massachusetts senator Charles Sumner agreed, but he imagined wartime confiscation and emancipation as transcendent symbols in the American epoch. Both measures "take from the Rebellion its mainspring of activity and strength" and "remove a motive and temptation to prolonged resistance," eliminating "forever that disturbing influence, which ... will keep this land a volcano ever ready to break forth anew." In targeting slavery, the United States had finally moved "from Barbarism to Civilization," claiming "Indemnity for the Past such as no nation ever before was able to win, and there will be Security for the Future such as no nation ever before enjoyed."[113]

Abraham Lincoln applied similar logic when he expanded his war powers delegated by the new law. Less than one week after the Second Confiscation Act went into effect, he issued an executive decree soon codified as War Department General Orders No. 109. Army commanders who operated in rebellious states could now "seize and use any property, real or personal, which may be necessary or convenient for their several commands for supplies or for other military purposes; and ... while property may be destroyed for proper military objects, none shall be destroyed in wantonness or malice." But for Lincoln, military necessity extended far beyond questions of property. The president also authorized commanders to "employ as laborers ... so many persons of African descent as can be advantageously used for military and naval purposes, giving them reasonable wages for their labor." In a single cluster of legalese, Lincoln unbound the entire premise of human bondage that American slaveholders had toiled for centuries to construct. Reminding the world that all individuals owned the fruits of their labor, the president exposed the pathetic conceit of slaveholding, thereby aligning the Union's military strategy with liberal nationalism. It was a testament to Lincoln's restraint, his ability to use the contingencies of war, constitutional sanction, and international law to undermine the Confederacy's tangible and symbolic claims to nationhood. Republicans now employed slavery, the cause of national balkanization and civil war, in the martial service and ideological reformation of Union.[114]

Lincoln had become persuaded about the military necessity of emancipation in wake of Union battlefield reverses during the early summer of 1862. He informed his cabinet then that he intended to issue a proclamation of emancipation, which he regarded as an essential wartime weapon. Waging war against the Constitution deprived Confederates of all legal protections to their property, especially enslaved people, whose peculiar presence somehow caused the war and whose unrequited labor damaged the Union war effort. "If the rebels persisted in their war upon the Government, it would be a necessity and a duty on our part to liberate their slaves," the president informed his advisers. The federal government "could not carry on a successful war by longer pursuing a temporizing and forbearing policy towards those who disregarded law and [the] Constitution, and were striving by every means to break up the

Union." To permit the army to strike more vigorous blows," to "strike at the heart of the rebellion," and to remove "an insuperable obstacle to peace," a policy of general emancipation served "a military necessity, absolutely essential to the preservation of the Union." The war's bloody indecision, Lincoln counseled, balanced the republic's precarious fate: "We must free the slaves or ourselves be subdued."[115]

Lincoln acted within the boundaries of congressional statute and his constitutional war powers to issue the preliminary Emancipation Proclamation in September 1862. In fact, much of the original document quoted from the Second Confiscation Act, a careful reminder that Congress had already approved of the president's stroke. But the law itself had bestowed broad executive discretion to customize the scope of wartime emancipation. While Lincoln never strayed from the legal justification of wartime necessity, the final Emancipation Proclamation, which went into effect on January 1, 1863, revealed a far more sweeping vision than Congress's limited confiscation decree. "An act of justice, warranted by the Constitution, upon military necessity," the proclamation declared "that all persons held as slaves within any State or designated part of a State, the people whereof shall then be in rebellion against the United States, shall be then, thenceforward, and forever free." The edict exempted the Border States and locales already undergoing processes of reconstruction, a testament to Lincoln's recognition that federal law barred the president from emancipating human property belonging to loyal citizens. Nevertheless, "the Executive government of the United States, including the military and naval authorities thereof, will recognize and maintain the freedom of" millions of people held in bondage throughout the Confederacy. And the executive order invited formerly enslaved men to enlist in the U.S. military. Union forces now unfolded the banner of freedom as they continued their march against armies of the Slave Power.[116]

To guard against accusations of wielding the unjust authority of a military dictator, Lincoln framed emancipation as a temporary wartime decree. The "proclamation has no constitutional or legal justification, except as a military measure," he explained. Exempting the Border States and areas already under Union occupation "were made because the military necessity did not apply to the exempted localities." To transgress legal boundaries and martial pragmatism, "would I not thus give up all footing upon constitution or law? Would I not thus be in the boundless field of absolutism?" During his December 1862 message to Congress, Lincoln framed wartime emancipation as a direct outgrowth of just war doctrine: the measure "secure[s] peace more speedily, and maintain[s] it more permanently than can be done by force alone." A wartime executive order, the proclamation expired at the termination of hostilities. Emancipation did not displace Union as the republic's wartime purpose insofar as it furnished lawful means to secure the nation from slaveholding militancy. "Other means may succeed; this could not fail. The way is plain, peaceful, generous, just," an "assurance [that] would end the struggle now, and save the Union forever." Lincoln thus implored Congress to institutionalize emancipation as a constitutional amendment, an act of peaceful democratic consensus that "would restore the national authority and national prosperity, and perpetuate both indefinitely."[117]

Wartime emancipation unfolded in August 1862, just as Dakota Sioux sparked a simultaneous belligerent challenge to Federal authority. Much of the loyal citizenry regarded the Dakota War as distinct from and secondary to Union's struggle against the Confederacy. But the ways in which the Union responded to the Native unrest in Minnesota underscored the loyal citizenry's conception of emancipation as a limited military measure in combating the Confederate rebellion. During the 1850s, the United States and Dakota forged two treaties in which the Natives surrendered tribal lands in exchange for trading rights, financial compensation, and material goods. The federal government soon reneged on these assurances, depriving the Sioux of critical sustenance. When Minnesota joined the Union in 1858, federal authorities reclaimed Sioux reservation lands to redistribute to white settlers. Overwhelmed by privation and suffering, the Natives channeled hostile resentment against the United States. In August 1862, Sioux warriors assailed white settlements, killed as many as eight hundred women, men, and children, and displaced thousands of civilians. State militia joined with U.S. volunteers to pacify the ethnic conflagration, which grew into a six-week war. Both sides targeted civilian noncombatants and engaged their armed foes with little restraint. Some reports charged the Dakota of committing murder and rape. Federal troops in turn scalped Indigenous warriors and mutilated their bodies.[118]

In the wake of the Union's humiliating August defeat at the battle of Second Bull Run, President Lincoln transferred Gen. John Pope to Minnesota to suppress the Dakota revolt. "It is my purpose utterly to exterminate the Sioux," Pope declared. "Destroy everything belonging to them and force them out to the plains, unless, as I suggest, you can capture them. They are to be treated as maniacs or wild beasts, and by no means as people with whom treaties or compromises can be made." Pope voiced the nearly universal outrage of white Minnesotans who demanded unlimited reprisals against the Sioux. Minnesota's governor and congressional delegation even assured Lincoln that his political fortunes would suffer if he did not authorize immediate executions of the captured Sioux warriors and order the summary removal of *all* Natives from the state. If the president did not respond in kind, warned the representatives, white Minnesotans would embark on campaigns of ruthless vigilantism to eradicate the Indigenous people. Though most loyal citizens elsewhere considered the Dakota War tangential to the Union's primary war against the Confederacy, stalwart feminist and abolitionist Jane Grey Swisshelm identified the two conflicts as inextricably linked. She condemned the

Sioux "as the allies of the South" and its aristocratic rebels, each aggressive, illegitimate impediments to the march of white American civilization. As a recent settler to Minnesota, Swisshelm believed that the Confederate rebellion had destabilized the Union's precarious western borderlands, inviting hostile Indians to stoke bitter domestic upheavals. "It was of course in the interests of the South," she remarked, "and meant to prevent [Federal] troops leaving the State" to battle rebellious slaveholders.[119]

When the Sioux surrendered in late September, Col. Henry H. Sibley assembled a military commission to try the captives as armed insurrectionists. Unaccustomed to Anglo laws of war and American jurisprudence, the Sioux suffered unambiguous show trials in which some convictions were rendered in mere minutes. Military authorities condemned 323 Sioux warriors—and sentenced 303 to execution—as illegitimate combatants who waged unlawful armed rebellion against the United States. The sentencings raised theoretical questions about the legitimacy of public combatants and the limits of state reprisal in wars of rebellion. Lincoln reviewed each of the Sioux convictions. He commuted all but 38 sentences on the premise that a preponderance of Sioux *were* lawful combatants due the full protection of the laws of war. The 38 condemned to execution, according to the president, had forfeited the shelter of international law when they illicitly murdered and raped noncombatants. On December 26, 1862, in the largest public execution in United States history, the convicted Dakota Sioux were hanged for war crimes.[120]

Lincoln's calculus judged prisoners of war to be fully entitled to critical wartime rights as formal belligerents, limiting the reprisals that a nation could exact against lawful combatants. "Anxious to not act with so much clemency as to encourage another outbreak on the one hand, nor with so much severity as to be real cruelty on the other," the president informed the Senate in December, "I caused a careful examination of the records of trials to be made, in view of first ordering the execution of such as had been proved guilty of violating females." Lincoln determined that only two Sioux had committed rape, and thirty-six had "proven to have participated in *massacres*, as distinguished from participation in *battles*." Such oblique logic reinforced the Union's restrained policy toward legitimate Confederate belligerents, who donned a formal uniform, marched beneath a national flag, and repudiated irregular conduct. The insurrectionary principle applied only to guerrillas and civilian combatants who themselves rejected the civilized laws of war. Excessive displays of retaliation, either against Confederate rebels or Dakota warriors, would trigger escalating cycles of retributive violence absent any limiting principle. Lincoln's secretary of the navy, Gideon Welles, decried "the savage wretches [who] have been guilty of great atrocities." But any nation that claimed the ostensible mantle of civilization could not respond in kind. "When the intelligent Representatives of a State can deliberately besiege the Government to take the lives of these ignorant barbarians by wholesale, after they have surrendered themselves prisoners, it would seem the sentiments of the Representatives were but slightly removed from the barbarians whom they would execute."[121]

Lincoln professed, "I could not afford to hang men for votes." He rejected the notion that wholesale capital punishment fell within executive powers as a just means to wage public war. In fact, long unsettled by the injustices of U.S. policy toward Native peoples, the president allegedly vowed, "If we get through this war [against Confederates], and I live, *this Indian system shall be reformed.*" Lincoln nevertheless also recognized that white Minnesotans "manifest much anxiety for the removal of the tribes beyond the limits of the State as a guarantee against future hostilities." Indeed, the Republican Congress in early 1863 nullified all treaties between the United States and the Dakota Sioux. Because the "Indians made an unprovoked, aggressive, and most savage war upon the United States," read a February law, the Sioux forfeited in Minnesota "all lands and rights of occupancy." Detribalizing Indigenous sovereignty, the Congress ordered the Indians removed to "tract[s] of unoccupied land outside the limits of any state." And the more than 260 Dakota whom Lincoln exonerated were condemned as prisoners of war and held for several years in debilitating and deadly conditions because their death sentences had not been fully commuted. The implication was clear: waging an ostensibly unjust war against federal authority yielded permanent expulsion from the nation. The western conflict suggested how the federal state shaped the borders of national inclusion in the wake of wars of rebellion. The government's violent displacement of the Dakota inaugurated its thirty-year campaign across the western plains to force Indigenous peoples to forfeit their tribal sovereignties to an aggressive Anglo-American republic that by 1890 controlled the continent.[122]

Federal responses to the Dakota and Confederate Wars illustrate subtle but critical distinctions in how white nineteenth-century Americans conceived of just war and military necessity. The Union's loyal citizenry, notes one scholar, "fought the 'civilized' enemy by customary means and the 'barbarous' enemy by suitably unpleasant means." Myriad white Americans regarded Indigenous people as uncivilized barbarians who did not merit the beneficent protection of law and martial restraint. Native Americans occupied the same realm as guerrillas, deprived of quarter, warranted for execution, their tribal sovereignty subject to dissolution. James Madison Bowler, a Union soldier transferred from service against the Confederacy to Minnesota in 1862 to combat the Dakota uprising, condemned Natives as "savages who have *not the least restraint, either moral physical, upon their conduct toward their victims.*" Indigenous warfare, he averred, was unbound from self-control, devoid of enlightenment, rooted only in "torture and outrage." Echoing his commanding general John Pope, Bowler concluded, "I believe I could yield my life willingly to see these savage devils exterminated."[123]

The Sand Creek Massacre in November 1864 testifies to the enormous racial gulf separating so-called civilized and illegitimate combatants. When colonel of United States volunteers John M. Chivington was tasked with subduing Native American resistance in the District of Colorado, he believed "the Cheyennes will have to be soundly whipped before they will be quiet." Such rhetoric was fairly consistent with that of Union soldiers who marched against the Confederacy. But Chivington continued: "If any of them are caught in your vicinity kill them, as that is the only way." Chivington led the First and Third Colorado Volunteers, the latter raised "to pursue, kill, and destroy all hostile Indians that infest the plains," against Cheyenne and Arapaho settlements. At Sand Creek, the white soldiers murdered and mutilated hundreds of innocent civilians. "I did not see a body of a man, woman, or child but was scalped," observed an officer of a New Mexico regiment, "and in many instances their bodies were mutilated in the most horrible manner—men, women, and children's privates cut out."[124]

Union armies never replicated a Sand Creek inside the Confederacy. "The central restraining force on the destructive abilities of Civil War soldiers," explains a leading historian, "was their visceral perceptions of racial identity." Unionists saw Confederates, no matter how violent or rebellious, as civilized belligerents who practiced war within the Anglo-American tradition. Unlike with the Dakota War, a civil war waged between white combatants *mandated* that former rebels reintegrate into the republic as constitutionally protected citizens. White southerners would not be explicitly displaced or have their membership in the national community stripped. United States military policy thus targeted *slavery* as the purpose and symbol of the Confederate rebellion—not the *people* who sparked or escalated the war. Secretary of War Edwin Stanton noted in August 1862 how slavery empowered "rebel armies [to] wage a cruel and murderous war." Wartime confiscation and emancipation "reduc[ed] the laboring strength of the rebels [and] their military power ... consistent with civilized warfare to weaken, harass, and annoy" the ability to prolong war. And when Federal forces pillaged, sacked, and burned Athens, Alabama; Barnwell, South Carolina; Darien, Georgia; and Fredericksburg, Virginia, to retaliate against irregular combatants and guerrilla conduct, such acts served as deterrents against future unlawful civilian activity. As William T. Sherman acknowledged in January 1863, "Our armies are devastating the land, and it is sad to see the destruction that attends our progress—we cannot help it. Farms disappear, houses are burned and plundered, and every living animal killed and eaten. General officers make feeble efforts to stay the disorder, but it is idle." White southerners invited military reprisals only by their own illicit actions, compelling the United States to activate the laws of war in combating threats to national sovereignty.[125]

To be sure, the United States waged a profoundly hard war, which produced acute suffering and displacement among civilian populations. However, Union armies did not deliberately target white southern civilians, a blatant violation of civilized custom, Federal policy, and international law. Prominent historian James M. McPherson, supported by calculations from statistician J. David Hacker, estimates that the conflict's fifty thousand civilian deaths resulted largely from the collateral damage of modern war and indirectly from Union military actions. McPherson writes, "Breakdowns in transportation, the loss of crops and livestock from army operations by both sides, from overcrowding refugees fleeing from war zones" all exacerbated the "shortages, fatigue, and malnutrition" endured by civilians who succumbed to disease. Though the international laws of war did not compel Union armies to announce their intention to bombard cities, Federal commanders in some cases *did* advise civilians of their martial aims. Civilians could then choose to remain in urban centers or flee from advancing United States forces. Union armies that besieged Confederate cities produced strikingly few civilian deaths. The 1862 Federal shelling of Fredericksburg killed four civilians; fewer than ten died in the forty-seven-day siege of Vicksburg in 1863; Sherman's bombardment of Atlanta in the summer of 1864 caused approximately twenty civilian fatalities; and the nine-month siege of Petersburg (1864–65) yielded nine citizen deaths. When compared to the enormous loss of civilian life during the sieges of medieval and early modern Europe, joined with the U.S. Army's intermittent destruction of mid-nineteenth-century Indigenous villages, rapes of Native women, and executions of Indian noncombatants, the wartime experiences of white southern citizens appears relatively mild.[126]

Tensions even permeated Federal ranks about the implications of the "directed severity" that Union armies visited upon the Confederate home front. Disgusted by the "vandalism" near Corinth, Mississippi, Brig. Gen. James W. Denver in 1862 condemned his troops, who "seem to be possessed with the idea that in order to carry on war men must throw aside civilization and become savages. . . . I do not see how men claiming to be enlightened and educated can do such things." From some soldiers stealing horses and carriages to others who "sweep the country as with the besom of destruction," Denver brooded, "instead of an army we will have an undisciplined mob. Self-preservation to say nothing of humanity requires that discipline be maintained." Cavalry officer Charles Wright Wills worried that his soldiers came to embody the very fringe guerrilla violence that they combated. "The army is becoming awfully depraved," he observed from Holly Springs, Mississippi. Pondering the unwarranted destruction of civilian property committed in the name of military necessity, Wills questioned "how the civilized home folks will ever be able to live with them after the war." For Wills, the once noble Union had "degenerate[d] into a nation of thieves" patterned by the shameful "example set by a fair portion of our army."[127]

For Col. Robert Gould Shaw, the adversity of counter-guerrilla warfare occasioned inward changes to otherwise virtuous soldiers. After transferring out of the Army of the Potomac, Shaw raised the Fifty-Fourth Massachusetts Volunteers, one of the Union's first regiments of African American soldiers.[128] Serving in the Department of the South and battling irregulars who disregarded martial civilization, Shaw admitted, "We are [also] outlawed, and therefore not bound by the rules of regular warfare." He argued that burning homes of known guerrillas, displacing communities suspected of sheltering irregular bands, and exacting reprisals against an immoral brand of warfare fundamentally changed the character of Union armies. Shaw imagined himself engaged in a "barbarous sort of warfare," one that plunged otherwise virtuous soldiers "into a plunderer or robber" until it became very difficult to distinguish a guerrilla from his opponent. "As the case stands, we are no better than 'Semmes,' who attacks and destroys defenceless vessels, and haven't even the poor excuse of gaining anything by it." A people's war was far different from a noble limited war between enlightened armies. "After going through the hard campaigning and hard fighting in Virginia, this makes me very much ashamed of myself." Guerrilla and counter-irregular operations are "an Indian ... mode of warfare," Shaw concluded, "I can't say I admire it. It isn't like a fair stand up such as our Potomac Army is accustomed to."[129]

Despite the reservations voiced by Denver, Wills, and Shaw, Edwin M. Stanton's idea of "civilized warfare" and William T. Sherman's notion of "progress" held specific meanings for a growing mass of Union soldiers. As they traversed the vast South, the synonymous symbols of rebellion and slaveholding greeted their march. All that fueled the revolutionary threat to Union had to be destroyed, the instigators christened into a new birth of freedom, liberated from the regressive decay of slavery. Myriad soldiers adopted a liberal reading of confiscation and counterinsurgency, understanding that they marched at once in the service of Union *and* in the deliverance of the South. Though pillaging and vandalism often exceeded the limits of congressional statute or executive authorization, Union troops regarded their conduct as just retaliations against the radicalism of disunion. Burning towns, confiscating agriculture, scorching fields, and liberating slaves all extinguished the *sources* of rebellion, circumventing more extreme measures such as battlefield retribution or the execution of civilians deemed unfit to inhabit the national community. Only then would the South finally be cleansed of the antiquated institutions that sustained an unscrupulous, regressive, and rebellious slaveholding ruling class.[130]

U.S. armies marched to emancipate the South from militant oligarchs whose machinations had long divorced the region from American civilization. "It is nearly a hundred years since our people first declared to the nations of the world that all men are born free, and still we have not made our declaration good," announced Brig. Gen. John W. Phelps in the summer of 1862 from his post in New Orleans. "Highly revolutionary means have since then been adopted" to reverse the Union's exceptional international standing, culminating in the terrible war of secession. "The danger of a violent revolution, over which we can have no control, must become more imminent every day" in which the global Slave Power continued to manipulate the American South. "It is clear that the public good requires slavery to be abolished" through military means because the institution has underwritten a government and society that are "not republican either in form or spirit." The modern world had long disavowed slavery, a corrosion to democracy whose accomplices "fasten upon the people an aristocracy or a despotism." The United States waged an increasingly violent but just war against slavery—and not necessarily against white southern civilians—to unite an egalitarian republic liberated from the "slave influences which are opposed to its character and its interests."[131]

Myriad soldiers came to understand that republican liberty and free-labor egalitarianism depended on wartime emancipation. Slaveholding reeked of degenerative licentiousness, undermining cherished virtues of progress and industry. Iowan William Legg Henderson commended central Alabama's "diversity of timber. . . . And yet with all those natural advantages the Southern Country is a Century behind the North in Architecture, Mechanics & Civilization." Slavery had stripped the region of any economic diversification, any chance at moral and material improvement, and any use of the land other than large-scale plantation agriculture. Acquiring thousands of acres and managing armies of slaves afforded opulent lifestyles for the precious few planters fortunate enough to exploit land and people to their personal advantage. Poor and middling whites were left with the agricultural scraps, eking out a mediocre existence devoid of economic prospects. Themselves drawn from a sizable cross-section of rural and agricultural life, Union volunteers bristled at the catastrophic effects wrought by slaveholding. As he traversed Virginia, a soldier in the Fourteenth Vermont protested how slavery had "impoverished the land, and reduced the people to the lowest state of misery and degradation, and has at last culminated in this wicked rebellion."[132]

Slavery had battered the land and barred the South's entrance into modernity. The institution had moreover created a culture of dependence not only among its victims but also among its administrators. Rufus Kinsley, who soldiered in the Eighth Vermont, served in Louisiana, and loathed slaveholders, looked with awe at the splendid cotton lands of the lower Mississippi River valley. "This country is rich beyond comprehension," he wrote. Clearly he held the region's natural resources in high regard, but he lamented that because white southerners had crafted their entire existence on an arrogant faith in slavery's everlasting fortunes, "an air of gloom at present overshadows everything. Desolation reigns supreme. Hunger stands guard at every door." Kinsley harbored little sympathy for white southerners whose power, opulence, and prestige had collapsed in their martial effort to defend slavery through disunion and war. Recognizing how the terrible swift sword had cut down so fiercely the South's entire basis for existence, Kinsley underscored the just influence of military emancipation in restructuring a society revolutionized by slavery. "Sad, and desolate, and fearful as it is, this is a picture on which I love to look." Much like his president, this soldier viewed the Civil War and its immense destruction as a sacrosanct cleansing, or, as he called it, a "harvest." The war "is the legitimate fruit of the seed we have sown." Union armies that waged this holy war spread the "seed[s] as shall bear to us National honor and permanent peace." All realms of life were directed by "a law of compensation, so accurately adjusted by Infinite wisdom, that no action or purpose can fail to receive its reward." At its most basic level, military emancipation and "directed severity" rendered slaveholding impotent, stunting any future rebellion against the Union.[133]

As the spring campaigns commenced in 1863, Henry W. Halleck assessed the scope of Union military conduct. The United States' foremost expert on the laws of war echoed his soldiers in the ranks: "The character of the war has very much changed within the last year. . . . There can be no peace but that which is forced by the sword. We must conquer the rebels or be conquered by them. The North must conquer the slave oligarchy or become slaves themselves . . . to Southern aristocrats." Though confiscation and emancipation functioned as legal and limited war measures, few contemporaries could ignore that "there is now no possible hope of reconciliation" with rebellious slaveholders. Such uncompromising rhetoric may suggest that military necessity had sanctioned Union armies to wage total war against the Confederacy. Yet as Halleck no doubt understood, conducting a truly unlimited contest would violate national claims to modernity, reason, and civilization, transforming the Union into an unrestrained state that visited arbitrary violence on its foes. Essential to democratic legitimacy, a civilized war demanded something more than congressional laws or executive orders that justified destructive conduct under the nebulous guise of military necessity. The concept of military necessity itself mandated codification and definition within the context of the Union's war. Only then could loyal citizens conduct an unhesitating but restricted contest.[134]

Halleck turned to his old friend Francis Lieber for advice on distinguishing the scope of military necessity. Reflecting on the transformative elements of modern war, in which the fates of civilians, nations, institutions, and humanity all converged against massive armies, Lieber probed the central question that legal theorists had asked for centuries: How do nations expand the scope of war and escalate conduct while maintaining critical restraints through law and moral reason? Lieber published his considerations in a lengthy treatise titled *Instructions for the Government of Armies of the United States in the Field*, which the federal government adopted in April 1863 as General Orders No. 100. "Lieber's Code," as it came to be known, advised that war was a profoundly human event which had to be conducted with relentless but compassionate severity. "The more vigorously wars are pursued, the better it is for humanity. Sharp wars are brief." Modern nation-states "related to one another in close intercourse. Peace is their normal condition; war is the exception. The ultimate object of all modern war is a renewed state of peace." Democracies particularly could not withstand incessant war; they required elastic means by which to forge lasting accord. Lieber's instructions codified scores of Republican wartime policies, including the suspension of habeas corpus, property confiscation, martial law, summary penalties for irregular conduct, and even emancipation. Lieber departed from Vattel to argue that modern belligerents related the aims of war with their national values to justify wartime conduct. "Ever since wars have become great national wars, war has come to be acknowledged not to be its own end, but the means to obtain great ends of state, or to consist in defense against wrong."[135]

The essence of the code hinged on Articles 14, 15, and 16, in which Lieber outlined military necessity. Framing the concept in purposeful contradictions, Lieber employed rhetorical paradox to guard against belligerents seizing the law to justify unlimited wartime conduct. At once affording salient leeway and imposing notable limitations on its practitioners, military necessity functioned in accordance with human reason and moral obligation. "As understood by modern civilized nations," stipulates Article 14, wartime obligation "consists in the necessity of those measures which are indispensable for securing the ends of the war, and which are lawful according to the modern law and usages of war." So continues Article 15: "Military necessity admits of all direct destruction of life and limb of *armed* enemies, and other persons whose destruction is incidentally *unavoidable* in the armed contests of the war." Yet "military necessity does not admit of cruelty—that is, the infliction of suffering for the sake of suffering or for revenge," explains Article 16. "In general, military necessity does not include any act of hostility which makes the return to peace unnecessarily difficult." Here Lieber updated Vattel's just war philosophy to link "what an army *did* in light of what it aimed to *achieve*." Indeed, as Article 15 concluded, "men who take up arms against one another in public war do not cease on this account to be moral beings, responsible to one another and to God."[136]

Military necessity held belligerents to critical ethical standards. "No conventional restriction of the modes adopted to injure the enemy is any longer admitted," Lieber explained, "but the law of war, imposes many limitations and restriction on principles of justice, faith, and honor." Among the foremost limiting principles was the distinction that Lieber drew between wars of rebellion and civil wars. The latter consisted "between two or more portions of a country or state, each contending for mastery of the whole, and each claiming to be the legitimate government." Such classifications did not apply to the American contest. The Confederacy had established a separate constitutional government, fielded uniformed armies, and sought international recognition separate and distinct from U.S. sovereignty. A rebellion, Lieber wrote in updating Vattel's eighteenth-century definitions, was "usually a war between the legitimate government of a country and portions of provinces of the same who seek to throw off their allegiance to it and set up a government of their own." Lieber thus affirmed that "humanity induces the adoption of the rules of regular war toward rebels," a recognition that did not "imply a partial or complete acknowledgement of their government" or an "independent or sovereign power." The United States treated the Confederacy according to "the law and usages of public war between sovereign belligerents," moderating conduct by holding captured soldiers as formal prisoners of war, acknowledging flags of truce, confiscating belligerent property, and declaring martial law.[137]

Lieber's Code reaffirmed to the world that the United States waged a civilized but limited contest of arms, conferring protections on formal enemy combatants and affording federal armies with necessary means of retaliation against any participant who violated the laws of war. Guerrillas endured particular scrutiny. Deemed "highway robbers or pirates," unlawful combatants were "not entitled to the privileges of prisoners of war," because they operated "without commission, without being part and portion of the organized hostile army." Regarded as barbaric savages whose violence flouted the rules of modern civilization, guerrillas qualified for just retaliation. "Civilized nations acknowledge retaliation as the sternest feature of war," reads Article 27. "A reckless enemy often leaves to his opponent no other means of securing himself against the repetition of barbarous outrage." Executing guerrillas, burning towns that concealed unlawful combatants, and confiscating property all functioned as lawful, civilized retaliations. Appreciating its violent implications, Lieber warned against retaliation "as a measure of mere revenge, but only as a means of protective retribution." Armies could not retaliate for acts not yet committed or against civilians *suspected* of being unlawful combatants. The threat of retaliation not only worked as a deterrent to uncivilized conduct but also permitted in-kind responses to illicit offenses. "Unjust or inconsiderate retaliation removes the belligerents farther and farther from the mitigating rules of regular war, and by rapid steps leads them nearer to the internecine wars of savages."[138]

Retaliation performed well beyond reprisals for unlawful conduct. It also codified claims for combating the entire Confederate insurrection, itself an unjust violation of democratic civilization. As Article 28 stipulates, "Retaliation shall only be resorted to after careful inquiry into the real occurrence, and the character of the misdeeds that may demand retribution." Here Lieber established a remarkably broad legal basis from which Union armies waged an incredibly destructive war against the Confederacy's military infrastructure and the incipient republic's principal institution, slavery. "Private property," announced Article 38, "can be seized only by way of military necessity, for the support or other benefit of the army or of the United States." Though the orders left to field commanders the prerogative of defining "military necessity" and "private property," Lieber's Code forbade on the penalty of death "all wanton violence committed against persons in the invaded country, all destruction of property not commanded by the authorized officer, all robbery, all pillage or sacking, even after taking a place by main force, all rape, wounding, maiming, or killing of such inhabitants." Under Lieber's watchful eye, Union armies would not deteriorate into the very barbarism that they claimed to combat. Soldiers who engaged in wanton, unsanctioned destruction would be held in the republic's contempt. Among its many geniuses, the code absolved the nation and its military forces of uncivilized crimes perpetrated by individuals who exceeded the lawful scope of military necessity.[139]

Lieber's Code upheld emancipation as a combination of martial pragmatism and enlightened humanitarianism. Military necessity demanded the morality of absolute of victory, cleansing the nation of the elements that sparked war in the first place. "The law of nature and nations has never acknowledged [slavery]," Lieber argued, citing Roman law holding "that 'so far as the law of nature is concerned, all men are equal.'" Democracies could never accommodate human bondage, an institution that deprived individual liberty and militarized its propagators. "In a war between the United States and a belligerent which admits of slavery," moral conscience demanded that civilized republics recognize "the rights and privileges of a freeman." Because it was impossible to "enslave any human being," justice necessitated that "a person so made free by the law of war is under the shield of the law of nations." As a reasoned measure of wartime progress, emancipation fell within the scope of military necessity, a tool to frustrate the ability of aristocratic oligarchs to wage current and future wars.[140]

While Lieber approved remarkable military power to combat the Confederacy, his code checked escalations in conduct with legal and rational restraints. "I do not know that any such thing as I design exists in any other country," he admitted about his code, "but in all other countries the Law of War is much more reduced to naked Force or Might, than we are willing to do it, especially now, perhaps, in this Civil War." The Confederacy's unjust bid for slaveholding independence necessitated an equivalent but ethical response, one that met the contingent demands of modern war without undercutting the Union's declaration of moral superiority. Lincoln embraced the same philosophy when he issued the Emancipation Proclamation, which he regarded as "the heaviest blow yet dealt to the rebellion," a logical and even radical war measure. "The constitution invests its commander-in-chief, with the law of war, in time of war," the president reminded a skeptic of emancipation. "Armies the world over, destroy enemies' property when they can not use it; and even destroy their own to keep it from the enemy. Civilized belligerents do all in their power to help themselves, or hurt the enemy, except a few things regarded as barbarous or cruel. Among the exceptions are the massacre of vanquished foes, and non-combatants." While an escalation away from the conciliatory conduct of 1861, emancipation took the place of mass citizen arrests, noncombatant prison camps, and civilian executions, demonstrating instead "that, among free men, there can be no successful appeal from the ballot to the bullet; and that they who take such appeal are sure to lose their case."[141]

Military necessity possessed a distinct political component. Loyal Democrats routinely advanced Vattel's writings to argue that Republicans had exceeded the limits of a just and civilized war. The suspension of habeas corpus, expansive executive authority, confiscation and emancipation, and General Orders No. 100 all reeked of antidemocratic profligacy, shattering the very liberties, political institutions, and social norms that a war for Union was supposed to uphold. Vattel, they charged, preached that civilized war required profound restraints lest the people's liberties be forever curtailed, conferring unprecedented power to a central state and embittering the process of postwar reconciliation. Democrats indicted Lincoln for using the veil of war to target political dissent, a cherished civil liberty in a free republic. Given that he jailed opponents "in the dead of night ... in a distant and unknown dungeon," protested the prominent Democratic organ *New York World*, "the President is as absolute a despot as the Sultan of Turkey." Whether they fell in with the War Democrats—who supported prosecuting the rebellion with moderate means—or the Peace Democrats—who favored immediate peace and reconciliation with white southerners on the status quo antebellum—a preponderance of the party consented that Republicans escalated an unjust war that defied their electoral mandate. "If to-day, we secure peace, and begin the work of reunion, we shall yet escape," announced Ohio representative Clement Vallandigham, the loudest voice of Peace Democratic opposition. "If not, I see nothing before us but universal political and social revolution, anarchy, and bloodshed, compared with which the Reign of Terror in France was a merciful visitation." Republicans had transformed an otherwise limited domestic political dispute into "one of the worst despotisms of the earth," embracing "an arbitrary power which neither the Czar of Russia, nor the Emperor of Austria dare exercise."[142]

Democratic critiques forced Republicans and even the Union army to test the legal and political limits of military necessity. As commander of the Department of Ohio, Gen. Ambrose E. Burnside acted within the bounds of General Orders No. 100 when he arrested Vallandigham in May 1863. Concerned that Vallandigham's incendiary rhetoric deterred the recruitment of new volunteers, Burnside justified the arrest within the scope of Article 155: "Disloyal citizens may further be classified into those citizens known to sympathize with the rebellion without positively aiding it, and those who, without taking up arms, give positive aid and comfort to the rebellious enemy." Vallandigham stood trial before a military commission, which found him guilty of violating martial law as defined by the "common law of nations," now codified for the Federal war effort as General Orders No. 100. The commission sentenced the

Ohio congressman to prison for the duration of the war, but Lincoln moderated the verdict, only expelling Vallandigham from the United States as a free man. The Supreme Court soon upheld the military commission and the president's judgment. Though a lifelong Democrat, Justice James Moore Wayne judged Burnside's conduct "in conformity with [Lieber's Code] approved by the President of the United States."[143]

Republicans had effectively wielded the rule of law to target excessive wartime dissent, which they claimed hindered efforts to conquer the rebellion. But as a critical feature of democratic moderation, Democrats remained a loyal political opposition, advancing reasoned arguments from which the people could decide which of the two parties should prosecute the war. "It is the mission of the Opposition party not to break down or enfeeble the federal government, but to get possession of it and administer it on constitutional principles," averred the *New York World*. "The function of an opposition party is negative. It is to expose administrative corruption, resist bad measures, and stand up against infractions of the Constitution." Yet Republicans maintained a nearly immortal resource: the broad discretion outlined in international law and the U.S. Constitution with which to wage war. "Some politicians seem to ignore the fact that there is a vast difference between war and peace, and insist that war shall be carried on just as we carry on peace. They do not comprehend that war, from its very nature, involves the exercise of powers, which, in times of peace, are unnecessary, and are prohibited," Oliver P. Morton, the Republican governor of Indiana, reminded Democratic dissidents. Enhanced war powers, echoed *Harper's Weekly*, were temporary expedients through which to combat an exceptionally hostile belligerent. "The president of the United States has ... been created Dictator, with almost supreme power over liberty, property, and life—a power nearly as extensive and as irresponsible as that wielded by the Emperors of Russia, France or China. And this is well. To succeed in a struggle such as we are waging a strong central Government is indispensable."[144]

Lincoln nonetheless remained sensitive to charges of dictatorship. At once to undercut Democratic critiques, to demonstrate the moderation of military necessity, and to underscore the purpose of Union, Lincoln in December 1863 issued the Proclamation of Amnesty and Reconstruction. "All persons who have, directly or by implication, participated in the existing rebellion ... a full pardon is hereby granted to them and each of them, with restoration of all rights of property, except as to slaves." Though it exempted high-ranking Confederate civil and military officials, the decree invited the great mass of civilians and common soldiers to renounce their loyalty to the false republic, swear devotion to the Union, and reclaim their full constitutional protections. Lincoln further outlined a remarkably conservative process of state restoration in which loyal citizens drafted new constitutions that outlawed slavery and disavowed secession. The states themselves would retain their original names, boundaries, and equitable position in the federal constellation. The proclamation reminded the world that the Union waged a moderate war for national restoration in which neither its armies nor their civilian authorities exacted unjust retribution upon conquered foes. Lincoln clarified these aims in his December 1864 message to Congress when he concluded, "In stating a single condition of peace I mean simply to say that the war will cease on the part of the Government whenever it shall have ceased on the part of those who began it."[145]

Lincoln did not conduct a naive overture of white reconciliation in offering amnesty. The executive pardon power was one of the foremost tools of political moderation in the constitutional tradition. In a world governed by reactionary rulers who wielded powerful monopolies on statecraft, a republic maintained its legitimacy by preserving vibrant political opposition and even pardoning treasonous rebels for heinous national crimes. Absolving domestic enemies of the state meant retaining them within a national community, which held civil and political equality in higher regard than partisan animus. Clemency stemmed insurrectionary spirits, forestalled bitter faction, and reunited the national family once divorced by fratricidal militance. A democratic government, Lincoln implied, *could* restrain its passions even in the most appalling national trials. Pursuing malice would render impossible a peaceful, lasting reunion. Amnesty transcended licentious violence, the sordid antithesis of republican liberty for which Union armies fought. Long concerned that base passions would overwhelm practical reason, Lincoln's proclamation underscored the precise purpose of just war and lawful retaliation: extend an olive branch so that any future hostility espoused by Confederates would expose slaveholding rebels before the world as violent opponents to peace. Enemies were punished, he explained, only insofar as their ability to practice war was impaired. The loyal citizenry and their armies "can properly have no motive of revenge, no purpose to punish merely for punishment's sake. While we must, by all available means, prevent the overthrow of the government, we should avoid planting and cultivating too many thorns in the bosom of society."[146]

Lincoln's cautious instructions permeated the ranks of Maj. Gen. William Tecumseh Sherman's Union armies, which conducted some of the American Civil War's most celebrated, infamous, and misunderstood campaigns. Few mid-nineteenth-century American military minds better comprehended the principle of just war and applied the concept of military necessity better than Sherman. At once relentless and restrained, his grand marches through Georgia and the Carolinas between the autumn of 1864 and the spring of 1865 organized the Union's broad array of military policies to target Confederate infrastructure and civilian psychology in search of a definitive peace. From the destruction of belligerent property, to the confiscation and redistribution of former slaveholders' lands to freedpeople, to Union armies cutting broad swaths of targeted devastation against the sources of rebellion, Sherman's actions were sanctioned by congressional statutes, executive order, Lieber's Code, and international law. Sometimes mischaracterized as the practitioner of modern total war, the figurehead whose seemingly ruthless excesses portended the unimaginable scale of twentieth-century warfare, Sherman instead acted in accordance with nineteenth-century notions of moral and civilized war.[147]

Several weeks before he forced the capitulation of Atlanta, an event that would safeguard the reelection of President Lincoln and initiate the imposing March to the Sea, Sherman corresponded in September 1864 with an old friend from Kentucky about the conditions of the American Civil War. Remembering that the rule of law and popular democracy had long governed domestic affairs, Sherman remarked, "Our hitherto political and private differences were settled by debate, or vote, or decree of a court." Yet the slaveholding South had "dared us to war" to resolve the irreconcilable entanglement between egalitarian and slaveholding civilizations. "We are still willing to return to that system"—the democratic-republican arrangement that had conceived an American Union that stood apart from the world's tyrannical monarchies—"but our adversaries say no, and appeal to war." In a turn of phrase that perhaps only Sherman could have concocted, he proclaimed, "War is the remedy our enemies have chosen.... I say let us give them all they want; not a word of argument, not a sign of let up, no cave in till we are whipped or they are." Peace would dawn only "when one or the other party gives in, [and] we will be the better friends."[148]

When he declared that "war is the remedy," Sherman voiced a consensual faith that free societies acquiesced to military solutions when politics miscarried and peaceful alternatives failed to reconcile incompatible differences. Contrary to postwar mythmaking, Sherman did not conceive of war in unlimited terms, nor did he see it as a senseless, interminable exercise that wrought needless destruction on society. Military affairs instead assumed critical roles in charting the course of nations. Nothing less than the future of a republic depended on the success or failure of armed conflict. Sherman deplored the "general anarchy" occasioned when free societies renounced reason, law, and ordered liberty. "The law is and should be our king," he observed during the secession winter of 1861; "we should obey it, not because it meets our approval but because it is necessary to every system of civilized government." Recognizing the democratic passions sparked by the ardor of liberty, he warned against "substitut[ing] mere opinions for law." Chaos and unrestricted bloodshed, the tools of local, national, and global despots, would supplant social stability and legal restraint if free societies did not check their militant democratic tendencies. War cured the internal infections that riddled a national body.[149]

Sherman's distaste of lawless anarchy permeated his wartime writings and shaped his military conduct. Echoing Lieber and Halleck, Sherman believed that ending war proved just as critical as waging war. Extinguishing the uncompromising elements that instigated armed conflict underscored the central purpose for any civilized belligerent. "We must have peace . . . in all America," he explained in 1864 to the mayor and city council of Atlanta. "To secure this, we must stop the war that now desolates our once happy and favored country. To stop war, we must defeat the rebel armies which are arrayed against the laws and Constitution that all must respect and obey." For Sherman, the alternative was clear. "You cannot have peace and a division of our country. If the United States submits to a division now, it will not stop, but will go on until we reap the fate of Mexico, which is eternal war." The Union could neither emulate unruly Central American nations nor embrace the populist radicals and central statists of Europe. If it did, the United States would join the world's failed republics that collapsed through anarchical civil violence. Waging a just war meant effecting a permanent peace that fashioned an everlasting national stability. War and division were thus the exceptions — not the rules — to the foundation of civilization. "This may not be war," he concluded, "but rather statesmanship." [150]

"Statesmanship" underscored Sherman's faith in conducting a just war. As he explained to the mayor of Atlanta, the United States did not seek irrevocable punishment for the South more than it sought to preserve the moderation of constitutional republicanism. The secessionist slaveholding aristocracy had to be held responsible, if not dismantled, for sparking the awful national conflagration. "Whilst I would not remit one job or title of our nation's right in peace or war, I do make allowances for past political errors or prejudices," Sherman wrote in January 1864, outlining his philosophy on martial retaliation. "To those who submit to the rightful law and authority all gentleness and forbearance, but to the petulant and persistent Secessionists, why, death is mercy." Those who returned to the Union would enjoy the bounties of civilization and the blessings of national accord. With regard to those white southerners who chose war, he professed, "We cannot change the hearts of those people, but we can make war so terrible that they will realize the fact that, however brave and gallant and devoted to their country, still they are mortal and should exhaust all peaceful remedies before they fly to war." Far from a war of vindictive annihilation against noncombatants, Sherman's rhetoric and military actions in Georgia and South Carolina complemented Vattel and Lieber's recognition that humans administered war to maintain peace. "War is hell," but "[it is] the grand machinery by which this world is governed" — an unpleasant but rational process of national restoration. [151]

A lasting peace came from a prodigious but targeted demonstration of force like the world had never before seen. As Lieber explained, civilized war demanded blunt martial dynamism to stem mounting tides of violence. "It is overwhelming to my mind that there are thousands of people abroad and in the South who reason thus," Sherman explained to U. S. Grant: "If the North can march an army right through the South, it is proof positive that the North can prevail." Hardly provincial and narrow-minded, Sherman considered his brand of warfare laden with global implications. The United States' battle against disputatious upheaval must be validated before an international community skeptical of democratic legitimacy. "If we can march a well-appointed army right through [Confederate] territory, it is a demonstration to the world, foreign and domestic, that we have a power which [Jefferson] Davis cannot resist." The fate of nations was secured on the field of battle. But for Sherman, the *legitimacy* of nations was sanctioned by order, stability, and control. And he was bent on demonstrating for the world the Confederacy's spurious claims of nationhood, showcasing the slaveholding republic's humiliating inability to maintain its territorial sovereignty and endure the very war of independence that it had foolishly instigated.[152]

Sherman did not possess a concept of "total war"; he recognized that careful restraints must balance the conduct of modern mid-nineteenth-century nation-states. Because he understood the Union's war as a contest to restore the promise of American civilization, Sherman never considered arbitrary or excessive abuse the obvious means of national restoration. He sensed that the American Civil War was somehow distinct from history's great conflicts. "In Europe, whence we derive our principles of war, wars are between kings or rulers through hired armies, and not between peoples." No matter how rebellious, no matter how terrible the war they wrought, the foes of Union were, in Sherman's estimation, *people*—and a free people at that. "Should we treat as absolute enemies all in the South who differ from us in opinion or prejudice, kill or banish them, or should we give them time to think and gradually change their conduct so as to conform to the new order of things which is slowly and gradually creeping into their country?" The answer was self-evident. "Let every thought of the mind, every feeling of the heart, every movement of a human muscle all be directed to one sole object, Successful War and consequent Peace, and you have the ideal I aim at," he professed. "God will not permit this fair land and this Brave People to subside into the anarchy and despotism that Jeff Davis had cut out for them." A just and civil war at once compelled the stunning use of force and disavowed gratuitous "anarchy and despotism."[153]

Given that the Civil War was waged of, by, and for democracies, Sherman distinguished the American contest from global conflicts. "This war differs from European wars in this particular," he disclosed in late 1864. "We are not only fighting hostile armies, but a hostile people, and must make old and young, rich and poor, feel the hard hand of war." Sherman nonetheless conducted his campaigns with attendant restraint, targeting Confederates' ability to make war and stifling their claims to nationhood. "War," he conceded in 1863, "at best is barbarism, but to involve all—children, women and helpless—is more than can be justified." His close friend U. S. Grant agreed. Although he deemed utter "conquest" the fruit of victory, Grant "regarded it as humane to both sides to protect the persons of those found at their homes, but to consume everything that could be used to support and supply the armies." Their collective campaigns through Tennessee, Mississippi, Georgia, and the Carolinas, joined with Union army commander Philip H. Sheridan's targeted devastation of Virginia's Shenandoah Valley in 1864, wrecked infrastructure, property, and food stocks used by Confederate civilians and armies to sustain their nation at war.[154]

Some might indict Sherman's armies ostensibly for introducing to the North American continent the infamous *chevauchée*, an Old World raiding strategy bound by few restraints. Pre-Enlightenment European armies pillaged and raped, torched landscapes, sullied food sources, murdered civilians, and obliterated sacred houses of worship. They left in their wake sacked cities, overwhelming refugee crises, and survivors who lived under the daunting weight of military tyrants. Yet, as historian Mark Grimsley notes, "the America of 1864–1865 witnessed a new *chevauchée*—as systematic and extensive as anything Europe had seen, yet also more enlightened, because it was conducted not by brutes but by men from good families, with strong moral values that stayed their hands as often as they impelled retribution." Sherman's just war philosophy infused the ranks of his armies. Union soldiers generally subscribed to their commanders' wishes as they foraged liberally, wrecked railroads, destroyed agriculture, and burned selected properties. They rarely cut swaths of subjective destruction that violated a broad understanding of military necessity, and they did not target civilians for summary punishment.[155]

Volunteer soldiers understood the intimate political work of wartime destruction. "Here is where treason began and, by God, here is where it shall end!" declared one of Sherman's soldiers as the army entered South Carolina in early 1865. The Palmetto State endured overwhelming abuse from Sherman's forces, who identified the state as the home of disunion, the locus of the nation's terrible strife, the source of death for hundreds of thousands of fellow Union soldiers. Unlike during their earlier marches through Georgia, Sherman's troops set South Carolina ablaze, burning private homes, fields, whole communities, and Columbia, the state capital. But there was a distinct purpose embedded in the terrible infernos: white southerners, one soldier concluded, "will never want to seceed again." And when the army later entered North Carolina, "not a house was burned," observed another soldier, "and the army gave to the people more than it took from them." Though complete in its destruction and transformative in its implication, military necessity furnished the legal means to rehabilitate the national political community, to assimilate violent, wayward rebels into peaceful and loyal citizens of the Union. As Sherman later recorded, "Though I never ordered [the burning of Columbia] and never wished it, I have never shed many tears over the events, because I believe it hastened what we all fought for, the end of the war."[156]

Civilized military conduct in the just war tradition contained its own subtle but critical limitations. The confiscation of property, military emancipation, and widespread devastation to infrastructure and communities did not trade legal restraints for gross atrocity. Executions, hangings, and flagrant acts against civilians and prisoners of war, while rare in the American conflict, tested the boundaries of civilization and functioned decidedly outside the international laws of war. "In the midst of a civil war of unequalled magnitude and severity," Lincoln recognized in his October 1863 Thanksgiving Proclamation, "peace has been preserved with all nations, order has been maintained, the laws have been respected and obeyed, and harmony has prevailed everywhere except in the theatre of military conflict." While Lincoln reflected on the scope and meaning of belligerent restraint, nineteenth-century Americans also understood just war itself largely as a cultural contract between *white* actors. George B. McClellan's "truly loyal men," "rebel masses," and "all foreign nations," joined by Lincoln's "civilized belligerents," defined public warfare as restricted contests framed by Anglo assumptions and practiced by Anglo institutions. As was so often the case in the exercise of American life, seen in the 1862 Dakota War and the 1864 Sand Creek Massacre, perceptions of racial barbarism injected impossibly complicated dimensions into the conduct of the American Civil War. Emancipation and African American wartime participation further challenged Union and Confederate moderation, as the lingering and seemingly irreconcilable specter of race came to fracture the very foundation of a just war.[157]

5
Insurrection
★ ★ ★

In the three decades since David Walker petitioned freed and enslaved people to unite against American slaveholders, the United States had grown into the world's uncontested slaveholding power. Fashioning the nation-state into the chief protectorate of human bondage, slaveholders had eyed the American West, the Caribbean, and Central and South America as sprawling lands in which to plant slavery's future. By the late 1850s, they were confident about their place in modern world. They had grown anxious, however, about their status in the Union. In response to the hemispheric emancipations well underway, John Brown's abolitionist raid on Harpers Ferry in 1859, and the election in 1860 of the antislavery restrictionist Abraham Lincoln to the presidency, slaveholders sparked a rapid series of events that, by 1861, broke the Union, removed the Deep South into the protective confines of a new slaveholding republic, and incited a massive war.[1]

The zealous black abolitionist Martin Delany also sensed the dramatic national shift. After witnessing the devastating effects of the 1850s on the African American community—the brutal Fugitive Slave Law, the rapid expansion of slaveholding power, and the demoralizing implications of the *Dred Scott* decision—Delany himself was disillusioned, seeking refuge for his people anywhere outside the United States. Conceiving of the entire Atlantic world as an interminable conflict between slavery and freedom, Delany published the first installments of a novel, which, though unintentionally, picked up where Walker's *Appeal* left off. In *Blake, or the Huts of America*, which appeared periodically between 1859 and 1861 in the *Weekly Anglo-African* newspaper, Delaney responded to the Slave Power's imperial designs throughout the 1850s, telling the cosmopolitan story of Henry Blake, an enslaved man in Mississippi whose wife is sold to a planter in Cuba. Outraged, Blake travels to Canada to organize recruits for a grand insurrection throughout the South and in the Caribbean. The novel imagines a sweeping global revolt against slavery, one originating in the American South, traveling to Cuba, collapsing the world's great slaveholding empires, and transforming Africa into a haven of black emigration.[2]

Delany understood the deeply entangled networks of hemispheric slaveholders. "Few people in the world lead such a life as the white inhabitants of Cuba, and those of the South now comprising the 'Southern Confederacy of America,'" he opined toward the end of the novel. "A dreamy existence of the

24th Regt. U.S. Colored Troops. Let Soldiers in War, Be Citizens in Peace, *ca. 1865.*
Approximately 180,000 African American men—many of whom were enslaved to
Confederates at the beginning of the war—marched in the Union army, symbolizing
the rapid wartime transformations in American social and political life. Their
service as legitimate volunteers in national military institutions justified their
demands for civil rights and equal citizenship in the very republic that once
endorsed their enslavement. Confederates defined and engaged the U.S. Colored
Troops as unlawful insurrectionists who waged an unjust war against the
slaveholding republic. (William A. Gladstone Collection, Library of Congress)

most fearful apprehensions, of dread, horror and dismay; suspicion and distrust, jealousy and envy continually pervade the community; and Havana, New Orleans, Charleston or Richmond may be thrown into consternation by an idle expression of the most trifling or ordinary ignorant black." Despite their seemingly firm grip on all aspects of life, hemispheric slaveholders appear deeply vulnerable in Delany's tale. "A sleeping wake or waking sleep," he continued, "a living death or tormented life is that of the Cuban and American slaveholder." The most potent threat to the Slave Power resided in the very enslaved people on whom the entire system of bondage functioned. Blake thus appears as David Walker prophesied in the *Appeal*, leading a slave army, cleansing through violence the lands of oppression. "I am for war—war upon the whites," Blake declares. "'I come to bring deliverance to the captive and freedom to the bond.' Your destiny is my destiny; the end of one will be the end of all." And the novel ends with Blake's ominous but prophetic avowal "Woe be unto those devils of whites, I say!"[3]

Delany's *Blake* framed the international context in which myriad African Americans regarded the Civil War, which began during the story's serial publication. Just as slaveholders imagined themselves as progressive cosmopolitans, African Americans regarded abolitionism as a global crusade. "They have no moral right to hold rule over us," Blake tells his compatriots on the eve of their uprising in Cuba. "What say you, brethren, shall we rise against our oppressors and strike for liberty, or will we remain in degradation and bondage?" The fate of Atlantic slavery would follow one of two paths: either slaveholders would yield to emancipation, or they would conquer a flagging hemisphere. Thus, for black Americans, the Civil War was much more than a political conflict over the contested meaning of Union. That wars accelerated social change portended that the battle between slavery and freedom would be forever settled in the conflict's wake. The history of the modern slaveholding world—from Haiti to Demerara, from Barbados to Jamaica, and from John Brown to Abraham Lincoln—demonstrated that only armed conflict provoked immediate and decisive antislavery action.[4]

After decades of political mobilization, militant resistance, and identification with both the Haitian and American revolutionary traditions, African Americans in 1861 acted out David Walker and Martin Delaney's prophecies when disunion sparked war. Seeing the conflict as an uncompromising Haitian-style referendum on slavery, enslaved and free people of color demanded an active role in shattering the institution and dismantling the slaveholding regime. But many also saw the war as an American-style referendum on democratic liberty, which they declared could be protected only within a constitutional Union finally cleansed of slaveholding. Honed throughout the antebellum era, African Americans' bold wartime dialogue and actions— particularly men's service in United States armies—shaped how emancipation unfolded, but also summoned uncertain and even terrified reactions from white Unionists and especially from Confederates. While myriad black Americans saw the war as the long-awaited moment to strike for freedom, other whites imagined the conflict deteriorating into the Atlantic world's largest and most chilling race war. By 1861, the Age of Revolution had collided with the Age of Emancipation. And although he did not live to see it, David Walker's war had finally come.[5]

Race, Union, and the Limits of Colonization

Spurred by an acute political awareness, African Americans embraced the Civil War as the seminal moment to strike a resolute, unconditional blow against slaveholding. In national pamphlets, public addresses, and novels, free people of color and their white allies called on the enslaved to redeem the Atlantic revolutionary past. For Osborn Perry Anderson, one of a handful of black men who aided John Brown's raid at Harpers Ferry, the war arrived as the Atlantic world's latest liberation movement. "There is an unbroken chain of sentiment and purpose," he declared, "from Moses of the Jews to John Brown of America; from Kossuth, and the liberators of France and Italy, to the untutored Gabriel, and the Denmark Veseys, Nat Turners and Madison Washingtons of the Southern American States." For Anderson, emancipation was not a gradual process. In fact, it was not even a process at all. It was humanity's natural state, depending on aggressive force to remain alive. The war, according to a free black Pennsylvanian, thus could not end "till every slave in the South is set free." From cracking whips to blood-soaked backs, the horrors of human bondage were relics of a barbaric past, destined to die on American battlefields. "In a Christian land—in the 19th century," concluded the writer, shocked that such a regressive institution could still live in the modern world, "oh, if there be a God of mercy and justice, how fearful is the crime of those who uphold slavery!"[6]

Haiti epitomized this revolutionary recognition. A contributor to the *Weekly Anglo-African* petitioned the enslaved to "emulate" the Haitian heroes, while writers from William Wells Brown to James Redpath to Martin Delany justified the violent conduct of Haiti's warriors on the grounds of slavery's inherent evil. Indeed, the central theme in *Blake* stresses that black mobilization and organization could yield successful insurrections throughout the slaveholding world. Cuba and the United States would transform just as "Hayti is a noble self-emancipated nation," a character in the novel explains. And Charles Sumner, a strident white abolitionist, even encouraged "SLAVE INSURRECTION" against Confederates, whose faith in human bondage warranted their destruction. "When they rose against a paternal government," Sumner wrote of secessionists, "they set the example of insurrection, which has carried death to so many firesides. They cannot complain if their slaves, with better reason, follow it."[7]

As soon as the war commenced, African Americans petitioned the government to serve in the ranks of freedom's army. Seeing the conflict as a contest between slavery and liberty, the war dawned as Providence's deliverance from bondage. "The set time has come when the numerous promises of God to Africa is about to be fulfilled," Henry Highland Garnet predicted while visiting London in September 1861. "The system of negro slavery is rapidly passing away, and ere long it will thunder to the ground." Steadying himself for the impending conflict, Garnet vowed "to renew my strength to enter the field ... for I am enlisted for the war." Yet other editors and contributors to black newspapers agreed that their brethren must approach the war with restraint, stemming a burning desire to set ablaze the Confederate nation. Only participation in national institutions, such as the U.S. Army, offered the most effective means of collapsing the slaveholding order. Despite the passionate Haitian-style rhetoric that encouraged insurrection against Confederates, black leaders urged moderation in the quest for emancipation. Forming sovereign bands of militant free and enslaved people would almost certainly align Confederates with nations of the world to crush such an obvious racial uprising, ending any hope of liberation. "Let the slaves and free colored people be called into service, and formed into a liberating army, to march into the South and raise the banner of Emancipation among the slaves," Frederick Douglass announced on the pages of his monthly digest. Uniting toward the promises of freedom and equality had to be tied to civic participation in organized public institutions guided by the legitimate standards of the state.[8]

Douglass understood that war produced the requisite instability to strike for immediate freedom, unlike the slow legislative processes of West Indian abolition. He did not have to look beyond his own hemisphere for proof of instant military emancipation. Douglass could not contain his excitement when Giuseppe Garibaldi, the freedom fighter who battled for Italian liberation in 1848 and subsequently led a campaign of emancipation in Brazil, petitioned the U.S. government for a generalship in the Union army. Pledging his own biracial army, Garibaldi requested only one condition of his service to the Union. "Tell me," he asked the Americans, "if this agitation is regarding the emancipation of the Negroes or not." Like Douglass, Garibaldi envisioned the Civil War sparking a series of emancipations that would consume all slaveholding lands from the American South to Brazil. And he assured the Union, which was in desperate need of his services in the summer of 1861, that "draw[ing] my sword for the cause of the United States, [would be] for the abolition of Slavery, full, unconditional." When Abraham Lincoln's government refused in early 1861 and the spring of 1862 to commit to a war for emancipation—and rejected petitions from hundreds of African Americans to serve in the military—Douglass could not restrain his incredulity. "Such a course ... would bring not only Garibaldi and his twenty thousand Italian braves to our side, but what is more important still, our own sense of right, and the sympathy of the enlightened and humane men throughout the world."[9]

Garibaldi's appeal, Douglass's exasperation, and Lincoln's refusal under-scored the yawning chasm separating abolitionists from moderates in their collective war for Union. While African Americans and their white allies saw the war as a moment for immediate emancipation, a path that would place the United States in orbit with the community of enlightened nations, they comprised a small fraction within the antislavery coalition. The Lincoln administration approached early questions of military emancipation with remarkable caution. From black rhetoric of a second Haitian Revolution to Garibaldi's bold promise for immediate liberation, Lincoln and moderate whites feared a limited contest for constitutional democracy spiraling into an uncontrollable race war. Dread of such an unthinkable insurrection joined Lincoln's pragmatic political concerns about alienating the fragile Border States, estranging skeptical Democrats from the Union war effort, aligning once loyal white southerners with Confederates in a death struggle against the enslaved, and summoning European intervention into an unmanageable war.[10]

Nonetheless, as early as 1861, thousands of enslaved people absconded from their plantations, destabilizing both the Confederate home front and the Union armies to which they fled. Societal disruptions caused great consternation among moderate whites. Would runaways enlist free people of color to massacre slaveholders? Would Confederates retaliate and trigger an internal civil war? Would the ballooning numbers of fugitives hamper ongoing Union military operations? In fact, did slavery have any meaning when those once held in bondage were so able to undermine the institution? White Unionists accepted, just as African Americans had long understood, that the rapid pace of war often shaped unanticipated and perhaps revolutionary moments of change. Worried about an escalating humanitarian crisis and concerned about an intensifying military struggle, the U.S. government responded to "slave politics" by legislating conditions of wartime liberation. From identifying runaways as "contraband" of war to recognizing the permanent freedom of those who reached Union armies, the federal government encouraged African Americans to pursue their own emancipation.[11]

Hoping to circumvent a second Haitian Revolution while aligning with the broader Atlantic's antislavery gradualism, the Union imposed moderate limits on black immediatism. At the heart of this effort stood colonization, Abraham Lincoln's preferred method to avoid overt racial revolution at the expense of a cautious emancipation. At the beginning of the war, Lincoln petitioned Border State slaveholders to forfeit their property through gradual emancipation with just financial compensation. Following in the long abolitionist tradition throughout the Atlantic world—in stark contrast to Haiti—Lincoln imagined a slow, decades-long emancipation unfolding in the United States. Only then would sectional toxicity finally be squelched and the extreme social implications wrought by the slaveholders' war carefully evaded. However, when the Border States rejected Lincoln's offer, the president then renewed his efforts toward colonization, a transnational solution to the domestic problem of race in a white republic.[12]

Colonization had long been the favored option among many moderate whites—including a sizable portion of slaveholders in the early republic—who feared the dangerous concentration of enslaved people inhabiting a rapidly expanding nation. Colonizationists conceded that a densely populated slave society would inevitably explode into a catastrophic race war. In 1814, Thomas Jefferson predicted an unavoidable black liberation, "whether brought on by the generous energy of our own minds; or by the bloody process of St. Domingo." As he acknowledged several years later, "Nothing is more certainly written in the book of fate than that these people are to be free." Jefferson alleged nonetheless that people of African descent could not be assimilated into a white republican civilization. That "the two races, equally free, cannot live in the same government" necessitated "an asylum to which we can, by degrees, send the whole of that population from among us, and establish them under our patronage and protection, as a separate, free and independent people, in some country and climate friendly to human life and happiness." Colonizationists believed, on the one hand, that seemingly pugnacious people of color were crafty enough to organize a massive insurrection, and, on the other, that enslaved people had seemingly not yet evolved enough to participate in a modern democracy. Only the deliberate, consistent, state-sponsored exodus of African Americans would exempt the United States from the horrors that once toppled thriving slave societies.[13]

Abraham Lincoln had endorsed Jefferson's brand of colonization throughout the 1850s, outlining his "first impulse" as "free[ing] all the slaves, and send[ing] them to Liberia." Emigration would cure the dangerous infection wrought by slavery to American social and political institutions. Indeed, "the separation of the races is the only perfect preventative of amalgamation," and "such separation ... must be effected by colonization." When Lincoln in 1852 eulogized Henry Clay, his personal hero and a foremost antebellum colonizationist, he charged that black emigration would "succeed in freeing our land from the dangerous presence of slavery; and at the same time, in restoring a captive people to their long-lost father-land, with bright prospects for the future." Only in Africa, so went the argument, could black Americans enjoy the full fruits of liberty, while sparing whites the strife of racial integration. The upheaval of civil war only expedited Lincoln's faith in colonization. During his annual message to Congress in December 1861, he advised that enslaved people "be at once deemed free," followed by colonization "at some place, or places, in a climate congenial to them. It might be well to consider too," the president counseled, "whether the free colored people already in the United States could not ... be included in such colonization."[14]

Perhaps discomfited by the bellicose rhetoric of African Americans who judged the war as a moment to strike for immediate liberation—"No nation has ever or ever will be emancipated from slavery," a black writer noted in October 1861, "but by the sword wielded too by their own strong arms"— Lincoln likely saw the advent of war as the zenith of colonizationist prophecy. Long fearing the collapse of social order and long convinced that black and white could not coexist socially, Lincoln judged colonization to be a useful tool to blunt rapid and violent wartime transformations. "On this whole proposition," he continued in his congressional message, "does not the expediency amount to absolute necessity—that, without which the government itself cannot be perpetuated?" For Lincoln, preservation of the Union was a multifaceted enterprise. Democracy had to be spared from reckless political revolutionaries who chose to rupture the nation rather than abide by the free electoral process. The Union also had to be protected from the unthinkable prospects of race war. But always the shrewd politician, Lincoln likewise advanced colonization to condition large swaths of the northern public to accept the possible reality of emancipation. Should slavery dissolve so swiftly through the tumult of war, colonization moderated the radical social changes brought to a white republic skeptical of black freedom.[15]

The twin fears of racial insurrection and national insecurity further informed Lincoln's colonization proposal. "In considering the policy to be adopted for suppressing the [war], I have been anxious and careful that the inevitable conflict for this purpose shall not degenerate into a violent and remorseless revolutionary struggle." The volatility of civil war necessitated judicious programs to diffuse slavery's fury. Early wartime emancipation policies—the "contraband order," the Confiscation Acts, and Lincoln's dalliance with colonization—encouraged the enslaved to pursue freedom all while abating insurrectionist tendencies. The dramatic act of escaping plantations hampered Confederate war-making abilities. Those who reached Union army lines would not be returned to slavery. The U.S. government would shelter and legitimize black freedom, no matter how limited or ambiguous that freedom was. And the ultimate removal to overseas locales deemed better fit for people of African descent would temper the rocky transition from slavery to freedom.[16]

Early experiments in wartime emancipation, including Lincoln's pursuit of colonization, grew from white fears that slavery had transformed African Americans into hostile belligerents. According to a *Harper's Weekly* writer deeply ambivalent about black bellicosity, any gesture toward emancipation, no matter how moderate or fledgling, needed to prevent the enslaved from rebelling outright while assuaging white fears about black liberation. Meeting enslaved resistance on its own terms—encouraging and channeling runaways' desires for freedom—cooled the bubbling cauldron of resentment within the enslaved community. The Haitian Revolution, the author explained, "was terrible, but it was not the result of emancipation.... It was the consequence of slavery." Countering the proslavery argument that any form of abolition would prompt a deadly race war, the author rejoined in April 1862 that the Caribbean uprising began three years *prior* to emancipation because "the trouble of insurrection springs from slavery, and not from liberty." Enslavement antagonized the raw yearning for freedom, flouted the laws of nature, and stoked the embers of vengeance. "The point for us all to remember," the editorial concluded, "is that it is always more dangerous to the public peace to treat men as brutes than as human beings." A restrained form of emancipation thus provided a safe, pragmatic alternative to enslaved bellicosity, forestalling a white civil war from transforming into a cataclysmic race war.[17]

From the earliest days of the struggle, the Lincoln administration pursued colonizationist options throughout the Atlantic triangle, citing Guatemala, Chiriqui (a region in modern-day Colombia), Haiti, and Liberia as ideal destinations. The Union even extended formal recognition to Haiti and Liberia, granting legitimacy to each as optimal termini for black émigrés. Colonization, Lincoln vowed in an August 1862 meeting with free black leaders at the White House, legitimized emancipation while checking the excesses of white and black integration. The conference, which took place during a critical military and diplomatic moment, sought to enlist African American support for colonization through executive assurances that emancipation thereafter would be a formal wartime policy. Lincoln hoped to demonstrate to the world that a relatively sudden emancipation—a key measure in hindering the Confederate war effort—would not shatter the stability of race and Union.[18]

The president acknowledged slavery's immorality and told the black delegates, "Your race are suffering, in my judgment, the greatest wrong inflicted on any people." Slaveholding severed the most sacred bonds of justice, divorcing all humanity from a natural equality. "You and we are different races," Lincoln explained. "We have between us a broader difference than exists between almost any other two races." However, the president believed that the unique and terrible circumstances of American slavery had imposed deleterious effects on both black and white, rendering each unfit to live abreast in the same republic. That unfortunate reality "affords a reason at least why we should be separated." Lincoln's formative years in Kentucky, Indiana, and Illinois had likely offered little evidence that the two races could coexist in any meaningful social equality. Despite the self-evident truth that all humans shared a common liberty, the president alleged that slavery had stunted the moral growth of former bondpeople who now sought inclusion within a republic. American civilization, already threatened by the weight of civil war, could not withstand the abrupt assimilation of a group ostensibly alien to the demands of virtuous citizenship. "Even when you cease to be slaves, you are yet far removed from being placed on an equality with the white race. You are cut off from many of the advantages which the other race enjoy." Lincoln argued that black "intellects are clouded by Slavery" and that "on this broad continent, not a single man of your race is made the equal of a single man of ours." While he recognized slavery's devastating implications for national harmony and reminded his audience of his personal hatred of the institution, Lincoln contended, "But for your race among us there could not be war," and "it is better for us both, therefore, to be separated."[19]

Lincoln further anticipated extending free labor throughout the hemisphere, undercutting the Confederacy's dream of a powerful empire of slavery. African Americans living abroad would thus spread American civilization to nations in desperate need of moral cultivation, especially in Central America, where "the political affairs . . . are not in quite as satisfactory condition as I wish." Allegedly predisposed to hot, humid environments and inured to hard labor, black people would thrive naturally in tropical climates, linking commercial enterprises along "a great highway from the Atlantic or Caribbean Sea to the Pacific Ocean." Only in a pan-hemispheric setting would black Americans be able to realize the promise of liberty denied them in the United States. Colonizationist outposts in Central America and the Caribbean contained the natural resources, land, and opportunities that only a people accustomed to arduous toil could exploit. And their commercial instincts, harnessed in the American capitalist tradition, would thrive because "whites as well as blacks look to their self-interest." The president concluded, "I see the means available for your self-reliance."[20]

Colonizationist efforts largely failed. Nearly all black leaders adamantly opposed the national expulsion of freedpeople. Preservation of the Union, they affirmed, demanded both emancipation *and* the equitable inclusion of all people. "This is our country by birth," resolved a black political meeting in New York, "this is the country of our choice, being our fathers' country. We love this land, and have contributed our share to its prosperity and wealth." Other adversaries considered colonization little better than slavery itself. After centuries of bondage, coercion, and subjugation, "to pull up stakes in a civilized and Christian nation, and to go to an uncivilized nation," protested a renowned Philadelphia orator, "is unreasonable and anti-Christian in the extreme." Colonizing African Americans abroad did not purify an exceptional land of its racial blemishes; removal *exposed* the Union as a conventional nation obsessed with ethnic purity. How could a president who pledged his full devotion to sustaining a nation conceived by divine Providence, asked Frederick Douglass, promote wartime doctrines that exposed the United States' base duplicity? Colonization displayed "all of Lincoln's inconsistencies, his pride of race and blood, his contempt for Negroes, and," Douglass concluded, "his canting hypocrisy." Prominent abolitionist Robert Purvis thus scolded Lincoln for "talk[ing] to me about 'two races' and their 'mutual antagonism'" because "this is our country just as much as it is yours, and we will not leave it."[21]

And leave it they did not. Rather than amassing volunteers to resettle abroad, black leaders organized opposition *against* colonization. Grassroots resistance, joined with inadequate funding, government incompetence, and international opponents of African Americans settling in their countries, ensured that only one colonizationist endeavor took place. In April 1863, nearly five hundred black émigrés relocated to Île-à-Vache, an island off the coast of Haiti. There they met with abject disaster, their ranks riddled by disease— approximately 20 percent perished. Those who survived found dreadful conditions for free labor. Less than a year after they arrived, the expatriates returned to the United States. Foreshadowing the disastrous experiment, A. P. Smith, a foremost African American opponent to colonization, asked Lincoln, "Is our right to a home in this country less than your own"? Smith scoffed at the empty prospects of international free labor: "Say, good Mr. President, why we, why anybody should swelter, digging coal, if there be any in Central America?" The colonizationist enterprise, long the dream of white Americans who trembled at the instability of racial strife, now seemed delegitimized in a nation careening toward universal emancipation and racial integration.[22]

By the late summer and early fall of 1862, when Lincoln made his strongest push for voluntary black emigration, stalwart Confederate military resistance had mired the Union war effort. Burdened with thousands of runaways who continued to flock to U.S. armies and threats from European powers to broker a peace between the American belligerents, Lincoln sought additional reinforcements for the Union's wartime arsenal. In July, he proposed to his cabinet a preliminary proclamation of emancipation, which declared that on January 1, 1863, the federal government would recognize the freedom of all enslaved people who resided in the rebellious states. The president explained that black liberation would undercut Confederate reliance on forced labor and align the United States with international sensibilities. Yet Lincoln did not entirely abandon colonization. He intended to balance the rapidity of emancipation with the voluntary emigration of freedpeople. Secretary of the Navy Gideon Welles confided to his diary that although "the president objected unequivocally to compulsion," he "thought it essential to provide an asylum for a race which we had emancipated, but which could never be recognized or admitted to be our equals." Perhaps convinced that racial separation assuaged the racial anxieties of a white society skeptical of unchecked black freedom, Lincoln proposed within the preliminary proclamation "the effort to colonize persons of African descent, with their consent, upon this continent, or elsewhere." And as he advised in his annual message to Congress in December, Lincoln envisioned "the voluntary emigration of" freedpeople "upon conditions which shall be equal, just, and humane." The president concluded, "Liberia and Hayti are as yet the only countries to which colonists of African descent from here could go with certainty of being received and adopted as citizens."[23]

As he had done so often in his public life, Lincoln imagined domestic emancipation within an international sphere. In the vein of voluntary emigration,

Lincoln embedded within the preliminary proclamation his faith in the enslaved to influence the scope of liberation. "The United States," the proclamation announced, "will recognize and maintain the freedom of such persons, and will do no act or acts to repress such persons ... in any efforts they may make for their actual freedom." Inviting runaways to seek permanent refuge in the free states, denying slaveholders access to their absconded property, and transforming Union armies into vessels of liberation, Lincoln recognized that the long trend of Atlantic abolition—no matter how cautious and measured, or violent and hasty—had originated, somehow, with the enslaved. Rooted in the natural yearning for liberty, their actions necessitated recognition, legitimation, and shelter. But only in the United States would their strikes toward freedom be moderated with a cautious eye toward national security and employed for national purposes. In catering both to black activism and white apprehension of widespread, precipitous abolition, the Union would achieve a feat enjoyed by no other nation in the nineteenth-century world: immediate wartime emancipation moderated by peaceful national order, joined, perhaps, by the deportation of the very people lately liberated from bondage.[24]

The preliminary proclamation, however, sparked vehement opposition. George B. McClellan, commander of the Union Army of the Potomac and ardent critic of abolition, warned of the edict "inaugurating servile war, emancipating the slaves, & at one stroke of the pen changing our free institutions into a despotism." And while parties of European abolitionists had long favored the American war as the decisive verdict on New World slavery, some observers in Great Britain interpreted the proclamation as a call to slave uprising. Disgusted that the Union would not guard against enslaved endeavors from which "they may make for their actual freedom," one critic alleged that the proclamation gave "direct encouragement to servile Insurrections." The world would be once more exposed to racial horrors not witnessed since the Haitian Revolution. The Republicans had seemingly unleashed emancipation onto an already devastating war, necessitating European intervention. "We may see reenacted some of the worst excesses of the French Revolution," another Briton cautioned, undoubtedly fearing the quagmire into which European powers would sink when brokering an impossible peace not only between warring nations but also between warring races. That horrific prospect once drew France, Spain, and Britain to the Haitian crisis of the 1790s, in which black rebels ousted the European powers. The same could well happen again during the American crisis of the 1860s.[25]

Lincoln justified issuing the proclamation in the wake of the September bloodletting at Antietam, a battle that seemed to confirm the war's interminable nature. While the Army of the Potomac had blunted the Confederate incursion into Maryland, the indecisive confrontation indicated that the Americans would interminably continue their devastating slaughter. European critics were now convinced that the American war had transformed into a bloody quagmire, especially once Robert E. Lee's Army of Northern Virginia had retreated safely into the Confederacy. And when seemingly rabid black insurrectionists joined the fray, the once powerful Union—and perhaps all of North America—would collapse into racial anarchy. The London *Times* detected gross cynicism in Lincoln's ploy to inject emancipation into the wake of the appalling autumn battle. "He will appeal to the black blood of the African; he will whisper of the pleasures of spoil and of the gratification of yet fiercer instincts; and when blood begins to flow and shrieks come piercing through the darkness, Mr. LINCOLN will wait till the rising flames tell that all is consummated, and then he will rub his hands and think that revenge is sweet." The world no longer regarded the American war as a limited constitutional struggle. Preserving the Union and toppling the Confederacy simply were no longer worth their price in blood. Intervention, for the sake of humanity, was imperative.[26]

Yet the British and French never intervened. A fortuitous blend of European politics, cold feet, and Lincoln's shrewd political acumen forestalled international mediation. Likely moved by interventionist threats, condemnations of the Union's endorsement of enslaved insurrection, and commitments to a just war, Lincoln revised the proclamation's rhetoric and scope in the months before its formal issuance on January 1, 1863. While he continued to invite enslaved people to pursue "their actual freedom," the final proclamation offered a caveat: "I hereby enjoin upon the people so declared to be free to abstain from all violence, unless in necessary self-defence." White critics might continue to sense an insurrectionary spirit among restive enslaved people seeking freedom. But the proclamation now absolved the United States from any complicity in black rebellion. Indeed, Lincoln's revisions quietly conceded the power of alleged black bellicosity, recognizing its inevitable infusion into the quest for self-emancipation. Yet rather than unleashing former bondpeople onto vulnerable slaveholders, the proclamation channeled supposed enslaved bloodlusts into restrained federal institutions. "And I further declare and make known," Lincoln continued in a remarkable invitation, "that such persons of suitable condition, will be received into the armed service of the United States to garrison forts, positions, stations, and other places, and to man vessels of all sorts in said service." That African Americans would be enlisted as soldiers into the U.S. military and regulated by the strict ethos of white martial institutions would temper any replication of the Haitian past.[27]

Ardent abolitionist generals John W. Phelps and David Hunter had earlier anticipated the president's international conception of black military enlistment. When Lincoln linked colonization with emancipation during the spring and summer of 1862, Phelps also recognized that "society in the South seems to be on the point of dissolution, and the best way of preventing the African from becoming instruments in a general state of anarchy, is to enlist him in the cause of the Republic." An ordered emancipation stemmed any chaos that might erupt in the unpredictable pursuit of black freedom. From his post in New Orleans, Phelps had witnessed the fast crumbling of slavery as Union armies advanced throughout the Mississippi Valley. He feared that the destabilization caused by such a sudden emancipation would inspire "any petty military chieftain" to rise and organize a devastating insurrection "for the purpose of robbery and plunder. It is for the interest of the South ... that the African should be permitted to offer his block for the temple of Freedom." Now only the U.S. government could sanction freedpeople's martial exploits, their belligerence ordered by federal institutions.[28]

Hunter also beheld the stunning rapidity with which slavery collapsed in South Carolina. But for Hunter, this swift emancipation appeared not to diminish within African American men "the curse of that ignorance which slavery fostered." Generations of servitude, he averred, nurtured lives of apathy and dependence, while also breeding justifiable resentment. According to Hunter, enslaved men did not emerge from bondage self-controlled, nor could they enter freedom as virtuous and reasoned citizens. Only "the discipline of military life will be the very safest and quickest school in which these enfranchised bondsmen can be elevated to the level of our higher intelligence and cultivation." Slavery imposed contradictory elements upon its victims, who were at once prepared for the rigors of "regular military organizations" but also allegedly inculcated with a dangerous thirst for vengeance. "Giving them in this manner a legitimate vent to their natural desire to prove themselves worthy of freedom," Hunter explained, "cannot fail to have the further good effect of rendering less likely mere servile insurrection, unrestrained by the comities and usages of civilized warfare."[29]

The specter of Haiti always haunted the Anglo-American imagination, and the Emancipation Proclamation attempted to defuse white fears of black insurrection. Often regarded as one of the Civil War's revolutionary transformations, a moment in which a conservative war for Union morphed into a progressive crusade, the document moderated the scope of black freedom. In calling for African American soldiers to serve in garrisons and auxiliary stations, Lincoln exposed his own doubts about the integration of black men into "civilized" republican military institutions. Mid-nineteenth-century military culture regarded "garrisons"—the operative word in the proclamation's invitation for black enlistment—as restricted, stifling outposts of permanent martial life. Garrisons smacked of military despotism, the loci of Old World standing armies. They housed not citizen-volunteers—the idealized republican soldier—but hapless mercenaries, wards of the state who were regulated by smothering military order, subjected to arbitrary punishment, and tasked with debilitating labor duties. Though their uniforms boasted an eagle and brandished the letters "U.S.," newly minted African American soldiers were to be largely relegated to a form of second-class military service.[30]

The Emancipation Proclamation is sometimes celebrated as a confirmation of Lincoln's evolution on race, a signal that he welcomed the seamless incorporation of black men into the institutions of American civilization. And there is good reason to read the proclamation in this manner: recommendations for voluntary colonization had been replaced with a revolutionary invitation to serve in the U.S. military. The landscape of war—indeed, the landscape of American life—appeared completely transformed as the proclamation's soldiering clause ripped apart the once impenetrable tapestry of the slaveholding republic. Yet the garrisoning concept suggested that Lincoln had not fully abandoned his faith in colonization, which he appeared to link to black military service. Segregated behind the lines in immobile garrisons, African American soldiers would be separated from mainstream republican military culture. They would replace disgruntled white volunteers who would instead march to the front, waging the glorious battles for Union. Black troops would be restricted from wreaking havoc on white progress, their alleged penchant for violence checked by strict labor and fatigue duties. The colonizationist dream now seemed a reality. "Will you [freedmen] go away if I venture to free you?" Wendell Phillips, an ardent white abolitionist, asked rhetorically of the proclamation's call for black soldiers. "May I colonize you among the sickly deserts of the vast jungles of South America?" he queried in a pointed reference to Lincoln's obsession with black emigration. Or, perhaps, "let me colonize you in the forts of the Union, and put rifles in your hands."[31]

Phillips's insight exposed how garrisoning aimed to defuse the potential racial chaos of emancipation. Rev. J. M. Sturtevant, president of Illinois College, a steadfast antislavery institution, typified the skepticism of many white northerners who remained apprehensive about an abrupt, universal manumission. "How can the public mind be assured that to emancipate the enslaved race, to confer on them all the moral rights of humanity," asked the Methodist abolitionist, "does not involve by any necessity, or even remote possibility, either an internecine war of races on our own soil, or the fusion of the two races into one homogenous people?" Garrisoning signaled to white Americans—it signaled to the *world*—that the United States could control rapid wartime social changes without succumbing to anarchy. Indeed, Lincoln informed his commanding generals that permanent Union holdings could "be garrisoned by colored troops, leaving the white forces now necessary at those places, to be employed elsewhere." The central battles in defense of the Union would be waged by "true" republican soldiers, the ostensible embodiment of American civilization.[32]

The U.S. Colored Troops (USCT) would thus colonize the garrisons dotting the subtropical Confederacy, relieving white troops from the debilitating malarial environments, swampy heat, and suffocating humidity to which they were not accustomed as fair northern men. As some Union generals claimed, black men's long subjection to the punishing labors of enslavement and natural conditioning to scorching southern climates somehow predisposed them to their new roles as soldiers. "I do not want the White men to do any work that can possibly be avoided during the hot months," Ulysses S. Grant explained from Vicksburg shortly after the Mississippi River fortress fell in July 1863. African American troops were best fit for the hard toil, rigid discipline, and steady immobility of service in the sultry South. "A nigger makes a good enough Soldier for garrison and guard duty," reported Harrison Soule, a white volunteer from Michigan, "but for Field Service a Hundred [white] men is worth a Thousand of them." Echoing the basic essence of Lincoln's garrisoning philosophy, Soule considered African American soldiers "only fit to help us in the capacity of Laborers and watchmen [because] they cant be trusted when there is the least danger."[33]

Soule's perspective underscored the central theme uniting garrisoning with colonization. That black men were ostensibly fit for lives of hard labor in sultry climates informed the notion of "isothermalism," a racialized understanding of biological aptitude that justified ethnic separation. As thousands of white soldiers garrisoned stifling locales from the Atlantic coast to the Mississippi River valley, the diseases incurred in the subtropical environs decimated their ranks. Black troops who hailed from these same regions would alleviate the suffering of white troops, fulfilling the roles once proposed for free black laborers who would colonize Central America and Africa. "Placing strong garrisons of thoroughly acclimated troops in the Southern forts and posts of this department," David Hunter advised from South Carolina, would relieve white soldiers from "being peculiarly liable to the ravages of climatic and epidemic diseases." Henry W. Halleck, the general-in-chief of Union armies, made even more explicit the federal government's new policy. We will "use the negroes of the South ... for the defence of forts, depots, &c.," he proposed in March 1863. Large "force[s] will be organized during the coming summer, & if they can be used to hold points on the Mississippi during the sickly season, it will afford much relief to our armies." So when Lincoln explained that "the colored population is the great *available* and yet *unavailed* of, force for restoring the Union," from which "the bare sight of fifty thousand armed, and drilled black soldiers on the banks of the Mississippi, would end the rebellion at once," he rooted his claims in distinct notions of racial difference, situating the Union within the broader "American Mediterranean."[34]

Garrisoning defined the USCT in much the same way that cautious whites across the Atlantic rim considered people of African ancestry: that they were somehow alien to civilization, conditioned only for use by whites in a hierarchical world. Raising regiments of black soldiers, and the distinct purposes for which they would be applied, was hardly unprecedented. White American commentators hailed Lincoln's garrisoning prescription, recognizing that it came from an Atlantic tradition of employing African-descended soldiers in auxiliary capacities. "In the peculiarities of this climate and Country they will prove invaluable auxiliaries," David Hunter predicted, "fully equal to the similar regiments so long and successfully used by the British Authorities in the West India Islands." William Winthrop, an American consul to Malta, also understood the garrisoning philosophy as a distinctly transnational phenomenon. Praising England's decision to escalate the number of black regiments in the West Indies, Winthrop averred that "in hot climates, and for garrison duty, not better soldiers can be found than the blacks." Indeed, the Spanish, Portuguese, Turks, and "Brazils" employed black units "to be stationed by themselves for the performance of particular duties."[35]

For Winthrop, the USCT would not only solve the problems of climate, military labor, and stationary service deemed so distasteful by white soldiers. Their deployment to the boundaries of national life would also thwart British and French imperial ambitions from encroaching into the Western Hemisphere. Stationing a "colored army of at least 75, to 80,000 men" on the Texas borderlands "would enable us to expel the French from Mexico ... and at the same time to meet the black regiments of England, whenever, and wherever they might be thrown our way." Winthrop considered "a colored army as absolutely necessary for the preservation of our whole Country." When enforcing the Monroe Doctrine, Winthrop pondered, "Why should we not have our colored regiments to meet [France's] black Zouaves, which she employed with such good effect." The USCT shielded the national periphery, standing on the front lines against hemispheric violations. And for Winthrop, they were at once native and alien, performing critical state functions but also somehow divorced from the national mainstream.[36]

By linking the enlistment of African American soldiers with existing ideas about race, whites came to see an otherwise overt racial revolution in relatively moderate terms. Because they would be regulated by the U.S. military and colonized on the fringes of the national landscape, black troops would not yield to the supposed violent tendencies embedded in their alleged anarchical character. The United States would be spared the humiliation and terror of racial strife, despite black men entering freedom under remarkably militaristic auspices. The *New York Times* considered racial disaster unlikely because "the negroes ... are robust, hardy and acclimated," already acquainted with the South, and already "submissive and very amenable to discipline," evident in their use "for many years by the British in garrisoning their West India Islands." Thus, the Union "could prove within the next year ... that the African race can defend themselves in arms[, and] we should have solved, in the eyes of the world, the great problem of their use and their destiny" because "the duty of solving this problem devolves in a great measure on us." Indeed, when the president delivered his annual message to Congress in December 1863, he rightly claimed that "no servile insurrection, or tendency to violence or cruelty, has marked the measures of emancipation and arming of the blacks."[37]

Perhaps Lincoln had occasioned what some whites had long thought impossible: diffusing black bellicosity during the chaos of war to fashion a conservative emancipation. Had immobile, permanent, subtropical, labor-intensive garrisons forestalled an otherwise inevitable racial insurrection? Was the *New York Times* correct in stating that only white Americans could decipher the impossible enigma of arming formerly enslaved men? In actuality, garrisoning, colonization, and white paternalism had little to do with averting an unrestrained race war. "For the noble struggle for country and liberty," proclaimed black Philadelphia abolitionist George E. Stephens in the pages of the *Weekly Anglo-African*, one of the nation's foremost black newspapers, "for the sake of honor, manhood and courage—in the name of God, of country, and or race, spit upon the base sycophants who thus dare to insult you." Colonization affronted the enduring ideals of Union. White "negrophobia," proclaimed Stephens, framed black men as little more than violent brutes who teamed with vengeful passion, a baseless charge that willfully ignored the ubiquitous appeals of African Americans to serve the republic as civilized volunteers. "We have more to gain, if victorious, or more to lose, if defeated, than any other class of men," he concluded. African American men thus welcomed the opportunity to mold—not to destroy through the devastations of racial insurrection—a new birth of freedom in *their* Union, a republic finally open to "our personal liberties."[38]

Marching in Freedom's Army

A week after the Emancipation Proclamation went into effect, African American abolitionist H. Ford Douglas could not ignore the moment's overwhelming implications. That "the slaves are *free*" rendered hollow "the claims of the impious Confederate States of America" and its "Government established upon the idea of the perpetual bondage of the Negro." For Douglas, the war had morphed into an unparalleled liberal crusade, portending that the United States would never again reign as the world's largest slaveholding republic. "Now by the fortunes of war" could people of color emerge "into the broad sunlight of our Republican civilization." Anything less than full national inclusion would delegitimize the war for Union. Douglas disparaged Abraham Lincoln's many colonization proposals, claiming that the "national duties and responsibilities of" *all* citizens could never "be colonized, they must be heroically met and religiously performed." He thus called on his close friend Frederick Douglass to assist in raising regiments of black volunteers to serve the Union's hallowed cause. Soldiering in the ranks of freedom's army rehabilitated the "mighty waste of manhood resulting from the dehumanizing character of slave institutions in America," conferring liberty "to the world through the patient toil and self-denial of this proud and haughty race."[39]

As a formerly enslaved man and foremost proponent of global freedom, Frederick Douglass framed the international symbolism of black soldiering during the American Civil War. Confederates "do not conceal the purpose of the war," now a world-historical event to settle the contested meaning of American civilization. "That purpose," Douglass reminded all enemies of enslavement, was "to make slavery of the African race universal and perpetual on this continent." Engaging Vice President Alexander H. Stephens's infamous "Cornerstone Address," Douglass condemned "the fundamental ideas of the Confederate Government," which were "based upon the idea that colored men are an inferior race, who may be enslaved and plundered forever." The Union, like modern egalitarian nations, "recognizes the natural and fundamental equality of all men." Although the United States lately grew into the world's largest slaveholding domain, the war had rehabilitated the Union into an international antislavery beacon. From the abolition of slavery in Washington, DC, to the banning of slavery in the western territories; from the termination of the international slave trade to emancipation in a preponderance of slaveholding states; and from the diplomatic recognition of Haiti to the slow march toward racial equality in some northern cities, aristocratic slaveholders no longer ruled the Union. The dawn of emancipation, Douglass argued, compelled U.S. armies to crush the Confederacy, extinguishing its pledge to spread human bondage across the hemisphere.[40]

Only African Americans themselves, Douglass advised, could complete the rejuvenation of national exceptionalism. "Nothing can be more plain, nothing more certain," he announced, than serving the Union and "burying rebellion and slavery in a common grave." The Confederacy, its racial hierarchy, its privilege, and its autocratic tyranny exhibited the regressive decay of the Old World. After centuries of bondage, a new birth of freedom lived within a Union committed to liberty's eternal security. "Never since the world began was a better chance offered to a long enslaved and oppressed people," Douglass declared. With military service, former bondmen could terminate the Confederacy, the last vestige of North American slavery, and transform the Union into a just, equitable, biracial civilization. By donning the Union blue and brandishing the weapons of war "we may blot out the hand-writing of ages against us," Douglass concluded. "Once let the black man get upon his person the brass letters U.S.; let him get an eagle on his button, and a musket on his shoulder, and bullets in his pocket, and there is no power on earth . . . which can deny that he has earned the right of citizenship in the United States."[41]

Douglass played an instrumental role in organizing regiments of African American soldiers. His recruitment efforts stressed a central theme within the Atlantic tradition of enslaved resistance: that defiance, no matter how subtle or even futile, one day would produce the moment to strike for freedom. Just as David Walker promised, just as Henry Highland Garnet anticipated, and just as Martin Delany imagined, "a new era is [finally] open to us," one of Douglass's 1863 recruiting posters read. "For generations we have suffered under the horrors of slavery, outrage and wrong; our manhood has been denied, our citizenship blotted out, our souls seared and burned, our spirits cowed and crushed, and the hopes of the future of our race involved in doubt and darkness." But the advent of war here, as throughout the Atlantic world, had changed "our relations to the white race." Now that the long anticipated moment had finally arrived, "let us Rush to Arms!" Only a collective effort would occasion a lasting liberty, because "the day that has seen an enslaved race in arms has, in all history, seen their last trial." "We must strike NOW.... We WILL Rise!" For "a nation or a people that cannot fight may be pitied, but cannot be respected."⁴²

Douglass's appeals denounced any pretense of racial chaos, reminding the nation that African Americans sought equitable and peaceful inclusion within the Union. The recruitment posters countered claims that black men were both too cowardly and too warlike to serve in national military institutions. The clear evidence that they craved liberty, that they desired national assimilation, suggested that they acted as any other citizen would when volunteering in the republic's defense. "More than a Million White Men have left Comfortable Homes and joined the Armies of the Union to save their Country," the recruitment poster explained. Whites did not possess a monopoly on republican virtue, the guiding ideal of all citizen-soldiers. "Cannot we leave ours, and swell the Hosts of the Union, to save our liberties ... and deserve well of our Country[?]" Federal armies comprised innumerable nationalities and ethnicities, all of which claimed the Union as the last best protectorate of international freedom. "If we are not lower in the scale of humanity than Englishmen, Irishmen, White Americans, and other Races, we can show it now." Defying long-standing allegations that they were unwelcome aliens within a captive nation, African American soldiers could justify the Union as "the soil of our birth," the only land in which equality truly thrived. "If we value liberty, if we wish to be free in this land, if we love our country ... [we] must show by our own right arms that we are worthy to be freemen." Displaying the virtue, dispassion, and moderation required of enlightened citizens would confirm the superiority of the Union as the once and future home of African Americans.⁴³

Testimony from Robert Hamilton, editor of the *Weekly Anglo-African,* and from a delegation of free New Yorkers of color underscored African American definitions of a just war for Union. Hamilton cited the war's overwhelming, zero-sum implication for black Americans. Regardless of the war's outcome, he averred, white volunteers could go home assured of their freedom and citizenship. They do not "have the same incentives to fight. Our life, our liberty, our country, our religious privileges, our family, OUR ALL, is at stake." If slaveholders triumphed in their unholy quest to consolidate racial bondage as *the* foundation of modern nationhood—indeed, "if the Union is overthrown"— "then a night of darkness and horror comes upon us, the like of which no people ever saw." The New York delegation likewise employed the providential language of Union to convince skeptical white northerners that black men should serve the national cause. The American contest was "one of the most justifiable wars that was ever inaugurated" because it pitted the eternal struggle "for the sacred rights of Man against the myrmidons of Hell itself. It is a battle for the right of self-government, true democracy, just republicanism, and righteous principles, against anarchy, misrule, barbarism, human slavery, despotism, and wrong." The war to preserve the Union necessitated a grand army of free black men who would collapse the Slave Power's obdurate claim to civilization. The world could ill afford the Union's demise, a proposition that "will forever stand as the synonym of American disgrace," signaling the permanent regression of "human society, civilization and democratic republican institutions."[44]

African American volunteers accordingly poured into the Union's blue ranks. Even Charles L. Remond, who once renounced the Union in the wake of the notorious *Dred Scott* decision, and Martin Delany, who long advocated an African American exodus from the United States, assumed vital roles in recruiting for and serving in black regiments intended to *preserve* the republic. Never had the United States legitimized biracial army service, once regarded as the limited prerogative of virtuous white men.[45] Regiments of the USCT comprised 180,000 soldiers, or 10 percent of the nation's military forces. The soldiers engaged Confederates in more than four hundred battles and skirmishes; they occupied scores of southern towns; and they dismantled the slaveholding regime wherever Union armies moved. No other conflict in the New World—except the Haitian Revolution—had witnessed such a dramatic collapse of slavery through war, joined by the demise of the globe's most influential order of slaveholders.[46] The "trusting Decendants of Africs Clime" understood that fundamental social and political change arrived at the point of the bayonet, James Henry Gooding, a volunteer in the Fifty-Fourth Massachusetts, explained to Abraham Lincoln, and they desired to serve only "in defense of Union, and Democracy." They, more than any other American, knew "the cruelties of the Iron heel of oppression" and therefore demanded that "our Patriotism, our enthusiasm will have a new impetus, to exert our energy more and more to aid Our Country." And though the Union had long "spurned us," obsessed more with international power than with a commitment to national ideals, "now we are sworn to serve her."[47]

African American soldiers did not soak their former plantations in the blood of slaveholding tyrants, nor did they topple the U.S. government that for so long had authorized their enslavement. The USCT considered their principal military duty the systematic dismantling of the Slave Power. They appropriated national military service to expand the once limited blessing of American civilization from white to black. More so than white loyal citizens, black men regarded slaveholders as unyielding tyrants whose power depended on human subjugation. If the very people long shackled by enslavement severed the chains of bondage, the once impenetrable system of American slavery would fast dissolve. When James Jones, a Rhode Island artilleryman who served in New Orleans, "walked fearlessly and boldly through the streets of a southern city," he scoffed at "those lordly princes of the sunny south, the planter's sons," who had "lost thy potent power." As Union armies blanketed the Confederacy, unfurling the banner of freedom with each march, black troops marveled at the rapid, unprecedented pace of slavery's destruction. The world's largest, most powerful, most aggressive, and most stable slave society had dissolved so suddenly under the weight of war. "What a change in Beaufort," exclaimed a chaplain in the Fifty-Fifth Massachusetts. "Here only a few years ago, slavery held undisputed sway." And shortly after entering the Confederate capital in Richmond, Virginia, John C. Brock commemorated "the mighty and progressive age in which we live. The hydra-headed monster slavery," which slaveholders had long heralded as a symbol of modernity, was now fast "dying under the scourging lash of Universal Freedom."[48]

That "scourging lash" was felt all across the southern landscape. But it was cracked in few places with more passion than in Virginia, the first Anglo settlement in the New World. There, as the First USCT arrived in the spring of 1864 on a sprawling plantation overlooking the James River, one soldier remarked that he stood "a few miles above Jamestown, the very spot where the first sons of Africa were landed" 245 years previously. On that terrible ground the New World had been corrupted, tarnished for centuries by the Old World's callous and lustful dominance. The planting of slavery in the virgin lands of North America had branded people of color "as an inferior race by all civilized nations." The advent of war, however, had finally agitated the stolid waters of slavery, the vessels of freedom now sailing unencumbered. "Behold what has been revealed in the past three or four years," the soldier remarked, "why the colored men has ascended upon a platform of equality." The once gloomy national panorama now boasted rays of hope, shattering once impenetrable castes. Witnessing his comrades "apply the lash to the tender flesh of [their former] master," the plantation's formerly enslaved reminded the now powerless master "that they were no longer his, but safely housed in Abraham's bosom, and under the protection of the Star Spangled Banner, and guarded by their own patriotic, though once down-trodden race." War had delivered emancipation to the United States, a lingering outpost of human bondage. "Oh, that I had the tongue to express my feelings," the soldier concluded, "while standing [in] the mother state of slavery, as a witness of such a sudden reverse!"[49]

Sgt. Charles W. Singer of the 107th USCT spoke for African American troops who considered international freedom tenuous until the Union fully emancipated itself from the chains of human bondage. Only in the United States, he professed, could liberty extend to *all* humans, flourishing as an untarnished beacon for the rest of the world to emulate. Appealing to the exceptionalist spirit voiced by H. Ford Douglas and Frederick Douglass, Singer affirmed that the war was "a great battle for the benefit not only of the country, but for ourselves and the whole of mankind. The eyes of the world are upon us," he vowed, in a perspective remarkably analogous to Abraham Lincoln's conception of Union. The guarantee of international freedom depended on the contest of arms now being waged in North America. "I recognize in the stability of this Government"—a stability marked by the guarantee of universal equality—"a source of strength to other nations." It was one thing to restore the United States on secure constitutional grounds. But it was another thing altogether for African Americans to wage the battle, "to show the whole world that we are willing to fight for our rights." Only then could the genius of Union shine as an unprecedented experiment in biracial liberty. "While this Government stands, there is hope for the most abject, disabled, and helpless of mankind."[50]

Waging war against slaveholders presented a unique moment for African American men to link the cause of Union to Atlantic abolitionism. A company of soldiers in the Fifty-Fourth Massachusetts Volunteers christened their unit the "Touissant Guards," named for the famed Haitian revolutionary hero Toussaint Louverture. In February 1863, two "natives of Africa" who, in 1858, had been unlawfully kidnapped from their homes along the Congo River and transported to the American South fled their Louisiana plantation at the approach of Union military forces. When they reached Federal lines, "in broken language [they] declared that they wanted to fight for the United States." Upon their enlistment in the Union's Second Louisiana Native Guards, a black recruiting officer named Robert H. Isabelle announced, "We want ten thousand more brave sons of Africa." Americans of African descent across the nation petitioned to serve the republic as stewards of global liberty. "We stand as ever on the side of the Government," resolved a black political organization in Ohio, "in its efforts to subdue the rebellion of the slave oligarchy of the country, in its determination to emancipate the slaves of all rebels." They predicted that wartime abolition would cleanse the republic and its vast western territories, long the contested locus of the national future. Emancipation would also radiate south and east "to welcome Hayti and Liberia to the great family of nations." The United States would never again greet the world as a daunting slaveholding empire. The refurbished egalitarian republic would anchor a new world of freedom, cordoned by "the colored soldiers, who, taking the American musket and bayonet, have gone forth at the call of their country to do and die for the Government and the Union."[51]

Enslaved Insurrection and the Confederate Just War
When the United States buckled under the weight of secession during the winter of 1860–61, Frederick Douglass anticipated that "the slave population of South Carolina may at last prove the most serious check upon disunion." The enslaved "cannot have failed to learn something from passing events," beckoning the waves of international abolition descending upon the fractured

Union. "*They* have a direct interest in the controversy" and might well "burst forth and spread havoc and death among slaveholders to an extent never surpassed even in the annals of St. Domingo." Douglass knew all too well the power of a slaveholding Union. He assumed that white southerners would rather relinquish temporary political influence in the wake of Abraham Lincoln's election than surrender the iron grip of federal authority that protected, regulated, and controlled their restive enslaved populations. The daily presence of insurrection, that discursive phantom of slaveholding paranoia, demanded a formidable military apparatus to forestall black men from slaughtering their unsuspecting masters.[52]

White southern opponents of disunion John Pendleton Kennedy and Sam Houston echoed Douglass's prediction. They warned that secession would spark a devastating civil war, bringing about slavery's violent and permanent death. "You are asked to plunge into a revolution," Houston vented, "but are you told how to get out of it?" The slaveholding Union, Kennedy explained, enjoyed great prestige because it marginalized radical abolitionism and promoted racial stability. Slavery, "a very appropriate and necessary agent in the interests of civilization," flourished best in peace, when sheltered from domestic volatility, external antagonism, and revolutionary turmoil. The South's rich bounty, harvested by enslaved legions, "is peculiarly exposed, not only to damage, but utter overthrow by the occurrence of war," a "common and inevitable weakness of all merely agricultural countries." Dissolution of the Union and the overt founding of a new republic of slavery, Houston concluded, would erase all slaveholding power, dismantle the institution's careful safeguards, turn the enslaved against their masters, and mobilize the United States through the "insidious arts of abolition emissaries, supported by foreign powers." The Union would wage a devastating war against slaveholders, their safety now "cursed by internal disorders and insurrections."[53]

Nevertheless, now that reckless "abolitionists" controlled the U.S. government and military, argued Senator Jefferson Davis, slaveholders had to reconsider their place in a hostile Union. On January 10, 1861—the day after his home state of Mississippi seceded, two weeks before he resigned his U.S. Senate seat, and one month before he was inaugurated as president of the Confederacy—Davis anticipated how Abraham Lincoln's Republican administration planned to foment insurrection throughout the South. Applying the lessons of Haiti to the current American crisis, Davis claimed that race wars occurred only when outside agitators stoked the enslaved into bloodthirsty action. Whenever "governments have tampered with slaves," and "bad men have gone among the ignorant and credulous people, and incited them to murder and arson," bondpeople erupted in mad fulmination. "San Domingo . . . is not a case where black heroes rose and acquired a Government," Davis instructed. "It was a case in which the French Government, trampling upon the rights and safety of a distant and feeble colony by sending troops among them, brought on a revolution." Enslaved people were allegedly incapable of pursuing freedom and building an independent nation. They could only be manipulated, their licentious ferocity channeled by devious whites. And thus "do you wonder," Davis concluded, "that we pause when we see this studied tendency to convert [our] Government into a military despotism? Do you wonder that we question the right of the President to send troops to execute the laws wherever he pleases, [given that] we remember the conduct of France," which had instigated Haiti's slaves into an irrepressible rebellion?[54]

Secession and the formation of the Confederacy occurred at a stunning pace *because* slaveholders so deeply feared enslaved militancy. They required a nation hospitable to slavery, a centralized government capable of thwarting domestic uprisings, and a military apparatus that defied armies of international abolitionists. The Confederate States of America stood in remarkable defiance to nineteenth-century emancipations, announcing to the world that democratic civilization thrived only on an unshakable foundation of slavery. The new republic would be the first Atlantic slave society not to collapse to the forces of insurrection or emancipation. The Haitian Revolution, a white critic wrote, proved "the madness which a sudden freedom from restraint begets—the overpowering burst of a long buried passion, the wild frenzy of revenge, and the savage lust for blood, all unite to give the warfare of liberated slaves, traits of cruelty and crime which nothing earthly can equal." Granting the enslaved the extraordinary power to shape the course of history through their alleged violent nature, the Confederacy charted an unprecedented destiny *against* African American bellicosity. Yet Confederates also believed that the enslaved would never organize, rebel, and strike against their benevolent masters. "The South can never be a St. Domingo, in spite of all that the ingenuity of Yankee hate can do," the *Richmond Examiner* explained in 1863, "for our negroes are better Christians and truer gentlemen than their would-be liberators." Only external agitation—free people of color, international abolitionists, or military forces—might seduce the enslaved to rise en masse.[55]

Riddled in striking paradox, the insurrection that white southerners had long feared came *because* of their hasty decision to secede and found a slaveholding republic. Though Confederates waged war to secure slavery, they instigated a conflict that destabilized the very civilization that their war sought to protect. The history of New World emancipation had proven that only war and revolution could shatter slavery so suddenly. Enslaved African Americans used the subsequent conflict to align with the United States and break their chains of bondage. Frederick Douglass may have misjudged the South's ultimate verdict on disunion. But John Pendleton Kennedy, Sam Houston, and Jefferson Davis's forecasts of insurrection proved prescient. While it is difficult to locate a true Haitian-style rebellion in the American Civil War, Confederates envisioned one unfolding every day in their quest for independence. For slaveholders, a shocking racial revolution dawned almost as soon as the first armies clashed in 1861. From increasing numbers of enslaved people deserting plantations, seeking refuge in Union armies, to the U.S. government legitimizing black freedom through congressional legislation and executive order, to free people of color aligning with the enslaved, the first two years of war developed unlike anything ever before experienced by the world's largest slave-holding society. Rather than expanding slavery's promise across the Western Hemisphere, it appeared that the Atlantic world had barricaded the tiny assemblage of slaveholders in the American South.[56]

An insurrection did not have to produce the mangled and bloodied corpses of white victims to devastate Confederate civilization. All it required was the Union aligning with the enslaved, each fomenting an internal collapse of the Confederacy. For example, when U.S. forces captured Georgia's coastal Sea Islands in the spring of 1862, enslaved people there, as elsewhere across the wartime landscape, absconded from their plantations and sought refuge among the blue-clad liberators. Panicked slaveholders reported to local authorities the immeasurable "injury inflicted upon the interests of the Confederate States by this now constant drain." Worried that "negroes occupy the position of spies" and "traitors," yielding a sudden "insecurity" to slavery, the petitioners claimed "that the United States have allowed their introduction into their Army and Navy, aiding the enemy by enlisting under his banners, and increasing his resources in men for our annoyance and destruction." A foreign military joined so effortlessly with the enslaved, portending that "the threat of an army of trained Africans for the coming fall and winter campaigns may become a reality."[57]

The white Georgians expressed utter shock that their seemingly docile and loyal bondpeople, who "constitute a part of the body politic," would transgress the laws of war and unite with invading armies. "They are perfectly aware that the act which they commit is one of rebellion against the power and authority of their owners and the Government under which they live." For Confederates, the enslaved constituted the unquestioned essence and secure foundation of the southern republic. Without slavery, the Confederacy was hardly an exceptional nation, indistinct from the rest of the world. "Our negroes are property, the agricultural class of the Confederacy," the lobbyists pleaded, "upon whose order and continuance so much depends." The implications were stark. Confederates confronted an internal enemy, one whom they never suspected of disloyalty, actively joining with an external antislavery nation. Indeed, the United States' superintendent of contrabands at Fort Monroe, Virginia, testified early the following year that enslaved people arrived to Union lines "from all about," aided by dynamic communication and transportation networks enmeshed within enslaved communities. By aiding Union armies, concluded the Confederate Georgians, "bringing in the foe upon us to kill and devastate," and weakening the slavery from within, the enslaved, whose bondage gave the Confederacy life, chiseled away the nascent republic's cornerstone.[58]

Confederates regarded the Union's recognition of black freedom in 1862 as a violation of the laws of civilized war. "By their emancipation and confiscation measures ... the Yankees have made this a war of extermination," confessed John B. Jones, a clerk in the Confederate War Department. Jones excoriated the United States for refusing to make war "only on men in arms, and spar[ing] private property, according to the usages of civilized nations." That unjust decision filled Confederates with "the same energy and determination to contest the last inch of soil with the cruel invader." Secretary of War James Seddon likewise indicted the Union army for transforming into an unjust tool of abolitionists, realizing long-standing slaveholder fears that foreign governments would turn human bondage against itself: "[Slaves'] employment by the enemy as soldiers converts them from valuable laborers into savage instruments of an atrocious war against our people and their institutions." Jefferson Davis sensed the same dynamic when he condemned the Union for provoking enslaved rebellion through emancipationist policies, which were "so atrocious as to insure ... the utter ruin of the entire population of these States." Meanwhile, some Union generals "are engaged, unchecked by their Government, in exciting servile insurrection, and in arming and training slaves for warfare against their masters," the president informed the Confederate Congress in August. "These passions have changed the character of the hostilities waged by our enemies, who are becoming daily less regardful of the usages of civilized war and the dictates of humanity."[59]

As their former bondmen enlisted in Union military forces, engaged slave owners on the field of battle, occupied conquered southern communities, and shattered slavery wherever they traveled, Confederates perceived a black army engulfing their increasingly isolated nation. Marching as liberated men, armed with the bayonet of freedom, and aligned against the Slave Power, the USCT fostered profound anxiety among Confederates, who saw emancipation as a fatal insurrection. Like the French stoking the embers of rebellion in Haiti during the 1790s, the Union during the 1860s prepared to unleash a second St. Domingue upon the Confederacy. "Will brave men quietly submit to Black Republican rule?" a woman from Arkansas wailed at the beginning of the war. "Shall our glorious South be made a second St. Domingo? Forbid it, soldiers! Forbid it, heaven!" To subdue the forces of emancipation, the Confederate military state had to fight *two* wars: one against Union armies and the other against their former bondpeople. When he recognized this impossible situation, an Alabama planter implored Jefferson Davis as early as May 1861 to limit the number of white soldiers entering the Confederate army. "We need the remainder of them to keep the slaves down, and save ourselves from the horrors of insurrection, which may be an incident of the war."[60]

According to Confederates, a war waged by two modern mid-nineteenth-century nations had now introduced a class of soldiers allegedly alien to the just war tradition. The seeming alteration of civilized war demanded a just reprisal against African American troops, whom Confederates regarded as unlawful insurgents. "Stern and exemplary punishment can and must be meted out to the murderers and felons who, disgracing the profession of arms," Davis advised the Confederate Congress, "seek to make of public war the occasion for the commission of the most monstrous crimes." That enslaved men were deemed unrestrained, violent, and destructive, while also forswearing their role as *the* lifeblood of Confederate civilization, necessitated a just and equal response to their unmitigated subversion. "Slaves in flagrant rebellion are subject to death by the laws of every slave holding State," read a November 1862 retaliatory proclamation from Confederate secretary of war James A. Seddon. "They cannot be recognized in anyway as soldiers subject to the rules of war," and thus "it is deemed essential that slaves in armed insurrection should meet condign punishment, summary execution must therefore be inflicted on those taken." Enslaved insurrection fell well outside laws of war; any retaliatory action that countered the immoral crimes against civilization were thus justified.[61]

Jefferson Davis affirmed Seddon's policy when he issued scathing rebukes of the preliminary Emancipation Proclamation. The president charged that "African slaves have not only been excited to insurrection by every license and encouragement, but numbers of them have actually been armed for a servile war — a war in its nature far exceeding in horrors the most merciless atrocities of the savages." American slaveholders had never before witnessed this kind of racial destabilization, having only translated the accounts of Caribbean rebellions in their paranoid minds. Davis reminded his constituents that white officers "found serving in company with armed slaves in insurrection" would not be "considered as soldiers engaged in honorable warfare, but as robbers and criminals, deserving death." The Confederate president refused to designate the USCT as uniformed soldiers of a foreign belligerent, categorizing them instead as "negro slaves captured in arms" to be conveyed to state authorities for prompt prosecution. In words that any slaveholder in the nineteenth-century world would have understood, Gen. Robert E. Lee derided the final Emancipation Proclamation as a "savage and brutal policy," a declaration of race war, "which leaves us no alternative but success or degradation worse than death." Only independence would stem the forces of international radicalism, Lee advised in January 1863, and "would save the honor of our families from pollution, our social system from destruction."[62]

According to seething Confederates, the Emancipation Proclamation's enlistment and arming of former slaves into Union armies confirmed the United States' radical degeneration. As Davis lamented, "Humanity shudders at the appalling atrocities which are being daily multiplied under the sanction of those who have obtained temporary possession of power in the United States, and who are fast making its once fair name a byword of reproach among civilized men." A Confederate cavalry officer in South Carolina decried a "raid by a mixed party of black and degraded whites [that] seems to have been de-signed only for plunder, robbery, and destruction of private property; in carry-ing it out they have disregarded all rules of civilized war, and have acted more as fiends than human beings." Deprecating emancipation as an "astounding stretch of power," North Carolina jurist James Rumley condemned an unscru-pulous Abraham Lincoln, who "designed to light the fires of insurrection." Not even in "a constitutional monarchy in Europe … would the sovereign, in peace or war, be allowed this prorogation." Rumley judged "the diabolical scheme" of enlisting black troops so unprecedented that "the civilized world appeared to be shocked at the thought of it." Davis thus invited "our fellow men of all countries to pass judgment on a measure by which several millions of human beings of an inferior race" had suddenly been transformed into armed war-riors. Scoffing at the proclamation's hollow counsel against fomenting vio-lence, Davis judged that the enslaved now had the means, authority, and sanc-tion "to a general assassination of their masters."[63]

Visions of a second Haitian Revolution showcased the well-rehearsed con-victions of a slaveholding civilization. Confederates did not speak in hyperbole when they considered that their new nation might succumb to unthinkable racial devastation. They had memorized the histories of Haiti, Demerara, and Jamaica. They had read David Walker's *Appeal*. They had once lived among Gabriel Prosser, Nat Turner, Denmark Vesey, and Frederick Douglass. They had ordered every aspect of life to guard their fragile white democracy from collapse. To prove that a slaveholding society could live independent from the New World's reckless flirtation with biracial freedom, a Texas newspaper thus called for "a war of extermination [against] every negro taken in arms against us." Long inundated by an enemy "inciting our slaves to insurrection," Mis-sissippi governor Charles Clark issued a warning to his citizens in November 1863: "Humbly submit yourselves to our hated foes, and they will offer you a reconstructed Constitution providing for the confiscation of your property, the immediate emancipation of your slaves, and the elevation of the black race to a position of equality," he cautioned, "aye, of superiority, that will make them your masters and rulers." And so when the same conditions that trig-gered the Haitian Revolution emerged in the wartime Confederacy—enslaved people's uneven but consistent mobilization; their steady drive to unite with freedpeople; their freedom recognized by a foreign nation with which they aligned militarily; and their enlisting in a foreign army—slaveholders did not wake from their nightmare. They were *living* an insurrectionist calamity.[64]

For Confederates, the USCT symbolized detestable traitors to the organic civilizing process of slavery. Their eagerness to don the uniform of a foreign nation and turn against their "benevolent" masters betrayed their seemingly unrefined ignorance of the natural world. "Think of it, armed negroes! Think what it means!" jeered prominent North Carolinian Catherine Edmonston. "And this is the nineteenth Century!" It was inconceivable to see black men released from bondage, transitioning into mercenaries charged with killing the very institution that refined their alleged barbarism, sanctioned white democracy, and organized the very civilization on which the modern world turned. "We all know what the negro is free and as a slave," divulged Confederate nurse Kate Cumming to her diary. In slavery, "he is better, morally and physically." The world had long displayed the ostensible imprudence of emancipation, which triggered "the degradation of the negro in the North and in the West India Islands." Volunteer soldiering in the American tradition embodied individual independence and the spirit of white masculine virtue, the fundamental antitheses of slavery. "The true character of this war," announced James Rumley soon after USCT occupied his town of New Bern, North Carolina, "is a grand crusade against African slavery." Only war and radical revolutionaries could facilitate the swift and arbitrary reconstruction of modern life. To declare loyalty to the new Union thus would be akin to "swear[ing] allegiance to the Negro government of Hayti, or the king of Dahomey," an absurd prospect for all remaining slaveholders in the Atlantic world.[65]

Acting swiftly to preserve its tenuous civilization, the Confederate Congress in May 1863 condemned the United States for seeking "to overthrow the institution of African slavery and bring[ing] on a servile war." Such violation of "the laws or usages of war among civilized nations" authorized "full and ample retaliation" against all who "excited a servile insurrection." White Union officers would be executed, and state authorities would try USCT as insurrectionists. Then, a joint congressional resolution passed in January 1864 labeled the war "a struggle for the preservation both of liberty and civilization," a contest to settle the fate of racial modernity. The conflict "has been marked by a brutality and disregard of the rules of civilized warfare that stand out in unexampled barbarity in the history of modern wars." The southern Congress petitioned an enlightened world to see emancipation as an invitation to destroy the sacred process of peaceful of self-determination. "President Lincoln has sought to convert the South into a San Domingo, by appealing to the cupidity, lusts, ambition, and ferocity of the slave." The resolutions compelled Confederates to resist a destructive war that portended a "sense of inferiority [by making] our condition abject and miserable beyond what freemen can imagine." Defeat in this war would fashion a new world entirely: "the destruction of our nationality [and] the equalization of whites and blacks."[66]

Confederates upheld Congress's dictates. When formerly enslaved men breached the sacred codes of a slaveholding society—leaving their plantations, fleeing to abolitionist armies, and enlisting as foreign soldiers—their conduct sanctioned reprisal no less than arrest and even death. The brazen violation of international and natural laws, Jefferson Davis declared, necessitated a "police force, sufficient to keep our negroes in control." The Confederate army would rebuff the white invaders *and* quell the enslaved insurrection sweeping the nascent republic. Functioning as the slaveholding state's inflexible arm, Confederate military forces routinely captured runaway slaves, kidnapped freedpeople and sent them south into slavery, or executed black soldiers regarded as unlawful insurgents. An Alabama officer ordered his command "to shoot, wherever & whenever captured, all negroes found armed & acting in concert with the abolition troops either as guides or brothers in arms." Condemning the Yankees for "instilling into [the enslaved] their hellish doctrin of insurrection," a soldier stationed near Helena, Arkansas, prayed, "God grant that we may be able to murder the last one of them." Edmund Kirby Smith, commander of the Trans-Mississippi department, advised "the propriety of giving no quarter to armed negroes and their officers. In this way," he concluded (no doubt having read the proclamations issued by the Confederate Congress, president, and secretary of war), "we may be relieved from a disagreeable dilemma." Thus, when the Army of Northern Virginia invaded the United States during the summer of 1863, culminating at the Battle of Gettysburg, General James Longstreet, R. E. Lee's principal subordinate officer, sent orders to his First Corps that "captured contrabands had better be brought along with you for further disposition." While campaigning north of the Confederacy, the army abducted and enslaved as many as 250 free people of color who lived in southern Pennsylvania. These were self-evident, natural, and practiced instincts long honed among the world's premier slaveholding class. Confederate armies *were* the Confederacy, each joined together in proving to the world the viability of a slaveholding civilization.[67]

It is little wonder that Confederate troops under the command of Nathan Bedford Forrest, one of the antebellum South's wealthiest slave traders, slayed nearly two hundred USCT and almost a hundred white Union soldiers who attempted to surrender Fort Pillow, their Mississippi River garrison near Memphis, Tennessee. The dreadful April 1864 racial massacre derived from the furious anxieties of a slaveholding republic that now confronted liberated and armed black men on the field of battle. Ignoring their pleas for clemency, Forrest's cavalrymen slaughtered the vulnerable U.S. soldiers in ways that few white Union troops had ever been engaged by Confederates. African American civilians likewise incurred the wrath of the rampaging soldiers. "There were also 2 negro women and 3 little children standing within 25 steps from me," a white Union soldier recalled, "when a rebel stepped up to them and said, 'Yes, God damn you, you thought you were free, did you?' and shot them all." All were killed instantly except one child, and the Confederate "knocked it in the head with the breech of his gun." The episode underscored the shocking intersection of perceived black insurrection and the unbending power of white mastery, both of which became entangled in a cataclysmic race war. "Very likely it is all *true* & I hope it is," Catherine Edmonston wrote after receiving news of Fort Pillow. "If they will steal our slaves & lead them on to murder and rapine, they must take the consequences!"[68]

Rivaling only Fort Pillow's infamy, the Battle of the Crater exposed the enduring racial hostility between slaveholding and egalitarian civilizations. In July 1864, Union engineers blew a giant hole in the middle of the stubborn siege lines outside Petersburg, Virginia, creating a massive crater into which white and black Federals poured. Confederate troops overlooking the cavernous basin then unleashed a devastating volley of fire upon the helpless Union soldiers. Meeting the Army of Northern Virginia for the first time, USCT regiments comprised many of the Federals trapped in this cauldron of death. One Confederate acknowledged how the presence of black soldiers "excited in the troops indignant malice" for which "they disregarded the rules of warfare which restrained them in battle with their own race, and brained and butchered the blacks until the slaughter was sickening." Once more denied quarter, USCT who attempted to surrender "were not allowed to do so," Confederate artilleryman William Pegram explained. "This was perfectly right, as a matter of policy," which had "a splendid effect on our men." Edward Porter Alexander, Robert E. Lee's chief artillerist, recalled that few black prisoners surrendered at the Crater. Because it was the Army of Northern Virginia's first encounter with black soldiers, "the general feeling of the men toward their employment was very bitter," Alexander commented. "The sympathy of the North for John Brown's memory was taken for proof of a desire that our slaves should rise in servile insurrection & massacre throughout the South, & the enlistment of Negro troops was regarded as advertisement of that desire & encouragement." Some estimates maintain that Confederates executed nearly one thousand USCT at the Crater.[69]

Confederates rarely extended quarter to black Union soldiers, ignoring the basic terms of surrender to which civilized belligerents pledged fealty. But from the Confederate perspective, this was *not* a civilized war. It was a war to prove the timeless, universal truth that some were born to rule and others were born to be ruled. African American soldiers defied and endangered this basic social tenet. Their presence signaled the breaking of slavery's chains, unleashing a dangerous, inexorable, and unjust birth of black freedom. Hangings and public displays of mutilated soldiers' bodies; kidnappings and reenslavement; and battlefield executions even after formal surrenders reminded even the most ambivalent observer of the Confederacy's overt claim to white supremacy. In a twisted way, one foreign to modern sensibilities, Confederates' response to African American Union soldiers was rational and conservative. When Vice President Alexander Stephens told the world in 1861 that his new nation's "cornerstone rests, upon the great truth that the negro is not equal to the white man; that slavery, subordination to the superior race, is his natural and moral condition," he underscored why black Union soldiers had to be neutralized. They, more than any other force, shattered the Confederate destiny. Only they could marshal the requisite power to dismantle a white slaveholding democracy. If they were taken prisoner, if they were regarded by the laws of war, if their humanity was even remotely recognized, the Confederate cornerstone would crumble. Confederates employed military necessity in what they defined as a just war to escape the horrors of racial barbarism and to stem the revolutionary tide of international abolitionism from overwhelming their exceptional civilization.[70]

Given that USCT soldiers served in a genuine state capacity, functioning as official public volunteers of the United States, Abraham Lincoln condemned Confederate policy toward black troops as a "relapse into barbarism, and a crime against the civilization of the age." The "law of nations and the usages and customs of war as carried on by civilized powers," the president continued, "permit no distinction as to color in the treatment of prisoners of war as public enemies." The moral bonds of public war would be forever shattered if one belligerent ignored the restraints imposed on enlightened conduct while the other belligerent silently countenanced the ethical breach. Loyal citizens of the Union likewise indicted the slaveholding republic as an unworthy and illegitimate member of the community of Western nations. "If we lead [black soldiers] into battle and even place them in its path," Francis Lieber had advised during the summer of 1863, "and then permit them to be butchered when captured and held as prisoners, the world will fully denounce our conduct as both criminal and cowardly." Accordingly, in July 1863 Lincoln issued a formal policy of retaliation that at once protected USCT as legitimate soldiers and situated the Confederacy as a disreputable foe. "For every one enslaved by the enemy or sold into slavery, a rebel soldier shall be placed at hard labor on the public works and continued at such labor until the other shall be released and receive the treatment due to a prisoner."[71]

According to the just war tradition, nations accused of waging uncivilized war would avoid retaliatory conduct out of fear of appearing dishonorable and barbaric. Neither side, the theory suggested, was willing to endure the violent retaliatory pressures wielded by their enemy. Threatening retaliation ensured that a careful balance of moderation would guide armed conflict, preventing the war from deteriorating into endless cycles of vicious reciprocity. But when Forrest's cavalrymen slaughtered the USCT attempting to surrender at Fort Pillow, Unionists howled in outrage. Confederates, they alleged, mocked the most basic wartime relations. "I know well the animus of the Southern soldiery," a disgusted William T. Sherman remarked after the episode, "and the truth is that they cannot be restrained." Candid Unionists understood why Fort Pillow happened: slavery had too long degraded the white southern master class, tarnishing its soul and devastating its moral compass. "The whole civilized world will be shocked by the great atrocity at Fort Pillow," commented an exasperated *Chicago Tribune*, "but in no respect does the act misrepresent the nature and precedents of Slavery." Slaveholding oligarchs' unrestrained violence and their shocking disregard for humanity had transformed a war waged between civilized belligerents into a trial of gross savagery.[72]

Retaliation against the Slave Power now became even more urgent. Lincoln promised that "retribution shall as surely come" when he addressed the Baltimore Sanitary Commission in April 1864, shortly after the Fort Pillow massacre. Congress's Committee on the Conduct of the War recommended man-for-man retaliation, which, advised Ohio senator Benjamin Wade, "has in all ages of the world been a means of bringing inhuman and savage foes to a sense of their duty." Indeed, General Orders No. 100, the code of military conduct adopted the previous year, stated that "the law of nations knows of no distinction of color." Thus, enemy nations could not reenslave people already liberated by another nation. Nor could belligerents in public war slay soldiers attempting to surrender. Lieber's Code challenged Confederate policies that justified executing captured USCT and their white officers. "It is against the usage of modern war to resolve, in hatred and revenge, to give no quarter," instructed Article 60. "Modern wars are not internecine wars, in which the killing of the enemy is the object," Article 68 concluded. "Unnecessary or revengeful destruction of life is not lawful." The laws of war held the United States to the highest retaliatory standard and justified legal, ethical, and retributive measures to protect the nation's soldiers. Moral imperatives compelled the Union to distinguish itself from the Confederacy's uncivilized violation of human rights. But Lieber also warned that retaliation promoted a kind of indiscriminate and even unrestrained violence. Retaliation, "as the sternest feature of war," he advised, should "never be resorted to as a measure of mere revenge, but only as a means of protective retribution." Though the Union possessed a righteous claim to shelter African American troops, "unjust or inconsiderate retaliation removes the belligerents farther and farther from the mitigating rules of war, and by rapid steps leads nearer to the internecine wars of savages."[73]

Lieber's careful wording placed the Lincoln administration in an impossible position. While legal and ethical, retaliation would likely trigger a series of devastating Confederate reprisals against black Union soldiers, igniting a truly dreadful racial inferno. Retaliation would also render the Union morally equivalent to the Confederacy, each nation escalating violent conduct. If the Union did *not* retaliate, Confederates could claim a moral victory and continue engaging African Americans in acts of uncivilized passion. "Every consideration due to our position in the family of nations—to humanity, to civilization should prompt us," concluded Secretary of the Interior John P. Usher, "in the existing condition of the country, to maintain an habitual and scrupulous observance of the usages of modern warfare." Against the cries of Radical Republicans who desired summary retribution against slaveholding tyrants, the administration retained its pledge of retaliation but did not act in kind. Even Charles Sumner, the ardent abolitionist senator from Massachusetts, disavowed retaliation, while acknowledging its legitimate purpose. The practice, he announced in January 1865 during a debate on limiting rations for Confederate prisoners of war, established "useless barbarism, having no other end than vengeance, which is forbidden alike to nations and men." Any emulation of "rebel barbarism," Sumner warned, "would be plainly impracticable, on account of its inconsistency in the prevailing sentiments of humanity among us." The United States would become just as corrupted as the Slave Power that it vowed to destroy. Retaliation "would be injurious at home, for it would barbarize the whole community," turning a once stable and moderate Union, on the global stage, into discordant warring racial factions.[74]

That the Union did not retaliate for the reenslavement of black civilians and the massacre of USCT underscored the commanding influence of civilization in the nineteenth-century American imagination. The mere threat of retaliation marginalized an increasingly isolated Confederacy, condemning the slaveholding republic as an antiquated relic of Old World savagery. Legitimizing but ultimately not acting on retaliation placed the United States on par with a progressive community of nations dedicated to human dignity. The Union considered retaliation only because Confederate policy toward the USCT compelled the loyal citizenry to recognize black men's full inclusion in the body politic. If African American soldiers were truly second-class residents, deemed fit only for "colonized" military service, loyal citizens never would have erupted in righteous outrage at the indiscriminate slaughter of black men. Indeed, the USCT had validated their claim to national integration. Serving with honor and restraint in public institutions, black men undermined the long-standing assertion that they would propagate brutal reprisals against whites. Although an anxious white officer alleged that black troops "are all eager ... to retaliate for the Fort Pillow massacre," independent, unauthorized, and insurgent revenge rarely occurred. Henry McNeal Turner, a chaplain in the First USCT, explained why: "True, the rebels have set the example, particularly in killing the colored soldiers; but it is a cruel one," he averred in the wake of Fort Pillow. "Such a course of warfare is an outrage upon civilization and nominal Christianity. And in as much as it was *presumed* that *we* would carry out a brutal warfare, let us disappoint our malicious anticipators, by showing the world that higher sentiments not only prevail, but actually predominate."[75]

The USCT respected the limits imposed on their public service to the state. They in turn enjoyed the shelter of a nation that had once certified their enslavement. The Union might have unleashed black soldiers in a true insurrection upon guilty slaveholders. But that never happened because it *could not* happen. African American men, like white loyal citizens, disavowed unrestrained violence, instead pledging fealty to the Union as a civilized idea. They saw military service as a means to an end—not a violent end unto itself. "We are now determined to hold every step which has been offered to us as citizens of the United States," explained Joseph E. Williams, who served in the Thirty-Fifth USCT. "We must learn deeply to realize the duty, the moral and political necessity for the benefit of our race," because "every consideration of honor, of interest, and of duty to God and man, requires that we should be true to our trust." Williams desired nothing more than any other nineteenth-century American: the freedom of self-determination and the liberty from state coercion. For all willing to acknowledge it, black military service broadened the scope of American civilization, populating the City on a Hill with a new class willing to defend—not to destroy—its fortresses.[76]

Abraham Lincoln also recognized how emancipation and African American military service "constitute[d] the heaviest blow yet dealt to the rebellion." By depriving the Confederacy of its essential slaveholding lifeblood, emancipation "weakened the enemy in his resistence" to the Union. Yet emancipation itself had even eclipsed the martial pragmatism of just war, embodying profound moral implications. "Negroes, like other people, act upon motives," the president reminded a Republican skeptic of African American troops. "Why should they do any thing for us, if we will do nothing for them? If they stake their lives for us, they must be prompted by the strongest motive—even the promise of freedom. And the promise being made, must be kept." Given that they marched as legitimate public defenders of the Union, "there is no way but to give [them] all the protection given to any other soldier." The war had occasioned powerful changes to the republic's once limited extension of unalienable rights, "hence we behold the processes by which thousands are daily passing from under the yoke of bondage, hailed by some as the advance of liberty, and bewailed by others as the destruction of all liberty." When Confederates joined their slaveholding nationalism to their disgusting policies that targeted black Union soldiers, they exposed themselves as shameful allies of global repression. In stark contrast to his earlier faith in colonization, Lincoln had come to believe that the enduring legitimacy of Union depended on black men serving alongside white men in a common cause "for the great republic—for the principle it lives by, and keeps alive—for man's vast future." Enlisted in the causes of democracy and human dignity, African Americans "have helped mankind on to this great consummation." Later, in remarks delivered from the White House on April 11, 1865, just days before his attendance at Ford's Theater, Lincoln advocated for freedpeople the elective franchise "now conferred on the very intelligent, and on those who serve our cause as soldiers." Through their honorable military service, African American soldiers had demonstrated the uncompromising necessity of a biracial republic committed to a common liberty.[77]

The United States had secured wartime emancipation without destroying itself in the process. But the same was not true for the Confederacy. By 1865, the experiment in slaveholding civilization had been wholly defeated. Biracial Union armies had crushed Confederate dreams of a new world ordered by racial hierarchy, racial stability, and racial slavery. Wealthy planter J. H. Stringfellow recognized this overwhelming reality when, in February 1865, he encouraged Jefferson Davis to consider emancipation as a stabilizing force against a deteriorating war effort. In a letter riddled with anxious disenchantment, Stringfellow admitted that the Confederacy had sown the seeds of its own destruction. Built on false premises and hubristic miscalculations, the world's largest slaveholding nation assumed that it could compel international recognition, prevent an enslaved uprising, resist abolitionist militancy, and forever prove the folly of free labor. The war had shattered each of these assumptions. "The Yankees have now in their service 200,000 of our ex-slaves," bemoaned Stringfellow, while "we have not *one* soldier from that source." Slavery's ardent defenders long disavowed the legitimacy of black soldiers, seeing them as embodiments of insurrectionist calamity. But "our enemies are creating," he gasped, "an auxiliary army of our escaped slaves," an army which would "at will, ravage and destroy our whole country, and we will be absolutely conquered by our own slaves." Stringfellow thus believed that Confederate emancipation could stem the flood of black men pouring into Union armies. Perhaps the promise of freedom would retain their ambivalent loyalty.[78]

Stringfellow echoed the appeals of Patrick Cleburne, a Confederate general who first urged his nation to emancipate and arm enslaved men. Condemning slavery as a national "embarrassment," the Irish immigrant saw the institution in early 1864 as "a source of great strength to the enemy" and "our most vulnerable point." Emancipation would retaliate against the Union's gross abuse of military necessity, which sanctioned undue war against the South's social institutions. The measure would also align the Confederacy with the antislavery community of nations, undermining the United States' claims to moral superiority. "There will be a complete change of front in our favor of the sympathies of the world," Cleburne predicted, that would "deprive the North of the moral and material aid which it now derives from the bitter prejudices with which foreigners view the institution." He even condemned slavery's alleged virtue. "The negro has been dreaming of freedom," a desire that could be harnessed in the quest for national independence. "Their hope of freedom is perhaps the only moral incentive that can be applied," enlisting black loyalty and tempering vengeful desires, which the Union had long used to its advantage. In a remarkable departure from slaveholding dogma, Cleburne cited the enslaved of St. Domingue and Jamaica as proof that bondpeople would fight for their liberty. "With the allurement of a higher reward," he concluded, "and led by those masters, they would submit to discipline and face dangers." Only then could Confederates achieve their experiment in national self-determination rather than succumbing to a new life "forced upon us by a conqueror."[79]

As much as he wanted to believe in Cleburne's vision, J. H. Stringfellow recognized that Confederate emancipation could not cure the national crisis. The world had long ago abandoned the slaveholding republic within its isolated part of North America. England and France did not plead for southern cotton; few of the world's aristocratic oligarchs sought common cause with Confederate elites; and the spirit of international liberalism seemed to scatter the ghosts of racial conservatism. "There can be no other reason," Stringfellow admitted, "than that we are exclusively & peculiarly a nation of slaveholders." The Confederacy was indeed exceptional. And the nineteenth-century world wanted little to do with a nation so acquiescent with, so casual about, and so dedicated to the proposition that all men were not created equal. Though Stringfellow also claimed that emancipation might redeem the national cause, proven in the shrewd ways the Union wielded emancipation against the Confederacy, he could not escape his tortured connection to slavery. "I have always believed & still believe that slavery is an institution sanctioned if not established by the Almighty and the most humane & beneficial relation that can exist between Labor & Capital." But in war, as slaveholding opponents to secession long ago anticipated, it had "proven an element of weakness," and thus *"to secure & perpetuate our independence we must emancipate the negro."*[80]

Stringfellow likely knew that Confederate emancipation would never— *could* never—happen. While the measure might help win a military struggle, it would erase the foundational principles and self-evident truths on which he and his fellow slaveholders organized their natural world. Emancipation might produce independence, but independence from what? In the absence of slavery, there would be no nation, no home, no civilization. Life would have little meaning, devoid of purpose, absent any direction. "The day you make soldiers of [enslaved men] is the beginning of the end of the revolution," protested Confederate general Howell Cobb. "If slaves will make good soldiers our whole theory of slavery is wrong." The very war that slaveholders waged to deliver their eternal salvation had instead furnished their permanent destruction.[81]

It was a just war, concluded Abraham Lincoln, that divine Providence had willed "until all the wealth piled by the bond-man's two hundred and fifty years of unrequited toil shall be sunk, and until every drop of blood drawn with the lash, shall be paid by another drawn with the sword, as was said three thousand years ago, so still it must be said 'the judgments of the Lord are true and righteous altogether.'" Like so many African American prophets before him, Frederick Douglass likewise understood war as the decisive catalyst for fundamental national rebirth, the very transformation that Stringfellow, Cobb, and Lincoln witnessed in 1865. "We are Americans, speaking the same language, adopting the same customs, holding the same general opinions," Douglass declared at the war's outset, "and shall rise and fall with Americans." Foreshadowing the roots of the Confederacy's demise and anticipating the United States' "progress and improvement," the famed abolitionist predicted, "The hope of the world is in Human Brotherhood; in the union of mankind, not in [the] exclusive nationalities" of race, blood, and soil. That union, that nation, that humanity entered a new world when the guns fell silent in 1865.[82]

6
Endings

★ ★ ★

Catherine Edmonston's world seemed to be collapsing all around her. For months she had received terrible news from across the wartime landscape of Confederate armies retreating, Union forces advancing, and even rumors that her Richmond government aimed to emancipate and arm enslaved men. For this wealthy North Carolina slaveholder, the quest for national independence seemed in grave danger. And then, in mid-April 1865, devastating reports arrived. "How can I write it?" she exclaimed. Could mere words "tell what has befallen us? *Gen Lee has surrendered!* Surrendered the remnant of his noble Army to an overwhelming horde of mercenary Yankee knaves & foreigners." But even capitulation of the slaveholding republic's premier national institution—Robert E. Lee's Army of Northern Virginia—might not spell complete defeat. Edmonston clung to reports that French fleets in the Gulf of Mexico threatened war against the United States. Perhaps the western community of nations would finally rescue her faltering republic. Yet even a committed rebel as she could "scarce credit it." As additional Confederate armies surrendered and the Richmond government collapsed, Edmonston acknowledged a once unthinkable reality. "We are *crushed*! subjugated! and I fear, O how I fear, *conquered*." She reported her fellow citizens utterly defeated, disavowing further resistance, and admitting that "we are out numbered [and] overrun"—"'The War is over.'"[1]

Like countless Confederates, Edmonston regarded slavery as the lifeblood of civilization, a beacon of progress, "the birthright of the South," the essence "of national honour," and the source of "true national prosperity." The Confederacy was the only major modern nation founded on the slaveholding standard: that human bondage and racial hierarchy promoted social stability, domestic affluence, and white democracy. "Slaveholders on principle, & those who hope one day to become slaveholders in their time," she explained several months before Lee's surrender, "will not tacitly yeild their property & their hopes & allow a degraded race to be placed at one stroke on a level with them." Now, a biracial army of "foreign mercenaries" had extinguished all that Edmonston claimed exceptional about her former republic. "We feel a deep & abiding resentment towards a nation who thus debases our sense of personal honour," she protested. In the wake of Confederate collapse, Edmonston faced an impossible dilemma: pledge loyalty to a new abolitionist Union, "or see yourself plundered alike by Yankees & negroes." Confederates charted a

The Last Offer of Reconciliation ... "The door is open for all," *ca. 1865,*
by Henry Thomas, depicts the conciliatory spirit of reunion in the wake of
Confederate surrender. In accordance with the martyred Abraham Lincoln's
wish "to bind up the nation's wounds" and forge "a just and lasting peace among
ourselves and with all nations," the United States welcomes former Confederates
and freed African Americans into the republic's fold. The Union's moderation
appears to stabilize and restrain the national future. (Library of Congress)

new national destiny in 1861 to avoid these dual disasters that had long transformed the Western Hemisphere. By 1865, the world had turned against the
American slaveholders and joined in the United States' triumph. "England,
France, & I beleive the rest of the habitable globe," Edmonston groaned, "so
inflated are they with their victory!" Leading an ostensible host of conquering
nations, the Union imposed the twin verdicts of the war—emancipation and
submission—upon a conquered nation and a prostrate people.[2]

Charles Pinckney Kirkland, a loyal citizen of the Union, also recognized the
momentous dissolution of the slaveholding republic. "After a contest of four
years of unexampled proportions," he exclaimed, "the glorious end has come;
reason, right, justice, liberty, humanity, have triumphed." The Union vindicated democracy through a gory contest of arms to prove "that 'man is capable
of self-government.'" U.S. legions occasioned "the unspeakable delight [in] the

utter extinction of Slavery in this land." The nation emerged in victory free from "the great disturbing cause of [t]his country's peace, the source of all the discord, heart-burnings and dangers of the Republic for the last half century." The United States now enjoyed "an elevated, influential and distinguished place among the nations." In Kirkland's estimation, no people ever expended more blood, treasure, and pluck in the sacred service of democracy. "The great cause of civilization, of free institutions, of civil and religious liberty, indeed of Humanity," had been preserved. Unburdened from slavery's draining yoke, the Union could now stand on behalf of the world's weary masses as a truly free, sovereign republic safe from internationalist subversions.[3]

While he took great pride in his nation's victory, Kirkland also warned his fellow citizens against levying excessive retribution against former Confederates. He did not hesitate to condemn the Confederacy's unrighteous pursuit of slaveholding independence, nor did he exonerate rebels' brutal wartime conduct. But they had been utterly vanquished; their cause was now dead, their unholy republic nonexistent. If loyal citizens waged war to prove democracy's eternal life, the triumphant republic mandated a temperate reunion. Unionists were prepared "to cast the veil of oblivion over the past; to pardon the grievous wrongs they have suffered as a people and as individuals, and to welcome back to brotherhood the people of the rebel States." Though he questioned the extent to which treasonous rebels should pay for their crimes, Kirkland believed that the United States' elevated standing in the world depended on "reason, justice and mercy" to bind the Union to "equally high and imperative considerations" of restraint and moderation.[4]

According to Kirkland, to execute a preponderance of rebels would betray the cause of Union. Justice demanded holding Confederate leaders accountable, while forgiving the multitude of misguided white southerners. "We are a civilized, a Christian, a humane people," Kirkland avowed. "As such we now owe a stern duty to ourselves, our posterity, *our* country and the world" to fashion an unconditional but moderate peace, one grounded only in Union and emancipation. Balancing moderation and force would stem future wars of rebellion. "Self-interest," Kirkland concluded, "demands of [white southerners] a full and honest acquiescence in the 'new' state of things." Relieving conquered Confederates from violent retribution would quell their rebellious spirit "and will place them as their fellow-citizens of the North are placed, in the perfect fruition of all the privileges of this, 'the best Government in the world.'"[5]

For Catherine Edmonston and Charles Kirkland, ending the American Civil War proved just as critical as waging the conflict. Each viewed the decisive events during the spring of 1865 as conclusive stages in the long course of American civilization. The rise and fall of nation-states, and with them the preservation of liberal democracy and the decimation of slaveholding, signaled an overwhelming end to ruinous war. Everything for which Edmonston's Confederacy stood now lay in smoldering ash. Yet she did not bathe in the serenity of peace. Rather, she cursed 1865 as the terrible birth of a distant, dreaded future, which her young nation had aimed—but failed—to abort. For Kirkland, that grand spring renewed the Union, revealing to the world that popular representative government could flourish free from internal anarchy. Now, in addition to an absolute triumph of arms, the Union could demonstrate how to end a civil war freed from callous retribution. Both Edmonston and Kirkland thus framed critical questions faced by their respective societies: Would former Confederates reject their national failure and promote a widespread insurgency? Would they seek aid and common cause abroad in hopes of reigniting their quest for independence? Would Unionists pursue a restrained peace astride the world's largest military establishment? And would they prevent the former Confederacy's international sympathizers from destabilizing the Union's continental hegemony?[6]

For the United States especially, the nineteenth-century just war tradition resided at the core of these questions. The legitimacy of Union victory depended on recognizing that the war had truly ended, that Confederate surrender divorced belligerents from state-sanctioned violence, and that the nation's distinct wartime scope had fundamentally changed with the close of public war. "The Rebellion is now ended in the only mode in which it could be ended," Kirkland advised, "by the total destruction of its military power." Only "'restoration' to the Union, in a practical sense, may well be predicated [on this] present condition," he instructed. The dissolution of one military state necessitated a relative demobilization of the other. Francis Lieber's wartime instructions echoed Kirkland's perspective: "Men who take up arms against one another in public war do not cease on this account to be moral beings," the German legalist wrote in his instructions to Union armies, "responsible to one another and to God." If morality guided war, it most certainly informed peace, safeguarding human dignity and preserving the nation in which that dignity rested.[7]

War waged to unify a democratic nation mandated a lenient and lasting peace. "Consider," Kirkland beseeched, "the genuine brotherly feeling toward the people of the rebel States which pervades the universal North; no one among us is actuated by a spirit of revenge; no one calls for indiscriminate punishment." A just peace demanded that white southerners "return to the fulfillment of those duties and obligations" but also permitted them "the enjoyment of those privileges" from which they once benefited as citizens. Disavowing secession, pledging loyalty to the Union, and accepting emancipation were just punishments for the crimes of rebellion and civil war. The American destiny and the international future depended on a republic reunited.[8]

Only in the rarest cases, then, did the United States prosecute and execute Confederates convicted of war crimes: Henry Wirz, commandant of the notorious Andersonville prison; Champ Ferguson, an infamous guerrilla alleged to have murdered more than a hundred Union soldiers and civilians; and the various conspirators who devised Abraham Lincoln's assassination. Among the 850,000 soldiers who served in the Confederate army, the federal government indicted only thirty-seven high-ranking generals. And although Jefferson Davis spent two years in prison, federal prosecutors eventually dropped his case. Northern abolitionists who desired an agreeable reconciliation then paid the former Confederate president's bail, releasing Davis to live the remainder of his life as a free man. A just war's emphasis on peace, combined with a uniting faith in American exceptionalism and white reconciliation, necessitated the reintegration of wayward southerners into the democratic fold with leadership provided by regional Unionists. With no martyrs to defend and no cause to reignite, loyal citizens claimed, embittered but defeated rebels would assist in restoring the Union.[9]

From Conciliation to Demobilization

When spring dawned in 1865, Union armies enjoyed strong military advantages over their Confederate foes. In late March, Abraham Lincoln conferred privately with his leading commanders—Ulysses S. Grant, William T. Sherman, and David D. Porter—to share his vision of peace. All anticipated the imminent capitulation of Confederate armies, and Lincoln presented his military chieftains with a clear and decisive but also a restrained vision: compel the unconditional surrender of the Confederacy and all of its armies, permit the officers and soldiers to return home unmolested, and refrain from "indulg[ing] in revenge." The dissolution of the Confederate state itself would soon follow. Lincoln urged that all former rebels be welcomed once again as fellow countrymen. Only the "most liberal and honorable terms," the president explained, should be offered. Federal armies would be barred from pursuing gross reprisals because "we want those people to return to their allegiance to the Union." If the war was a contest to preserve liberal democracy, then it logically followed that American citizens—no matter how rebellious and destructive—had to be treated with just equanimity. A once democratic Union could not emerge from the throes of civil war with a rigid hierarchy composed of victors and vanquished, citizens and subjects. Lincoln had transmitted this same message a few weeks earlier to the American people. "With malice toward none; with charity for all," he concluded in his second inaugural address, "let us strive on to finish the work we are in; to bind up the nation's wounds," in hopes that "a just, and lasting peace, among ourselves, and with all nations," would follow.[10]

Union generals extended the desires of their civilian commander in chief. On April 9, 1865, fewer than three weeks after the president met with his military leaders, Robert E. Lee's Army of Northern Virginia surrendered to Ulysses S. Grant at Appomattox Court House. "I am equally anxious for peace," Grant informed Lee. "By the South laying down their Arms, they will hasten that most desirable event, save thousands of human lives and hundreds of Millions of property not yet destroyed." Grant demanded that Confederates surrender unconditionally, pledging their undying loyalty to and promising never again to rebel against the federal government. Eschewing any hint of degrading malevolence, Grant permitted Confederates to be paroled and advised them to go home; he also commanded his own army to abstain from any form of celebration. "The War is over," Grant declared shortly thereafter. "The rebels are our countrymen again." Grant assured Lee privately that "each officer and man will be allowed to return to their homes, not to be disturbed by United States authority as long as they observe their parole and the laws in force where they may reside." While numerous Confederate armies still remained in the field—only to surrender in the coming weeks—Appomattox struck a symbolic chord with Americans of all persuasions as the war's definitive end.[11]

The Union's citizen-soldiers identified Confederate surrender as the war's long-awaited climax. For young men steeped in the language of American civilization, who saw the war as a public crusade in the name of national exceptionalism and hailed from a culture that identified military contests as determinants of national destiny, the capitulation of Confederate armies confirmed the permanent security of the American republic. "Glory to God in the highest. Peace on earth, good will to men! Thank God Lee has surrendered," Rhode Islander Elisha Hunt Rhodes extolled from his camp in the triumphant Army of the Potomac. "I have seen the end of the Rebellion." At the end of April he reported "news that [Joseph E.] Johnston has at last surrendered," which "is good news, and the war is certainly over." As he reflected on the devastating trial in Virginia to which he had long been witness, Rhodes commented in May that finally "here all is peace, and the war is over." John F. Brobst, who marched in William T. Sherman's western Union army that forced Johnston's surrender in North Carolina, also celebrated the "permanent peace and the re-establishment of the laws of the Union again. We all think and believe that this cruel war has reached its end at last."[12]

The demise of rebel armies appeared to unbind the slaveholders' stubborn grip on democracy. Private Wilbur Fisk, who soldiered in the Army of the Potomac, regarded Appomattox as the dawn of a new American epoch. "It is hardly possible for anything to take place now that will compare with what has already taken place," he wrote in May 1865. With "the complete overthrow of Gen. Lee and his rebel host, that had so long withstood us," Fisk opined, "we knew that the great serpent of secession whose poisonous fangs had been struck at the nation's life, was about to lose its power for evil forevermore." Fisk indicted the slaveholders' rebellion as the greatest transgression ever perpetrated on humanity, one that could die a violent death only by the might of a superior and enlightened nation committed to its eternal destruction. "It did not die until it had exhibited to all the world, the infernal spirit which has ruled its every action, but committing a crime, the atrocity of which shows a depth of depravity and wickedness without parallel in modern history."[13]

With the collapse of the Confederate state, loyal citizens imagined the Union's national banner once again hugging a united republic. "The rebellion is broken—crushed—our national flag will float the country over," Missouri Unionist Franklin Archibald Dick reported on the day after Appomattox. Now that "our Nation is preserved—Slaughter and wounds will cease—peace & tranquility will be restored," radiating liberal democracy to all corners of the continent. Few impediments now blocked a manifest American destiny: "The surrender of Lee leaves really nothing in the field against us." The Slave Power's long reign as the obstacle to national progress had been decimated. The war and its dramatic conclusion thus served an ominous warning both to opponents of democratic republicanism and to the Confederacy's international sympathizers. "The olive branch will flourish, and the old Banner of freedom will wave over a once more united people," Iowa soldier Charles O. Musser anticipated. "And we will let foreign nations know that our flag cannot be insulted with impunity by any one. We will let them now that man is capable of Self-Government." The war's end confirmed that the will of a free people, the moderation of popular democracy, and the providential blessings of liberty would always triumph against the corrupted forces of slaveholding internationalism. "Our country is surely safe now," a volunteer reported from the Grand Review of Union armies in May. "There is not a doubt in regard to the ability of our great and good government to crush all rebellions that may spring up."[14]

Volunteer Union soldiers cited Appomattox as the signal feat of national purpose. Understanding that military events guided national fortune, citizens of modern mid-nineteenth-century nation-states looked to their military establishments to direct, shape, and secure the national destiny. When he reminded the American people during his second inaugural address that "the progress of our arms, upon which all else chiefly depends," Abraham Lincoln articulated a self-evident principle of the just war tradition. Only formal militaries engaged in public war determined the fate of belligerent nations. Only the triumph of state-sanctioned arms could shape a new birth of democratic liberalism, neutralizing the internal and external foes of American civilization. The newspaper for the Sixth Corps of the Army of the Potomac printed a poem in early May 1865 that captured the implications of military triumph: Union soldiers have "*conquered* us Peace and have shown to the world that tyranny's flag must in darkness be furled." The events of April 1865 served as *the* gateway to national restoration. Dissolution of the Confederacy, and with it a powerful military apparatus and political oligarchy, signaled the evaporation of the slaveholding republic's existential purpose: national independence through the disintegration of the United States. The conditions of war thus gave way to a new peace.[15]

That the United States claimed to be among the world's most civilized nations compelled the loyal citizenry to measure their conduct with humble restraint and moderate passion. Victorious nations pledged to waging a just war no doubt enjoyed certain privileges and responsibilities to command permanent submission of the defeated. But the Union demanded only that former Confederates pledge their national loyalty and recognize emancipation. Abraham Lincoln calculated that generous and lenient terms would entice former Confederates to participate fully as citizens within a steady and functioning republic, rather than again staking their future on radical separatist movements. Long anxious about the dangers of an unrestrained war guided by unbridled passion, Lincoln maintained that summary punishments would compel rebel troops "not to return to their homes to accept citizenship under a hated rule; and with nothing but desolation and want through the South, the disbanded Confederate soldiers would be tempted to lawlessness and anarchy." At the center of this equation stood the Union itself. Democracies could not tolerate continued states of war, much less endure the chaos of insurgencies. Without a clearly defined end to the war—the collapse of Confederate nation and the complete disbanding of its armies—all participants would be engulfed in infinite cycles of retributive violence. A once stable Union might well tear into fragile warring factions, a condition far different from the limited, organized, public war waged between nation-states. "Let them once surrender and reach their homes," Lincoln predicted, "[and] they won't take up arms again."[16]

Ulysses S. Grant agreed that reprisals, military compulsion, and summary punishment would likely provoke former Confederates into an irregular and chaotic insurgency. In this scenario, the war would never end, assuming new and deadly forms, defying any kind of ordered restoration. The immediate wake of Appomattox convinced Grant that the mass of white southerners "are anxious to see peace restored so that further devastation need not take place in the country." He endorsed a moderate peace that eschewed "further retaliation and punishment," aware "of the suffering endured already" by countless Confederates. Though favoring strict penalties for rebel leaders, Grant argued that imprisoning thousands of former Confederates, pursuing mass prosecutions, and holding public trials would only convince white southerners of their ever precarious and marginalized place in the new Union. He also recognized that the overwhelming mass of young white southern men who had been trained in the militaristic art of modern war could reignite devastating pockets of violence throughout the South. After all, what did they have to lose if the federal government pledged prodigious reprisals? "I made certain terms with Lee," Grant explained years later, "the best and only terms. If I had told him and his army that their liberty would be invaded, that they would be open to arrest, trial, and execution for treason, Lee would never have surrendered, and we should have lost many lives in destroying him." Being allowed to return home with their horses and sidearms, absolved from public prosecution, and free to rejoin the American Union "will have the best possible effect upon the men," Lee informed Grant. "It will be very gratifying and will do much toward conciliating our people."[17]

Appomattox otherwise might have been a bloody turning point in a continuing war, transforming a once stable Union into a cauldron of fanatic militancy. One week before Lee's army surrendered, Jefferson Davis informed Confederate citizens that they "now entered upon a new phase of a struggle." The president proposed that Lee's Army of Northern Virginia might break from its entrenchments at Petersburg and wage a war of maneuver to "strike in detail detachments and garrisons of the enemy, operating on the interior of our own country." Though Davis disavowed guerrilla resistance, merely hours before the surrender on April 9 Lee's chief artillery officer, Edward Porter Alexander, begged Lee "to spare us the mortification of" surrender by dispersing the army to "scatter like rabbits and partridges in the woods." An incessant, pestering, irregular resistance might exhaust the Union's resolve, compelling recognition of Confederate independence. But Lee rejected Alexander's proposal. Like Davis, as a product of American military professionalism, Lee understood that military affairs were tied to the limited dictates and purposes of the nation-state. "The surrender of this army is the end of the Confederacy," he replied to Alexander. "I've never believed we could gain our independence except by our own arms." The capitulation of his state-sanctioned army, joined by the collapse of national authority, undermined legitimate resistance. The Confederacy could no longer live as a member of the community of nations, a reality that an insurgency could not cure.[18]

Lee predicted that guerrilla resistance would further transform his citizen-soldiers into barbaric hordes whose shameful conduct would invite their own destruction. "They are already demoralized by four years of war" and scarred by the devastations of armed conflict. Unshackled from the controls of national military institutions, young men would deteriorate into "lawless bands," preying on the countryside and exciting a violent "state of society . . . from which it would take the country years to recover." Rather than obliging the Union to concede the slaveholding republic's independence, federal military forces would "pursue in the hopes of catching the principal officers, and wherever they went there would be fresh rapine and destruction." Union armies would likely engulf the South in flames, a just response to Confederates' gross breach of the laws of war. White southerners would be regarded thereafter as a people who willfully discarded the restraints of civilization. "A partisan war may be continued," Lee reminded Davis, but a prolonged insurgency would produce "individual suffering and the devastation of the country" without ever occasioning "a separate independence." Only the "suspension of hostilities and the restoration of peace" could prevent unchecked violence, ensure the safety of former Confederates, and forestall the South's eternal destruction.[19]

Other Confederates initially disavowed Lee's recommendations, viewing the collapse of their nation with unmitigated shock. Riddled with anxiety, overcome with despair, burdened by fear, and yet dismissive, defiant, and pugnacious, Confederates struggled to concede the meaning of Appomattox. It was at once a decisive and impossible moment, one that defied the natural course of history but that had obvious implications. "We can't realize the truth of the astounding events that are transpiring so rapidly," an exasperated Alabamian in Lee's army wrote during the flight to Appomattox. "Oh! can it be possible that after all sacrifices made—immolation of so many noble heroes it is not to end in our favor—that we are to lose our independence & be in subjection to the Yankees!" How could a slaveholding republic, long the promise of American civilization, collapse in such a devastating and absolute manner? How could a people so committed to waging a noble war against the furious forces of international abolitionism fall prey to the world's largest armies of emancipation? And how could a nation evaporate so violently and with such little warning, forcing its wayward citizens into an unknown but long-dreaded future?[20]

Confederates reasoned that the suddenness of national collapse had rarely before devastated a chosen and exceptional people. Few societies in modern history—excluding Haiti, which white southerners were loath to forget—had undergone such rapid, transformative wartime change. As the ashes of defeat settled on the southern landscape, some intransigent Confederates initially rejected Robert E. Lee's warnings against insurgent warfare, the only mode of resistance that might mitigate if not reverse their nation's hopeless destiny. Despite the weight of military defeat, especially at the hands of an allegedly barbaric and inhuman foe, and despite the chaotic vacuum energized by the evaporation of state legitimacy, insurgent dreams convinced some that independence might still be salvaged. Clusters of defiant rebels might not achieve national sovereignty, mainly because the Confederate state no longer existed. But perhaps they could harass Union armies, kill Union soldiers, and inflict such discouraging misery on the Union itself that the world would recognize the United States' pitiful inability to maintain *its* sovereignty. When Charles Huston sensed the impending surrender of his Army of Tennessee, he proposed scattering myriad bands to wreak "utter annihilation" against Union detachments. "Living on the country as we pass through and leaving a desert behind us," he reckoned, "would secure peace on *our* terms very promptly." It mattered little whether Lee or Joseph Johnston surrendered. The cause of an independent slaveholding republic was too great, too pure, and too exceptional to abandon with the mere capitulation of armies.[21]

Jared Sanders, a Louisiana soldier who served in the Confederacy's Trans-Mississippi forces, also endorsed "a partizan warfare, as Sumpter and Marion of the old revolution." Indeed, a "disorganized resistance" would demoralize the Union, debilitating the blue-clad invaders' indefinite, expensive, and dispiriting military occupation. Sanders prophesied that his society would "draw encouragement & confidence in our final success from history," following "the rise of Grecian republics—from the foundation of the Dutch Republic—Holland contested for eighty years & at last won her independence from the Spaniards." He also recalled that glorious past, embedded in the minds of all Americans, when "our fathers forced recognition from the haughty invincible Britons." Deliverance rested in the near beyond, Sanders concluded. "We finally must succeed if we fight it to the Last."[22]

Although Huston and Sanders were brash and defiant, a remarkable sense of loss pervaded their faith in a successful insurgency. They hoped that a people's war would spawn lasting independence. But what *kind* of independence would emerge, and at what cost? While Huston, Sanders, and scores of other Confederates may have pledged eternal resistance against the Union, their proposals to wage a chaotic partisan war betrayed the absolute weight of Confederate defeat. Insurgent warfare functioned well beyond the purview of modern mid-nineteenth-century nation-states and ignored their standards of respectability. It stood in abject defiance of republican military traditions and mocked a democracy's claim of legitimacy. Success required nearly universal commitment, crossing delicate class lines and slaveholding interests. Most fundamentally, it undermined the very stability that a caste-based society needed for survival. And Huston admitted as much. He predicted that the Union, and perhaps even the international community, would be compelled to recognize the southern dissidents, "especially if we carry negro troops with us." Yet nothing was more antithetical to a democratic slaveholding civilization. And by 1865, slavery began dissolving at a rapid pace, never again to be revived in a North American nation.[23]

Even if guerrilla resistance succeeded in forcing Union armies to withdraw, the South would emerge thereafter only as ravaged, unstable, disorganized, and smoldering states unbound from any nation, detached from any government, and exposed before the world as little more than liberated but besieged militants. An insurgent war would transform once civilized belligerents into anarchical savages. "We were engaged in a just and holy war," a Virginia Confederate explained, but "we have failed in our efforts to establish a separate nationality." With no nation, former Confederates who continued to wage war would reveal themselves as lawless insurrectionists, beckoning the United States to exact punishing reprisals. Echoing Lee's warnings, even a former wartime guerrilla believed an insurgency "would not only be fruitless of any good, but be a source of serious injury to the people by inviting retaliatory measures." The future had to be shaped within the constitutional boundaries of Union—not within the uncertain and limitless sphere of an erratic insurgency.[24]

Testimony from three Confederates suggests how indignant passion in the wake of national collapse failed to translate into partisan resistance. Samuel T.

Foster, a cavalry officer who soldiered in the Army of Tennessee, questioned why white southerners would even consider defying an absolute defeat. "What were we fighting for," he asked at the end of April after his army surrendered, "the principles of slavery? And now the slaves are all freed, and the Confederacy has to be dissolved." Resistance was futile because Foster's nation, its overt purpose, and its basic objective now lay in ruins. A guerrilla war might channel the humiliation and rage of defeat, but it could not resurrect the Confederacy, the national safeguard of a slaveholding civilization. Foster even sensed a marked alteration transpiring among his comrades. "Men who have not only been taught from their infancy that the institution of slavery was right," he observed with disgust, "have now changed in their opinions regarding slavery." Confederate defeat shattered the slaveholding foundation—humanity's presumed natural inequality—which now possessed a "meaning different from the definition [we] had been taught." For Foster, "no more fighting, no more war. It is all over." But it was still left to see whether white southerners would so easily give up the "natural" prerogatives of white supremacy that slaveholding logically conferred.[25]

James Rumley, a demoralized civilian who lived on North Carolina's eastern shore, also implied that the overwhelming burden of defeat could never be cured by an insurgency. Not content with a peaceful restoration, Rumley viewed the Union as bent on the South's eternal destruction. Yet no matter how defiant, no matter how committed to their cause, white southerners could not contest the seemingly despicable brand of war that Unionists had perpetrated upon the Confederacy. In pursuit of ruthless conquest, the United States had sullied its national banner, now "the bloody ensign of a tribe of brutal fanatics and tyrants." That once great flag "was now polluted by bands of armed negroes who had been taken from masters who had spent their lives in upholding and sustaining the Union it was intended to symbolize." Armed resistance could not stem the crushing revolution that befell Rumley's world, which now lay prostrate before "runaway slaves [who] were enlisted and armed against their masters ... prostitut[ing] to the vilest purposes that ever disgraced a civilized nation." The slaveholding republic once stood as the only bulwark against this unthinkable upheaval. But by the end of April 1865, "the fate of the Confederacy is sealed," Rumley conceded. "Its sun has set forever."[26]

Kate Stone, who hailed from a prominent family of Louisiana slaveholders, echoed Foster's and Rumley's deflation. Sensing that military institutions settled the fates of quarreling nations, Stone confided to her diary in May 1865 "words that burn into my heart": "Conquered, Submission, Subjugation." While defiant, she also wrote with striking finality, never envisaging a distant independence, but seeing instead a dark and definite future. "Our Confederacy will be a Nation no longer," she worried, and "we will be slaves, yes slaves, of the Yankee government." The image of enslavement was hardly metaphorical. It captured the unbearable failure of war to secure slaveholding within what Stone considered the world's foremost civilized nation-state. That "glorious struggle," she protested, mixed with "the torrents of noble blood that have been shed for our loved Country," have all been "in vain." Indeed, "we have given up hope ... and all are humiliated, crushed to the earth." Not even the prospects of a punishing insurgency could cure "a future without hope." Stone anticipated that "if we make a stand, it would only delay the inevitable with the loss of many valuable lives. The leaders say the country is too much disheartened to withstand the power of a victorious Yankee army flushed with victory."[27]

Though the Union's surrender terms were unconditional, they nevertheless acted as a negotiated compromise, offering former Confederates a decisive yet restrained peace. That both belligerents subscribed to the international laws of war meant that each was committed to the threat of retaliation for any breach of "enlightened" conduct. Neither side could afford to violate the verdicts rendered on the fields of battle. On a grand autumn tour of the former Confederacy in late 1865, Ulysses S. Grant acknowledged that "the mass of thinking men of the South accept the present situation of affairs in good faith." White southerners professed their loyalty and disavowed slavery and secession, which "they regard as having been settled forever, by the highest tribunal, arms, that man can resort to." While the Union's just war seemed to have triumphed, Grant advocated that a small military presence stabilize the region "until such time as labor returns to its proper channel and civil authority is fully established." The general-in-chief nevertheless emphasized "that the citizens of the Southern states are anxious to return to self government," pleading that the Union forgo any action "humiliating to them as citizens." As far as Grant was concerned, moderation in the wake of civil war facilitated a consensual reunion of white citizens into the national body.[28]

Robert E. Lee responded favorably to the Union's magnanimity, urging his compatriots "to unite in the restoration of the country, and the reestablishment of peace and harmony." He advised, "It should be the object of all to avoid controversy, to allay passion, give full scope to reason and every kindly feeling." A lasting restoration, one built on energy and enterprise, should never succumb to "thoughts of the past & fears of the future." Such a course guaranteed that "our country will not only be restored in material prosperity, but will be advanced in science, in virtue, and in religion." Submission to federal authority—no matter how grudging or distasteful—offered white southerners an opportunity to exist free from state-sanctioned abuse. As Lee well understood, and Grant himself confirmed, if former Confederates restrained the bitter passions of defeat, the federal government would not impose strict penalties for the crime of disunion. If white southerners rejected guerrilla warfare, they could escape uncompromising reprisals, thereby reconstructing the region on *their* terms. The implication was clear: a moderate surrender permitted former Confederates to return home and reestablish rigid racial and labor regimes predicated on white supremacy. When Lee later admitted his "oppos[ition] to any system of laws that would place the political power of the country in the hands of the negro race," there was little doubt that he interpreted the leniency of Appomattox as license to rebuild as much of the Old South's civilization as possible.[29]

It might be tempting to appraise Abraham Lincoln's mercy, Ulysses S. Grant's moderation, and Robert E. Lee's gratification as foolish approaches to white reconciliation. When also reading of Confederates' unapologetic vengeance, one can almost foresee the slaveholders' rebellion never dying at Appomattox, slinking instead into a deep hibernation and only later to resurrect the Confederacy's old cornerstone. But the measured surrenders in 1865 testified to the commanding influence of civilized restraint in the nineteenth-century American imagination. Americans of all persuasions believed they lived in a world riddled with oppressive, state-sanctioned violence. Fearful that the forces of internationalization always impinged on their civilization, and worried that they would exude the very global radicalism that they claimed to oppose, the transition from war to peace persuaded these Americans that military surrenders could not function in a barbaric manner. Only the stability and moderation of the nation-state, either in guiding a peaceful reunion or in discouraging a stateless people's insurgency, could promote some kind of lasting accord.[30]

In obliging an unconditional but merciful surrender, the Union's loyal citizenry sought to demonstrate to the world how civilized republics practiced peaceful restraint. If the United States claimed to be the exception to violent degeneracy, merciless retribution against white domestic enemies delegitimized American democracy. "Rightly will more forbearance be required from the North than the South, for the North is the victor," Herman Melville recorded in a postwar reflection. "May we all have moderation; may we all show candor," because only "the time of peace may test the sincerity of our faith in democracy." Reprisals would fail to distinguish the Union from the violent internationalist Slave Power that it had just conquered. Even steadfast abolitionist Wendell Phillips warned that overt castigation of slaveholders would "sink our civilization to the level of Southern barbarism. It would forfeit our right to supersede the Southern system, which right is based on ours being better than theirs." Peace required checking retributive violence. Though Maj. Gen. William T. Sherman detested the radicalism of disunion, in May 1865 he reasoned, "We cannot combat existing ideas with force." Sherman urged the moderate, lenient, "slower and not less sure means of statesmanship." Otherwise, the Union risked "imitating the French, whose political revolutions have been bloody and have actually retarded the development of freedom."[31]

Sherman offered a provocative counterpoint to the premise of a restrained but unconditional surrender. He believed that military commanders, rather than tremulous politicians, best possessed the dispassion to negotiate the end of war and establish the terms of peace. Any hint of retribution, any insinuation of punishment, portended a "great danger that the Confederate armies will dissolve and fill the whole land with robbers and assassins." U.S. armies would then be tasked with combating a widespread insurgency that might take years to quell, soaking the nation in overwhelming bloodshed. Sherman alleged that lingering Confederates "admitted that Slavery was dead" and that all white southerners "want Peace and I do not believe they will resort to war again during this century." His negotiated terms for Joseph E. Johnston's Confederate army in North Carolina thus stipulated that the army disband and its soldiers return home, recognized once again by the U.S. government as full, equal citizens. The terms at once granted "amnesty" to Confederates, whom Sherman ordered to resume their "peaceful pursuits," and reinstated to white southerners "their political rights and franchises, as well as their rights of person and property as defined by the Constitution of the United States and of the States respectively."[32]

Sherman's terms of surrender posed profound implications to the Union's definition of unconditional surrender and just war. He superseded civilian control of the military to establish the political conditions of peace, the scope of white southern citizenship, and the functions of local civil government, processes reserved only to federal civil authorities. And Sherman explicitly reinstated slavery into the fabric of southern life when he authorized former Confederates to reclaim "their rights of person and property." Stalwart Republicans condemned Sherman's careless act as treasonous and called for the immediate nullification of the surrender terms. To cool the national tension, Ulysses S. Grant visited Sherman personally and convinced his old friend to draft new terms that mirrored the Appomattox agreement, which reserved matters of statecraft to elected officials. To obviate future wars of secession, the Union of 1865 *had* to stand necessarily changed from the Union of 1861. Slavery had to die unequivocally, and U.S. military forces had to occupy the South in the region's stateless transition from war to peace. Sherman consented, but not without protest. A policy of "physical power," he warned, "will produce new war, and one which from its desultory character will be more bloody and destructive than the last." That same power, Sherman predicted, would invariably produce African American citizenship and suffrage. These seemingly unjust acts exceeded the Union's wartime purpose, imposing an undue burden on the white South. "To give all loyal negroes the same political status as white 'voters' will revive the war," Sherman imagined. "Why not, therefore, trust to the slower and not less sure means of statesmanship," relying on the moderation of constitutional deliberation, "instead of imitating the French, whose political revolutions have been bloody and have actually retarded the development of political freedom?" In their distinct readings of surrender and national purpose, Grant and Sherman encountered a stark paradox of exceptionalist conviction: how to balance moderation and force alongside Union and emancipation to preserve and stabilize the republic. This question would soon become the paramount theme of the postwar era.[33]

That same question acquired even greater currency in April 1865, when Abraham Lincoln's assassination provoked widespread calls for retribution. No other nation, Charles Pinckney Kirkland declared, was more justified than the United States in exacting copious reprisals for the crimes of secession, war, and Lincoln's slaying. "It is an undoubted fact that the Rebellion, from its beginning to its end, has been conducted by the rebels in a spirit of savage barbarity." Rending the nation in the name of slaveholding unleashed anarchical violence across the American landscape. Yet few white southerners beyond the handful charged with the president's murder incurred punishment. The errant "slave aristocrat" and "the commonest of 'white trash,'" "in our willingness to receive them again into the common fold," Kirkland opined, "they will see a spirit of elevated magnanimity and of true Christian love, of which the world has as yet furnished few of any examples." Stripping revolutionary disorder from national life, a peaceful but decisive reunion required sober restraint. A far more just punishment than retaliatory executions compelled former slaveholders to *live within* a new Union cleansed by the blood of a martyred antislavery president. Lincoln's senseless death stemmed from the "barbarisms" long performed by the Slave Power. "The revenge we shall take for the murder of Lincoln will be, to raise the loyal black population of the South not only to the position of freemen, but of voters," predicted a Boston theologian, "to shut out from power forever the leaders of the rebellion; to re-admit no Southern State into the Union until it has adopted a free-state constitution, and passed [an] antislavery amendment so dear to Abraham Lincoln's heart."[34]

The rapid demobilization of Union armies testified to the loyal citizenry's commitment to an antimilitaristic peace. The United States' blue legions halted their imposing march when rebel armies evaporated and the Confederate state disintegrated. Democratic republics forswore large military states sustained by overbearing centralized compulsion. Composed overwhelmingly of private citizens who wielded nearly unchecked political power, Union armies themselves bowed to the prevailing ethos of republicanism secured by battlefield victory. A condition of constant war, the persistent anxieties of violence, and "a garrison state" always pulsating to the strides of warrior hosts defied claims of national exceptionalism. A just and lasting peace would dawn only if the loyal citizenry no longer considered *themselves* in a status of mobilized public war, no longer regarded former Confederates as enemies of the state, and no longer brandished the tools of militaristic state power. "As the grave necessity that called [Union volunteers] to the field has passed away, there is nothing left for them but to return to the quiet pursuits of peaceable life," reported the *New York Herald*. "Let all these servants of the republic be employed in public as well as in private establishments." The demobilization of the Union's million-man army thus underscored the enduring democratic image the United States had long presented to the world: that popular representative government could be upheld only by the strong arms of its own citizens, who in turn relinquished their state-sanctioned military dominion.[35]

The Union's citizen-soldiers linked the surrender of Confederate armies and the republic's survival to the end of their own military careers. U.S. forces comprised common citizens—not professional mercenaries—who demanded immediate discharges from the stifling confines of army life. They longed for a return to their peaceful civilian pursuits. "We offered our services to our country to help put down the rebellion," Charles O. Musser explained. "That object has been accomplished, and our time is out, and we are no longer needed." Nothing affronted democratic sensibilities more than military service, Joseph Fisk remarked. "If [a man] becomes a soldier, [he] must for the time being suspend his claims to its privileges, and surrender himself on the requirements of military life, absolutely and entirely." But in July 1865, Fisk rejoiced that the shackles of military compulsion had finally had been lifted, that "our old regiment no longer exists as an organization among the powers that be, but must henceforth be reckoned as among the powers that were." "Now that the war is over," he concluded, "I am no longer a soldier." Minnesotan Madison Bowler voiced the same sentiment from his post in Arkansas. "Peace *must follow soon*. What a grand glorious result of four years of strife!" he cheered. "I do not consider myself under the least obligation to the Gov't."[36]

Serving in temporary military roles to sustain an enduring liberal democracy necessitated that the citizenry remain sovereign in the wake of formal hostilities. On his grand tour of the United States in 1831, Alexis de Tocqueville foreshadowed Union volunteers' demands to be relieved of service. "Among soldiers who compose a democratic army," the young French aristocrat observed of the citizen-soldier ethos, "the greater number, thus brought to serve under the flag despite themselves and always ready to return to their homes, do not consider themselves seriously engaged in a military career and think only of leaving it." Governed by fierce individualism but also moved by a collective duty to safeguard the promise of American liberty, citizen-soldiers served the state with provisional passion. Their service mandated that the nation, on entering a new era of security and stability, sustain private citizens' autonomy. The alluring power of an antimilitaristic democracy captivated Tocqueville, who witnessed volunteers whose "souls remain attached to the interests and desires they were filled with in civil life." Never discarding their identities as citizens, volunteers did not march as militaristic wards of the nation-state. They instead retained a persistent image of peace, that distant moment when they would return to their homes, practice their civilian trades, pursue economic independence, and live free from the sequestered trappings of martial life.[37]

Federal armies thus dissolved at a remarkable pace, almost at the behest of Walt Whitman's graceful petition. "Melt, melt away ye armies—disperse ye blue-clad soldiers; / Resolve ye back again, give up for good your deadly arms," America's poet called. "Other the arms the fields henceforth for you, or South or North; / With saner wars, sweet wars, life-giving wars." By November 1865, more than 800,000 volunteers had been discharged, followed by an additional 190,000 by the spring of 1866. Congress then limited the army's size in July 1866 to 54,302 soldiers, a number that dwindled to 37,313 by 1869, and shrank to 27,472 in 1876. The Union retained a small professional force that resumed its marginal influence in American life. By the mid-1870s, most soldiers patrolled the coastlines and battled Native Americans in the West, while several thousand troops maintained social and political stability in the postwar South. By contrast, the grand armies of Europe, even during moments of peace, ballooned in size, with Prussia and France boasting more than 1 million soldiers combined in 1890.[38]

Disbanding the world's largest and most lethal military force signaled to the community of nations that the United States would not trade democracy for an expensive military state. Nor would the newly preserved Union flaunt a highly nationalized bureaucracy that wielded martial power in the name of national stability. Proponents of American civilization long accused centralized military states of stemming modernity's progress and stanching liberty. Maintaining a million-man army would invite corruption and retard national development, enslaving a free citizenry to the state. Union general John Schofield pointed to these "most important lessons taught by the late American war" when he spoke in Paris in December 1865. The conflict spawned a striking irony: "People who have always enjoyed so great a degree of personal liberty as to be almost unconscious of even the existence of a Government over them in time of peace, have found this mild Government to be in time of civil war the strongest in the world." Few nations had ever mobilized so completely and waged so decisively a massive war in the name of self-preservation. And yet, though the citizenry was stirred by the ardor and devastation of war, "what is grandest of all," he concluded, "these vast armies, when their work was done, quietly disbanded, and ... returned to the avocations of peace." No longer a soldier, the Union's democratic warrior now emerged "in all respects a better *citizen* than he was before."[39]

Drawn from a society skeptical of massive standing armies that threatened constitutional and economic liberty, soldiers transitioning to citizens embodied the decentralization of the federal state. Private civilians who once marched as national warriors were now relieved from the debilitating effects of unremitting war. In May, as he welcomed home his state's "war-stained and battle-scarred veterans," New York governor Reuben Fenton showered praise upon his fellow citizens who had battled "in the cause of liberty." Dispassionate civilians, whose own freedom depended on the preservation of unfettered democratic institutions, had met their country's call to don the Union blue and dismantle the rebellious slaveholding menace. With the laurels of a grateful nation crowning their momentous feat, Fenton implored his dear soldiers "to throw off their uniform, and abandon the weapons of dreadful war for the implements of peace." Only then would they "prove to the world that American soldiers could be peaceful citizens." The corrupting scales of war would thereafter fall away, relieving peaceful citizens of their once fleeting careers as soldiers. Unlike the yoked mercenaries in Europe's crowded legions, peaceful and private citizens, restrained again by martial skepticism, checked the Union from forging an unbroken chain of war.[40]

Unionists praised demobilization as a moral imperative. Disbanding federal armies preserved American democracy from a military force unparalleled by any ever before assembled on the North American continent. Even the trial of civil war would not transform the Union into a rigid militaristic state. Democracy endured, opined a *Harper's Weekly* editorial, because "when the people are the army their liberties are pretty safe." Because it was an army of and by the people, because it waged war to secure peace, "during its existence it was not a public danger, but a public defense." The citizen-soldier ethos undermined any budding Napoleon from seizing the army to use for his own petty ambition. This same institution, "with which Washington secured our national existence, and that with which Grant maintained it, dissolved in the moment of victory." Because the soldier was always a citizen, "the instruments with which he has done his military work disappear, and only the gratitude and admiration which his work excited remain." The nation did not reward the soldier with "a peerage, nor an estate." To tempt human passions with the bounties of military fortune would be to legitimize the most corrupted and furious elements of unrestrained and unmeaning war. The citizen entered the military untrained in the art of killing, and he left desirous never again to brandish the sword. "A profound confidence springs in the popular heart," *Harper's* concluded, "which makes it willing to trust the same wisdom in untried spheres."[41]

Although demobilization aimed to return a republican Union to its antimilitaristic disposition, peace also required a dynamic military occupation of the former Confederacy. Enacting the national will, maintaining civil accord, and enforcing the dictates of emancipation, the peacetime army performed critical domestic functions while also sparking fears of centralized tyranny, democracy's fatal contaminant. Only federal armies could transition the fractured Union into a stable peace, securing the permanent fruits of victory. But large, standing military forces could appear unambiguously coercive, compelling loyalty unto themselves. Would democracy thrive—indeed, could democracy even *exist*—if federal armies indefinitely managed civil affairs, influenced politics, and marginalized the Union's opponents? Could peace flourish, could war end, when armies still roamed the domestic landscape?[42]

Few institutions wrought more fear during the immediate postsurrender period than the specter of a standing army shattering the republic's democratic foundation. *Harper's Weekly* warned that no domestic institution invited greater despotic temptations than "the standing army which is the enemy of Liberty." Worrying less about the army instigating a coup, but instead imagining military authority replacing popular government, even the most ardent supporters of biracial egalitarianism cautioned against the fraught implications of European-style standing armies of occupation. John William DeForest, a former Union officer and Freedmen's Bureau agent in South Carolina, recognized the federal government's imperative role in shaping a legitimate postemancipation landscape. The preservation of liberal democracy would mean little, DeForest explained, if former slaveholders regained control over their former bondpeople's labor, from which they extracted arbitrary political power. African Americans and white southerners would be caught once again in a stifling web of dependence where neither enjoyed the natural fruits of self-determination. Standing as a blunt impediment against the Slave Power, DeForest "believe[d] that my first and great duty lay in raising the blacks and restoring the whites of my district to a confidence in civil law, and thus fitting both as rapidly for citizenship." Yet he posed an impossible question: "If the military power were to rule them forever—if it were to settle all their difficulties without demanding of them any exercise of judgment or self-control," DeForest asked, "how could they ever be, in any profound and lasting sense, 'reconstructed?'"[43]

Republicans like DeForest harbored intense anxieties about tyrannical slaveholders *and* centralized governing institutions. They waged war against the Slave Power to cleanse from the continent the forces of international despotism, but they also dreaded unchecked revolutions spawned within a democratic republic. While the loyal citizenry cheered demobilization as the triumph of representative government, those same voices charged that an excessive military occupation might destabilize popular democracy. Yet only a demobilized but occupying army—to be sure, a contradictory manifestation—could shape a lasting, legitimate, and civilized peace. Carl Schurz outlined the dilemma. "Although the war is over," he worried, "the country is not yet at peace." Discomfited by the unashamed violence that white southerners exacted on freedpeople, and uneasy with former Confederates' gross defiance of federal authority, Schurz observed that "the *spirit of persecution* has shown itself so strong as to make the protection of the freedmen by the military arm of the Government in many localities necessary." He paused, however, when recognizing that "as speedily as possible all the attributes of our democratic system of government should be restored," because "this Republic rests upon the right of the people to control their local concerns."[44]

A refugee from the European revolutions of 1848, Schurz naturally opposed the American Slave Power, which he saw as a pernicious extension of European oligarchy. Though the Union triumphed against revolutionary slave-holders, Schurz wondered how democratic liberalism would replace the Slave Power. "The interference of the national government in the local concerns of the States lately in rebellion is argued against by many as inconsistent with the spirit of our federal institutions. Nothing is more foreign to my ways of thinking in political matters than a fondness for centralization or military government." As a personal witness to state-sponsored despotism, he concluded, "nobody can value the blessings of local self-government more highly than I do." Yet Schurz recognized "the exceptional circumstances" in which the Union found itself. If the nation abandoned the promise of emancipation, he imagined former slaveholders once again regaining power and "provoking new and repeated acts of direct practical interference." Such a course, Schurz concluded with touch of anxiety, "would not pass over without most seriously affecting the political organism of the Republic."[45]

Carl Schurz's forecast stemmed from his familiarity with the excesses of state power. Convinced that a standing army of occupation at once guaranteed a biracial national restoration *and* undermined American exceptionalism, Schurz saw the Union wielding the legitimate tools of victory while at the same time planting the potential seeds of its own destruction. He posed the same question asked by John W. DeForest: Could popular sovereignty be truly sovereign if bolstered by the strong arm of the bayonet? The army assured biracial democracy *but* threatened to undermine it; certified the preservation of the Union *but* threatened its legitimacy; eliminated the Slave Power *but* emboldened its Democratic allies; sheltered emancipation *but* artificially sustained African American freedom. "It is not in accordance either with our national interest or the principles of our government, to keep up a heavy standing army in time of peace," a Republican newspaper responded. "As the standing armies of the Old World despotism are virtually a standing menace to other powers, as well as their own discontented subjects, so the absence of a great army in the Republic of the United States, is a token of our independence."[46]

The Union enjoyed few alternatives to the necessary evil of military occupation. Only the U.S. Army could ensure a lasting emancipation, collapse the slaveholders' republic, and preserve American democracy. And only robust and persistent military power could ensure the Union's wartime purpose *and* shape an enduring peace. Yet how could the Union maintain its exceptional disposition while also wielding the tools of a powerful military apparatus to compel obedience from the vanquished? In a celebrated public speech delivered at Boston's Faneuil Hall in June 1865, prominent U.S. district attorney Richard Henry Dana outlined a robust but restrained course of military occupation. Guided by international law, Dana proposed that the Union could hold the defeated rebels within a "grasp of war." That "we have been in a condition of public and perfect war" necessitated that "the government has a right to exercise, at its discretion, every belligerent power." The United States possessed the moral authority to employ the same war powers used to conquer Confederate armies into insisting the conditions on which the rebel states would return to the Union. Maintaining a broad yet constitutional "state of war" would constrain former Confederates from breaching federal mandates. "We hold each State in the grasp of war until the State does what we have a right to require of her," Dana outlined in the tradition of just war doctrine. "When one nation has conquered another in war, the victorious nation does not retreat from the country and give up possession of it.... No; it holds the conquered enemy in the grasp of war until it has secured whatever it has a right to require."[47]

Wartime victory meant precious little if a triumphant nation could not pursue peace on its own unquestioned terms. To exercise war powers in the absence of formal combat, and even in the wake of the Confederacy's demise, might well suggest a continuation of war by other means. For Dana, however, prolonging the army's war powers served the ultimate *end* of peace. How else would the Union uproot the causes of the war—slaveholding and secession— from the American landscape? An "adequate military occupation" forestalled Confederates from "com[ing] back at once, without condition, into the exercise of all their State functions" to resurrect the dangerous "corner-stone" of their former country. "When a nation goes into a war," it does so "to secure an end, and the war does not cease until the end is secured." An occupying army imposed rigid barriers against former rebels regaining political power, and thus in any "military occupation of the country, the political relations of its citizens are suspended." A lasting, stable, and civilized peace, as "the principle that governs war between nations," obliged a temporary occupation to ensure the full fruition of democracy and emancipation. "There must be an abolition of the slave system," or else the dangerous germ of disunion would again grip the republic. Occupying the states in a grasp of war indeed meant suspending "the political relations of these people to their State governments," because "we require" societal and political "changes [which] must be fundamental." Only the army, retaining its powerful hold on the conquered states, could forge an integrated and enduring Union.[48]

Dana outlined the constitutional limits of military compulsion. The Confederacy once lived as a legitimate nation-state and then died through public war. "Let no man say that I overlook the distinction between a civil or domestic war and a war between recognized nations," Dana warned. "We have fought against an empire established within the limits of this republic—a complete de facto government, perfected in all its parts; and if we had not destroyed it by war, it would have remained and stood a completed government." No civilized nation could therefore wield indefinite military power "to require our conquered foe to adopt all our notions, our opinions, our systems, however much we may be attached to them." Instead, war powers had to be utilized in a moderate, antimilitaristic manner to restore republican governments to the former Confederate states—not erase their essential democratic character. Indeed, only the true flourishing of American democracy would unleash a lasting peace and conclude the military occupation.[49]

Dana explored the profoundly foreign nature of military occupation in the nineteenth-century American disposition. While he fully endorsed the wide latitude available to victors in war, he also recognized that the grasp of war functioned within the limits of a democratic republic. "The conqueror must choose between two courses," he advised, "to permit the political institutions, the body politic, to go on, and treat with it, or obliterate it. Now, we mean to adhere to the first course." Within the American context, the dissolution of the Confederacy ushered in a new set of circumstances from which the United States no longer could operate as a fully mobilized body engaged in public war. Holding the defeated South in a perpetual state of occupation—and thus in a perpetual state of war—undermined basic republican ideals for which the Union waged war in the first place. "It would be the most dangerous course for us," Dana cautioned. He then reiterated Grant's concerns of overbearing coercion: "If we should undertake to exercise sovereign civil jurisdiction over those States, it would be as great a peril to our system as it would be a hardship upon them." Here Dana referred to the proper ways of shaping *peace*, in which each state would again live equally in the Union, governed by republican constitutions and administered by a new political class. Otherwise the nation would balkanize, inflaming the embittered wounds of war and consuming the people within endless flares of militaristic violence. "We have never been willing to try the experiment of a consolidated democratic republic," he reminded his audience. Such a course would place the Union in an endless condition of war, which defied the necessities and purposes of democratic restoration.[50]

In a remarkable way, the grasp of war functioned in concert with demobilization. Although it is tempting to read Dana's theory as a seamless continuation of war, in which Appomattox functioned as a mere turning point, his proposal revealed the transformative power of Confederate surrender. The total dissolution of the slaveholding republic sparked extraordinary changes in how the loyal citizenry conceived of war, curbed the sway of militarism, and aimed to restore peacetime relations both with the southern states and with the international community. Viewing Appomattox, demobilization, and the grasp of war through the scope of just war doctrine reveals how mid-nineteenth-century Americans embraced clearly distinct notions of war and peace; delineated the purposes of military institutions during war and peace; conceived of separate wartime and peacetime processes of national restoration; and envisioned the stark ways in which the United States allied with the world during war and peace.[51]

The Confederacy's death indicated that the Union no longer operated as a true belligerent nation, itself now detached from formal public war and reoriented fundamentally with the rest of the world. The naval blockade of southern ports ended; foreign nations no longer could claim the mantle of neutrality, nor could they regard the Confederacy as a legitimate entity; property confiscation programs were terminated; prisoners of war were released; and any person caught rebelling against the federal government would be considered a civil criminal and not a soldier engaged in public war, because a state of public war no longer existed. Thereafter, in the midst of its own rampant demobilization, federal authorities used the U.S. Army in a highly specialized constabulary manner to oversee the chaotic transition from Confederate authority to new civil jurisdiction, with an eye toward returning the southern states as quickly as possible to the democratic fold. Employing a moderate occupation concomitant with demobilization demonstrated to the world how civilized republics ended civil wars.[52]

Extinguishing the Flame of Hemispheric Rebellion

The surrender of Confederate armies did not bring absolute peace to the North American continent, nor did it signal the death of imperial ambition there. As the slaveholding republic collapsed, France's monarchical adventure in Mexico persisted in civil war between national liberals and Maximilian's imperialists. If Appomattox was a turning point in any conflict, it was within the continental crisis that continued to embroil the Western Hemisphere. Unionists and Confederates both considered the Mexican affair an intimate referendum on the American Civil War. Each event beckoned to the enduring struggle between republican civilization and aristocratic internationalization. While the Union's loyal citizenry branded the Confederate Slave Power a dangerous global agent bent on shattering American exceptionalism, Maximilian's monarchical presence granted continued legitimacy to the failed slaveholding nation. For the United States, the death of the Confederacy meant little if aristocratic privilege, oligarchical clout, and unbounded monarchy took root in Mexico. Antirepublicanism could well spread to all corners of the hemisphere, inviting hungry European nations—and perhaps even disgruntled Confederates—to join with Maximilian's legions to live in imperial defiance of the weak republican Union. For dazed and disillusioned Confederates, Mexico symbolized a flickering hope for their failed national destiny. The American Civil War thus could not end until the entire "North American crisis" also came to a decisive finale.[53]

As their nation teetered on the edge of collapse, some Confederates looked to Mexico in hopes of reigniting war against the United States, gaining international recognition, and achieving independence. Slaveholders had long dreamed of a hemispheric empire; now they hoped for a desperate continental rescue. Rumors pervaded the crumbling republic that French armies assembled on the Mexican border to invade Texas, declare war against the United States, and ally with the Confederacy. Thereafter, "this country will be [a] separate and distinct nation from the U.S. and so recognized by one or more of the European powers," Confederate soldier Hugh Montgomery predicted in March. When Confederate armies surrendered several weeks later, other white southerners placed increasing faith in a possible French incursion. "England and France have CERTAINLY recognized the Confederate States," Texan William Heartsill declared in the wake of Joseph E. Johnston's capitulation to William T. Sherman. "The Emperor Napoleon has landed a large Army on the Texas Coast." Although numb from the news of Lee's surrender, Lizzie Hardin, a Kentucky exile who lived in Georgia in 1865, heard reports "that France had recognized us, and even that she had sent a fleet which had whipped the Yankees in the Mississippi."[54]

Although it might be sensible to dismiss the fanciful image of French fleets landing in the Gulf of Mexico to aid the fallen Confederacy, Montgomery, Heartsill, and Hardin all voiced well-rehearsed articulations of the American slaveholding worldview. Few episodes were more inconceivable than the sudden and absolute collapse of a civilization built on slavery. Because much of the world had embraced abolition, proslavery theorists long argued, once powerful empires now existed on the global margins. Thus the Confederate nation simply could not fail. It stood not as a *place*, but as an *idea*, boasting the self-evident notion that all humans were *not* created equal, that "slavery, subordination to the superior race," as Alexander H. Stephens once declared, "is [the negro's] natural and moral condition." The Confederacy was "the first, in the history of the world, based upon this great physical, philosophical, and moral truth." That the slaveholding republic no longer existed in 1865 did *not* mean that its eternal promise had faded. It only made sense that the allies of hierarchical stability and political conservativism—embodied by France's Napoleon III and Austria's Maximilian—would rescue Confederates from their national and military crises.[55]

Although slaveholding republicanism no longer thrived inside a North American nation, perhaps former Confederates could transplant its enduring promise to a sympathetic world. Lizzie Hardin truly believed that "if we cannot be independent I hope at least we may be a province of France or England or Mexico or anything rather than to go back into the Union." Aligning with the same forces that opposed the United States' liberal democracy presented the only alternative to life in the abolitionist republic. "Even if this last humiliation awaits us," she averred, "we can go to some foreign land and wait with hope for another struggle for freedom." Slavery had to exist *elsewhere* lest it die *everywhere*. When Samuel Foster, an officer from Texas, also heard rumors that the United States demanded that Confederates "go back into the Union," he asked, "what have we been fighting all these years for? Oh no— no more Union for us." The war would instead assume a new guise, "a war of some Magnitude," in which "France Austria Mexico and the Confederacy on one side, against England Russia and the US on the other." Once France declared war against the United States, Confederates would "take the oath of Allegiance to France, and our soldiers will enlist under French colors."[56]

For Hardin and Foster, a nationality distinguished by allegiance to a government and restricted by physical borders mattered little. Any nation seemingly sympathetic to the Confederate ideal, any nation willing to preserve the promise of slaveholding civilization, earned the fidelity of some white southerners who traversed international boundaries in search of deliverance. Indeed, shortly after Appomattox a Virginia planter envisioned "a new life in South America," a safe refuge from "Yankee rule." Approximately ten thousand former Confederates absconded from their disintegrated nation, fleeing to Mexico, South America, the Caribbean, Europe, and even Egypt. Some, like Confederate generals Jubal Early and Jo Shelby, who petitioned Maximilian to forge a joint Confederate-Mexican invasion of the United States, hoped to enlist international aid in resuscitating their failed nation. In an ironic way, military defeat stimulated the most dynamic export of Confederate ideals across the world. "We are turning our eyes to the little Confederate colonies of Mexico as future homes for exiles from the oppression of the Yankees," admitted a former Alabama slaveholder. Preserving the slaveholding principle meant forging an international consensus, continuing the struggle through legitimate state-sanctioned institutions, and advocating for formal public war waged between nation-states. Attempting to resurrect the same kind of conflict that they waged against the Union, these Confederates understood the enduring necessity of international approval. Only a war sanctioned by the community of nations and waged in the name of slaveholding could achieve what Confederate armies had failed to.[57]

Dreams of planting slavery's future abroad (even though Mexico had outlawed slavery) underscored the power of wartime emancipation in the United States. For white southerners, who once populated the world's most dominant, most abundant, and most sprawling empire of slavery, the Confederacy's demise forced slaveholders to decide between new lives overseas or a daunting new existence within a revolutionized Union. For those thousands of southerners who trekked to new lands, life in a foreign country presented a satisfying alternative to an alien existence in the United States. Eliza Frances Andrews, a young woman who hailed from a prominent Georgia slaveholding family, struggled to explain this dilemma. "The demoralization is complete. We are whipped, there is no doubt about it. Everybody feels it, and there is no use for the men to try to fight any longer," she conceded in mid-April. "Our cause [is] doomed" and "the spell of invincibility has left us." Now, as "the heavy battalions of the enemy" forged a new biracial utopia on "our poor, doomed, Confederacy," Andrews imagined a new garrison state rising from the ashes of her tarnished republic. The South's fertile lands "will give place to Yankee barracks, and our dear old Confederate gray will be no more."[58]

No greater calamity had infected a slaveholding civilization more than emancipation; no greater refuge could be found than in the world's monarchies and aristocracies. "The men are all talking about going to Mexico and Brazil," Andrews noted about those who sought to align with Maximilian or forge a new slaveholding future in South America. While a beacon of hope, Andrews nevertheless sensed an inherent danger in expatriation. "If all emigrate who say they are going to, we shall have a nation made up of women, negroes, and Yankees," an amalgamation that spelled utter disaster. Life abroad offered affable sanctuary for some. But for white southerners who could not leave their region, life in an abolitionist military state guaranteed the strife of race war and federal coercion. "Everybody is cast down and humiliated, and we are all waiting in suspense to know what our cruel masters will do with us," Andrews feared. "A race war is sure to come," she forecasted later in the summer. "If insurrections take place," would the federal government obstruct or encourage the devastating massacres? After all, "our conquerors can protect themselves, but would they protect us, 'rebels and outlaws'?" Would the Union of John Brown, Abraham Lincoln, and Frederick Douglass finally cleanse the nation of white southerners? "They have disarmed our men, so that we are at their mercy." Mexico, Central America, and the Caribbean thus beckoned.[59]

For good reason, the United States also saw Mexico as an extension of the slaveholders' war. Confederate migrations to the tropics, southern alliances with powerful monarchs, and slaveholding visions of hemispheric empire convinced myriad loyal citizens that their effort to preserve liberal democracy could not triumph until the forces of radical internationalization had been neutralized. "I regard the act of attempting to establish a monarchical government on this continent in Mexico by foreign bayonets as an act of hostility against the Government of the United States," Ulysses S. Grant informed President Andrew Johnson in June. Hardly relishing his victory over the Confederacy, Grant saw the rebellion continuing in a different guise. If the French presence in Mexico survived, if the enemies of republicanism secured a permanent continental foothold, "I see nothing before us but a long, expensive, and bloody war," which "will be joined by tens of thousands of disciplined [Confederate] soldiers, embittered against their Government by the experience of the last four years." The Confederacy had moved across porous borders, summoning a true international war. "Rebels in arms have been allowed to take refuge on Mexican soil, protected by French bayonets," which in Grant's estimation demanded a categorical military response.[60]

Republicans had long opposed France's incursion into Mexico. Maximilian's reign violated the Monroe Doctrine, which forbade European meddling in the Western Hemisphere, and defied the Union's triumph over the Confederacy. Each belligerent nation posed the same danger: replacing continental republicanism with monarchy and oligarchy. The Republican National Convention in 1864 opposed European designs "to obtain new footholds for monarchical governments, sustained by foreign military force in near proximity to the United States." Secretary of State William Seward advised that same year "that the destinies of the American continent are not to be permanently controlled by political arrangements that can be made in the political capitals of Europe." Confederate aristocrats and European monarchs united to betray the American Union. "We have had no craftier enemy than LOUIS NAPOLEON," a *Harper's Weekly* correspondent opined shortly after Appomattox. "His operations in Mexico were meant as a powerful flank movement for the rebellion. They were leveled at the United States, and the United States are not likely to forget it." The French emperor grossly flouted "the traditional policy of the United States upon this continent, which is unrelenting hostility to the planting of monarchies along our borders by European arms." One of Grant's premier lieutenants, Philip Sheridan, considered France's "expedition to subvert the Republic of Mexico" to be in league with the slaveholders' war, demonstrating to the world "that republicanism was not a success." Indeed, "we never will have a restored union till the French leave Mexico," a nation to which "the malcontents of the South" looked for hope. Thus, "the occupation of Mexico was [always] part of the rebellion," and given that "the contest in our own country was for the vindication of republicanism, I did not think that the vindication would be complete until Maximilian was compelled to leave."[61]

Although hardly desirous of a war with Mexico, U. S. Grant believed that only an invasion could preserve both the Union and continental stability. Because France and Austria had hijacked Mexico to plant "monarchy upon our continent, thus threatening our peace at home," Grant "regarded this as a direct act of war against the United States" and "would treat it as such when [our] hands were free to strike." To neutralize the French threat and to thwart any alliances between disgruntled Confederates and Mexican armies, Grant deployed Philip Sheridan and twenty-five thousand Union soldiers— including the XXV Corps, composed largely of U.S. Colored Troops—to the Texas border to stand as an imposing military presence. "It will not do to remain quiet," Grant argued, "and theorize that by showing a strict neutrality, all foreign force will be compelled to leave Mexican soil." Sheridan's army supplied weapons to Benito Juarez's liberal resistance and executed military demonstrations across the permeable national borders. Only by declaring war against Mexico, traversing the national frontier, occupying the sprawling southern nations, and defusing the enemies of republicanism could the Union preserve its hemispheric inviolability.[62]

A formal war never materialized, thanks in part to William H. Seward's deft diplomacy. Forecasting that the American people likely would not countenance another prolonged military conflict, Seward orchestrated a nimble diplomatic enterprise to convince the French to abandon North America. As he had done throughout the Civil War, Seward employed the power of rhetoric, deployed spectacular threats, and marginalized France and Austria on the international stage. "The United States," he expounded in an unashamed public address, "must continue to exercise a just and beneficent influence in the international conduct of foreign states, particularly those which are near to us on this continent." No doubt aiming his words at Maximilian's French puppeteers, Seward informed his audience of his expectation "that we shall see republican institutions, wherever they have been heretofore established throughout the American continent, speedily vindicated, renewed, and reinvigorated."[63]

The formidable U.S. military presence and Seward's capable diplomacy assisted Juarez in his liberal resistance against the imperialists. "It is now believed here that Maximilian will have to leave Mexico," a loyal Unionist predicted in August 1865. "Our people are determined that the Monroe Doctrine shall be enforced, that European nations shall not interfere with the political affairs of our American continent, nor be permitted to substitute their system of government for ours." The following summer, imperialist forces incurred a series of military defeats, relinquished control of most cities, and succumbed to international diplomatic coercion, prompting Napoleon III to extract his remaining armies. By the spring of 1867, devoid of allies and surrounded by Mexican national forces, Maximilian's government collapsed. Juarez's liberals soon captured the disgraced Austrian monarch, and on June 19, 1867, they executed him. The loyal citizenry celebrated the preservation of republicanism, citing the tangible power of the Monroe Doctrine and the enduring symbol of American civilization as impenetrable bulwarks against hemispheric internationalization. Global elites, declared a New York newspaper, "will conclude that the rebellion is absolutely and unequivocally put down; and these European Powers will suddenly begin to inquire in what position the close of the struggle leaves with respect to the newly discovered giant on this side of the water." Confederate slaveholders, French imperialists, and Austrian monarchs could not withstand the providential destiny of a liberal American Union.[64]

Numerous implications arose from the United States' linking a monarchical Mexico to the Confederate rebellion. First, despite Ulysses S. Grant's blunt military posturing and even his proposal to invade Mexico, neither he nor most of the loyal citizenry desired international war. Armed conflict in the draining wake of Appomattox promised to spread U.S. armies across much of the continent, placing the nation on a perpetual war footing. The great danger, warned the *New York Herald*, stemmed from rousing democratic passions in the name of hemispheric conquest. "After Mexico will come Canada, and after Canada will come Cuba." War against Mexico might even compel the United States to incorporate a people long deemed unbefitting of republicanism. "There cannot be a man in the Union whose heart does not sympathize with the cause of Republicanism in Mexico as well as in any other part of the world," remarked William J. Potts, a U.S. Army officer stationed near Matamoros in November 1865. "But the Question arises, who are these for whom we would risk the peace of our country," he asked of the Mexican republicans battling French monarchists. They "have no sympathy with our cherished institutions. Their system of warfare is that of robbers and they subsist in predatory bands. The peculiar character of the Mexican unfits them for stable Government and representation." Entering a war with Mexico might well barbarize U.S. armies trained in the martial arts of civilized restraint.[65]

An invasion of Mexico sparked the same anxieties of centralized militarism posed by an indefinite military occupation of the former Confederacy. Citizen-soldiers recently returned from American battlefields, living in pursuit of peaceful civilian trades, might again populate the ranks of federal armies. Would they morph into European mercenaries, impervious agents of the state, conquerors whose sole purpose was killing and marauding? John Nicolay and John Hay, two of Abraham Lincoln's closest confidants, pondered whether "a million men, with arms in their hands, flushed with intoxicating victory, led by officers schooled in battle," could ever return to civilian life if the seductions of war teased their basest passions. "Would [they] consent to disband and to go to work again," and would "these myriad warriors ... lay down their arms and melt away in the everyday life of citizens?" American antimilitarism drew strength from deep-seated fears that citizens and the democratic republic—at once the lifeblood of civilized liberty and the fountainhead of restrained stability—would be forever tainted by war, corrupted by violence, and consumed by depravity.[66]

Invading and occupying Mexico would ostensibly transform the Union into the very kind of imperial European-Confederate state that the loyal citizenry aimed to extricate from the continent. Rampant militarism and bloody international crusades undermined American republicanism from standing as the envy of civilized nations. U.S. policy had long opposed hemispheric encroachment because oligarchs, monarchs, and emperors wielded the tools of war to secure their imperial designs. An able republic and a sovereign citizenry stood as powerful antidotes to militaristic aggrandizement. Thomas Corwin, the American ambassador to Mexico, argued that if the United States abandoned republicanism, if it pursed aggressive continental consolidations, no other nation could adopt and unfurl the American example. "The United States are the only safe guardians of independence and true civilization of this Continent," he declared. "It is their mission and they should fulfill it." A robust American influence, Corwin explained in unsubtle racial tones, taught Mexicans "lessons in morals, religion and politicks ... which alone are wanting to make them proper citizens of a free Republick. Let it be remembered that Mexico is our *neighbour*, and enlightened self-interest requires that we should not be indifferent to the welfare of such."[67]

As Corwin suggested, only liberal progress and popular sovereignty could inspire Mexico's republican salvation. Yet his racialized framing betrayed an elusive uncertainty about the Mexican capacity for republicanism. John

Bigelow, the American minister to France, also questioned a bold militaristic posturing, claiming that a republican transformation of Mexico might take decades to complete and might fail altogether. Could such a nation, which so easily permitted a European monarchy to seize its government, Bigelow asked, possess the requisite stability to fashion a lasting democracy? Imposing regime and cultural changes at the bayonet's point exceeded the prerogatives of American civilization, particularly when considering Mexico's allegedly long-standing inability to maintain a stable, independent republic. "The Spanish race in our hemisphere will require for many years a much more centralized government than we can offer them under our present condition," Bigelow advised Seward. Invasion, war, and occupation were "hardly worth our while, under pretext of defending republican institutions." Armed conflict would marginalize the United States among the international community, inviting Old World powers to descend on the Western Hemisphere, broker a truce between the warring insurgents, and shape a peace in the European interest. The continental balkanization that Americans long feared might well transpire in their efforts to shape—and not inspire—hemispheric reform.[68]

Corwin and Bigelow's racial anxieties framed the second implication of Unionists linking Confederate collapse with a monarchical Mexico. To contest the French hemispheric threat, the Union high command dispatched ten thousand U.S. Colored Troops from the XXV Army Corps to serve as a borderland army of observation. Occupying the Rio Grande, the USCT personified the striking militaristic and racial considerations that sprang from Confederate surrender, French imperialism, Mexican republicanism, and American emancipation. With one year remaining on the service contracts of African American soldiers, Union authorities regarded them as ideal guardians of hemispheric stability. While white citizen-volunteers poured out of Union armies, the USCT defended vital American interests on the international frontier. Worried that black soldiers provoked dangerous volatility from their occupation of the defeated Confederacy, Ulysses S. Grant advocated "the withdrawel of Colored troops from the interior of the Southern states to avoid unnecessary irritation." He envisioned the USCT staged along the Texas border to thwart Maximilian's imperial ambitions, while their departure from the Union's interior improved the conditions for a moderate restoration between the United States and white southerners.[69]

Grant surmised that the USCT best represented the Union's continental ambitions. African Americans, the commanding general suggested, augured the nation's future, populating and improving the boundless West. Black soldiers should be "sent as far West as possible," Grant argued, because "these troops will do very well on the Plains, much better than dissatisfied Volunteers." And once discharged from the military, they "may also furnish labor hereafter for our railroads and mining interests." Hardly riddled with the anxieties about black freedom that paralyzed so many white Americans—

indeed, few greater champions of African American soldiers existed among the loyal citizenry—Grant envisioned the USCT guarding the nation's borders, securing American seaboards, and boasting a powerful American image to the globe. "It is highly important that we should have a strong foothold upon the Rio Grande," Grant reminded a subordinate, while to another he advised, "Colored troops can garrison the sea coast entirely." Though perhaps stationed on the national margins, coastal, western, and borderland service planted African American men-in-arms as the Union's gateway to the world.[70]

The Union high command assumed that African American soldiers sympathized with Mexico's contested liberalism. Philip Sheridan informed Grant of "a great desire on the part of the colored troops to go to that country if discharged." Reports indicated that Mexico presented a far more tolerant haven for freedpeople than the American South. Matías Romero, the liberal Mexican government's minister to Washington, cheered the June arrival of "colored soldiers," whom he anticipated would "cross over to us ... because of the advantages they will enjoy in Mexico, where the Negro race is not the victim of prejudice." Long opposed to slavery and deeply skeptical of tyrannical elites, Mexican liberals welcomed expanding the boundaries of American emancipation in assisting the project of New World liberation.[71]

Although hundreds of USCT protested and even mutinied against their transfer to the Rio Grande, outraged to be removed from families who relied on their protection in the precarious wake of emancipation, others viewed Mexico as a referendum on freedom itself. Aware that thousands of former Confederates sought refuge within Maximilian's dominion, the USCT stifled trade between white southerners and imperialists, and even spanned the border to occupy Mexican towns suspected of harboring Confederates. Sheridan recounted the near impossibility of "restrain[ing] officers and men from crossing the Rio Grande with hostile purpose." African American soldiers opposed former Confederates reigniting the slaveholders' rebellion "in the aid of the Imperialists," sensing that an emancipated Union depended on a republican Mexico. "We, the National Guard who by the General-in-Chief and War Department were selected to establish a new picket line on the Rio Grande," Garland H. White of the Twenty-Eighth USCT explained, thus "look after the welfare of the whole nation." The fate of Union, the fate of emancipation, and the fate of hemispheric stability rested on the sturdy shoulders of formerly enslaved men, who, perhaps more than anyone else, depended on a perpetual international freedom.[72]

But that very freedom seemed limited by borderland military service. Although African American troops contributed to the Union's sincere efforts to stifle European monarchy, the USCT functioned in the same capacity as black soldiers from across the Atlantic rim. Mid-nineteenth-century military powers, including France, England, Brazil, Portugal, and the United States, all deployed black troops in the service of international ambition. Considered immune to debilitating tropical climates, allegedly ripe for strenuous labor duties, and seemingly conditioned for indefinite, stagnant military service, soldiers of African descent marched in the lead columns of global empire. European powers, particularly Napoleon III in Mexico and the British on their Caribbean islands, utilized African soldiers "in the performance of particular duties" to consolidate their New World holdings. Thus, when the USCT formed in 1863, William D. Kelley, a founding member of the Republican Party and fierce advocate of a biracial army, declared that black troops would "warn any European government that would interfere in our affairs that we will overrun it with black soldiers if need be." And Joseph Hooker, a former general of the Army of the Potomac, "predicated that after the rebellion was subdued, it would be necessary for the United States to send an army into Mexico. This army would be composed largely of colored men."[73]

The American political traditions of limitation, moderation, and restraint informed the third implication of negotiating Confederate surrender and European hemispheric incursions. Unionists had to look no further than their own continent to see the onerous civil violence that they claimed to oppose. "Mexico," scoffed a derisive William T. Sherman in 1865, was a "country cursed with anarchy & civil war." White American democrats recoiled at the gross atrocities committed by France's monarchical Mexican government. Transpiring almost simultaneously with the transition from war to peace in the United States, Maximilian's infamous "Black Decree" offered the loyal citizenry a useful counterpoint when brokering peace with Confederates. Issued in October 1865, the decree announced that any soldier—even one donning an official military uniform—rebelling against the monarchy would be promptly executed. Aimed to crush the resistance from Benito Juarez's liberal counterrevolutionaries, the Black Decree openly breached the international laws of war and sanctioned devastating cycles of retributive violence. Secretary of State Seward denounced the decree as "a system of warfare so little in consonance with the usages of enlightened states." White Americans had long branded Mexico the antithesis of modernity, progress, and stability, viewing its mixed-race populations as poor candidates for republican civilization. American exceptionalists claimed that any society seduced by the trappings of Old World centralization would inevitably revert to barbarism. France's effortless installation of a puppet monarchy testified to Mexico's alleged volatility. Mexico was thus a "false" republic, always consumed by war and violence, riddled by fractious political chaos, and too weak to maintain its own sovereignty.[74]

Even before the decree was issued, Amzi Wood, an American representative in Mexico, condemned the vulnerable nation's rampant militarism. Wood accused Juarez's liberals of hanging captured imperialists "by the feet & [leaving] them to die & rot . . . along the road side." Hardly the means by which to shape a lasting peace, Wood judged the atrocious violence an obvious sign of Mexico's alleged antiquated savagery. "How long this state of things will continue, depends upon the fact, whether the United States government will take this infernal motley crew of beings under their protecting care," he scoffed. Only an Anglo civilization steeped in moral restraint could bring order to a society devoid of republican tranquility. For Wood, the Black Decree reflected appalling brutality committed by both imperialists and liberals. "The people are no more capable of self government than the animals nor are they capable of any uniform government," he concluded.[75]

Critics saw the civil and political violence engulfing Mexico as an ominous reminder that overt militarism, unconcealed retribution, and centralized tyranny were cancerous to peaceful democratic progress. With the dissolution of the Confederacy and its armies, the United States could either retain its claim as the world's "last best hope" or inject its own Black Decree into the process of national restoration. No former Confederate stood more obviously at this precarious intersection than Jefferson Davis. Fleeing Richmond just before Appomattox, Davis intended to resurrect Confederate fortunes in Texas, Mexico, or even Cuba. But Union forces captured his presidential caravan in May 1865, thwarting any international refuge. The disgraced president then languished for the next two years as a prisoner of war at Fort Monroe, Virginia, awaiting what seemed to be an inevitable trial for treason. Many loyal citizens even called for Davis's prompt execution, which they cited as the proper response to waging an unjust war against the United States. Exonerating Jefferson Davis, *The Nation* averred in May 1867, would legitimize treason, regularize civil strife, and approve violent anarchy as the only solutions to democratic disputes. "We can never expect to be entirely free from elements of danger," the editorialist argued, unless we eliminate "all doubt as to the allegiance of American citizens and the perpetuity of our Government." For this reason, "we should desire to see Jefferson Davis fairly tried."[76]

When Mexican liberals conquered the imperialist threat and promptly executed Maximilian in June 1867, sympathetic Americans could not help but link the slain monarch with the former Confederate president. Both Maximilian and Jefferson Davis, explained the *New York Times*, equally flouted the progress of New World civilization. Each symbolized discredited relics of Old World absolutism, social privilege, and aristocratic license. And each had been defeated by the armies of democratic liberalism. "The treason of DAVIS was open, notorious, and proved by the whole people of the United States," the *Times* opined. "He should have been tried by a court-martial and shot, as MAXIMILIAN was." When France's Napoleon III "looked about to find some royal scion to put upon the throne of a people who abhorred the idea" of monarchy, he found no better dupe than the dashing Austrian. In "usurping the throne of a country which wanted no throne," and in "issu[ing] a proclamation denouncing and consigning to death the Mexican patriots," Maximilian's execution "was not only just, but necessary to justice." The message was clear: Maximilian and Davis were both illegitimate war criminals who waged indiscriminate battles to perpetuate monarchy and slaveholding, which civilized republics roundly denounced.[77]

The *Times* published its editorial in July 1867, immediately following Maximilian's execution *and* Davis's bailed release from prison. Remarkably, the former president would no longer remain shackled, would not face trial, and "escapes the hangman." For some of the loyal citizenry, Davis's liberation seemed to vindicate the Confederacy's unholy war and foreshadowed a future of endless strife. "It will be for history to decide how far a silly sympathy with crime is compatible with justice to the American people," scoffed the *Times*. The Union appeared bereft of political legitimacy and devoid of moral superiority. The writer struggled to understand this monstrous injustice. How could the United States ignore Mexico's patent example, forsaking the punishment of a traitor whose reign had killed hundreds of thousands, occasioned untold destruction, and sundered a once unified people? "Human justice is at best very imperfect," the author sighed, "but why should we make it more so by utterly refusing to enforce our own laws"? Guided by political and legal prudence, federal prosecutors countered that Davis's treason trial might offer an unchecked platform on which the former president could vindicate the legality of secession and Confederate nation-building. To complicate matters, the trial would have been held in Richmond, Virginia, the former capital of the Confederacy, portending a jury pool partially sympathetic to Davis and his late slaveholding nation. Even though U.S. armies had crushed the nascent southern republic's bid for independence, Davis still posed a legal and symbolic threat to the legitimacy of Union. The government ultimately terminated Davis's prosecution in 1868.[78]

A surprising cast of northerners—them all self-described radical abolitionists—collected and paid Davis's bail. Horace Greeley, Gerrit Smith, Henry Ward Beecher, William Lloyd Garrison, and Lydia Maria Child joined fellow reformers to support the former Confederate president. Few Americans more loudly protested Jefferson Davis's world, opposed his slaveholding nation, and welcomed war to destroy his livelihood. However, Smith reminded northerners that the United States had not waged a true civil war against unorganized bands of rebels, those whom the Constitution recognized as genuine traitors unbefitting the protections of the laws of war. Instead, the Union regarded the Confederacy as a belligerent state whose aim was "the Southernizing of the whole nation." The Confederacy thus had to be eliminated as a member of the community of nations so that the Union might again live as a cohesive body. The laws of war, the pragmatism of emancipation, and the providence of American civilization necessarily prohibited blanket executions and mass incarcerations. "Our Generals, in the terms of the surrender of the Southern armies, recognized this bargain"—the Union's offer to former Confederates to live in peace in exchange for their loyalty—"that we should treat each other not as traitors under Constitutional law, but as belligerents under the law of war."[79]

To violate "this bargain" now, to pursue Davis's trial and potential execution, would inflame old passions and summon white southerners again to war. "How it dims the glory and reduces the value of victory! The shame of defeat is nothing compared with the shame of abusing the power of success," Smith exclaimed. He measured Davis's fate within the Mexican context. Smith reasoned that encouraging former rebels to rejoin the nation as equal citizens promoted national stability and obviated future wars far more than executions and summary punishments would. "The present conquering party in Mexico," he advised, "hold[s] the contrary of this doctrine." Retribution, coercion, and redress would never stabilize a fractured nation. "A sounder philosophy teaches that they will exasperate and brutalize, and thus tend to multiply wars," the terrible condition to which Mexico always reduced itself. Only reconciliation "would soften the nation's heart, and prepare it to receive the seed of that higher civilization amongst whose fruits are the enduring Peace and established order for the lack of which Mexico ... is still so unprosperous and unhappy."[80]

According to Smith, constant states of war never produced justice; instead they recycled the devastating tumult that undermined civilized republics. Executing Davis would absolve the former president to live in a new nation conceived in abolition and dedicated, perhaps, to biracial suffrage. True justice stripped from Davis all that once made him powerful, ripping slavery from the national fabric and "removing the occasion for another and a speedy war." Slaying former Confederates would further signal national weakness, revealing to the world that mass slaughter supplied the Union's only recourse against internal rebellion. As they had so often in their short national past, Americans eyed the southern reaches of their hemisphere to proclaim the exceptionalism of their Union. Executing enemies of the state would "Mexicanize" the American republic. Punitive violence reduced civilized peoples to the level of their foes. As Lydia Maria Child explained, state-sponsored penalties of death stimulated "a brutalizing influence on the public mind, and does not tend to diminish crime, as is generally supposed. I consider it a remnant of barbarism, with which the world will dispense as it advances in civilization." For mid-nineteenth-century abolitionists, slavery and civil violence retarded societal progress. The former could never be employed to rectify the latter. Aversion to civil retribution framed their understanding of a just war and foreshadowed how the permanent restoration of Union should unfold. Peace, as the natural condition of civilization, would flourish in the United States, a nation lately justified and cleansed through war and emancipation.[81]

The permanent abolition of slavery, institutionalized in the Thirteenth Amendment to the U.S. Constitution, marked the final implication of the

Union's twin conflicts against the Confederacy and Mexico. Abraham Lincoln had earlier interpreted his 1864 reelection as a democratic mandate to remove slavery from American life. "It is the voice of the people now, for the first time, heard upon the question. In a great national crisis, like ours, unanimity of action among those seeking a common end is very desirable—almost indispensable," he explained after his electoral triumph. "In this case the common end is the maintenance of the Union; and, among the means to secure that end, such will, through the election, is most dearly declared in favor of such constitutional amendment." By 1865, emancipation no longer served merely as a war measure to defeat the international Slave Power. It now functioned as the decisive referendum on the Union itself. If Republicans failed to enshrine abolition within the Constitution, the Union risked ruthless oligarchs again seizing undue political power and severing the nation. Loyal citizens could thus expect the Union to emulate the weak New World republics that routinely ruptured from the turmoil of disputed, fraudulent elections. "Peace with an unchanged Constitution would leave us to stand like Mexico," predicted Wendell Phillips in 1861. "States married, not matched; chained together, not melted into one; foreign nations aware of our hostility, and interfering to embroil, rob, and control us." Only removing slaveholding obstructions to popular consent would stabilize the Union as a strong and legitimate republic. *Harper's Weekly* likewise concluded that the amendment would conquer "all the assaults upon the principles of our institutions, all the signal overthrow of personal and political rights."[82]

In January 1865, Congress passed the Thirteenth Amendment, which President Lincoln hailed as a "great moral victory" for "the country and the whole world." The amendment's foremost supporters likewise interpreted the measure as the principal salvation of the republic, an epic moment that perfected the American mission. Indiana abolitionist congressman George W. Julian considered the amendment "the greatest event of this century." The Constitution would never again genuflect to the barbaric institution of slavery, which affronted the self-evident laws of nature upheld in the Declaration of Independence. Essential to securing a more perfect Union, one that privileged an antislavery consensus and the rule of law over anarchical balkanization, the Thirteenth Amendment marginalized international enemies of republican egalitarianism. No longer would slavery prostitute the Union "to the jealousy and cupidity of tyrants, despots, and adventurers of foreign countries," declared Henry Highland Garnet, the first African American to address Congress, in February 1865. Permanent abolition closed the "door through which a usurper, a perjured but powerful prince, might stealthily enter and build an empire on the golden borders of our south-western frontier, and which is but a steppingstone to further and unlimited conquests on this continent." The Thirteenth Amendment marked the dawning of a new age in which "people of other countries, who are standing tiptoe on the shores of every ocean, earnestly looking to see the end of this amazing conflict," concluded Garnet, "behold a Republic that is sufficiently strong to outlive the ruin and desolations of civil war." By December 1865, a preponderance of the states had ratified the amendment.[83]

In the brief wake of Appomattox, the newly founded *Nation* magazine captured the meaning of war's end. "The issue of the war marks an epoch by the consolidation of nationality under democratic forms.... This territorial, political, and historical oneness of the nation is now ratified by the blood of thousands of her sons.... The prime issue of the war was between nationality one and indivisible, and the loose and changeable federation of independent states." As they triumphed on the fields of battle, U.S. armies had assured the perpetuity of Union. But *The Nation*'s "oneness" seemed uncertain. The ten thousand Confederates who emigrated, hoping they might find remnants of their slaveholding destiny in nations abroad, combined with those millions of defiant and embittered white southerners who remained at home, stood as blunt impediments to national restoration. For slaveholders, the Union of 1865 represented a twisted amalgamation of their worst nightmares. Yet *only* ten thousand white southerners fled the United States, leaving behind a preponderance who would join with loyal citizens and freedpeople in once more charting the nation's vast future. Americans had waged civil war to test the eternal endurance of their civilization. And in that fateful spring and summer of 1865, they faced extraordinary questions: What kind of civilization would be restored in the wake of war? What kind of civilization would the United States boast to the world? The Union had been preserved. But the reconstruction of national sovereignty had just begun.[84]

PART III
Shall Not Perish from the Earth

*Americans frequently change the laws,
but the foundation of the Constitution is respected.
... It is to be feared that men will in the end consider
the republic as an inconvenient way of living in
society; the evil resulting from the instability of
secondary laws would then put the existence of
fundamental laws in question, and would
indirectly bring a revolution; but that period
is still very far from us.*

ALEXIS DE TOCQUEVILLE,
Democracy in America

7

Consequences

★ ★ ★

In early April 1865, when his regiment of U.S. Colored Troops (USCT) entered the conquered Confederate citadel of Richmond, Virginia, Garland H. White, a formerly enslaved man and now a chaplain in the Twenty-Eighth USCT, could not contain his emotions. Urged by his comrades to address the throngs of freedpeople who lined the streets, White "proclaimed for the first time in that city freedom to all mankind." Shortly thereafter, "slave pens were thrown open, and thousands came out shouting and praising God, and Father, or Master Abe." With tears streaming down his face, White watched families and friends reunite, even as he, for the first time in twenty years, embraced his own mother. "I never saw so many colored people in all my life," White exclaimed. "The excitement of this period was unabated." As the capital of the world's largest slaveholding republic dissolved, the day was not seen as the fitting end to centuries of bondage. It was instead an extraordinary beginning, a new birth of freedom, a leap into a future unknown but somehow foretold. Now that slavery had finally collapsed in the United States, White concluded, the institution would fall everywhere else it still lingered. Just as he and his fellow USCT were among the first to enter Richmond and sign slavery's death certificate, so too would they march "until freedom is proclaimed throughout the world. Yes, we will follow this race of men in search of liberty through the whole Island of Cuba." Freedom was now national, and it was destined to thrive internationally.[1]

Paul Ambrose, a loyal white citizen of the Union, also reflected on the historic occasion of the Confederacy's demise. "The collapse of the rebellion, in the surrender of its armies and the submission of its leaders," he wrote in July 1865, signaled an everlasting change to the United States' national disposition. No longer would Americans be roiled by "that long-vexed question of Slavery," forever the bitter and violent source of domestic instability. "Slavery has performed its mission in the world," Ambrose advised, "and is soon to be reckoned amongst the spent forces that have disturbed or assisted the progress of civilization." The southern "Slave Power," that inhibitor of modernity and the kernel of despotism, was now extinct. The United States may have arrived late to the postemancipation world, but those who waged war to spread the eternal flame of liberty tossed the cursed institution "into the great storehouse of things finished upon earth, and to be henceforth committed to the accusing record of history." Like Garland White, Ambrose sensed the moment as a new

323

Reconstruction, *ca. 1867, by John Lawrence Giles. Union functions at the center of postwar Reconstruction, in which loyal citizens join with former Confederates and formerly enslaved African Americans to rebuild a government freed from dangerous slaveholding political obstructions. Ghosts of the American past join Justice and Liberty in watching the postwar generation forge a new republic of true equality and liberty, united on an edifice of law, education, commerce, and free labor.* (Library of Congress)

dawn when the Union would chart an unencumbered course among the community of nations. Constitutional democracy, the fountainhead of national exceptionalism, could now be truly perfected, forever marginalizing the dangers of internationalization once posed by radical slaveholders.[2]

Farther south, in North Carolina, James Rumley, an orthodox Confederate and now former slaveholder, ruminated on the very events celebrated by White and Ambrose. Devastated at his nascent republic's passing, Rumley also gazed into the future. But it was a terrifying reality in which the horrors of a postemancipation world engulfed the American South. Rumley's civilization, once secured upon the delicate foundation of racial hierarchy, now lay on the ash heap of the Atlantic world's decimated slave societies. He now lived in the swirling midst of what he believed to be the nineteenth century's most cataclysmic revolution. Not content with a peaceful restoration of the antebellum status quo, Federal radicals instead demanded that James Rumley succumb to a new existence that defied everything he understood to be natural, orderly, and timeless. He thus indicted the "Emancipation Proclamation, calculated, and no doubt designed, to upheave and ruin the whole mass of Southern society, by insurrections with all their attendant horrors." The United States had overwhelmed the South's slaveholding civilization, imposing, Rumley feared, a perverse substitute for American exceptionalism. "For three years past, we have dreaded, as one of the results of subjugation, that the north would insist on placing the negroes on an equality with the white man at the ballot box." Rumley no longer lived "under a white man's government," once the undying guarantee provided by slavery. He now faced the uncertain "dread of this revolting degradation [which] has long darkened our hopes of the future." Once the envy of the world, American civilization, at least as James Rumley conceived of it, was dead.[3]

The violent wartime death of a slaveholding society had occurred only one other time in the modern Atlantic world. With the collapse of the Confederate States of America, the United States joined Haiti as the only countries to defeat a powerful slaveocracy through a decisive contest of arms. Abraham Lincoln captured the nearly unprecedented nature of this moment in March 1865, in his second inaugural address. The president recalled the situation four years earlier, when "all thoughts were anxiously directed to an impending civil-war," which most Americans feared and sought to avoid. Though "both parties deprecated war ... one of them would *make* war rather than let the nation survive; and the other would *accept* war rather than let it perish. And the war came." Only war could occasion, as White, Ambrose, and Rumley well understood, a decisive outcome to the crisis of American civilization. Thus, the conflict's scope and verdict produced universal astonishment. "Neither party expected for the war, the magnitude, or the duration, which it has already attained. Neither anticipated that the *cause* of the conflict"—"slaves," the president reminded his audience, who "constituted a peculiar and powerful interest"—"might cease with, or even before, the conflict itself should cease. Each looked for an easier triumph, and a result less fundamental and astounding."[4]

That "a result less fundamental and astounding" never occurred—perhaps, according to White, Ambrose, and Rumley, it never *could* have occurred—confronted the United States with questions that most other fractured societies faced in the wake of civil conflict. To what extent would former rebels incur punishment? How would the republic safeguard against radical elements spawning future internal conflicts? What role would freedpeople play in a postemancipation society? Although bitter wars had long plagued the world, the United States was wholly unique in the way it transitioned from civil war to civil peace. The restoration of a constitutional republic within a world seemingly hostile to political moderation distinguished the United States' postwar reconstruction. With few exceptions, former Confederates did not face summary punishment, nor would they be barred en masse from the democratic political system. The tremendous faith in liberal democracy necessitated moderation, restraint, and leniency in shaping a mild peace. Any other path would undermine the very purpose for which the war for Union had been waged. If the loyal citizenry extended massive reprisals against their enemies, if an imperial Union colonized a vanquished American South, or if the formerly enslaved were shunted into an uncertain and immobile freedom, the very forces of instability, resentment, and radicalism that had caused the war might well again overwhelm the Union. Loyal citizens feared that the permanent collapse of state authority would splinter the fragile republic into incessant warring factions. Only an enduring popular democracy, freed from slaveholding obstruction and yet reconstructed together with white and perhaps even black southerners, could maintain the Union.[5]

The Limits of Self-Restoration

When Alexis de Tocqueville toured the early American republic, the young French aristocrat "avow[ed] that I do not consider the abolition of servitude as a means of delaying the struggle between the two races in the southern states." Freedom, Tocqueville surmised, was not itself enough to confer liberty. "Negroes can long remain slaves without complaint; but having joined the number of free men, they will soon become indignant at being deprived of almost all the rights of citizens; and not being able to become the equals of the whites, they will not be slow to show themselves the enemies." If former slaveholders retained political authority and curtailed the freedom of lately enslaved people, an emancipated republic would remain rigidly hierarchical, dependent, and combustive. "The period which follows the abolition of slavery has therefore always been a time of uneasiness and social difficulty," the Frenchman later instructed a national commission that in 1839 was pondering emancipation for France's Caribbean colonies. For Tocqueville, freedom distinguished humanity's organic state, while liberty unchained the individual to live independent from oppressive coercion. To stabilize post-emancipation societies, governments had to erase all vestiges of slaveholding, a system predicated entirely on mastery over the individual. The formerly enslaved could not be divested of natural rights, nor could they be compelled to labor for erstwhile masters. "When the last traces of servitude disappear, and the Negro is raised to the rank of a free man, when he has already tasted absolute independence and believes that he has nothing more to expect and little to fear from the magistrate, social power loses its authority over his will, his opinions, and his habits."[6]

Tocqueville expressed concern about the Atlantic world's turbulent transitions from slavery to freedom. He warned that British West Indian emancipation in 1834 had produced a hierarchical society, limiting freedpeople's rights, blunting their access to land and capital, and implementing brutal labor regimes, which created a landless and aggrieved proletariat. Such limits on freedom forced the formerly enslaved into apprenticeships with white masters determined to extract agricultural labor. In the British Caribbean a state of pseudo-slavery coexisted with a pseudo-freedom, producing a new world riddled with economic stagnation, rampant social instability, and dangerous racial volatility. "This seems to be the only danger we have to fear," Tocqueville professed, "but it is a serious one and must be avoided at all costs." Postemancipation societies had to guard against the inherent tumult wrought from a limited freedom by dismantling the unmatched political authority of ruling elites. "The Government, therefore, after having acted on the planter by means of an indemnity, should then act on the slave by wise and prudent legislation, which will first show him and then, if necessary, pressure him into the arduous and manly habits of liberty."[7]

When the American Civil War produced the largest emancipation in the nineteenth-century world, the United States faced the precise issues that Tocqueville raised during the 1830s. Yet the American context differed substantially from European emancipations in the New World. Abolition in British, Dutch, and French colonies transpired with gradual, compensated deliberation, furnishing the white ruling class with steady and coerced labor regimes. The colonial-metropolitan relationship itself maintained natural hierarchies that stemmed the chaos of abrupt social transformation. However, an immediate and decisive wartime emancipation in the United States shattered the world's largest slaveholding regime. A war sparked by the Slave Power, waged over the democratic meaning of Union, and ultimately compelling slavery's necessary destruction forever settled the place of human bondage in the American republic. An enduring restoration of the world's foremost democracy nonetheless depended on the abolition of slavery *and* the equitable participation of former slaveholders in realigning the rebellious states within the federal system. While the Union's loyal citizenry demanded a unifying peace based on emancipation, they also consented that democratic restoration required negotiation, compromise, and moderation with former Confederates.[8]

Abraham Lincoln championed the self-restoration of the South. "Reconstruction," the president announced in an April 1865 address from the White House, three days before his visit to Ford's Theater, "is pressed much more closely upon our attention." For Lincoln, reconstruction held one overriding objective: unite and strengthen the democratic bonds of Union to prevent any future national dissolution. "We simply must begin with, and mould from, disorganized and discordant elements" to orchestrate "the proper practical relation between [the rebellious] states and the Union." This was not a continuation of civil war by other means, nor a conflict "between independent nations." Reconstruction was conceived as the civil process of peace, nurtured by moderate Republicans, trustworthy Democrats, and loyal white southerners who had opposed disunion. Though Lincoln acknowledged "the new and unprecedented" nature of the moment, "important principles may, and must, be inflexible." His steadfast faith in governance of, by, and for the people guided this reasoning. Under the presidential plan of reconstruction, rebellious states would rejoin the Union when 10 percent of a state's Unionist voters who cast a ballot in the 1860 election devised a new constitution, disavowed secession, and endorsed emancipation. Lincoln's lenient course favored the South's loyal, anti–Slave Power residents, privileging democratic moderation and favoring efficient national reunion. Even "the colored man too, in seeing all united for him, is inspired with vigilance, and energy, and daring, to the same end," remarked Lincoln. Emancipation would thrive in a Union no longer managed by slaveholders, permitting freedpeople to pursue enriching lives of independence and perhaps achieving formal inclusion in the body politic. Only the fiercest champions of Union, and those who defied the slaveholders' rebellion, could ensure that oligarchic cabals never again severed the nation against the people's democratic will.[9]

American abolitionists renounced Lincoln's temperate measures, echoing Tocqueville's warnings about the turbulence wrought from incomplete emancipations. Congressman Thaddeus Stevens, considered among the most radical of Republicans, cited the abolition of Russian serfdom as an instructive model for American freedom. Stevens praised the czar's confiscation and redistribution of land, which provided "homesteads upon the very soil which [the serfs] had tilled." Although Stevens hailed the Russian case as "a perfect success," the project suffered from insufficient land plots, crushing debt, and deficient social mobility. Worried that formerly enslaved Americans had "nothing but freedom," Stevens wanted the federal government to seize slaveholders' lands and transfer them to former bondpeople. He favored land and capital as the principal tools with which freedpeople could assemble independent lives. "The whole fabric of southern society *must* be changed," Stevens charged. "How can republican institutions, free schools, free churches, free social intercourse exist in a mingled community of nabobs and serfs?" Stevens desired the same end as President Lincoln: a reconstructed South freed from the apathetic, enervating, and archaic culture of slavery. But Stevens vowed that a modern South depended above all on the elevation of freedpeople into the civilizing institutions of American life. Only an egalitarian republicanism, and even equal citizenship, would erase the devastations of slaveholding and forestall the resurrection of the old white ruling class. "If the South is ever to be made a safe republic let her lands be cultivated by the toil of the owners," Stevens concluded, assuring that universal liberty endowed national security and global modernity.[10]

Prominent African American abolitionist Frederick Douglass endorsed Stevens's appeal to call for the "immediate, unconditional, and universal enfranchisement of the black man." Like Tocqueville, Douglass claimed that freedom without liberty mocked the natural rights due *all* humans, thereby sullying the Union's international standing. "You declare before the world that we are unfit to exercise the elective franchise," he argued, condemning white Americans for the empty gesture of undefined freedom. The entire basis of American civilization hinged on the nation finally upholding the self-evident truths on which the United States distinguished itself from the global community. "Ours is a peculiar government, based upon a peculiar idea," which "is universal suffrage." As the essence of Old World aristocracy and oligarchic privilege, the Confederacy had existed but failed to prove the veracity of race-based social hierarchies and political exclusion. If the United States, "where universal suffrage is the rule, where that is the fundamental idea of Government," did not confer black citizenship and the elective franchise, the Union would restore the old Confederate cornerstone to the bedrock of American life. "If I were in a monarchical government, or an autocratic or aristocratic government," Douglass bellowed, "where the few bore rule and the many were subject, there would be no special stigma resting upon me." He thus scoffed at the notion that white southerners could reconstruct their splintered region. "I want the franchise for the black man," the only judicious alternative to racial oppression and social deterioration.[11]

Much of the loyal citizenry at first rejected the proposals from Stevens and Douglass. They believed that massive revolutionary property redistributions and African American voting rights would not be necessary. The allure of democratic moderation and white self-determination—indeed, of *Union*— were far too essential to the moderate process of self-restoration. Even the most committed Republicans anticipated former Confederates willfully rejoining the republic to live again as part of the world's paramount democracy. Welcoming the wayward rebels as chastised siblings, and assigning them the challenging task of reconstruction, "is beyond doubt," Charles Pinckney Kirkland advised, "indispensable to the present harmony and future safety of the Republic." The unequivocal death of slavery removed undemocratic slaveholding privileges that had long fractured the Union. With very little remaining for which to fight, joined with the "'leaven' of loyalty in every rebel State," former Confederates would "perform well their duties as citizens of a Republic, in which a political and social aristocracy, founded on Negro slavery, will no more be known for ever." Preserving federalism freed the Union from the suffocating manipulation of slaveholders and obviated the balkanization of civil war. Republicans thus did not see prolonged military coercion or a revolution in civil rights as inevitable outgrowths of Union victory. Their wartime objectives had been fully secured. "By our true moderation," opined *Harper's Weekly* in July 1865, "we are to show that in no point of a secure and economical and free government is a republic inferior to the most cunningly balanced aristocracy and paternal monarchy."[12]

Transformation of the slaveholding Union nonetheless mandated that all residents of a free republic enjoy equitable independence. The federal government did not entirely consider a notional emancipation, unlike in post-slavery Caribbean societies. With the charter of the Freedmen's Bureau in the spring of 1865, the United States pledged that freedpeople would emerge from slavery industrious and self-sufficient. Administered by the U.S. Army, the bureau aimed to transition the formerly enslaved into productive and autonomous free laborers. "Every effort will be made to render the people self-supporting," announced the agency's chief administrator, Gen. Oliver O. Howard. While the bureau provided education, assisted in securing free labor contracts, and offered medical care, its founders envisioned only temporary assistance "to enable destitute persons speedily to support themselves." Conferring black citizenship would have revolutionized American life during the delicate transition away from slavery, alienating white southerners and fracturing a Union composed of an overwhelming white population skeptical of black equality. Former slaves, the idea went, had to prove themselves capable of thriving in a free-labor system because slavery stunted individual improvement. By demonstrating "a knowledge of personal and moral responsibility," instructed in "the necessary rudiments of civilization," and "enlightened to think and provide for themselves," advocated an early wartime proponent of free labor, African Americans would have to demonstrate their *eventual* fitness for citizenship. Restrained in scope but progressive in implication, the Freedmen's Bureau moderated the restoration of the world's newest anti-slavery republic.[13]

In the wake of Abraham Lincoln's murder in April 1865, Vice President Andrew Johnson assumed the presidency. Johnson had joined Lincoln's re-election campaign in 1864 as the embodiment of bipartisan moderation to obtain northern Democratic votes and affirm the need for sectional reconciliation. The South's only Democratic senator to oppose secession and renounce the Confederacy, Johnson detested elite slaveholding aristocrats and favored a modest national restoration. Reared in eastern Tennessee in abject poverty, Johnson always blamed oligarchic slaveholders for manipulating government to feed their privileged interests. Slavery created unfair class distinctions, preventing poor southern whites like himself from enjoying true political, economic, and social equality. And when those same aristocrats shattered the Union in the name of slaveholding, Johnson disavowed their unrighteous crusade. "A great monopoly ... existed," he announced shortly after the war, "that of slavery," on which "rested an aristocracy." The dissolution of "the monopoly slavery," the president averred, secured the Union and ensured white egalitarianism. Like Lincoln, and all but the most radical Republicans, Johnson never believed that the southern states had left the nation. To be reconstructed, the states had to follow Lincoln's plan of restoration, elect new representatives, devise new constitutions, and appeal to Congress for readmission. Meanwhile, Johnson demanded that the leaders of the rebellion—the slaveholders whom he most despised—plead personally to him for amnesty. Signing nearly fourteen thousand pardons tendered the kind of power over slaveholders Johnson long craved. With the states realigned, with slaveholders crushed, and with the Union moving toward an efficient preservation, Reconstruction under Johnson seemed a painless endeavor.[14]

Andrew Johnson was nevertheless a striking paradox. While he declared that "treason must be made odious," and while he delighted in crippling the slaveholding class, Johnson viewed the world as governed by a stable racial hierarchy. The American Union, he argued, privileged universal equality for all *white* citizens, those imbued with the virtuous restraint essential for modern civilization. "I am for a white man's government, and in favor of free white qualified voters controlling this country, without regard to negroes," he disclosed in 1864. Johnson navigated the postwar moment as a reactionary demagogue. Though he endorsed the Thirteenth Amendment as a necessary consequence of the war, emancipation overturned the basic laws of nature, he maintained, placing black people in a contrived, unrestricted freedom. For Johnson, slavery regulated social evolution, civilizing African Americans and limiting their allegedly degraded, primitive dispositions. "Can it be reasonably supposed that they posses the requisite qualifications to entitle them to all the privileges and immunities of citizens of the United States?" he asked. The absolute immediacy of national emancipation undermined American republicanism with "persons who are strangers to and unfamiliar with our institutions and our laws." Like most Democrats, Johnson insisted that only the states, acting in sober deliberation reminiscent of Caribbean slave societies, could set the time and place for abolition. Individual state action—not federal decree or equal citizenship—moderated "the tumult of emotions" wrought "by the suddenness of the social change" engendered by war.[15]

Johnson's racial worldview mirrored the anxieties of a former slave society burdened by a devastating sense of loss. Emancipation manifested a catastrophic new world that heretofore dwelt only in the white southern imagination. Former Confederates witnessed their once unwavering and rich society now seemingly infested with barbarism, chaos, and stagnation. "The *abolition of slavery* immediately by military order, is the most marked feature of this conquest of the South," pronounced one white southerner. The universal emancipation, "when it has borne its fruits and the passions of the hour have passed away," will prove to be "the greatest social crime ever committed on the earth." George Fitzhugh likewise observed that "abolition was a great crime," one sure to spark "a war of races." Foreign revolutionaries now aligned with freedpeople who plotted black insurrection throughout the South. "The consequence is they are becoming careless, & impudent," one planter reported, "told by the [USCT] that they are as good as the whites." Emancipation was merely the first step toward erecting a new black republic in the Haitian image, banishing white refugees across an Africanized continent. Removed from the restraints of bondage, "we are in frequent dread of an insurrection among the negroes" sparking "another and worse war, we believe to be inevitable," reported a Virginia woman. White southerners "have most pressing, grave and responsible duties to perform," Fitzhugh concluded, to forestall "that internecine war of races."[16]

In the late autumn of 1865, news arrived of an October revolt in Jamaica, which traumatized the American South. The Morant Bay Rebellion sprung from long-simmering grievances among Jamaica's black peasants, who suffered from debilitating limits on their freedom. Barred from political participation, contracted as laborers for ruthless landlords, burdened by excessive taxation, and thwarted in terms of economic and social mobility, black Jamaicans objected to the impossibly unequal demands of manumission. Violence erupted "when a crowd of blacks stormed a courthouse to protest the harsh sentences being meted out to squatters by local magistrates who were also prominent planters." The uprising killed nearly twenty government officials, spawning hundreds of fatal retaliations, and many hamlets of black peasants were destroyed. White southerners interpreted Morant Bay as proof that emancipation unleashed people of color into fits of uncontrollable violence. Soon, predicted a Virginia newspaper, the horrid aftershocks of Atlantic abolition would spill onto American shores, bringing "the scenes of Jamaica and San Domingo to the Southern States of this Union." Morant Bay proved the alleged economic and social instability of abolition, leaving white southerners "to think of what would be the effect of these incendiary teachings in the lately populous slave regions of the South." The slaveholding South had long withstood the Atlantic world's flirtation with emancipation, even seceding from the Union and charting a new national destiny to thwart global abolitionists. But with the death of the Confederacy and emancipations sweeping the hemisphere, the specter of black insurrection and economic collapse appeared imminent.[17]

White southerners forecasted an American reenactment of Morant Bay for Christmas Day 1865. In the uncertain months after the Confederate collapse, paranoid white citizens reported "suspicious activities" among their former slaves, who appeared to be mobilizing in small parties, skulking through the countryside, conducting secret meetings, and collecting firearms. The USCT plotted with such insubordinate freedpeople, alleged a white Louisianan, maintaining "a vexatious & perilous agitation." To avoid reenslavement, testified a Mississippi planter, "they are urged to begin at an early day, perhaps about Christmas, a massacre of the whites, in order to ensure their freedom." Christmas indeed seemed the obvious moment at which "to rise in insurrection and murder all the white habitants." The holiday customarily arrived not as the annual feast of good tidings but as a foreboding day in which slave-holders had formerly eased the restraints of bondage and permitted the en-slaved a degree of autonomy. Restive freedpeople would "grow more & more insolent & will without a doubt ... turn this fair land into another Hayti," con-suming the South in "Anarchy and bloodshed." With Morant Bay transpiring so close to Christmas, and with seething black southerners already assembling to plot revenge, one former Confederate anticipated that the "horrible scenes [of Jamaica] may be reenacted in this country," while another regarded the smoldering Caribbean island as a "rehearsal for the South's Armageddon."[18]

Although the Christmas Day massacre never materialized, white southern-ers mobilized an aggressive campaign to neuter black freedom and save their battered civilization. They had to contest the ongoing Caribbeanization of the South, in which the chaos of emancipation disrupted a cherished social order, shattered labor relations, and obstructed progress. From his prison cell at Fort Monroe in Virginia, Jefferson Davis recognized that emancipation could not devastate the American South as it had the Atlantic world. "If those who can-not shut their eyes to the evils involved in the social change which has been so suddenly wrought," he informed his wife Varina in November, "or vainly attempt to resist a tide which cannot now be arrested, the direction of affairs must fall into incompetent or corrupt hands and accumulating disasters must be the result." Davis hoped for "the kind relations heretofore existing between the races, when a life long common interest united them," with "the inferior race" affixed to a permanent, subordinate status. The suddenness of emanci-pation had revolutionized the South, casting enslaved people into what North Carolinian Catherine Edmonston termed "the unknown sea of freedom." Once the rich envy of the world, the American South was now a feral land consumed with recalcitrant freedpeople who would, a former planter prophesied, "defy our authority, remain a subject of continual agitation for fanatics, and dis-courage and utterly hinder the introduction here of a better class of laborers." Only a "deeper degree of destruction and want is inevitable."[19]

The American South seemed to be undergoing a revolution of unprece-dented scale. Former Confederates, explained a Texas newspaper, could thus "feel but little interest or sympathy in the struggles" of people across the Atlantic world who suffered state-sponsored oppression. The crisis at home was too grave. "Moral goodness is all that is now required to restore our gov-ernment to its former glory and prosperity." White southerners therefore used federally sanctioned democratic self-restoration to reinstate as much of the old order as possible. They elected local, state, and federal officials who real-ized the imperative reconstruction of white supremacy. And they drew inspi-ration from Andrew Johnson, "a southern man by birth and education, who knows too much of mental incapacity of the negro," opined one southerner. A critical bulwark against racial revolution, the president would never "attempt to force the bitter cup of negro suffrage down the throats of his conquered and afflicted countrymen." Johnson's tacit endorsement of local white rule comforted southern whites devastated by emancipation. To achieve, as he put it, the "perfect restoration of fraternal affection ... transmit[ted] by our great inheritance of State governments," Johnson appointed provisional governors to rehabilitate civil administration throughout the South. To be reconstructed and readmitted into the federal Union, while maintaining a fragile but natural racial hierarchy, the southern states ratified the new Thirteenth Amendment *and* passed a series of restrictive laws, known as the Black Codes, which curbed African American freedom and mobility. By the end of 1865, ten of the eleven former Confederate states had complied with Johnson's reconstruction program, while populating state houses and congressional delegations with former Confederates and slaveholders.[20]

The Black Codes embodied the fundamental purpose of white southern reconstruction. The radicalism of emancipation must be "limited, controlled, and surrounded with such safeguards as will make the changes as slight as possible," explained South Carolinian Edmund Rhett. "The general interest of both the white man and the negro requires that he should be kept as near to his former condition as Law can keep him." Southern state legislatures imitated Caribbean restrictions on black freedom, using the force of law to prohibit vagrancy, to enact curfews, to forge labor relations between black laborers and former masters, and to control access to firearms. The laws uniformly regulated African American autonomy, stemming possible insurrections and averting moribund labor. As a prominent advocate of the Black Codes argued, "The course pursued by the South in regard to this unfortunate class of people is liberal, generous, and altogether as humane and equitable as the legislation of any country in the world." The codes restrained an alleged racial revolution from sweeping the South. In addition, their authors contended, the laws compelled freedpeople to labor under the supervision of civilized white managers, their former masters, who curtailed the economic stagnation that typically befell emancipated societies. Just as slaveholders once justified secession as a conservative reaction against Republican internationalization, they now vindicated the Black Codes as a rational and racialized democratic check against emancipation.[21]

Republicans objected to what they perceived as the violent resurrection of the aristocratic slavocracy. On an autumn 1865 tour of the war-torn South, Carl Schurz described the rapidity with which former Confederates were reconstructing their devastated society. In a report to the president and Congress, Schurz echoed Alexis de Tocqueville's predictions of American emancipation, chronicling how planters considered abolition nothing more than the nonexistence of slavery. Restrictive laws on freedom and hierarchical labor regimes still regulated society, just as they did in the British and French Caribbean. Schurz noted that for freedpeople, the resentments of slavery, fused with the antipathies from a false liberty, "would inflict terrible calamities upon both whites and blacks, and present to the world the spectacle of atrocities which ought to be foreign to civilized nations." Indeed, "insurrection or anarchy" were the inevitable outcomes of self-reconstruction, racial control, and unchecked white political authority. "Nothing renders a society more restless than a social revolution but half accomplished," he noted in implicit Tocquevillian fashion. Yet Schurz warned *against* revolution, advocating for political moderation and social stability. Every facet of slaveholding, from plantation labor contracts to racial hegemony, had to be eliminated. For Schurz, slavery had long fostered a foreign, revolutionary, premodern society that retarded national progress. The Union would never be preserved if the vital essence of bondage, "which for so long a time has kept the southern people back while the world besides was moving," remained intact.[22]

A reconstructed Union could not coexist with the lingering spirit of human bondage. An Illinois journalist named Sydney Andrews toured Georgia and the Carolinas throughout late 1865 and observed that myriad white southerners accepted the end of slavery but "appear to believe that they still have the right to exercise over [freedpeople] the old control." Andrews acknowledged how the enduring sway of aristocracy still infected southern life. "Even the best men hold that each State must have a negro code" to coerce labor, limit mobility, and curtail freedom. "They acknowledge the overthrow of the special servitude of man to man, but seek through these codes to establish the general servitude of man to the Commonwealth." The implications were startling. "I everywhere found a condition of affairs" in which "idleness, not occupation, seemed the normal state," a condition "likely to continue indefinitely." The stagnant ethos of slaveholding molded the postwar South into a languid hierarchy, affixing a pseudo-freedom to a tired dormancy. Was this the sacred republic that three hundred thousand loyal citizens had died to preserve? "The war will not have borne proper fruit if our peace does not speedily bring respect for labor as well as respect for man," Andrews echoed of the mass of loyal citizens who were deeply offended by the white South's pugnacious obstinacy. To fulfill the ideal of free-labor egalitarianism, to justify the Union's preservation, loyal citizens would have to secure the blessing of liberty for *all* Americans, regardless of race. Only then "shall we have noble cause for glorying in our country," meriting "true warrant for exulting that our flag floats over no slave."[23]

African Americans also protested their curtailed liberties through state-sanctioned oppression. Freedpeople disavowed insurrection and race war as solutions to second-class freedom. They petitioned governments through independent political conventions, organizations such as the Union League, and individual entreaties. Only biracial citizenship and equitable inclusion in national life supplied the surest means of marginalizing former slaveholders and upholding the inherent logic of American constitutionalism. Citizenship would secure the republic, they argued; it would broaden the Republican Party's free-labor coalition and forestall the Slave Power from again procuring undue political and economic monopolies. More fundamentally, civil equality ensured freedpeople the political liberty to access land, to pursue economic independence, to secure education, and to safeguard the right of conscience through suffrage. "God in his wisdom designed that the colored man should be a man on this continent," declared a USCT veteran on the pages of an African American newspaper. "We have been released from a worse-than-Egyptian bondage, not that we might colonize Liberia nor migrate to Mexico, but that we might engage in the great struggle and assist in making this a Republic." The death of slavery shattered legalized racial distinctions; equal citizenship validated an egalitarian Union unbeholden to aristocratic license, oligarchic influence, or ethnic privilege. "An abridgement of the liberties of the black, will have for effect, the strengthening of the hands, of the enemies of our beloved country," warned a meeting of freedpeople in New Orleans. Failure to link emancipation with liberty would "damag[e] before the world, the honor and the social cause of the American Union."[24]

By 1866, a preponderance of Republicans had declared southern self-reconstruction a failure. Though the states had complied with presidential directives, the restored South resembled the very society that seceded in 1861. Former slaveholders maintained a monopoly of political power; newly elected representatives arrived in Washington wearing their Confederate uniforms; the plantation system burgeoned with coerced labor; and restrictive laws upheld immobile social hierarchies in tying black Americans to the state. During the spring of 1866, whites even murdered scores of freedpeople in Memphis and New Orleans, joining the pugnacious Ku Klux Klan in policing African American autonomy through overt civil violence. "Southern arrogance and brutality have revived, lifted up their ugly heads, and seem nearly as rank as ever," New York diarist George Templeton Strong recorded in July. "The First Southern War may prove not the last." And President Johnson seemed to conciliate the escalating chaos. "The spirit which was baffled in the rebellion will seek to achieve its ends by political alliances and intrigues," scoffed an editor regarding Johnson's unscrupulous ways. The South was like a Caribbean island fuming with racial resentment, robbed of stability and governed by a white ruling class obsessed with power and control. "The practical difficulty in emancipation always proceeds from the masters, not from the slaves," Harper's Weekly observed. "This has been curiously illustrated in some parts of the British West Indies" and replicated in the late Confederacy.[25]

The Morant Bay Rebellion startled Republicans as much as it did former slaveholders. They saw in Jamaica and the American South postemancipationist societies that failed to reconstruct properly, each riddled by brutal abuses of freedom. Senator Charles Sumner wondered when an insurrection like that waged by Jamaica's formerly enslaved would consume the southern states. "The freedmen among us are not unlike the freedmen of San Domingo or Jamaica," broken by "the Barbarism of slavery" and excluded from the fruits of liberty. Only "enfranchisement" would distinguish the United States from its Caribbean neighbors. The measure functioned "as an act of justice," which "has a necessity of its own." Sumner believed that the horrors of slavery instilled in its victims a poisonous but justified vengeance. Conferring to freed-people "the promises of the Republic," those sacred inalienable rights accessible only in the United States, would "avoid insurrection and servile war." The American South was not a colonized outpost, its white and black residents not wards of a metropolitan state. Unlike in the Caribbean, it was impossible to confer *degrees* of freedom in the Union. At some point, the natural yearning for liberty would compel African Americans to embark on a revolutionary crusade to secure their manifest equality. Only citizenship, suffrage, and civil dignity—the hallmarks of democratic civilization—would obviate racial "calamity" and pave "the way for the great triumphs of the future, when through assured peace there shall be tranquillity, prosperity, and reconciliation."[26]

Sumner's perspective framed a remarkable alteration of the Republican Party's approach to Reconstruction. From the intransigent Andrew Johnson to the Caribbeanization of the South, congressional Republicans consented by 1866 that only biracial political equality could secure the republic. In reauthorizing the Freedmen's Bureau and especially in passing the Civil Rights Act of 1866, the Republican Congress conferred civil liberties upon all freedpeople, initiating an unprecedented experiment in the history of Atlantic emancipations. No other nation in the New World used the force of law to guarantee biracial citizenship. "All persons born in the United States and not subject to any foreign power," the act affirmed, "are hereby declared to be citizens of the United States," regardless of "every race and color" or "previous condition of slavery or involuntary servitude." Each citizen now possessed "full and equal benefit of all laws and proceedings for the securing of person and property, as is enjoyed by white citizens." The measure was "unparalleled in the history of nations," noted one congressman. "France and England emancipated their slaves, but the emancipated never dreamed that they should have letters of nobility, or should be elevated to the woolsack." Republicans gave the federal government consummate authority to regulate state-sanctioned discrimination, targeting the Black Codes, outlawing unfree labor contracts, and tempering white racial dispensation. That emancipation and the preservation of Union transpired in a republic mandated that nothing less than equality before the law guide postwar restoration. American Reconstruction was thus distinct from any other Atlantic society transitioning from slavery to freedom. African Americans had obtained full civil equality in the postemancipation Union from the very state that once certified human bondage.[27]

Andrew Johnson vetoed both the Freedmen's Bureau reauthorization bill and the Civil Rights Act. The president alleged that each law violated the restraints of confederated governance, weaponizing the federal system by stripping delicate checks from the states. Underwritten "by acts of caprice, injustice, and passion," renewal of the Freedmen's Bureau, because it was managed by the army, "declar[ed] to the American people and to the world that the United States are still in a condition of civil war." The bureau encouraged a purported military despotism, employing the army as a radical tool of social change "over which there is no legal supervision." Only the states, guided by their own laws and regulations, could moderate the transition from slavery to freedom, acting within their reserved constitutional prerogatives. Here the president gave latent validation to the Black Codes, which he likely saw as requisite screens against the abruptness of emancipation. Even more repugnant to Johnson, the Civil Rights Act manifested unequal racial distinctions by "establish[ing] for the security of the colored race safeguards which go infinitely beyond any that the General Government has ever provided for the white race." Civil rights, Johnson argued, fostered "centralization and the concentration of all legislative powers in the national government." Because the act granted federal oversight against state action, and supposedly privileged one race over another, "the bill must be to resuscitate the spirit of rebellion" and shatter "the bonds of union and peace."[28]

Then, in August 1866, Johnson proclaimed the formal end of Reconstruction, citing the successful restoration of civil authority throughout the former Confederate states. Peace had finally dawned across the Union, the spirit of rebellion seemingly replaced with democratic stability. The nation now stood before the world united despite its late fratricidal strife. Johnson celebrated the United States for not emerging from civil war splintered into warring factions or coerced by an intimidating military state. Cloaked in comforting exceptionalist rhetoric, the president's declaration of peace hailed "a fundamental principle of government" that encouraged former rebels to return voluntarily to the Union, lest "they must be held by absolute military power or devastated so as to prevent them from ever again doing harm as enemies." Such "policy is abhorrent," smacking of Old World despotism. Given that "standing armies, military occupation, martial law, military tribunals, and the suspension of the writ of habeas corpus are in time of peace dangerous to public liberty," Reconstruction had succeeded only through the democratic (and white) "genius and spirit of our free institutions." The prodigal states had returned home, their dissident citizens repentant of their wayward deeds. The "insurrection is at an end," Johnson meditated, and "peace, order, tranquility and civil authority now exist in and throughout the whole of the United States of America."[29]

Republicans objected to what they considered the bastardization of reunion. Andrew Johnson had encouraged the reconstruction of white southern supremacy into a regional hierarchy built on coerced labor, political privilege, and racial subordination. The verdicts at Appomattox meant little if southern aristocrats and slaveholding oligarchs emerged triumphant once more to destabilize the republic. Diarist George Templeton Strong expressed the frustrations of myriad white citizens when he declared in March 1866, "We must not be too nice and scrupulous about the Constitution in dealing with these barbaric, half-subdued rebel communities, or we shall soon find that there is no Constitution left." To preserve the Constitution from Johnson's unhinged presidency required, perhaps, sweeping changes to the Constitution itself. Strong also voiced the inherent tension gripping the ranks of stalwart Republicans. "Though on the whole I prefer the policy of Congress to that of the President," he concluded in September, "I do not want to take part in proceedings that will doubtless endorse an extreme 'radical' policy." But what exactly signified the limits of radicalism?[30]

Republicans overrode Johnson's vetoes of the Freedmen's Bureau and Civil Rights Act, enshrining the federal government—and not the individual states—as the principal arbiter of national restoration and natural rights. They indicted the president's reactionary scheme to impose European confederated supremacy on the American landscape. And they countered that biracial citizenship did not rupture—but instead fortified—American republicanism. Civil rights expanded the republic's constitutional order, joining freedom and equality in a marriage essential to an enduring Union. The southern states preserved their equal place in the federal system, the mass of former Confederates retained the privileges and immunities of citizenship, and the government had not transformed into a militarized state to chasten the conquered rebels. During the November 1866 midterm elections, a striking majority of loyal citizens endorsed these extensive alterations, mandating that Republicans forever neuter the white South's outmoded ideas of confederated governance and racial supremacy. The Republican ascendency commenced a new era in which Americans battled over the kind of Union they would present to the world.[31]

The Reconstruction of American Democracy

The Thirteenth Amendment and the Civil Rights Act failed to stem the alarming democratic imbalances that plagued the American South. Former slaveholders still ruled the region, leveraging racial control to obtain political influence. Though slavery no longer lived, democracy itself did not exist in its natural form, giving undue advantage to white southerners by placing the formerly enslaved in a liminal freedom. "The feeling of caste," worried a Republican editor, continued to organize the South into an Old World ethnic hierarchy that mocked the Union's liberal democracy. "The European doctrine," explained New England abolitionist minister Henry Ward Beecher, "is that rights and prerogatives belong to the better classes," delegated only by a privileged few. "In a free republic," however, "it is far more dangerous to have a large under-class of ignorant and disfranchised men who are neither stimulated, educated, nor ennobled by the exercise of the vote." It was one thing for the federal government to regulate state-sanctioned oppression, targeting the white privileges wrought by slavery and the Black Codes. But it was another thing altogether, Beecher explained, to integrate *all* free people into the constitutional orbit to disrupt the balkanization imposed by an oligarchic ruling class. "The safety of the State consists in the virtue, liberty, and power of its whole citizenship," by "ensuring that all rights and prerogatives belong to the whole people."[32]

By 1866, a preponderance of Republicans consented that a successful national restoration—one in which the republic was secured from future sectional ruptures—depended on universal citizenship to marginalize the resurgent white southern aristocracy. Even before the passage of the Civil Rights Act and their overwhelming midterm electoral victories, Republicans recommended a new amendment to the Constitution that they believed would convey for international audiences the true meaning of Union. The proposed Fourteenth Amendment would confer formal citizenship on all people born in the United States, guaranteeing to *all* citizens the due process and equal protection of law. The republic would thereafter stand as the only nineteenth-century nation to recognize birthright citizenship as the universal prerogative of national inclusions. Artificial ethnic privileges would no longer establish exclusionary societal distinctions. For the first time in American history, the Constitution defined, regulated, and enforced this criteria for citizenship, previously a hazy concept delineated by the states. The amendment targeted the Supreme Court's notorious holding in *Dred Scott* (1857), which deemed African Americans unqualified for inclusion in the body politic. For slaveholders on the Court, citizenship was reserved only for white people, the force of law used to disconnect American life based on race, creed, servitude, or ethnicity. "The object of the amendment is to punish arbitrary deprivation of political power, based upon race or color, by reduced representation," explained one Republican, "and no object could be more laudable." The amendment also deprived former Confederate leaders from holding political office, thereby dismantling Andrew Johnson's program of self-reconstruction, while also absolving the federal government from compensating slaveholders for "for the loss or emancipation of any slave."[33]

The architects of the Fourteenth Amendment envisioned the measure within the scope of a just war to preserve the Union. Regardless of the constitutional right to secession, explained the Congressional Joint Committee on Reconstruction, oligarchic slaveholders "did, in fact, withdraw from the Union and make themselves subject to another government of their own creation." They waged "a long, bloody, and wasting war, [and] were compelled by utter exhaustion to lay down their arms." Though defeated in public war, the South was still gripped by the radical, destabilizing spirit of disunion, and "treason, defeated in the field, has only to take possession of Congress and the cabinet." Therefore, "the people waging [the war] were necessarily subject to all the rules which, by the law of nations, control a contest of that character, and to all the legitimate consequences following it." The victorious party in a public war conducted between consenting states possessed the privilege and duty "to exact indemnity done, and security against the recurrence of such outrages in the future." Republicans insisted on loyalty to the Union and government, the abolishment of all institutions and practices that threatened national cohesion, and a democratized share of power between political factions. "It is most desirable that the Union of all the States should become perfect at the earliest moment consistent with the peace and welfare of the nation," concluded the committee. "The possession and exercise of more than its just share of power by any section is injurious, as well to that section as to all the others. Its tendency is degrading and demoralizing." Only the constitutionally sanctioned rule of law could obviate future national calamities.[34]

Although the amendment portended a striking transfer of power from the states to the federal government, the act did not alter the essence of federalism. In fact, the amendment did not give the national government explicit new powers. It instead blocked the states from administering laws unequally, permitting Congress to act as a body of last resort in protecting individual rights against state coercion. "From this it is easy to gather an understanding that civil rights are the natural rights of man," explained Iowa senator James F. Wilson, a foremost proponent of the amendment, which "protect[ed] every citizen in the enjoyment of [rights] throughout the entire dominion of the Republic." Moreover, as a constitutional amendment, the act relied on the consent of the governed for its ultimate sanction. The people, through sober and judicious reflection, would be compelled to recognize the amendment as an enduring feature of national life, and not as a statute imperiled by judicial review, congressional obstruction, or executive ambivalence. The Civil Rights Act could well be overturned at the whim of Democratic electoral triumph or at the swift behest of the Supreme Court. As a permanent appendage of the Constitution, the Fourteenth Amendment could not be soon annulled. "The political system of this Republic rests upon the right of the people to control their local concerns in the several states," explained Republican Carl Schurz. "This system was not to be changed in the work of reconstruction."[35]

The Fourteenth Amendment codified the manifest truths outlined in the Declaration of the Independence. The failure of southern self-reconstruction had convinced enough Republicans that freedom had to join with universal citizenship to afford all Americans the liberty to live unburdened from state-sanctioned coercion. According to Ohio congressman John Bingham, one of the amendment's principal authors, the measure bolstered "the essential provisions" housed in the republic's national charters, "divine in their justice, sublime in their humility, which declare that all men are equal in the rights of life and liberty before the majesty of American law." At its core, the amendment furnished freedpeople with the civil protections to secure their own equitable place in national life. "If the Union be a nation, and not a confederation, as the blacks have helped to prove by the most conclusive of arguments," read an endorsement from *The Nation*, "our Government owes to those who can get it in no other way that one thing for which all governments exist": "security for person and property." Through their industrious quests for self and civic improvement, through their past service in republican institutions, and through their free-labor tendencies, freedpeople had qualified to join the Union's progressive march. Liberated from the pressures of white supremacist governance, African Americans now possessed the independence to chart their own destinies shielded—rather than coerced—by the rule of law. The amendment thus offered "an immense step in advance along the path of civilization."[36]

Frederick Douglass saw the Fourteenth Amendment as *the* tool to restore the exceptional idea of Union. The United States, he believed, was unlike any nation in the world, established on an immutable, self-evident principle: "a Government founded upon justice, and recognizing the equal rights of all men; claiming higher authority for existence, or sanction for its laws, than nature, reason, and the regularly ascertained will of the people." Any human who pledged fealty to the national creed thus pledged loyalty to the republic itself, forging a democratic immunity to international subversion. The Union represented "the most conspicuous example of composite nationality in the world. Our people defy all the ethnological and logical classifications." Yet "the real trouble with us was never our system or form of Government, or the principles underlying it; but the peculiar composition of our people, the relations existing between them and the compromising spirit which controlled the ruling power of the country." Slaveholders had long defied the American ideal to impose an ethno-nationalist hierarchy upon an otherwise egalitarian constitutional order. They displayed "little sympathy with our Emancipated and progressive Republic, or with the triumphs of liberty anywhere." That the concept of Union was rooted in natural law meant that it could never again pretend to model the privileges of blood, soil, or race. Contrary to the delusions of slaveholders as "the owners of this great continent to the exclusion of all other races," Douglass envisioned a diverse citizenry now sustaining the Union's international standing. "I want a home here not only for the negro, the mulatto and the Latin races; but I want the Asiatic to find a home here in the United States, and feel at home here, both for his sake and for ours. Right wrongs no man."[37]

When the Republican Congress passed the amendment in the summer of 1866, a chorus of former slaveholders protested an "Africanized" national landscape. Elite white southerners accused Republicans of altering the racial stability of American life, stripping the South of its lawful sovereignty, and spawning unchecked black political radicalism. Racial revolutionaries now conspired to transform the Union and turn former slaveholders into helpless wards of their former bondmen. South Carolina governor Benjamin Perry predicted an inevitable "war of races" if "the negro will be invested with all political power." Civilization had been ostensibly overturned to unleash complete social anarchy in the name of racial equality. "This Government has been the white man's government, both Federal and State. It was formed by white men and for white men exclusively," Perry said about the exceptionalism of southern civilization. "The history of the world shows ... that the negro is inferior to the white man." The radicalization of universal equality, coerced by a powerful central state, deprived former slaveholders of their natural right to order a racialized world. The Union, once the secure guarantor of white liberty, had declined "at mercy of the maddened tide of fanaticism and being drifted to irretrievable ruin," moaned a devastated Herschel Johnson. "We are undone and constitutional liberty gone forever."[38]

Opposition to the Fourteenth Amendment exposed a vital conceit of white southern civilization: that racial control and ethnic identity eclipsed slavery as the critical determinant of American exceptionalism. Indeed, human bondage was an expendable means of enforcing the natural order of white supremacy. Edward Pollard, the outspoken editor of the *Richmond Examiner*, worried that radical Republicans would "compel the South [to] lose its moral and intellectual distinctiveness as a people, and cease to assert its well-known superiourity." Pollard praised white southerners for acquiescing "fairly and truthfully to *what the war has properly decided*": "the restoration of the Union and excision of slavery." Though embittered by defeat, former Confederates were satisfied to reconstruct their shattered society within the United States as long as the natural law of racial subordination governed the process of restoration. Because "the war did not decide negro equality" or even "negro suffrage," Republicans could not oblige the South to forfeit "the forms of her thought, and in the style of her manners, her peculiar civilization." Such unconscionable demands violated the just and limited terms of Confederate surrender. For Pollard, Republican coercion had revolutionized the Union into an allegedly barbarous nation, one that white southerners never agreed at Appomattox to restore. Ratification of the Fourteenth Amendment thus portended utter disaster for the entire republic. "For it is the South," once bolstered by the stability of racial subordination, that stimulated the national intellect and distinguished the republic before the world. "That superiourity the war has not conquered or lowered," Pollard concluded, "and the South will do right to claim and to cherish it."[39]

Andrew Johnson further stoked white southern hostility to the Fourteenth Amendment. Though he detested disloyal slaveholders, Johnson also considered racial equality an affront to civilized progress. On a whirlwind tour of the South, the president urged his sympathetic constituents to defy Republican excess and block ratification. Infusing the idea of American exceptionalism with the rhetoric of white supremacy, Johnson extolled "the glory of white men" who "buil[t] upon this continent a great political fabric ... while in every other part of the world all similar experiments have failed." Now, with the specter of racial equality, the Republican Party threatened to undo the United States' unique origins. "In the progress of nations Negroes have shown less capacity for government than any other race of people. No independent government of any form has ever been successful in their hands." Given that they did not possess civic virtue, and thus are "so utterly ignorant of public affairs," the president argued, African Americans could not partake in republican governance. One need look no further than the Caribbean, Johnson implied, to see the failure of black freedom. Slavery so stunted intellectual growth, so damaged the industrious spirit, that "it may be doubted whether as a class they know more than their ancestors how to organize and regulate civil society." Lives spent in abject dependence had supposedly deprived freedpeople of the "intelligence, patriotism, and a proper appreciation of our free institutions." Such untested people, who "have shown a constant tendency to relapse into barbarism," could not be trusted with the enlightened reins of democracy.[40]

Republicans sensed that the old white southern oligarchy still maintained shocking degrees of political influence, spearheaded by the president himself. Mobilized to oppose Reconstruction through the antagonisms of Andrew Johnson, too many white southerners appeared to scorn a lasting national peace; some even targeted southern Unionists and freedpeople with clandestine terrorism. Mob violence churned the American South as white vigilante groups, whom Gen. Philip H. Sheridan called "revolutionary men," mocked the rule of law and jeered federal authority. The loyal citizenry condemned the gross enmity flaunted against the Constitution, the Union, and emancipation. "The butcheries and atrocities perpetuated scarcely have a parallel in history," commented Illinois congressman Elihu Washburne from Memphis. Although the Fourteenth Amendment criminalized state-sanctioned abuse and proscribed unequal application of the laws, its dictates meant little if a preponderance of the states failed to ratify the measure. And by late 1866, ten of the former Confederate states had rejected the amendment. Republicans conceded the utter failure of Reconstruction. Why, many began to ask, had three hundred thousand Union soldiers given their last full measures of devotion to preserve a republic roiled by lawless anarchy, one governed by a recalcitrant president? American civilization hung in a precarious balance, its delicate threads snapping with each presidential veto, each act of white terrorism, each former slaveholder regaining political power, and each southern state reconstructing into a dreadful image of its antebellum self.[41]

When Republicans commandeered Reconstruction in the wake of their midterm triumph, Frederick Douglass framed the party's consensus on renovating the Union in the image of the Fourteenth Amendment. A preponderance of Republicans agreed that "whatever may be tolerated in monarchical and despotic governments," republics could not endure when "a privileged class" deprived others of equality. "The late Rebellion is the highly instructive disclosure it made of the true source of danger to republican government," Douglass wrote of the dueling visions of American civilization that competed for supremacy in the federal Union. Even in peace, the political vitality of southern aristocrats, reinforced by the political stasis of freedpeople, portended further national ruptures if former slaveholders retained unchecked power. Loyal Americans thus "demand such a reconstruction as shall put an end to the present anarchical state of things in the late rebellious States." Douglass once again advanced the full enfranchisement of *all* citizens as the only way to realize the war's true verdict: "a solid nation, entirely delivered from all contradictions and social antagonisms, based upon loyalty, liberty, and equality." Otherwise, if those most loyal to Union could not freely shape its future through the electoral process, the republic's wartime triumph "shall pass into history a miserable failure, barren of permanent results," offering "no value to liberty or civilization."[42]

Republicans disagreed on the means by which to secure Douglass's vision. Congressman Thaddeus Stevens had long advocated stripping the rebel states of their sovereignty and colonizing them as provisional territories. "The Slave Power made war upon the nation" and "declared themselves a foreign nation, alien to this republic," Stevens reminded his fellow citizens. Every vestige of slaveholding life thus had to be extinguished to reconstruct southern "municipal institutions as to make them republican in spirit as well as in name." Moderate ends mandated radical means. Indiana congressman George W. Julian likewise endorsed a robust military occupation that held the former Confederacy in an indefinite state of martial law. "The power of the great landed aristocracy in these regions, if unrestrained by power from without, would inevitably assert itself" in hostile ways that went well beyond current local self-reconstruction measures. "What these regions need, above all things, is not an easy and quick return to their forfeited rights in the Union, but *government*, the strong arm of power, outstretched from the central authority here in Washington." For Julian, the matter was not merely political. Reconstruction posed global implications for the Union's standing as the world's foremost democracy. Paradoxically, only robust military oversight would make "it safe for the freedmen of the South, safe for her loyal white men, safe for emigrants from the Old World and from the Northern States ... safe for Northern capital and labor, Northern energy and enterprise, and Northern ideas to set up their habitation in peace, and thus found a Christian civilization and a living democracy amid the ruins of the past."[43]

Moderates howled that Julian's prescriptions shattered the Union's republican foundation, transforming a limited government into a coercive, centralized military state. "We can supply either by the provision of a good police or by the admission of the blacks to such a share in the management of state affairs that they can provide a police for themselves," countered *The Nation*, a reliable organ of Republican moderation. "The former of these courses is not strictly in accordance with our institutions; the latter is." Though hardly a moderate, Douglass agreed with Julian and *The Nation*. "Armed with despotic power, to blot out State authority, and to station a Federal officer at every cross-road," the Union could again fight southern tyranny with military sway. "This, of course, cannot be done, and ought not even if it could" because such a course would delegitimize American republicanism before the world. Or the Union could exercise democracy against the foes of liberty, making "our government entirely consistent with itself," giving "to every loyal citizen the elective franchise," which "will form a wall of fire for his protection." Republicans faced the enduring quandary of constitutional governance: how to exercise power in the service of liberty without succumbing to excessive coercion. At the heart of the impasse stood nineteenth-century American fears of revolution in which radical factions disavowed constitutional restraints to wield unlawful power, or in which government itself became corrupt and exceeded its constitutional mandates. "Radical" Republicans maintained that white southerners had occasioned the former, while moderates insisted that the latter would dawn with the advent of widespread military occupation.[44]

Republicans negotiated a series of laws that integrated both the moderate and radical positions. The subsequent Reconstruction Acts of 1867 fundamentally altered the course of national restoration. Unparalleled in their scope and implication, the acts joined the pending Fourteenth Amendment to embody most of the sweeping reforms for which Thaddeus Stevens and Frederick Douglass had called in 1865. Because "no legal State governments or adequate protection for life or property now exists in the rebel States," Republicans pledged that "peace and good order should be enforced ... until loyal and republican State governments can be legally established." The acts divested the former Confederate states of their civil sovereignty and assigned each state to one of five military districts commanded by a general of the U.S. Army, populating the South with more than twenty thousand soldiers. The acts compelled the military to oversee the formation of a wholly new biracial southern political order that favored coalitions of freedpeople and loyal whites to reconstruct their battered region. In an extraordinary, transformative, and radical moment in the history of the republic, the acts enfranchised African American males, while disbarring from the democratic process formerly high-ranking Confederate officials and disloyal white southerners. The unprecedented danger to the Union mandated unprecedented measures to save the Union. For Congress to consider states "reconstructed" and fit for readmission to the Union, new biracial electorates had to convene constitutional conventions; draft state charters that outlawed the Black Codes and other forms of racial discrimination; elect truly loyal officials; and ratify the Fourteenth Amendment, all under the army's supervision.[45]

Augmented with uncommon civil and political power—at least in the American tradition—the U.S. Army registered voters; called and oversaw constitutional conventions; acted as the states' judicial body; policed unruly civilians; and intervened on behalf of harassed freedpeople. Individual commanders even wielded the power "to remove from office ... all persons who are disloyal to the government of the United States." While this was military occupation in the truest sense, the Reconstruction Acts encouraged southerners — African Americans and Unionists, to be sure — to *end* military occupation at their own bidding. The states could remain indefinitely under military rule, or they could comply with Republican standards and rejoin the Union on par with the existing states. Commander of the Second District Daniel Sickles explained the democratic *restraints* of occupation: "The commanding general, desiring to preserve tranquility and order by means and agencies most congenial to the people, solicits the zealous and cordial cooperation of civil officers in the discharge of their duties, and the aid of all good citizens in preventing conduct to disturb the peace." Rather than acting as coercive instruments of government, the acts mobilized a new southern electorate to marginalize former Confederates who had commandeered political power under Andrew Johnson's blatant consent. "Far from desiring centralization repulsive to the genius of this country, it is in the distinct interest of local self-government and legitimate State rights that we urge these propositions," especially biracial suffrage, noted Senator Carl Schurz. "Nothing can be more certain than that this is the only way in which a dangerous centralization of power in the hands of our general government can be prevented."[46]

Though the army played a central role in restoring democracy, its presence on the front lines of social and political change fueled great consternation among professional soldiers. "I am exceedingly anxious to see reconstruction effected and Military rule put an end to," a cautious Ulysses S. Grant confided about employing militaristic power in civic life. "Politicians should be perfectly satisfied with the temperate manner with which the Military have used authority thus far," he averred in the autumn of 1867, "but if there is a necessity for continuing it too long there is great danger of a reaction against the Army. The best way ... to secure a speedy termination of Military rule is to execute all the laws of Congress in the spirit in which they were conceived, firmly but without passion." The U.S. Army operated in a postwar milieu largely foreign to its institutional purpose and distinct from the nineteenth-century American antimilitaristic character. "The military are the servants of the laws, and are for the benefit of the people," explained a commander in the Fourth Military District. "The assumption that a party of soldiers can, at their own option, forcibly destroy a citizen's property, and commit a gross violation of the public peace, would not be tolerated under a Napoleon." Sensing the unprecedented nature of the moment, former Union general John Logan warned of "the iron bands of power" wielded by the army. Without a swift, conscious effort to replace military occupation with democratic self-determination, "this country shall be subverted into the hands of powerful military men who are to become aristocrats as they are in Europe." In a paradoxical way, Military Reconstruction aimed to return a republican Union to its antimilitaristic disposition.[47]

The new Republican program made democracy more competitive by disassembling the South's confederated governance and by dismantling the region's once legalized racial distinctions. From the Fourteenth Amendment to the Reconstruction Acts, the rehabilitation of American constitutionalism had ostensibly settled the nation's long-standing debate about the locus of governing power. Former Confederates "say that this is a blow at State rights," averred *Harper's Weekly*, but "they forget that they are speaking from the old and now obsolete Southern theory that the Constitution is a mere treaty between sovereign States and the Union a common servant of many masters. They must now understand that the people of the Union have decided by the last appeal that it is a national power." Republicans intended to bring to the American South that which never before existed: true political equality in which the democratic will of *all* male citizens could influence the Union. "You must enfranchise all the loyal men, black as well as white," commented Carl Schurz, "thus effecting a safe reconstruction of the whole Republic by enlarging the democratic base of our political system." Removing aristocratic and oligarchic obstructions permitted common citizens to moderate elites' manipulation of government, forever blocking a radical secessionist class from again sundering the republic. Preserving and enforcing the unalienable rights of individual sovereignty and conscience, regardless of ethnicity and happenstance of birth, are "the only safe basis for democratic institutions to rest upon," Schurz concluded. "These are the fundamental conditions of democratic republicanism according to the enlightened philosophy of this age, and they are the life-element of American civilization."[48]

For the mass of white loyal citizens, the Reconstruction Acts were less an idealistic gesture of racial progress and more a pragmatic measure to secure the Union. In an unprecedented and sweeping act of democratic governance, Republicans expanded the base of democracy along a multiethnic, crosssectional, constitutional consensus. Only two-party competition and democratic consent could ensure national equilibrium. Because "the Constitution of the United States knows no distinction between citizens on account of color," explained Frederick Douglass, the southern political order could not be reserved only for white Democratic planters. In tempering competing claims to American civilization, the striking moment reaffirmed the Union's commitment to government of and by the people, signaling Reconstruction as a transformative enterprise in biracial democracy. It was an attempt to do something that the world had never before accomplished, including the United States prior to its civil war: join universal liberty to universal freedom in the service of lasting national accord. "You do not extinguish Slavery; you do not trample out the Rebellion, until the vital truth declared by our Fathers is established and nature in her law is obeyed," Charles Sumner wrote in 1867.

"Liberty has been won; Equality must also be won." The Atlantic world's many revolutions had failed to sponsor the self-evident idea that governments derived their just power from the people's consent. "In England, there is Liberty without Equality; in France, Equality without Liberty." The moment was ripe for the United States to stand as the true international exemplar of democratic republicanism. "The two together must be ours," moderating governing authority against loyal, popular self-determination.[49]

The Fourteenth Amendment and the Reconstruction Acts underscored the entire purpose of Republican Reconstruction. Aggrieved populations subject to new social norms, like southern whites, typically rebelled against what they considered the fundamental redefinition of custom, of language, of civilization. To enforce an unparalleled social end like racial equality thus required centralized coercion and perhaps even state-sanctioned violence to reeducate and intimidate insubordinate parties. Yet the Republican program of Reconstruction, which relied on the rule of law and the competence of African Americans to chart their own destinies, was not a zero-sum game. Unlike the exclusionary legalism that once bolstered the slaveholding republic, the elevation of one class of formerly oppressed people did not entirely subjugate white southerners or hold them in fixed abeyance by the federal state. "No people ... that ever attempted by revolution and force of arms to break up, disintegrate, and destroy their Government and failed, in the whole world's history," remarked a white Alabama Unionist, "was ever so generously treated ... with so little punishment, and so soon, restored to all the rights, privileges, and immunities of the Government." Slavery stunted the growth of nations and corrupted free societies, but so too did centralized duress and uniformity of thought. Though some Republicans called for it, a true European-style military occupation of the former Confederacy never occurred because it *could not* have occurred, lest the entire legitimacy of Union rupture in the process. *"All legal* distinctions between the races are now abolished," declared an African American Union League in Alabama. *"Color can no longer be pleaded for the purpose of curtailing privileges, and every public right,"* permitting all citizens to chart unfettered lives of their own conscious making. "The law no longer knows white nor black, but simply men."[50]

Republicans thus unleashed one of the great democratic transformations anywhere in the nineteenth-century Atlantic world. The United States was among the Western Hemisphere's final slaveholding societies to eradicate human bondage, yet the Union was unique in its transition from a slaveholding nation into an egalitarian republic. No other country or colonial outpost had so rapidly and so entirely equipped former bondpeople with civil and political equality. No longer trapped in slavery nor marginalized by freedom, African Americans were now mandated to stimulate national life as active political citizens. The seeds of biracial democracy grew in the fading wake of slaveholding, from which freedpeople emerged as truly dynamic civil actors.

In 1867, 90 percent of eligible southern African American men registered as voters. Military occupation was thus a means to the end of preserving the Union through democracy. Freedpeople and Republicans, rather than the army, transformed the South by participating in constitutional conventions and voting for the champions of Union, including approximately 1,500 African Americans elected into local, state, and federal offices. Formerly enslaved men now functioned as county sheriffs, cast ballots as state legislators, and trod the halls of Congress. Those who toiled in slavery not five years prior now played remarkable roles in cleansing the final vestiges of slaveholding from the United States. Apart from civil war, no moment so uniformly shattered the Slave Power's unrivaled dominance of national life.[51]

The constitutional conventions of 1867 faced a simple proposition. Shall the states, asked white Republican and former Union army officer Albion Tourgée, "have an Oligarchy or a Republic? An aristocracy or a Democracy?" Freedmen assumed a signal function in answering Tourgée's questions, drafting new state charters to replace slaveholding privilege with legal systems of equitable justice and protection. The rule of law had to rip out the cancerous remnants of slavery from the body politic so that no southerner—white or black—was again shackled by the dependence, lethargy, and vice imposed by human bondage. "We claim exactly *the same rights, privileges and immunities as are enjoyed by white men*—we ask nothing more and will be content with nothing less," resolved a black Union League meeting. Biracial constitutional conventions rehabilitated American republicanism to favor individual aptitude rather than exclusive ethnic privilege. "The proposition of the Republican party," acknowledged formerly enslaved man Abraham Galloway, "is to allow every man in the nation to be his own *master*." Tourgée further elaborated: "The principles of equal and exact justice to all men" enfranchised the broadest possible electorate, institutionalized the cause of public education, and guaranteed the shared rights of citizenship. Indeed, procuring the fruits of one's labor, enjoying the legal protections of marriage, entering into contracts, and acquiring private property all strengthened American republicanism. The liberty to pursue happiness and the independence to improve one's condition validated the "justice, humanity and patriotism" of the American mission, bringing to the South a new birth of civilized freedom.[52]

Republicans envisioned Reconstruction as an antiaristocratic counterrevolution in free labor. For centuries, the South had stagnated under the feudal rule of landed elites who extracted exorbitant wealth and political power from their bound laborers and land domination. With slaveholding a distant relic, the region could modernize through industry and economic diversification. Adelbert Ames, a Union army veteran appointed in 1868 as the provisional governor of Mississippi, averred that the "carpetbagger"—progressive antislavery northerners who settled in the postwar South—"represents northern civilization, northern liberty and has a hold on the hearts of the colored people that nothing can destroy. He is the positive element of the party and if the south is to be redeemed from the way of slavery it must be done by him." Dismantling retrograde class and racial hierarchies sought to transform an institutionalized southern oligarchy into a liberal, biracial democracy. "No republic is safe that tolerates a privileged class, or denies to any of its citizens equal rights and equal means to maintain them," Frederick Douglass explained. The Southern Homestead Act (1866) thus aimed to turn public lands into autonomous plots for white and black farmers to secure "liberty and independence," an egalitarian renovation of the privileged monopolization of acreage and labor.[53]

The essential American creed could now be restored to a region long divorced from the national ideal. "The United States is truly the land—the very paradise of labor," announced a wartime pamphleteer. "In no country on the face of the earth is labor more prized and honored." A republic governed by the popular will had to protect the rights of *all* citizens to pursue economic independence, the only true guarantee of individual autonomy. *"Free Labor—* that is to say, the equal right of all men to the pursuit of happiness—has been recognized as the first natural and inalienable right." Formerly enslaved Virginian Bayley Wyatt likewise explained the enduring implication of free labor. "We now, as a people, desires to be elevated, and we desires to do all we can to be educated," he declared in 1866 before a meeting of freedpeople at Yorktown. Eager for an independent life of "honest, hard work," Wyatt lambasted the base immorality of slavery. Not only had his people "been bought and sold like horses; dey has been kept in ignorance; dey has been sold for lands, for horses, for carriages, and for every thing their old masters had." Their unfree labor had also furnished the ill-gotten wealth for thousands of white aristocrats. "Didn't we clear the land, and raise de crops of corn, ob cotton, ob tobacco, ob rice, ob sugar, ob ebery ting. And den didn't dem large cities in de North grow up on de cotton and de sugars and de rice dat we made? Yes! ... I say dey has grown rich, and my people is poor." The right to claim the fruits of one's sovereign labor militated against a noble ruling class again seizing regional power and threatening national stability. But for Bayley Wyatt and millions of freedpeople, it also meant securing the self-evident liberties to which all humans were entitled.[54]

The experience of Francis Rollin, a free woman of color born in South Carolina who came of age in the vibrant intellectual circles of Philadelphia, testified to the dynamic ways in which African American women also shaped the contours of democratic freedom. At the dawn of Reconstruction, she relocated to Charleston and educated the formerly enslaved as a teacher for the Freedmen's Bureau. There she met Martin Delany, the passionate black abolitionist, emigrationist, and Union army veteran. Struck by Delany's remarkable life, Rollin soon moved to Boston to pursue a literary vocation and pen Delany's biography, published in 1868 as *Life and Public Services of Martin R.*

Delany. Rollin performed important political and intellectual work in shaping a positive public image of African American men's right to citizenship. "A race before persecuted, slandered, and brutalized, ostracized, socially and politically," she wrote, "have scattered the false theories of their enemies, and proved in every way their claim and identity to American citizenship in its every particular." Though advocating for the exclusionary right to male citizenship, Rollin's writing and framing of history were themselves powerful modes of political work that confronted the rigid gender and racial barriers of her era. As a public figure—an African American woman, no less—she joined the ranks of prominent nineteenth-century white male historians to narrate a biracial national story, even as her private role as an educator of freedpeople conformed to more conventional gender functions. Rollin's biography documented the swift transformation for African American men, while the *act* of biography authorship itself featured unparalleled public prospects for free women of color.[55]

Diehard adherents to slaveholding civilization indicted Republican Reconstruction as the most cataclysmic revolution ever to befall the Atlantic world. Since their political inception, Republicans appeared to have upheaved the natural order one plank at a time: first pledging to restrict the spread of slavery, then waging a war of emancipation, then allegedly reneging on the promise of a moderate restoration to enact civil rights legislation, revolutionize the Constitution, and even transform laws of nature through universal racial equality. No government—including those of the bloody French revolutionaries, the European monarchs of 1848, or even Haiti itself—had ever seemingly coerced their people with such swift, unprecedented radicalism. A Georgian warned in 1868, "[Rebellious] sentiments are gaining strength, and even ripening into a determination to resist forcibly ... the consummation of Negro supremacy. We will never submit to such degredation." Republicans had shattered the white supremacist stability of constitutional governance. They "are determined to retain[power] even at the risk of destroying the country & of putting an end to republican government," Robert E. Lee confided privately. Edward Pollard even probed the necessity of national disintegration to forestall any further racial revolutions emanating from Washington. It would be "far better that the States should disband into petty republics still preserving their institutions of local government, than pass into imperial despotism, disfigured, too, by Negro rule."[56]

Mississippi Democrats spoke for myriad white southerners when they condemned in 1868 "the nefarious design of the republican party ... to place the white men of the Southern States under the governmental control of their late slaves." To "degrad[e] the Caucasian race as the inferior of the African negro, is a crime against the civilization of the age, which has only to be mentioned to be scorned by all intelligent men." The Mississippians called on fellow white southerners "to vindicate alike the superiority of their race over the negro and their political power, and to maintain constitutional liberty." The postwar United States too closely resembled an "uncivilized" world obsessed with emancipation and infatuated with racial liberalism. Any acts in 1868 to combat crimes against civilization were just as warranted as secession was in 1861 to combat a seemingly radical Republican Party bent on racial amalgamation and race war. Brandishing the language of the Mississippi Democrats, white terrorist groups throughout the South sought to cleanse the new Union from racial corruption. Pledging to restore a civilization of white supremacy, organizations like the Ku Klux Klan disrupted the constitutional conventions and aimed to terminate, through armed intimidation and murder, the South's biracial ruling class. The Confederate republic may have been killed through war, but its legacy had to endure within the United States.[57]

Desperate for legitimacy following years of political marginalization, the Democratic Party channeled white southern outrage during the presidential campaign of 1868. A feckless President Johnson fueled opposition to Republican Reconstruction, condemning the radicals who "must now resort to a revolution changing the whole organic system of our Government." Johnson blasted Republicans for occasioning unchecked social and political changes via a standing army, an unaccountable institution that at any moment could effect a coup. "The temptation to join in a revolutionary enterprise for the overthrow of our institutions is extremely strong," warned the lame duck president, firing anxieties of national centralization. Even Francis P. Blair, the Democratic vice presidential nominee, denounced the "Africanization" of the South, pledging his party to contest "a semi-barbarous race of blacks who are worshippers of fetishes and poligamists." For Blair, such rhetoric was hardly political posturing. Racial equality seemingly retarded both national and human progress, mongrelizing white Americans into a debased species on par with Native peoples, Mormons, and atheists. As they always had, prominent Democrats co-opted for their political advantage the rhetoric and tactics of the former Slave Power. They appealed to political and racial reaction to oppose the Reconstruction program, positioning their party as the only national institution capable of stemming the excesses of democracy and stabilizing white supremacy.[58]

Republicans sensed the Democrats again stoking the embers of rebellion. Unable to claim legitimacy from the political process, Democrats had embraced seemingly extraconstitutional tactics to seize power. And in their nefarious schemes, the Union was expendable. National collapse seemed more likely in 1868 than it had been at any point since Appomattox. But the next civil war would not resemble the organized conflict between consenting nation-states. A political war between Republicans and Democrats knew no sectional devotion, reeking of Old World conflicts between factions of government, political loyalties, and ethnic identities. Constitutional restraints would be meaningless, and with few limiting principles or institutions, an ideological civil war might roil the nation for decades. In the wake of a devastating Klan massacre in Camilla, Georgia, Republicans charged that Democrats had exchanged the rule of law for civil violence and racial murder. "The rebel leaders of the South have commenced their work for persecution of Union, white as well as black," announced a Republican newspaper, animated by presidential candidates who "would again establish their Confederacy." It was imperative for Republicans to defeat a political party inimical to constitutional consensus, sympathetic to national balkanization, and hostile to liberal pluralism. Republicans thus framed the election as a contest between democracy and anarchy in which only the true party of Union could affirm the republic as the world's arbiter of ordered liberty. "Upon this we offer peace to the country," pledged Carl Schurz. "We confidently and proudly appeal to the enlightened judgment of the American people and the sympathies of mankind."[59]

No Democrat continued to defy the post-Appomattox consensus more than Andrew Johnson. Republicans viewed the president as the foremost impediment to reconstructing a moderate, egalitarian Union built on the rule of law and unbeholden to repressive demagoguery. Johnson's hostility to constitutional norms "tramples upon [the] law, defies the authority of Congress, and claims to exercise absolute and despotic power," opined the *New York Tribune*. His overt resentment toward the popular will, his refusal to sanction or enforce the laws of Congress, fueled a dangerous and unchecked autocracy. When he fired Secretary of War Edwin M. Stanton, Johnson violated a statute that barred the president from removing executive officials without Senate approval, a measure designed to stabilize the government in the wake of Abraham Lincoln's assassination. "For the right to do as he pleases with any law," the *Tribune* continued, "to assume to be its sole arbiter and judge, may become a tyranny more absolute than that of the Emperor of Russia." Johnson moreover legitimized the resurrection of the southern white supremacist order, blessing oligarchs as they rebuilt an ethno-nationalist South loyal only to race, caste, and Johnson himself. "The President of the United States has so singular a combination of defects for the office of a constitutional magistrate," averred a scathing editorial in *The Atlantic*. "Insincere as well as stubborn, cunning as well as unreasonable, vain as well as ill-tempered, greedy of popularity as well as arbitrary in disposition, veering in his mind as well as fixed in his will, he unites in his character the seemingly opposite qualities of demagogue and autocrat, and converts the Presidential chair into a stump or a throne, according as the impulse seizes him to cajole or to command."[60]

Johnson's obstinacy gave rise to Republican anxieties about a political civil war. The *New York Times* reported in late 1867 that Democrats boasted of Johnson tacitly endorsing a coup against Congress. Though the president assured his cabinet that he would never cater to the "demands of illegal and revolutionary violence" and never "surrender his office to a usurper," myriad Republicans imagined militant operatives organizing scattered remnants of the old Confederate army to descend on Washington. Enough loyal citizens well understood that the history of the Atlantic world had proven that "civil wars often pile atop one another, fragility spawning new fragilities." An enduring peace was hardly guaranteed. If the nineteenth-century world offered any indication, the United States was far more likely to experience persistent civil strife if Johnson continued to reign as a Central American caudillo. "Had it not been for his treachery, there would have been little difficulty in settling the terms of peace, so as to avoid all causes for future war," scoffed *The Atlantic*. "But, from the time he quarreled with Congress, he has been the great stirrer-up of disaffection at the South, and the virtual leader of the Southern reactionary party." Republicans thus interpreted their 1866 electoral triumph as a mandate to impeach the president. As the *New York Tribune* explained of its multifaceted purpose, "The impeachment of Andrew Johnson will not merely be commended because he tried to evade the law, but because he degraded his office, and brought his country to shame, and made it a scandal among the nations." Employing the moderation of constitutional mechanisms, the House of Representatives in February 1868 impeached Johnson, marginalizing a disgraced president who defied the basic norms of democratic stability.[61]

Johnson's impeachment underscored the election of 1868 as a referendum on the meaning of Union. "It is part of our thirty years' effort to place the country in harmony with the age, and to make her what she ought to be—a leader, and not a mere follower, in the pathway of civilization," Frederick Douglass explained. The election portended the final political battle against the Slave Power: "Rebellion has been subdued, slavery abolished, and peace proclaimed; and yet our work is not done," Douglass continued. Only after the Union cleansed itself from the "enemy of liberty and progress" could the republic "shake off an old but worn-out system of barbarism," standing unfettered as the world's last best hope. African Americans thus well understood the world-historical implications of the election, the first formal political contest in which they had ever participated in widespread numbers. "We have nothing to fear in the great battle now waged for our rights on this continent," reported a black editor, "if we play a faithful part in the drama of American reform." Only the democratic political system could secure the promises of liberty, and only the Republican Party could assure the civil protections of self-determination. Though threatened and intimidated by astonishing levels of violence, freedpeople descended on the polls in overwhelming numbers. Their critical contributions sealed the electoral triumph of Ulysses S. Grant, the Union's premier war hero and the Republican candidate who promised a new dawn of peace. The very people whose enslavement had for so long guaranteed slaveholders' political hegemony were the ones whose new freedom guaranteed the Democrats' 1868 political demise.[62]

A meditation on Grant's electoral victory published in *The Atlantic* explored "the moral significance of the Republican triumph," which signaled "the crowning victory of the War of the Rebellion." Defeating the Confederate republic through a just war had killed the Slave Power, but democracy itself had to exterminate slavery's lingering contamination. Republicans had learned that the death of slavery did not naturally facilitate national loyalty among its ardent devotees, but instead organized the foes of "humanity and freedom, of reason and justice, of good morals and good sense." The loyal citizenry possessed no other option than to channel against the Slave Power its most cherished ideal: a subordinated racial class. The Fourteenth Amendment and black suffrage were hardly inevitable products of Union victory because "the form which reconstruction eventually took . . . was necessary to insure the safety and honor of the nation." A preponderance of Republicans came to understand that African Americans' "interests, hopes, and passion, their very right to own themselves, were all bound up in the national cause." Racial equality was less a noble, progressive endeavor than it was a pragmatic rebaptism of Union. *The Atlantic*, doubtlessly like millions of Unionists, could not escape the paradoxical moment. "The immense achievement of emancipating four millions of slaves, and placing them on an equality of civil and political rights with their former masters" stemmed exclusively from slaveholders' rebelling against the very nation that once certified their cherished institution. No other nation had transformed with such unintended contingency. Yet no other nation had so fully realized its self-ascribed mission.[63]

Grant's ascension to the presidency guaranteed the full implementation of Republican Reconstruction. The U.S. Army continued to occupy the recalcitrant states, monitoring constitutional conventions and protecting black self-determination. Biracial coalitions of loyal citizens rehabilitated southern life and implanted free-labor democracy to a region that for so long had disavowed true egalitarianism. The Slave Power had been killed, the Fourteenth Amendment, ratified in July 1868, fortified the Constitution, and national endurance depended on the will of free and equal citizens. Grant thus entered the presidency with the same cautious moderation that he had displayed since Appomattox. Because "a great debt has been contracted in securing to us, and our posterity, the Union," the wake of rebellion demanded that government approach national questions "calmly, without prejudice, hate, or sectional pride." The new president praised equality before the law, which compelled the "security of person, property, and for religious and political opinion in every part of our common country, without regard to local prejudice." The reconstructed Union would not comprise privileged citizens and subjugated vassals, nor would it colonize lands of former slaveholders deemed unworthy of national inclusion. It seemed that the loyal citizenry had finally triumphed in their nearly decade-long struggle to eliminate internal threats to the Union.[64]

President Grant encouraged Republicans to advance one final initiative in their Reconstruction program, which he believed would mitigate any future breach of national sovereignty: a constitutional assurance of suffrage for all male citizens. Institutionalizing the supreme right of conscience would perfect the Union in the same manner that the Fourteenth Amendment enshrined the natural condition of equality. Republicans who advocated the Fifteenth Amendment considered the measure a critical buffer against the kind of tactics slaveholders once used to procure and maintain political power. It would prevent obstinate, manipulative state factions from controlling and depriving free citizens of their democratic prerogatives. White southerners who intimidated black voters and blocked Republican access to the polls delegitimized democracy and privileged one class at the expense of another. Grant demanded immediate action from his fellow Republicans. "The question of suffrage is one which is likely to agitate the public so long as a portion of the citizens of the nation are excluded from its privileges," he explained. After all, the Reconstruction Acts, which granted African American suffrage, expired once the individual states complied with Congress's demands and reentered the Union.[65]

Myriad Republicans considered suffrage essential to the Union's security and international legitimacy. The United States could not claim itself an archetype of liberal equality if its own citizens lived in contested states of independence. "The right of suffrage is fundamental to republics," declared James Wilson. It distinguished the Union from a global community committed to regulating thought and compelling state-sanctioned behavior. "Republics can only stand when the ballot-box is secured to the poor as well as the rich," alleviating revolutionary tensions among aggrieved classes, an Indiana representative explained. To assure the Union "in her present proud rank among nations," outlined another Republican, "we will have no disfranchised, disaffected, clamoring classes always ready and ripe for tumult, rebellion, and revolution. Then the will of the people, legally and peacefully expressed, will have a weight and a power which will command and insure universal acquiescence and obedience." The proposed Fifteenth Amendment thus emerged from the same goal as the Fourteenth: to prevent the formation of a Caribbeanized postemancipation society in which freedpeople lived powerless to protect themselves by voting freely in their own self-interest. The amendment, according to one senator, would unveil "that state of society toward which the nations have been struggling since the beginning of Christian civilization." Indeed, it would be the final tool used to renovate a nation once committed to human bondage, reaffirming itself by 1870 as the world's foremost bastion of consensual governance.[66]

President Grant regarded ratification of the Fifteenth Amendment as the Union's signal achievement. It was "a measure of grander importance than any other one act of the kind from the foundation of our free government to the present day." The amendment "completes the greatest civil change, and constitutes the most important event that has occurred since the nation came into life." To contest the "revolution begun in hostility to the Union," argued the *New York Times*, the Fifteenth Amendment "secures political equality" as the enduring basis of an antislavery republic: "The measure was the completion of the work of which emancipation was the commencement. It purges the Union of the last taint of slavery, and makes Reconstruction national." The following year, Georgia reentered the Union as the final state to complete the Republican program of Reconstruction. For a preponderance of like-minded Unionists, the jubilant events closed the devastating era of civil war. By 1871, the United States appeared to have accomplished its mission set forth in the spring of 1861: securing a democratic Union from dangerous rebellious factions bent on sundering the republic. Loyal Americans had bled, toiled, and labored to realize the Union's enduring principle of democracy by equal consent—not oligarchy for the unchecked few. Though devoted citizens considered their Constitution now inviolable, the question remained whether the reinvigorated old charter could withstand the stormy future.[67]

Peace

★ ★ ★

The newly inaugurated president Ulysses S. Grant carried a trying burden as he stood in 1869 before his fellow citizens. The gory wake of Appomattox defied Grant's once optimistic hope for an orderly reunion between warring Americans. Though he campaigned to "let us have peace," the Union's premier war hero surveyed the bloody national terrain and wondered if domestic accord could ever flourish despite the Confederate banner's everlasting interment. Like Abraham Lincoln, Grant had to assure the viability of a Union of and by the people. He had to prove that God's chosen republic still prevailed amid a world consumed by fractious violence. While he did not enjoy Lincoln's poetic aptitude, Grant possessed a general's pragmatism, which he deployed with consummate skill. "The country having just emerged from a great rebellion, many questions will come before it for settlement in the next four years, which preceding Administrations have never had to deal with," he appealed in his inaugural address. Sober restraint in the pursuit of national unity demanded "the greatest good to the greatest number," enveloping "our common country, without regard to local prejudice."[1]

As a political moderate, Grant understood that an enduring but limited peace depended on constitutional moderation and on realigning the Union as a beacon of international republicanism. Loyal citizens had enacted necessary defenses against future national convulsions by outlawing slavery, guaranteeing biracial citizenship and civil equality, and enshrining the right of universal male suffrage. Their efforts capped a near decade-long project of removing from national life the international radicalism embodied by the American Slave Power. When Grant delivered his *second* inaugural address four years later, he boasted of the United States' confident and secure global position. Finally liberated from antidemocratic obstructions, "our own great republic is destined to be the guiding star to all others." Following a half century of bitter sectional disputes about the national future, Grant viewed the Union now standing unfettered as the world's eminent democracy. With the restoration of "harmony, public credit, commerce, and all the arts of peace and progress" to the federal Union, "the civilized world is tending towards republicanism." The triumph of liberal democracy over oligarchic subversion charted a new era, reorienting the United States with the North American continent, the Western Hemisphere, and the Atlantic and Pacific worlds.[2]

Relieved from civil war and absolved from the pressures of national res-

The "Strong" Government, 1869–1877, by James A. Wales, 1880, is part of a two-framed denunciation of Republican Reconstruction policies. For Wales, a decade of allegedly oppressive military occupation, propped up by the strong centralizing policies of Ulysses S. Grant's presidency, burdens the white postwar South. In his negative depiction, the U.S. Army has stunted democracy by "Europeanizing" the American landscape. The second frame features a yeoman President Rutherford B. Hayes plowing over his predecessor's ostensibly misguided policy of "bayonet rule," replaced instead with a new policy of "let 'em alone." (Library of Congress)

toration, the United States now possessed a simple mission: demonstrate to the world how democratic republicanism privileged the peaceful competence of citizens over state centralization, radical militarism, and oligarchic exploitation. The Union could now model an exceptional civilization unburdened from supporting a European military leviathan and discharged from supervising the former Confederate states. While Grant believed that the world would emulate the American image, some Republicans also favored a peaceful arbitration between Cuban rebels and Spanish imperialists, acquiring Canada, and annexing Santo Domingo, a Caribbean republic dedicated to free labor. The vast continental West also beckoned Americans, fluent in the language of civilization and progress, to consolidate an antislavery continent. With formerly enslaved people already transitioning into adept citizens, the republic was now compelled "to bring the Aborigines of the country under the benign influence of education and civilization," saturating the West with civic institutions, the rule of law, and the right of property. "If the effort is made, in good faith," toward Native peoples to make them "a useful and productive member of society," Grant believed, "we will stand better before the civilized nations of the earth."[3]

Nineteenth-century Americans considered it their providential obligation to cleanse antirepublican toxins from the national soul. If the Union tilted the globe toward a republican future, many Americans welcomed a central role in shaping that prospect. With its own slaveocracy marginalized, the United States would now republicanize the continent and the hemisphere. "I believe that our Great Maker is preparing the world, in His own good time, to become one nation, speaking one language," Grant announced in classic exceptionalist rhetoric. By 1870, the international Slave Power and its monarchical, aristocratic, and imperial associates began to sound hemispheric retreats as an egalitarian Union eyed the Caribbean and the American West as its departure points toward global prominence. The triumph of American democracy seemed to coincide with failing European ambitions in both the Old and New Worlds. Antirepublican forces had long encroached upon the Union, legitimized by the Confederacy's rise but devastated by its overwhelming fall. The preservation of Union thus forestalled France's desultory attempt to install a puppet monarchy in Mexico, confronted British influence in Canada, challenged Spanish imperialism in South America and Cuba, and marginalized human bondage in Brazil.[4]

Yet the newly triumphant biracial and egalitarian Union rested on a shaky edifice. Republicans had long contended that slaveholding and democracy could not coexist. But in the long wake of slavery's destruction, democratic republicanism came to mean different things to different loyal citizens. For so-called radical Republicans and African Americans, an authentic republic depended on a strong federal state and a military apparatus willing to enforce its own ideals of civil equality. The Fourteenth and Fifteenth Amendments meant little if their universal principles could not be executed. Government possessed a duty to ensure liberty if white southerners continued to terrorize freedpeople's natural right to self-determination. However, for moderate and conservative Republicans, some of whom populated a new movement known as Liberal Republicanism, American civilization depended on a decentralized and antimilitaristic Union that did not employ federal force in the service of civil liberties. The great threat to liberty itself stemmed from centralized states that compelled thought, regulated behavior, or promoted one constituency at the expense of another. The progress of democratic republicanism spread by example, not through force, privileging individual ability over ambivalent compulsion.[5]

After decades of political instability, social anarchy, and civil war, by 1871 the Union was preserved. Americans now faced the question of how to secure, as Grant put it, "the very existence of the nation" against any future dissolution. Republics could not manage the rapid assimilation of new peoples and provinces, sustain perpetual states of war, or tolerate the chaos of insurgencies. Yet those very dynamics confronted the loyal citizenry throughout the 1870s. As the United States sought new territorial acquisitions and aimed to pacify the continent and manage a biracial democracy, white southerners accused Republicans of exploiting the black franchise to procure illegitimate and excessive political power. Former Confederates instigated a devastating paramilitary counterrevolution against Republican Reconstruction and African American political equality. The palpable anxiety about the Union's place in the world informed an emergent Republican coalition that preached against the instability of political institutions, the persistent threat of civil war, and the fear of impending coups. Europe, the Americas, and Latin America, so many in the United States believed, had proved incapable of perfecting democracy, embroiled by radical factions and ruptured by political absolutisms.[6]

The seeming fragility of international states underscored Republican resistance to this so-called Mexicanization, the inability of Latin American nations to ensure governing legitimacy and territorial stability. Republics survived by channeling hostile factions into a democratic consensus. Growing numbers of moderate Republicans interpreted their domestic volatility as moving dangerously close to European militarism, French socialism, and Mexican disintegration. Republican policy throughout the 1870s remained guarded and conservative, searching for ways to resist the internationalization of the republic against the dual forces of revolutionary destabilization and despotic centralization. Near the end of the decade, one Republican thus captured an ominous logic likely embedded in the hearts of many Americans: "The lesson of the war that should never depart from us is, that the American people have no exemption from the ordinary fate of humanity. If we sin, we must suffer for our sins, like the Empires that are tottering and the Nations that have perished."[7]

The Limits of Hemispheric Civilization

Loyal citizens celebrated their triumph over aristocratic slaveholders and oligarchic revolutionaries when the southern states realigned by 1871 within the federal orbit. Yet the fate of global republicanism and the progress of civilization seemed ambiguous. The British consolidated an imperial footprint in Canada, Spanish colonizers attempted to quash Cuban liberation movements, unrest spread across Ireland, devastating civil wars consumed China, labor riots sprouted throughout Paris, and France and Germany militarized for another round of continental war. The loyal citizenry faced a delicate uncertainty: how to fortify the Union against the hemisphere's radical, destabilizing, and revolutionary tendencies. For prominent Republicans who assumed decisive roles in defining the United States' war against national dissolution, the answer lay in emancipating the world's captive populations from tyrannical suppression. "This great nation," announced congressman and former Union general Nathaniel P. Banks, "was intended to hold liberty ... in trust for all mankind." The republic "is destined to enlighten and civilize the rest of the world." Hamilton Fish, the secretary of state for President Grant, likewise believed that Americans "occupy of necessity a prominent position on this continent, which they neither can nor should abdicate." The stability of American institutions and the moderation of constitutional restraint beckoned oppressed populaces. "As the United States is the freest of all nations," Grant proclaimed, the American republic "sympathise[s] with all peoples struggling for liberty and self government."[8]

The moral superiority of their liberal democracy obliged Americans to direct the world's progressive march toward civilization. Few Republicans embraced this national commitment more than William H. Seward did. Abraham Lincoln's former secretary of state embodied an unyielding faith in republican progress, seeing the world as entangled in persistent struggles between liberty and oppression. A civilized nation was independent and prosperous, its citizens competent and energetic, "enjoy[ing] peace at home and abroad." War, civil strife, absolutism, and slavery, "incompatible with a successful republic," subverted the dynamism of free thought, free expression, and free labor. With the death of the American Slave Power and the rehabilitation of constitutional liberty, loyal citizens possessed a critical burden to expel lingering international impurities from the hemisphere. "The permanent continuance of European or monarchical government in the American hemisphere would be injurious and dangerous to the United States," he announced in 1869. Seward thus advocated rapid hemispheric expansion not to satiate imperial lusts but to fortify the Union against an autocratic world.[9]

Seward's internationalist dreams knew few bounds. He advocated acquiring Cuba, the Dominican Republic, the Dutch West Indies, the Fiji Islands, and Hawaii, while also imagining a canal directing American economic ambitions through Central America toward Asia. Above all, he prioritized aligning the North American continent as the physical buffer against European encroachment, a desire that led in, 1867, to the United States' purchase of Alaska from Russia. The vast snowy landscape was far more than a seemingly uninhabited wilderness far removed from the influences of civilization. For Seward, it was the foundation of civilization itself. Appropriating the immense territory expanded American republicanism, thereby frustrating the encroachments of global monarchists. "When European monopoly is broken down and United States free trade is being introduced within the Territory," Seward declared, Alaska "will prove a worthy constituency of the Republic." He argued for the stability inherent in vast territorial acquisitions. "True in its republican instincts and loyal to the American Union," Alaska contained a wealth of natural resources to facilitate a free-labor empire. The territory would attract only the most ambitious, independent, and energetic settlers, and they would forge a consensual bond with easterners, whose collective liberty depended on a Union committed to *all* free citizens. Consolidating the continent thwarted balkanization, "foster[ing] and cultivat[ing] harmony and peace equally throughout the whole Republic."[10]

Alaska symbolized the Republican Party's long-standing ideals of Union: the hemispheric triumph of free labor, the perpetuation of republican institutions, and the expulsion of foreign contamination. This same vision influenced how like-minded Republicans sympathized with the plight of Cuba, one of the New World's lingering outposts of human slavery. When Cuban rebels revolted in 1868 against Spanish colonial rule, Spain responded with devastating brutality. Grant condemned Spain's "barbarous and cruel" conduct in the subsequent Ten Years' War (1868–78), which pitted the monarchical power's authoritative control of labor against Cuban planters' desire for independence. The war embroiled imperial and colonial belligerents in shocking cycles of atrocity and reprisal, compelling the United States to sympathize with Cuban liberation from Old World hierarchy, Catholic authority, and monarchical authority. Just as the American example had proven, the presence of slavery anywhere invited imperial corruption, stoked violent hostility, and ruptured internal stability. In order that the Spanish "know the United States control their destinies," the Grant administration summoned Spain to join the "governments of the old world that are preparing their colonies for independence and self-government." Cuban independence would maintain the republican rehabilitation of the Western Hemisphere, complementing the collapses of the aristocratic Confederacy and monarchical Mexico.[11]

Yet pragmatic and equally powerful ideological considerations barred American involvement in the Ten Years' War. Aiding the Cubans against a powerful European belligerent could well spark war between the United States and Spain, a conflict that the healing Union could ill afford to wage. Some Republicans also wondered whether the wake of a successful liberation would compel the United States to annex Cuba, a prospect antagonized by the racial dynamics of American Reconstruction. "The public good sense of this country will decide whether, when we have recently and properly admitted so many new citizens in the late rebel states," commented *Harper's Weekly* in 1870, "it is desirable to violate our honorable policy and interfere in the troubles of another country." The United States had waged civil war, reformed the Constitution, and reconstructed democracy to expel international pollutants from the republic. African Americans had proven qualified for citizenship by virtue of their long lineage in the United States, their capacity for free labor, and their military service in national institutions. But Cubans were allegedly unfit for national inclusion. As a leading voice of Republican moderation, *Harper's* cautioned against the impulsive and "inevitable consequences of such interference" in Caribbean affairs, especially "for the purpose of adding to our population more than a million and a half people wholly alien from us in principles, language and traditions, a third of whom are barbarously ignorant." Simply rebelling against European colonialism did not confer upon Cubans the inevitable fitness for republican civilization. Seemingly burdened by centuries of colonial rule and allergic to ordered liberty, Cubans might well disturb the United States' own republican convalescence. Perceived notions of racial difference, cultural oddity, and the ineffectiveness of Caribbean peoples to practice democratic governance negated any serious attempt to fold Cuba into the Union.[12]

Alaska and Cuba framed how the United States negotiated two subsequent international events, which both posed direct referendums on the limited purpose of domestic Reconstruction. First, the American desire to avoid war with European powers resulted in diplomatic tensions—and ultimately resolution—between the United States and Great Britain. Emerging mutually distrustful from the American Civil War, both nations waged a diplomatic proxy war in Canada over continental supremacy. In 1866 and 1870, the Fenian Brotherhood, a clandestine Irish American league of former Union soldiers, staged illicit invasions of Canada from bases in New York and Vermont. They intended to deflect British attention away from ongoing independence crusades in Ireland, hoping to assist in the deliverance of the Emerald Isle. Meanwhile, homegrown liberation movements sprouted in western Canada, led in 1869–70 by local Native leader Louis Riel. Grant and Fish sympathized with the swelling aspirations for Canadian independence, a spirit that could be harnessed to American advantage. Though stiff British resistance, in concert with arrests made by U.S. marshals, crushed the Fenians and Riel, the president and secretary of state supported Irish independence and even favored annexing Canada. Both triumphs would continue to republicanize the Atlantic rim, neuter Great Britain's hemispheric imprint, and temper the colonial destabilization on the northern American border. "That the events of the late war showed what a menace and threat the British possessions on our borders are the constant danger of annoyance and even collision resulting therefrom," Fish scolded the British ambassador Edward Thornton, "if Great Britain would make the Provinces independent, all that cause of irritation and of possible complication would be removed."[13]

While Fish imagined Canada one day joining the United States, he also considered war against Great Britain a dangerous means of national expansion. Fish hailed England and the United States as the world's greatest civilized nations, and he convinced Grant to pursue diplomatic alternatives to armed conflict, perhaps even arbitrating a peaceful settlement to obtain Canada. Massachusetts senator Charles Sumner agreed that pursuing negotiations to purchase the British territories seemed far more palatable than stoking internal rebellions against royal authority. In a notorious public speech, Sumner accused the British of bestowing tacit wartime legitimacy on the Confederacy and of genuflecting to the American slaveholders' unholy cause. Moreover, English shipbuilders had manufactured numerous Confederate commerce raiders, including the infamous CSS *Alabama*, which departed from British ports and exacted vast economic devastation on the Union's maritime trade. This gross abuse of neutrality, Sumner charged, violated the laws of war by extending belligerent rights to the Confederacy. "It was in no just sense a commercial transaction, but an act of war." Sumner demanded that Great Britain compensate the United States for the financial costs attendant to the *Alabama*'s brief but ruinous wartime career. Above all, he concluded, "when civilization was fighting a last battle with Slavery, England gave her name, her influence, her material resources to the wicked cause, and flung a sword into the scale with Slavery."[14]

Sumner's indictment provoked fiery responses among the British and American publics. *The Times* (London) blasted a careless demagogue's invective "of that intuitive sort which has been common in all the tribunals of despotism." Conversely, Americans who hailed Sumner's speech considered Canada a fitting exchange to account for wartime transgressions wrought by the *Alabama*. While Sumner never publicly posed the idea, Grant and Fish toyed with the notion of using the *Alabama* claims to negotiate for Great Britain's northern territories. But despite the passions roused by Sumner's grandiloquence, British liberals and American moderates forged a compromise to avert armed conflict. Indeed, pressuring Great Britain to relinquish Canada as the price for maritime offenses nearly led to international war. Fish surrendered the seductions of Canadian annexation, instead forming trade deals, establishing continental markets, and brokering an arbitration between the United States and Great Britain. In a tribute to diplomatic restraint, the British agreed at the subsequent Geneva Arbitration of 1872 to pay for the wartime damages incurred by Confederate ships assembled in metropolitan boatyards. Both sides heralded the moment as a victory for moderation and compromise in which civilized sobriety checked the impulses of radical militarism. "It is a noble thing for the two great protestant Christian nations of the earth to settle by a *tribunal* difficulties and differences," observed Republican senator Frederick T. Frelinghuysen. "It is a great thing for the course of ... civilization that while the Latin races and the Germans are consolidating their nationality, the Anglo-Saxons are strengthening themselves and their influence by establishing more intimate relations."[15]

Maintaining a peaceful republic domestically and globally stood among Reconstruction's principal purposes. War stemmed progress, yoked citizens to a centralized state, and corrupted virtuous liberty. Republicans thus arranged the process of national restoration and international affairs to subvert armed conflict. Although Americans indeed looked abroad in search of territorial acquisitions, aggressive imperialism was simply not worth the cost of national destabilization. Cuba and Canada might have been easily attained from Spain and Great Britain, but their procurements might also have militarized the United States into a perpetual wartime footing to defend its vast international holdings. But what if the United States could expand peacefully, avoiding costly entanglements with European powers by planting the free-labor seeds of American civilization beyond national borders? What if the restrained and sober influence of Union could extend beyond the Union itself, helping to prevent an aggressive, revolutionary world from corrupting the American republic?[16]

Such questions lay behind Ulysses S. Grant's desire to annex Santo Domingo, a sovereign Caribbean nation that symbolized the second international referendum on domestic Reconstruction. In 1844, Santo Domingo declared independence from Haiti, but by 1861 it had come under the imperial purview of Spain. After four years of bitter resistance, the Dominican Republic emerged as an independent nation concomitant with Confederate surrender and the Union's ongoing efforts to topple Napoleon's Mexican monarchy. When he assumed the presidency in 1869, Grant advanced the annexation as a signal policy initiative of Republican Reconstruction. The president outlined how the small Caribbean nation joined with the United States as the hemisphere's foremost champions of free-labor egalitarianism. In the same way that Republicans advertised the Fourteenth and Fifteenth Amendments, Grant promoted annexation as a moderate, anti-imperialist expansion of democracy in the name of national security. A friendly Caribbean territory would enhance the United States' hemispheric presence, ensure the viability of free labor, reaffirm anticolonial commitments, and spread American democracy abroad. "Its acquisition is carrying out Manifest destiny," the president announced in 1870. "I believe it will redound greatly to the glory of the two countries interested, to civilization, and to the extirpation of the institution of slavery" throughout the hemisphere.[17]

Santo Domingo would assist in the Union's ongoing antislavery rehabilitation, which Grant claimed extended beyond the republic itself. Dominicans complemented the American character and shared "in entire sympathy with our institutions, anxious to join their fortunes to ours," Grant outlined in 1870.

The president celebrated the locals' embrace of free labor, which erased the arbitrary privileges of slaveholding and ethnic caste. Their tolerance "as to the religious, or political views of their neighbors" revealed a penchant for ordered liberty, which deserved "the protection of our free institutions and laws, our progress and civilization." The United States did not retain a monopoly on natural rights. The republic instead embraced peoples who shared American passions for constitutional restraint, democratic pluralism, and "receiving the reward of [one's] own labor." Grant thus imagined Santo Domingo as a haven to which African Americans could emigrate and labor unfettered from "the prejudice to color" that still haunted the former Confederacy. Freedpeople's ability to thrive in a hospitable Caribbean sanctuary would demonstrate to cynical white southerners their competence, thereby "bringing all parts of the United States to a happy unity." Though he condemned racial bigotry as "senseless," Grant predicted that with "a refuge like San Domingo [the freedman's] worth here would soon be discovered, and he would soon receive such recognition as to induce him to stay." The endurance of domestic harmony, as the limited aim of Reconstruction, depended on expanding American democracy into the Caribbean.[18]

Annexing an archetype of free-labor egalitarianism marginalized the Western Hemisphere's lingering slaveholding provinces. Grant criticized the United States as "the largest supporter of that institution" of human bondage because Americans imported vast agricultural goods harvested by enslaved peoples in Brazil, Cuba, and Puerto Rico. "Our imports of tropical products, and products of slave labor" diminished the Union's antislavery commitment, thereby ensuring the institution's global perpetuation. If Americans continued to patronize Cuban and Brazilian commerce, "an export duty is charged to support slavery and Monarchy." But Santo Domingo's lush soils "of great productiveness," its favorable climate, and its abundance of "tobacco, tropical fruits, dyes, and all the imports of the equatorial region" would militate against the United States' troubling reliance on international bondage. Annexation "would make slave labor unprofitable and would soon extinguish that hated system of enforced labor," isolating slaveholding colonies to an "insupportable" fate. For Grant and like-minded Republicans, emancipation in the United States was merely one step in the nineteenth century's long march toward an antislavery future. The security of the Union depended on slavery's global eradication. "The acquisition of St. Doming is an adherence to the 'Monroe Doctrine,'" Grant advised. "It is a measure of national protection," imposing a stifling barrier against European imperialists who, in the guise of Confederate oligarchs, descended on the hemisphere in search of ill-gotten bounty extracted from enslaved laborers. To forestall a "cordon" of European territories, Santo Domingo fit as the first piece in "a Confederation of all the Islands of the Caribian Sea, and Gulf of Mexico, under a protectorate ... of the United States."[19]

Prominent African American leaders, including newly elected congress-men and senators, also supported annexation. And when President Grant in December 1870 named Frederick Douglass a special envoy to the Dominican Republic, the great abolitionist also championed its acquisition. While Grant envisioned the Caribbean republic as a natural economic ally, Douglass con-sidered it "vastly more important to know what we can do, and ought to do, for Santo Domingo." Witnessing how bondage had devastated the island with privation and lethargy, Douglass endorsed the reconstruction of Caribbean slave societies into republican outposts. As the world's foremost antislavery nation, the United States possessed a moral obligation to transition former slave colonies "at home in the interest of civilization." The triumph of Ameri-can emancipation meant only so much if emancipation abroad yielded "the measureless depth of ignorance, weakness, and barbarism." By dismantling the hierarchical constraints of Old World colonialism, annexation would re-vitalize Santo Domingo from "Latin and Catholic rule," thus "strik[ing] a blow at slavery wherever it may exist in the tropics." Only then would the "millions of treasure and rivers of blood to abolish" slavery in the United States "put an end to the wars of rival chiefs" within a volatile hemisphere. Ultimately, the fate of an exceptional, antislavery, egalitarian Union was at stake. "If we are really in favor of freedom and free institutions, if we would be as a nation a grand civilizing force among the nations of the earth, and bless the world as well as ourselves," concluded Douglass, "we want Santo Domingo as one in-strument of power in carrying out the beneficent mission" of Union.[20]

The conditions of Reconstruction that incentivized annexation—securing the Union, strengthening republicanism, and institutionalizing free labor—were the very issues that sparked opposition among skeptical white Republi-cans and Democrats. Antiannexation presented an intriguing counterpoint to the extant faith in biracial democracy, foreshadowing how some antislavery activists—including some abolitionists—negotiated the forthcoming domes-tic trials of the 1870s. Carl Schurz, a foremost champion of wartime emanci-pation *and* a steadfast opponent of annexation, framed the liberal Republi-can *and* the Democratic critique of Santo Domingo. The Missouri senator predicted during a lengthy public diatribe in 1870 that Caribbean acquisi-tions would destabilize the Union's long struggle to secure a moderate democ-racy. "Once started in that course" of integrating "the American tropics in our political system," he warned, "you will not be able to control yourselves." Hardly content with one Caribbean acquisition, avaricious colonizers would fix their hungry gaze on Cuba, Haiti, Mexico, Puerto Rico, and the West Indies "until we have everything down to the Isthmus of Darien." The speculation and corruption attendant to annexation shredded the virtuous fabric of re-publicanism. Enticed by power, profit, and mastery, annexationists inevitably "encroach[ed] upon the rights of the laborer" to feed their rapacious appe-tites. The new Union of ordered liberty would transform into the very exploitative, oligarchic state once ruled by slaveholders, forcing Americans again "to choose between a tyrannical policy, hostile to the great principles upon which this Republic now stands."[21]

Multiple Caribbean possessions internationalized the Union with racial constituents hostile to white American civilization. Schurz rejected the notion that "that part of the globe and the people inhabiting it" suited "the integrity, safety, perpetuity and progressive development of our institutions." The region's harsh tropical climates and wretched environmental conditions sapped energy, barred improvement, and promoted radical politics. Labor routinely devolved "in the direction of slavery" because the heat and humidity from "the tropical sun inflames the imagination to inordinate activity and develops the government of the passions." Hopeless lethargy naturally invited "government by force instead of by argument," obstructing the sober deliberations necessary for democratic republicanism. Thus, Central American and Caribbean "revolutions are of common occurrence," stoked from "two extremes— liberty which there means anarchy, and order which there means despotism." Though rehabilitated politically and constitutionally, the subtropical and once slaveholding American South had long degenerated from similar tyrannies of climate and absolutism. Now, "fancy ten or twelve tropical States added to the Southern States we already possess," fretted Schurz, "people of the Latin race mixed with Indian and African blood," having "neither language nor traditions nor habits nor political institutions nor morals in common with us." The United States would be more Caribbeanized in emancipation than it was during slavery. The "prejudices and passions" once symptomatic of the slaveholders' nation and forever common in the Caribbean imperiled "the destinies of this Republic."[22]

For Schurz, appending turbulent tropical locales to the United States undermined national stability. Santo Domingo was merely the first piece in a series of Caribbean procurements that would affix in the Union the very elements that once sparked secession and civil war. The monarchical "traditions of slavery" reinstated "the old spirit of violence, the old impatience of adverse opinions, the old propensity to use force in preference to patient reason." Schurz thus warned that the tropics would "introduce a poison ... which may become fatal to the very life of this Republic." That "poison" was twofold. First, like "the Central and South American Republics," Dominicans, approximating their Haitian neighbors, had failed to establish "stable political system[s]" based on constitutional democracy. Their anarchical "history of revolutions" would compel the federal government to assume unprecedented powers to forestall insurgent rebellions, unmooring the republic's constitutional foundation. "Our political life will tend to the arbitrary assumption of power by the National Government, and perhaps to military usurpation," he envisioned, in rhetoric consistent with his old aversion to the Slave Power. "The very acquisition of that territory would put us on the high road to military rule."[23]

Conservative Senate Republicans joined with Democrats to spoil the Santo Domingo annexation treaty from passing with the requisite two-thirds majority. Though following in wake of the ratification of the Fifteenth Amendment, the failure of annexation in 1871 sprang in part from Liberal Republicans like Carl Schurz, who privileged domestic stability over global dominance. Swift annexations in the Caribbean and Central America reeked of the corrupt imperialism once sponsored by slaveholding expansionists. The consolidated militarism likely required to regulate and defend international protectorates undermined the decade-long effort to reform the republic into a limited, decentralized democracy. And perhaps most damning, the revolutionary specter of racial contamination informed how "foreign affairs could not be separated from the tensions arising from Reconstruction itself." A growing preponderance of white Republicans consented that the fate of American civilization depended only on constitutional reforms at home designed to banish the radical excesses of oligarchic privilege, ostracize the conceit of aristocracy, and maintain moderate political and racial cultures friendly to republican progress. Internationalizing the republic in the wake of national restoration would subvert the Union, perhaps even collapsing the new amendments intended to forestall future civil strife.[24]

The limits of hemispheric imperialism underscored the Union as a *symbol* of civilization for the world to emulate—not as the active *instrument* of global authority. As the *Chicago Tribune* noted, "The best mode of propagating Republicanism among other nations is by teaching them that our own Republic is [merely] intent on securing the welfare of its own people." African American skeptics of Republican moderation sensed a troubling prospect embedded within overtures of national progress. Henry Highland Garnet recognized the consequences of American vacillation toward Cuba, and, by extension, Santo Domingo. The Union gleamed as a symbol of international liberty only insofar as it *acted* on its commitment to equality. "The struggle for freedom and equal rights," which "culminated in the complete overthrow of despotism in the United States," was part of the same global conflict that now enmeshed Cuba. "We regret," Garnet told an assemblage of Cuban refugees, "that we cannot give you that material aid we would wish to afford you." The delicate balance of international diplomacy barred the United States from antagonizing Spain. But "if our relations with Spain retard the progress of liberty in Cuba," Garnet concluded, liberty in the United States would also be imperiled. To equivocate on emancipation abroad endangered the republic's domestic commitment to human rights. For Henry Highland Garnet, the promise of American Reconstruction depended entirely on the United States' moral and physical stature in the world *and* at home.[25]

Far more than even the Caribbean or any other hemispheric domain, the American West fueled white imaginations of domestic progress. The vast region that played such a decisive role in sparking the antebellum crisis of national sovereignty informed the postwar Union's continental integrity. The American future had always dwelt in the West, explained William Seward, yet despotic slaveholders long held the region hostage to "material improvement and national progress." With the slaveocracy dead, "the political power of the United States and the American continent is rapidly" kindling a new "national energy in the prosecution of internal improvements." An unimpeded West "opens a bright and glorious prospect" in "the spread of republican institutions over the whole American Continent, involving by absolute necessity a regeneration of civilization." Between 1861 and 1896, eleven of the twelve states that joined the Union resided in the American West, their swift national entry freed from the once debilitating sectional quarrels over slavery's expansion. Railroads and telegraphs could now unite the great republic. Boundless land beckoned competent settlers to pursue economic independence. Natural resources facilitated technological advancements. And access to new markets in Asia promised unprecedented commercial opportunity. Consolidating the Union's continental reach, concluded Seward, would "foster and cultivate harmony and peace equally throughout the whole Republic, and harmony and peace equally with all foreign nations." In the essential vein of Reconstruction, the West functioned as "part of a broader national effort to solidify the territorial sovereignty of the United States," preserving the Union against any latent national ruptures and liberating American democracy from internationalist subversions.[26]

Republicans of the 1870s envisioned the West in ways that white nineteenth-century Americans had always anticipated the vast frontier: an uncorrupted, uninhabited land of opportunity waiting patiently for industrious and independent white pilgrims to exploit its rich and abundant assets. Though it had once played a central role in fomenting sectional discord, the vast West now beckoned a triumphant Union to ensure middle-class, free-labor economic prosperity. President Grant captured this quixotic continental promise when he declared, "We are blessed with peace at home and are without entangling alliances abroad to forebode trouble." A "free people, all speaking one language" could now pursue unobstructed independence strengthened by a united "country extending from the Atlantic to the Pacific." Seemingly devoid of sectional tension and racial strife, and absolved from the devastations of civil war, the West was cleansed from eastern corruptions. "With facilities for every mortal to acquire an education; with institutions closing to none the avenues to fame or any blessing of fortune that may be coveted; with freedom of the pulpit, the press, and the school," *all* Americans could partake in the continent's bountiful liberty. A republic of itinerant free laborers could now share in the rewards of economic progress. "Manufactures hitherto unknown in our country are springing up in all sections," continued the president, "producing a degree of national independence unequaled by that of any other power." The West was thus the final piece in forging an expansive free-labor democracy, connecting the rehabilitated South to the industrious North, channeling a civilized, progressive upward mobility for all citizens.[27]

Republicans heralded the inevitable planting "of free labor civilization to every corner of North America." Yet blunt reality confronted the romantic visions of a West untainted by peoples, uncorrupted by foreign elements, and unimproved by earnest independence. Diverse Native populations, whose presence had long antagonized the Union's providential errand, arrested the westward proliferation of progress. How would Native Americans, who typically existed outside the boundaries of national life, whose embrace of communal tribalism rejected the system of free labor, integrate into the civilizing project of continental republicanism? When Grant acknowledged how "the building of railroads, and the access thereby given to all the agricultural and mineral regions of the country" brought "civilized settlements in contact with all the tribes of Indians," he voiced an overwhelming white consensus that Indigenous people were impediments to national growth. "The original inhabitants of this Continent" remained stagnant fixtures of a bygone time, failing to advance with the swift currents of modernity. As one historian explains, they were "both domestic and foreign, both in but not of the United States," whose destiny rested, Grant assumed, "under the benign influences of education and civilization." Americans' "superiority of strength, and advantages of civilization, should make us lenient," until "the Indian be made a useful and productive member of society by proper teaching and treatment." The president thus encouraged respectful conduct toward Natives, especially "any course toward them which tends to their civilization and ultimate citizenship," a course that would place the United States "before the civilized nations of the earth." Grant shuddered at the obvious alternative: "It is either this or war of extermination."[28]

In a similar scenario to the postemancipation South, the presence of western Natives compelled the federal government to define the limits of citizenship and the scope of national sovereignty. The authors of the Fourteenth Amendment explicitly omitted Indians from the constitutional definition of citizenship, depriving them of critical protections, immunities, and privileges afforded to an otherwise legitimate body politic. Remarkable implications of this meaning of Union sprang from a Wisconsin Republican's allegation that Indians were "not quite constitutionalized." Indigenous peoples existed outside constitutional boundaries because they adhered to cultures seemingly foreign to American civilization. Tribalism rejected the rule of law, disavowed notions of private property, and considered land a collective, stationary place rather than the foundation of individual economic improvement. The absence of formal education further stunted intellectual growth, facilitating a uniform and stagnant group identity, obstructing individual uniqueness, technological innovation, or entrepreneurial initiative. Native peoples ostensibly did not encourage democratic pluralism, nor did they govern by enlightened consent.

Their false "nations" blocked federal access to western land, the essential core of progressive free labor, thwarting the mobility of ambitious citizens. Native Americans thus lived seemingly as illegitimate international coalitions within the Union.[29]

In the same way that slaveholders once commandeered and drained vast agricultural territories of energy, development, and growth, the tribalization of western lands inhibited free labor and republican institutions from spreading across the continent. As noncitizens, Indians were denied constitutional safeguards, their tribal grounds subject to federal confiscation and redistribution to "civilized" Americans who would perfect the terrain with capitalist institutions. This sequestration practice informed President Grant's "Peace Policy," the process by which Natives relinquished their land, lived as territorial wards of the federal state, and underwent a "civilizing" education in preparation for citizenship. Grant condemned any "system which looks to the extinction of a race" as a cruel "disregard for human life and the rights of others." The inevitable march of progress therefore compelled white Americans to place "all the Indians on large reservations, as rapidly as it can be done, and giving them absolute protection." Dependent on federal largesse to provide small parcels of land, and inculcated with Christian philanthropy and Protestant ethics, Natives were expected to shed their tribal loyalties, assimilating as competent, productive individuals fit for the market economy and the constitutional order. To oversee detribalization and assimilation, in 1869 Grant appointed his trusted army aid and Seneca native Ely S. Parker as commissioner of Indian affairs. Parker encouraged federal Indian commissioners and secular philanthropists to exercise restraint and patience and to honor existing treaties. Yet he cautiously echoed prevailing white attitudes regarding the reservation system, from which "the government [could] more readily control [Native Americans] and more economically press and carry out plans for their improvement and civilization."[30]

The "Peace Policy" reflected the federal state's remarkable power to exert authority, shape the borders of national inclusion, and dismantle autonomous communities to forge continental unity. The limited yet potent conception of "civilization" informed irreconcilable white notions of tribal and American sovereignty. "Hereafter," Congress announced in 1871, "no Indian nation or tribe within the territory of the United States shall be acknowledged or recognized as an independent nation, tribe, or power, with whom the United States may contract by treaty." The American West would transform in the same manner as the old American Southeast, displacing outmoded Natives with energetic citizens of a modern nation-state. No power could halt the inevitable parade of civilization; no authority could derail the Union's rendezvous with progress. Federal force necessarily compelled Natives to adopt new habits, new customs, and new identities that enhanced their ostensibly bleak existence, while also ensuring the American republic's manifest destiny. "We do not contest the ever ready argument," read a report of Indian peace commissioners, "that civilization must not be arrested in its progress by a handful of savages.... The Indian must not stand in the way." Any repudiation of the "Peace Policy," any refusal to relocate to reservations, any obstacle to the construction of railroads or telegraphs, any barriers to the settlement of lands, and any reluctance to detribalize flouted the inevitable march of modernity. "If the savage resists," concluded the commissioners, "civilization, with the ten commandants in one hand and the sword in the other, demands his immediate extermination."[31]

Detribalization depended on Native consent, but willing agreements rarely materialized between white Americans and Indigenous people. The government after 1871 no longer considered western tribes "semi sovereign nations"; instead it categorized Indians as dependent wards whose illegitimate land claims and outright hostility signaled an explicit rebellion against federal authority. Washington regarded Natives who did not occupy reservations by the mid-1870s as antagonistic, stateless insurgents waging an unlawful rebellion against the government. The U.S. Army emerged as a critical institution to enforce federal legitimacy and to dismantle tribal sovereignties. At the same moment that the army retreated to the margins of the American South in the wake of Military Reconstruction, soldiers targeted Indigenous communities to direct the long march toward "civilization." Gen.-in-Chief William Tecumseh Sherman and his foremost lieutenant, Philip H. Sheridan, established the "just" reprisals against Natives who resisted. Only "annihilation, obliteration, and complete destruction" of food supplies and natural resources, explained Sheridan in 1873, would either force submission to federal authority or yield infinite extermination. "Peaceful Indians have by me, and by all the army, always been treated with the utmost kindness, but the hostile savages," Sherman remarked in 1876, "must feel the superior power of the Government, before they can realize that they must not kill, must not steal, and must not continue to carry into practice their savage instincts and customs."[32]

Though spread thin across tiny frontier garrisons, the army directed intermittent campaigns of "ruthless total war" against Indigenous populations. That Native insurrectionists supposedly rejected American beneficence, standing foolishly athwart the tide of progress, justified their removal from national life. The Union's sovereignty depended on the ability to exert federal authority over subversive dissidents, whether they materialized as aristocratic secessionists or as hostile Indians. Yet the Indian wars between 1870 and 1890 revealed striking distinctions between the consolidation of the West and the reconstruction of the South. The United States' war against slaveholding secessionists assumed that former Confederates, who identified as republican citizens and shared a common Anglo heritage, deserved restoration to the federal Union. Reconstruction of the American South was aimed at bringing true democracy to a region long drained of authentic, egalitarian representation. A southern coalition of loyal whites and blacks ostensibly secured the region and the republic from revolutionary aristocrats. The same moderate rationale was not extended to Native Americans, whose very presence defied any "potential political community." As one leading scholar explains, "The denial of community between whites and Indians except on white terms made it easy to define Indian resistance as illegitimate and to employ tactics that would have seemed barbaric, extreme, and unthinkable if employed against Southern whites" and former Confederates. Through military campaigns and federal decree, by 1890 the government had eliminated Indigenous sovereignties from within national borders, securing the West for burgeoning railroad networks and bequeathing millions of public acres to white free laborers who populated the vast frontier.[33]

Republicans did not consider Indigenous populations the only western obstructions to the progress of American civilization. Utah Territory burgeoned with Mormonism, a uniquely American yet seemingly fallacious corruption of Protestantism. Federal military coercion pushed Mormons to the far West prior to the Civil War, and the Republican Congress used the war itself to regulate religion in the territories. The 1862 Morrill Act, which reserved western public lands for free-labor settlement and vocational education, banned polygamy, a custom that many Republicans identified with the immorality of slaveholding. Like human bondage, the suspicious marriage practice affronted constitutional liberty by affording arbitrary patriarchal privilege at the expense of subservient victims. Republican James F. Rusling voiced the party consensus when he condemned in 1867 all "'peculiar Institutions,' whether slavery or polygamy, [which] breed the same results, whether in South Carolina or Utah." Polygamy resurrected the ghost of human bondage, in which unyielding, autocratic Mormon men acted "as our southern slave lords used to speak of their 'likely young niggers.'" Mormonism undermined the Union's progressive future because "the whole thing is simply an organized insult to Christianity and an outrage against the civilization of the age." That polygamy served as "slavery's hideous and exquisite 'twin relic of barbarism'" demanded the elimination of false religions that drew power from the same hierarchical and state-sponsored exploitation as slaveholding. To secure personal sovereignty, independent mobility, and freedom of thought, "let us then begin by guarding against every enemy threatening the perpetuity of free republican institutions," Ulysses S. Grant concluded in an 1875 speech to Union veterans. Though he never explicitly condemned Mormonism, Grant implicitly nodded to the era's anti-Mormon tenor when he advocated the strict separation of church and state joined by a system of public education "unmixed with sectarian, pagan or atheistical tenets."[34]

Mormon barbarism had to be cleansed from the American West in the same manner that emancipation had erased slaveholding despotism from the American South. Any illiberal, reactionary faction had to be dismantled to facilitate republican progress and national unity. Mormons thus joined with Indigenous people, who propagated "pagan" religions on providential western lands designated for civilized Americans. To maintain "sovereign powers over the territories," the Republican Party pledged in the mid-1870s "to prohibit and extirpate . . . that relic of barbarism, polygamy." Only then would flourish the "supremacy of American institutions" that protected individual liberty and human dignity. Believing that Mormonism compelled universal loyalty to a church rather than to the republic, Congress in 1874 issued the Poland Act, which gave federal courts the remarkable power to adjudicate marriage practices. But did not anti-Mormonism shatter the First Amendment's sacred protections of religious liberty and freedom of conscience? In a dramatic ruling that underscored the Republican vision of Union and consolidated federal authority over local, state, and territorial matters, the Supreme Court proscribed polygamy in *Reynolds v. United States* (1879). Outlawing this false religious habit did not violate the Constitution, reasoned the Court, because the republican ideal of marriage, one uncorrupted by power or mastery, mandated protections against compulsive state religions. *Reynolds* embodied a Republican faith that enlightened, restrained, democratic institutions would eventually overwhelm Mormonism, in much the same way that they had destroyed slavery.[35]

The specter of foreign others populating the West with odd customs, heathen ways, and barbaric practices also informed Republican appraisals of the Chinese immigrants whose semi-coerced labor improved the western frontier. At first Republicans welcomed the Pacific workers who toiled for cheap wages in mines, on ranches, and aboard the transcontinental railroad. The Burlingame Treaty of 1868 even encouraged unlimited Chinese immigration to fulfill endless demands on labor to meet exponential western development. The question of Chinese citizenship soon consumed debates over the meaning of republican inclusion and the boundaries of national sovereignty. Some western Republicans coalesced against Chinese citizenship, arguing that peoples of Asiatic descent, no matter how valuable their labor, weakened the American disposition. Nevada senator William Stewart, a leading sponsor of the Fifteenth Amendment, warned that Chinese "devotion to pagan despotism" and "hostil[ity] to free institutions" threatened Christian integrity and republican legitimacy. "We are charged with the duty of preserving these liberties for mankind," he continued. "America is the palladium of free institutions, and we are but the trustees to guard those rights." Echoing Carl Schurz's critique of Dominican citizenship, Stewart warned, "We must not incorporate any foreign element which is hostile to free institutions." In this vein, California refused a vote on the Fourteenth Amendment and repudiated the Fifteenth. Oregon initially ratified the former in 1866, but two years later annulled ratification, while Nevada barely passed the latter. Ultimately, the Naturalization Act of 1870 denied Chinese citizenship, recognizing only people of white and African descent, while the Page Act of 1875 limited Chinese immigration entirely. In ways they seemingly always had done, white Americans defined "civilization" in distinct racial and ethnic terms.[36]

The American West and the American South facilitated the unification of continental sovereignty. Republicans emerged from the Civil War committed to extinguishing radical, revolutionary, antidemocratic internationalism from the republic. Only continental stability and the rule of law could guard the nation against international factions, among them the Slave Power, Indigenous nations, false religions, and suspicious ethnicities. "The resultant disorders of a great war," read the 1872 party platform, joined the death of the Confederate rebellion, the triumph of emancipation, and the fruition of biracial equality with "a wise and humane policy toward the Indians," while introducing "the Pacific railroad and similar vast enterprises" into western "public lands." Consolidating the continent under a banner of Americanized free labor allegedly barred antirepublican schisms from again sundering national accord, instead enabling "peace and plenty ... throughout the land." The struggles to extinguish the once imposing menace of disunion and establish national stability "have been peacefully and honorably composed," assuring "the honor and power of the nation kept in high respect throughout the world." By reconstructing the Union's broad territorial reach, Republicans guaranteed that "the people will not intrust the Government to any party or combination of men composed chiefly of those who have resisted every step of this beneficent progress."[37]

It is worth remembering, however, that the Reconstruction South and the American West underwent distinct processes of federal authority and force, each reflecting distinct dimensions of national purpose. Racialized notions of civilization and one's continental relationship to the federal state determined how individuals and regional groups experienced national power. "Does the Declaration of Independence mean that Chinese coolies, that the Bushmen of south Africa, that the Hottentots, the Digger Indians, heathen, pagan, and cannibal, shall have equal political rights under this Government with citizens of the United States?" asked Oregon Republican George Henry Wilson. "Sir, that is the absurd and foolish interpretation." Republicans never viewed all white southerners as foreigners unworthy of inclusion in the nation's body politic. Reunion in the wake of a civil war waged between white democratic Americans demanded "unparalleled magnanimity," the party declared, and "warmly welcomed all who proved loyalty" to the republic. As equal constituents of the federal system, the former Confederate states profited from political moderation and an extant faith in popular sovereignty. Repressive coercions unleashed against such constitutionally protected citizens—even those who once waged a massive war of rebellion that truly endangered national sovereignty—would have undermined the enduring purpose of Union. And when the Fourteenth and Fifteenth Amendments conferred constitutional citizenship on African Americans, while denying the same privileges to Indigenous populations, Mormons, and Chinese, Republicans acknowledged that white *and* black Americans imbued with republican virtue, democratic proclivities, a free-labor acumen, and Protestant enlightenment could assure the progress of civilization. Though federal power had reshaped the Constitution, reordered the continent, and expanded the concept of "citizen," the centrality of federalism in the orbit of democratic republicanism limited the reconstruction of the South from transforming into the violent, unbridled reorganization of the West.[38]

Insurgency, Internationalism, and the Compromise of Reconstruction

As Republicans used the postwar state to restore the Union, reform the Constitution, negotiate international diplomacy, and consolidate the continent, former Confederates emerged violently disillusioned from what they deemed the utter collapse of civilization. From the Reconstruction Acts to the Fourteenth and Fifteenth Amendments, to the rising tide of black political activism, to a seemingly oppressive bayonet rule, few slaveholding societies like the American South had experienced the abruptness of emancipation and the decisiveness of civil equality conferred upon former bondpeople. For a preponderance of southern whites, Reconstruction had unleashed an unholy racial revolution. "All is lost, and a long dark night settles on our beloved State," ruminated Jefferson Davis when a new class of white and African American Republicans claimed political authority of his cherished Mississippi. "I have not been so depressed by any public event which has transpired since the surrender of Confederate Armies." The once hopeful dream of a thriving, independent, slaveholding republic was, by 1870, a distant memory shattered by unremitting nightmares. Indeed, the seat that Davis once occupied in the U.S. Senate—the very institution that safeguarded the slaveholding Union—had been claimed by Hiram Revels, a free man of color, "a representative of the race that Mr. Davis intended to be the cornerstone" of the Confederate nation.[39]

White southerners strained to make sense of the carnage, grasping for any kind of meaning. Their society had been conquered ostensibly not through sober, deliberate, legislative reflection but, rather, through the unjust coercion of a consolidated military state. Only martial compulsion could so unnaturally rearrange a society once conceived by divine Providence. "A negro legislature, negro militia, negro justices, constables, and policemen—the whole power of the State committed to the hands of carpet-baggers and negroes," observed a crestfallen South Carolinian in 1871. "Shame upon the party that, with Federal bayonets, forced such a government upon ... men of their own race and country." Radical Republicans seemed to have morphed into monarchical Europeans who scoffed at the pleas of their helpless subjects amid the devastating application of imperial might. Military compulsion stood as "a reproach to the civilization of the age," in which liberal whites were "ruled by the former slaves." Yet Republicans had also seemingly unleashed French revolutionary Jacobinism by elevating a people so "corrupted and debased by slavery," averred an Alabamian. That "a state of slavery cannot be eradicated by a legislative enactment, nor a by a constitutional provision" signaled that uneducated, passionate, and degraded freedpeople now controlled republican institutions. "The purity of the ballot-box is the great perseverance of freedom in our country." Yet "when the great body of our electors ... are ignorant blacks," manipulated by military "agents" and seduced by white Republicans, "the grossest corruption in our elections" had transpired, the sacred "liberty of choice" forever lost.[40]

Reconstruction signified to former Confederates that the United States had followed a disturbing nineteenth-century trajectory in which seemingly oppressed peoples rebelled against despotism only to lose their liberty at the behest of coercive central states. "The South is no more a real partner in the so-called Union than Poland is a part of Russia, or India of England, or Cuba of Spain," decried Randolph Abbott Shotwell. "Why then should this country be called a Union? The very term signifies equality of parts. Let it be called Yankeeland." The American South appeared completely balkanized, detached from its once safe place in the federal Union, overrun by blue-coated mercenaries, and despoiled by racial inferiors. "If we are not to become Mexicanized and lose sight of civilization," declared Jonathan Worth, once a stalwart opponent of disunion but an adherent nonetheless to racial hierarchy, "we must put down the proposed Constitution" of North Carolina. White southerners, the sovereign guardians of racial republicanism, had been stripped of all legitimacy, and their wayward region was now fractured by anarchy. "Resistance on the part of individuals is the inevitable consequence of such outrages," acknowledged a South Carolinian who warned that fellow whites would pursue "various paths of peace" to combat "a thousand acts of injustice and tyranny."[41]

Yet white southerners hardly chose a peaceful path of resistance. The transformative consequences of Republican Reconstruction occasioned a widespread insurgency that aimed to cleanse a liberal South of its alleged racial corruption. Political and racial violence had long plagued the postwar landscape, and white insurgents consented on an unambiguous purpose: to use informal militancy to restore the South's racial hierarchy, to consolidate white control of land and labor, and to reclaim political power. To secure those ends, insurgents populated various institutions that evolved in complexity and purpose. During the late 1860s, clandestine and somewhat unorganized vigilante groups, such as the Ku Klux Klan, targeted specific Republicans and individual freedpeople, aiming to rebalance the southern political landscape altered by Congress and grassroots black political activism. More systematized paramilitary units, which comprised hundreds of former Confederate soldiers, grew during the early 1870s to conduct public guerrilla operations against politicians, African American political organizations, and elections. By the middle of the decade, paramilitary groups instigated counterrevolutions against Republican state governments in Arkansas, Louisiana, Mississippi, and South Carolina. Civil violence manipulated the electoral process in favor of white southern Democrats, sparking "organized coup[s] d'tat" to "redeem" the South from Republican and African American political authority.[42]

The white southern insurgency conducted during the 1870s was not a continuation of the struggle from 1861 to 1865 nor even a "second Civil War." It was, as all insurgencies are, an internal scheme of political and social terrorism deployed to alter existing domestic conditions. Using unconventional but institutionalized violence, including political assassinations and racial intimidation, paramilitary insurgents pursued distinctly dogmatic ends: realigning the American South within a political and social ethos of white racial supremacy. If elections could be unsettled, if black and white Republicans could be cowed into submission, white southerners could reconstruct a society built on racial subordination and Democratic Party political hegemony. Unlike the Confederate rebellion; postwar diplomatic conflicts with Mexico, Great Britain, and Canada; or even hostile interactions with Native Americans, the paramilitary counterrevolution purposely did not challenge the United States' sovereignty. Insurgents instead sought to *preserve* the Union from radical internationalization imposed by anarchical abolitionists. "We are living," declared an exasperated Edward Pollard, "in the solemnity of Revolution," one "unusually remarkable" and "so extreme as to claim a particular notice." The reconstructed Union had become Europeanized through military compulsion, Africanized through racial barbarism, and Mexicanized through illegitimate and corrupted state governments. "The Union may be more effectually destroyed by Consolidation than by Secession," the Virginia editor explained. "The first is more odious, and especially at the present instance, with the stripe of Negro government in it." Insurgents did not campaign to sunder the republic and establish a new slaveholding nation, an enterprise that failed at Appomattox. The "appeal we put up is *the Union*," concluded Pollard, "that for which the war was fought, and which for three generations has symbolized our greatness, and assured our prosperity."[43]

Republicans sensed that the insurgency portended a radical danger to the republic. They had assembled Reconstruction with an optimistic faith that constitutional rehabilitation would obviate domestic strife, compelling *all* southerners to participate equally in the blessings of limited American governance. And they had assumed that civil equality, the rule of law, and a revitalized democracy would stabilize the postwar South and furnish freedpeople with the tools of self-preservation. As stalwart Alabama Unionist John A. Minnis acknowledged, "In the present century, the civilization of the world arrayed itself against slavery," an institution "valuable, and interwoven into" all white southerners. Minnis thus hailed the Fourteenth and Fifteenth Amendments as "right in principle [and] made for the best purposes and from the purest motives, the safety and security of the Government." For Minnis, Reconstruction succeeded in forging a sturdy foundation of antislavery republicanism without revolutionizing the Union. The restrained, rational process knew no "parallel in the history of the world." Bestowed with "the rights, privileges, and immunities of citizens," freedpeople "have conducted themselves [as] orderly, law-abiding, and worthy of the privileges." Yet few Republicans, concluded Minnis, had appreciated the delicacy of the new laws themselves, both in protecting freedpeople and in earning the consent of former Confederates. "The southern people generally regard [Reconstruction] as created to punish and humiliate," justifying a disgraceful insurgency that defied the natural progress of civilization, defied the Union's moderation, and defied American faith in democratic self-determination.[44]

The white counterrevolution exposed a deeply embedded conceit that few Republicans anticipated. The Slave Power's poisonous spirit seemed to linger in the same troubling ways in slavery's *absence* as it did when slaveholding oligarchs held power. Threatened with widespread intimidation and violence, African Americans and white southern Unionists could not pursue the promises of liberty guaranteed by the Fourteenth and Fifteenth Amendments. "We know that when the old aristocracy and ruling power of this state get into power," announced a delegation of black South Carolinians, "they will take precious good care that the colored people shall never be enlightened." Indeed, Maj. Lewis Merrill of the Seventh U.S. Cavalry observed that violence in the Palmetto State "has no parallel, either in wanton and brutal cruelties inflicted ... or in the utter deadening of the moral sense in large parts of white communities reputed and believed to be far removed from the barbarism of savages." White southerners again appeared in rebellion against the Constitution and the republic. "For four years the National Government conducted a war for the perpetuity of the Union and the establishment and preservation of the Liberty of the people," wrote a dejected southern Unionist to President Grant, "and those who were its opponents throughout that desperate struggle are the same class of men who now resist its policy."[45]

The paramilitary insurgency called into question the federal state's role in protecting individual liberty from militant coercion. "Whenever there is a refusal to obey the laws made by the majority in due form, and whenever popular opinion in any community can override laws, then there is no longer a republican Government," acknowledged Senator John Sherman. "It is anarchy first, and despotism afterward." The Union appeared as unstable as the Atlantic world's tremulous republics, notably the Third Republic of France, which promised to restore the French monarchy in accordance with popular will. However, in early 1871, a militant alliance of utopian socialists, budding Marxists, and antiaristocrats known as the Paris Commune rejected the legitimacy of the new republic, seizing the national capitol with military force supplied by the National Guard. Although Americans celebrated the new republic's birth—the United States was the first nation to recognize the new French regime—many also saw the French as turbulent radical democrats who did not possess dispassionate self-determination. Skeptical Americans interpreted the commune as a militant hazard to the rule of law, the respect for private property, and the validity of state authority. When the commune exploded into a violent insurgency for social and economic equality, Congressman Elihu Washburne warned of its "frightful excesses," which "have brought reproach upon the sacred name of the Republic, and the good name of Republicanism suffers."[46]

Some Republicans wondered whether such so-called republics could claim authenticity when violent factions like the Paris Commune spurned national consensus. "The preference of rural France, and of the middle class in the cities, is monarchical," explained *Harper's Weekly* regarding the French populace's overwhelming support of the Third Republic. "To them the republic is not *démocratique* only, it is *sociale*; and [it was] sheer anarchy" when a minority cabal—"the mob of Paris"—attempted to overthrow the people's will. The commune portended the collapse of ordered liberty and exposed the problem of majority consensus in a free society. "It is an insurrection, then, not more against political government than against social organization," wrote Henry Ward Beecher, who recognized how the commune rejected reason, restraint, and religion "to make an experiment on a magnificent scale of the reconstruction of men's relations to each other." The comparative implications for the United States were inescapable. Though he warned against the hazards of a society fomenting stark class distinctions, Beecher also asked whether "we, on this side, [are] in danger of similar insurrections." Revolutionary internationalization always sprang from "different parts of the population antagonistic to each other."[47]

Within two months, more than 150,000 French national military forces eradicated the commune in much the same way that the democratic revolutions of 1848 collapsed under state-sanctioned reprisal. Thousands of civilians perished in chaotic street battles. As Beecher observed, "Paris is soaked in blood," "festering corpses lie along the streets," and "the scenes of the hideous French Revolution are enacted again." The ubiquity of social upheaval hardly surprised the conservative pastor, who cautioned against "look[ing] upon this with mere exclamatory feeling. Still less should we congratulate ourselves upon our own safety and superiority. We may not always be secure." The Paris Commune, like the paramilitary insurgency engulfing the American South, compelled republics to determine the proper response to violent resistance against the rule of law and the consent of the governed. As Beecher implied, French internationalization might well descend on the United States either in the form of radical stateless insurgents or in the devastating retaliations executed by the central state itself. But the limited, peacetime conditions of American Reconstruction—a context far different from the state of public war that closed in 1865—mandated significant restraints on government power, especially where issues of military centralization and race were concerned.[48]

In 1870–71 Congress passed the Enforcement Acts, a series of laws that outlawed Klan activity, criminalized the deprivation of constitutional rights, and authorized the president to use federal military force to quell domestic lawlessness. The acts even permitted the government to punish state crimes such as murder. Congressional Republicans and President Grant exercised federal force to uphold the Fourteenth and Fifteenth Amendments, protecting civil rights when state governors and militias simply could not withstand the onslaught of white terrorism. Though military commanders could advance only at the request of civil authorities, the U.S. Army nonetheless waged the unprecedented counterinsurgent campaigns with remarkable acumen. Fewer than ten thousand soldiers occupied the former Confederacy in 1871, a number that trended downward through the remainder of the decade. Still, the army conducted hundreds of cavalry expeditions to clean out pockets of paramilitary resistance, helping civil authorities to enforce federal and state laws. Despite its dwindling numbers and the constitutional limitations imposed on its scope and reach, the army succeeded in stemming violence and convincing white dissidents of federal supremacy.[49]

Employing national military forces to combat civil violence and administer federal supremacy were extraordinary tasks for the U.S. Army. The military retreated to the margins of civil and political life in 1871, when the former Confederate states had complied with Republican Reconstruction and established democratically elected biracial electorates. Yet only federal power could stem insurgent violence from dismantling the Republican state governments, and the Enforcement Acts placed the army in an unparalleled position. General-in-Chief Sherman regarded the military's law enforcement function as "dirty work" because "it [is] wrong to bolster up weak State governments by our troops." "We should keep the peace always," he opined, "but not act as bailiff constables and catch thieves." Even President Grant, among the principal supporters of enforcement, acknowledged its entirely foreign character. "I am well aware that any military interference by the officers or troops of the United States with the organization of the State legislature," he advised the Senate, "or with any civil department of the Government, is repugnant to our ideas of government." And though he implemented the letter of the acts and supported Grant's Reconstruction program, Gen. Alfred Terry wrote from his post in Georgia, "The pressure upon me ... is very great and I would not again go through with a job of this kind even if it would make me a Marshal of France."[50]

Still, the army achieved great success. Military forces neutralized Klan activity in 1871 in South Carolina, the embroiled state that inspired the Enforcement Acts; forestalled coups in Louisiana in 1871 and 1872; and imposed the will of President Grant in 1874, when he selected the victor of a guerrilla-infested election in Arkansas. But the central question is not whether enforcement measures worked. Instead, why did scores of moderate Republicans scorn the Enforcement Acts? Why did they imagine the Union fast transforming into a centralized European state in response to Klan violence? Anti-Klan measures in the United States occurred at roughly the same moment as the Paris Commune, pushing some Republicans to wonder whether the Union had traded federalism for centralized militarism in combating rogue civil criminals. "I agree that the wicked organizations should be put down," announced Senator Lyman Trumbull, but "the people of this country prize their liberties too highly to trust anybody with this power of military despotism, except when pressed by invasion or rebellion." The acts permitted the president to suspend the writ of habeas corpus, which Grant did in nine South Carolina counties, worrying scores of Republicans that the federal state and its military apparatus would thereafter monitor social conditions and regulate civic life under the auspices of "domestic rebellion." The Enforcement Acts and Grant's simultaneous efforts to acquire Santo Domingo compelled Henry Adams to admit, "I see no constitutional government any longer possible." Republican critics alleged that the swift centralization of the federal state posed grave dangers to constitutional separation of powers and the Union's anti-militaristic disposition. Could the South ever stand truly reconstructed if the military always remained on guard to intervene at the threat of civil disruption? Federalism thereafter would have little meaning, transforming a limited American republic into a commonplace European military leviathan.[51]

Testimony from Congressman James Garfield and *The Nation* exemplify the internationalist context in which moderate Republicans condemned alleged extremes of federal enforcement. In April 1871, Garfield heralded the American republic as one of the world's only nations ever to balance independent localism with national authority. Most nations, averred the Ohio representative, either succumb to "that despotism which swallows and absorbs all power in a single-central government" or collapse from extreme "local sovereignty which makes nationality impossible and resolves a general government into anarchy and chaos." The war for Union "vindicated the centripetal power of the nation." Yet excessive postwar federal power imposed "the destruction or serious crippling of the principle of local government," a result "as fatal to liberty as secession would have been fatal to the Union." Garfield looked to France as an archetype of monarchical centralization that routinely devolved into riotous democracy. The collective "despotism" of Louis XIV and Napoleon III inspired reactionary "reign[s] of terror, when liberty had run mad," producing "vast scene[s] of blood and ruin." Now "the communes of France [have been] crushed, and local liberty exist[s] no longer." Only "the swords of the citizens of that new republic are now wet with each other's blood."[52]

Garfield called on white Americans to uphold the Union's national stability while ensuring that the "centrifugal force" of federalism retained its "grand and beautiful equipoise." Though he detested the "wide-spread secret organization" in the South that threatened the sanctity of voting, equality, and the rule of law, Garfield was concerned about the federal government's response to insurgent terrorism. He worried that the Enforcement Acts conferred seemingly unchecked power on the commander in chief, who could routinely suspend habeas corpus, declare martial law, and activate federal military forces within the states. "When we provide by congressional enactment to punish a mere violation of a State law," no less in the name of civil unrest, "we pass the line of constitutional authority." The implications were startling. "When other men with other purposes may desire to confer this power on another President for purposes that may not aid in securing public liberty and public peace," few restraints existed against an executive declaring arbitrary states of civil war, holding citizens indefinitely as prisoners, and imposing armed forces to consolidate personal political power. What if, Garfield implied, federal military enforcement not only transformed a limited republic of consent into a centralized military state, but also escalated the already fierce and violent resistance to federal authority? As in France, interminable cycles of compulsion, faction, and grievance would litter the streets of shattered cities with dead bodies, while in the process undoing all constitutional boundaries on government power.[53]

The Nation, though founded as a pro-Republican, antislavery supporter of biracial civil rights, emerged in the 1870s as a foremost critic of Reconstruction's seeming internationalist excesses. Editor E. L. Godkin lamented "the outrages committed by what are called the Ku-klux on the negroes and Unionists at the South." Commending the "social revolution" in which "the negroes and Unionists [were] guaranteed a voice in the Government" and "were secured in the exclusive control of it," Godkin argued that Reconstruction had furnished "common civil rights ... without having recourse to pure military coercion." Although the Ku Klux Klan had "taken the field against the new regime," threatening to dismantle the Union's robust constitutional modifications, *The Nation* criticized the South's biracial coalitions as "the worst specimens" of democracy, hapless amateurs who could not ensure domestic tranquility and regulate ruthless felons. They instead had to petition the federal government to protect their state with military force, inviting certain despotism and threatening to rearrange the balance of popular sovereignty. "To impose the duty of protecting life and property on the Federal Government is" a "distinct and well-marked novelty." The Enforcement Acts adopted "the machinery in use under the arbitrary and centralized governments of Europe—that is, the withdrawal of criminal cases from the jury, and their committal to single judges appointed by the central authority and armed with extraordinary powers."[54]

The Europeanization of American constitutionalism underscored *The Nation*'s central critique. "There is this to be said for the means to which European governments resort for the protection of life and property," Godkin remarked sardonically—"they work." The French, Prussian, British, and Russian governments were all too happy to "send as many troops into the disturbed districts as will police them accordingly." Indeed, "if dealing with the South, they would occupy it with at least 100,000 men, they would patrol the roads with clouds of cavalry, and fill the streets with swarms of police." And though the "evil-doers" might be subdued "and, though liberty might suffer, honest people would sleep in peace." Was security worth the price of liberty? The Klan was just as destructive and dangerous as French socialists, each practicing perverted brands of democracy. But the greater threat ostensibly stemmed from centralized reaction, the chief menace to democracy itself, once embodied by the American Slave Power and militaristic European monarchs. "If we once get into the habit of treating the Constitution as a mere expression of opinion, to be set aside whenever its observance seems inconvenient, we shall have substituted a Gallic Republic for an American one." At that point "we have sown the seeds of anarchy," we have declared "the whole American system a mistake," and thus "we cannot interfere effectively, and had better not interfere at all."[55]

To comprehend the ambivalence of Republicans who feared the awesome scope of military power, one must appreciate the ways in which nineteenth-century Americans distinguished war from peace. Reconstruction was always a limited process to secure and maintain lasting accord; it was not a moment of continued warfare. Formal, public, and just wars in the nineteenth century typically featured nation-states battling for limited objectives. In the American context, the republic enlisted private citizens to wage war on behalf of the public interest. The wake of Military Reconstruction—and indeed, all of Reconstruction—was a fundamentally different kind of conflict that few Americans would have identified as a prerequisite for military mobilization. African American political and social equality unquestionably depended on an occupying army big enough to enforce the Fourteenth and Fifteenth Amendments. More than 1 million Union soldiers occupied only portions of the Confederacy in April 1865, an impossible number to replicate during peacetime. Planting a permanent army indefinitely in the South, acknowledged Senator Carl Schurz, would "protect the rights of some" while "break[ing] down the bulwarks of the citizens against arbitrary authority, and by transgressing all Constitutional limitations of power." The unprecedented mobilization of military forces to serve a regional political agenda would have consolidated on American soil a standing army, the dreaded specter of tyranny that coerced free citizens to pledge loyalty to military institutions and political programs. The United States would still exist, these Republicans charged, but it would no longer be a Union of, by, and for the people.[56]

Antimilitarism privileged a restrained federal state. When he pledged military force to execute federal laws, President Grant claimed that the inability "of local communities" to protect themselves "imposed upon the National Government the duty of putting forth all its energies for the protection of its citizens of every race and color, and for the restoration of peace and order throughout the entire country." Willfully suspending habeas corpus and declaring martial law in parts of South Carolina reflected Grant's disgust about the deprivation of common civil rights and his desire "that all traces of our late unhappy civil strife may be speedily removed." Yet he also admitted his "relunctan[ce] to call into exercise any of the extraordinary powers thereby conferred upon me," favoring "the people of those parts of the country to suppress all such combinations by their own voluntary efforts." Indeed, "social equality is not a subject to be legislated upon nor shall I ask that anything be done to advance the social status of the colored man except to give him a fair chance to develop what there is good in him." The United States would not transform into a military leviathan under Grant's purview, even though he employed the army in temporary and extraordinary measures. Though the military stood as the foremost institution to enforce civil rights, "under our republic," Grant heralded, "we support an Army less than that of any European Power of any standing."[57]

Grant was correct. By 1872, fewer than eight thousand federal troops patrolled the American South, a landmass the size of Western Europe. Meanwhile by 1880, Russia, France, Germany, Great Britain, Austria-Hungary, and Italy boasted median standing armies of nearly four hundred thousand professional soldiers, products of highly bureaucratized and belligerent governments. Former diplomat John Lothrop Motley spoke for much of the white loyal citizenry when he described the United States' antimilitaristic relationship to the rest of the world. "Progress must be fettered and halting everywhere, under the military rule prevailing over continental Europe," he averred. Motley interpreted Europe's large standing armies as troubling signs of societal stagnation. A republic maintained its legitimacy only when "every citizen becomes a soldier" temporarily to defend the national interest and "great armies resolve themselves again into the mass of the people." European citizenries in contrast served as mercenaries to "every monarchy." While Motley recognized the abounding spirit of democracy among the European masses, he also asked, "Is it really the final result of European civilization to decide which nation shall have the most populous armies and the biggest guns?" For Motley, civilization progressed only at the behest of the popular will, not through the barrel of a gun.[58]

Recently elected African American congressional representatives and senators listened with shock as their Republican allies seemed far more concerned about esoteric constitutional transgressions and lofty antimilitaristic aspirations than the protection of basic human rights. The fate of American civilization, they charged, hinged on whether the federal government would defend the Union's sacred commitment to natural equality and universal liberty, each threatened by white terrorists *and* conservative Republicans. "In the dawn of our freedom our young Republic was widely recognized and proudly proclaimed to the world [as] the refuge, the safe asylum of the oppressed of all lands," declared South Carolina congressman Joseph Rainey. The real peril to constitutional legitimacy stemmed not from excessive federal enforcement but, rather, from too *little* application of the laws. "What will it be but a proof to all men that we are utterly unfit for our glorious mission, unworthy our noble privileges, as the greatest of republics, the champions of freedom for all men?" Rainey's fellow representative Robert B. Elliott likewise announced, "The great paramount duty of the Republic [is] to protect its citizens wherever the flag has the right to wave." If Republicans permitted white southerners to hijack the political process and reestablish their pathetic racial hierarchy, the promise of Union, as the world's last best hope, would be forever lost. "The best Government is that under which the humblest citizen is not beneath the protection of the laws, or the highest above the reach of their authority."[59]

Elliott leveled one of the most powerful African American critiques against Republican ambivalence toward federal enforcement. Though excluded from the nation's founding, black Americans had never been "inactive or unconcerned spectator[s]" of national growth. They maintained a powerful stake in the meaning and progress of Union. And they had performed critical work in helping to preserve the republic from slaveholding obstructions. It was "to that Government [the formerly enslaved] now appeals; that Constitution he now invokes for protection against outrage and unjust prejudices founded upon caste." To countenance the reign of terror sweeping the southern states affronted the rivers of blood shed in the cause of Union. To tolerate the gross violation of civil rights mocked the Fourteenth and Fifteenth Amendments' collapse of the old slaveholding order. To relinquish control of land coerced free black laborers into dependent wards of white planters. To abide the same violent insurgents who once sought "the overthrow of civil and political liberty on this continent" reignited the old "cancer of slavery," which again held the republic hostage to its evil demands. The rule of law and even morality itself now mandated the nation "to enforce the constitutional guarantee against inequality and discrimination." The debate was over, the long national trial complete. "The result of the war, as seen in reconstruction, have settled forever the political status of my race," Elliott concluded. Either the United States was an exceptional beacon in the world, or it was not. After decades of shortcomings, trials, and errors, the time had come to complete "the grandest [experiment] which the world has ever seen, realizing the most sanguine expectations and the highest hopes of those who, in the name of equal impartial, and universal liberty, laid the foundation stones."[60]

White skepticism about federal military enforcement nevertheless informed a growing opposition within the Republican Party to President Grant's seeming perversion of national power. The disillusioned Liberal Republicans—spearheaded by Carl Schurz and *The Nation*—alleged that Grant's policies reintroduced into the Union the very revolutionary toxins once cleansed through civil war, emancipation, and constitutional reform. Liberal Republicans joined Democrats in painting Grant as a corrupt tyrant whose unchecked militarism stoked white southern insurgents. That Grant's imperial appetite relied on military power to prop up unpopular southern state governments both shattered individual, state, and national sovereignties and reeked of oligarchic slaveholding tactics. The U.S. Army functioned as a disgraceful political arm of the Republican Party, wielding the bayonet "to sustain in power the very adventurers who by their revolting system of plunder were violently keeping alive the spirit of disorder which [Reconstruction] legislation was to repress." The experiment in biracial democracy had seemingly failed. To be sure, Schurz very much opposed this unfortunate reality, because state governments would "fall into the hands of those classes which, to a great extent, stood against us during the civil war." That situation "cannot be avoided, unless you adopt a system of interference which will subvert the most essential principles of our government." Schurz thus condemned Grant for never "appreciate[ing] the difference between military command and the complex duties and responsibilities of civil administration." Preservation of the Union now depended on removing a budding Napoleon who had ostensibly rejected the virtue of Lincoln. "Grant's reelection appeared to me so heavily fraught with danger to the future of our republican institutions," concluded Schurz, "that I could not, even indirectly, favor his success."[61]

The Liberal Republicans nominated Horace Greeley, editor of the *New York Tribune*, as the party's candidate for president in 1872. The party pledged to uphold the great constitutional amendments "acquired through our late bloody convulsion." And they advocated that no citizen—black or white—could be deprived of suffrage or an equal voice in political deliberation. Only then would "long estranged people shall reunite and fraternize upon the broad basis of Universal Amnesty." The essence of Liberal Republicanism emphasized "local self-government, and not at centralization; that the civil authority should be supreme over the military." Liberals vowed to untangle the consolidated martial state spun under Grant's purview, instead promoting individual freedom, state sovereignty, and constitutional restraint as the lifeblood of ordered liberty. Greeley ultimately sponsored national reconciliation to discard the "jealousies, strifes, and hates" which for so long had forestalled "Peace, Fraternity, and Mutual Good Will." The Liberal Republicans pledged a future seemingly rejected by Grant's Republican Party: a unity "of our countrymen, North and South, [who] are eager to clasp hands across the bloody chasm which has too long divided them." Their message too seductive to oppose, Liberals earned the endorsement of the Democratic Party, aligning malcontent Republicans with ambitious Democrats. Nonetheless, Grant won a decisive victory, earning 56 percent of the popular vote.[62]

Although the Liberal Republican Party dissolved with electoral defeat, its internationalist critique of American life resonated. By 1872 and 1873, skeptical Republicans began questioning the capacity of African Americans to contribute competently and equitably to national progress. Liberal Republicanism had always exuded a deeply sinister racial undertone, which appealed to like-minded Democrats who rejected the Republicans' seemingly naive faith in biracial government. "The rule of unprincipled and rapacious leaders at the head of the colored population," which controlled many southern state legislatures, "has resulted in a government of corruption and plunder," Schurz declared. And when the national economy collapsed in 1873, resulting in a widespread panic, bank runs, failed businesses, and shuttered industries, disgruntled Americans, in search of an enemy to blame, placed hapless freedpeople at the center of their condemnation. The Panic of 1873 resulted in devastating levels of unemployment from which mobs of resentful workers fueled widespread labor strikes to demand government restitution or to seek vengeance against corporate aristocrats. Democratic newspapers and sympathetic Republicans joined forces to print reports of riotous black workers sacking urban industries and rural plantations. The *Boston Evening Transcript*, a reliable supporter of President Grant, reproduced one story from Tennessee that claimed, "The blacks, as people, are unfitted for the proper exercise of political duties." The first generation of freedpeople necessitated "a period of probation and of instruction ... to have forgotten something of [their] condition as a slave and learned much of the true method of gaining honorable subsistence and of performing the duties of any position to which [they] might aspire."[63]

The Panic of 1873 convinced some conservatives that Republican Reconstruction governments had failed to transform African Americans into liberal free laborers. European socialism now seemed to blanket the American South. Corrupted state legislatures seemingly morphed into Parisian communes directed by venal black lawmakers who imposed excessive taxation and confiscated and redistributed private property from prostrate whites to slothful constituents. "The French Reds, like their brethren, the black Radicals of this country, are appealing to a higher law to justify their crimes," roared the Democratic *Charlottesville Weekly Chronicle*. "They threaten the guillotine in Paris," just as black and white abolitionists "would send halters to the leading men of the South. One set is as bad as the other." James S. Pike, once a stalwart Radical Republican turned disenchanted Liberal, reported in 1873 on the predominantly African American South Carolina legislature, which he labeled "the spectacle of a society suddenly turned bottom side up." Black legislators, "invested with the functions of government," practiced "the rude form of the most ignorant democracy." Former dependence on slaveholding masters had transformed into dependence on government to steal money, reallocate land, and plunder private holdings. "This is what socialism has done for South Carolina," scoffed *The Nation*. "The only question remaining to be settled is how long it will take to make the once 'sovereign State' of South Carolina a truly loyal, truly Republican, truly African San Domingo."[64]

A growing chorus of Republicans joined with white southerners and Democrats in claiming that the exhausting duration and misplaced assumptions of Reconstruction had internationalized the nation. The progress of civilization, once emboldened by emancipation, shaped by civil rights, and enhanced by the Constitution, had, alleged Pike, "descen[ded] into barbarism." Cries from the Democratic press of "military despotism" and "bayonet rule" struck a devastating chord among some Republicans, who envisioned that their political handiwork had spawned corrupt governments propped up only by strong-armed military force in defiance of democratic consensus. Moderate Republican Thomas Cooley disagreed with the baseless charges leveled by Pike and *The Nation*. But he still acknowledged, "To concede to the Federal government authority to take itself State powers, on an assumption that the people of a State have shown themselves incapable of self-government, and must consequently be ruled by the strong hand of central power, would be to conceded the failure of the American experiment in government."[65]

Cooley's indictment spoke to a troubling implication of federal enforcement. Though the swift application of federal law dismantled broad swaths of clandestine terrorism, enforcement itself compelled white southerners to change their insurrectionary tactics. By the mid-1870s, white insurgents no longer conducted secret night-riding operations against individual black and white Republicans. Now, fully formed paramilitary institutions and "rifle clubs" descended on southern communities in overt support of Democratic redemption. The White League of Louisiana, the Red Shirts of South Carolina, and the White Line of Mississippi all possessed an insidiously simple mission: overthrow "unlawful" Republican state governments through anarchical violence. "Carry the election peaceably if we can," read a Democratic campaign slogan, "forcibly if we must." Paramilitary organizations, populated largely with former Confederate soldiers, marched as the public, political, enforcement arm of the Democratic Party, defying any pretense of law, order, or electoral legitimacy. And they slayed hundreds of African American civilians and militiamen in bloody confrontations in Colfax, Louisiana; Hamburg, South Carolina; and Vicksburg, Mississippi. When they turned their attention to Republican-held states, paramilitaries "proclaim their purpose to seize the government by violence, depose the Executive, by assassination if necessary, and drive from the state all leading republicans." Only through murderous force could white southerners undo the profane racial revolution that had befallen their once providential civilization.[66]

Paramilitary counterrevolutions in Louisiana and Mississippi testify to Reconstruction's escalating internationalization. The 1874 elections in Louisiana yielded competing claimants to local and state offices. When six elected Republicans near Shreveport assumed their seats, White League insurgents coerced each of the elected officials from office, subsequently murdering them all. Meanwhile, though Democrats claimed victory in the Louisiana House, a Republican electoral certification board rejected the outcome on grounds that terroristic threats intimidated enough black and white Republicans from voting. When the legislature convened in January 1875, Democrats forcibly commandeered the lower chamber, compelling Republican governor William P. Kellogg to petition federal troops to remove the political dissidents. Grant condemned the Democrats' "lawless and revolutionary proceedings," in which illegitimate claimants "undertook to seize" the legislature "by fraud and violence." The president promptly approved Kellogg's request for military force. "I am well aware that any military interference by the officers and troops of the United States ... is repugnant to our ideas of government," Grant acknowledged. But "if a mob ... of unauthorized persons seize and hold the legislative hall in a tumultuous and riotous manner," he declared, no doubt anticipating the inevitable critiques forthcoming from fellow Republicans, "any exercise of power would only be justifiable under most extraordinary circumstances." The setting was indeed astonishing. The Democratic Party, aided by its White League allies, appeared to have repudiated the sacred consent of the governed, trading republicanism for irregular military force to contest the electoral process.[67]

Republicans ultimately maintained control of the Louisiana legislature, but the White League succeeded in devious ways. Its tactics forced Republicans yet again to employ military force to uphold a fragile democracy, sparking ever-increasing doubt about the legitimacy of "reconstructed" state governments. Lt. Gen. Philip Sheridan, who commanded U.S. Army forces in Louisiana, even recommended that paramilitary insurgents be treated as "banditti" and "tried by military commission." However, the image of federal troops removing Democratic politicians from office, and the army holding civilian criminals subject to the laws of war, stoked deep-seated fears of standing armies manipulating civic life on behalf of tyrannical dictators. The sight of "United States soldiery marched into the hall of a State legislature," blasted Senator Carl Schurz, "to do the bidding of a State governor," unbound "our time-honored Constitutional principles." Such tactics no doubt "keep peace and order," demonstrated by "singular success in Russia, and may be in other countries." Thus, "if such things be sustained by Congress, how long will it be before it can be done in Massachusetts and in Ohio? How long before the Constitutional rights of all the States and the self-government of all the people may be trampled under foot? How long before a general of the Army" seizes Congress and supplants democratic deliberation with martial law? "That method would have been effective for its purpose" in stemming anarchical terrorism, "but it would have been a cruel stroke of irony after all this to call this still a republic."[68]

Mississippi followed a similar insurgent trajectory. Republicans reconstructed the late antebellum South's wealthiest slaveholding state through competent biracial governance, public education, and labor reform. Elected in 1874, Governor Adelbert Ames, a former Union army officer and committed champion of African American equality, hailed the state's restoration as a testament to "northern civilization [and] northern liberty," which "has a hold on the hearts of the colored people that nothing can destroy." But that very "hold" underscored the foaming resentment of white Mississippians who alleged that a rapacious black political majority held prostrate landowners hostage through excessive taxation and property redistribution. The notorious White Line emerged as the state's paramilitary organization to topple the Republicans' contrived and blasphemous crusade in racial equality. "It is through indolence and votes that we see our noble State falling into ruin," declared the *Forest Register*. "Run the white line and save your State and estate." Racial violence combated the perverted revolution that Republicans had foisted upon the South. "Every effort [to civilize African Americans] tends to bestialize his nature, and by obfuscating his little brain unfits him for the duties assigned him as a hewer of wood and drawer of water," the *Forest Register* continued. "The effort makes him a demon of wild, fanatical destruction, and consigns him to the fatal shot of the white man."[69]

The White Line embarked on shocking campaigns of murder, destruction, and intimidation. Its adherents pledged not only to dismantle the state's Republican government but also to reinstate the natural order of racial subservience. "In the contest on which they have entered they mean something more than the election of certain men to office," reported the *Columbus Democrat* in 1875. "They mean the preservation of their constitution, their laws, their institutions, their civilization from impending ruin. They mean that white men shall rule Mississippi." The course of history had vindicated white supremacy. Though temporarily impeded by the folly of emancipation and civil rights, the White Line would assist in realigning the American South as the envy of global racial stability. Paramilitary insurgents thus systematically disrupted Republican political organizations, interfered in elections, and coerced black and white officials from office on the threat and application of murder. Known as the "Mississippi Plan," the White Line's reign of terror convinced enough Republicans of both races not to vote and to resign their public offices, thereby swinging subsequent elections to mercenary Democrats. "The terrorism was so intense," acknowledged African American representative John Roy Lynch, "as in my judgment to make life, liberty, and happiness perfectly insecure except to democrats. I do not think there is any such thing as law in that society." In the wake of his forced resignation of the governorship, Ames proclaimed the "chief duty of all Governments" to be "the protection of the citizen." As governor, he called on his close friend and ally President Grant to deploy federal troops to Mississippi, an act that "never interfered with any man's rights" but "only prevented wrongs." Otherwise, "if an American citizen cannot rightfully demand protection from his Government, what is the use of Government?"[70]

Though despondent, Grant replied in the only manner available to him by the mid-1870s. "The whole public are tired out with these annual autumnal outbreaks at the South," he confided, "and the great majority are ready to condemn any interference on the part of the Government." Ames never received federal support, and the White Line completed its "redemption" of Republican rule. Such tactics, mixed with profound ambivalence from northern Republicans, established a pattern from which Democratic paramilitaries in other southern states toppled so-called negro governments. But as Grant alluded, white Republicans, exhausted by the seemingly pointless endeavor of reconstructing the hopelessly unreconstructable, came to interpret the white southern insurgency as a reaction both against a biracial democracy incapable of neutering civil violence *and* against the military's activism in propping up alleged unpopular governments. Like Grant, Ames responded in the only way available to him: "A *revolution* has taken place—by force of arms—and a race are disenfranchised—they are to be returned to a condition of serfdom—an era of second slavery.... The nation should have acted but," Ames concluded with biting sarcasm, "*it* was '*tired* of the annual autumnal outbreaks in the South.'"[71]

While Congress passed in 1875 a new round of Force Acts and a Civil Rights Act designed to safeguard constitutional protections, the gestures clashed against the utter inability and desire to enforce federal authority. The dilemma stemmed from an ailment identified by scores of Republicans as "the Mexicanization of American politics." The paramilitary revolution produced factional cycles of civil combustion in which insurgents and their Democratic allies disregarded the restraint of law and the consent of the governed. State elections routinely yielded rival claimants to governorships and legislatures, bolstered by the U.S. Army, on the one hand, and sustained by paramilitary institutions, on the other. Politics now reeked of fragile Central and South American republics that struggled to maintain legitimacy. Indiana senator Oliver P. Morton indicted "the late pretended election in Mississippi [as] an armed revolution, characterized by fraud, murder, and violence." Mirroring the nineteenth-century revolutions that decimated much of the New World, Democrats embraced "the violation of law, and the trampling under foot of the dearest rights of great masses of men" to quench their bloody thirst for power. Such "revolutions which have distinguished the states of Mexico and the countries of South America" had now militarized a Union ostensibly committed to democratic consent and electoral restraint.[72]

"Mexicanization" spoke to a democracy's violent collapse of territorial integrity and constitutional legitimacy. *The Nation* outlined the concept as "a particular state of mind," a conscious judgment to employ "armed force to decide political contests." Ordered liberty demanded moderation, restraint, and consent, which "do not succeed in France and Mexico ... for want of habits of legality." Mexicanization exposed the uncivilized instinct for "seizing the public offices and public records, and placing armed men in possession of" government. It was the essence of radical internationalization, against which the United States stood as an exceptional beacon. "Such proceedings are necessarily in the direction of substituting for [constitutional] republicanism," opined legal theorist Thomas Cooley, "a different republicanism whose manifestations as we witness them in the neighboring republic of Mexico are not assuring to those who have faith in government by the people." As he watched Democratic insurgents descend on the South Carolina statehouse in 1876, William J. Balentine exclaimed, "Is it not revolutionary for persons to attempt to exercise the functions of governor, legislators, and other state offices without authority?" Indeed it was. But as *The Nation* concluded, Mexicanization "exists in greater or less degree all over the South." Republicans had failed to instill "the manners and customs and ideas of good and free government, and abate party passions to such a degree as to make them manageable by constitutional forms." Speaking for numerous Republicans by 1876, Balentine conceded, "I am tired of this mexican style of government, and hope that a way will be soon found to put a stop to it."[73]

Moderate Republicans came to the sober conclusion that retreating from the enforcement of Reconstruction was the only path toward preserving national stability and constitutional integrity. As *Harper's Weekly* acknowledged, "The presence of the troops has not preserved the Republican party in the other Southern States." Any state government "which can be upheld only by the national army is not in the American sense a government of the people." The United States could not endure as a "Mexicanized" republic that compelled behavior through military compulsion only to confront persistent, violent resistance from anarchical factions. "There are wrongs [in the South] that we can never reach in this Hall until we have changed the Constitution of the United States," explained Connecticut representative Joseph Hawley. "There is a social, and educational, and moral reconstruction of the South needed that will never come from any legislative halls, State or national; it must be the growth of time, of education, and of Christianity." The reconstruction of a republic could never transpire through coercion or force, because "we cannot put justice, liberty, and equality into the hearts of a people" whose own freedom stemmed from divine self-determination. But Senator John Sherman, among so many conflicted Republicans, cited the devastating implication. White southerners "may submit to the democratic party and produce a kind of peace," but it was "not the peace of equality of rights; it is not the peace that your Constitution guarantees to every man; it is the peace of despotism."[74]

A nation splintered by endless faction and severed by contested elections could never stand as a civilized republic. What might happen if the Mexicanization of Louisiana, Mississippi, Arkansas, and South Carolina infected the federal level with the same ailments that plagued the South? What if rival claimants to the presidency and Congress rejected the will of the people and exercised military force to contest *and* assert governing legitimacy? The Union might well collapse into civil wars and military coups far more devastating than the conflict of 1861, toppling fifteen years of cultural, political, and constitutional reforms designed to forestall that very occurrence. With the presidential election of 1876 looming ever near, Republican Murat Halstead predicted that the Democratic Party would mobilize the old Confederate Army and coerce "a disputed Presidential election, which would reduce the American Republic to the grade of Mexico." Even if Republicans triumphed, Halstead envisioned "the old Confederate politicians" arming 'to occupy and possess' all the departments of National authority," a scenario "far more menacing to all of us than when the same politicians twenty years ago attempted ... to nationalize the peculiar institution." The Old and New Worlds had long confronted the militant chaos of democracy *and* heavy-handed coercion. Thus, "the American people have no exemption from the ordinary fate of humanity." Halstead warned, "If we sin, we must suffer for our sins, like the Empires that are tottering and the Nations that have perished." The election did not merely pose a referendum on Reconstruction; rather, it unveiled the delicate providence of American civilization.[75]

Halstead's prediction transpired. Although Democratic candidate Samuel J. Tilden seemed to have secured the White House, Republican electoral commissioners in Florida, Louisiana, and South Carolina annulled each state's electoral ballots based on rampant fraud and violence committed by white insurgents. This unprecedented act swung a razor-thin electoral college majority to Republican Rutherford B. Hayes. Democrats and white southerners howled accusations of chicanery, some threatening to march on Washington to install Tilden as the rightful president. "The excitement in the South over the presidential election is literally frightful," reported the *Atlantic Monthly*. House Democrats might well "cause an explosion in the South so terrific that the outbreak of 1860–61 will be almost forgotten." *Harper's Weekly* likewise worried "that this republic shall fall into a Mexican row, not over any principle whatever, but simply over a disputed method of counting the electoral votes," producing "a catastrophe no less grotesque than tragical." The Mexicanization of the South had seemingly consumed the entire republic. "In the present dispute over the Presidency there are actually signs, not only that we have not cured the South, but that, by nursing and manipulating the South, we have ourselves caught the contagion," observed *The Nation*. "The Mexican poison has reached us."[76]

Only moderation, restraint, and compromise, the long-regarded hallmarks of American political exceptionalism, could assuage bitter faction. President-elect Hayes called for "people of ardent temperatures ... to return to our better wisdom and judgment" and reject the Mexicanization of national life. "I have too much faith in the saving common sense of the American people to think that they desire to see in their country a Mexicanized Government," he announced shortly after the election. "We are now afforded an opportunity of giving to the world an example of the value of republican government." In 1877, Hayes negotiated a compromise in which he would retain the presidency in exchange for Democratic governors in Florida, South Carolina, and Louisiana maintaining their seats. The new president also pledged that Republicans no longer would employ federal soldiers to monitor state elections and intervene in social affairs on behalf of freedpeople. Though the U.S. Army retained small numbers of troops in the South, they would be barred from ever again enforcing Reconstruction policy. The federal government was obliged instead to secure "the interests of both races carefully and equally," never employing centralized institutions to regulate a free society. The South "has been arrested by the social and political revolution through which it has passed, and now needs and deserves the considerate care of the National Government within the just limits prescribed by the Constitution." The Reconstruction Amendments were ostensibly far more enduring and consistent with the American character than sustained martial oversight. Yet white southern terrorists had brutalized citizens and the law to repel a regional, free labor, biracial democracy.[77]

Hayes greeted compromise as a triumph of political moderation. Demilitarizing the South—both from the presence of the army and from paramilitary organizations—would seemingly stabilize American democracy. He draped the Compromise of 1877 in the same pragmatism with which Abraham Lincoln in 1861 outlined the Union's wartime purpose: that legitimate republics endured only by the autonomous consent of the governed. Any effort to undermine the electoral process, any impediment to a free people's will, confirmed before the world the failure of American institutions. So-called bayonet rule appeared to disgrace the American mission as much as slaveholding secessionists had done. "Upon one point there is entire unanimity," Hayes announced: "that conflicting claims to the Presidency must be amicably and peaceably adjusted" because the republic "has been reserved for a Government of the people." Even "in the midst of a struggle of opposing parties for power," the United States was compelled to demonstrate peaceful transitions of governance. The Union was again preserved. But the price of peace was the restoration of the old planter elite to southern political and economic authority. After centuries of slavery, the South's soil was free. But its labor and its people were not fully liberated. Yet those same people finally constituted the republic's citizenry. In a not-too-distant future, they would prolong the struggle to achieve a more perfect Union.[78]

Epilogue

THE PARADOX OF CIVILIZATION

In a public address delivered in 1880 to commemorate the First of August—
the day on which Parliament in 1834 abolished British West Indian slavery—
Frederick Douglass reflected on the United States' era of civil war and restoration. Three years removed from President Hayes's conspicuous compromise
with white Democrats, Douglass had digested the profound, if not devastating, and wholly exceptional circumstances of American life. "English emancipation has one advantage over American emancipation," he reasoned in comparing the death of slavery in the British Caribbean to the climax of abolition
in the United States: "The freedom of the negro [in the Union] has no birthday." At the same moment that the English public during the early nineteenth
century had crested a humanitarian wave that overwhelmed human bondage,
the United States had consolidated its slaveholding power and augmented the
Atlantic world's dominant slave nation. The ultimate collapse of American
bondage and the origin of biracial civil rights sprouted from the contingencies
of a massive modern war and an unprecedented process of national restoration. "History does not furnish an example of emancipation under conditions
less friendly to the emancipated class than this American example," professed
the great abolitionist. "Liberty came to the freedmen of the United States not
in mercy, but in wrath, not by moral choice but by military necessity, not by
the generous action of the people among whom they were to live, and whose
good-will was essential to the success of the measure, but by strangers, foreigners, invaders, trespassers, aliens, and enemies."[1]

Only "the tempest and whirlwind of war" had shattered the impenetrable
force of American slavery, a belligerent process designed to extinguish the
source of war itself. Occasioning "an end to the entire cause of that calamity" of
disunion required "forever putting away the system of slavery and all its incidents" by ensuring that "the negro was made free, made a citizen, made eligible to hold office." Douglass heralded the broad extension of liberal equality,
that natural, self-evident prerogative unmoored from racial distinctions. Unlike the wake of West Indian slavery, with the advent of great constitutional
reforms in the United States "we have declared before all the world that there
shall be no denial of rights on account of race, color, or previous condition of
servitude." Nowhere else on earth, Douglass commended, had a formerly enslaved class emerged as equal civil partners alongside former slaveholders,
each participating in democratic self-determination. "It is a great thing to
have the supreme law of the land on the side of justice and liberty," he averred.

Thomas Nast, Victory, *appeared as the frontispiece for volume 3 of Robert Tomes and Benjamin G. Smith,* The Great Civil War *(3 vols.; New York: R. Worthington, 1867). Nast centers Union as the era's principal theme, with white United States soldiers welcoming defeated Confederates into the reunited republic. A lone African American Union soldier assists a barefooted enslaved man toward freedom. The Goddess of Liberty watches from above as an angel consecrates the flag, while a dove of peace blesses everyone, all of whom are represented as patriotic American exceptionalists.*

"It is the line up to which the nation is destined to march—the law to which the nation's life must conform."[2]

Yet Douglass questioned whether "the cause of freedom and humanity" in the United States had been ever truly a cause at all. In "the eager desire to have the Union restored, there was more care for the sublime superstructure of the republic than for the solid foundation upon which it could alone be upheld." The incomparable processes of American emancipation had always been subordinated to the cause of Union. "To the freedmen was given the machinery of liberty, but there was denied to them the steam to put it in motion. They were given the uniform of soldiers, but no arms; they were called citizens but left subjects; they were called free but left almost slaves." The inability and unwillingness to enforce the law had "virtually nullified" the Reconstruction amendments. Broadening the base of citizenship and proclaiming the equal rights of all Americans without securing a sturdy federal administration compelled "the old master class" to "employ every power and means in their reach to make the great measure of emancipation unsuccessful and utterly odious." Unlike the Hebrews of ancient Egypt or the serfs of modern Russia, "who were given three acres of ground upon which they could live and make a living," American freedpeople "were sent away empty-handed, without money, without friends and without a foot of land upon which to stand." White Americans might have argued that the formerly enslaved had been bestowed with a gift far more sacred than worldly redistributions: equitable inclusion in a liberal, multiracial, exceptional republic. And thus, Douglass countered unequivocally, "our reconstruction measures were radically defective" because they assumed that a moderate, decentralized state could accommodate the formally enslaved *and* the former slaveholders in an equitable bastion of democracy.[3]

As Douglass suggested with bitter paradox, emancipation had secured a republic whose lasting life depended on a compromise with civil rights. When the white northern idealist Albion Tourgée surveyed the bloody wake of Reconstruction, he reiterated Douglass's indictment. In a popular novel that traces the wartime and postbellum feats of Comfort Servosse, a committed Union soldier and visionary "carpetbag" politician who believed in a fundamentally reconstructed South, Tourgée excoriated what he deemed the United States' tepid conciliatory reunion with white southerners at the expense of biracial equality. Servosse functions as Tourgée himself, divulging the Ohioan's carefully constructed racial sensibilities, his declining faith in Union, and his disillusion with the American creed. In one revealing passage Servosse offers a blunt appraisal of national restoration. "A great deal was gained by" Reconstruction. "It gave us a construction of 'we the people' in the preamble of our Federal Constitution which gave the lie to that which had formerly prevailed. It recognized and formulated the universality of manhood in governmental power, and, in one phase or another of its development, compelled the formal assent of all sections and parties."[4]

A true republic could stand only on the basis of liberal equality, the rule of law, and colorblind justice. But in that regard, Servosse declares, echoing Douglass, "Reconstruction was a failure so far as it attempted to unify the nation." For Servosse and Tourgée, the principal obstruction against restoring the Union was the Union itself. If the foundation of American civilization rested on the sacred consent of the governed, no group—white or black, freedpeople or elites, Republican or Democrat, northerner or southerner—could be excluded from national democracy. But that, for Tourgée, was the fundamental problem. "The North and the South are simply convenient names for two distinct, hostile, and irreconcilable ideas,—two civilizations." Yet the two had to be reunited to legitimize the republic's preservation. "These two must always be in conflict until the one prevails, and the other falls," he continues. "To uproot one, and plant the other in its stead, is not the work of a moment or a day," or even the product of transformative, modern war. "We presumed, that, by the suppression of rebellion, the Southern white man had become identical with the Caucasian of the North in thought and sentiment; and that the slave, by emancipation, had become a saint and a Solomon at once. So we tried to build up communities there which should be identical in thought, sentiment, growth, and development, with those of the North. It was a FOOL'S ERRAND."[5]

The Civil War era had always featured incompatible civilizations competing for democratic supremacy in the federal Union. Servosse acknowledges that too many white northerners saw that in the wake of Confederate collapse "slavery as a formal state of society was at an end." Thus, they presumed, the radical kernel of disunion would never again threaten the republic. But "as a force, a power, a moral element, it was just as active as before." And he was right. Though Rutherford B. Hayes in 1877 hailed "the act of emancipation" as "a wise, just, and providential act, fraught with good," he also acknowledged that the same sentiment "is not generally conceded throughout the country." This was an understatement, as Servosse and Douglass knew full well. "Was all this justifiable?" asked Robert Wallace Shand, a leader of the South Carolina Red Shirts who waged the devastating white southern paramilitary counterrevolution of 1876. "Yes—for unlike elections at other times our very civilization was at stake. We could not live in South Carolina if negro rule continued," he admitted. "Our plan of campaign was an evil, but its success overcame a greater evil." President Hayes had insisted that only American democracy could remedy these hostile forces of civilization. "The evils which afflict the Southern States," explained the president, "can only be removed or remedied by the united and harmonious efforts of both races actuated by motives of mutual sympathy and regard." Servosse and Shand, however, knew that discordant civilizations could never harmonize *because* they cohabited in the same Union. "The battle must be fought out. If there is to remain one nation on the territory we now occupy, it must be either a nation unified in sentiment and civilization," concluded the disillusioned Servosse, "or the one civilization must dominate and control the other."[6]

The unending battles for civilization manifested themselves in a resurgent Democratic Party campaigning against civil rights and securing control of the House of Representatives in 1874. The shifting national mood compelled increasing numbers of white Republicans to begin suspending the enforcement of Reconstruction. The party pledged in 1876 "the permanent pacification of the Southern sections of the Union and the complete protection of all its citizens." And "we sincerely deprecate all sectional feeling and tendencies," which "would reopen sectional strife and imperil national honor and human rights." But the very act of federal administration in the service of civil rights fueled the endless war that Servosse witnessed, that Robert Wallace Shand welcomed, that Frederick Douglass dreaded, and that President Hayes feared. "My judgment was that the time had come to put an end to bayonet rule," Hayes remarked in 1880. "My task was to wipe out the color line, to abolish sectionalism, to end the war and bring peace.... The army was withdrawn because I believed it a constitutional duty and a wise thing to do." Thus, Hayes's civilization—a moderate republic that rejected "Mexicanization," coercion, and militarism—triumphed alongside Shand's civilization—a moderate republic that fast consolidated around racial caste and white supremacy.[7]

In remaining a republic, realizing the paramount purpose of Reconstruction, the United States offered to African Americans, as Douglass observed, only a "legal and theoretical condition" of liberty. The era's revolutionary transformations occasioned by the death of slavery and the expansion of individual rights had been enshrined in the United States Constitution. But John Roy Lynch, a formerly enslaved man and Republican congressman elected from Mississippi in the great waves of biracial voting during the early 1870s, agreed with Douglass that, no matter how foundational and metamorphic, constitutional reform meant little if the citizenry remained unwilling to enforce the guarantees and protections embedded in the great national charter. "It is not social rights that we desire. We have enough of that already," Lynch declared. "What we ask is protection in the enjoyment of public rights." As Abraham Lincoln had warned nearly four decades earlier at the Young Men's Lyceum, Lynch believed that rejecting the rule of law undermined any national claim to global exceptionalism. A republic could not long endure fractious civil violence and antidemocratic mob rule. "If this unjust discrimination is to be longer tolerated by the American people ... then I can only say with sorrow and regret that our boasted civilization is a fraud; our republican institutions a failure; our social system a disgrace; and our religion a complete hypocrisy."[8]

A preponderance of the white loyal citizenry regarded emancipation and biracial civil rights as essential, unprecedented, and even moral means to the end of preserving the Union from any future national balkanization. When contrasted alongside Lynch's assessment of Reconstruction, this view might appear as a distinction with few differences. However, a vast gulf separated each interpretation of the era's meaning and purpose. Millions of white loyal citizens had conducted war against a militant slaveholding oligarchy and shaped the subsequent peace to prove to an antidemocratic world the inviolability of a people's republic. International elites had long scorned the United States as a pathetic and foolish experiment in democracy, one destined to dissolve in the chaos of civil war. "Monarchical Europe generally believed that our republic was a rope of sand that would part the moment the slightest strain was brought upon it," Ulysses S. Grant reflected in his memoirs. To demonstrate that they were not subject to the inevitable forces of history, loyal citizens, just as Lincoln petitioned at Gettysburg, pledged their "full measure of devotion" to ensuring that the republic "shall not perish from the earth."[9]

Lincoln's hallowed address framed the cause of Union—both in war and in peace—as "a new birth of freedom" from autocratic slaveholding factions that threatened national unity and the popular democratic will. This calculus mandated enslaved people never again toiling as unwilling accomplices to the disloyal Slave Power's unchecked aristocratic authority. Through emancipation and the civil liberties afforded by citizenship and male suffrage, white Americans welcomed free people of color as vital allies in sustaining the United States as a beacon of global democracy. The natural right of *all* people to rise or fall equally in society, liberated from the arbitrary privileges or coercions of slaveholding, upheld the nation's founding ideal. "It is in part to the aid of the negro in freedom that the country owes its success in its movement of regeneration, that the world of mankind owes the continuance of the United States as the example of a Republic," heralded the famed historian George Bancroft in June 1865. The war and its long tortuous aftermath confirmed to much of the white citizenry that they had indeed succeeded in their quest to secure the republic from its foremost existential threat of disunion. "The war has made us a nation of great power and intelligence," Grant believed. With the preservation of the Union, emancipation, and constitutional rehabilitation complete, "We have but little to do to preserve peace, happiness and prosperity at home, and the respect of other nations." Now that the United States' "institutions [have] become homogenous," finally relieved from slaveholding obstructions, concluded Bancroft, the exceptional symbol of Union could radiate across the world, "with one wing touching the waters of the Atlantic and the other on the Pacific," evolving "into a greatness of which the past has no parallel."[10]

Ulysses S. Grant unbound the many tangled tensions between civil rights and the concept of Union. To be sure, Grant was disgusted, if not deeply depressed, that many of his fellow white citizens could not see the prudent and moral imperative that sustaining African American equality impressed on the republic. Grant condemned as an unequivocal failure any democratic "Government that cannot give protection to the life, property and all guaranteed civil rights" to its citizenry. To abandon constitutional "privileges or protection" was to invite a "bloody revolution" upon the entire experiment in representative government. "Looking back over the whole policy of reconstruction," the former president reflected in 1879, "it seems to me that the wisest thing would have been to have continued for some time the military rule," which "would have been just to all, to the negro who wanted freedom, the white man who wanted protection, the Northern man who wanted Union." Perhaps even holding the former Confederacy in a continued state of war "as a mild penalty for the stupendous crime of treason" would have reconstructed the recalcitrant states "not on their own terms but upon ours," thereby rendering "universal suffrage" unnecessary.[11]

An ardent champion of African American civil equality, Grant nevertheless deemed it "unjust to the negro to throw upon him the responsibilities of citizenship, and expect him to be on even terms with his white neighbor." White southerners had proven incapable of tolerating black freedom and civil equality, combating each with a kind of social violence "such as would scarcely be accredited to savages, much less to a civilized and christian people." If only Republicans had had the judgment to foresee the shortcomings of their policies, to deflect the devastating insurgency that would later assail black freedom and civil rights. "I am clear now that it would have been better for the North to have postponed suffrage, reconstruction, State governments, for ten years, and held the South in a territorial condition," he acknowledged with striking honesty. "The men who had made war upon us should be powerless in a political sense forever." But now the republic confronted "the political triumph of the men who led [the South] into secession," their power sustained through terror, intimidation, and disfranchisement.[12]

Though lured by the benefit of hindsight, Grant recognized that his personal desires were restricted by the limitations of nineteenth-century American exceptionalism. Reconstruction policies that would have obstructed an efficient national restoration, balkanized the republic, abandoned conciliatory moderation, and deprived political liberty for both formerly enslaved people and former slaveholders would have undermined the entire concept of Union for which Grant fought so passionately to preserve. "We made our scheme," he concluded, "and must do what we can with it. Suffrage once given can never be taken away, and all that remains for us now is to make good that gift by protecting those who have received it." But paradoxes abounded. Only a powerful centralized government could uphold civil liberties and guarantees of racial equality. Only a citizenry willing to enforce the ideal of human rights could redeem Reconstruction's noble ambition. However, as a majority of the democratic populace, most white Americans favored a stable and demobilized constitutional republic that did not reflect the world's volatile and compulsive military states. "The trouble about military rule in the South was that our people did not like it," Grant admitted. "It was not in accordance with our institutions." The smoldering wake of civil war demanded a temporary occupation to ensure peace. And the new constitutional amendments depended on a federal state equipped and ready to apply swift, consistent force in the service of African American civil rights. But military occupation and centralized governance themselves dwelled as foreign agents in the national psyche. Seen as toxic cancers to democracy, standing armies embedded in politics, civil institutions, and social relationships undermined the moderation of popular sovereignty, the essential and abiding basis of Union. And herein lay the central tension of Reconstruction, and perhaps the whole of nineteenth-century America: the constitutional republic that loyal citizens went to war in 1861 to conserve was the very symbol that precluded Reconstruction from satisfying its biracial ideal.[13]

In their triumphant restoration of the Union, Republicans pursued an exceptional but irreconcilable objective: maintaining a moderate antimilitaristic republic within a fully functional biracial democracy nonetheless gripped by white supremacy. There is little question that the scope of Reconstruction deprived African Americans of their due rights of life, liberty, and happiness. But perhaps the tepid federal response to white Reconstruction terrorism was less about ambivalence toward racial equality—though some Republicans certainly grew ambivalent about using federal force to protect civil rights— and more about conserving a stable peacetime Union that emerged from the unprecedented upheaval of civil war and national restoration. Perhaps the moderating processes of Reconstruction aimed to prevent the republic from transforming into a military leviathan or even from collapsing altogether into warring factions from which all constitutional liberties might thereafter dissolve. Perhaps the pernicious white counterrevolution against a free labor, biracial republic testified to Reconstruction's uncommon though fleeting triumph of liberal democracy. Perhaps Reconstruction was an exceptional moment marked by hostile and often irreconcilable values and shaped by incompatible understandings of the United States' place in a terribly volatile Atlantic world. Yet the era concluded in similar ways to other nineteenth-century liberal crusades: with regional overlords consolidating their power over labor, land, and political rights.[14]

The epoch of the United States' Civil War ended in perhaps the only way it could end: through a negotiated compromise among white Americans. Compromise ensured the continuity of Union, preserved the democratic system, and upheld national stability, while at the same time exposing a painful conceit about the nineteenth-century United States: that whites, somehow, would govern the republic. To withstand the permanent internationalization of American life, Republicans handed control of the South to Democrats, an act that erased escalations in political "Mexicanization." The enduring concept of Union, the aura of federalism, and the faith in political moderation—

indeed, the sacred, unremitting ingredients of American civilization—would never be traded for authentic racial equality, seen by many white Americans as an ideal at best and a curse at worst. Though white southern terrorists held the nation hostage to their local demands, in a terrible paradox, loyal citizens would not countenance or deploy a weaponized central state—one that resembled the old slaveholding Confederacy—to combat unlawful insurgents. Hayes prayed in his inaugural address for his "fellow-citizens, here and everywhere, to unite with me in an earnest effort to secure to our country the blessings, not only of material prosperity, but of justice, peace, and union—a union depending not upon the constraint of force, but upon the loving devotion of a free people." Such exceptionalist rhetoric infused the American soul, compelling enough Republicans to compromise with a resurgent Slave Power.[15]

Slavery had long ago died, and the Slave Power assumed a new form during the 1870s, but it employed the devious tactics of old: threatening the republic, defying federal authority, and flouting the rule of law to extract from the nation critical protections for a peculiar society. To maintain a conservative Union, to ensure a limited but lasting peace, Republicans once more catered to white southerners rather than sundering the very republic that they had dedicated their full measures of devotion to preserve. Though peace endured, a forthright Frederick Douglass asked, "What will peace among the whites bring?" The subsequent decades, even down to the present day, would answer the great abolitionist's question, informing the lasting but contested legacies of the U.S. Civil War era.[16]

ACKNOWLEDGMENTS

At breakfast one morning at the 2015 Meeting of the Southern Historical Association, Michael Parrish invited me to author the final volume of the Littlefield History of the Civil War Era, a project that he had conceived and long deeply contemplated. I was then an assistant professor only in the second year on the tenure track, and I had never expected to receive such a humbling proposition. Though I had not yet completed my first book, I could not pass up the opportunity to join the ranks of esteemed scholars who had already published remarkable, field-defining texts for the Littlefield Series. Producing *A Contest of Civilizations* has been the most challenging and most gratifying experience of my professional life. Mike has been an unceasing champion of my career for more than a decade, and I have valued our close collaborative relationship on this project. Mike was gracious in sharing sources and ideas that he had been collecting for many years. He read multiple drafts of each chapter, dedicated long phone calls to critiquing and improving the manuscript, prepared much of the bibliography on my behalf, and procured the Thomas Nast sketch featured in the epilogue. His bold, interpretative imagination, careful editorial eye, and unyielding consideration to language, even down to single words, augmented this book in immeasurable ways. I will cherish our partnership, for I have learned much from his expertise and insight into notions of exceptionalism, moderation, restraint, and fears of internationalism as hallmarks of the American past. And so, Mike, thank you for taking a chance on me. I hope that what I have produced fulfills your vision of what you always imagined this book to be.

This project would not have been possible without the steadfast support from Gary W. Gallagher, Mark Simpson-Vos, and Jay Mazzocchi. Few scholars have influenced my historical awareness and philosophy more than Gary. His blunt criticism and trademark attention to detail made the manuscript immensely better. But more importantly, his steady encouragement, positive endorsements of my ideas, and faith in the project allowed me to push forward with confidence. In these ways, he and Mike make a fine editorial team. It is little wonder that they have influenced the profession in such positive and enduring ways. Likewise, the professional relationship I have forged with Mark Simpson-Vos at the University of North Carolina (UNC) Press has been among the great rewards of working on this project. Mark is a model editor and exemplar of everything good about the enterprise of scholarly publishing. Leaving me alone to write but always available for a phone call, tolerating my misinformed submission projections while always encouraging quality over haste, Mark has been a source of stability and kindness. We should all be so fortunate as to work with such a consummate and compassionate professional. Finally, I am greatly indebted to Jay Mazzocchi, assistant managing editor at UNC Press. With patient, kind assistance, Jay permitted me to make numerous last-minute revisions to the manuscript. The final form of this book is, in large measure, a testament to Jay's courtesy.

In addition to Gary's reading and formal report of the manuscript, Mark solicited two outside referees to scrutinize the project. I am grateful for the time and attention that these reviewers dedicated in offering long, careful, and often chastening critiques of the work. Their insightful commentary improved the final product considerably.

Many friends and colleagues assisted me at various stages of this project. Many thanks to Caroline E. Janney and Kevin R. Caprice at the University of Virginia and W. Caleb McDaniel at Rice University for sending me several sources that I could not easily obtain. Ryan Semmes, Ian Davis, and Stephen Powell, three of my doctoral students at Mississippi State University; James Hill, a friend and former colleague at Mississippi State; and Jonathan Lande, a fast-rising star in Civil War history at Purdue University, all recommended important primary and secondary sources. Aaron Sheehan-Dean (Louisiana State University), D. H. Dilbeck (Yale University), and Lorien Foote (Texas A&M University) offered perceptive insights into just war theory and notions of civilized warfare during their participation at a symposium held at Mississippi State in early 2017. Lorien even shared with me an early draft of an essay she later published. Andrew Bledsoe, Carl Paulus, and Sarah Bischoff Paulus—among my closest friends from graduate school and excellent historians in their own right—suggested obscure sources and conversed almost daily about ideas, history, federalism, and politics. I am grateful for their professional influence and personal friendships. My first academic mentor, Randolph B. "Mike" Campbell, read an early draft of the introduction. John B. Boles, who directed my doctoral studies at Rice University, read portions of chapter 1. Mike and John's enduring inspirational counsel shapes each page of this text. I benefited from the excellent work of two graduate research assistants at Mississippi State, Sarah Lewin and Christina Baxter. I hope you both came to value *Harper's Weekly* and *The Nation* as much as I do. At Mississippi State, my colleague Mark Hersey listened to my ideas and offered very helpful feedback on various sections of the manuscript. Finally, my department head, Alan Marcus, approved three separate teaching releases so that I could focus on writing. These remarkably generous arrangements testify to Alan's emphasis on quality scholarship and his faith in the Mississippi State history faculty.

Special thanks are due to Louisiana State University Press and UNC Press for generously granting permission to republish portions of my earlier work. Portions of Andrew S. Bledsoe and Andrew F. Lang, "Military History and the American Civil War," and Andrew F. Lang, "The Limits of American Exceptionalism: Military Occupation, Emancipation, and the Preservation of Union," were originally published in *Upon the Fields of Battle: Essays on the Military History of America's Civil War*, pp. 3–19, 183–204, edited by Andrew S. Bledsoe and Andrew F. Lang (Louisiana State University Press, 2018), and are reprinted with permission. Portions of this manuscript were previously published in different form in Andrew F. Lang, "Union Demobilization and the Boundaries of War and Peace," *Journal of the Civil War Era* 9, no. 2 (June 2019): 178–95, and are reprinted with permission of UNC Press.

A Contest of Civilizations is principally a narrative history of mid-nineteenth-century America and the Civil War era. I would be remiss not to thank the countless scholars, both past and present, who have shaped our field and our understanding of the United States' great national trauma. Their tireless efforts, diverse research agendas, and impressive and sometimes revolutionary conclusions informed this book and my thinking in incalculable ways.

This book would not have been possible without the patience, stability, and love of my wife, Anne. I have been an unpleasant person to be around for much of the last five years. From completing my first book, coediting another, and penning numerous essays, to finalizing the myriad requirements for tenure, all the while writing this book, I have been grumpy, tired, and distant. And even as she listened to my ideas, assuaged my worries, and always offered helpful advice and encouragement, Anne maintained her own professional career and gave birth to two beautiful children. Today marks the beginning of the next five years. I am looking forward to them.

The challenge in writing this book proved to be nothing compared to the profound test in becoming a father, a life-changing experience that coincided almost with the entirety of this project. But nothing has been more rewarding or humbling than parenthood. Margaret and Jamie, this book will always remind me of your earliest years, your little laughs, your sweet smiles, and your perfect innocence. You are rays of light in a troubled world, and I am honored to dedicate this book, and my life, to you.

NOTES

Abbreviations

CWL   Roy P. Basler, ed. *Collected Works of Abraham Lincoln.* 9 vols. New Brunswick, NJ: Rutgers University Press, 1953–55.

OR   War Department. *The War of the Rebellion: A Compilation of the Official Records of the Union and Confederate Armies.* 128 vols. Washington, DC: Government Printing Office, 1880–1901.

PAJ   LeRoy P. Graf, Paul H. Bergeron, and Ralph W. Haskins et al., eds. *The Papers of Andrew Johnson.* 16 vols. Knoxville: University of Tennessee Press, 1967–2000.

PJD   Lynda L. Crist et al., eds. *The Papers of Jefferson Davis.* 14 vols. Baton Rouge: Louisiana State University Press, 1971–2015.

PUSG   John Y. Simon et al., eds. *The Papers of Ulysses S. Grant.* 32 vols. Carbondale: Southern Illinois University Press, 1967–present.

Prologue

1. Lincoln, Address before the Young Men's Lyceum of Springfield, Illinois, "The Perpetuation of Our Political Institutions" (hereafter cited as Lyceum Address), January 27, 1838, *CWL*, 1:108–15. My interpretation of the Lyceum Address is drawn from Donald, *Lincoln*, 80–83; Neely, *Last Best Hope of Earth*, 15–17; J. H. Baker, "Lincoln's Narrative of American Exceptionalism," 35–37; Porter, "'Last, Best Hope of Earth'"; Strozier, "On the Verge of Greatness"; and Carwardine, "Lincoln's Horizons," 29–31. For synthetic treatments of early nineteenth-century America, see Sellers, *Market Revolution*; Wilentz, *Rise of American Democracy*; Howe, *What Hath God Wrought*; Feller, *Jacksonian Promise*; and Watson, *Liberty and Power*.

2. Lyceum Address, *CWL*, 1:108.

3. Lyceum Address, *CWL*, 1:109.

4. Lyceum Address, *CWL*, 1:109, 110.

5. Lyceum Address, *CWL*, 1:111.

6. Lyceum Address, *CWL*, 1:111–12, 113–14.

7. Lyceum Address, *CWL*, 1:113, 112. See also A. I. P. Smith, *Stormy Present*, 3–13, 31–32, 44–48, 59–64, 82–84, 239n42; and C. Phillips, *Rivers Ran Backward*.

8. Lyceum Address, *CWL*, 1:115.

9. Lyceum Address, *CWL*, 1:115, 113.

10. Lincoln, First Inaugural Address, March 4, 1861, *CWL*, 4:268.

Introduction

1. Molho and Wood, introduction to *Imagined Histories*, 3–18 (quotation, p. 4); Rodgers, "Exceptionalism"; Fredrickson, "Nineteenth-Century American History"; Kammen, "Problem of American Exceptionalism"; J. P. Greene, *Intellectual Construction of America*, 45, 64, 8, 96, 101, 114–26, 130, 142–45, 150–61, 167–70, 177, 197–209; Hoogenboom, "American Exceptionalism"; Madsen, *American Exceptionalism*, 16–40,

70–99; Wilsey, *American Exceptionalism and Civil Religion*, 13–63, 91–119; Litke, *Twilight of the Republic*, 5–18, 23–24, 46–49, 85–90; Onuf, "American Exceptionalism and National Identity"; Restad, *American Exceptionalism*, 43–48; Ross, "American Exceptionalism," 22–23; Ross, "American Modernities, Past and Present"; Ross, "Historical Consciousness in Nineteenth-Century America"; Parish, "Exception to Most of the Rules"; von Beyme, *America as a Model*; Billias, *American Constitutionalism Heard Round the World*; Eric Foner, "American Exceptionalism, American Freedom"; Mansfield, "To the Heart of American Exceptionalism"; Tocqueville, *Democracy in America* (ed. Mansfield and Winthrop). Portions of this introduction draw from and are inspired by an early book proposal drafted by T. Michael Parrish.

2. Lang, "Limits of American Exceptionalism," 183–84. For examples of Cold War–era historiography that framed an exceptional American past, see Boorstin, *Genius of American Politics*; Potter, *People of Plenty*; Hartz, *Liberal Tradition in America*; Tuveson, *Redeemer Nation*; and Lipset, *American Exceptionalism*. For historiographic critiques of American exceptionalism, see Tyrrell, "American Exceptionalism in an Age of International History"; McGerr, "Price of the 'New Transnational History'" (a historiographic response to Tyrrell); Tyrrell, "Ian Tyrrell Responds"; Hodgson, *Myth of American Exceptionalism*; Thelen, "Making History and Making the United States"; Pease, "Anglo-American Exceptionalisms"; and Pease, *New American Exceptionalism*. For transnational approaches to American history, see Bender, *Rethinking American History in a Global Age*; Bender, *Nation among Nations*; Tyrrell, *Transnational Nation*; and Hahn, *Nation without Borders*. For histories that subsume the United States within a global nineteenth century, see Osterhammel, *Transformation of the World*; Bayly, *Birth of the Modern World*; and Osterhammel, "In Search of a Nineteenth Century."

3. Kammen, "Problem of American Exceptionalism," 6; Paine, *Common Sense*, in *Common Sense and Other Writings*, 33; J. P. Greene, *Intellectual Construction of America*, 136 (second Paine quotation), 130–51; Findley, *History of the Insurrection*, vi (final quotation); Lang, "Limits of American Exceptionalism," 183–84; Bright and Geyer, "Where in the World Is America?," 71–74; Nagel, *One Nation Indivisible*, 3–9, 281–88; Bailyn, *Ideological Origins of the American Revolution*, 79–92, 172–74, 233–35, 273–84, 316–18; Wood, *Creation of the American Republic*, 24–28, 70–73, 163–64, 370–72, 479–80, 483–99, 506–17, 527–32, 571–98, 603–4; E. Foner, *Tom Paine and Revolutionary America*, 131–44, 188–92; Waldstreicher, *In the Midst of Perpetual Fetes*, 3–10, 49–52, 85–113, 141–42, 178–94, 202–16; Israel, *Expanding Blaze*, 3–24, 71–79, 90, 112, 128, 425; A. Taylor, *American Revolutions*, 155–62, 353–480; Polasky, *Revolutions without Borders*, 3–5, 18–26, 34–50, 57–58, 103, 121–27, 266–78; Park, *American Nationalisms*, 12–16.

4. A vast literature exists on the relation of nineteenth-century America to global revolutions. Recent titles include Armitage, *Declaration of Independence*; Park, *American Nationalisms*; Cleves, *Reign of Terror in America*; McDaniel, *Problem of Democracy in the Age of Slavery*; C. L. Paulus, *Slaveholding Crisis*; Sharp, *American Politics in the Early Republic*; Calhoon, *Political Moderation in America's First Two Centuries*; R. Huston, "Rethinking the Origins of Partisan Democracy in the United States"; Berkin, *A Sovereign People*; Waldstreicher, *In the Midst of Perpetual Fetes*; Fitz, *Our Sister Republics*; Hunt, *Haiti's Influence on Antebellum America*; Roberts, *Distant Revolutions*; Morrison, *Slavery and the American West*; Dzelzainis and Livesey, *American Experiment and the Idea of Democracy in British Culture*; Quigley, *Shifting Grounds*;

Fleche, *Revolution of 1861*, Doyle, *Cause of All Nations*; Sexton, *Monroe Doctrine*; Varon, *Disunion!*; A. I. P. Smith, *Stormy Present*; Prior, *Between Freedom and Progress*; G. P. Downs, *Second American Revolution*; Eichhorn, *Liberty and Slavery*; Sheehan-Dean, *Reckoning with Rebellion*; and Tucker, *Newest Born of Nations*.

5. Lincoln, "Annual Message to Congress," December 1, 1862, and "Address Delivered at the Dedication of the Cemetery at Gettysburg," November 19, 1863, *CWL*, 5:537, 7:17–18; McPherson, "'Whole Family of Man,'"; Restad, *American Exceptionalism*, 41–43; Ross, "Historical Consciousness in Nineteenth-Century America"; Mansfield, "To the Heart of American Exceptionalism"; Hietala, *Manifest Design*; Litke, *Twilight of the Republic*, 5–22, 85–114; Hess, *Liberty, Virtue, and Progress*, 1–80; Gallagher, *Union War*, 1–6, 36–37, 40–49, 50–54, 60–69, 70–78, 116–19, 132, 139, 156–59, 160–62; Feller, *Jacksonian Promise*; Bonner, *Mastering America*, 1–213; Quigley, *Shifting Grounds*; Barnes, Schoen, and Towers, *Old South's Modern Worlds*; Potter, *Impending Crisis*, 1–17; Armitage et al., "Interchange"; McDaniel and Johnson, "New Approaches to Internationalizing the History of the Civil War Era"; Onuf and Onuf, *Nations, Markets, and War*, 176–80, 219; Wood, *Empire of Liberty*, 8–11, 20–22, 146, 348, 485–90; S.-M. Grant, *North over South*, 15, 82, 114–17, 129, 141–49; Morgan, *American Slavery, American Freedom*, 363–87.

6. Emerson, "American Civilization," *Atlantic Monthly*, April 1862, 502, 504. Ideas on the concept of "civilization" are derived from J. P. Greene, *Intellectual Construction of America*, 151–61; Onuf and Onuf, *Nations, Markets, and War*, 79–108; Bowden, *Empire of Civilization*, 14–16, 44–69, 72–73, 116–17, 146–73, 176–95, 197–201; Wilsey, *American Exceptionalism and Civil Religion*, 29, 44, 56–60, 75–78, 119, 130–36, 146–67, 176–79, 188; Ninkovich, *Global Dawn*, 8–23, 33–34, 40–46, 80–82, 137–40; Adas, *Dominance by Design*, 106, 123–24; Prior, "Civilization, Republic, Nation"; Sexton, "William H. Seward in the World"; Chang, "Whose 'Barbarism'? Whose 'Treachery'?"; Winterer, *American Enlightenments*, 2–6, 74–83, 253–56; Foote, "Civilization and Savagery in the American Civil War"; and Prior, *Between Freedom and Progress*, 7–12, 36–43, 109, 124, 147–49, 157–60.

7. Emerson, "American Civilization," *Atlantic Monthly*, April 1862, 502, 504;W. D. Jordan, *White over Black*, 24–46, 228–36, 253, 286–307, 542–72; Fredrickson, *Black Image in the White Mind*, 47–50, 98–100, 135–52; Berkhofer, *White Man's Indian*, 33–60, 92–94, 126–94; Lee, *Barbarians and Brothers*, 128–29, 164; G. P. Downs, "Mexicanization of American Politics"; Beasley, *Victorian Reinvention of Race*.

8. For important works that engage how the inconsistencies of Union and American exceptionalism worked to limit liberty, see Madsen, *American Exceptionalism*, 41–69, 83–89, 100–121; Parkinson, *Common Cause*; Hahn, *Nation without Borders*; A. Taylor, *American Revolutions*.

9. Motley, *Historic Progress and American Democracy*, 5–6; Conlin, "Dangerous *Isms* and the Fanatical *Ists*"; Eaton, *Civilization of the Old South*, 209–26.

10. "American Conservatism," *Harper's Weekly*, December 3, 1859, 770. My understanding of mid-nineteenth-century American conservatism as a political discourse and mode of political behavior derives from A. I. P. Smith, *Stormy Present*, 1–22, 59–63, 134–38, 156, 177, 192, 228–29. See also Benedict, "Preserving the Constitution"; Elazar, "Civil War and the Preservation of American Federalism"; S. B. Paulus, "America's Long Eulogy for Compromise"; Bender, *Nation among Nations*, 116–81; and Calhoon, *Political Moderation in America's First Two Centuries*. "Positive nationalism" is attributed to T. Michael Parrish.

11. Quotations from Onuf and Onuf, *Nations, Markets, and War*, 81; Lincoln, "A House Divided," June 16, 1858, *CWL*, 2:461. An older but still relevant version of this argument is made in McPherson, "Antebellum Southern Exceptionalism."

12. Lincoln, Second Inaugural Address, March 4, 1865, *CWL*, 8:332; Neely, *Lincoln and the Triumph of the Nation*, 29–62; Butler, *Critical Americans*.

13. "American Conservatism," *Harper's Weekly*, December 3, 1859, 770; A. I. P. Smith, *Stormy Present*, 1–22; Conlin, "Dangerous *Isms* and the Fanatical *Ists*."

14. Surveys of the respective national causes include Hess, *Liberty, Virtue, and Progress*; McPherson, *Battle Cry of Freedom*; Guelzo, *Fateful Lightning*; Varon, *Armies of Deliverance*; McCurry, *Confederate Reckoning*; S.-M. Grant, *North over South*; Gallagher, *Union War*; Gallagher, *Confederate War*; Bonner, *Mastering America*; Quigley, *Shifting Grounds*; and Doyle, *Cause of All Nations*. On the transformative implications of wartime military conduct, see Grimsley, *Hard Hand of War*; and Sheehan-Dean, *Calculus of Violence*. On the revolutionary nature of Reconstruction, see E. Foner, *Reconstruction*; Hahn, *Nation under Our Feet*; G. P. Downs, *After Appomattox*; G. P. Downs, *Second American Revolution*; and E. Foner, *Second Founding*.

15. For a comprehensive historiographic treatment and bibliography of the literature on of the American Civil War era in a global context, see Doyle, "Global Civil War." See also Armitage et al., "Interchange"; Kelly, "European Revolutions of 1848"; and Sexton, "Toward a Synthesis of Foreign Relations in the Civil War Era." For a sampling of individual studies, see Potter, "Civil War in the History of the Modern World"; May, *Union, the Confederacy, and the Atlantic Rim*; Bender, *Nation among Nations*, 116–81; Kelly, "North American Crisis of the 1860s"; Clavin, *Toussaint Louverture and the American Civil War*; Fleche, *Revolution of 1861*; Fleche, "Civil War in the Age of Revolution"; Onuf and Onuf, *Nations, Markets, and War*; Doyle, *Cause of All Nations*; Doyle, *American Civil Wars*; Prior, *Between Freedom and Progress*; G. P. Downs, *Second American Revolution*; Eichhorn, *Liberty and Slavery*; Sheehan-Dean, *Reckoning with Rebellion*; and Tucker, *Newest Born of Nations*.

16. Nagel, *One Nation Indivisible*, 3–9, 21–31, 68–87, 112–22, 124–42, 157–75; Wood, *Radicalism of the American Revolution*, 177–80, 213–15, 229–34, 240–43, 257–58, 278–86, 300, 318; J. L. Huston, "American Revolutionaries, the Political Economy of Aristocracy, and the American Concept of the Distribution of Wealth"; E. Foner, "Meaning of Freedom in the Age of Emancipation," 439–40; E. Foner, "American Freedom in a Global Age," 1–9; Polasky, *Revolutions without Borders*, 17–47; S.-M. Grant, *North over South*, 157–67.

17. A sampling of scholarship includes Glaude, *Exodus!*; Blackett, *Building an Antislavery Wall*; Hahn, *Nation under Our Feet*; Haynes, *Divine Destiny*; Kerr-Ritchie, *Rites of August First*; Ball, *To Live an Antislavery Life*; Cameron, *To Plead Our Own Cause*; Shulman, *American Prophecy*; Waldstreicher, *In the Midst of Perpetual Fetes*; Moody, *Sentimental Confessions*; Kachun, *Festivals of Freedom*; Kantrowitz, *More Than Freedom*; Horton and Horton, *In Hope of Liberty*; Rael, *Black Identity and Black Protest*; D. B. Davis, *Problem of Slavery in the Age of Emancipation*; Fagan, *Black Newspaper and the Chosen Nation*; Ernest, *Liberation Historiography*; M. S. Jones, *Birthright Citizens*; Sinha, *Slave's Cause*; Sidbury, *Ploughshares in Swords*; Egerton, *Gabriel's Rebellion*; Breen, *The Land Shall Be Deluged in Blood*; Twitty, *Before* Dred Scott; Kennington, *In the Shadow of* Dred Scott; P. G. Foreman, *Activist Sentiments*; Byrd, *Black Republic*; and Lande, "'Lighting Up the Path of Liberty and Justice.'" On nineteenth-century women, see Clinton, *Other Civil War*; DuBois, *Feminism and Suf-*

frage; Dublin, *Women at Work*; Kelley, *Private Women, Public Stage*; Wellman, *Road to Seneca Falls*; Welter, "Cult of True Womanhood"; McCurry, *Masters of Small Worlds*; Sterling, *We Are Your Sisters*; D. G. White, *Ar'n't I a Woman?*; Jensen, *Loosening the Bonds*; Fox-Genovese, *Within the Plantation Household*; Boydston, *Home and Work*; and Camp, *Closer to Freedom*. Primary source testimony of African American attitudes can be found in Ripley, *Black Abolitionist Papers*, vols. 3–5.

18. Lincoln, "Speech at Peoria, Illinois, October 16, 1854," *CWL*, 2:275; Rael, *Eighty-Eight Years*, 1, 26, 62–79, 117, 123–37; Berlin, *Long Emancipation*, 41–52, 59–71, 90–96, 147; Wilentz, *No Property in Man*, 103–6, 198–205, 229–30; Harrold, *American Abolitionism*, 18–60, 71–72, 84–85, 129–48; McPherson, *Battle Cry of Freedom*, 127; Douglass, "West India Emancipation" (1880), in Douglass, *Life and Times*, 607.

19. A sampling of literature includes Campbell, "Excess of Isolation," 174; Nye, "Slave Power Conspiracy"; Potter, "Historian's Use of Nationalism and Vice Versa"; Potter, *Impending Crisis*, 1–50, 448–84; Richards, *Slave Power*; Malvasi, "Old Republic and the Sectional Crisis"; Kornblith, "Rethinking the Coming of the Civil War"; Brettle, "Struggling to Realize a Vast Future"; Onuf, "Antebellum Southerners and the National Idea"; Rael, *Black Identity and Black Protest*; Rugemer, *Problem of Emancipation*; McDaniel, *Problem of Democracy in the Age of Slavery*; Kelly, "European Revolutions of 1848"; Onuf and Onuf, *Nations, Markets, and War*, 81; Restad, *American Exceptionalism*, 41–42; Conlin, "Dangerous *Isms* and the Fanatical *Ists*"; Roberts, "'Revolutions Have Become the Bloody Toy of the Multitude'"; Morrison, "American Reaction to European Revolutions"; S.-M. Grant, *North over South*; and A. I. P. Smith, *Stormy Present*.

20. See the works in the next note.

21. Potter, *Impending Crisis*; Gallagher, *Confederate War*; Dew, *Apostles of Disunion*; C. L. Paulus, *Slaveholding Crisis*; Eichhorn, *Liberty and Slavery*. Works on the "slaveholders' Union" include Bonner, *Mastering America*; Quigley, *Shifting Grounds*; Waldstreicher, *Slavery's Constitution*; Van Cleve, *Slaveholders' Union*; Mason, *Slavery and Politics in the Early American Republic*; and Fehrenbacher, *Slaveholding Republic*. Important rejoinders to these works can be found in Wilentz, *No Property in Man*; and Nabors, *From Oligarchy to Republicanism*.

22. Davis, Speech to the Confederate Congress, April 29, 1861, *OR*, ser. 4, vol. 1, pp. 258–59; Thornwell, *Our Danger and Our Duty*, 5; Fleche, *Revolution of 1861*, 80–106; Doyle, *Cause of All Nations*, 27–49; E. M. Thomas, "Jefferson Davis and the American Revolutionary Tradition"; Quigley, "Secessionists in an Age of Secession;" Rubin, *Shattered Nation*; McCurry, Confederate Reckoning.

23. Lincoln, "Speech at New Haven, Connecticut," March 6, 1860, and Second Inaugural Address, March 4, 1865, both in *CWL*, 4:27, 8:332; Crofts, *Lincoln and the Politics of Slavery*, 208–33, 264–68, 272–75; A. I. P. Smith, *Stormy Present*, 64, 76, 125–39, 144–65.

24. Lincoln, Second Inaugural Address, March 4, 1865, Annual Message to Congress, December 3, 1861, and Annual Message to Congress, December 1, 1862, all in *CWL*, 8:332, 5:53, 537; Fleche, *Revolution of 1861*, 38–79, 107–31; Doyle, *Cause of All Nations*, 50–82, 240–56; Gallagher, *Union War*, 1–4, 33–36, 47–66, 73–88, 116–19; Hess, *Liberty, Virtue, and Progress*, 4–55; S.-M. Grant, *North over South*, 153–72; A. I. P. Smith, *Stormy Present*, 166–225; Butler, *Critical Americans*, 52–86.

25. Lincoln, Annual Message to Congress, December 1, 1862, and "Proclamation of Thanksgiving," October 3, 1863, *CWL*, 5:536, 537, 6:497; McPherson, "Last Best

Hope for What?," 1–14. Gallagher, *Union War*, and Hess, *Liberty, Virtue, and Progress*, provide comprehensive interpretations of the white loyal citizenry's understanding of emancipation.

26. "No Gradual Emancipation," *New York Times*, February 25, 1864; Smith, *Stormy Present*, 189–94. I credit Berry, "Future of Civil War Era Studies," for use of the *Times* passage.

27. Speech of Dr. J. W. C. Pennington, August 14, 1863, *Principia*, January 7 and 14, 1864, quoted in McPherson, *Negro's Civil War*, 76; Matthews, *Caribbean Slave Revolts and the British Abolitionist Movement*; Rugemer, *Problem of Emancipation*; Clavin, *Toussaint Louverture and the American Civil War*; D. B. Davis, *Problem of Slavery in the Age of Emancipation*; Sinha, *Slave's Cause*; Rael, *Eighty-Eight Years*; Berlin, *Long Emancipation*; Kantrowitz, *More Than Freedom*; Manning, *What This Cruel War Was Over*; Hahn, *Nation under Our Feet*; Hahn, *Political Worlds of Slavery and Freedom*; Taylor, *Embattled Freedom*; Reidy, *Illusions of Emancipation*.

28. General Orders No. 100, Articles 15 and 29, *OR*, ser. 3, vol. 3, pp. 150, 151. Literature that emphasizes restraint, law, and "civilization" within Civil War military conduct includes Neely, "Was the Civil War a Total War?"; Grimsley, *Hard Hand of War*; Neely, *Civil War and the Limits of Destruction*; Neff, *Justice in Blue and Gray*; Dilbeck, *More Civil War*; Lang, *In the Wake of War*; Foote, "Civilization and Savagery in the American Civil War"; and Sheehan-Dean, *Calculus of Violence*.

29. Bancroft, "Place of Abraham Lincoln in History," *Atlantic Monthly*, June 1865, 764; McCurry, *Confederate Reckoning*; Lang, *In the Wake of War*; Sheehan-Dean, *Calculus of Violence*.

30. McCurry, *Confederate Reckoning*; Lang, *In the Wake of War*; Sheehan-Dean, *Calculus of Violence*.

31. These themes are pursued most comprehensively in E. Foner, *Reconstruction*; Summers, *Ordeal of the Reunion*; and Gallagher, *Union War*.

32. Rugemer, *Problem of Emancipation*, 291–301; E. Foner, *Nothing but Freedom*, 26–27; C. L. Paulus, *Slaveholding Crisis*, 236–37. Works that treat Reconstruction as a continuation of the Civil War include G. P. Downs, *After Appomattox*; Grimsley, "Wars for the American South"; and Blair, "Finding the Ending of America's Civil War."

33. For debates on the revolutionary nature of Reconstruction, see Benedict, "Preserving the Constitution"; E. Foner, *Reconstruction*; Hahn, *Nation under Our Feet*; H. C. Richardson, *Death of Reconstruction*; Summers, *Ordeal of the Reunion*; G. P. Downs, *After Appomattox*; Parsons, *Ku-Klux*; Lang, *In the Wake of War*; Guelzo, *Reconstruction*; G. P. Downs, *Second American Revolution*; and E. Foner, *Second Founding*.

34. Lynch, "Political Status of the Colored Race," August 12, 1876, in Middleton, *Black Congressmen during Reconstruction*, 189; E. Foner, *Reconstruction*; Edwards, *Gendered Strife and Confusion*; Stanley, *From Bondage to Contract*; Schmidt, *Free to Work*; Hahn, *Nation under Our Feet*; K. E. Williams, *They Left Great Marks on Me*; Rosen, *Terror in the Heart of Freedom*; Emberton, *Beyond Redemption*; Hunter, *Bound in Wedlock*; McDaniel, *Sweet Taste of Liberty*; Schweninger, *Appealing for Liberty*.

35. Lang, "Union Demobilization and the Boundaries of War and Peace," 188–89; G. P. Downs, "Palace That Will Fall upon Them"; G. P. Downs, *After Appomattox*, 40–51, 247–53.

Chapter 1

1. Lincoln, "Fragment on the Constitution and Union," [January 1861], *CWL*, 4:168–69; Guelzo, *Abraham Lincoln as a Man of Ideas*, 73–86, 105–24.

2. Lincoln, "Fragment on the Constitution and Union," [January 1861], *CWL*, 4:169.

3. Lincoln, "Fragment on the Constitution and Union," [January 1861], *CWL*, 4:169; Williams, Bader, and Blais, "Apple of Gold and Picture of Silver"; Guelzo, *Abraham Lincoln as a Man of Ideas*, 105–24.

4. Lincoln, "Fragment on the Constitution and Union," [January 1861], *CWL*, 4:169; Letter from John Adams to Abigail Adams, April 14, 1776, Adams Family Papers: An Electronic Archive, Massachusetts Historical Society, https://www.masshist.org/digital adams/archive/doc?id=L17760414ja; "From John Adams to James Sullivan, 26 May 1776," *Founders Online*, National Archives, accessed April 11, 2019, https://founders .archives.gov/documents/Adams/06-04-02-0091 (original source: *The Adams Papers, Papers of John Adams*, vol. 4, February–August 1776, ed. Robert J. Taylor [Cambridge, MA: Harvard University Press, 1979], 208–13). Both Adams quotations are drawn from A. Taylor, *American Revolutions*, 437–38; Wood, *Radicalism of the American Revolution*.

5. Hoogenboom, "American Exceptionalism," 45, 43 (first quotations); "Permanency of the American Union," *Niles' Weekly Register*, June 7, 1817; J. Q. Adams, *An Address ... Celebrating the Anniversary of Independence*, July 4, 1821, 3; Lincoln, "Address to Springfield Washington Temperance Society," February 22, 1842, *CWL*, 1:278; *New York Daily Tribune*, November 7, 1854, quoted in S.-M. Grant, *North over South*, 19; Nagel, *One Nation Indivisible*, 3–9, 13–25, 54–55, 68–87, 109–22, 170–75, 281–88; Kammen, "Problem of American Exceptionalism," 7; Madsen, *American Exceptionalism*, 34–38; Wood, *Radicalism of the American Revolution*, 3–8, 30, 169, 175–79, 189, 230–38; Berthoff, *Republic of the Dispossessed*, 38; Suri, *Liberty's Surest Guardian*, 4, 20–26; Gallagher, *Union War*, 3–4, 34–51, 62–70; Appleby, *Inheriting the Revolution*, 26–59, 133–37, 239–68.

6. Tocqueville, *Democracy in America* (ed. Mansfield and Winthrop), 430, 488; Restad, *American Exceptionalism*, 44 ("proximity from Europe"; "social egalitarianism"; "meritocratic tendencies"); Mansfield, "To the Heart of American Exceptionalism"; E. Foner, "American Freedom in a Global Age," 8; Ross, "American Exceptionalism,"; Howe, *What Hath God Wrought*, 306; Litke, *Twilight of the Republic*, 10–12; Tyrrell, *Transnational Nation*, 45–46; Wilsey, *American Exceptionalism and Civil Religion*, 28–30; Howe, *What Hath God Wrought*, 305–6.

7. Hamilton to Edward Carrington, May 26, 1792, in Holloway and Wilson, *Political Writings of Alexander Hamilton*, 2:133; Tocqueville, *Democracy in America* (ed. Mansfield and Winthrop), 3; Osterhammel, *Transformation of the World*, 416 (third quotation); Story, *Familiar Exposition of the Constitution of the United States*, 270; Wood, *Creation of the American Republic*, 47, 72, 84, 100–112, 135–44, 205–15, 237–45, 489–509; J. L. Huston, "American Revolutionaries, the Political Economy of Aristocracy, and the American Concept of the Distribution of Wealth"; Howe, *What Hath God Wrought*, 306.

8. Paine, *Common Sense*, in *Collected Writings*, 52, 36; Kammen, "Problem of American Exceptionalism," 7 (Bostonian quotation); N. Mitchell, *Oration Delivered before the Fourth of July Association* (1848), 16; Ross, "Historical Consciousness in Nineteenth-Century America"; Persons, "Cyclical Theory of History in Eighteenth

Century America," 147–63; Rodgers, "Republicanism"; Quigley, *Shifting Grounds*, 21–30.

9. Ross, "Historical Consciousness in Nineteenth-Century America," 911; Melville, *White-Jacket*, 237–38; diary entry, November 8, 1854, in Nevins and Thomas, *Diary of George Templeton Strong*, 2:196–97; Restad, *American Exceptionalism*, 45–46; S.-M. Grant, *North over South*, 26; Bright and Geyer, "Where in the World Is America?," 71–73; Onuf and Onuf, *Nations, Markets, and War*, 179–80, 220–23; Feller, *Jacksonian Promise*, 7–11; Ross, "American Modernities, Past and Present."

10. Jefferson to the Citizens of Washington, DC, March 4, 1809, *Founders Online*, National Archives, https://founders.archives.gov/documents/Jefferson/03-01 -02-0006; Hamilton, *Federalist Papers: No. 1*, Avalon Project, accessed May 5, 2020, https://avalon.law.yale.edu/18th_century/fed01.asp; "First Inaugural Address of George Washington," April 30, 1789, Avalon Project, accessed May 5, 2020, https:// avalon.law.yale.edu/18th_century/wash1.asp; Everett, "Speech at Yellow Springs, Ohio," June 29, 1829, in Everett, *Orations and Speeches*, 4:199; Breckinridge, *An Address, Delivered July 15, 1835, before the Eucleian and Philomathean Societies*, 9, 34; Noll, *America's God*, 74.

11. Noll, *America's God*, 9 (quotations), 17, 64–72, 203–19, 247–52, 367, 424, 426, 441–43; "Washington's Farewell Address," 1796, Avalon Project, accessed May 5, 2020, https://avalon.law.yale.edu/18th_century/washing.asp; Boles, *Great Revival*, 106–7 (Furman quotation), 101–7; Melville, *White-Jacket*, 238–39; Tocqueville, *Democracy in America* (ed. Mansfield and Winthrop), 280; Tuveson, *Redeemer Nation*, 34, 59–73, 87–90, 108–15, 127–33, 154–59, 193–94, 213–14; Parish, *North and the Nation in the Era of the Civil War*, 171–74; Rable, *God's Almost Chosen Peoples*, 3, 21, 25; Wright and Dresser, *Apocalypse and the Millennium in the American Civil War Era*, 1–11; Wilsey, *American Exceptionalism and Civil Religion*, 17–28; Restad, *American Exceptionalism*, 45.

12. W. E. Channing, "The Union" (1829), in *Works of William E. Channing*, 1:337; Hamilton, *Federalist Papers: No. 9*, Avalon Project, accessed May 5, 2020, https:// avalon.law.yale.edu/18th_century/fed09.asp; Varon, *Disunion!*, 1–16, passim (final quotation, p. 15); Bayly, *Birth of the Modern World*, 125–28; Wiebe, "Framing U.S. History"; Nagel, *One Nation Indivisible*, 23, 93–95, 114–21, 130–31, 140, 187; Donald, *Liberty and Union*, 3–30.

13. Madison, *Federalist Papers: No. 10*, Avalon Project, https://avalon.law.yale .edu/18th_century/fed10.asp; Washington's Farewell Address, 1796, Avalon Project, accessed May 5, 2020, https://avalon.law.yale.edu/18th_century/washing.asp; Hamilton, *Federalist Papers: No. 1*, Avalon Project, accessed May 5, 2020, https://avalon.law .yale.edu/18th_century/fed01.asp.

14. Donald, *Liberty and Union*, 30 (Everett quotation); Webster, "Second Reply to Hayne"; Hamilton, *Federalist Papers: No. 8*, Avalon Project, accessed May 5, 2020, https://avalon.law.yale.edu/18th_century/fed08.asp; Nagel, *One Nation Indivisible*, 264, 258 (Dallas quotation); Cleves, *Reign of Terror in America*, 42–43; Sexton, *Monroe Doctrine*, 26–28.

15. Cleves, *Reign of Terror in America*, 9–27, 32–37, 40–43, 73–81, 84–86; Bellamy, *Massacres and Morality*, 70; Tyrrell, *Transnational Nation*, 11–17; Israel, *Expanding Blaze*, 331–47; Bell, *First Total War*, 91–92, 128–29, 183–84; Blackman, *Foreign Fanaticism and American Constitutional Values*, 63–76; Kramer, "French Revolution and the Creation of American Political Culture"; D. B. Davis, "Impact of the

French and Haitian Revolutions," 3–10; Newman, "American Political Culture and the French and Haitian Revolutions"; Wood, *Empire of Liberty*, 162–63, 174–77; Sharp, *American Politics in the Early Republic*, 73–74, 81–87, 90, 104–5.

16. "Washington's Farewell Address," 1796, Avalon Project, accessed May 5, 2020, https://avalon.law.yale.edu/18th_century/washing.asp; "From John Adams to Massachusetts Militia, 11 October 1798," *Founders Online*, National Archives, accessed May 2, 2017, https://founders.archives.gov/documents/Adams/99-02-02-3102; Kramer, "French Revolution and the Creation of American Political Culture," 54.

17. Madison, *Federalist Papers: No. 51*, Avalon Project, accessed May 5, 2020, https://avalon.law.yale.edu/18th_century/fed51.asp; Blackman, *Foreign Fanaticism and American Constitutional Values*, 31, 34–45; Maslowski, "To the Edge of Greatness," 205–41; Bayly, *Birth of the Modern World*, 139–47; Wood, *Empire of Liberty*, 7, 31–36, 182.

18. Bailyn, *Ideological Origins of the American Revolution*, 366 (first quotation); Madison, *Federalist Papers: No. 10*, Avalon Project, accessed May 5, 2020, https://avalon.law.yale.edu/18th_century/fed10.asp; Rush, "Information to Europeans Who Are Disposed to Migrate to the United States of America" (1790), in *Essays, Literary, Moral and Philosophical*, 204; Sheehan, *Mind of James Madison*, 42–46, 77, 86–88; Banning, *Sacred Fire of Liberty*, 6–7, 101–2, 129–37, 202–17, 227–28, 351–55; Rakove, *Original Meanings*, 35–56, 161–243; Park, *American Nationalisms*, 57–68.

19. Tocqueville, *Democracy in America* (ed. Mansfield and Winthrop), 153, 154; Seward, "True Greatness of Our Country" (1844), in G. E. Baker, *Works of William H. Seward*, 3:18; Parish, *North and the Nation in the Era of the Civil War*, 96–97; Nagel, *One Nation Indivisible*, 93–94; Potter, "Historian's Use of Nationalism and Vice Versa"; Donald, *Liberty and Union*, 27; Cleves, *Reign of Terror in America*, 41–43, 203; S.-M. Grant, *North over South*, 19–36.

20. "Inaugural Address of John Adams," March 4, 1797, Avalon Project, accessed May 5, 2020, https://avalon.law.yale.edu/18th_century/adams.asp; Jefferson, "First Inaugural Address," March 4, 1801, Avalon Project, accessed May 5, 2020, https://avalon.law.yale.edu/19th_century/jefinau1.asp; Madison to Andrew Bigelow, April 2, 1836, in Mattern, *James Madison's "Advice to My Country,"* 105; Sharp, *American Politics in the Early Republic*, 187–275; Calhoon, *Political Moderation in America's First Two Centuries*.

21. W. E. Channing, "The Union" (1829), in *Works of William E. Channing*, 1:337; Davis, "Speech in U.S. Senate," August 13, 1850, in Cooper, *Jefferson Davis: Essential Writings*, 84; Varon, *Disunion!*, 11–16, 24–45, 87–100, 209–10; Nagel, *One Nation Indivisible*, 114–21, 130, 233–34, 268–69, 274–80; Guelzo, *Fateful Lightning*, 8–12.

22. Osterhammel, *Transformation of the World*, 61, 601–3; Tyrrell, *Transnational Nation*, 45–46; Wilsey, *American Exceptionalism and Civil Religion*, 27–30; Hodgson, *Myth of American Exceptionalism*, 34–37, 40–45; Onuf, "Antebellum Southerners and the National Idea," 26; Bayly, *Birth of the Modern World*, 139–47; Wiebe, "Framing U.S. History"; Wilentz, *Rise of American Democracy*, xvii–xviii, 3–19, 29–30, 70–75, 82–83, 96–98, 186–205, 309–10, 341–45; Gallagher, *Union War*, 4–5; Berthoff, *Republic of the Dispossessed*, 38–42.

23. Tocqueville, *Democracy in America* (ed. Mansfield and Winthrop), 482; J. L. Huston, "American Revolutionaries, the Political Economy of Aristocracy, and the American Concept of the Distribution of Wealth," 1083, 1084 (final two quotations); Bailyn, *Ideological Origins of the American Revolution*, 319; Wood, *Radicalism of the*

American Revolution, 187–89, 233–43, 305–19, 327–36; Pocock, *Machiavellian Moment*, 527–46; Lerner, "Commerce and Character."

24. McPherson, *Battle Cry of Freedom*, 29; A. Smith, *An Inquiry into the Nature and Causes of the Wealth of Nations*, 286; Emerson, "The Young American" (1844), in Johannsen, *Democracy on Trial*, 10; E. Foner, "Meaning of Freedom in the Age of Emancipation," 442; Glickstein, *American Exceptionalism, American Anxiety*, 13; J. L. Huston, "American Revolutionaries, the Political Economy of Aristocracy, and the American Concept of the Distribution of Wealth," 1095; Guelzo, *Fateful Lightning*, 12–15; Onuf and Onuf, *Nations, Markets, and War*, 187–218; Howe, *What Hath God Wrought*, 5, 44–45, 81, 252, 271–72, 359–60, 463, 501–6, 850; Bayly, *Birth of the Modern World*, 131–32; J. L. Huston, *British Gentry, the Southern Planter, and the Northern Family Farmer*, 17, 26, 85, 126–28, 192, 202–3; Tyrrell, *Transnational Nation*, 23–44. For debates on the advent of a "market revolution," see Sellers, *Market Revolution*; Post, *American Road to Capitalism*, 1–183; Clark, *Roots of Rural Capitalism*, 9–17, 318–26; Feller, "Market Revolution Ate My Homework"; Lamoreaux, "Rethinking the Transition to Capitalism in the Early American Northeast"; and Bruegel, *Farm, Shop, Landing*, 1–2, 57–62, 66–77, 88, 131–66, 220.

25. J. L. Huston, "American Revolutionaries, the Political Economy of Aristocracy, and the American Concept of the Distribution of Wealth," 1097 (first quotation); Donald, *Liberty and Union*, 28, 29 (final quotations), 3–33; Wilentz, *Rise of American Democracy*, xxi; Howe, *What Hath God Wrought*, 304–7; Earle, *Jacksonian Antislavery and the Politics of Free Soil*.

26. "President Jackson's Veto Message regarding the Bank of the United States," July 10, 1832, Avalon Project, accessed May 5, 2020, https://avalon.law.yale.edu/19th _century/ajveto01.asp; Wilentz, *Rise of American Democracy*, 203–14, 244–45, 253, 308, 357–72; Sellers, *Market Revolution*, 281, 312–16, 346–57.

27. Clay, *Speech in Support of an American System*, 17, 31; Howe, *What Hath God Wrought*, 211–12, 270–75, 377–91, 533, 557; Howe, *Making the American Self*, 1–9, 80–84, 114–35, 263–68; Howe, *Political Culture of the American Whigs*, 117–22, 140–41, 136–49, 213–18; Wilentz, *Rise of American Democracy*, 482–518.

28. McPherson, *Battle Cry of Freedom*, 15 (first quotation), 9, 11, 13; Lincoln to the People of Sangamo County, March 9, 1832, *CWL*, 1:8; Hoogenboom, "American Exceptionalism," 53–55 (Mann quotation, p. 53); Parish, *North and the Nation in the Era of the Civil War*, 59; Hodgson, *Myth of American Exceptionalism*, 34–37; Glickstein, *American Exceptionalism, American Anxiety*, 41–49; Henkin, *Postal Age*, 1–92.

29. "Thomas Jefferson to James Madison, 27 April 1809," *Founders Online*, National Archives, accessed April 11, 2019, https://founders.archives.gov/documents /Jefferson/03-01-020140 (original source: *The Papers of Thomas Jefferson*, Retirement Series, vol. 1, *4 March 1809 to 15 November 1809*, ed. J. Jefferson Looney [Princeton, NJ: Princeton University Press, 2004], 168–70); Jefferson, First Inaugural Address, March 4, 1801, Avalon Project, accessed May 5, 2020, https://avalon.law.yale .edu/19th_century/jefinau1.asp; "From Thomas Jefferson to William Ludlow, 6 September 1824," *Founders Online*, National Archives, accessed April 11, 2019, https:// founders.archives.gov/documents/Jefferson/98-01-02-4523; Webster, "The Bunker Hill Monument."

30. Sampson, *John L. O'Sullivan and His Times*, 194 (O'Sullivan [1845] quotation); Polk, Third Annual Message to Congress, December 7, 1847, in J. D. Richardson, *Compilation of the Messages and Papers of the Presidents*, 4:533; Nagel, *One Nation In-*

divisible, 152 (Walker quotation); "To John Adams from John Quincy Adams, 31 August 1811," *Founders Online*, National Archives, https://founders.archives.gov/documents/Adams/99-03-02-2020; Emerson, "The Young American" (1844), in Johannsen, *Democracy on Trial*, 7; Wilsey, *American Exceptionalism and Civil Religion*, 64–90; Wilentz, *Rise of American Democracy*, 562–85, 605–11, 664–71; Hietala, *Manifest Design*, 2–9, 39–40, 50, 68, 111–25, 132, 184–97, 255–71.

31. Tocqueville, *Democracy in America* (ed. Mansfield and Winthrop), 395; "Brother Jonathan," *United States Review* (May 1853), reprinted in Johannsen, *Democracy on Trial*, 22–23; Osterhammel, *Transformation of the World*, 331–39; McPherson, *Battle Cry of Freedom*, 6, 9; Huston, *British Gentry, the Southern Planter, and the Northern Family Farmer*, xv; Dean, *Agrarian Republic*, 1–10.

32. Motley, *Historic Progress and American Democracy*, 4; Emerson, "American Civilization," *Atlantic Monthly*, April 1862, 502; Swisshelm, *Half a Century*, 225; Hietala, *Manifest Design*, 2–9, 135–52, 193–207, 255–71; Limerick, *Legacy of Conquest*, 18–19, 45–48, 51–58, 78–83, 94, 175–81, 203–11; DuVal, "Independence for Whom?"; R. Huston, "Land Conflict and Land Policy in the United States," 324–45; Watson, *Liberty and Power*, 13–14, 53–54, 105–13, 135.

33. Jackson, Second Annual Message to Congress, December 6, 1830, in J. D. Richardson, *Compilation of the Messages and Papers of the Presidents*, 3:1084, 1085; Hietala, *Manifest Design*, 148 (Indian affairs agent quotations); Seward, "True Greatness of Our Country" (1844), in G. E. Baker, *Works of William H. Seward*, 3:14; Wallace, *Long, Bitter Trail*, 47–102, 121–24; DuVal, "Independence for Whom?"; Watson, *Liberty and Power*, 13–14, 53–54, 105–13, 135.

34. Boudinot, *An Address to the Whites* (1826), 7, 14, 15; Madsen, *American Exceptionalism*, 48–53 (Wannuaucon quotation, p. 51); Wallace, *Long, Bitter Trail*, 73–102; C. Snyder, "Rise and Fall and Rise of Civilizations"; Perdue, *Cherokee Removal*, 1–21; Pairns, *Literacy and Intellectual Life in the Cherokee Nation*, 51; Cumfer, *Separate Peoples, One Land*, 101–24; Deloria, "American Master Narratives and the Problem of Indian Citizenship in the Gilded Age and Progressive Era," 3–12; Maddox, *Citizen Indians*; Limerick, *Legacy of Conquest*, 188–200; Osterhammel, *Transformation of the World*, 791–92.

35. Lieber, *On Civil Liberty and Self-Government*, 177; Prior, "Civilization, Republic, Nation"; Fluhman, *"A Peculiar People,"* 103–26; Parkinson, *Common Cause*; Hernández, *Mexican American Colonization during the Nineteenth Century*; Mora, *Border Dilemmas*; Madsen, *American Exceptionalism*, 100–121.

36. Berlin, *Many Thousands Gone*, 7–13, 95–108; Osterhammel, *Transformation of the World*, 699; Rugemer, "Why Civil War?," 16; Rael, *Eighty-Eight Years*, 3–26; Mintz, "American Slavery in Comparative Perspective."

37. Berlin, *Many Thousands Gone*, 9–11 (quotation, p. 9); Mintz, "American Slavery in Comparative Perspective"; W. D. Jordan, *White over Black*; Blackburn, *Making of New World Slavery*, 12–20, 33–34, 53–83, 103–5, 112–14, 123, 134–56, 179–80, 235–61, 322–25, 350–63, 583–90; D. B. Davis, *Inhuman Bondage*, 27–140; Cottrol, *Long Lingering Shadow*; Degler, *Neither Black nor White*.

38. W. Johnson, *River of Dark Dreams*, 18–45 (first quotation, p. 27); Wright, *Slavery and American Economic Development*, 15 (second quotation); Onuf, "Empire of Liberty," 195–211; Rothman, *Slave Country*, 1–72; Rael, *Eighty-Eight Years*, 11, 103, 158, 172–73.

39. Madison, *Federalist Papers: No. 10*, Avalon Project, accessed May 23, 2020,

https://avalon.law.yale.edu/18th_century/fed10.asp; Madison, *Federalist Papers: No. 54*, Avalon Project, accessed May 23, 2020, https://avalon.law.yale.edu/18th_century /fed54.asp; Onuf and Onuf, *Nations, Markets, and War*, 103–4; Rael, *Eighty-Eight Years*, 69–79; Fehrenbacher, *Slaveholding Republic*, 37–47, 80, 224–44; Van Cleve, *Slaveholders' Union*, 103–85; Wilentz, *No Property in Man*, 1–20, 97–99, 166, 196.

40. Mintz, "American Slavery in Comparative Perspective"; *Historical Statistics of the United States*, 1:14; Kolchin, *Sphinx on the American Land*, 76–77 (quotation); Tyrrell, *Transnational Nation*, 75–76; Kolchin, *American Slavery*, 37–38; Rael, *Eighty-Eight Years*, 7–8, 11–12, 23–24; Bergad, *Comparative Histories of Slavery in Brazil, Cuba, and the United States*.

41. Kolchin, *American Slavery*, 101 (first quotation), 76–77, 100–103, 153; Faust, *James Henry Hammond*, 134 (Hammond [1847 and 1848] quotations); Blackburn, *Making of New World Slavery*, 406–69, 536–43.

42. Deyle, *Carry Me Back*, 172–73 (first quotation); W. Johnson, *River of Dark Dreams*, 32 (second quotation); Osterhammel, *Transformation of the World*, 846 (final quotation); Guelzo, *Fateful Lightning*, 35; J. L. Huston, *Calculating the Value of Union*, 30–38; Kaye, "Second Slavery," 633–35; Rugemer, "Why Civil War?," 18; Wright, *Slavery and American Economic Development*, 13–15; W. Johnson, *Soul by Soul*, 13–52; L. K. Ford, *Deliver Us from Evil*, 81–139. For a primer on the debates regarding British abolition, see E. Williams, *Capitalism and Slavery*; Matthews, *Caribbean Slave Revolts and the British Abolitionist Movement*; and C. L. Brown, *Moral Capital*.

43. McPherson, *Battle Cry of Freedom*, 39 (first and fourth quotations); Forbes, *Missouri Compromise and Its Aftermath*, 206 (Hayne quotation); Gilmer, "Address to the Agricultural Association of the Slaveholding States" (1853), in Cloud, *American Cotton Planter*, 2:222 (third quotation); Ransom, "Economics of the Civil War" (penultimate quotation); Deyle, *Carry Me Back*, 59 (final quotation), 60; Howe, *What Hath God Wrought*, 125–63, esp. 131–32; Beckert, "Emancipation and Empire"; Schoen, *Fragile Fabric of Union*, 48–49, 95–97, 146–96, 203–8, 226–29, 253–54. Rockman, "Slavery and Capitalism," organizes the recent historiographic literature on slavery and capitalism and also provided inspiration for the geographic connections of American and global cities listed in this paragraph.

44. Dain, *Hideous Monster of the Mind*, 82–93; Rugemer, *Problem of Emancipation*, 42–53, 92–93, 107–8, 300–301; D. B. Davis, *Problem of Slavery in the Age of Emancipation*, 74–82, 83–90, 105–66; Osterhammel, *Transformation of the World*, 699; Berlin, *Many Thousands Gone*, 11; Bayly, *Birth of the Modern World*, 99; Dun, *Dangerous Neighbors*, 38–79, 90–133, 145–65. Dubois, *Avengers of the New World*, presents a comprehensive interpretation of the revolution and its aftermath.

45. E. Foner, *Nothing but Freedom*, 11–14, 40–43; Davis, D. B. *Problem of Slavery in the Age of Emancipation*, 45–48; Rugemer, *Problem of Emancipation*, 17–95, 107–8; Guterl, *American Mediterranean*, 40–43; Dubois, *Avengers of the New World*; Geggus and Fiering, *World of the Haitian Revolution*; Dun, *Dangerous Neighbors*, 2–4, 31–55, 148–54, 159–65, 214–26; Polasky, *Revolutions without Borders*, 147–49, 152–58, 164–68.

46. First two Jefferson quotations in "Jefferson's Attitudes toward Slavery," Monticello, accessed May 27, 2019, https://www.monticello.org/thomas-jefferson/jefferson -slavery/jefferson-s-attitudes-toward-slavery/; "captive nation" adopted from Onuf, "'To Declare Them a Free and Independent People,'" 4, passim; Jefferson, *Notes on*

the State of Virginia, 169, 145; Boles, *Jefferson*, 170–80, 181–82, 470–77, 503–5; Onuf, "Empire of Liberty," 207–12.

47. Jefferson, *Notes on the State of Virginia*, 150–51; 145; Onuf, "'To Declare Them a Free and Independent People'"; E. Foner, "Meaning of Freedom in the Age of Emancipation," 444; Wolf, *Race and Liberty in the New Nation*, 102–9, 165–66; Dain, *Hideous Monster of the Mind*, 20, 31–35, 91–108; Boles, *Jefferson*, 77–78, 177–79, 470–77, 504–5, 599.

48. L. K. Ford, *Deliver Us from Evil*, 144, 195, 201–2; Kolchin, *American Slavery*, 181; E. Foner, "Meaning of Freedom in the Age of Emancipation," 441–42; D. B. Davis, *Problem of Slavery in Western Culture*, 370–71, 393–400, 412–19, 438–41; Parkinson, *Common Cause*, 241–47, 251–63, 583–88; Dain, *Hideous Monster of the Mind*, 17–39, 85–86; Wolf, *Race and Liberty in the New Nation*, 1–38, 191–93; Holcomb, "Abolitionist Movement"; Stewart, *Holy Warriors*, 30–31; Burin, *Slavery and the Peculiar Solution*; Tocqueville, *Democracy in America* (ed. Nolla, trans. Schleifer); Morgan, *American Slavery, American Freedom*, 363–87; Morgan, "Slavery and Freedom."

49. Clay, *Speech of Mr. Clay … on the Subject of Abolitionist Petitions*, 16; McCord, "Slavery and Political Economy" (1856), in Lounsbury, *Louisa S. McCord*, 431; Onuf and Onuf, *Nations, Markets, and War*, 184–85; Tise, *Proslavery*, 3–11, 41–179; Faust, *Ideology of Slavery*, 1–20.

50. McCord, "Diversity of the Races" (1851), in Lounsbury, *Louisa S. McCord*, 173, 174, 175; letter from Robert E. Lee to Mary Randolph Custis Lee (December 27, 1856), Lee Family Digital Archive, accessed June 29, 2019, https://www.encyclopedia virginia.org/Letter_from_Robert_E_Lee_to_Mary_Randolph_Custis_Lee_Decem ber_27_1856; *Richmond Enquirer*, April 15, 1856, quoted in Oakes, *Ruling Race*, 141; E. B. Pryor, *Reading the Man*, 123–54.

51. Buchanan, *Oration upon the Moral and Political Evil of Slavery* (1793), quoted in Waldstreicher, *In the Midst of Perpetual Fetes*, 311–12; Rugemer, "Why Civil War?," 24–25; Dun, "Atlantic Antislavery, American Ambition"; Newman, "Pendulum Swings"; E. Foner, "Meaning of Freedom in the Age of Emancipation," 448–52; McDaniel, *Problem of Democracy in the Age of Slavery*, 5–14, 96, 139–42, 159–61, 206–9; Laurie, *Beyond Garrison*; Newman, *Transformation of American Abolitionism*.

52. Speech by William Wells Brown, Cincinnati Anti-slavery Convention, April 25, 1855, in Ripley, *Black Abolitionist Papers*, 4:287; M. S. Jones, *Birthright Citizens*, 1, 21–33, 68–98, 90–102; E. S. Pryor, *Colored Travelers*, 3–6, 45–74, 75–82; Sinha, *Slave's Cause*, 71–89, 154–60, 316–30; Van Cleve, *Slaveholders' Union*, 166–205.

53. Kachun, "Antebellum African Americans, Public Commemoration, and the Haitian Revolution," 253 (Bostonians quotations); Delany, *Condition, Elevation, Emigration, and Destiny of the Colored People of the United States*, 160, 12; Ross, "'Are We a Nation,'" 336; Fagan, *Black Newspaper and the Chosen Nation*, 5–6, 107, 113, 136; D. B. Davis, *Problem of Slavery in the Age of Emancipation*, 45–47, 51–52, 76–83, 105, 178, 120–36, 352–53; Gosse, "'As a Nation, the English Are Our Friends'"; Waldstreicher, *In the Midst of Perpetual Fetes*, 328–31; Dun, *Dangerous Neighbors*, 17–18, 84–85, 121–33; Dubois, "Avenging America"; Sepinwall, "Specter of Saint-Domingue"; Tyrrell, *Transnational Nation*, 74–75; Hunt, *Haiti's Influence on Antebellum America*, 147–88; Sidbury, "Saint Domingue in Virginia"; Fanning, "Roots of Early Black Nationalism"; L. Alexander, "Black Republic," 57–80; and Byrd, *Black Republic*.

54. D. B. Davis, *Problem of Slavery in the Age of Emancipation*, 129 (first quotation), 121–22, 129–32, 176; "New England Colored Citizens' Convention," *The Libera-*

tor, August 26, 1859; Douglass, "Colonization," *North Star*, January 26, 1849, in Foner and Taylor, *Frederick Douglass*, 126; Blight, *Frederick Douglass*, 370–80; M. S. Jones, *Birthright Citizens*, 1–12, 29–40, 60–62, 74–87, 90–91.

55. Douglass, "The Meaning of the Fourth of July for the Negro," July 5, 1852, in Foner and Taylor, *Frederick Douglass*, 191; Blight, *Frederick Douglass*, 229–36.

56. Douglass, "Meaning of the Fourth of July for the Negro," 194, 196.

57. Douglass, "Meaning of the Fourth of July for the Negro," 195, 197; Ray, "Frederick Douglass on the Lyceum Circuit."

58. Douglass, "Meaning of the Fourth of July for the Negro," 202, 203.

59. Speech by Charles L. Remond, May 13, 1858, in Ripley, *Black Abolitionist Papers*, 4:386, 387; M. S. Jones, *Birthright Citizens*, 9–13, 128–45; Sinha, *Slave's Cause*, 238, 289–91, 318–22, 352–54, 522–25, 534, 560–71; Kantrowitz, *More Than Freedom*, 237–38.

60. Rael, *Black Identity and Black Protest*, 237–78 (quotations, pp. 255, 257, 266); Glaude, *Exodus!*; Haynes, *Divine Destiny*; Kerr-Ritchie, *Rites of August First*; Ball, *To Live an Antislavery Life*; Shulman, *American Prophecy*; Moody, *Sentimental Confessions*; Kachun, *Festivals of Freedom*; Kantrowitz, *More Than Freedom*; Blackett, *Building an Antislavery Wall*; Horton and Horton, *In Hope of Liberty*; Fagan, *Black Newspaper and the Chosen Nation*; Ernest, *Liberation Historiography*; M. S. Jones, *Birthright Citizens*; Sinha, *Slave's Cause*; Twitty, *Before* Dred Scott; Kennington, *In the Shadow of* Dred Scott; P. G. Foreman, *Activist Sentiments*; Hahn, *Nation under Our Feet*.

61. Douglass, "Meaning of the Fourth of July for the Negro," 204; "Resolutions by a Meeting of Chicago Blacks," December 26, 1853, in Ripley, *Black Abolitionist Papers*, 4:181; "New England Convention of Colored Citizens," *The Liberator*, August 26, 1859.

62. "New England Convention of Colored Citizens," *The Liberator*, August 26, 1859; Jacobs, *Incidents in the Life of a Slave Girl*, 68, 69; Blackett, *Building an Antislavery Wall*, 3–78.

63. Clinton, *Harriet Tubman*, 140 (Tubman quotations), 36–37, 61–76; Hahn, *Nation under Our Feet*, 3–4, 15–19, 37–68; Camp, *Closer to Freedom*, 3, 50–51, 127; Kaye, *Joining Places*, 7–9, 13–19, 42–44, 50–53, 74–78, 116–17, 129–36, 146–60, 178, 185–91, 209; W. Johnson, "On Agency," 113–24.

64. Sarah M. Grimke to My Dear Sister, September 6, 1837, in Grimke, *Letters on the Equality of the Sexes, and the Condition of Women* (1838), 74; Edwards, "Gender and the Changing Roles of Women," 223–25 (penultimate quotation, p. 224); Clinton, *Other Civil War*, 72 (Child quotation), 40, 68–69, 77–78; Cott, *Bonds of Womanhood*, 1–10, 64–74, 84–100; DuBois, *Feminism and Suffrage*, 27–37.

65. "Declaration of Sentiments," July 20, 1848, in Stanton et al., *History of Woman Suffrage*, 1:70; McPherson, *Battle Cry of Freedom*, 33–37 (first quotation, p. 35); Clinton, *Other Civil War*, 21–32, 45, 73–76, 153–57; Edwards, "Gender and the Changing Roles of Women," 225–27; DuBois, *Feminism and Suffrage*, 21–23, 40–48, 87–88, 119, 148–49, 181; Dublin, *Women at Work*, 31–49, 151–53, 167–82; Kelley, *Private Women, Public Stage*; Wilentz, *Chants Democratic*, 10–11, 51, 117, 248–49, 350–51; Wellman, *Road to Seneca Falls*, 10–11, 177, 186–208; Howe, *What Hath God Wrought*, 234, 450, 463, 536–47, 837–55, 603–9.

66. "Address by Elizabeth Cady Stanton on Woman's Rights," [September 1848], in Gordon, *Selected Papers of Elizabeth Cady Stanton and Susan B. Anthony*, 1:97, 105; Wellman, *Road to Seneca Falls*, 210–15.

67. W. E. Channing, "The Union" (1829), in *Works of William Ellery Channing*, 1:335; Israel, *Expanding Blaze*, 3–9, 13–24, 54, 75–97, 128, 219–23, 423–26, 435, 471–76, 489–92, 506–9, 548–49; Armitage, *Declaration of Independence*, 95–96, 104–29, 131–38.

68. Fitz, "Hemispheric Dimensions of Early U.S. Nationalism," 362 (first quotation); Robertson, "Recognition of the Hispanic American Nations by the United States," 254 (Clay quotation); Tyrrell, *Transnational Nation*, 17; Fitz, *Our Sister Republics*, 1–155; J. E. Lewis, *American Union and the Problem of the Neighborhood*, 2–8, 13–15, 80–81, 97–98, 102–15, 119–27, 136–43, 150–204, 210–13; Howe, *What Hath God Wrought*, 111; Kelly, "Lost Continent of Abraham Lincoln," 225–27.

69. "Thomas Jefferson to Tadeusz Kosciuszko, 16 April 1811," *Founders Online*, National Archives, accessed April 11, 2019, https://founders.archives.gov/documents /Jefferson/03-03-02-0439 (original source: *The Papers of Thomas Jefferson*, Retirement Series, vol. 3, *12 August 1810 to 17 June 1811*, ed. J. Jefferson Looney [Princeton, NJ: Princeton University Press, 2006], 565–67); Sexton, *Monroe Doctrine*, 37; Robertson, "Recognition of the Hispanic American Nations by the United States," 254 (first Adams quotation); Adams diary entry, March 9, 1821, quoted in C. F. Adams, *Memoirs of John Quincy Adams*, 5:325; Fitz, *Our Sister Republics*, 33–35, 181; Osterhammel, *Transformation of the World*, 532–37; Bayly, *Birth of the Modern World*, 126, 141–42, 147.

70. Webster, "The Bunker Hill Monument"; Tocqueville, *Democracy in America* (ed. Mansfield and Winthrop), 293; Osterhammel, *Transformation of the World*, 532–37; Bayly, *Birth of the Modern World*, 126, 141–42, 147; Doyle, "Global Civil War," 2:1104 (final quotation).

71. Tennery diary entry, November 21, 1846, in Livingston-Little, *Mexican War Diary of Thomas D. Tennery*, 37–38; Neely, *Civil War and the Limits of Destruction*, 17 (Pennsylvanian quotation); Tocqueville, *Democracy in America* (ed. Mansfield and Winthrop), 156; G. P. Downs, "Mexicanization of American Politics," 393; Doyle, "Global Civil War," 2:1104; Fitz, *Our Sister Republics*, 42–44, 110–39; J. E. Lewis, *American Union and the Problem of the Neighborhood*, 145–98, 201–12; Thelan, "Rethinking History and the Nation-State."

72. Adams diary entry, November 26, 1823, in C. F. Adams, *Memoirs of John Quincy Adams*, 6:207; "Monroe Doctrine, December 2, 1823," Avalon Project, accessed July 16, 2019, https://avalon.law.yale.edu/19th_century/monroe.asp; Sexton, *Monroe Doctrine*, 56–58; Howe, *What Hath God Wrought*, 107–16; Hahn, *Nation without Borders*, 25–26; Fitz, *Our Sister Republics*, 122–24, 158–60, 189–92, 243–44, 294, 304, 312–13.

73. Everett, "Speech at Yellow Springs, Ohio," June 29, 1829, in Everett, *Orations and Speeches*, 4:199; Bright and Geyer, "Where in the World Is America?," 74–79; Rugemer, "Why Civil War?," 16–17; Sexton, *Monroe Doctrine*, 3–45; E. Foner, "American Freedom in a Global Age," 8; Hahn, *Nation without Borders*, 11–42, 114–91.

74. N. Mitchell, *Oration Delivered before the Fourth of July Association* (1848), 15, 24, 21; Curti, "Impact of the Revolutions of 1848 on American Thought," 209; Bayly, *Birth of the Modern World*, 155–60; Roberts, *Distant Revolutions*, 1–104; Morrison, "American Reaction to European Revolutions"; Israel, *Expanding Blaze*, 547–99; Stearns, *Revolutions of 1848*; Evans and Von Strandmann, eds., *Revolutions in Europe, 1848–1849*; Sperber, *European Revolutions, 1848–1851*.

75. Diary entry, April 9, 1848, in Nevins and Thomas, *Diary of George Templeton Strong*, 1:316; Roberts, *Distant Revolutions*, 30 (correspondent quotations), 4–6,

21–40, 77, 82–83, 98; Curti, "Impact of the Revolutions of 1848 on American Thought," 210–11.

76. Lester, *My Consulship*, 2:226–27; Gemme, *Domesticating Foreign Struggles*, 53; Roberts, "'Revolutions Have Become the Bloody Toy of the Multitude,'" 266; Bayly, *Birth of the Modern World*, 155–60; Curti, "Impact of the Revolutions of 1848 on American Thought," 209.

77. Roberts, "Now the Enemy Is within Our Borders," 205 (Scott quotation); Morrison, "American Reaction to European Revolutions," 121 (Ticknor quotation); Pierce, Inaugural Address, March 4, 1853, in J. D. Richardson, *Compilation of the Messages and Papers of the Presidents*, 7:2730–32; Campbell, "Excess of Isolation"; Messer-Kruse, *Yankee International*, 1–26; Glickstein, *American Exceptionalism, American Anxiety*, 41–49; Conlin, "Dangerous *Isms* and the Fanatical *Ists*."

78. Curti, "Impact of the Revolutions of 1848 on American Thought," 212–15 (Greeley quotation, p. 213); Potter, "Civil War in the History of the Modern World," 292; Roberts, *Distant Revolutions*, 146–67; Morrison, "American Reaction to European Revolutions," 123–24.

79. Lincoln, "Resolutions in Behalf of Hungarian Freedom," January 9, 1852, *CWL*, 2:115–16; Morrison, "American Reaction to European Revolutions," 123–30; Roberts, *Distant Revolutions*, 146–67.

80. Morrison, "American Reaction to European Revolutions," 129 (Bell quotation); Know-Nothing Party Platform, *America Votes: Presidential Campaign Memorabilia*, Duke University Special Collections Library, accessed July 28, 2019, https://library .duke.edu/rubenstein/scriptorium/americavotes/know-nothing.html; Messer-Kruse, *Yankee International*, 12; Parish, *North and the Nation in the Era of the Civil War*, 7; Howe, *What Hath God Wrought*, 827; Wilentz, *Rise of American Democracy*, 682–702; Anbinder, *Nativism and Slavery*, 3–126; Wellman, *Road to Seneca Falls*, 183–240; B. S. Anderson, "Lid Comes Off."

81. Donald, *Liberty and Union*, 14 (first two quotations); Parish, *North and the Nation in the Era of the Civil War*, 8 (Beecher quotation); Lincoln, "Speech at Chicago, Illinois," July 10, 1858, *CWL*, 2:499–500; McPherson, *Battle Cry of Freedom*, 133–39.

82. Lincoln, "Speech at Chicago, Illinois," July 10, 1858, *CWL*, 2:499–500.

83. Lincoln, "Speech at Chicago, Illinois," July 10, 1858, *CWL*, 2:500.

84. Lincoln, "Speech at Edwardsville, Illinois," September 11, 1858, and "Definition of Democracy," [August 1, 1858?] ("As I would not be a *slave*" quotation), *CWL*, 3:95, 2:532.

85. Lincoln, "Speech at Chicago, Illinois," July 10, 1858, *CWL*, 2:501.

Chapter 2

1. Lincoln, "Address at Sanitary Fair," April 18, 1864, *CWL*, 7:301.

2. Lincoln, "Address at Sanitary Fair," April 18, 1864, *CWL*, 7:301–2.

3. Lincoln, "Address at Sanitary Fair," April 18, 1864, *CWL*, 7:302. In the service of transparency, I should note that Lincoln delivered his speech shortly after the 1864 Confederate massacre of U.S. Colored Troops at Fort Pillow. This unjust wartime act committed against recently emancipated African American men who enlisted as Union soldiers undoubtedly shaped Lincoln's rhetoric regarding liberty and tyranny. Here Lincoln did not probe the causes of the Civil War, but he had also used myriad occasions in his public life to explore the contested meanings of liberty. See McPherson, *Abraham Lincoln and the Second American Revolution*, 43–64; Carwardine, "Lin-

coln's Horizons"; Porter, "'Last, Best Hope of Earth'"; and J. H. Baker, "Lincoln's Narrative of American Exceptionalism," 33–44.

4. On the meaning of nineteenth-century American liberty, see Hess, *Liberty, Virtue, and Progress*, 5–17.

5. Campbell, "Excess of Isolation"; Potter, *Impending Crisis*, 1–50, 448–84; Morrison, *Slavery and the American West*; Morrison, "American Reaction to European Revolutions"; Roberts, *Distant Revolutions*; Bender, *Nation among Nations*, 116–81; Varon, *Disunion!*; E. Foner, *Free Soil, Free Labor, Free Men*.

6. There is little room available here to catalog the massive literature on Civil War causation. For an introduction to the literature and historiographical schools, see Towers, "Partisans, New History, and Modernization"; and Woods, "What Twenty-First-Century Historians Have Said about the Causes of Disunion." This chapter draws on a recent and vibrant literature that places the early national United States in its broader global context. See Onuf and Onuf, *Nations, Markets, and War*; Guterl, *American Mediterranean*; Rugemer, *Problem of Emancipation*; Roberts, *Distant Revolutions*; Clavin, *Toussaint Louverture and the American Civil War*; Bonner, *Mastering America*; Quigley, *Shifting Grounds*; Schoen, *Fragile Fabric of Union*; McDaniel, *Problem of Democracy in the Age of Slavery*; C. L. Paulus, *Slaveholding Crisis*; Fleche, *Revolution of 1861*; J. L. Huston, *British Gentry, the Southern Planter, and the Northern Family Farmer*; and Eichhorn, *Liberty and Slavery*. On the "slaveholding Union," see Waldstreicher, *Slavery's Constitution*; Van Cleve, *Slaveholders' Union*; Mason, *Slavery and Politics in the Early American Republic*; and Fehrenbacher, *Slaveholding Republic*. For earlier conversations on whether the antebellum North and South were "irreconcilable civilizations," see Campbell, "Excess of Isolation"; Potter, *Impending Crisis*, 1–50, 448–84; McPherson, "Antebellum Southern Exceptionalism"; and Pessen, "How Different from Each Other Were the Antebellum North and South?," 1119–49.

7. On the "Slave Power" conspiracy, see D. B. Davis, *Slave Power Conspiracy and the Paranoid Style*; Richards, *Slave Power*; Slap, *Doom of Reconstruction*, 51–72; Fehrenbacher, *Slaveholding Republic*; Pfau, *Political Style of Conspiracy*; and S.-M. Grant, *North over South*.

8. Hahn, *Political Worlds of Slavery and Freedom*; Rugemer, *Problem of Emancipation*, 25, 42–53; Hunt, *Haiti's Influence on Antebellum America*, 9–19, 21, 34–37, 44, passim; Cleves, *Reign of Terror in America*, 105, 135, 146–49. On the Haitian Revolution, see Dubois, *Avengers of the New World*; Geggus and Fiering, *World of the Haitian Revolution*; Cleves, *Reign of Terror in America*, 9; Kramer, "French Revolution and the Creation of American Political Culture"; Tyrrell, *Transnational Nation*, 12–16; Rugemer, *Problem of Emancipation*; D. B. Davis, *Problem of Slavery in the Age of Emancipation*; C. L. Paulus, *Slaveholding Crisis*; Dun, *Dangerous Neighbors*; Egerton, *Gabriel's Rebellion*; and Sidbury, *Ploughshares into Swords*. Rothman, *Slave Country*; Mason, *Slavery and Politics in the Early American Republic*; and Kornblith, *Slavery and Sectional Strife in the Early American Republic*, all position American sectionalism at the republic's founding rather than with the Missouri Crisis.

9. "Reflections on the Slavery of the Negroes," *Rural Magazine, or Vermont Repository*, June 1796, quoted in Cleves, *Reign of Terror in America*, 135, 104–52; Jay to Elias Boudinot, November 17, 1819, in Jay, *Life of John Jay*, 1:453.

10. McDaniel, *Problem of Democracy in the Age of Slavery*, 33 (Tallmadge quotation); Adams diary entry, November 29, 1820, in Waldstreicher and Mason, *John Quincy Adams and the Politics of Slavery*, 94, 95; Rugemer, *Problem of Emancipation*,

76–77. On the Atlantic abolitionist reform tradition, see Matthews, *Caribbean Slave Revolts and the British Abolitionist Movement*; C. L. Brown, *Moral Capital*; and D. B. Davis, *Problem of Slavery in the Age of Emancipation*. The most recent treatment of the Missouri Crisis is Forbes, *Missouri Compromise and Its Aftermath*, which emphasizes the Union's tradition of political moderation and compromise.

11. Hunt, *Haiti's Influence on Antebellum America*, 127 (both quotations); Rugemer, *Problem of Emancipation*, 45–57, 77–78; L. K. Ford, *Deliver Us from Evil*, 73–75, 106–11, 385–89, 402, 447.

12. Rugemer, *Problem of Emancipation*, 78 (Tallmadge quotation); Varon, *Disunion!*, 39–48; Hunt, *Haiti's Influence on Antebellum America*, 1–8; McDaniel, *Problem of Democracy in the Age of Slavery*, 33–34. For a sampling of the role of race in American politics prior to the Missouri Crisis, see Mason, *Slavery and Politics in the Early American Republic*; Wilentz, *No Property in Man*; and Fehrenbacher, *Slaveholding Republic*.

13. McDaniel, *Problem of Democracy in the Age of Slavery*, 8 (Garrison quotation); Sinha, *Slave's Cause*, 454 (Ray quotation); Hunt, *Haiti's Influence on Antebellum America*, 37–83; Clavin, *Toussaint Louverture and the American Civil War*, 11–29; Dun, *Dangerous Neighbors*, 17–19, 40–51, 77–79, 90–93, 99–120, 125–37, 147–48, 182–99, 201–8, 212–22.

14. Whitemarsh Seabrook, *Concise View of the Critical Situation, and Future Prospects of the Slave-Holding States* (1825), quoted in Varon, *Disunion!*, 52, 50–53; Hunt, *Haiti's Influence on Antebellum America*, 190–20; Rugemer, "Why Civil War?," 18–20; Freehling, *Prelude to Civil War*, 53–69; Sinha, *Counterrevolution of Slavery*, 1–94.

15. Walker, *Walker's Appeal*, 5; Hinks, *To Awaken My Afflicted Brethren*, 1–21, 63–90; Rugemer, *Problem of Emancipation*, 105–8; D. B. Davis, *Problem of Slavery in the Age of Emancipation*, 209–16; C. L. Paulus, *Slaveholding Crisis*, 51–60; Bender, *Nation among Nations*, 93–100.

16. Walker, *Walker's Appeal*, 5, 6, 23.

17. Walker, *Walker's Appeal*, 24, 14; C. L. Paulus, *Slaveholding Crisis*, 54; da Costa, *Crowns of Glory, Tears of Blood*; Kytle and Roberts, *Denmark Vesey's Garden*.

18. Walker, *Walker's Appeal*, 82, 84, 62, 74–75; Bender, *Nation among Nations*, 93–100.

19. Walker, *Walker's Appeal*, 35; D. B. Davis, *Problem of Slavery in the Age of Emancipation*, 209–16.

20. C. L. Paulus, *Slaveholding Crisis*, 68 (Virginian quotation); Onuf, "'To Declare Them a Free and Independent People,'" 33 (Jefferson quotation); Cooper, *Liberty and Slavery*, 178–84; Breen, *Land Shall Be Deluged in Blood*.

21. Hunt, *Haiti's Influence on Antebellum America*, 129 (Legare quotation); Varon, *Disunion!*, 119–20 (Preston quotation); E. Foner, *Nothing but Freedom*, 40–41; C. L. Brown, *Moral Capital*, 165–70, 185–87, 213–14, 217–20, 228–51; Matthews, *Caribbean Slave Revolts and the British Abolitionist Movement*, chaps. 3 and 4; Rugemer, *Problem of Emancipation*, 110–13, 132–42; McDaniel, *Problem of Democracy in the Age of Slavery*, 49–53; Schoen, *Fragile Fabric of Union*, 161–68, 186–87; Karp, *This Vast Southern Empire*, 10–31.

22. Jefferson to St. George Tucker, August 28, 1797, in Geggus, *Haitian Revolution*, 196; W. Johnson, *River of Dark Dreams*, 32; Onuf, "'To Declare Them a Free and Independent People'"; Roberts-Miller, *Fanatical Schemes*, 1–17, 72–102; Rugemer, *Problem of Emancipation*, 148.

23. Cooper, *Liberty and Slavery*, vi, 30–32, 117–19, 136–37, 179–81, 208–10, 219–21, 267–68; Cooper, *South and the Politics of Slavery*, 23–98; Onuf, "Antebellum Southerners and the National Idea," 38–39; O'Brien, *Conjectures of Order*, 2:938–59; Fox-Genovese and Genovese, *Mind of the Master Class*, 88–122, 473–527; Faust, *James Henry Hammond*, 176–77, 201–3; Karp, *This Vast Southern Empire*, 150–72. On colonization as a favored option among moderate slaveholders of the Upper South, see L. K. Ford, *Deliver Us from Evil*, 5–18, 46–48, 55–77, 317–26; Freehling, *Road to Disunion: Secessionists at Bay*, 126–27, 157–61, 188–89, 194–95; and W. Johnson, *River of Dark Dreams*, 151–208.

24. "Harper on Slavery," in *Pro-slavery Argument*, 4, 62, 61, 72, 87, 88 (an abridged version of Harper's writing was also consulted in Gienapp, *Civil War and Reconstruction*, 18–21); W. Johnson, *River of Dark Dreams*, 203–8; Towers, "Partisans, New History, and Modernization," 247–48. Eugene D. Genovese's work on the slaveholding worldview is critical to understanding the shift in slaveholders' arguments. See his *Political Economy of Slavery*; *World the Slaveholders Made*; and especially Fox-Genovese and Genovese, *Mind of the Master Class*.

25. Hammond, "Speech on the Justice of Receiving Petitions for the Abolition of Slavery in the District of Columbia" (1836), 19, 29. C. L. Paulus, *Slaveholding Crisis*, 118–19, instructed on this use of Hammond. See also Faust, *James Henry Hammond*, 48–49, 161–62, 176–77, 194–203, 245–59, 267–85, 291–94.

26. Hammond, "Speech on the Justice of Receiving Petitions for the Abolition of Slavery in the District of Columbia" (1836), 31, 40; C. L. Paulus, *Slaveholding Crisis*, 119–23; Thornton, *Politics and Power in a Slave Society*; L. K. Ford, *Origins of Southern Radicalism*, 99–104, 185–86; Freehling, *Road to Disunion: Secessionists at Bay*, 39–58, 164, 223, 270; Watson, "Conflict and Collaboration"; Quigley, *Shifting Grounds*, 102–5; Towers, "Partisans, New History, and Modernization," 249; McCurry, *Masters of Small Worlds*, 93, 232, 240, 251.

27. Rugemer, "Why Civil War?," 18–26 (quotations, pp. 24, 25); Karp, *This Vast Southern Empire*, 150–72.

28. Rugemer, "Why Civil War?," 20, 23–26. The presidential listing is adopted from Hahn, *Political Worlds of Slavery and Freedom*, 13–14; Fehrenbacher, *Slaveholding Republic*, 15–133, esp. 21–44; Van Cleve, *Slaveholders' Union*, 103–266; Waldstreicher, *Slavery's Constitution*, 4–16, 83–90, 114–24, 144–46; Rothman, *Slave Country*; W. Johnson, *River of Dark Dreams*, 18–45; Karp, *This Vast Southern Empire*, 10–102; Onuf and Onuf, *Nations, Markets, and War*, 103–4; Rael, *Eighty-Eight Years*, 69–79; and Wilentz, *No Property in Man*, 1–20, 97–99, 166, 196.

29. Bonner, *Mastering America*, 5, 25–26 (Chesnut and Hunt quotations); Karp, *This Vast Southern Empire*, 10–69.

30. W. Johnson, *River of Dark Dreams*, 34 (Jackson quotation), 18–45; E. Brown, *Notes on the Origin and Necessity of Slavery*, 5–7; L. K. Ford, *Deliver Us from Evil*, 509–15; Genovese, *Slaveholders' Dilemma*, 80–83.

31. Fehrenbacher, *Slaveholding Republic*, 116–17 (Legare ["moderate" southerner] quotation); Rugemer, *Problem of Emancipation*, 141–42 (Hammond quotation); Cleves, *Reign of Terror in America*, 254–55; Roberts-Miller, *Fanatical Schemes*, 1–4, 11–12, 18–26, 187–88, 191–95, 227–33.

32. Hietala, *Manifest Design*, 67 (Sevier quotation), 10–54, 67–70, 76; Schoen, *Fragile Fabric of Union*, 146–96; Bonner, *Mastering America*, 23–32; Torget, *Seeds of Empire*, 137–218; Silbey, *Storm over Texas*, 6–27.

33. Hietala, *Manifest Design*, 19, 24 (Green and Calhoun quotations).

34. Hietala, *Manifest Design*, 35 (Calhoun quotation).

35. First Adams quotation, diary entry, June 10, 1844, in C. F. Adams, *Memoirs of John Quincy Adams*, 12:49; subsequent Adams quotations in Wilentz, *Rise of American Democracy*, 561; and Sexton, *Monroe Doctrine*, 92–93. Adams's complex views on slavery, abolition, and Union are surveyed in Waldstreicher and Mason, *John Quincy Adams and the Politics of Slavery*; Richards, *Life and Times of Congressman John Quincy Adams*, 54, 88, 152–71, 185–92; Nagel, *John Quincy Adams*, 354–66, 371–92; Parsons, *John Quincy Adams*, 125–26, 143, 160–62, 214–15, 222–33; Cooper, *Lost Founding Father*, 73–77, 170–77, 333–75, 396–417.

36. *Mr. Adams' Speech, on War with Great Britain and Mexico* (1842), 33–35; Oakes, *Freedom National*, 35–40; Carnahan, *Act of Justice*, 6–16, 22–23; Cooper, *Lost Founding Father*, 318, 326, 333, 358.

37. Floan, *South in Northern Eyes*, 55 (Emerson quotation); Morrison, *Slavery and the American West*, 19–25 (remaining quotations, pp. 20, 22).

38. Morrison, *Slavery and the American West*, 14–19 (quotations, p. 19).

39. Emerson, "The Young American" (1844), in Johannsen, *Democracy on Trial*, 10; Howe, *What Hath God Wrought*, 853.

40. *Illinois State Register*, July 17, 1846, quoted in McCaffrey, *Army of Manifest Destiny*, 69; Whitman (May 1846) quoted in Greenberg, *Wicked War*, 96; Neely, *Civil War and the Limits of Destruction*, 6–40; Foos, *Short, Offhand, Killing Affair*.

41. Stephens (1846) quoted in Schroeder, *Mr. Polk's War*, 28; and Howe, *Political Culture of the American Whigs*, 93; Holt, *Rise and Fall of the American Whig Party*, 253–55, McPherson, *Battle Cry of Freedom*, 48–49; Greenberg, *Wicked War*, 188–99, 236–37, 247, 260.

42. Potter, *Impending Crisis*, 6; Bayly, *Birth of the Modern World*, 139; Geyer and Bright, "Where in the World Is America?," 71–79; Bender, *Nation among Nations*, 122–30; Hahn, *Nation without Borders*, 127–69.

43. Bender, *Nation among Nations*, 122–30 (quotation p. 123); Tocqueville, *Democracy in America* (ed. Mansfield and Winthrop), 368–69; McPherson, *Battle Cry of Freedom*, 51 (Emerson quotation); Bayly, *Birth of the Modern World*, 134–47; Potter, *Impending Crisis*, 14–17; Kelly, "European Revolutions of 1848"; Bright, "Where in the World Is America?," 71–79; Hahn, *Nation without Borders*, 127–69.

44. *Congressional Globe*, 29th Congress, 2nd sess., 1847, Appendix, pp. 314–17; McPherson, *Battle Cry of Freedom*, 55; Varon, *Disunion!*, 180–86; Bender, *Nation among Nations*, 116–19; C. L. Paulus, *Slaveholding Crisis*, 185–87.

45. Clay, "Henry Clay's Advice to His Countrymen Relative to the War with Mexico"; Greenberg, *Wicked War*, 222, 233, 263–65.

46. *North Star*, January 21, 1848, in P. Foner, *Life and Writings of Frederick Douglass*, 1:291–96.

47. Calhoun, "Speech and Resolutions on the Restriction of Slavery from the Territories," February 19, 1847, in Wilson and Cook, *Papers of John C. Calhoun*, 24:170, 172, 175; Davis to Malcolm D. Haynes, August 18, 1849, *PJD*, 4:32; C. L. Paulus, *Slaveholding Crisis*, 181–82; Varon, *Disunion!*, 191–94.

48. Calhoun, "Speech and Resolutions on the Restriction of Slavery from the Territories," February 19, 1847, in Wilson and Cook, *Papers of John C. Calhoun*, 24:172, 175; C. L. Paulus, *Slaveholding Crisis*, 181–82; Rugemer, *Problem of Emancipation*, 42–53, 135–36; Roberts-Miller, *Fanatical Schemes*, 28–29, 82–85, 123–29, 151–52.

49. Morrison, "American Reaction to European Revolutions," 118–19, 120 (Calhoun quotations); Genovese, *Slaveholders' Dilemma*, 29 (Huston quotation); Fleche, *Revolution of 1861*, 17–20; Roberts, *Distant Revolutions*, 1–43; Potter, *Impending Crisis*, 15–16; Howe, *What Hath God Wrought*, 792–96.

50. Potter, "Civil War in the History of the Modern World," 292; Tocqueville, *Democracy in America* (ed. Mansfield and Winthrop), 482, 369; Onuf, "Antebellum Southerners and the National Idea," 25–28.

51. Tocqueville, *Democracy in America* (ed. Mansfield and Winthrop), 237, 241; McDaniel, *Problem of Democracy in the Age of Slavery*, 97–99; Howe, *What Hath God Wrought*, 306; Onuf, "Antebellum Southerners and the National Idea," 25–28; Mansfield, "To the Heart of American Exceptionalism."

52. Hahn, *Political Worlds of Slavery and Freedom*, 16 (quotation); Potter, *Impending Crisis*, 1–50, 448–84; Quigley, *Shifting Grounds*; Bonner, *Mastering America*; Morrison, *Slavery and the American West*.

53. A vast literature exists on the Crisis and Compromise of 1850. Leading primers include Potter, *Impending Crisis*, chaps. 3 and 4; Morrison, *Slavery and the American West*, 96–125; Varon, *Disunion!*, 199–231; Bordewich, *America's Great Debate*; and Maizlish, *Strife of Tongues*.

54. Quotation in Morrison, *Slavery and the American West*, 114; J. L. Huston, *British Gentry, the Southern Planter, and the Northern Family Farmer*, 175–82.

55. First quotation in Roberts, "'Revolutions Have Become the Bloody Toy of the Multitude,'" 226; Davis Senate speech, January 26, 1860, in Rowland, *Jefferson Davis, Constitutionalist*, 4:183; Roberts, *Distant Revolutions*, 125–45; Fleche, *Revolution of 1861*, 22–37; Conlin, "Dangerous *Isms* and the Fanatical *Ists*"; Honeck, *We Are the Revolutionists*, 13–37; Levine, *Spirit of 1848*, chaps. 1–3; K. L. Anderson, *Abolitionizing Missouri*, 34–47, 58–70; Messer-Kruse, *Yankee International*, 25, 12.

56. "Speech of Jefferson Davis in Senate Feb. 13 and 14, 1850, on Slavery in the Territories," in Rowland, *Jefferson Davis, Constitutionalist*, 1:265, 266, 299, 300.

57. "Speech of Jefferson Davis in Senate Feb. 13 and 14, 1850, on Slavery in the Territories," in Rowland, *Jefferson Davis, Constitutionalist*, 1:279, 284, 289–90, 303.

58. Adams quoted in Slap, *Doom of Reconstruction*, 52, 51–72; *Weekly Wisconsin* (1848), quoted in J. L. Huston, *British Gentry, the Southern Planter, and the Northern Family Farmer*, 217, 75–128, 160–207, 213–19; Fleche, "Civil War in the Age of Revolution," 10; Honeck, *We Are the Revolutionists*, 10–11, 24–33, 42–79, 109–42; K. L. Anderson, *Abolitionizing Missouri*, 34–47, 60–70. The classic study of free labor is Eric Foner, *Free Soil, Free Labor, Free Men*. An updated account of northern perceptions of the South is S.-M. Grant, *North over South*.

59. Salmon P. Chase to Charles Sumner, September 19, 1849, quoted in Roberts, *Distant Revolutions*, 80, 63–80; Montgomery Blair et al., *Address to the Democracy of Missouri* (1850), quoted in Morrison, *Slavery and the American West*, 111; Gienapp, *Origins of the Republican Party*, 364–72; E. Foner, *Free Soil, Free Labor, Free Men*, 11–39, 73–102; S.-M. Grant, *North over South*, 34, 44, 74–75, 92–94, 99–103, 108, 116, 124–25, 132–49.

60. "William H. Seward's Higher Law Speech," March 11, 1850, in Rozwenc, *Compromise of 1850*, 45–47.

61. "Irrepressible Conflict," October 25, 1858, in G. E. Baker, *Works of William H. Seward*, 4:290, 291, 292, 294, 302.

62. William Gilmore Simms, "Southern Convention—Second Session," and Benja-

min C. Pressley, *Reasons for Dissolution of the Union*, both quoted in Quigley, *Shifting Grounds*, 59, 92; Jennings, *Nashville Convention*, 57–79; Freehling, *Road to Disunion: Secessionists at Bay*, 479–86; Bordewich, *America's Great Debate*, 256–60; Varon, *Disunion!*, 223–30.

63. *Philadelphia Public Ledger*, February 20, 25, 1850, quoted in Varon, *Disunion!*, 215, 210–17; Johnson quoted in Nagel, *One Nation Indivisible*, 266–67.

64. First quotations in Roberts, *Distant Revolutions*, 143, 134–45; Davis to F. H. Elmore, April 13, 1850, in Rowland, *Jefferson Davis, Constitutionalist*, 1:323.

65. Daniel Webster, "Seventh of March Speech," reprinted in Rozwenc, *Compromise of 1850*, 39–41.

66. First Clay quotations in Rozwenc, *Compromise of 1850*, 27; final Clay quotation in Bordewich, *America's Great Debate*, 7, 183–88, 195–96, 205–10, 303–26, 345–46; Remini, *At the Edge of the Precipice*, 68–70, 116–55; Maizlish, *Strife of Tongues*, 16, 28–34, 72–75, 118–19, 127–30, 220–21. A vast literature exists on the Compromise of 1850. For a comprehensive historiographical treatment, see Woods, "Compromise of 1850 and the Search for a Usable Past."

67. Fillmore, Second Annual Message to Congress, December 2, 1851, in Richardson, *Messages of the Presidents*, 5:139; final Fillmore quotations (beginning with "we must endure") in Bordewich, *America's Great Debate*, 356.

68. Potter, *Impending Crisis*, 90–128; Freehling, *Road to Disunion: Secessionists at Bay*, 487–510.

69. Guelzo, *Fateful Lightning*, 72–73; Fehrenbacher, *Slaveholding Republic*, 205–51 (quotation, p. 233); Blackett, *Captive's Quest for Freedom*, 3–134.

70. Floan, *South in Northern Eyes*, 58 (Emerson quotation).

71. Forten journal entries, July 5, 1857, and July 14, 1855, in Stevenson, *Journals of Charlotte Forten Grimké*, 235, 136; D. B. Davis, *Problem of Slavery in the Age of Emancipation*, 130 (Delany quotation); Rael, *Black Identity and Black Protest*, 264 (Douglas quotation).

72. Sinha, *Slave's Cause*, 419 (Garnet quotation); "Christian Anti-slavery Convention," *The Liberator*, August 26, 1859 (remaining quotations); Hahn, *Nation under Our Feet*, 57–75.

73. *The Liberator*, August 26, 1859 (first quotations); Rael, *Black Identity and Black Protest*, 258 (second quotation); Kantrowitz, *More Than Freedom*, 3 (third quotation), 1–9, 171–231. Leading recent works on antebellum African American resistance and identity include Hahn, *Nation under Our Feet*; Rael, *Black Identity and Black Protest*; Rael, *Eighty-Eight Years*; Sinha, *Slave's Cause*; Berlin, *Long Emancipation*; and Blackett, *Captive's Quest for Freedom*.

74. Kerr-Ritchie, "Rehearsal for War," 16; Kerr-Ritchie, *Rites of August First*, 164–89.

75. Sinha, *Slave's Cause*, 381–460 (Garnet quotation, p. 419).

76. Joseph Lumpkin to Howell Cobb (1848), quoted in Bonner, *Mastering America*, 103; North Carolina newspaper quoted in Potter, *Impending Crisis*, 473; H. C. Richardson, *To Make Men Free*, 6; Barney, *Road to Secession*, 109, 121.

77. McCord, "Charity Which Does Not Begin at Home" and "Slavery and Political Economy," in Lounsbury, *Louisa S. McCord*, 325, 456; Fitzhugh, *Sociology for the South*, 226, 230, 236, 244, 245, 246; Quigley, *Shifting Grounds*, 83–86; Kaye, "Second Slavery"; Schoen, *Fragile Fabric of Union*, 197–237; Onuf and Onuf, *Nations, Markets, and War*, 244–77, 309–10, 322–33; Karp, *This Vast Southern Empire*, 103–24, 150–72; Huston, "Theory's Failure."

78. "The Future of the South," *DeBow's Review*, February 1851, 132 (quotations), 132–46; Guelzo, *Fateful Lightning*, 40 (penultimate quotation); "Speech of Hon. James H. Hammond," March 4, 1858, *Northern Visions of Race, Region, and Reform*, accessed November 30, 2018, https://www.americanantiquarian.org/Freedmen/Manu scripts/cottonisking.html; Bonner, *Mastering America*, 4. See also "Stability of the Union," *DeBow's Review*, April 1850, 348–63; "The Black Race in North America," *DeBow's Review*, March 1856, 290–315; W. Johnson, *River of Dark Dreams*, 151–302; Karp, "King Cotton, Emperor Slavery"; Onuf, "Antebellum Southerners and the National Idea"; Mason, "World Safe for Modernity"; Morrison, *Slavery and the American West*, 175–79; May, *Southern Dream of a Caribbean Empire*, 3–76; and Schoen, *Fragile Fabric of Union*, 197–259.

79. "Cotton and Its Prospects," *DeBow's Review*, September 1851, 11:312; May, *Southern Dream of a Caribbean Empire*, 3–76 (Brown quotation, p. 9); Guterl, *American Mediterranean*, 12–46 ("dreams and nightmares" quotation, p. 16), esp. 35–40; May, "'Southern Strategy' for the 1850s"; Bordewich, *America's Great Debate*, 395; Bonner, *Mastering America*, 3–213; Karp, *This Vast Southern Empire*, 50–102, 142–48.

80. Matthew Karp calculates that "men from the future Confederate state served as secretary of war for eleven of fourteen years and secretary of the navy for nine." Meanwhile, slaveholding southerners "occupied nearly three-quarters of the key federal positions in the formulation of military policy" (Karp, *This Vast Southern Empire*, 199, 200–201).

81. Davis to William R. Cannon, December 7, 1855, in Cooper, *Jefferson Davis: Essential Writings*, 115, 116; Karp, *This Vast Southern Empire*, 199–225; Waite, "Jefferson Davis and Proslavery Visions of Empire in the Far West"; Waite, "Slave South in the Far West," 72–124.

82. Quitman (1856) quoted in Guterl, *American Mediterranean*, 24–25, 12–43; Davis to Malcolm D. Haynes, August 18, 1849, *PJD*, 4:44; May, *John A. Quitman*, 236–37, 272–78, 288–96; Sexton, *Monroe Doctrine*, 97–98; W. Johnson, *River of Dark Dreams*, 303–65; Karp, *This Vast Southern Empire*, 50–69, 103–24, 199–225.

83. Cobb (1858) quoted in Guterl, *American Mediterranean*, 36; Douglas (1854) quoted in Morrison, *Slavery and the American West*, 146–47, 142–56.

84. Roberts, *Distant Revolutions*, 172–86; Roberts, "European Revolutions of 1848 and Antebellum Violence in Kansas," 58–68; Richardson, *To Make Men Free*, 6–23.

85. Weston and final quotations in S.-M. Grant, *North over South*, 145, 147; Cleves, *Reign of Terror in America*, 262–63; Roberts, *Distant Revolutions*, 180; Woods, *Emotional and Sectional Conflict*, 152–69; Etcheson, *Bleeding Kansas*, 89–189; Malvasi, "Old Republic and the Sectional Crisis," 466–67; Phillips, *Rivers Ran Backward*, 46–48, 62–88; McDaniel, *Problem of Democracy in the Age of Slavery*, 53–60, 72–73, 100–107.

86. Sumner, *Crime against Kansas*, 5, 30, 29, 31.

87. Sam Houston Senate speech, February 15, 1854, quoted in Williams and Barker, *Writings of Sam Houston*, 5:502; Longfellow quoted in Floan, *South in Northern Eyes*, 73; Lawrence quoted in Abbott, *Cotton and Capital*, 26; Maltz, *Fugitive Slave on Trial*, 54, 65.

88. Gienapp, *Origins of the Republican Party*, 192 (Seward quotation), 71–77, 82–87, 113–14, 131–50, 189–237, 256–68; Potter, *Impending Crisis*, 225–48; Howe, *Political Culture of the American Whigs*, 275–92; E. Foner, *Politics and Ideology in the Age of the Civil War*, 26, 47–53, 73–76, 148–49; Holt, *Rise and Fall of the American Whig Party*, 804–985; Bonner, *Mastering America*, 39, 56, 189, 211.

89. British economist (1862) quoted in Towers, "Partisans, New History, and Modernization," 241; *Five Years' Progress of the Slave Power* (1852) quoted in Nye, "Slave Power Conspiracy," 263; Michigan Republican (1860), quoted in Malvasi, "Old Republic and the Sectional Crisis," 466, 465–68; final quotation from Republican Party Platform of 1856, American Presidency Project, accessed May 5, 2020, https://www.presidency.ucsb.edu/node/273293; McPherson, "What Caused the Civil War?," 17; Kornblith, "Rethinking the Coming of the Civil War," 99; Richards, *Slave Power*; E. Foner, *Free Soil, Free Labor, Free Men*, 97–102; Morrison, *Slavery and the American West*, 165–69, 182–83; D. B. Davis, *Slave Power Conspiracy and the Paranoid Style*; Pfau, *Political Style of Conspiracy*; Woods, *Emotional and Sectional Conflict*, 18, 119–20, 138–41, 146–47, 170; J. L. Huston, *British Gentry, the Southern Planter, and the Northern Family Farmer*, 219–20; S.-M. Grant, *North over South*, 146–74.

90. *Cincinnati Daily Commercial* (1857) quoted in Nye, "Slave Power Conspiracy," 264; Wade quoted in Morrison, *Slavery and the American West*, 163–64; Connecticut congressman quoted in E. Foner, *Free Soil, Free Labor, Free Men*, 101; Wilson, *History of the Rise and Fall of the Slave Power in America*, 1:2; Karp, *This Vast Southern Empire*, 32–69, 173–250; M. S. Jones, *Birthright Citizens*, 131–45.

91. Olmsted, *Cotton Kingdom*, 2:234; Charles Sumner to Francis Bird, September 11, 1857, and Carl Schurz speech, August 1, 1860, both quoted in E. Foner, *Free Soil, Free Labor, Free Men*, 72; J. L. Huston, *British Gentry, the Southern Planter, and the Northern Family Farmer*, 185–239; S.-M. Grant, *North over South*, 12–13, 103–7; Glickstein, *American Exceptionalism, American Anxiety*, 3–9.

92. Gienapp, *Origins of the Republican Party*, 210 (first quotation). The "cordon of freedom" is best captured in recent works by James Oakes. See his *Freedom National*, 25–26, 31–40, 256–300; *Scorpion's Sting*, 13–18, 22–50, 155–56, 175–76; and "When Everybody Knew," 104–16 (Julian quotation, p. 110).

93. D. B. Davis, *Problem of Slavery in the Age of Emancipation*, 317.

94. D. B. Davis, *Problem of Slavery in the Age of Emancipation*, 126–34 (Garnet quotations, p. 129); Kantrowitz, *More Than Freedom*, 3 (final quotation), 253–62.

95. Lincoln at Alton, Illinois, October 15, 1858, and "Eulogy on Henry Clay," July 6, 1852, *CWL*, 3:312, 315, 2:131; Potter, *Impending Crisis*, 339; Porter, "'Last, Best Hope of Earth,'" 213; S. B. Paulus, "America's Long Eulogy for Compromise"; E. Foner, *Fiery Trial*, 60–62; H. C. Richardson, *To Make Men Free*, 1–24.

96. Lincoln, "Resolutions on Behalf of Hungarian Freedom," January 9, 1852, "Debate at Galesburg, Illinois," October 7, 1858, and "Speech at New Haven, Connecticut," March 6, 1860, *CWL*, 2:116, 3:235, 4:24; J. H. Baker, "Lincoln's Narrative of American Exceptionalism," 38 (penultimate quotation); Porter, "'Last, Best Hope of Earth,'" 214; May, *Slavery, Race, and Conquest in the Tropics*, 149–50; Bender, *Nation among Nations*, 121–22, 152, 158–61.

97. Lincoln to Joshua F. Speed, August 24, 1855, *CWL*, 2:323; Guelzo, "Democracy and Nobility"; Paludan, "Emancipating the Republic," 22–24.

98. Lincoln, Peoria Address, October 16, 1854; Speech at Edwardsville, Illinois, September 11, 1858; and Debate with Douglas at Alton, Illinois, October 15, 1858, all in *CWL*, 2:276, 255, 3:92, 307, 308; E. Foner, *Fiery Trial*, 63–73, 104–42.

99. Lincoln, Peoria Address, October 16, 1854; "A House Divided," June 16, 1858; and "Speech at New Haven, Connecticut," March 6, 1860, *CWL*, 2:276, 255, 461, 4:16; J. H. Baker, "Lincoln's Narrative of American Exceptionalism," 38–39.

100. Republican Party Platform of 1856, American Presidency Project, accessed

May 5, 2020, https://www.presidency.ucsb.edu/node/273293; "Fremont and Dayton," *Frederick Douglass's Paper*, August 15, 1856, in Foner and Taylor, *Frederick Douglass*, 339, 342; McPherson, *Battle Cry of Freedom*, 162; Crofts, *Lincoln and the Politics of Slavery*, 53.

101. [John Tyler Jr.], "The Relative Political Statues of North and South," *DeBow's Review*, February 1857, quoted in Bonner, *Mastering America*, 191, 188–91, 205–13; Nicholas W. Battle to R. E. B. Baylor, December 1860, Robert Emmett Bledsoe Baylor Papers, Star of the Republic Museum, Washington, Texas; *Charleston Mercury*, July 13, 1857, quoted in Morrison, *Slavery and the American West*, 174; Messer-Kruse, *Yankee International*, 25–26; Conlin, "Dangerous *Isms* and the Fanatical *Ists*"; Rugemer, "Why Civil War?," 23–26; Egerton, "Slaves' Election"; Rable, "Fighting for Reunion."

102. Powers, "'Worst of All Barbarism,'" 139, 142 (Calhoun quotation); final quotations (1850) in Hunt, *Haiti's Influence on Antebellum America*, 131; and Cleves, *Reign of Terror in America*.

103. W. Johnson, *River of Dark Dreams*, 303–420 (Butler quotation, p. 318); May, *Southern Dream of a Caribbean Empire*, 6 (Alabama periodical quotation), 1–21, 22–189; Freehling, *Road to Disunion: Secessionists Triumphant*, 144, 148, 152, 160–67, 177–84; D. B. Davis, *Problem of Slavery in the Age of Emancipation*, 325–28; Hahn, *Nation without Borders*, 44–77, 156–81, 185–91; Karp, *This Vast Southern Empire*, 173–225; Horne, *Deepest South*, 85–150; Fleche, "Civil War in the Age of Revolution," 13–14.

104. The subhead above is derived from Sidbury, "Saint Domingue in Virginia."

105. W. W. Brown, *St. Domingo*, 32, 38, 37; Guterl, *American Mediterranean*, 41; Kantrowitz, *More Than Freedom*, 238–39; Sinha, *Slave's Cause*, 454–55.

106. W. W. Brown, *St. Domingo*, 37, 38; Guterl, *American Mediterranean*, 41; Kantrowitz, *More Than Freedom*, 238–39; Sinha, *Slave's Cause*, 454–55.

107. Varon, *Disunion!*, 326–35.

108. "Speech of William Lloyd Garrison," December 2, 1859, *The Liberator*, December 16, 1859; McDaniel, *Problem of Democracy in the Age of Slavery*, 225–31.

109. "The Haytians and John Brown," *New York Times*, August 8, 1860, quoted in Guterl, *American Mediterranean*, 40; Redpath quoted in Sinha, *Slave's Cause*, 562, 563; Von Frank, "John Brown, James Redpath, and the Idea of Revolution"; Nudelman, *John Brown's Body*, 14–39.

110. Walther, *Fire-Eaters*, 153, 184, 185 (Rhett and Keitt quotations); Clavin, *Toussaint Louverture and the American Civil War*, 33–54; Quigley, *Shifting Grounds*, 63–77, 103–10; C. V. Woodward, *Burden of Southern History*, 61–68.

111. *Richmond Enquirer*, October 23, 1859; Charles Eliot Norton to Mrs. Edward Twisleton, December 13, 1859, in Norton and Howe, *Letters of Charles Eliot Norton*, 1:201, 197–202 (both sources drawn from Gienapp, *Civil War and Reconstruction*, 53–55); Lincoln, "Speech at New Haven, Connecticut," March 6, 1860, *CWL*, 4:14; Drescher, "Servile Insurrection and John Brown's Body in Europe," 266–69; Varon, *Disunion!*, 326–35; Powers, "'Worst of All Barbarism'"; Sinha, "Revolution or Counterrevolution?"

Chapter 3

1. "Declaration of Immediate Causes Which Induce and Justify the Secession of South Carolina from the Federal Union, December 24, 1860," Avalon Project, accessed May 5, 2020, http://avalon.law.yale.edu/19th_century/csa_scarsec.asp; Stephens, "Cornerstone Address," in Wakelyn, *Southern Pamphlets on Secession*, 402–12. Sinha,

Counterrevolution of Slavery, 187–258; McCurry, *Confederate Reckoning*, 1–37; and Freehling, *Road to Disunion: Secessionists Triumphant*, all argue for the undemocratic nature of secession.

2. Stephens, "Cornerstone Address," in Wakelyn, *Southern Pamphlets on Secession*, 406, 407, 405; McPherson, "Antebellum Southern Exceptionalism"; E. M. Thomas, *Confederacy as a Revolutionary Experience*, 32–57.

3. Lincoln, Annual Address to Congress, December 1, 1862, *CWL*, 5:537.

4. Lincoln, Annual Address to Congress, December 1, 1862, and Special Message to Congress, July 4, 1861, *CWL*, 5:537, 4:426; McPherson, "'Whole Family of Man.'"

5. McPherson, "'Whole Family of Man,'" 208–9; Fleche, *Revolution of 1861*; Doyle, *Cause of All Nations*; Armitage et al., "Interchange"; Fleche, "Civil War in the Age of Revolution."

6. McCurry, *Confederate Reckoning*, 7, 12–13; Potter, "Civil War in the History of the Modern World"; Onuf, "Antebellum Southerners and the National Idea," 25–28; Bender, *Nation among Nations*, 116–75; Fleche, *Revolution of 1861*, 1–8; Doyle, *Cause of All Nations*, 6–7, 88–105; H. Jones, *Blue and Gray Diplomacy*, 28; Bowman, *At the Precipice*, 11.

7. Thomas J. Wharton to Tennessee Legislature (Spring 1861), quoted in Bonner, *Mastering America*, 219, 217–20; Potter, *Impending Crisis*, 448–84; Dew, *Apostles of Disunion*, 74–81; Quigley, *Shifting Grounds*, 106–14, 125–27; Clavin, "Second Haitian Revolution"; Sinha, "Revolution or Counterrevolution?"

8. Curry, "The Perils and Duty of the South," November 26, 1860, in Wakelyn, *Southern Pamphlets on Secession*, 37–38, 39.

9. Curry, "The Perils and Duty of the South," November 26, 1860, in Wakelyn, *Southern Pamphlets on Secession*, 40–42, 46; Bowman, *At the Precipice*, 43–44. On last-minute efforts toward compromise, see Crofts, *Lincoln and the Politics of Slavery*.

10. Curry, "The Perils and Duty of the South," November 26, 1860, in Wakelyn, *Southern Pamphlets on Secession*, 40–42, 46; McPherson, "Antebellum Southern Exceptionalism"; Onuf, "Antebellum Southerners and the National Idea"; Karp, "King Cotton, Emperor Slavery."

11. "A Declaration of the Immediate Causes Which Induce and Justify the Secession of the State of Mississippi from the Federal Union," January 26, 1861, Avalon Project, accessed May 5, 2020, http://avalon.law.yale.edu/19th_century/csa_missec .asp; Rable, *Confederate Republic*, 24–25; Karp, *This Vast Southern Empire*, 235–36.

12. Jonathan Worth to D. G. Worth, May 15, 1861, in J. G. Hamilton, *Correspondence of Jonathan Worth*, 1:144; Rives, "Speech on the Proceedings of the Peace Conference and the State of the Union," March 8, 1861, in Wakelyn, *Southern Pamphlets on Secession*, 372; Stephens, "Speech against Secession," November 14, 1860, in Cleveland, *Alexander H. Stephens*, 699; G. P. Downs, "Mexicanization of American Politics." Freehling, *Road to Disunion: Secessionists at Bay* and *Road to Disunion: Secessionists Triumphant*, provide the most comprehensive treatments on the lack of white southern consensus regarding secession. See also Rable, *Confederate Republic*, 20–38.

13. Sam Houston to H. M. Watkins and Others, November 20, 1860, in Williams and Barker, *Writings of Sam Houston*, 8:195–97; Jonathan Worth to D. G. Worth, May 15, 1861, in J. G. Hamilton, *Correspondence of Jonathan Worth*, 1:144; J. P. Kennedy, *Border States*, 224–25.

14. Rhett, December 24, 1860, quoted in Victor, *History, Civil, Political and Military of the Southern Rebellion*, 1:107; Palmer, "The South: Her Peril and Duty," Novem-

ber 29, 1860, in Wakelyn, *Southern Pamphlets on Secession*, 75, 77; S. A. Channing, *Crisis of Fear*, 281–93; McCurry, *Confederate Reckoning*, 7–13; C. L. Paulus, *Slaveholding Crisis*, 228–34.

15. Davis to the Confederate Congress, April 29, 1861, *OR*, ser. 4, vol. 1, pp. 258–59; "Address of William L. Harris," December 17, 1860, and "Letter of Stephen F. Hale," December 27, 1860, both reproduced in full in Dew, *Apostles of Disunion*, 85, 97–98, 99 (see also 83–103).

16. "George Wythe Randolph's Secessionist Speech," March 16, 1861, in Freehling and Simpson, *Showdown in Virginia*, 59; "Terrors of Submission," *Charleston Mercury*, October 11, 1860, in Dumond, *Southern Editorials on Secession*, 181; Clavin, *Toussaint Louverture and the American Civil War*, 55–73, esp. 62; C. L. Paulus, *Slaveholding Crisis*, 228–34.

17. William H. Holcombe, "A Separate Nationality, or the Africanization of the South" (February 1861), quoted in Guterl, *American Mediterranean*, 66; "James Holcombe's Secessionist Speech," March 20, 1861, in Freehling and Simpson, *Showdown in Virginia*, 65–66; C. L. Paulus, *Slaveholding Crisis*, 11, 198–234.

18. Davis, Inaugural Address as Provisional President, February 18, 1861, in Cooper, *Jefferson Davis: Essential Writings*, 198–99, 202; E. M. Thomas, "Jefferson Davis and the American Revolutionary Tradition"; Fleche, *Revolution of 1861*, 3–4, 80–89; Quigley, *Shifting Grounds*, 131–39; Quigley, "Secessionists in an Age of Secession"; Bowman, *At the Precipice*, 20, 29–30; Tucker, *Newest Born of Nations*.

19. Benjamin, "The Right of Secession," December 31, 1860, and Thornwell, "The State of the Country," January 1861, both in Wakelyn, *Southern Pamphlets on Secession*, 101, 178; Meade, *Address on the Day of Fasting and Prayer* (1861), quoted in Rubin, *Shattered Nation*, 17; Cooper, *Jefferson Davis, American*, 7–8, 338–40, 347–48.

20. Lincoln, First Inaugural Address, March 4, 1861, and Message to Congress in Special Session, July 4, 1861 (penultimate quotation), *CWL*, 4:270, 268, 271, 434; Neely, *Lincoln and the Triumph of the Nation*, 37–56; Gienapp, *Abraham Lincoln and Civil War America*, 78–79; Hess, *Liberty, Virtue, and Progress*, 18–27; Gallagher, *Union War*, 58–59; McClintock, *Lincoln and the Decision for War*, 172–73, 181–89, 195–96, 247–52; Guelzo, "Democracy and Nobility."

21. Diary entry, November 29, 1861, in Nevins and Thomas, *Diary of George Templeton Strong*, 3:66; M. B. Anderson, "Issues of the Civil War" (1861), 136, 137; S.-M. Grant, "'How a Free People Conduct a Long War,'" 136; Fleche, *Revolution of 1861*, 70–75; G. P. Downs, "Mexicanization of American Politics," 393–94; Doyle, "Global Civil War," 2:1104; May, *Slavery, Race, and Conquest in the Tropics*, 227.

22. Lincoln to James T. Hale, January 11, 1861 (first quotation), and Lincoln to William H. Seward, February 1, 1861 (second quotation), both in May, *Slavery, Race, and Conquest in the Tropics*, 215, 199–229; Crofts, *Lincoln and the Politics of Slavery*, 108–10.

23. Lincoln to J. T. Hale, January 11, 1861, in Gienapp, *This Fiery Trial*, 87; Buchanan, Fourth Annual Message to Congress, December 3, 1860, in J. D. Richardson, *Compilation of the Messages and Papers of the Presidents*, 5:627; Paludan, *"People's Contest,"* 12 (final quotation); Hess, *Liberty, Virtue, and Progress*, 4–31; McClintock, *Lincoln and the Decision for War*, 79, 88, 92–95, 101, 124, 143, 171–76, 189–99; Neely, *Lincoln and the Democrats*, 161; Silbey, *Respectable Minority*, 30–40.

24. Earl of Shrewsbury quoted in McPherson, "'Whole Family of Man,'" 214; French official quoted in "Important from Paris," *New York Times*, March 29, 1861 (source de-

rived from Doyle, *Cause of All Nations*, 1, 321n1); *Boston Post*, May 16, 1861, quoted in S.-M. Grant, *North over South*, 153, 153–72, esp. 155; Gallagher, *Union War*, 1–6, 45, 71–74; Doyle, *Cause of All Nations*, 98–105; Blackett, *Divided Hearts*, 89–122; O'Connor, *American Sectionalism in the British Mind*, 122–86; Dubrulle, *Ambivalent Nation*.

25. "The People and the Issue," *New York Times*, April 15, 1861, in Simpson, Sears, and Sheehan-Dean, *Civil War: First Year*, 277; Fleche, *Revolution of 1861*, 60–79; Onuf and Onuf, *Nations, Markets, and War*, 278–307.

26. "The Principle of Civilization," *Harper's Weekly*, April 13, 1861, 226; Clay letter published in *Times* (London), May 20, 1861, quoted in Fleche, *Revolution of 1861*, 67.

27. "Our Southern Rebellion," *New York Herald*, April 20, 1861, quoted in Cleves, *Reign of Terror in America*, 265; Lincoln, Special Message to Congress, July 4, 1861, *CWL*, 4:439; Hess, *Liberty, Virtue, and Progress*, 26; Bowman, *At the Precipice*, 261–87.

28. Doyle, *Cause of All Nations*, 6–7, 88–105; H. Jones, *Blue and Gray Diplomacy*, 28; Bowman, *At the Precipice*, 11; Fleche, *Revolution of 1861*; Sinha, "Revolution or Counterrevolution?"

29. Davis, "Speech in U.S. Senate (Farewell Address), January 21, 1861," in Cooper, *Jefferson Davis: Essential Writings*, 193, 194; Sinha, "Revolution or Counterrevolution?"

30. Davis, First Inaugural Address, February 18, 1861, *PJD*, 7:47 (first and second quotations); Davis, Second Inaugural Address, February 22, 1862, in Cooper, *Jefferson Davis: Essential Writings*, 198–203; McCurry, *Confederate Reckoning*, 11–37.

31. Davis, Second Inaugural Address, in Cooper, *Jefferson Davis: Essential Writings*, 198–203 (first, fourth, and fifth quotations); Davis, First Inaugural Address, *PJD*, 7:49, 46 (second and third quotations); Davis, Speech at Richmond, January 5, 1863, *PJD*, 9:11; Cooper, *Jefferson Davis, American*, 353–55; E. M. Thomas, "Jefferson Davis and the American Revolutionary Tradition," 6–7; Quigley, "Secessionists in an Age of Secession"; Sinha, "Revolution or Counterrevolution?"

32. Jimerson, *Private Civil War*, 8–26 (Hoyt quotation, p. 16); Stephens, Address at Crawfordville, Georgia, November 1, 1862, in Cleveland, *Alexander H. Stephens*, 753–54; Doyle, *Cause of All Nations*, 43; Rubin, "Seventy-Six and Sixty-One," 86–87; Rubin, *Shattered Nation*, 14–25, esp. 17–18; Faust, *Creation of Confederate Nationalism*, 15–16, 21–29; Quigley, *Shifting Grounds*, 128–96.

33. "A Northern Revolution," *Index*, August 27, 1863 (first quotation), and *Richmond Enquirer*, February 11, 1863 (second writer), both quoted in Fleche, *Revolution of 1861*, 102, 103 (see also 80–106); Albert Pike, "State or Province? Bond or Free?" (1861), in Wakelyn, *Southern Pamphlets on Secession*, 348; Quigley, *Shifting Grounds*, 63–77, 128–70; Fleche, *Revolution of 1861*, 80–106; Fleche, "Civil War in the Age of Revolution," 12–14.

34. Robert Toombs to William L. Yancey, Pierre A. Rost, and A. Dudley Mann, March 16, 1861, *Official Records of the Union and Confederate Navies in the War of the Rebellion*, ser. 2, vol. 3, pp. 191–95.

35. "Constitution of the Confederate States, March 11, 1861," Avalon Project, accessed June 12, 2018, http://avalon.law.yale.edu/19th_century/csa_csa.asp; E. M. Thomas, *Confederate Nation*, 62–66; Rable, *Confederate Republic*, 43–63. Hahn, *Nation without Borders*, 4, regards "the 'Confederacy' as a rogue rather than a legitimate state, in good part because no other state power in the world ever recognized it."

36. Davis, Second Inaugural Address, February 22, 1862, in Cooper, *Jefferson Davis: Essential Writings*, 225; Stephens, "Cornerstone Address," in Wakelyn, *Southern Pamphlets on Secession*, 405–7; Stephens, "Speech before the Virginia Secession Convention," April 23, 1861, in Cleveland, *Alexander H. Stephens*, 739.

37. "Our Position and That of Our Enemies," *DeBow's Review*, July 1861, 35; "The Non-slaveholders of the South," *DeBow's Review*, January 1861, 73; "The Future of Our Confederation," *DeBow's Review*, July 1861, 36, 41; W. R. Smith, *History and Debates of the Convention of the People of Alabama* (1861), 223 (Dowdell quotation); McCurry, *Confederate Reckoning*, 11–14, 80; Guterl, *American Mediterranean*, 63–67; Onuf, "Antebellum Southerners and the National Idea," 28–33, 37–42; Onuf and Onuf, *Nations, Markets, and War*, 332–38; Fleche, *Revolution of 1861*, 132–50.

38. Elliott, *Our Cause in Harmony with the Purposes of God in Christ Jesus*, 12–13; Guterl, *American Mediterranean*, 59, 60–71; Rubin, *Shattered Nation*, 100–101; McCurry, *Confederate Reckoning*, 81–84, 218–22; Onuf and Onuf, *Nations, Markets, and War*, 178–79, 338–41.

39. Fitzhugh, "Revolutions of 1776 and 1861 Contrasted," 719, 721, 722, 723; Rubin, "Seventy-Six and Sixty-One," 88–91; Clavin, *Toussaint Louverture and the American Civil War*, 73; Bowman, *At the Precipice*, 65; Onuf, "Antebellum Southerners and the National Idea," 37–42; Bonner, *Mastering America*, 270–87; Fleche, *Revolution of 1861*, 132–50; Onuf and Onuf, *Nations, Markets, and War*, 332–38; E. M. Thomas, *Confederacy as a Revolutionary Experience*, 23–42.

40. Thornwell, *Our Danger and Our Duty*, 3–5; McPherson, "Antebellum Southern Exceptionalism," esp. 431–33; McPherson, *Battle Cry of Freedom*, 234–75; Brettle, "Struggling to Realize a Vast Future," 268–85.

41. Chesnut diary entry, October 1, 1861, in C. V. Woodward, *Mary Chesnut's Civil War*, 204; McCurry, *Confederate Reckoning*, 1–12, 24–40, 78–82, 142, 215–19.

42. My interpretation relies on McCurry, *Confederate Reckoning*, 133–217 (quotation, p. 215). See also Clinton, *Other Civil War*, 81–96; Faust, "Altars of Sacrifice"; Rable, "'Missing in Action'"; Faust, *Mothers of Invention*, 3–7, 17–18, 23–24, 51–78, 93–96, 135–37, 215–19, 231–33; Silber, *Gender and the Sectional Conflict*, 13–20, 41–46, 75–76; and Jones-Rogers, *They Were Her Property*, 151–80. Two recent synthetic treatments include Glymph, *Women's Fight*, and McCurry, *Women's War*.

43. "The Non-slaveholders of the South," *DeBow's Review*, January 1861, 77. E. M. Thomas, *Confederacy as a Revolutionary Experience*; E. M. Thomas, *Confederate Nation*; Gallagher, *Confederate War*; Rubin, *Shattered Nation*; Bernath, *Confederate Minds*; and J. Phillips, *Diehard Rebels*, all demonstrate how Confederates regarded their nation as modern and progressive. See also Majewski, *Modernizing a Slave Economy*, 108–61, esp. 151–55; Bernath, "Confederacy as a Moment of Possibility"; Slap and Towers, introduction to *Confederate Cities*; Gallman, "Regionalism and Urbanism as Problems in Confederate Urban History"; and Moltke-Hansen, "Urban Processes in the Confederacy's Development, Experience, and Consequences."

44. W. C. Davis, *Rhett*, 401 (Rhett quotation); Davis, "Speech at Atlanta," February 16, 1861, *PJD*, 7:44; Bonner, *Mastering America*, 228–41; Guterl, *American Mediterranean*, 54–56; Karp, *This Vast Southern Empire*, 240–50; Waite, "Slave South in the Far West"; Zvengrowski, "They Stood Like the Old Guard of Napoleon"; Brettle, "Fortunes of War."

45. Karp, *This Vast Southern Empire*, 238–50 (Toombs quotation, p. 247); Davis, First Inaugural Address, February 18, 1861, in Cooper, *Jefferson Davis: Essential Writ-*

ings, 200; Waite, "Jefferson Davis and Proslavery Visions of Empire in the Far West"; Frazier, *Blood and Treasure*, 3–22, 48–72; Kerby, *Kirby Smith's Confederacy*, 12–13; Masich, *Civil War in the Southwest Borderlands*, 50–52, 72, 80–82.

46. Stephens, Address at Crawfordville, Georgia, November 1, 1862, in Cleveland, *Alexander H. Stephens*, 755–56; Davis, Message to the Confederate Congress, November 18, 1861, in Cooper, *Jefferson Davis: Essential Writings*, 222; *Charleston Mercury*, June 4, 1861, quoted in H. Jones, *Blue and Gray Diplomacy*, 49 (see also 2–3, 9–20, 31–32, 49, 84, 307, 322); Owsley, *King Cotton Diplomacy*; Crook, *North, the South, and the Powers*, 4–9, 16–21; Schoen, *Fragile Fabric of Union*, 260–69; Fry, *Dixie Looks Abroad*, 76–77; Beckert, *Empire of Cotton*, 242–73, 292–96; Karp, *This Vast Southern Empire*, 226–50.

47. Sexton, *Monroe Doctrine*, 123–39 (Bagby quotation, p. 138); Fitzhugh, "Hayti and the Monroe Doctrine," *DeBow's Review*, August 1861, 131–32; May, *Union, the Confederacy, and the Atlantic Rim*, 1–2; Bonner, *Mastering America*, 298–311; Kelly, "North American Crisis of the 1860s."

48. Kelly, "North American Crisis of the 1860s"; Sexton, *Monroe Doctrine*, 137; Doyle, *Cause of All Nations*, 118–30; H. Jones, *Blue and Gray Diplomacy*, 75–81; Cunningham, *Mexico and the Foreign Policy of Napoleon III*, 1–58. Mexico incurred serious debts from England, France, and Spain during the decades following its independence. All three powers unified in late 1861 as the Tripartite Alliance, sending armed forces to Mexico to collect the unpaid debts. Although Great Britain and Spain ultimately retreated from the continent, fearing war with the United States, the French remained behind. Napoleon admitted in July 1862 that the debt crisis, in concert with the American Civil War, was merely a ruse to justify French intervention in Mexico.

49. Napoleon III (1863), quoted in Schoonover, "Napoleon Is Coming! Maximilian Is Coming?," 117; Hanna and Hanna, *Napoleon III and Mexico*, 3–9, 84–95, 116–43; H. Jones, *Blue and Gray Diplomacy*, 75–81; Doyle, *Cause of All Nations*, 125–30.

50. J. Williams, *Rise and Fall of the Model Republic*, 25–26; Slidell to Mason, June 6, 1862, quoted in Kelly, "North American Crisis of the 1860s," 349, 343–49; Schoonover, *Dollars over Dominion*, 25–47, 78–100; Crook, *North, the South, and the Powers*, 247–48; H. Jones, *Blue and Gray Diplomacy*, 79–80, 294, 307.

51. Fitzhugh, "Hayti and the Monroe Doctrine," *DeBow's Review*, August 1861, 131; Henry St. Paul, *Our Home and Foreign Policy* (1863), quoted in Bonner, *Mastering America*, 304–5; Fry, *Dixie Looks Abroad*, 99; Kelly, "North American Crisis of the 1860s," 353–56. Hess, *Liberty, Virtue, and Progress*; S.-M. Grant, *North over South*; Gallagher, *Union War*; and A. I. P. Smith, *Stormy Present*, are all leading works on the ideological meaning of Union.

52. Lincoln, First Inaugural Address, March 4, 1861, *CWL*, 4:271; final quotation in McPherson, "Introduction: Last Best Hope for What?," 3.

53. Lincoln, First Inaugural Address, March 4, 1861, "Message to Congress in Special Session," July 4, 1861, and First Annual Message to Congress, December 3, 1861, all in *CWL*, 4:268, 438, 5:51; J. H. Baker, "Lincoln's Narrative of American Exceptionalism," 40–41; Gallagher, *Union War*, 48–50.

54. Lincoln, "Message to Congress in Special Session," July 4, 1861, *CWL*, 4:426; McPherson, "'Whole Family of Man,'"; Doyle, *Cause of All Nations*, 51–55; Fleche, *Revolution of 1861*, 60–79; McPherson, "'For a Vast Future Also.'"

55. Lincoln, Second Annual Message to Congress, December 1, 1861, *CWL*, 5:537; "Garibaldi and His Braves," *New York Times*, October 5, 1862, quoted in Doyle, "Global

Civil War," 2:1105–6, 1103–14; Doyle, *Cause of All Nations*, 93–98; McPherson, "Introduction: Last Best Hope for What?"; Gallagher, *Union War*, 2–4, 37, 48–53; Onuf and Onuf, *Nations, Markets, and War*, 1–8, 173–81, 340, 352; Potter, "Civil War in the History of the Modern World," 289, 295–99; Fleche, *Revolution of 1861*, 60–79, 107–31; Bender, *Nation among Nations*, 150–64.

56. "Why Immigration Increases," *Harper's Weekly*, May 23, 1863, 322; Gallagher, *Union War*, 72–73; Fleche, *Revolution of 1861*, 60–79, 107–31; S.-M. Grant, *North over South*, 153–72.

57. Hess, *Liberty, Virtue, and Progress*, 18–31 (Child quotations, p. 27).

58. Shedd, *Union and the War*, 24; Lieber, *What Is Our Constitution?*, 12; Grant, "'How a Free People Conduct a Long War,'" 136–37, 142.

59. Lieber, *What Is Our Constitution?*, 33; Grant, "'How a Free People Conduct a Long War,'" 136–37, 142.

60. Lincoln, First Inaugural Address, March 4, 1861, *CWL*, 4:268; Doyle, *Cause of All Nations*, 54–55; Fleche, *Revolution of 1861*, 65–69.

61. William H. Seward to Cassius M. Clay, May 6, 1861, and to William L. Dayton, April 22, 1861, in G. E. Baker, *Works of William H. Seward*, 5:250–51 (first quotation), 228 (second quotation); final Seward quotation (1862) in Fleche, *Revolution of 1861*, 73, 69–70, 73; Bowman, *At the Precipice*, 85.

62. First Seward quotation in Sexton, *Monroe Doctrine*, 123; Seward to Cassius M. Clay, May 6, 1861, in G. E. Baker, *Works of William H. Seward*, 5:250–51 (remaining quotations); Doyle, *Cause of All Nations*, 50–82; H. Jones, *Blue and Gray Diplomacy*, 20–31, 58; Bayly, *Birth of the Modern World*, 162.

63. Schurz to William H. Seward, September 14, 1861, in Bancroft, *Speeches, Correspondence and Political Papers of Carl Schurz*, 1:184, 186–88; Doyle, *Cause of All Nations*, 69–71.

64. Lincoln, First Inaugural Address, March 4, 1861, and Annual Message to Congress, December 3, 1861, *CWL*, 4:263, 5:49; Doyle, *Cause of All Nations*, 69; Fleche, *Revolution of 1861*, 60–79, 107–10; Crofts, *Lincoln and the Politics of Slavery*, 1–16, 235–39, 264–68.

65. Schurz to William H. Seward, September 14, 1861, in Bancroft, *Speeches, Correspondence and Political Papers of Carl Schurz*, 1:186, 190; Doyle, *Cause of All Nations*, 69.

66. Douglass, "How to End the War" (May 1861), in Simpson, Sears, and Sheehan-Dean, *Civil War: First Year*, 333–35 (first three quotations); Douglass, "The War and How to End It" (March 25, 1862), in Sears, *Civil War: Second Year*, 144–54 (remaining quotations).

67. H. Jones, *Blue and Gray Diplomacy*, 113–213 (British critic quotation, p. 133), 253.

68. Motley to William H. Seward, August 26, 1862, in Sears, *Civil War: Second Year*, 377–81; Lincoln, "Reply to Emancipation Memorial Presented by Chicago Christians of all Denominations," September 13, 1862, *CWL*, 5:424; "'Conservatism,'" *Harper's Weekly*, July 30, 1864, 482; A. I. P. Smith, *Stormy Present*, 190–99.

69. Lincoln to Horace Greeley, August 22, 1862, *CWL*, 5:388; Gallagher, "Civil War Watershed"; Gallagher, *Union War*, 88–90; McPherson, *Battle Cry of Freedom*, 857–58; Brasher, *Peninsula Campaign and the Necessity of Emancipation*, 68–71, 179–80, 197–216; Fredrickson, *Big Enough to Be Inconsistent*, 98–100; E. Foner, *Fiery Trial*, 208–36; Guelzo, *Lincoln's Emancipation Proclamation*, 3–10, 22, 201.

70. Lincoln, Annual Message to Congress, December 1, 1862, and "Reply to Emancipation Memorial Presented by Chicago Christians of All Denominations," September 13, 1862, *CWL*, 5:537, 536, 423–24. See chapter 4 for an extended discussion of emancipation as "military necessity."

71. Lincoln, Annual Message to Congress, December 1, 1862, *CWL*, 5:537; Gallagher, *Union War*, 50–52; Potter, "Civil War in the History of the Modern World," 289, 295–98; A. I. P. Smith, *Stormy Present*; Ross, "Historical Consciousness in Nineteenth-Century America," 910; Ross, "Lincoln and the Ethics of Emancipation."

72. Lester, *Light and Dark of the Rebellion*, 10; "The Irrepressible Conflict Again," *Harper's Weekly*, February 21, 1863, 114; Schurz, "Peace, Liberty, and Empire," September 16, 1864, in Bancroft, *Speeches, Correspondence and Political Papers of Carl Schurz*, 1:308; Fleche, *Revolution of 1861*, 118–31; Bender, *Nation among Nations*, 168–69; Doyle, *Cause of All Nations*, 245; Gallagher, *Union War*, 67; Hess, *Liberty, Virtue, and Progress*, 67.

73. Douglass, "Emancipation Proclaimed" (October 1862), in Foner and Taylor, *Frederick Douglass*, 517, 520; Shedd, *Union and the War*, 31, 32; Emerson, "American Civilization," *Atlantic Monthly*, April 1862, 509, 511.

74. "Recognition of Haytian and Liberian Independence a Step in Advance," *New York Times*, February 5, 1862, 4; H. C. Richardson, *Greatest Nation of the Earth*, 213–19, 221–25; H. Jones, *Blue and Gray Diplomacy*, 161; Guelzo, *Fateful Lightning*, 176–77; Hahn, *Nation without Borders*, 252–55, 275, 304–5; K. Masur, *Example for All the Land*.

75. Lincoln, First Annual Message to Congress, December 3, 1861, *CWL*, 5:52–53; Guelzo, *Fateful Lightning*, 230–31 (final quotation, p. 231); H. C. Richardson, *Greatest Nation of the Earth*, 144–49, 154–62, 176–87, 196–98, 202–6; Doyle, *Cause of All Nations*, 176–81; Brettle, "Struggling to Realize a Vast Future," 268–85.

76. "The Work Done by Congress," *Harper's Weekly*, March 14, 1863, 162; McPherson, "Introduction: Last Best Hope for What?," 8 (Lincoln quotation); Henry Adams to Charles Francis Adams Jr., January 23, 1863, in W. C. Ford, *Cycle of Adams Letters*, 1:243; McPherson, "'Whole Family of Man,'" 217–22; Doyle, *Cause of All Nations*, 213–15; H. Jones, *Blue and Gray Diplomacy*, 123–24.

77. Stillé, *Northern Interests and Southern Independence*, 7, 6; Lincoln, Annual Message to Congress, December 1, 1862, *CWL*, 5:521; Kelly, "Lost Continent of Abraham Lincoln," 223–48, esp. 223–26.

78. Lincoln to the Workingmen of Manchester, England, January 19, 1863; to Ohio regiments, August 18 and 22, 1864; and Annual Message to Congress, December 1, 1861, all in *CWL*, 6:64, 7:505, 512, 5:52–53; Potter, "Civil War in the History of the Modern World"; Fleche, *Revolution of 1861*, 107–11; Neely, *Last Best Hope of Earth*, 112–13; McPherson, "'Whole Family of Man,'" 217–22; Doyle, *Cause of All Nations*, 213–15; H. Jones, *Blue and Gray Diplomacy*, 123–24; Brettle, "Struggling to Realize a Vast Future," 268–85; Blackburn, "Lincoln and Marx"; Blackburn, *An Unfinished Revolution*.

79. Johnson to Lincoln, July 31, 1863, in Simpson, *Civil War: Third Year*, 426; Jacobs to Lydia Maria Child, March 18, 1863, in Ripley, *Black Abolitionist Papers*, 5:193, 194; J. Downs, *Sick from Freedom*, 18–41; A. M. Taylor, *Embattled Freedom*, 8–9, 22, 44–49, 78–84, 108–12, 122, 133–58, 201–10, 233–35; R. Newman, "Grammar of Emancipation."

80. These ideas are explored in greater detail in chapters 5 and 7. Jacobs to Lydia

Maria Child, March 18, 1863, in Ripley, *Black Abolitionist Papers*, 5:193; Clinton, *Other Civil War*, 88 (Forten quotation); Litwack, *Been in the Storm So Long*, 19–27, 41–63, 169–78, 212–40, 286–87, 292–302, 327–34, 468–500; Berlin, *Long Emancipation*, 52–66, 161–65; Glymph, *Out of the House of Bondage*, 87–149, 206–23; Sinha, *Slave's Cause*, 564–85; Hunter, *Bound in Wedlock*, 137–51, 184–95; Stevenson, "'Us Never Had No Big Funerals or Weddin's on de Place,'" and Glymph, "Black Women and Children in the Civil War," both in Blight and Downs, *Beyond Freedom*, 39–59, 121–35; A. M. Taylor, *Embattled Freedom*, 19–20, 27–40, 41–46, 53–54, 113–14, 126–37, 176–82, 192–200, 211–20, 245–46; Rose, *Rehearsal for Reconstruction*, 21–30, 78, 85–89, 93, 161–89, 200–236, 272–96, 305–6, 331–35, 353–58, 372–74; Glymph, *Women's Fight*, 87–122, 221–50.

81. Giesberg, *Army at Home*, 13 (quotation), 8–15, 20–34, 68–91, 120–26, 136–42; Clinton, *Other Civil War*, 81–96; McPherson, *Battle Cry of Freedom*, 480–83; Silber, *Daughters of the Union*, 115, 162–63, 174–213.

82. Stanton and Anthony, "Appeal to the Women of the Republic," March 1863, in Stanton et al., *History of Woman Suffrage*, 2:53; Silber, *Gender and the Sectional Conflict*, 25–66 (quotation, p. 42); R. Mitchell, *Vacant Chair*, 72–75, 102–3, 153–66; Silber, *Daughters of the Union*, 2–40, 170–272; Glymph, *Women's Fight*, 127–95.

83. "Foreign Intervention in American Affairs," *New York Times*, April 1, 1861; "Colonization of Discrowned Heads in America," *New York Times*, March 5, 1862, quoted in Doyle, *Cause of All Nations*, 118; Schoonover, *Dollars over Dominion*, 101–77 (Stevens quotation, p. 118); Joshua Leavitt (northern reformer), July 19, 1865, quoted in Kelly, "North American Crisis of the 1860s," 339; Bayly, *Birth of the Modern World*, 162; Sexton, *Monroe Doctrine*, 143–44; Crook, *North, the South, and the Powers*, 262–65, 331–43; Hanna and Hanna, *Napoleon III and Mexico*, 47–68, 116–43, 199–208; H. Jones, *Blue and Gray Diplomacy*, 75–80, 126–30, 146, 167–75, 255–67; 297–99, 306–19.

84. H. Jones, *Blue and Gray Diplomacy*, 20–31, 58, 285–320 (Seward quotation, p. 311); Kelly, "North American Crisis of the 1860s"; Townsend, *Yankee Invasion of Texas*, 107–22; Schoonover, *Dollars over Dominion*, 140–77; Masich, *Civil War in the Southwest Borderlands*, 107, 203; Sexton, *Monroe Doctrine*, 123.

85. Lincoln, Gettysburg Address, November 19, 1863, *CWL*, 7:23; Doyle, *Cause of All Nations*, 281–84; Kelly, "Lost Continent of Abraham Lincoln," 223–26, 238–48; E. Foner, *Free Soil, Free Labor, Free Men*, 72; Litke, *Twilight of the Republic*, 99–108; Fredrickson, *Big Enough to Be Inconsistent*, 123–24.

86. Lincoln, Gettysburg Address, November 19, 1863, *CWL*, 7:23; Doyle, *Cause of All Nations*, 281–84; Litke, *Twilight of the Republic*, 99–108; Fredrickson, *Big Enough to Be Inconsistent*, 123–24; Gallagher, *Union War*, 85–87.

87. Lincoln, "Memorandum Concerning His Probable Failure of Re-election," August 23, 1864, *CWL*, 7:514; McClellan to Democratic Nomination Committee, September 8, 1864, in Sears, *Civil War Papers of George B. McClellan*, 595; Neely, *Last Best Hope of Earth*, 157–81; Gienapp, *Abraham Lincoln and Civil War America*, 165–76; Guelzo, *Fateful Lightning*, 462–64.

88. Gallagher and Waugh, *American War*, 130 (Republican campaign poster quotation); Lieber, "Lincoln or McClellan: Appeal to German Americans" (October 1864), in Sheehan-Dean, *Civil War: Final Year*, 450–53; Letter of "Africano," September 2, 1864, in Redkey, *Grand Army of Black Men*, 213; Silbey, *Respectable Minority*, 118–57; Paludan, *"People's Contest,"* 92–93, 245–57, 311–12; Gallagher, *Union War*, 60, 64, 77, 91, 108.

89. Lincoln, "Response to a Serenade," November 10, 1864, *CWL*, 8:100–101;

McClellan to Samuel L. M. Barlow, November 10, 1864, and to Robert C. Winthrop, November 16, 1864, both in Sears, *Civil War Papers of George B. McClellan*, 618, 622; Neely, *Last Best Hope of Earth*, 173–74; J. W. White, *Emancipation, the Union Army, and the Reelection of Abraham Lincoln*, 98–128.

Chapter 4

1. Winfield Scott to William H. Seward, March 3, 1861, in W. Scott, *Memoirs of Lieut.-General Scott*, 2:627; Grimsley, *Hard Hand of War*, 26–27.

2. Diary entries, April 17 and 22, 1861, in J. B. Jones, *Rebel War Clerk's Diary*, 1:22, 25, 26.

3. McClellan to Abraham Lincoln, July 7, 1862, *OR*, ser. 1, vol. 11, pt. 1, pp. 73–74.

4. Lincoln to James C. Conkling, August 20, 1863, *CWL*, 6:408.

5. Hsieh, *West Pointers and the Civil War*; Foote, "Civilization and Savagery in the American Civil War"; Sheehan-Dean, *Calculus of Violence*.

6. Hsieh, *West Pointers and the Civil War*; Gallagher, *Confederate War*, 126–28, 142–53; Gallagher, *Union War*, 119–50; Gallagher and Meier, "Coming to Terms with Civil War Military History," 488, 492–93; Neely, *Civil War and the Limits of Destruction*; Hsieh, "Total War and the American Civil War Reconsidered"; Foote, "Civilization and Savagery in the American Civil War"; Dilbeck, *More Civil War*; Lang, *In the Wake of War*; and Sheehan-Dean, *Calculus of Violence*. Andrew Zimmerman provides a useful counterpoint to my argument in demonstrating how German "Forty-Eighters" who settled in the United States in the wake of the 1848 revolutions employed radical war-making tactics to target private property and subvert the rule of law to dismantle the American and Confederate slave power. In this way, stalwart egalitarians and even European socialists radicalized the Union war effort. See Zimmerman, "From the Rhine to the Mississippi"; Zimmerman, "From the Second American Revolution to the First International and Back Again"; and Fleche, *Revolution of 1861*, 144–47.

7. McPherson, "From Limited to Total War in America," 298, 295–309. See also Paludan, *Victims*; Stout, *Upon the Altar of the Nation*; Royster, *Destructive War*; Faust, *This Republic of Suffering*; Stout, *Upon the Altar of the Nation*; Nelson, *Ruin Nation*; and Sternhell, "Revisionism Reinvented?" My argument derives from Mark E. Neely's contention that "what at first may seem … [like] the degeneration of warfare, in fact proves the belief of the protagonists in rules and codes of civilized behavior which have in the twentieth century long since vanished from the world's battlefields. The real point is that Union and Confederate authorities were in substantial agreement about the laws of war, and they usually tried to stay within them" ("Was the Civil War a Total War?," esp. 13). Hsieh, "Total War and the American Civil War Reconsidered," esp. 395–96; Lee, *Barbarians and Brothers*, 1–11, 232–45; Lee, "Mind and Matter"; Dilbeck, *More Civil War*; Sheehan-Dean, *Calculus of Violence*.

8. Wayne E. Lee argues, "Only rarely is war truly unrestrained, fought without let or hindrance." Indeed, "no single atrocity defines the violence of an entire war" (Lee, *Barbarians and Brothers*, 10). Wayne Hsieh also observes, "Historians still resort too readily to broad-brush narratives such as the rise of total war, obscuring the limitations on and the political context of Civil War violence" ("Total War and the American Civil War Reconsidered," 396). Grimsley, *Hard Hand of War*, remains the standard interpretation of the "hard war" thesis, while Sheehan-Dean, *Calculus of Violence*, sets the standard for contextualizing the culture, scope, and meaning of Civil War–era mili-

tary conduct. On the Civil War as unjust, see Rosenberg, "Toward a New Civil War Revisionism"; and Stout, *Upon the Altar of the Nation*.

9. Geyer and Bright, "Global Violence and Nationalizing Wars in Eurasia and America," 638–43; J. Q. Whitman, *Verdict of Battle*, 1–24, esp. 22; Black, *War in the Nineteenth Century*, 1–4, 5–59.

10. Bellamy, *Massacres and Morality*, 42–98 (quotations, p. 70); Black, *War in the Nineteenth Century*, 1–5, 34, 42, 52–59; Geyer and Bright, "Global Violence and Nationalizing Wars in Eurasia and America," 622, 626–28, 638–43; Bender, *Nation among Nations*, 131–33; Maslowski, "300-Years War"; Egerton, "Rethinking Atlantic Historiography in a Postcolonial Era"; Fleche, "Civil War in the Age of Revolution"; Tyrrell, *Transnational Nation*, 95–106.

11. J. T. Johnson, *Just War Tradition*, 8–9, 78–94, 102, 112, 149; Preston, Roland, and Wise, *Men in Arms*, 175–79; Neff, *War and the Law of Nations*, 87–98, 100–108, 112–17, 122–25, 139, 147, 151–54; Lee, *Barbarians and Brothers*, 188–93, 201–2, 223, 234; Bender, *Nation among Nations*, 130–33; Sheehan-Dean, *Calculus of Violence*, 35–40.

12. Vattel, *Law of Nations*, 283, 295; Neff, *War and the Law of Nations*, 114, 112; Sheehan-Dean, *Calculus of Violence*, 17, 35–41.

13. Förster and Nagler, *On the Road to Total War*, 4–5; J. Q. Whitman, *Verdict of Battle*, 1–24, 234–37; J. T. Johnson, *Just War Tradition*, xxii–xxiii; McPherson, "Was It a Just War?," 16–18; Sheehan-Dean, *Calculus of Violence*, 26–35.

14. Halleck, *International Law*, 327; J. T. Johnson, *Just War Tradition*, 299 (Lieber quotation); Dilbeck, *More Civil War*, 5; Sheehan-Dean, *Calculus of Violence*, 16–17, 27–32. My discussion of Halleck and Lieber relies heavily on J. T. Johnson, *Just War Tradition*.

15. Halleck, *International Law*, 427; J. T. Johnson, *Just War Tradition*, 300–301 (Lieber quotation).

16. Halleck, *International Law*, 464, 399, 466; J. T. Johnson, *Just War Tradition*, 302 (Lieber quotation); Hennessy, "Looting and Bombardment of Fredericksburg," 132, 141.

17. Foote, "Civilization and Savagery in the American Civil War," 23; Sheehan-Dean, *Calculus of Violence*, 9–10, 27–45, 63–66, 67–72, 356; Hsieh, "Total War and the American Civil War Reconsidered," 400–402; Dilbeck, *More Civil War*, 1–11; Neely, *Civil War and the Limits of Destruction*, 1–5, 198–220; D. B. Davis, *Revolutions*, chaps. 2–3; Gemme, *Domesticating Foreign Struggles*.

18. Lincoln, Second Inaugural Address, March 4, 1865, and First Annual Message to Congress, December 3, 1861, both in *CWL*, 8:332, 5:51; "By the President of the United States: A Proclamation," April 15, 1861, *OR*, ser. 3, vol. 1, pp. 67–68; McClintock, *Lincoln and the Decision for War*, 226–80; A. I. P. Smith, *Stormy Present*, 173–78; Sheehan-Dean, *Calculus of Violence*, 34.

19. Shedd, *Union and the War*, 15, 16; Bishop John Joseph Hughes to Patrick Neeson Lynch, 1861, in Freidel, *Union Pamphlets*, 1:124; Stillé, *How a Free People Conduct a Long War*, 3, 39–40; Sheehan-Dean, *Calculus of Violence*, 66.

20. Emerson, "American Civilization," *Atlantic Monthly*, April 1862, 507; *Preservation of the Union*, 6, 7; James Shields to George B. McClellan, January 10, 1862, *OR*, ser. 1, vol. 5, p. 702; Grimsley, *Hard Hand of War*, 9–10; Fleche, *Revolution of 1861*, 125–31.

21. Jefferson Davis, First Inaugural Address, February 18, 1861, and Second Inaugural Address, February 22, 1862, both in Cooper, *Jefferson Davis: Essential Writings*, 200, 226.

22. Davis, Speech to the Confederate Congress, April 29, 1861, *OR*, ser. 4, vol. 1, p. 268.

23. Joint Resolutions of the Confederate Congress, January 22, 1864, *OR*, ser. 4, vol. 3, pp. 126–28; Kate Cumming diary entry, September 13, 1863, in Harwell, *Kate*, 142; Lee to Davis, July 6, 1864, in Dowdey and Manarin, *Wartime Papers of Robert E. Lee*, 816; Quigley, *Shifting Grounds*, 181–87.

24. Parish, *North and the Nation in the Era of the Civil War*, 171–95; Dilbeck, *More Civil War*, 6–7, 78–80, 99–100, 123–27; Rable, *God's Almost Chosen Peoples*, 52–56; Miller, Stout, and Wilson, *Religion and the American Civil War*, 3–19; Paludan, "Religion and the American Civil War"; Stout, *Upon the Altar of the Nation*, xiii–xiv, 186, 259–60, 457; Wright and Dresser, *Apocalypse and the Millennium in the American Civil War Era*, 1–12; Noll, *Civil War as a Theological Crisis*, 14–16, 159–62; Faust, *This Republic of Suffering*, 32–60.

25. Lincoln, Second Inaugural, March 4, 1865, Avalon Project, accessed February 2, 2018, http://avalon.law.yale.edu/19th_century/lincoln2.asp; W. O. White, *"Our Struggle Righteous in the Sight of God"*; Noll, *America's God*, 6–7, 425–35; White, "Lincoln's Sermon on the Mount," in Miller, Stout, and Wilson, *Religion and the American Civil War*, 208–27.

26. Bellows, *State and the Nation*, 4, 5, 12, 13, 14; Lincoln, "Proclamation Appointing a National Fast Day," March 30, 1863, *CWL*, 6:155–56; Rable, *God's Almost Chosen Peoples*, 56; Parish, *North and the Nation in the Era of the Civil War*, 174–75, 181; Noll, *Civil War as a Theological Crisis*, 18, 20, 61, 87–90; Fredrickson, "Coming of the Lord," in Miller, Stout, and Wilson, *Religion and the American Civil War*, 110–30; Gamble, *Fiery Gospel*, 50–52, 65–67, 70–78.

27. Bushnell, "Our Obligations to the Dead" (July 26, 1865), 319, 341, 355; Faust, *This Republic of Suffering*, 3–60, 190–91, 211–12; Rable, *God's Almost Chosen Peoples*, 89, 359.

28. Davis, Second Inaugural Address, February 22, 1862, in Cooper, *Jefferson Davis: Essential Writings*, 228–29; Luker, "God, Man and the World of James Warley Miles," 101 (Thornwell quotation); Rubin, *Shattered Nation*, 37–38; Conlin, "Dangerous *Isms* and the Fanatical *Ists*."

29. Elliott, *Our Cause in Harmony with the Purposes of God in Christ Jesus*, 6–7; Rable, *God's Almost Chosen Peoples*, 47, 59, 76, 188, 190; Faust, *Creation of Confederate Nationalism*, 23–31, 60–62, 75–77, 82–83; Rubin, *Shattered Nation*, 61–64; Noll, *Civil War as a Theological Crisis*, 37–39.

30. First Miles quotation in Rable, *God's Almost Chosen Peoples*, 54, 52–56; Miles, *God in History*, March 29, 1863, 24, 26; Harlow, *Religion, Race, and the Making of Confederate Kentucky*, 166–71; Noll, *Civil War as a Theological Crisis*, 51–74, 81–84, 119–20.

31. Sheehan-Dean, *Calculus of Violence*, 26–43; Neely, "Was the Civil War a Total War?"; Neely, "'Civilized Belligerents,'" 3–23; Foote, "Civilization and Savagery in the American Civil War."

32. Vattel, *Law of Nations*, 339, 336–40; Neff, *War and the Law of Nations*, 250–61, 272–73, 362–65, 375–76; Onuf and Onuf, *Nations, Markets, and War*, 345–46; Sheehan-Dean, *Calculus of Violence*, 12–43.

33. "The Necessity of War," *Harper's Weekly*, August 17, 1861, 514; diary entry, August 17, 1862, in Welles, *Diary of Gideon Welles*, 1:86.

34. Lincoln, Annual Message to Congress, December 3, 1861, *CWL*, 5:49; Dilbeck, *More Civil War*, 8–9 (Senator Thomas A. Hendricks quotation); Neff, *War and the Law of Nations*, 249–64; Grimsley, *Hard Hand of War*, 11–22, 30; Blair, *With Malice toward Some*, 66–99, esp. 67, 86; Carnahan, *Lincoln on Trial*, 9–34; Neff, *Justice in Blue and Gray*, 4–5, 19–21, 28, 113–26, 193–94, 210–11; Sheehan-Dean, *Calculus of Violence*, 28–32.

35. Seward to Charles Francis Adams, May 21, 1861, *CWL*, 4:379; *Prize Cases* (1863) quotation and final quotation in Neff, *War and the Law of Nations*, 259, 257–64; Paludan, *"People's Contest,"* 304; Blair, *With Malice toward Some*, 73–79, 85–89, 95–99; Neff, *Justice in Blue and Gray*, 24–28, 32–34; Sheehan-Dean, *Calculus of Violence*, 28–32; "Blockade of Confederate Ports," Office of the Historian, U.S. Department of State, accessed May 3, 2019, https://history.state.gov/milestones/1861-1865/blockade; Onuf and Onuf, *Nations, Markets, and War*, 346. On the *Trent* Affair, see H. Jones, *Blue and Gray Diplomacy*, 83–92, 341–42; Doyle, *Cause of All Nations*, 47–48, 76–81, 145–48; A. Foreman, *World on Fire*, 172–98.

36. "Notes of the Rebellion," *New York Times*, July 1, 1861; "Democracy on Trial," May 10, 1862, 290, "The State and National Governments," September 19, 1863, 594, and "Fighting for Our Foes," July 30, 1864, 483, all in *Harper's Weekly*; Grimsley, *Hard Hand of War*, 30; Varon, *Armies of Deliverance*, 1–14, 105–62, 235–36, 298–324, 358–59.

37. Bledsoe, *Citizen-Officers*, 1–24; Herrera, *For Liberty and the Republic*, 1–26; Gallagher, *Union War*, 3, 16–17, 23–27, 120–24; McPherson, *For Cause and Comrades*, 30–36; Gallagher and Meier, "Coming to Terms with Civil War Military History," 498–99; Lang, *In the Wake of War*, 1–14; Grimsley, "Surviving Military Revolution," 78–79; Coffman, "Duality of the American Military Tradition."

38. Grimsley, *Hard Hand of War*, 185–86, 222–25; R. Mitchell, *Civil War Soldiers*, 1–23; R. C. Snyder, *Citizen-Soldiers and Manly Warriors*, 1–13; McPherson, *For Cause and Comrades*, 1–29, 90–116; Hess, *Liberty, Virtue, and Progress*, 56–80; Jimerson, *Private Civil War*, 8–49; Clarke, "'Let All Nations See,'" 82–86; Carmichael, *War for the Common Soldier*, 1–16.

39. "Washington City in November" (1861), quoted in J. Clarke, *Autobiography, Diary and Correspondence*, 278; "The Draft," *Harper's Weekly*, September 6, 1862, 562; Grimsley, *Hard Hand of War*, 224 (first Lincoln quotation), 225; Lincoln to Agénor-Etienne de Gasparin, August 4, 1862, *CWL*, 5:355; U. S. Grant, *Personal Memoirs*, 749–50; Gamble, *Fiery Gospel*, 33–34; Katz, *From Appomattox to Montmartre*, 8; Herrera, *For Liberty and the Republic*, 1–26; Gallagher, *Union War*, 2–3, 16–17, 26–28, 124–28, 200n20; Royster, *Destructive War*, 152.

40. Gallagher, *Union War*, 1–6 (Seward quotation, p. 2); Hepworth, *Whip, Hoe, and Sword*, 224; final two soldiers quoted in McPherson, "'Whole Family of Man,'" in May, ed., *Union, the Confederacy, and the Atlantic Rim*, 134; "Second Inaugural Address of Abraham Lincoln," March 4, 1865, Avalon Project, accessed June 1, 2017, http://avalon.law.yale.edu/19th_century/lincoln2.asp; McPherson, *For Cause and Comrades*, 17–18, 90–102, 170–76; Hess, *Union Soldier in Battle*, ix–xi, passim; Carmichael, *War for the Common Soldier*, 20–26, 31–32, 88–90, 94–98, 104–7, 170–72; Clarke, "'Let All Nations See,'" 81–93; Gallagher and Meier, "Coming to Terms with Civil War Military History," 487.

41. Sullivan Ballou to My Very Dear Wife, July 14, 1861, National Park Service, accessed April 19, 2018, https://www.nps.gov/resources/story.htm%3Fid%3D253; John Wilson to Dear Kate, December 23, 1862, quoted in Hennessy, "Looting and Bombardment of Fredericksburg," 154; Gallagher, *Union War*, 54–71, 100–106.

42. Ofele, *True Sons of the Republic*, 70 (quotation); Gallagher, *Union War*, 2, 4–5, 71–73; Samito, *Becoming American under Fire*, 1–12, 26–35, 114–18, 125–32, 173–74, 185–92; Fleche, *Revolution of 1861*, 60–68; Doyle, *Cause of All Nations*, 1–11, 15–26, 91–105; Osterhammel, *Transformation of the World*, 60–61, 331–33.

43. Adolph Frick to Dear Mother and Sisters, May 11, 1862, and Magnus Brucker to Dear Wife, September 18, 1864, both in Kamphoefner and Helbich, *Germans in the Civil War*, 350, 268, 251.

44. Peter Welsh to Patrick Prendergast, June 1, 1863, in Kohl and Richard, *Irish Green and Union Blue*, 100–101; Edward Rolfe to My Dear Boy, July 4, 1865, and to Dear Charlotte, December 24, 1863, in Lillibridge, *Hard Marches, Hard Crackers, and Hard Beds*, 173, 99; McPherson, *For Cause and Comrades*, 113 (Cadman quotation).

45. "New Laws for Volunteers," *Richmond Enquirer*, December 14, 1861 (many thanks to Caroline E. Janney and Kevin Caprice at the University of Virginia for procuring this source for me); McPherson, *For Cause and Comrades*, 106 (citizen-officer quotation); Joint Resolutions of the Confederate Congress, January 22, 1864, *OR*, ser. 4, vol. 3, p. 129; Bonner, *Mastering America*, 294–95.

46. R. A. Pierson to W. H. Pierson, January 31, 1862, in Cutrer and Parrish, *Brothers in Gray*, 77; William C. Nelson to My Dearest Mother, October 29, 1862, in J. W. Ford, *Hour of Our Nation's Agony*, 102.

47. Davis to P. G. T. Beauregard, October 16, 1861, in Cooper, *Jefferson Davis: Essential Writings*, 216; "The War of Revenge," *Charlottesville Review*, April 19, 1861, and "Tennesseans to the Rescue of Tennessee," April 20, 1861, both reprinted in Dumond, *Southern Editorials on Secession*, 505, 507; Rable, *Damn Yankees!*, 68–99; Neely, "Guerrilla Warfare, Slavery, and the Hopes of the Confederacy"; Myers, "Partisan Ranger Petitions and the Confederacy's Authorized *Petite Guerre* Service," 13–15; Sheehan-Dean, *Calculus of Violence*, 110–11. Sutherland, "Guerrilla Warfare, Democracy, and the Fate of the Confederacy," 259–68, was essential to informing my argument and locating key primary sources for this and the subsequent paragraphs.

48. Davis to Wiley P. Harris, December 3, 1861, *PJD*, 7:434; Davis, First Inaugural Address, February 18, 1861, in Cooper, *Jefferson Davis: Essential Writings*, 201; Hsieh, *West Pointers and the Civil War*, 1–3, 10, 94, 111–13, 123–24, 140, 195–98; E. M. Thomas, *Confederacy as a Revolutionary Experience*, 53–57; Gallagher, *Confederate War*, 120–27, 140–53; Hess, "Civil War Guerrillas in a Global, Comparative Context"; Sutherland, "Guerrilla Warfare, Democracy, and the Fate of the Confederacy," 273–77; Fredrickson, *Why the Confederacy Did Not Fight a Guerrilla War after the Fall of Richmond*, 7–29.

49. Benjamin to R. G. Barkham, March 19, 1862, and Albert T. Bledsoe to D. M. K. Campbell, August 5, 1861, both in *OR*, ser. 4, vol. 1, pp. 1008, 532–33; Sutherland, "Guerrilla Warfare, Democracy, and the Fate of the Confederacy," 281.

50. Hsieh, *West Pointers and the Civil War*, 1–10, passim; Neff, *War and the Law of Nations*, 186–91; Sheehan-Dean, *Calculus of Violence*, 3 (quotation), 12–43, 314–51; Lee, *Barbarians and Brothers*, 121–67; Grenier, *First Way of War*, 14–19, 33–37; Neely, *Civil War and the Limits of Destruction*, 53–58, 140–66; Strang, "Violence, Ethnicity, and Human Remains during the Second Seminole War"; Hirsch, "Collision of Military

Cultures in Seventeenth-Century New England"; Millett, Maslowski, and Feis, *For the Common Defense*, 1–19, 23–44, 91–98.

51. Sherman to Ellen Ewing Sherman, July 28, 1861, in Simpson, Sears, and Sheehan-Dean, *Civil War: First Year*, 530, 529; Lee to Philip St. George Cocke, May 10, 1861, and General Orders No. 73, June 27, 1863, both in Dowdey and Manarin, *Wartime Papers of Robert E. Lee*, 23, 534; Hsieh, *West Pointers and the Civil War*, 125–45, 198–200; Skelton, *American Profession of Arms*, 318–25, 345–47; Herrera, *For Liberty and the Republic*, 1–26, 158–62.

52. Higginson, "Regular and Volunteer Officers," *Atlantic Monthly*, September 1864, 349–50; Bledsoe, *Citizen-Officers*, 62–71, 75–86, 94–109.

53. Hsieh, *West Pointers and the Civil War*, 3 (quotation), 95–96, 107–8, 125–26, 136–45, 198–200; Scott to George B. McClellan, May 3, 1861, *OR*, ser. 1, vol. 51, pt. 1, pp. 369–70; Reardon, *With a Sword in One Hand and Jomini in the Other*, 9–15, 19–25; Maslowski, "To the Edge of Greatness," 234–41; A. Jones, *Art of War in the Western World*, 409–18.

54. Scott to George B. McClellan, May 3, 1861, *OR*, ser. 1, vol. 51, pt. 1, pp. 369–70; McClellan to Simon Cameron, September 8, 1861, in Sears, *Civil War Papers of George B. McClellan*, 96–97; T. H. Williams, "Military Leadership of the North and the South," 43; Reardon, *With a Sword in One Hand and Jomini in the Other*, 5–8, 25–29.

55. McClellan quotations in Moten, *Delafield Commission and the Military Profession*, 148–49; Sears, *George B. McClellan: Young Napoleon*, 44–49, 74–76, 85, 91, 98–100, 110–15, 138–39, 149–50, 180–83, 200–207, 265–67; T. H. Williams, "Military Leadership of the North and the South," 45–49; Paludan, *"A People's Contest,"* 67–69.

56. McClellan to Mary Ellen McClellan, June 2, 1862, in Sears, *Civil War Papers of George B. McClellan*, 288; Sears, *George B. McClellan: Young Napoleon*, 164–89, 200–225; Stoker, *Grand Design*, 54–60, 77–87, 140–52.

57. Maslowski, "To the Edge of Greatness," 238; Young, *Around the World with General Grant*, 2:352–53; Garfield to My Dear Corydon, May 4, 1863, in E. E. Brown, *Life and Public Services of James A. Garfield*, 348; Reardon, *With a Sword in One Hand and Jomini in the Other*, 47–53; T. H. Williams, "Military Leadership of the North and the South," 55; Simpson, *Ulysses S. Grant: Triumph over Adversity*, 458; Stoker, *Grand Design*, 109–11, 211–12, 351–68.

58. Brinton, *Personal Memoirs of John H. Brinton*, 239 (Grant quotation); Grant to Julia Dent Grant, February 24, 1862, *PUSG*, 4:284; Weigley, *American Way of War*, 80, 128–52.

59. Lee to Davis, June 25, 1863, and to Gustavus W. Smith, January 4, 1863, both in Dowdey and Manarin, *Wartime Papers of Robert E. Lee*, 532, 384; E. M. Thomas, "Ambivalent Visions of Victory," 31, 43; Gallagher, *Confederate War*, 115–53; Hsieh, *West Pointers and the Civil War*, 1–10, 111–95; Guelzo, *Fateful Lightning*, 338; Stoker, *Grand Design*, 152–67, 230–31, 278–81.

60. Lee, "Battle Report on the Seven Days," March 6, 1863; to Wife, July 9, 1862; to James A. Seddon, June 8, 1863; to Jefferson Davis, June 10, 1863; and to Jefferson Davis, June 25, 1863, in Dowdey and Manarin, *Wartime Papers of Robert E. Lee*, 221, 230, 504, 507, 530; Gallagher, *Confederate War*, 58–65, 85–89; Weigley, *American Way of War*, 92–127; Gallagher, *Lee and His Army in Confederate History*, 151–90; Guelzo, *Fateful Lightning*, 337–40.

61. Chernow, *Grant*, 407 (Grant quotation); Weigley, *American Way of War*, 92–152; Stoker, *Grand Design*, 362–73.

62. Dawson, "First of the Modern Wars?," 64–68; Faust, *This Republic of Suffering*, 271 (quotation); Grimsley, "Surviving Military Revolution," 75–79; McPherson, "From Limited to Total War in America," 295–309; Engerman and Gallman, "Civil War Economy," 217–47; Bayly, *Birth of the Modern World*, 165; Tyrrell, *Transnational Nation*, 97–98; Royster, *Destructive War*; Stout, *Upon the Altar of the Nation*. For important retorts to this thesis, see Hsieh, "Total War and the American Civil War Reconsidered"; Murray and Hsieh, *Savage War*; Sheehan-Dean, *Calculus of Violence*.

63. Guelzo, "Democracy and Nobility"; Hess, *Rifle Musket in Civil War Combat*, 7–8, 197–208 (quotation, p. 202); Guelzo, *Fateful Lightning*, 200–202, 248–57; Grimsley, "Surviving Military Revolution," 76; Griffith, *Battle Tactics of the Civil War*, 74–75, 146–49, 191–92.

64. Hsieh, "Total War and the American Civil War Reconsidered," 403 (first quotation); "equilibrium of competence" adopted from Hsieh, *West Pointers and the Civil War*, 9, 133, 159, 240; Luvaas, *Military Legacy of the Civil War*, 17, 27 (Fletcher and Hewett quotations); Sherman, *Memoirs of Gen. William T. Sherman*, 2:394; Guelzo, *Fateful Lightning*, 247, 256; G. Phillips, "Military Morality Transformed"; Hattaway and Jones, *How the North Won*, 348, 390, 419–20, 468, 478, 683–702. Hsieh and Guelzo deserve special recognition for my framing and acquisition of sources for this section.

65. Hess, *Rifle Musket in Civil War Combat*, 205 (quotation); Chernow, *Grant*, 408 (Grant quotation); Lee to wife, December 25, 1862, in Dowdey and Manarin, *Wartime Papers of Robert E. Lee*, 380; Hsieh, "Total War and the American Civil War Reconsidered," 401–2; G. Phillips, "Military Morality Transformed"; Rable, *Fredericksburg! Fredericksburg!*, 343–44, 433.

66. Hsieh, "Total War and the American Civil War Reconsidered," 401–2 (quotation). Bass, "American Civil War and the Idea of Civil Supremacy over the Military," and Parrish, "Jeff Davis Rules," inform much of the subsequent chronological framing and anecdotes on civil-military relations. In a complex statistical analysis of Civil War deaths based on calculations drawn from the U.S. census, J. David Hacker estimates that between 650,000 and 850,000 soldiers died in the conflict (Hacker, "Census-Based Count of the Civil War Dead"). For a rejoinder to Hacker's thesis, see Marshall, "Great Exaggeration." See also Weigley, "American Military and the Principle of Civilian Control from McClellan to Powell"; Huntington, *Soldier and the State*, 2–3, 94–96, 212–13; Bell, *First Total War*; Geyer and Bright, "Global Violence and Nationalizing Wars in Eurasia and America," 654–57; Small and Singer, *Resort to Arms*, 59–60, 82–99, 223–32, 297–30; McPherson, "Was It a Just War?," 18; and Sheehan-Dean, *Calculus of Violence*, 1–11; Samet, *Willing Obedience*.

67. Bass, "American Civil War and the Idea of Civil Supremacy over the Military," 50; Hess, *Liberty, Virtue, and Progress*, 81–95; Hsieh, *West Pointers and the Civil War*, 163–64; Skelton, *American Profession of Arms*, 284–87, 295–97; Coffman, *Old Army*, 34, 87–103, 243–45; Tap, *Over Lincoln's Shoulder*, 5–7, 32–36, 54–55, 69–70, 74–75, 96–97, 163–64; Silbey, *Respectable Minority*, 68.

68. McClellan to Mary Ellen McClellan, October 31, 1861, in Sears, *Civil War Papers of George B. McClellan*, 113–14; Sears, *George B. McClellan: Young Napoleon*, xii, 58–59, 65–66, 117–18, 136–44, 175–76, 221–30, 324–27, 351–61.

69. Bass, "American Civil War and the Idea of Civil Supremacy over the Military," 52–53.

70. Burlingame, *Abraham Lincoln: Observations of John G. Nicolay and John Hay*, 106–7 (Key quotations); Bass, "American Civil War and the Idea of Civil Su-

premacy over the Military," 52–53; Hyman, "Ulysses S. Grant I, Emperor of America?," 177; Sears, *George B. McClellan: Young Napoleon*, 331; Tap, *Over Lincoln's Shoulder*, 109–24.

71. First quotation in Burlingame, *Abraham Lincoln: Observations of John G. Nicolay and John Hay*, 106; Lincoln to Key, November 24, 1862, *CWL*, 5:508; Nevins, *Diary of Battle*, 125–26 (Wainwright quotation); Bass, "American Civil War and the Idea of Civil Supremacy over the Military," 54; Sears, *George B. McClellan: Young Napoleon*, 331–32, 337–43; Tap, *Over Lincoln's Shoulder*, 152–53.

72. First McClellan quotation in Hillard, *Life and Campaigns of George B. McClellan*, 29; Farewell Address, November 7, 1862, in Sears, *Civil War Papers of George B. McClellan*, 521; Bass, "American Civil War and the Idea of Civil Supremacy over the Military," 54.

73. Sears, *Chancellorsville*, 21 (Correspondent William Swinton quotation); McPherson, *Battle Cry of Freedom*, 571–74, 584–85.

74. Lincoln to Hooker, January 26, 1863, *CWL*, 6:78–79; Bass, "American Civil War and the Idea of Civil Supremacy over the Military," 54.

75. Ideas in this paragraph are attributed entirely to Parrish, "Jeff Davis Rules," 47–48, 54–60 (Beauregard to Charles Villere, January 13, 1863, quoted on p. 59).

76. Ideas in this paragraph are attributed entirely to Parrish, "Jeff Davis Rules," 54–55 (quotation), 62–64. See also Sheehan-Dean, *Calculus of Violence*, 3, 6; Cooper, *Jefferson Davis, American*, 443, 565, 571, 670–71; and McPherson, *Tried by War*, 77–80, 141–42, 181. For counterarguments, see Sternhell, "Revisionism Reinvented?," 239–56; Fellman, *In the Name of God and Country*, 57–96; M. C. C. Adams, *Living Hell*; and Stout, *Upon the Altar of the Nation*. See chapter 6 for an interpretation of the Lincoln assassination.

77. This section addresses the United States' conceptions of military necessity. See chapter 5 for interpretations of Confederate just war theory and military necessity.

78. Lincoln, First Inaugural Address, March 4, 1861, *CWL*, 4:265; Guelzo, "Statesmanship and Mr. Lincoln"; Neely, *Fate of Liberty*, xi, 3, 22.

79. Lincoln to John M. Schofield, May 27, 1863, and First Inaugural Address, March 4, 1861, *CWL*, 6:234, 4:440; J. T. Johnson, *Just War Tradition*, 7–9, 25–26, 79–94.

80. Lincoln to Horatio Seymour, August 7, 1863, *CWL*, 6:370; L. A. Williams, "Northern Intellectual Reaction to Military Rule during the Civil War," 334–35; Carnahan, "Lincoln, Lieber and the Laws of War," 213–31.

81. Lincoln to Erastus Corning and Others, June 12, 1863, and "Proclamation Suspending the Writ of Habeas Corpus," September 24, 1862, both in *CWL*, 6:264, 263, 5:437; Neely, *Fate of Liberty*, xiii–xvi, 4–13, 32–37, 53–57, 64–65, 67, 70–74, 90–92, 191–92; Carnahan, *Lincoln on Trial*, 102; Neff, *Justice in Blue and Gray*, 34–39, 151–60; Neely, *Lincoln and the Triumph of the Nation*, 63–112.

82. Lincoln, Special Message to Congress, July 4, 1861, to Erastus Corning and Others, June 12, 1863, and to Edward Bates, May 30, 1861, *CWL*, 4:429–30, 6:267, 4:390n1 (Bates quotation); Guelzo, "Statesmanship and Mr. Lincoln"; Neff, *Justice in Blue and Gray*, 38–39, 153–54; Neely, *Fate of Liberty*, 11, 14, 68–69, 87, 161, 197, 202–3; Blair, *With Malice toward Some*, 91–92, 112, 167–79.

83. Diary of Hester Ann Wilkins Davis, May 7, 1861, Hester Ann Wilkins Davis Manuscript Collection, Maryland Historical Society [transcript]; Journal of Samuel A. Harrison, June 17, 1861, Harrison Collection, Maryland Historical Society; McPherson,

Battle Cry of Freedom, 284–87; Phillips, *Rivers Ran Backward*, 11–12, 145, 184–99, 211, 221; Silbey, *Respectable Minority*, 51–52, 72–77; Neely, *Lincoln and the Democrats*, 136–71; Ingersoll, "Personal Liberty and Martial Law" (1862), in Freidel, *Union Pamphlets*, 1:253–94. I am indebted to Stephen Powell, one of my doctoral candidates at Mississippi State University, for sharing transcripts and images of the Davis and Harrison sources from his dissertation research.

84. Emerson, "American Civilization," *Atlantic Monthly*, April 1862, 508; Stillé, *Northern Interests and Southern Independence*, 43; "Habeas Corpus and Martial Law," *North American Review*, October 1861, 518. All sources are derived from L. A. Williams, "Northern Intellectual Reaction to Military Rule during the Civil War," 337, 340, 346. See also Binney, "Privilege of the Writ of Habeas Corpus under the Constitution" (1862), in Freidel, *Union Pamphlets*, 1:199–252.

85. "Proclamation Made to the People of North Carolina," February 16, 1862, *OR*, ser. 1, vol. 9, pp. 363–64; Ash, *When the Yankees Came*, 13–37; Grimsley, *Hard Hand of War*, 2–3, 23–35, 47–68, 75–80; Lang, *In the Wake of War*, 38–42.

86. General Orders No. 32, December 22, 1861, and Halleck to John Pope, December 31, 1861, both in *OR*, ser. 2, vol. 1, pp. 237, 242; Marcy to Winfield Scott, October 6, 1847, *House Ex. Doc. No. 56*, 30th Congress, 1st sess., 197; Sutherland, "Guerrilla Warfare, Democracy, and the Fate of the Confederacy," 280; Neely, *Civil War and the Limits of Destruction*, 89.

87. Butler to Richard Taylor, September 10, 1862, in Butler, *Private and Official Correspondence of Gen. Benjamin F. Butler*, 2:267–68; Rosecrans to the Loyal Citizens of Western Virginia, August 20, 1861, *OR*, ser. 1, vol. 5, p. 576; *Frank Leslie's Illustrated Newspaper*, December 6, 1862, p. 164; Dilbeck, *More Civil War*, 37; Lang, *In the Wake of War*, 110–11; Sutherland, *Savage Conflict*, 28–29, 47–52.

88. General Orders No. 13, December 4, 1861, *OR*, ser. 2, vol. 1, pp. 234, 235; C. Phillips, "Lincoln's Grasp of War," 184–210, esp. 193–94; Grimsley, *Hard Hand of War*, 149.

89. "Gen. Fremont's Proclamation," August 30, 1861, in Moore, *Rebellion Record*, 3:33; Hunter proclamation, May 9, 1862, quoted in Sears, *Civil War: Second Year*, 215; Sutherland, "Guerrilla Warfare, Democracy, and the Fate of the Confederacy," 280; Carnahan, *Lincoln on Trial*, 29.

90. Lincoln to O. H. Browning, September 22, 1861, *CWL*, 4:531; Carnahan, "Lincoln, Lieber and the Laws of War," 220, 216; Witt, *Lincoln's Code*, 197–99.

91. Lincoln, Annual Message to Congress, December 3, 1861, *CWL*, 5:49; Witt, *Lincoln's Code*, 199 (quotation); quotations of Frémont critics in M. T. Smith, *Enemy Within*, 84–86; M. T. Smith, "Corruption European Style"; Dilbeck, *More Civil War*, 21–22; Fleche, *Revolution of 1861*, 60–63; Zimmerman, "From the Rhine to the Mississippi."

92. Brasher, *Peninsula Campaign and the Necessity of Emancipation*, 5–9, 22–29, 43–44, 50–53, 76–79, 86–87, 93–95, 111–15; A. M. Taylor, *Embattled Freedom*, 25–56; Grimsley, *Hard Hand of War*, 122–23.

93. Butler to Simon Cameron, July 30, 1861, in Butler, *Private and Official Correspondence of Gen. Benjamin F. Butler*, 1:185–88; Brasher, *Peninsula Campaign and the Necessity of Emancipation*, 33–39, 58–60; Grimsley, *Hard Hand of War*, 52, 210; Witt, *Lincoln's Code*, 202–7.

94. "An Act to Confiscate Property Used for Insurrectionary Purposes," August 6,

1861, *Statutes at Large*, 12:319; Siddali, *From Property to Person*, 76–87, 91–97, 106–14, 126–28, 153–57; Neff, *Justice in Blue and Gray*, 117–20; D. W. Hamilton, *Limits of Sovereignty*, 91–92, 142–44.

95. Sherman to John Sherman, August 26, 1862, in Simpson and Berlin, *Sherman's Civil War*, 292; Sutherland, *American Civil War Guerrillas*, 12 (Pennsylvania soldier quotation); U. S. Grant, *Personal Memoirs*, 225; General Orders No. 13, December 4, 1861, *OR*, ser. 2, vol. 1, p. 235.

96. C. Phillips, *Rivers Ran Backward*, 156 (Ohio volunteer [Noyes] quotation); Musser to Sister Hester, April 24, 1863, and to Dear Father and Mother, April 29, 1863, in Popchuck, *Soldier Boy*, 47, 49; Lincoln to Dear Wife, December 22, 1862, Benjamin C. Lincoln Papers, Schoff Civil War Collection, Clements Library, University of Michigan; Grimsley, *Hard Hand of War*, 35–46, 67–95; D. W. Hamilton, *Limits of Sovereignty*, 143–44, 146, 153; Bradley and Dahlen, *From Conciliation to Conquest*, 71–108; Danielson, *War's Desolating Scourge*, 75–77, 83–90, 122–23.

97. McClellan to Edwin M. Stanton, February 11, 1862, in Sears, *Civil War Papers of George B. McClellan*, 177; diary entry, May 14, 1862, in Nevins, *Diary of Battle*, 62.

98. "An Act to Organize Bands of Partisan Rangers," April 21, 1862, *Documenting the American South*, accessed May 29, 2019, https://docsouth.unc.edu/imls/statutes /statutes.html; Sutherland, "Guerrilla Warfare, Democracy, and the Fate of the Confederacy," 281 (quotation); Sutherland, *Savage Conflict*, 67–71, 93–117; Myers, "Partisan Ranger Petitions and the Confederacy's Authorized *Petite Guerre* Service," 15; Hess, "Civil War Guerrillas in a Global, Comparative Context."

99. Myers, "Partisan Ranger Petitions and the Confederacy's Authorized *Petite Guerre* Service," 26 (petitioner quotation); Seddon to Jefferson Davis, November 26, 1863, *OR*, ser. 4, vol. 2, p. 1003; Sutherland, "Guerrilla Warfare, Democracy, and the Fate of the Confederacy," 282–87; Sutherland, *Savage Conflict*, 136–88; C. Phillips, *Rivers Ran Backward*, 204–5, 250–62.

100. Lee to Samuel Cooper, April 1, 1864, in Dowdey and Manarin, *Wartime Papers of Robert E. Lee*, 688–89; Butler to Richard Taylor, September 10, 1862, in Butler, *Private and Official Correspondence of Gen. Benjamin F. Butler*, 2:268; Lieber, *Guerrilla Parties*, 12; Sutherland, *Savage Conflict*, 93–94, 171–72, 187–90, 237–38; Sutherland, "Guerrilla Warfare, Democracy, and the Fate of the Confederacy," 287–92; Sutherland, "Union's Counterguerrilla War"; Hess, "Civil War Guerrillas in a Global, Comparative Context," 337–40; Sheehan-Dean, *Calculus of Violence*, 315, 340–49. Albert Castel once appraised the number of Civil War guerrillas as 26,550. Daniel E. Sutherland, a leading authority on the subject, counters, "That number is surely low, perhaps by as much as half" (Sutherland, *Savage Conflict*, xii; Sutherland, "Sideshow No Longer," 14–15).

101. Hennessy, "Looting and Bombardment of Fredericksburg," 129 (Pope quotation); Matsui, *First Republican Army*, 1–9, 32, 46, 51–56, 60–66, 91–93, 100–105; Grimsley, *Hard Hand of War*, 67–68, 85–91; Sutherland, "Abraham Lincoln, John Pope, and the Origins of Total War."

102. General Orders No. 5, July 18, 1862, and General Orders No. 19, August 14, 1862, *OR*, ser. 1, vol. 12, pt. 2, p. 50, pt. 3, p. 573; Matsui, *First Republican Army*, 49–50, 111–24, 130–39.

103. General Orders No. 7, July 10, 1862, and General Orders No. 11, July 23, 1862, *OR*, ser. 1, vol. 12, pt. 2, pp. 50, 52.

104. War Dept. Exec. Order, July 22, 1862, *OR*, ser. 1, vol. 11, pt. 3, p. 383; Lincoln to Cuthbert Bullitt, July 28, 1862, *CWL*, 5:345–46; Grimsley, *Hard Hand of War*, 87–88; Sutherland, "Abraham Lincoln, John Pope, and the Origins of Total War."

105. Douglass, "The War and How to End It," March 25, 1862, in Foner and Taylor, *Frederick Douglass*, 488, 486; Julian, *Cause and Cure of Our National Troubles*, 3.

106. Julian, *Cause and Cure of Our National Troubles*, 7, 8; Blair, *With Malice toward Some*, 85–86.

107. Emerson, "American Civilization," *Atlantic Monthly*, April 1862, 509, 510; A. I. P. Smith, *Stormy Present*, 190–94; McCurry, *Confederate Reckoning*, 218–309; Lang, "Union Demobilization and the Boundaries of War and Peace," 182.

108. Douglass, "War and How to End It," 492; Adams to Charles Francis Adams Jr., September 5, 1862, in W. C. Ford, *Cycle of Adams Letters*, 1:182–83; Julian, *Cause and Cure of Our National Troubles*, 7.

109. Curtis to E. A. Carr, October 21, 1862, *OR*, ser. 1, vol. 13, p. 756; Letter of Stephen O. Himoe (Ohio officer), June 26, 1862, in Kuhns, "Army Surgeon's Letters to His Wife," 311; Teters, *Practical Liberators*, 66 (Landrum quotation); McPherson, *For Cause and Comrades*, 117–30, esp. 120; Gallagher, *Union War*, 40–41, 70–82, 101–14, 142–47; Manning, *What This Cruel War Was Over*, 13–15, 44–49, 72–95, 118–25, 147–57, 191–93; Brasher, *Peninsula Campaign and the Necessity of Emancipation*, 77, 110–13, 142–48, 193–94.

110. Fisk to *Green Mountain Freeman*, April 7, 1864, in Rosenblatt, *Hard Marching Every Day*, 206–7; Willoughby to My Dear Wife, January 22, 1863, in Silber and Sievens, *Yankee Correspondence*, 98; Jimerson, *Private Civil War*, 37 (Webb quotation).

111. Second Confiscation Act, July 17, 1862, *Statutes at Large*, 12:589; Bradley and Dahlen, *From Conciliation to Conquest*, 175 (Enos quotation); Gallagher, "Civil War Watershed"; Brasher, *Peninsula Campaign and the Necessity of Emancipation*, 71–85, 116–18, 151–56, 178–89, 194–214, 226–28; Siddali, *From Property to Person*, 120–44, 213–50; Oakes, *Freedom National*, 216–36.

112. Second Confiscation Act, *Statutes at Large*, 12:589–93; Witt, *Lincoln's Code*, 211–12; Neff, *Justice in Blue and Gray*, 123–27; Siddali, *From Property to Person*, 220–47; Oakes, *Freedom National*, 225–35; A. M. Taylor, *Embattled Freedom*, 13–14, 45–55, 61–66, 92–97, 106–7, 208–11, 241, 247–48.

113. Grimes, "Speech on the Surrender of Slaves by the Army," April 14, 1862, in Salter, *Life of James W. Grimes*, 188–89; Lowery, "Commander-in-Chief" (1863), in Freidel, *Union Pamphlets*, 1:484–85; Sumner, "Indemnity for the Past and Security for the Future," May 19, 1862, in Sumner, *Complete Works*, 9:76–77; Reidy, *Illusions of Emancipation*, 93; Brasher, *Peninsula Campaign and the Necessity of Emancipation*, 17; Oakes, *Freedom National*, 231–36.

114. General Orders No. 109, August 16, 1862, *OR*, ser. 3, vol. 2, p. 397.

115. Lincoln quotations in Welles, *History of Emancipation*, 842–43; McPherson, "Who Freed the Slaves?," 6–7; E. Foner, *Fiery Trial*, 216–21.

116. "By the President of the United States: A Proclamation," January 1, 1863, National Archives, accessed May 21, 2019, https://www.archives.gov/exhibits/featured -documents/emancipation-proclamation/transcript.html; Oakes, *Freedom National*, 225–31, 301–39; E. Foner, *Fiery Trial*, 230–33, 238–42. See chapter 5 for an extended discussion of the Emancipation Proclamation and the African American soldiering experience.

117. Lincoln to Salmon P. Chase, September 2, 1863, and Annual Address to Con-

gress, December 1, 1862, *CWL*, 6:428–29, 5:537; Carnahan, *Act of Justice*, 1–2, 79–80, 96–97, 106–7, 117, 126–30, 139–41.

118. Burlingame, *Abraham Lincoln: A Life*, 2:480; Soodalter, "Lincoln and the Sioux"; Stern, "War Is Cruelty"; Varon, *Armies of Deliverance*, 133–34; Berg, *38 Nooses*, 111–13, 203–4, 290–95; G. C. Anderson, *Massacre in Minnesota*, 47–160.

119. Pope to Henry H. Sibley, September 28, 1862, *OR*, ser. 1, vol. 13, p. 686; Swisshelm, *Half a Century*, 226, 229; Burlingame, *Abraham Lincoln: A Life*, 2:481–82; R. White, "Winning of the West"; Utley, *Frontiersmen in Blue*, 262–70; Gallagher, "Fighting on Multiple Fronts." It is likely that Pope employed the literal definition of "exterminate" when advancing his Sioux military policy. The first entry in the *Oxford English Dictionary* defines the term as "to drive, force (a person or thing) *from, of, out of* the boundaries or limits of (a place, region, community, state, etc.); to drive away, banish, put to flight" (s.v. "exterminate, v.," *OED Online*, September 2019, https://www.oed.com/view/Entry/66983?redirectedFrom=exterminate).

120. Witt, *Lincoln's Code*, 330–36; H. C. Richardson, "Largest Mass Execution in American History"; Herbert, "Explaining the Sioux Military Commission of 1862," 743–47; Berg, *38 Nooses*, 179; Finkelman, "Lincoln the Lawyer, Humanitarian Concerns, and the Dakota Pardons," 409–13, 424–32.

121. Lincoln to the Senate, December 11, 1862, *CWL*, 5:551; diary entry, December 4, 1862, in Welles, *Diary of Gideon Welles*, 1:186; Burlingame, *Abraham Lincoln: A Life*, 2:482; Finkelman, "Lincoln the Lawyer, Humanitarian Concerns, and the Dakota Pardons," 442–46; Berg, *38 Nooses*, 206–7, 220; Nichols, "Other Civil War."

122. Donald, *Lincoln*, 395 (first Lincoln quotation); Lincoln, Second Annual Message to Congress, December 1, 1862, *CWL*, 5:525–26; Nichols, "Other Civil War," 9–11 (Lincoln's promise for reform quoted on p. 9); "An Act for the Relief of Persons for Damages Sustained by Reason of Depredations and Injuries by … Sioux Indians," February 16, 1863, and "An Act for the Removal of … Sioux or Dakota Indians," March 3, 1863, both from 37th Congress, 3rd sess., in *Statutes at Large*, 12:652, 819; Berg, *38 Nooses*, 237–38; Witt, *Lincoln's Code*, 330–36; H. C. Richardson, "Largest Mass Execution in American History"; Stern, "War Is Cruelty"; Soodalter, "Lincoln and the Sioux"; Gallagher, "Fighting on Multiple Fronts"; Utley, *Frontiersmen in Blue*, 270–80, 341–49; Berg, *38 Nooses*, 282–83.

123. Neely, *Civil War and the Limits of Destruction*, 50 (first quotation); Bowler to My Dear Lizzie, September 27, 1862, in Foroughi, *Go If You Think It Your Duty*, 124; Grimsley, "'Rebels' and 'Redskins'"; Lee, *Barbarians and Brothers*, 1–11, 232–46.

124. Neely, *Civil War and the Limits of Destruction*, 140–69; Chivington to E. W. Wynkoop, May 31, 1864, *OR*, ser. 1, vol. 34, pt. 4, p. 151; Bartek, "Rhetoric of Destruction," 455 (New Mexico officer quotation); Grimsley, "'Rebels' and 'Redskins'"; Kelman, *Misplaced Massacre*, 8–18, 40–52, 67–89, 191–95.

125. Neely, *Civil War and the Limits of Destruction*, 219 (first quotation); Stanton to Rufus Saxton, August 25, 1862, *OR*, ser. 1, vol. 14, p. 378; William T. Sherman to John Sherman, January 25, 1863, in Simpson and Berlin, *Sherman's Civil War*, 373. Confederates *did* replicate a kind of Sand Creek in their massacre of white civilians at Lawrence, Kansas, in August 1863. There, Confederate raiders killed nearly two hundred civilian noncombatants (C. Phillips, *Rivers Ran Backward*, 13–14, 237–40; Sheehan-Dean, *Calculus of Violence*, 207–17).

126. McPherson, "Was It a Just War?," 18; Hacker, "Census-Based Count of the Civil War Dead," 309–10, 326–29, 344–48; Sheehan-Dean, *Calculus of Violence*, 191,

298–303; Rable, *Fredericksburg! Fredericksburg!*, 166; Wills, *Inglorious Passages*, 263; A. W. Greene, *Civil War Petersburg*, 315n4; Neely, *Civil War and the Limits of Destruction*, 140–69; Grimsley, *Hard Hand of War*, 186–90; Neely, "Was the Civil War a Total War?," 11–12, 18–20, 27–28; Sternhell, *Routes of War*, 64–68, 81–89, 135–51. See Grimsley, "'Rebels' and 'Redskins,'" 141–42, 150–53, for discussions of and evidence for the rapes of Native women and executions of civilians.

127. Sherman to John Sherman, January 25, 1863, in Thorndike, *Sherman Letters*, 185; Denver to My Dear Wife, November 29, 1862, James W. Denver Letter, Harrisburg Civil War Roundtable Collection, United States Army Military Heritage Institute, Carlisle Barracks; Charles Wright Wills diary entry, December 12, 1862, in Kellogg, *Army Life of an Illinois Soldier*, 136; Lang, *In the Wake of War*, 70–71, 112–13; Grimsley, "'Rebels' and 'Redskins.'" "Directed severity" adopted from Grimsley, *Hard Hand of War*, 105, 152, 157, 175, 218; Neely, *Civil War and the Limits of Destruction*, 1–5, 198–220.

128. See chapter 5 for an extended discussion of African American Union soldiers.

129. Shaw to My Dearest Annie, June 9, 1863, and to Dear Father, June 5, 1863, in Duncan, *Blue-Eyed Child of Fortune*, 343, 339; Lang, "Challenging the Union Citizen-Soldier Ideal," 326–28.

130. Grimsley, *Hard Hand of War*, 96–119; Varon, *Armies of Deliverance*, 2, 6, 10, 97–106, 163–71.

131. Phelps to R. S. Davis, June 16, 1862, *OR*, ser. 1, vol. 15, pp. 486–90; Grimsley, *Hard Hand of War*, 120–41; Teters, *Practical Liberators*, 31; Varon, *Armies of Deliverance*, 200–210, 233–38.

132. "Henderson Journal 06, November 8, 1864–May 14, 1865," April 23, 1865, William Legg Henderson Civil War Diaries, Civil War Diaries and Letters Digital Collection, University of Iowa Libraries, Special Collections Department, Iowa Digital Library, http://digital.lib.uiowa.edu/cdm/compoundobject/collection/cwd/id/26810/rec/2; Fleche, *Revolution of 1861*, 60–79, 107–31; Ash, "Poor Whites in the Occupied South," 47; Dean, *Agrarian Republic*, 101–7 (final quotation, p. 103); R. Mitchell, *Civil War Soldiers*, 97–107; Ash, *When the Yankees Came*, 171–73; Lang, "Limits of American Exceptionalism," 196.

133. Kinsley diary entry, August 31, 1862, in Rankin, *Diary of a Christian Soldier*, 105–6; Lang, "Limits of American Exceptionalism," 197; Varon, *Armies of Deliverance*, 200–210, 233–38.

134. Halleck to Ulysses S. Grant, March 31, 1863, *OR*, ser. 1, vol. 24, pt. 3, pp. 156–57.

135. General Orders No. 100, Articles 29 and 30, *OR*, ser. 3, vol. 3, p. 151; Dilbeck, *More Civil War*, 76–87, 88; Dilbeck, "'Genesis of This Little Tablet with My Name'"; C. Phillips, *Rivers Ran Backward*, 249; Witt, *Lincoln's Code*, 231–71. A gendered interpretation of Lieber's Code appears in McCurry, *Women's War*, 4–6, 15–19, 45–60.

136. General Orders No. 100, Articles 14, 15, 16, *OR*, ser. 3, vol. 3, p. 150; Carnahan, "Lincoln, Lieber and the Laws of War," 215–19; Neff, *Justice in Blue and Gray*, 60–64; Dilbeck, *More Civil War*, 87–96; Witt, *Lincoln's Code*, 183–84, 234–37.

137. General Orders No. 100, Articles 30 and 150–53, *OR*, ser. 3, vol. 3, pp. 151, 163; Onuf and Onuf, *Nations, Markets, and War*, 346–47.

138. General Orders No. 100, Articles 82, 27, 28, *OR*, ser. 3, vol. 3, pp. 157, 151; Dilbeck, *More Civil War*, 92–93; Foote, "Civilization and Savagery in the American Civil War," 26–27.

139. General Orders No. 100, Articles 28, 38, 44, *OR*, ser. 3, vol. 3, pp. 151, 152, 153; Lang, *In the Wake of War*, 123.

140. General Orders No. 100, Articles 42 and 43, *OR*, ser. 3, vol. 3, p. 153; Dilbeck, "'Genesis of This Little Tablet with My Name'"; Mancini, "Francis Lieber, Slavery, and the 'Genesis' of the Laws of War"; Witt, *Lincoln's Code*, 226–28, 234–37.

141. Dilbeck, *More Civil War*, 86 (Lieber quotation); Lincoln to James C. Conkling, August 20, 1863, *CWL*, 6:409, 408, 410.

142. *New York World*, March 3, 1863, quoted in L. A. Williams, "Northern Intellectual Reaction to Military Rule during the Civil War," 341; Vallandigham, "Great Civil War in America," January 14, 1863, in Freidel, *Union Pamphlets*, 2:737–38, 707, 710; Silbey, *Respectable Minority*, 24–28, 70–99, 114–15, 136–39, 189–94; Neely, *Lincoln and the Democrats*, 86–96; Blair, *With Malice toward Some*, 89; Neely, *Fate of Liberty*, 65–68, 105–7, 187–99, 203–5; Weber, *Copperheads*, 39–40, 71–81, 201–17.

143. General Orders No. 100, Article 155, *OR*, ser. 3, vol. 3, pp. 163–64; Witt, *Lincoln's Code*, 271–73 (final two quotations); Klement, *Limits of Dissent*, 138–54.

144. *New York World*, February 19, 1863, quoted in Neely, *Lincoln and the Democrats*, 73; Morton, *Speech of Gov. Oliver P. Morton*, February 23, 1864, 14; "The Work Done by Congress," *Harper's Weekly*, March 14, 1863, 162; Kent, "Constitution and the Laws of War during the Civil War," 1850; L. A. Williams, "Northern Intellectual Reaction to Military Rule during the Civil War," 347; Neely, "Civil War and the Two-Party System."

145. Lincoln, "Proclamation of Amnesty and Reconstruction," December 8, 1863, and "Annual Message to Congress," December 6, 1864, both in *CWL*, 7:53–56, 8:152; E. Foner, *Reconstruction*, 35–37, 60–61. See chapter 7 for a discussion of Lincoln's plan for Reconstruction.

146. Lincoln to Stanton, March 18, 1864, *CWL*, 7:255; Carnahan, *Lincoln on Trial*, 45; Neely, "'Civilized Belligerents,'" 12–16; Neff, *Justice in Blue and Gray*, 222–24; Dorris, *Pardon and Amnesty under Lincoln and Johnson*, 67–73.

147. Dilbeck, *More Civil War*, 128–30; Royster, *Destructive War*, 188–89, 324–47, 355–59; J. Q. Whitman, *Verdict of Battle*, 3–22, 211–15; Neely, "Was the Civil War a Total War?"; Sheehan-Dean, *Calculus of Violence*, 294–313; Grimsley, *Hard Hand of War*, 171–204.

148. Sherman to James Guthrie, August 14, 1864, *OR*, ser. 1, vol. 39, pt. 2, p. 248; Bledsoe and Lang, "Military History and the American Civil War," 3; Grimsley, *Hard Hand of War*, 186–90.

149. Sherman to G. M. Graham, January 5, 1861, in Simpson and Berlin, *Sherman's Civil War*, 30; Paludan, *"People's Contest,"* 289–91; Marszalek, *Sherman*, 182–96, 230–36, 250–62, 280–96, 301–33; Royster, *Destructive War*, 89, 119–20, 128, 135–39; Bledsoe and Lang, "Military History and the American Civil War," 3–4.

150. Sherman to James M. Calhoun, E. E. Rawson, and S. C. Wells, September 12, 1864, and Sherman to U. S. Grant, November 6, 1864, both in *OR*, ser. 1, vol. 39, pt. 2, pp. 418–19, and vol. 39, pt. 3, pp. 660; Royster, *Destructive War*, 270–71, 352–59; Marszalek, *Sherman*, 295–333.

151. Sherman to R. M. Sawyer, January 31, 1864, and Sherman to Grant, October 4, 1862, *OR*, ser. 1, vol. 32, pt. 2, p. 281, and vol. 17, pt. 2, p. 261; Marszalek, *Sherman*, 477 (final quotation), 133–47. For early treatments of Sherman as a progenitor of total war, see Walters, *Merchant of Terror* and "General William T. Sherman and Total War."

152. Sherman to U. S. Grant, November 6, 1864, *OR*, ser. 1, vol. 39, pt. 3, p. 660; Royster, *Destructive War*, 89, 119–20, 128, 135–39, 188–89, 327–30; Marszalek, *Sherman*, 290–316.

153. Sherman to R. M. Sawyer, January 31, 1864, *OR*, ser. 1, vol. 32, pt. 2, pp. 278–81; Sherman to Rev. Joseph P. Thompson, October 21, 1864, in Simpson and Berlin, *Sherman's Civil War*, 739–40; Marszalek, *Sherman*, 296.

154. Sherman to Henry W. Halleck, December 24, 1864, in Simpson and Berlin, *Sherman's Civil War*, 703; Sherman to Frederick Steele, April 19, 1863, *OR*, ser. 1, vol. 24, pt. 3, p. 209; U. S. Grant, *Personal Memoirs*, 251; Foote, "Civilization and Savagery in the American Civil War," 27–28; Neely, *Civil War and the Limits of Destruction*, 109–39; W. G. Thomas, "Nothing Ought to Astonish Us"; Dilbeck, *More Civil War*, 130–56; Grimsley, *Hard Hand of War*, 153, 171–204.

155. Grimsley, *Hard Hand of War*, 190–91, 203–4, 214 (quotation p. 204).

156. McPherson, *Battle Cry of Freedom*, 826 (Union soldiers quotations); J. F. Rhodes, "Who Burned Columbia?," 489 (Sherman quotation); Glatthaar, *March to the Sea and Beyond*, 134–55, esp. 143–46; Grimsley, *Hard Hand of War*, 203–4, 205–25; Dawson, "First of the Modern Wars?," 74–78.

157. Lincoln, "Proclamation of Thanksgiving," October 3, 1863, *CWL*, 6:496; Grimsley, *Hard Hand of War*, 222–25; Neely, *Civil War and the Limits of Destruction*, 1–5, 198–215; Lee, *Barbarians and Brothers*, 1–11, 232–45; Grimsley, "'Rebels' and 'Redskins'"; Sheehan-Dean, *Calculus of Violence*, 352–58.

Chapter 5

1. Guterl, *American Mediterranean*, 1–78; Bonner, *Mastering America*, 1–213; Kaye, "Second Slavery"; Karp, *This Vast Southern Empire*; Hahn, *Nation without Borders*, 2–4, 64–69, 185–91, 205–10.

2. Delany, *Blake*; Guterl, *American Mediterranean*, 41–42; Sinha, *Slave's Cause*, 455–56; Fagin, *Black Newspaper and the Chosen Nation*, 119, 134–37; G. P. Downs, *Second American Revolution*, 18, 75.

3. Delany, *Blake*, 305; Hahn, *Political Worlds of Slavery and Freedom*, 45–47.

4. Delany, *Blake*, 288; Matthews, *Caribbean Slave Revolts and the British Abolitionist Movement*; Rugemer, *Problem of Emancipation*, 140–41, 156–60, 261–76; Clavin, *Toussaint Louverture and the American Civil War*, 1–33, 121–43; D. B. Davis, *Problem of Slavery in the Age of Emancipation*, 3–7, 43–44, 48–52, 74–83, 116–24, 137–39, 210; C. L. Paulus, *Slaveholding Crisis*, 24–32, 42–45, 51–63, 77–78, 62–71, 187–94, 220–26; Sinha, *Slave's Cause*, 34–36, 53–67, 345, 373–74.

5. Kantrowitz, *More Than Freedom*, 235–39, 264, 279–94; Clavin, *Toussaint Louverture and the American Civil War*, 77–118; J. D. Smith, *Black Soldiers in Blue*; Manning, *What This Cruel War Was Over*, 95–96, 125–27, 140–41, 147–48, 153–57, 169–70, 175–76; J. Phillips, *Diehard Rebels*, 47–48, 54–55, 57–58, 66–68; Hahn, *Political Worlds of Slavery and Freedom*, 55–114; Sheehan-Dean, *Calculus of Violence*, 170–73; Fagan, *Black Newspaper and the Chosen Nation*, 119.

6. Gemme, *Domesticating Foreign Struggles*, 109–10, 114–24 (Anderson quotation, p. 123); letter of William H. Watson (a free black Pennsylvanian), February 14, 1865, in Redkey, *Grand Army of Black Men*, 153; Hahn, *Nation under Our Feet*, 1–159; Berlin, *Long Emancipation*, 9, 14–16, 19–25, 28–29, 32–41, 118–20; Rael, *Eighty-Eight Years*, 49–50, 126–97; Sinha, *Slave's Cause*, 1–5, 41–47, 113–60, 195–96, 218–19, 229–338, 450–51.

7. Hahn, *Political Worlds of Slavery and Freedom*, 55–114 (first quotation, p. 98); Delany, *Blake*, 289 (second quotation); Clavin, *Toussaint Louverture and the American Civil War*, 105 (Sumner quotation), 77–78, 83–94, 105–7; Guterl, *American Mediterranean*, 41–42; Byrd, "Black Republicans, Black Republic"; Sheehan-Dean, *Calculus of Violence*, 170–73.

8. Henry Highland Garnet to Henry M. Wilson, September 27, 1861, reprinted in Ripley, *Black Abolitionist Papers*, 1:502, 503; Fagan, *Black Newspaper and the Chosen Nation*, 119–41 (Douglass quotation, p. 121); McPherson, *Negro's Civil War*, 19–36; Berlin, Reidy, and Rowland, *Freedom's Soldiers*, 37–278; Glatthaar, *Forged in Battle*, 11–33, 61–80; Kantrowitz, *More Than Freedom*, 274–82.

9. Doyle, *Cause of All Nations*, 15–26 (Garibaldi quotations, pp. 20, 25); Gemme, *Domesticating Foreign Struggles*, 127–30 (Douglass quotation, p. 129).

10. Escott, *"What Shall We Do with the Negro?,"* 3–6, 18, 32–34, 41, 48, 52–54, 58–60, 63–67; Ash, *When the Yankees Came*, 13–37; Crofts, *Lincoln and the Politics of Slavery*, 11, 18–19, 56–80, 184–89, 191–93, 237–39, 240, 257–61, 275–79; Harris, *Lincoln and the Border States*, 11–158; C. Phillips, *Rivers Ran Backward*.

11. Hahn, *Nation under Our Feet*, 13–159; Hahn, *Political Worlds of Slavery and Freedom*, 55–114, esp. 58–61; Oakes, *Freedom National*, 192–223; Sinha, *Slave's Cause*, 543–85; Berlin, *Long Emancipation*, 18–20, 158–65; Rael, *Eighty-Eight Years*, 239–79; McCurry, *Confederate Reckoning*, 218–309; A. M. Taylor, *Embattled Freedom*, 25–100.

12. Fredrickson, *Big Enough to Be Inconsistent*, 13–15, 21–22, 26–28, 57–61, 93–94, 101–14, 117; Oakes, *Freedom National*, 157–65, 175–76, 274–83; Escott, *"What Shall We Do with the Negro?,"* 25–29, 35–39, 41–45, 50–65; Harris, *Lincoln and the Border States*, 159–93.

13. Onuf, "'To Declare Them a Free and Independent People,'" 6–7, 33 (Jefferson quotations); Dain, *Hideous Monster of the Mind*, 81–83, 98–101, 103–8; D. B. Davis, *Problem of Slavery in the Age of Emancipation*, xiv–xv, 74–82, 83–90, 105–66; Freehling, *Road to Disunion: Secessionists at Bay*, 126–27, 157–61, 188–95; L. K. Ford, *Deliver Us from Evil*, 299–359.

14. Lincoln, Peoria, Illinois, Address, October 16, 1854; Eulogy on Henry Clay, July 6, 1852; and Annual Message to Congress, December 3, 1861, all in *CWL*, 2:255, 132, 5:48 (first, third, and final quotations); Speech on the Dred Scott Decision, July 26, 1857, Teaching American History, accessed May 7, 2020, https://teachingamerican history.org/library/document/speech-on-the-dred-scott-decision/; Fredrickson, *Big Enough to Be Inconsistent*, 57; Rael, *Eighty-Eight Years*, 266; S. B. Paulus, "America's Long Eulogy for Compromise."

15. First quotation in Fagan, *Black Newspaper and the Chosen Nation*, 130; Lincoln, Annual Message to Congress, December 3, 1861, *CWL*, 5:48; Dain, *Hideous Monster of the Mind*, 82–93; Rugemer, *Problem of Emancipation*, 42–53, 92–93, 107–8, 300–301; D. B. Davis, *Problem of Slavery in the Age of Emancipation*, 74–82, 83–90, 105–66; C. L. Paulus, *Slaveholding Crisis*, 48; McPherson, *Ordeal By Fire*, 277.

16. Lincoln, First Annual Message to Congress, December 3, 1861, *CWL*, 5:48–49; Siddali, *From Property to Person*, 70–94, 120–44; E. Foner, *Fiery Trial*, 123–34, 175–91, 184–86, 215–22, 228–46; Hahn, *Nation under Our Feet*, 66–73; McCurry, *Confederate Reckoning*, 218–62; Oakes, *Freedom National*, 119–38, 224–35.

17. "A Common Error," *Harper's Weekly*, April 19, 1862, 242–43.

18. May, *Slavery, Race, and Conquest in the Tropics*, 230–76; Hahn, *Political Worlds of Slavery and Freedom*, 50–51; H. Jones, *Blue and Gray Diplomacy*, 120–21, 178;

Fredrickson, *Big Enough to Be Inconsistent*, 93–114; Escott, *"What Shall We Do with the Negro?,"* 51–55.

19. Lincoln, "Address on Colonization to a Deputation of Negroes," August 14, 1862, *CWL*, 5:371–72.

20. Lincoln, "Address on Colonization to a Deputation of Negroes," August 14, 1862, *CWL*, 5:373–74; Magness and Page, *Colonization after Emancipation*, 43–72; Fredrickson, "Man but Not a Brother"; Neely, "Abraham Lincoln and Black Colonization."

21. McPherson, *Negro's Civil War*, 79–99 (all quotations, pp. 94–98); Egerton, *Wars of Reconstruction*, 185; Escott, *"What Shall We Do with the Negro?,"* 51–65; Rael, *Black Identity and Black Protest*, 237–78; May, *Slavery, Race, and Conquest in the Tropics*, 230–76.

22. McPherson, *Negro's Civil War*, 95 (Smith quotation); May, *Slavery, Race, and Conquest in the Tropics*, 230–34; E. Foner, *Fiery Trial*, 239–40, 259–60; Magness, "The Île-à-Vache."

23. Diary entry, September 26, 1862, in Welles, *Diary of Gideon Welles*, 1:152; Lincoln, "Preliminary Emancipation Proclamation," September 22, 1862, and Annual Message to Congress, December 1, 1862, *CWL*, 5:434, 520; E. Foner, *Fiery Trial*, 230–42; L. P. Masur, *Lincoln's Hundred Days*, 126, 197; McPherson, "Who Freed the Slaves?"; Magness and Page, *Colonization after Emancipation*, 104–28. Lincoln ultimately abandoned his Chiriqui colonization proposal, instead favoring treaties with foreign nations to establish colonies in which African Americans might relocate freely (Vorenberg, "Abraham Lincoln and the Politics of Black Colonization," 36–38). Comprehensive converge and context of the Preliminary Proclamation is found in Oakes, *Freedom National*, 301–39.

24. Lincoln, "Preliminary Emancipation Proclamation," September 22, 1862, *CWL*, 5:434; Rael, *Eighty-Eight Years*, 266–71.

25. McClellan to William H. Aspinwall, September 26, 1862, in Sears, *Civil War Papers of George B. McClellan*, 482; Guelzo, *Lincoln's Emancipation Proclamation*, 178–79, 225–27; H. Jones, *Blue and Gray Diplomacy*, 231 (second and third quotations), 120–23, 146–49, 178–85, 228–32, 240–43; O'Connor, *American Sectionalism in the British Mind*, 180–81; Blackett, *Divided Hearts*, 27–30; Carnahan, *Act of Justice*, 127.

26. H. Jones, *Blue and Gray Diplomacy*, 120–21, 215–51, esp. 233–35 (*Times* quotation, p. 235); Crook, *North, the South, and the Powers*, 224–25, 236–40, 371–75; Doyle, *Cause of All Nations*, 216–20; D. B. Davis, *Problem of Slavery in the Age of Emancipation*, 321–32.

27. Emancipation Proclamation, January 1, 1863, National Archives, accessed June 14, 2017, https://www.archives.gov/exhibits/featured-documents/emancipation-proclamation/transcript.html; Guelzo, *Lincoln's Emancipation Proclamation*, 160–62; Fredrickson, *Big Enough to Be Inconsistent*, 101, 108; E. Foner, *Fiery Trial*, 216–21, 240–55, 265, 268–74, 288, 292, 299, 301, 314, 333; L. P. Masur, *Lincoln's Hundred Days*, 197–99, 219; Rael, *Eighty-Eight Years*, 262–68, 270–71; H. Jones, *Blue and Gray Diplomacy*, 215–320; Oakes, *Freedom National*, 340–92.

28. Brig. Gen. J. W. Phelps to Captain R. S. Davis, July 30, 1862, in Berlin, Reidy, and Rowland, *Freedom's Soldiers*, 62.

29. General Orders No. 17, Department of the South, March 6, 1863, *OR*, ser. 1, vol. 14, p. 1021.

30. Skelton, *American Profession of Arms*, 184–90, 260–81; Freehling, *South vs. the*

South, 119–20, 150–51. This argument and many of the following sources are derived and expanded from Lang, *In the Wake of War*, 7–8, 9–14, 129–57.

31. Paludan, *Presidency of Abraham Lincoln*, 189 (Phillips quotation); in Freehling, *South vs. the South*, 119; and in Lang, *In the Wake of War*, 138; Guyatt, "'An Impossible Idea?,'" 234–63; Oakes, *Freedom National*, 340–92; Gallagher, *Union War*, 2–3, 50–53, 75–76, 79–95, 101–9, 116–19, 141–50. See Fredrickson, *Big Enough to Be Inconsistent*, and E. Foner, *Fiery Trial*, for the leading treatment of Lincoln's views on race.

32. Emberton, *Beyond Redemption*, 71 (Sturtevant quotation); Lincoln to John A. Dix, January 14, 1863, *CWL*, 6:56; Lang, *In the Wake of War*, 136–38; Freehling, *South vs. the South*, 119–20.

33. Grant to Henry W. Halleck, July 24, 1863, *PUSG*, 9:110; Harrison Soule to his father, January 26, 1864, Soule Papers, Bentley Historical Library, University of Michigan; Lang, *In the Wake of War*, 144–53, 156.

34. General Orders No. 17, Department of the South, March 6, 1863, *OR*, ser. 1, vol. 14, p. 1020 (Hunter quotation); Halleck to Grant, March 30, 1863, *PUSG*, 8:93; Lincoln to Andrew Johnson, March 26, 1863, *CWL*, 6:149; Neely, "Colonization and the Myth That Lincoln Prepared the People for Emancipation," 64–65; Dain, *Hideous Monster of the Mind*, 1–39; Lang, *In the Wake of War*, 137–38, 146–48; Guterl, *American Mediterranean*.

35. Hunter to Edwin M. Stanton, June 23, 1862, in Berlin, Reidy, and Rowland, *Freedom's Soldiers*, 52; Winthrop to Frederick Seward, August 25, 1863, in *Negro in the Military Service of the United States*, reel 2, vol. 3, pp. 1528–30; J. E. Johnson, "Race, Foreign Armies and United States Colored Troops"; Lang, *In the Wake of War*, 145–46; Voelz, *Slave and Soldier*, 33–58, 85–88, 161–62.

36. Winthrop to Frederick Seward, August 25, 1863, in *Negro in the Military Service of the United States*, reel 2, vol. 3, pp. 1528–30; J. E. Johnson, "Race, Foreign Armies and United States Colored Troops"; Voelz, *Slave and Soldier*, 33–58, 85–88, 161–62; Lang, *In the Wake of War*, 145–46.

37. "Employment of Enfranchised Negroes as Soldiers," *New York Times*, January 9, 1863; Lincoln, Third Annual Message to Congress, December 8, 1863, *CWL*, 7:50; D. B. Davis, *Problem of Slavery in the Age of Emancipation*, 321.

38. George E. Stephens to Robert Hamilton, April 2, 1863, in *Weekly Anglo-African*, April 11, 1863, reprinted in Ripley, *Black Abolitionist Papers*, 5:199–200, 201, 202; Sheehan-Dean, *Calculus of Violence*, 285–88.

39. H. Ford Douglas to Frederick Douglass, January 8, 1863, reprinted in Redkey, *Grand Army of Black Men*, 24–25.

40. "Address for the Promotion of Colored Enlistments," July 6, 1863, in P. Foner, *Life and Writings of Frederick Douglass*, 3:534–37.

41. "Address for the Promotion of Colored Enlistments," 3:534–37.

42. *Men of Color to Arms! Now or Never!* (1863 poster, photograph), Library of Congress, accessed May 29, 2017, https://www.loc.gov/item/scsm000556/.

43. *Men of Color to Arms! Now or Never!*

44. "Editorial by Robert Hamilton," June 20, 1863, and "Manifesto of the Colored Citizens of the State of New York," July 16, 1863, both in Ripley, *Black Abolitionist Papers*, 5:218, 224–25.

45. African American sailors had always served in integrated crews in the U.S. Navy. Approximately eighteen thousand served during the Civil War. Bennett, *Union Jacks*, 12; Bolster, *Black Jacks*, 7–44, 131–57.

46. It is worth noting that approximately 3 million African Americans remained enslaved throughout the Confederacy in April 1865. Emancipation would come slowly over the next months as Union armies occupied the region. G. P. Downs, *After Appomattox*, 39–45; Berlin et al., *Freedom*, ser. 1, vol. 1: *Destruction of Slavery*, xii; Berlin et al., *Freedom*, ser. 1, vol. 3: *Wartime Genesis of Free Labor*, 77–80; Gallagher, *Union War*, 147–50.

47. Gooding to Abraham Lincoln, September 28, 1863, quoted in Berlin, Reidy, and Rowland, *Freedom's Soldiers*, 385–86, 1–34; Manning, *What This Cruel War Was Over*, 126; Fleche, "African-American Soldiering," in Sheehan-Dean, *Companion to the U.S. Civil War*, 1:297–315; Horton, "Defending the Manhood of the Race," 7; and Redkey, "Brave Black Volunteers," 22.

48. Letter of James Jones, May 8, 1864, quoted in Redkey, *Grand Army of Black Men*, 142–43; final two quotations in Manning, *What This Cruel War Was Over*, 197; Lang, *In the Wake of War*, 158–81; Sheehan-Dean, *Calculus of Violence*, 287–88.

49. Letter of George W. Hatton, May 10, 1864, reprinted in Redkey, *Grand Army of Black Men*, 95–96.

50. Letter of Charles W. Singer, September 18, 1864, reprinted in Redkey, *Grand Army of Black Men*, 213–15.

51. Herschthal, "Dreaming of Haiti" ("Touissant Guards"); Letter of Robert H. Isabelle, February 27, 1863, reprinted in Redkey, *Grand Army of Black Men*, 140; Ohio delegation quoted in *The Liberator*, September 4, 1863, reprinted in McPherson, *Negro's Civil War*, 182–83. I am grateful to Ian Davis, one of my doctoral candidates at Mississippi State University, for bringing the Isabelle letter to my attention.

52. "Dissolution of the American Union," *Douglass' Monthly*, January 1861, quoted in Foner and Taylor, *Frederick Douglass*, 427–28; Rael, *Eighty-Eight Years*, 271–72.

53. Houston, "Address at the Union Mass Meeting, Austin, Texas," September 22, 1860, in Williams and Barker, *Writings of Sam Houston*, 8:145–60; Kennedy, "The Border States: Their Power and Duty in the Present Disordered Condition of the Country," (1861), quoted in Wakelyn, *Southern Pamphlets on Secession*, 231–32, 240.

54. "Remarks of Jefferson Davis on the Special Message on Affairs in South Carolina," January 10, 1861, quoted in Rowland, *Jefferson Davis, Constitutionalist*, 5:30; C. L. Paulus, *Slaveholding Crisis*, 230–34; D. B. Davis, *Problem of Slavery in the Age of Emancipation*, 46–54.

55. *Richmond Examiner*, November 4, 1863, quoted in Bonner, *Mastering America*, 278 (see also 273–85); D. B. Davis, *Problem of Slavery in the Age of Emancipation*, 325–26; Bender, *Nation among Nations*, 132.

56. For compelling endorsements of the idea that the Civil War constituted an authentic enslaved rebellion, see Hahn, *Nation under Our Feet*, 64–73, 82–102; Hahn, *Political Worlds of Slavery and Freedom*, 55–114; McCurry, *Confederate Reckoning*, 218–309.

57. "Georgia Slaveholders to the Commander of the 3 Division of the Confederate District of Georgia," August 1, 1862, in Berlin et al., *Freedom*, ser. 1, vol. 1: *Destruction of Slavery*, 795–98; McCurry, *Confederate Reckoning*, 290–91.

58. "Georgia Slaveholders to the Commander of the 3 Division of the Confederate District of Georgia"; "Charles B. Wilder: Testimony before the American Freedmen's Inquiry Commission," May 9, 1863, in Simpson, *Civil War: Third Year*, 213; McCurry, *Confederate Reckoning*, 290–91; Hahn, *Nation under Our Feet*, 41–43, 57–61, 66–68.

59. Diary entry, July 4, 1862, in J. B. Jones, *Rebel War Clerk's Diary*, 1:141–42; Sed-

don to Jefferson Davis, November 26, 1863, *OR*, ser. 4, vol. 2, p. 999; Davis to the Confederate Congress, August 18, 1862, *OR*, ser. 4, vol. 2, pp. 53, 52; Grimsley, *Hard Hand of War*, 211–12.

60. Clavin, *Toussaint Louverture and the American Civil War*, 147 (Arkansas woman quotation); G. W. Gayle to Jefferson Davis, May 22, 1861, in Berlin et al., *Freedom*, ser. 1, vol. 1: *Destruction of Slavery*, 781; McCurry, *Confederate Reckoning*, 238–47.

61. Davis to the Confederate Congress, August 18, 1862, *OR*, ser. 4, vol. 2, p. 53; Seddon to Gen. G. T. Beauregard, November 30, 1862, in Berlin, Reidy, and Rowland, *Freedom's Soldiers*, 571–72; Bartek, "Rhetoric of Destruction," 235–97.

62. General Orders No. 111 (Proclamation of Jefferson Davis), December 24, 1862, *OR*, ser. 1, vol. 15, pp. 907–8; Lee to James A. Seddon, January 10, 1863, quoted in Dowdey and Manarin, *Wartime Papers of Robert E. Lee*, 390; Glatthaar, *Forged in Battle*, 201–4.

63. Davis to the Confederate Congress, January 12, 1863, *OR*, ser. 4, vol. 2, p. 345 (see also 336–50); Report of Capt. John S. Lay, June 24, 1863, *OR*, ser. 1, vol. 14, p. 306; Rumley diary entries, January 1 and May 30, 1863, in Browning, *Southern Mind under Union Rule*, 53–54, 70; McCurry, *Confederate Reckoning*, 257–59; Rable, *Damn Yankees!*, 78–79, 84–94, 107–14, 121–26.

64. *San Antonio Semi-Weekly News*, August 11, 1862, quoted in Bartek, "Rhetoric of Destruction," 264; Charles Clark to Citizens of Columbus, Mississippi, November 16, 1863, *OR*, ser. 4, vol. 2, pp. 960, 961; J. Phillips, *Diehard Rebels*, 54–55; Clavin, *Toussaint Louverture and the American Civil War*, 144–61; Rugemer, *Problem of Emancipation*, 57–65, 86–93, 105–8, 189–94, 218–20; C. L. Paulus, *Slaveholding Crisis*, 20–32, 40–45, 187–94, 220–26.

65. Edmonston diary entry, February 10, 1863, quoted in Crabtree and Patton, *"Journal of a Secesh Lady,"* 357; Cumming diary entry, October 6, 1863, quoted in Harwell, *Kate*, 158; Rumley diary entries, August 4 and June 1, 1863, quoted in Browning, *Southern Mind under Union Rule*, 85, 70; McCurry, *Confederate Reckoning*, 31–33, 222, 241, 287–93.

66. Joint Resolutions of the Confederate Congress, May 1, 1863, and January 22, 1864, *OR*, ser. 2, vol. 5, pp. 940–41, and ser. 4, vol. 3, pp. 126, 131, 133, 134; Clavin, *Toussaint Louverture and the American Civil War*, 148–51.

67. Davis, "Speech in Jackson, Mississippi, December 26, 1862," in Cooper, *Jefferson Davis: Essential Writings*, 279–80; Col. John R. F. Tattnall to Capt. S. Croom, November 8, 1862, quoted in Berlin, Reidy, and Rowland, *Freedom's Soldiers*, 570–71; J. W. Paup to My Dear Wife, June 29, 1863, quoted in Schieffler, "A 'Sickly, Pestilential, Crowded Post,'" cited with permission from the author; Smith quoted in Guelzo, *Fateful Lightning*, 377; Longstreet orders, July 1, 1863, *OR*, ser. 1, vol. 51, pt. 2, pp. 733; Alexander, "Regular Slave Hunt," 84–88; Urwin, "We Cannot Treat Negroes . . . as Prisoners of War"; Guelzo, *Gettysburg*, 72–74, 105–6; C. E. Woodward, *Marching Masters*, 104–53; Burkhardt, *Confederate Rage, Yankee Wrath*, 12–55; McCurry, *Confederate Reckoning*, 289–98.

68. Guelzo, *Fateful Lightning*, 378 (first quotations); Edmonston diary entry, April 22, 1864, quoted in Crabtree and Patton, *"Journal of a Secesh Lady,"* 549–50; Burkhardt, *Confederate Rage, Yankee Wrath*, 105–17; C. E. Woodward, *Marching Masters*, 7–8, 143–48, 187–99; Castel, "Fort Pillow Massacre"; Bennett, "Black Flag and Confederate Soldiers"; Sheehan-Dean, *Calculus of Violence*, 272–85; Silkenat, *Raising the White Flag*, 154–64, 175–79.

69. Bartek, "Rhetoric of Destruction," 292, 291 (first two quotations); Gallagher, *Fighting for the Confederacy*, 462 (Alexander quotation); Levin, *Remembering the Battle of the Crater*, 7–32; Silkenat, *Raising the White Flag*, 179–84.

70. Stephens, "Cornerstone Address," quoted in Wakelyn, *Southern Pamphlets on Secession*, 406; Bennett, "Black Flag and Confederate Soldiers"; Grimsley, "'Very Long Shadow'"; Manning, *What This Cruel War Was Over*, 140–41, 169–70, 175–76; Bartek, "Rhetoric of Destruction," 275–91; Grimsley, "'Very Long Shadow,'" 232. For an instructive postbattle report on the treatment of USCT prisoners, see Report of Col. Lewis Johnson, 44 USCT, October 17, 1864, *OR*, ser. 1, vol. 39, pt. 1, pp. 717–21.

71. Lincoln, "Order of Retaliation," July 30, 1863, *CWL*, 6:357; Dilbeck, *More Civil War*, 103–4 (Lieber quotation).

72. Sherman and *Chicago Tribune* both quoted in Tap, "'These Devils Are Not Fit to Live on God's Earth,'" 118; Dilbeck, *More Civil War*, 92–98, 102–8, 123–27; Sheehan-Dean, "*Lex Talionis* in the U.S. Civil War."

73. Lincoln, "Address at Sanitary Fair," April 18, 1864, *CWL*, 7:303; Tap, "'These Devils Are Not Fit to Live on God's Earth,'" 131 (Wade quotation); General Orders No. 100, Articles 58, 60, 68, 27, and 28 (quotations), and Articles 23, 42, 43 (on slavery and emancipation), *1863 Laws of War*, pp. 39, 38, 43, 46, 47, 48; Dilbeck, *More Civil War*, 102–8.

74. John P. Usher to Abraham Lincoln, May 6, 1864, *Abraham Lincoln Papers*, ser. 1, *General Correspondence*, Library of Congress, accessed February 22, 2019, https://www.loc.gov/item/mal3291800; Neely, *Civil War and the Limits of Destruction*, 181 (Sumner quotation), 179–97; Sheehan-Dean, *Calculus of Violence*, 356; Dilbeck, *More Civil War*, 102–8.

75. Letter of George W. Reed, May [14], 1864, in Redkey, *Grand Army of Black Men*, 273; K. W. Lewis, *Curse upon the Nation*, 184 (Turner quotation); Sheehan-Dean, *Calculus of Violence*, 285–88; Neely, *Civil War and the Limits of Destruction*, 179–97; Dilbeck, *More Civil War*, 102–8; Sheehan-Dean, "*Lex Talionis* in the U.S. Civil War," 180–83; Burkhardt, *Confederate Rage, Yankee Wrath*, 121–22.

76. Letter of Joseph E. Williams, June 23, 1863, quoted in Redkey, *Grand Army of Black Men*, 90–91.

77. Lincoln to James C. Conkling, August 26, 1863, *CWL*, 6:409–10; Lincoln, Address at Baltimore Sanitary Fair, April 18, 1864, *CWL*, 7:302; Lincoln, Last Public Address, April 11, 1865, *CWL*, 8:403; L. P. Masur, *Lincoln's Last Speech*, 164–69; Foner, *Fiery Trial*, 258–61, 330–33; Fredrickson, *Big Enough to Be Inconsistent*, 113–19.

78. Stringfellow to Davis, February 8, 1865, quoted in Berlin, Reidy, and Rowland, *Freedom's Soldiers*, 291–96; McCurry, *Confederate Reckoning*, 310–57, esp. 342; Levine, *Confederate Emancipation*, 89–147, esp. 99–102.

79. Cleburne [and others] to Joseph E. Johnston, January 2, 1864, *OR*, ser. 1, vol. 52, pt. 2, pp. 586–92; Levine, *Confederate Emancipation*, 27–40, 83–94; C. E. Woodward, *Marching Masters*, 155–79; McCurry, *Confederate Reckoning*, 310–57.

80. Stringfellow to Davis, February 8, 1865, quoted in Berlin, Reidy, and Rowland, *Freedom's Soldiers*, 291–96; Bonner, *Mastering America*, 311–22.

81. Cobb to James A. Seddon, January 8, 1865, *OR*, ser. 4, vol. 3, p. 1009; Levine, *Confederate Emancipation*, 129–47; McCurry, *Confederate Reckoning*, 350–61.

82. Lincoln, Second Inaugural Address, March 4, 1865, *CWL*, 8:333; Douglass (June 1861), quoted in McPherson, *Negro's Civil War*, 84–85.

Chapter 6

1. Edmonston diary entries, April 16, 20, and May 7, 1865, in Crabtree and Patton, *"Journal of a Secesh Lady,"* 694, 702, 708; Gallagher, *Confederate War*, 157–72; Rubin, *Shattered Nation*, 112–39; J. Phillips, *Diehard Rebels*, 147–77; Varon, *Appomattox*, 48–134.

2. Edmonston diary entries, January 9, June 26, July 28, and May 7, 1865, in Crabtree and Patton, *"Journal of a Secesh Lady,"* 652–53, 713, 716, 709. For important treatments of women as slaveholders, see Faust, *Mothers of Invention*, 6–7, 61–78, 187; and Jones-Rogers, *They Were Her Property*, 4–17, 60–88, 149–50, 196.

3. Kirkland, *Letter to Peter Cooper*, 5.

4. Kirkland, *Letter to Peter Cooper*, 16, 18; Blight, *Race and Reunion*, 6–30; Janney, *Remembering the Civil War*, 40–72; Blair, *With Malice toward Some*, 7–8, 234–303.

5. Kirkland, *Letter to Peter Cooper*, 20, 44.

6. C. V. Woodward, *Burden of Southern History*, 3–26; Blight, *Race and Reunion*, 6–30; Janney, *Remembering the Civil War*, 40–72; Blair, *With Malice toward Some*, 7–8, 234–303.

7. Kirkland, *Letter to Peter Cooper*, 40; General Orders No. 100, Article 15, in *1863 Laws of War*, 119; Lang, "Union Demobilization and the Boundaries of War and Peace," 180.

8. Kirkland, *Letter to Peter Cooper*, 45; Dilbeck, *More Civil War*, 157–62.

9. Blair, *With Malice toward Some*, 235–44, 251–62; Cooper, *Jefferson Davis, American*, 579–620; Leonard, *Lincoln's Avengers*, 67–136, 137–64; McKnight, *Confederate Outlaw*, 160, 176–78; Marvel, *Andersonville*, 241–47, 307–8; Blair, "Reconciliation as a Political Strategy," 217–31.

10. Donald, *Lincoln*, 574 (first quotations); Lincoln, Second Inaugural Address, March 4, 1865, Avalon Project, accessed May 5, 2020, http://avalon.law.yale.edu/19th _century/lincoln2.asp (final quotation); Waugh, "'I Only Knew What Was in My Mind,'" 320–31.

11. Grant to Lee, April 9, 1865, *PUSG*, 14:371, 373–74; Simpson, Graf, and Muldowny, *Advice after Appomattox*, xxi (second Grant quotation). For recent debates on Appomattox as the war's definitive end, see Waugh, "'I Only Knew What Was in My Mind,'" 320–31; Waugh, *U. S. Grant*, 90–101; Varon, *Appomattox*; and G. P. Downs, *After Appomattox*.

12. Rhodes diary entries, April 9, 28, and May 12, 1865, in R. H. Rhodes, *All for the Union*, 221–22, 226, 230; John F. Brobst to Mary Brobst, April 22, 1865, in Roth, *Well Mary*, 135; Lang, *In the Wake of War*, 185–89; G. P. Downs, *After Appomattox*, 11–38.

13. Fisk letter, May 19, 1865, in Rosenblatt and Rosenblatt, *Hard Marching Every Day*, 326–27; Lang, *In the Wake of War*, 186–87; Varon, *Appomattox*, 79–101.

14. Dick diary entries, April 10, 1865, in G. Carter, *Troubled State*, 190–92; Musser to Dear Father, May 14, 1865, in Popchuck, *Soldier Boy*, 205; John F. Brobst to Mary Brobst, May 27, 1865, in Roth, *Well Mary*, 205.

15. Lincoln, Second Inaugural Address, March 4, 1865, *CWL*, 8:332; "Salutatory," *The Sixth Corps*, May 5, 1865, New York State Military Museum and Veterans Research Center, accessed January 27, 2019, https://dmna.ny.gov/historic/reghist/civil /infantry/77thInf/6thCorpsNews/SixthCorpsNewsV1N8_5May1865_front.htm; Dilbeck, *More Civil War*, 157–61; Neff, *War and the Law of Nations*, 116–18, 194–95; Hsieh, *West Pointers and the Civil War*, 94.

16. Donald, *Lincoln*, 574 (Lincoln quotation); Waugh, "'I Only Knew What Was in My Mind,'" 321.

17. U. S. Grant to Julia Grant, April 25, 1865, *PUSG*, 14:433; Grant, interview with *New York Herald*, July 24, 1878, *PUSG*, 28:421; Lee quoted in Winik, *April 1865*, 189; Simpson, *Let Us Have Peace*, 86–109; Waugh, "'I Only Knew What Was in My Mind,'" 326; Blair, *With Malice toward Some*, 243. For compelling arguments that endorse the war continuing beyond Confederate surrender, see G. P. Downs, *After Appomattox*, 1–10, passim; Grimsley, "Wars for the American South," 6–22; and Blair, "Finding the Ending of America's Civil War," 1753–66.

18. Davis, "To the People of the Confederate States of America," April 4, 1865, in Cooper, *Jefferson Davis: Essential Writings*, 363–65; Gallagher, *Fighting for the Confederacy*, 532 (Alexander and Lee quotations); Hsieh, *West Pointers and the Civil War*, 1–3, 10–19, 111–13, 123–24; Gallagher, *Confederate War*, 140–44.

19. Gallagher, *Fighting for the Confederacy*, 532 (first four Lee quotations); Lee to Davis, April 20, 1865, in Dowdey and Manarin, *Wartime Papers of Robert E. Lee*, 939; E. M. Thomas, "Ambivalent Visions of Victory," 32–34; Varon, *Appomattox*, 88–89; Fredrickson, *Why the Confederacy Did Not Fight a Guerrilla War after the Fall of Richmond*, 7–29.

20. Sam Pickens diary entries, April 11 and 12, 1865, in Hubbs, *Voices from Company D*, 370–71; J. Phillips, *Diehard Rebels*, 171–74; Gallagher, *Confederate War*, 157–72; Varon, *Appomattox*, 157–66; Rubin, *Shattered Nation*, 117–38.

21. Charles Huston, April 1865, quoted in Rubin, *Shattered Nation*, 131–32.

22. Jared Sanders, May 1865, quoted in Rubin, *Shattered Nation*, 132–33.

23. Rubin, *Shattered Nation*, 131–32 (Huston and Sanders quotations); Gallagher, *Confederate War*, 120–27, 140–53; Fredrickson, *Why the Confederacy Did Not Fight a Guerrilla War after the Fall of Richmond*, 7–29; Hess, "Civil War Guerrillas in a Global, Comparative Context," 348–50.

24. James A. Scott (Virginia Confederate) quoted in Gallagher, *Confederate War*, 163; Confederate guerrilla quoted in Sutherland, *Savage Conflict*, 269.

25. Foster diary entries, April 28 and 30, May 3, 1865, in N. D. Brown, *One of Cleburne's Command*, 170, 171, 173.

26. Rumley diary entries, April 26 and 27, 1865, in Browning, *Southern Mind under Union Rule*, 173–74.

27. Stone diary entry, May 15, 1865, in Anderson, *Brokenburn*, 339–40.

28. Grant to Andrew Johnson, December 18, 1865, *PUSG*, 15:434–37; Silkenat, *Raising the White Flag*, 15–19, 184–85, 274–97.

29. E. B. Pryor, *Reading the Man*, 434, 453 (Lee quotations); Waugh, *U. S. Grant*, 100.

30. Waugh, "'I Only Knew What Was in My Mind,'" 320–31; Sheehan-Dean, *Calculus of Violence*, 344–51; Silkenat, *Raising the White Flag*, 1–4, 189–259, 295–98.

31. Melville, *Battle-Pieces and Aspects of the War*, 271, 265; Varon, *Appomattox*, 149 (Phillips quotation); Sherman to Salmon P. Chase, May 6, 1865, *OR*, ser. 1, vol. 47, pt. 3, pp. 410–11; Blair, "Reconciliation as a Political Strategy," 217–31.

32. Sherman to Joseph D. Webster, April 17, 1865, Sherman to Henry W. Halleck, April 18, 1865, and Memorandum of Surrender Agreement, April 18, 1865, all in Simpson and Berlin, *Sherman's Civil War*, 863–65; G. P. Downs, *After Appomattox*, 15–19; Silkenat, *Raising the White Flag*, 221–46; Marszalek, *Sherman*, 341–59; Bradley, *Bluecoats and Tar Heels*, 14–22.

33. Sherman to Salmon P. Chase, May 6, 1865, in Simpson and Berlin, *Sherman's Civil War*, 888–89; G. P. Downs, *After Appomattox*, 15–19.

34. Kirkland, *Letter to Peter Cooper*, 11, 16; Sermon of Rev. James Freeman Clarke, in *Sermons Preached in Boston on the Death of Abraham Lincoln*, 101; Blair, *With Malice toward Some*, 256–57, 268.

35. "Defenders of the Union," *New York Herald*, reprinted in *The Sixth Corps*, May 11, 1865, New York State Military Museum and Veterans Research Center, accessed January 27, 2019, https://dmna.ny.gov/historic/reghist/civil/infantry/77thInf/6thCorpsNews /SixthCorpsNewsV1N13_11May1865_front.htm; Holberton, *Homeward Bound*, xiii, 7–16, 31–38, 53–80; Clarke, "'Let All Nations See,'" 81–93; Emberton, *Beyond Redemption*, 13–14; Summers, *Ordeal of the Reunion*, 13–17, 36–37 (quotation, p. 36); Newell and Shrader, "U.S. Army's Transition to Peace"; Lang, "Union Demobilization and the Boundaries of War and Peace," 180.

36. Musser to Dear Father, July 15, 1865, in Popchuck, *Soldier Boy*, 215; Fisk to *Green Mountain Freeman*, June 25, and July 26, 1865, in Rosenblatt, *Hard Marching Every Day*, 336, 342; Madison Bowler to Lizzie Bowler, May 16, and June 3, 1865, in Foroughi, *Go If You Think It Your Duty*, 288, 296; Lang, *In the Wake of War*, 186.

37. Tocqueville, *Democracy in America* (ed. Mansfield and Winthrop), 623; Holberton, *Homeward Bound*, 9.

38. Whitman, "Return of the Heroes" (1867), in *Complete Writings of Walt Whitman*, 2:132; Gallagher, *Union War*, 124–25; Holberton, *Homeward Bound*, 7–16, 53–80; Kreidberg and Henry, *History of Mobilization in the United States Army*, 141; P. Kennedy, *Rise and Fall of the Great Powers*, 203; Lang, "Union Demobilization and the Boundaries of War and Peace," 181. Demobilization was also the result of rancorous political debates between Republicans and Democrats. So-called Radical Republicans demanded a much stronger postwar military presence, while moderates and Democrats favored a stark reduction in federal military power. This debate would continue well into the 1870s, until "the question of the army's role [began] fracturing the Republican Party in new ways" (G. P. Downs, *After Appomattox*, 223 [quotation], 89–106, 141–53, 188–89, 223–33; Newell and Shrader, "U.S. Army's Transition to Peace"). The implications of military occupation are explored later in this chapter and in chapters 7 and 8.

39. Clarke, "'Let All Nations See,'" 92 (Schofield quotation); Summers, *Ordeal of the Reunion*, 36–40; Gallagher, *Union War*, 27–30, 124–26; Lang, "Union Demobilization and the Boundaries of War and Peace," 181–82.

40. Quotations in *Report of Vincent*, 16–17, derived from B. M. Jordan, *Marching Home*, 41–42; Gallagher, *Union War*, 125–29.

41. "General Grant and His Advisors," *Harper's Weekly*, November 2, 1867, 690; Lang, *In the Wake of War*, 198.

42. "General Grant and His Advisors," *Harper's Weekly*, November 2, 1867, 690. These questions are pursued in G. P. Downs, *After Appomattox*; Summers, *Ordeal of the Reunion*; and Lang, *In the Wake of War*.

43. "General Grant and His Advisors," *Harper's Weekly*, November 2, 1867, 690; De Forest, *Union Officer in the Reconstruction*, 153; Lang, *In the Wake of War*, 60–81, 182–98, esp. 196–97; Lang, "Union Demobilization and the Boundaries of War and Peace," 184.

44. Schurz, "The Logical Results of the War," September 8, 1866 (first, third, and fourth quotations), and "Report on the Condition of the South," December 19, 1865

(second quotation), in Bancroft, *Speeches, Correspondence and Political Papers of Carl Schurz*, 1:377, 318, 379, 378; Slap, *Doom of Reconstruction*, 8–13, 73–106, esp. 76–78, 84–86; Blair, "Use of Military Force"; Lang, "Republicanism, Race, and Reconstruction"; G. P. Downs, *After Appomattox*, 94–100; Summers, *Ordeal of the Reunion*, 36–68.

45. Schurz, "Report on the Condition of the South," in Bancroft, *Speeches, Correspondence and Political Papers of Carl Schurz*, 1:364–65; Slap, *Doom of Reconstruction*, 76–77.

46. *Cincinnati Commercial*, December 16, 1865, quoted in Slap, *Doom of Reconstruction*, 76.

47. "Speech of Richard Henry Dana," *New York Times*, June 24, 1865, 8.

48. "Speech of Richard Henry Dana"; Lang, "Union Demobilization and the Boundaries of War and Peace," 183–84.

49. "Speech of Richard Henry Dana."

50. "Speech of Richard Henry Dana"; Blair, "Use of Military Force"; Lang, "Republicanism, Race, and Reconstruction"; Downs, *After Appomattox*, 67–69.

51. Lang, "Union Demobilization and the Boundaries of War and Peace," 184. On the grasp of war as a continuation of the Civil War, see Benedict, "Preserving the Constitution," 72–74; G. P. Downs, *After Appomattox*, 67; Blair, "Finding the Ending of America's Civil War," 1761–62; and McPherson, *War That Forged a Nation*, 175.

52. Neff, *Justice in Blue and Gray*, 204–8; Glatthaar, "Civil War"; Edwards, *Legal History of the Civil War and Reconstruction*, 54–63, 79–81; "Rebel Belligerent Rights Withdrawn," *Harper's Weekly*, July 1, 1865, 403.

53. Kelly, "North American Crisis of the 1860s"; Schoonover, *Dollars over Dominion*, 95–100, 126–39, 178–211; Schoonover, "Napoleon Is Coming! Maximilian Is Coming?"; Crook, *North, the South, and the Powers*, 345–70; H. Jones, *Blue and Gray Diplomacy*, 285–320.

54. J. Phillips, *Diehard Rebels*, 158–59, 172–73 (Montgomery quotation, p. 159); Heartsill diary entry, May 6, 1865, in Heartsill, *Fourteen Hundred and 91 Days in the Confederate Army*, 241; Hardin diary entry, April 25, 1865, in Clift, *Private War of Lizzie Hardin*, 233.

55. Stephens, "Cornerstone Address," March 21, 1861, in Wakelyn, *Southern Pamphlets on Secession*, 402–12; Hanna and Hanna, *Napoleon III and Mexico*, 118–20.

56. Hardin diary entry, April 25, 1865, in Clift, *Private War of Lizzie Hardin*, 233; Foster diary entries, April 19, 21, and 24, 1865, in Brown, *One of Cleburne's Command*, 166–67; J. Phillips, *Diehard Rebels*, 172–73; Rubin, *Shattered Nation*, 123–25.

57. Roark, *Masters without Slaves*, 121–32 (Virginian quotation, p. 122); Sutherland, "Exiles, Emigrants, and Sojourners," 244 (Alabamian quotation); Rolle, *Lost Cause*, 9; J. Phillips, *Diehard Rebels*, 180–81; Guterl, *American Mediterranean*, 71–113; Hanna and Hanna, *Confederate Exiles*; Weaver, "Confederate Emigration to Brazil"; Hanna and Hanna, *Napoleon III and Mexico*, 221–35; Arthur, *General Jo Shelby's March*, 65–194.

58. Diary entries, April 18 and 25, 1865, in E. F. Andrews, *War-Time Journal of a Georgia Girl*, 153, 184; Guterl, *American Mediterranean*, 77–78; Rolle, *Lost Cause*, 9.

59. Diary entries, April 25 and June 27, 1865, in E. F. Andrews, *War-Time Journal of a Georgia Girl*, 184, 316, 317; Guterl, *American Mediterranean*, 77–78; May, *Southern Dream of a Caribbean Empire*, 257.

60. Grant to Andrew Johnson, June 19, 1865, *OR*, ser. 1, vol. 48, pt. 2, pp. 923–24.

61. Republican National Convention and Seward both quoted in Crook, *North, the South, and the Powers*, 354; "Our French-Mexican Relations," *Harper's Weekly*, December 9, 1865, 771; Report of Philip H. Sheridan, November 14, 1866, *OR*, ser. 1, vol. 48, pt. 1, p. 300; Schoonover, *Dollars over Dominion*, 198 (third and fourth Sheridan quotations); Kelly, "North American Crisis of the 1860s," 337.

62. U. S. Grant, *Personal Memoirs*, 758; Grant to Andrew Johnson, June 19, 1865, *OR*, ser. 1, vol. 48, pt. 2, pp. 923–24; Kelly, "North American Crisis of the 1860s," 360–62.

63. Speech of William H. Seward, October 20, 1865, in G. E. Baker, *Works of William H. Seward*, 5:528; Sexton, *Monroe Doctrine*, 151–57.

64. Thomas J. Anderson to James H. Anderson, August 2, 1865, in Anderson and Anderson, *Life and Letters of Judge Thomas J. Anderson*, 451; "European Situation with Reference to the United States and War," *New York Herald*, May 2, 1865, reprinted in *The Sixth Corps*, May 6, 1865, New York State Military Museum and Veterans Research Center, accessed January 27, 2019, https://dmna.ny.gov/historic/reghist/civil/infantry/77thInf/6thCorpsNews/SixthCorpsNewsV1N9_6May1865_back.htm; Kelly, "North American Crisis of the 1860s," 360–62; Hanna and Hanna, *Napoleon III and Mexico*, 236–307.

65. *New York Herald*, August 1, 1865, quoted in Crook, *North, the South, and the Powers*, 361; Potts to William H. Seward, November 21, 1865, quoted in Neely, *Civil War and the Limits of Destruction*, 90.

66. Nicolay and Hay quoted in Abbott, "Civil War and the Crime Wave," 68 (source derived from Emberton, *Beyond Redemption*, 29–30); B. M. Jordan, *Marching Home*, 41–66.

67. Corwin quoted in Schoonover, *Dollars over Dominion*, 57; and in Sexton, *Monroe Doctrine*, 143–44.

68. Crook, *North, the South, and the Powers*, 366 (Bigelow quotation).

69. Grant to George H. Thomas, March 28, 1866, *PUSG*, 16:139–40; Simpson, *Let Us Have Peace*, 113; Dobak, *Freedom by the Sword*, 425–54; Lang, *In the Wake of War*, 206–9.

70. Grant to William T. Sherman, October 31, 1865, to Frederick Steele, May 21, 1865, and to George H. Thomas, November 4, 1865, all in *PUSG*, 15:377–38, 80–81, 390; Simpson, "Quandaries of Command," 136–37; Zalimas, "Black Union Soldiers in the Postwar South," 100–106; Dobak, *Freedom by the Sword*, 425–54.

71. Sheridan to Grant, November 20, 1865, *PUSG*, 15:425; Report of Matías Romero, June 18, 1865, in Schoonover, *Mexican Lobby*, 69; Work, "United States Colored Troops in Texas," 343–44; Simpson, "Quandaries of Command," 136.

72. Sheridan, *Personal Memoirs of P. H. Sheridan*, 217–18; White letter, September 19, 1865, in Redkey, *Grand Army of Black Men*, 201; Work, "United States Colored Troops in Texas," 343–44; Glatthaar, *Forged in Battle*, 218–19.

73. William Winthrop to Frederick Seward, August 25, 1863, in *Negro in the Military Service of the United States*, reel 2, vol. 3, pp. 1528–30; Kelley quoted in J. E. Johnson, "Race, Foreign Armies and United States Colored Troops" (Johnson's essay was critical in framing my argument and for locating sources); Hooker quoted in Wilson, *Black Phalanx*, 295.

74. Sherman to Salmon P. Chase, May 6, 1865, in Simpson and Berlin, *Sherman's Civil War*, 890; Hanna and Hanna, *Napoleon III and Mexico*, 261–62; Neely, *Civil War and the Limits of Destruction*, 72–108 (Seward quotation, p. 100); G. P. Downs, "Mexicanization of American Politics."

75. Quotations in Neely, *Civil War and the Limits of Destruction*, 100.

76. "The Release of Jefferson Davis," *The Nation*, May 16, 1867, 397; Cooper, *Jefferson Davis, American*, 540–610.

77. "Maximilian and Jefferson Davis," *New York Times*, July 17, 1867. My interpretation of Davis's capture and nontrial is drawn from Guterl, *American Mediterranean*, 72–78.

78. "Maximilian and Jefferson Davis"; Guterl, *American Mediterranean*, 72–73; Rubin, *Shattered Nation*, 201–7; Janney, *Remembering the Civil War*, 61, 74, 80–83; Varon, *Appomattox*, 110, 188–89, 192; Nicoletti, *Secession on Trial*, 6–7, 23–25, 63–79, 129, 153–64, 308–9; Icenhauer-Ramirez, *Treason on Trial*, 226–92.

79. G. Smith, "Gerrit Smith on the Bailing of Jefferson Davis," 1–2; Guterl, *American Mediterranean*, 74; Blair, *With Malice toward Some*, 251–54.

80. G. Smith, "Gerrit Smith on the Bailing of Jefferson Davis," 1–2.

81. G. Smith, "Gerrit Smith on the Bailing of Jefferson Davis," 2; Blair, *With Malice toward Some*, 257–58 (Child quotation); G. P. Downs, "Mexicanization of American Politics"; Dilbeck, *More Civil War*, 157–62; Kelly, "Lost Continent of Abraham Lincoln," 225–26.

82. Lincoln, Annual Message to Congress, December 6, 1864, *CWL*, 8:149; Samito, *Lincoln and the Thirteenth Amendment*, 125 (Phillips quotation); "Consolidation," *Harper's Weekly*, December 9, 1865, 771.

83. Lincoln, "Response to a Serenade," February 1, 1865, *CWL*, 8:255; Julian journal entry, February 1, 1865, and Garnet, "Let the Monster Perish," February 12, 1865, in Sheehan-Dean, *Civil War: Final Year*, 570, 588, 597; Vorenberg, *Final Freedom*, 29–30, 53–71, 89–114, 127–42, 171–97, 211–33, 208.

84. *The Nation*, July 13, 1865, quoted in E. Foner, *Reconstruction*, 24–25; J. Phillips, *Diehard Rebels*, 181–82.

Chapter 7

1. White letter, April 12, 1865, quoted in Redkey, *Grand Army of Black Men*, 175–78.

2. Paul Ambrose [John Pendleton Kennedy] to William Winston Seaton, July 1865, in J. P. Kennedy, *Mr. Ambrose's Letters on the Rebellion*, 239–40. Paul Ambrose was the pen name used by Marylander John Pendleton Kennedy.

3. Rumley diary entries, April 21, June 11, and June 5, 1865, quoted in Browning, *Southern Mind under Union Rule*, 172, 180, 177.

4. Lincoln, Second Inaugural Address, March 4, 1865, *CWL*, 8:332–33.

5. Osterhammel, *Transformation of the World*, 417; Summers, *Ordeal of the Reunion*, 1–6, 58–106; Summers, *Dangerous Stir*.

6. Tocqueville, *Democracy in America* (ed. Mansfield and Winthrop), 345–46; Tocqueville, "Report on Abolition," July 23, 1839, in Drescher, *Tocqueville and Beaumont on Social Reform*, 109, 130 (see also 99–136). E. Foner, *Nothing but Freedom*, 29–36, instructed on the use of Tocqueville.

7. Tocqueville, "Report on Abolition," in Drescher, *Tocqueville and Beaumont on Social Reform*, 117; E. Foner, *Nothing but Freedom*, 14–24; Rael, *Eighty-Eight Years*, 286–95.

8. Rael, *Eighty-Eight Years*, 280–95.

9. Lincoln, Last Public Address, April 11, 1865, *CWL*, 8:400–401, 403, 404, 405; Lincoln, "Proclamation of Amnesty and Reconstruction," December 8, 1863, *CWL*,

7:53–56; L. P. Masur, *Lincoln's Last Speech*, 11, 16–17, 32, 107–8, 153, 189; E. Foner, *Reconstruction*, 35–37, 60–61, 66, 73, 192; Summers, *Ordeal of the Reunion*, 10–12, 14–16, 20–26, 30–31.

10. E. Foner, *Nothing but Freedom*, 8–9; E. Foner, *Short History of Reconstruction*, 107 (second Stevens quotation); E. Foner, *Reconstruction*, 222, 235–37, 241–46, 308–10, 330; Guelzo, *Fateful Lightning*, 485; Kolchin, "Comparative Perspectives on Emancipation in the U.S. South"; Kolchin, *Unfree Labor*.

11. Douglass, "What the Black Man Wants," January 26, 1865, in McKivigan, *Douglass Papers*, ser. 1, 4:62, 63 (see also 59–69).

12. Kirkland, *Letter to Peter Cooper*, 44–45; "What Europe Thinks," *Harper's Weekly*, July 8, 1865, 418; Elazar, "Civil War and the Preservation of American Federalism"; Benedict, "Preserving the Constitution," 81; E. Foner, *Nothing but Freedom*, 39–46; Gallagher, *Union War*, 151–53; D. T. Carter, *When the War Was Over*, 24–60; E. Foner, *Short History of Reconstruction*, 133.

13. Circular No. 5 (General Howard), May 30, 1865, *House Ex. Docs.*, 39th Congress, 1st sess., 1865–66, pp. 45–46; Letter of T. W. Sherman, January 15, 1862, *OR*, ser. 2, vol. 1, pp. 802–3; Rael, *Eighty-Eight Years*, 283–84 (Rael was essential in framing my argument); Rose, *Rehearsal for Reconstruction*, 204–26, 298–313, 337–56, 374–77; E. Foner, *Reconstruction*, 68–70, 142–44, 151–68; Summers, *Ordeal of the Reunion*, 54–57; Guelzo, *Reconstruction*, 42–44.

14. Johnson, "Interview with Pennsylvania Delegation," May 3, 1865, *PAJ*, 8:20; Perman, *Reunion without Compromise*, 68–80, 95–109.

15. Johnson, "Remarks on the Fall of Richmond," April 3, 1865, "Veto of Civil Rights Bill," March 27, 1866, and "Annual Message to Congress," December 4, 1865, all in *PAJ*, 7:545, 10:313, 9:474; "Speech on the Restoration of State Government" (1864), in Wakelyn, *Southern Unionist Pamphlets and the Civil War*, 260 (second quotation).

16. Gallagher, *Confederate War*, 162 (first quotation); Fitzhugh, "Justice to the Negro," *DeBow's Review*, July 1866, 91; Sarah Whittlesey to Andrew Johnson, October 12, 1865, in Simpson, *Reconstruction*, 123; Hahn, *Nation under Our Feet*, 173–75; Rable, *But There Was No Peace*, 26; Zuczek, *State of Rebellion*, 173–75; Emberton, *Beyond Redemption*, 32–33; Lang, *In the Wake of War*, 204–7.

17. E. Foner, *Nothing but Freedom*, 26–27 (first quotation, p. 27); Rugemer, *Problem of Emancipation*, 295 (second and third quotations, from *Lynchburg Daily Virginian*, November 11, 1865), 291–301; C. L. Paulus, *Slaveholding Crisis*, 236–37.

18. D. T. Carter, "Anatomy of Fear," 353, 357 (first and final quotations); Hugh P. Kennedy (Louisianan) to Johnson, July 21, 1865, *PAJ*, 8:653–54; E. G. Baker to Citizens of Panola, Mississippi, October 22, 1865, in Berlin et al., *Free at Last*, 519–21; D. T. Carter, *When the War Was Over*, 24–95; Rable, *But There Was No Peace*, 16–32; Williams, "Symbols of Defeat," in Urwin, *Black Flag over Dixie*, 210–30; Hahn, *Nation under Our Feet*, 146–54; Summers, *Dangerous Stir*, 49–68; C. L. Paulus, *Slaveholding Crisis*, 232–33; Lang, *In the Wake of War*, 204–6.

19. Jefferson Davis to Varina Davis, November 21, 1865, *PJD*, 12:53; Edmonston diary entry, May 13, 1865, in Crabtree and Patton, "*Journal of a Secesh Lady*," 711; Roark, *Masters without Slaves*, 123 (planter quotation).

20. *Dallas Herald*, December 29, 1866; James Rumley diary entry, June 5, 1865, in Browning, *Southern Mind under Union Rule*, 178; Johnson, "Annual Message to Congress," December 4, 1865, *PAJ*, 9:484; E. Foner, *Reconstruction*, 66–67, 199–209.

21. Zuczek, *State of Rebellion*, 15 (Rhett quotation); "Department of the Freedmen," *DeBow's Review*, September 1866, 309; E. Foner, *Nothing but Freedom*, 17, 24, 49, 52–54, 59, 66.

22. Schurz, "Report on the Condition of the South," 35–39, 41; E. Foner, "Meaning of Freedom in the Age of Emancipation," 452–55; H. C. Richardson, *Death of Reconstruction*, 15–25.

23. S. Andrews, *South since the War*, 398, 400; Janney, *Remembering the Civil War*, 12–24, 104–26.

24. Letter of W. A. Freeman, May 1865, quoted in Redkey, *Grand Army of Black Men*, 225–26; Resolutions of New Orleans Freedpeople, March 21, 1865, in Berlin et al., *Free at Last*, 319–21; Emberton, *Beyond Redemption*, 130; Egerton, *Wars of Reconstruction*, 110; Hahn, *Nation under Our Feet*, 180–84.

25. Diary entry, July 2, 1866, in Nevins and Thomas, *Diary of George Templeton Strong*, 4:92; "Securing Peace," *Harper's Weekly*, December 2, 1865, 754; "Labor at the South," *Harper's Weekly*, May 20, 1865, 307; E. Foner, *Reconstruction*, 176–227; D. T. Carter, *When the War Was Over*, 176–231; Rable, *But There Was No Peace*, 33–58; Ash, *Massacre in Memphis*, 93–158; Hogue, *Uncivil War*, 31–52.

26. Sumner, "Equal Rights of All," in Sumner, *Complete Works*, 13:131–33; Rugemer, *Problem of Emancipation*, 295–300; Emberton, *Beyond Redemption*, 33–34; Eudell, *Political Languages of Emancipation in the British Caribbean and the U.S. South*, 131–66; Rugemer, "Jamaica's Morant Bay Rebellion and the Making of Radical Reconstruction."

27. Civil Rights Act, April 9, 1866, *Statutes at Large*, vol. 14, 39th Congress, 1st sess., 1866, p. 27; Rugemer, *Problem of Emancipation*, 295–300; E. Foner, *Reconstruction*, 118–19, 142–51, 243–51, 257–59; E. Foner, *Nothing but Freedom*, 3, 40–46 (congressman quotation, p. 46); E. Foner, "Meaning of Freedom in the Age of Emancipation," 457; Rael, *Eighty-Eight Years*, 301, 304–5; Rugemer, "Jamaica's Morant Bay Rebellion and the Making of Radical Reconstruction."

28. Johnson, "Freedmen's Bureau Veto Message," February 19, 1866, and "Veto of Civil Rights Bill," March 27, 1866, both in *PAJ*, 10:121, 122, 319, 320.

29. Johnson, "Proclamation re End of Insurrection," August 20, 1866, *PAJ*, 11:102, 103; G. P. Downs, *After Appomattox*, 146–51.

30. Diary entries, March 23 and September 3, 1866, in Nevins and Thomas, *Diary of George Templeton Strong*, 4:75, 100; Nicoletti, *Secession on Trial*, 2; Benedict, "Preserving the Constitution."

31. E. Foner, *Reconstruction*, 239–80; E. Foner, "Meaning of Freedom in the Age of Emancipation," 457–58; E. Foner, *Nothing but Freedom*, 42.

32. "The Constitutional Amendment," *Harper's Weekly*, February 17, 1866, 98; Beecher, *Universal Suffrage*, 5–7; Emberton, *Beyond Redemption*, 130–31.

33. "The Constitutional Amendment," *Harper's Weekly*, February 17, 1866, 98; E. Foner, "Birthright Citizenship Is the Good Kind of American Exceptionalism"; E. Foner, *Reconstruction*, 251–61; Edwards, "Reconstruction and the History of Governance," 30, 35, 39; Nabors, *From Oligarchy to Republicanism*, 16; M. S. Jones, *Birthright Citizens*, 1–9, 153.

34. U.S. Congress, *Report of the Joint Committee on Reconstruction*, xi, xii.

35. Kaczorowski, "Searching for the Intent of the Framers of the Fourteenth Amendment," 377–78 (Wilson quotation); Benedict, "Preserving the Constitution," 76–78 (Schurz quotation, p. 77); Elazar, "Civil War and the Preservation of American

Federalism"; Lyons, *Statesmanship and Reconstruction*, 73–74; Rael, *Eighty-Eight Years*, 307–9.

36. Bingham, February 28, 1866, quoted in Lyons, *Statesmanship and Reconstruction*, 55, 55–84; "Universal Suffrage and Universal Amnesty," *The Nation*, November 29, 1866, 430; Benedict, "Preserving the Constitution," 83–84.

37. Douglass, "Our Composite Nationality," December 8, 1869, in Buccola, *Essential Douglass*, 218; Fried, "Thomas Nast's Thanksgiving Vision of American Identity."

38. Zuczek, *State of Rebellion*, 36–37 (Perry quotation); Rable, *But There Was No Peace*, 8 (Johnson quotation), 74–75; Emberton, *Beyond Redemption*, 156–58.

39. Pollard, *Lost Cause*, 751, 752; Emberton, *Beyond Redemption*, 65–67.

40. Johnson, "Third Annual Message to Congress," December 3, 1867, *PAJ*, 13:287; E. Foner, *Reconstruction*, 264–71; Summers, *Dangerous Stir*, 140–43; Rael, *Eighty-Eight Years*, 297.

41. Sheridan to Ulysses S. Grant, August 1, 1866, and Washburne to Thaddeus Stevens, May 24, 1866, both in Simpson, *Reconstruction*, 270, 252; Rable, *But There Was No Peace*, 33–58; Hogue, *Uncivil War*, 31–52; Ash, *Massacre in Memphis*, 3–8, 177–85.

42. Douglass, "Reconstruction," *Atlantic Monthly*, December 1866, 762, 764, 761; Benedict, *Compromise of Principle*, 188–243; E. Foner, *Reconstruction*, 261–80.

43. Stevens, "Speech at Lancaster," September 6, 1865, in Simpson, *Reconstruction*, 105, 92–93; Julian, "Regeneration before Reconstruction," January 28, 1867, in Julian, *Speeches on Political Questions*, 352–53.

44. "Universal Suffrage and Universal Amnesty," *The Nation*, November 29, 1866, 430; Douglass, "Reconstruction," *Atlantic Monthly*, December 1866, 762; Benedict, *Compromise of Principle*, 210–43; Benedict, "Preserving the Constitution," 80–85; G. P. Downs, *After Appomattox*, 89–112; Edwards, *Legal History of the Civil War and Reconstruction*, 90–173; Edwards, "Reconstruction and the History of Governance"; Lang, "Union Demobilization and the Boundaries of War and Peace," 185.

45. "An Act to Provide for the More Efficient Government of the Rebel States," March 2, 1867, Texas State Library and Archives Commission, accessed October 30, 2018, https://www.tsl.texas.gov/ref/abouttx/secession/reconstruction.html; Benedict, "Preserving the Constitution," 82–83; G. P. Downs, *After Appomattox*, 137–78; E. Foner, *Reconstruction*, 271–91; Lyons, *Statesmanship and Reconstruction*, 85–125; Blair, "Use of Military Force," 395–96. The Reconstruction Acts exempted Tennessee, which ratified the Fourteenth Amendment in 1866.

46. "An Act to Provide for the More Efficient Government of the Rebel States," March 2, 1867, Texas State Library and Archives Commission, accessed October 30, 2018, https://www.tsl.texas.gov/ref/abouttx/secession/reconstruction.html; Sickles, General Orders No. 9, Second Military District, March 21, 1867, quoted in Sefton, *United States Army and Reconstruction*, 119; Benedict, "Preserving the Constitution," 83–85 (Schurz quotation, p. 84); Summers, *Ordeal of the Reunion*, 116; Lang, "Union Demobilization and the Boundaries of War and Peace," 186.

47. Grant to Edward O. C. Ord, September 22, 1867, *PUSG*, 17:354; Pfanz, "Soldiering in the South," 485 (second quotation); G. P. Downs, *After Appomattox*, 223 (Logan quotation); Lang, *In the Wake of War*, 220–25; Sefton, *United States Army and Reconstruction*, ix, 41–49, 59, 253; Richter, "'Outside My Profession,'" 5–21; Dawson, *Army Generals and Reconstruction*, 44–62; Bradley, *Bluecoats and Tar Heels*, 5, 135–88; Summers, *Ordeal of the Reunion*, 109, 116.

48. "The Amendment at the South," *Harper's Weekly*, December 1, 1866, 754; Schurz to Heinrich Meyer, June 10, 1866, quoted in Bancroft, *Speeches, Correspondence and Political Papers of Carl Schurz*, 1:403; Schurz, "The True Problem," *Atlantic Monthly*, March 1867, 375–76; Slap, *Doom of Reconstruction*, 83–89.

49. Douglass, "Reconstruction," *Atlantic Monthly*, December 1866, 765; Sumner, *Are We a Nation?*, November 19, 1867, 35; B. Thomas, "Unfinished Task of Grounding Reconstruction's Promise," 33–34; Benedict, "Preserving the Constitution," 82–86; Summers, *Ordeal of the Reunion*, 115–16, 119–24.

50. Testimony of John A. Minnis, October 20, 1871, in U.S. Congress, *Report of the Joint Select Committee to Inquire into the Condition of Affairs in the Late Insurrectionary States: Alabama*, 8:570; "Address of the Colored Convention to the People of Alabama," *Montgomery Daily State Sentinel*, May 21, 1867, in Perman and Taylor, *Major Problems in the Civil War and Reconstruction*, 395; Summers, *Ordeal of the Reunion*, 115–16; Lyons, *Statesmanship and Reconstruction*, 57.

51. Hahn, *Nation under Our Feet*, 163–65, 180, 198, 199–207, 217–20, 237–41; Rael, *Eighty-Eight Years*, 307–12; E. Foner, *Nothing but Freedom*, 1, 44–45, 55–58; Kolchin, *American Slavery*, 214; Blair, "Use of Military Force," 395.

52. "Albion Tourgée to the Voters of Guilford," October 1867, quoted in Simpson, *Reconstruction*, 315–17; "Address of the Colored Convention to the People of Alabama," *Montgomery Daily State Sentinel*, May 21, 1867, quoted in Perman and Taylor, *Major Problems in the Civil War and Reconstruction*, 395; Hahn, *Nation under Our Feet*, 203 (Galloway quotation), 163–264; E. Foner, *Reconstruction*, 77–123, 281–307, 316–411; Hunter, *Bound in Wedlock*, 196–260; Stanley, *From Bondage to Contract*, 28–59, 74–89, 136–53, 172–99, 203–17, 233–40, 255, 68.

53. Rable, *But There Was No Peace*, 144 (Ames quotation); Douglass, "Reconstruction," *Atlantic Monthly*, December 1866, 762; Guelzo, "Reconstruction as a Pure Bourgeois Revolution"; Dean, *Agrarian Republic*, 154–55; E. Foner, *Reconstruction*, 104–6, 228–39.

54. *Preservation of the Union*, 5–6; "Report of a Speech by a Virginia Freedman," December 15, 1866, in Hayden et al., *Freedom*, ser. 3, vol. 2, *Land and Labor*, 336–41; E. Foner, *Reconstruction*, 234–36, 525, 563.

55. Rollin, *Life and Public Services of Martin R. Delany*, 8; Gatewood, "'Remarkable Misses Rollin,'" 172–88; M. S. Jones, *Birthright Citizens*, 122–35. Ideas in this paragraph are attributed entirely to Jonathan Lande, who introduced me to Francis Rollin. His paper "'Nature Marked Him for Combat'" joins his forthcoming work to further develop these insights.

56. J. A. Stewart (January 1868), quoted in Russ, "Was There Danger of a Second Civil War during Reconstruction?," 49; Lee to Edward Childe Lee, January 16, 1868, Lee Family Digital Archive, Stratford Hall, accessed May 2, 2019, https://www.encyclopediavirginia.org/Letter_from_Robert_E_Lee_to_Edward_Lee_Childe_January_16_1868; Pollard, *Lost Cause Regained*, 211, 58.

57. Democratic Party of Mississippi platform, January 15, 1868, in U.S. Congress, *Report of the Select Committee to Inquire into the Mississippi Election of 1875*, 1:518.

58. Andrew Johnson to the Cabinet, November 30, 1867, *PAJ*, 13:269; Summers, *Dangerous Stir*, 94 (Blair quotation), 175–222; E. Foner, *Reconstruction*, 340, 330–36.

59. Egerton, *Wars of Reconstruction*, 236 (Republican newspaper quotation); Schurz, "The Road to Peace—a Solid, Durable Peace," September 19, 1868, in Bancroft, *Speeches, Correspondence and Political Papers of Carl Schurz*, 1:429; Hahn, *Nation*

under *Our Feet*, 289–92; Rable, *But There Was No Peace*, 73–74; Summers, *Dangerous Stir*, 223–43; Russ, "Was There Danger of a Second Civil War during Reconstruction?"

60. *New York Tribune*, February 24, 1868, in Simpson, *Reconstruction*, 329–30; E. P. Whipple, "The Johnson Party," *Atlantic Monthly*, September 1866, 374; E. Foner, *Reconstruction*, 333–36; Appelbaum, "Impeach Donald Trump."

61. Cabinet Meeting of Andrew Johnson, November 30, 1867, *PAJ*, 13:270; Russ, "Was There Danger of a Second Civil War during Reconstruction?," 43–44; G. P. Downs, "Mexicanization of American Politics," 391 (third quotation); E. P. Whipple, "The Johnson Party," *Atlantic Monthly*, September 1866, 379; *New York Tribune*, February 24, 1868, quoted in Simpson, *Reconstruction*, 336; E. Foner, *Reconstruction*, 333–36; Summers, *Dangerous Stir*, 1–3, 108–20, 134–61, 189–97, 201–10; Guelzo, *Reconstruction*, 51–55.

62. Douglass, "The Work before Us," *The Independent*, August 27, 1868, quoted in Simpson, *Reconstruction*, 352–56; editor (1868) quoted in Egerton, *Wars of Reconstruction*, 244; Behrend, *Reconstructing Democracy*, 84–100, 106–18; E. Foner, *Reconstruction*, 332–45; Hahn, *Nation under Our Feet*, 216–64.

63. "Moral Significance of the Republican Triumph," *Atlantic Monthly*, January 1869, 124–28; Summers, *Ordeal of the Reunion*, 141–52; Calhoun, *Conceiving a New Republic*, 7–12.

64. Grant, First Inaugural Address, March 4, 1869, *PUSG*, 19:140; Simpson, *Let Us Have Peace*, 245–64; G. P. Downs, *After Appomattox*, 206–10; Summers, *Ordeal of the Reunion*, 151–52.

65. Grant, First Inaugural Address, March 4, 1869, *PUSG*, 19:142; Benedict, *Compromise of Principle*, 325–27; Calhoun, *Conceiving a New Republic*, 10, 18–19; Simpson, *Let Us Have Peace*, 253.

66. All quotations in Calhoun, *Conceiving a New Republic*, 15, 16, 13 (see also 10–19); Benedict, *Compromise of Principle*, 325–36; E. Foner, *Reconstruction*, 446–55.

67. Grant, Message to Congress, March 30, 1870, *PUSG*, 20:130–31; "Reconstruction Nationalized," *New York Times*, February 21, 1870, in Simpson, *Reconstruction*, 379–80; Gillette, *Retreat from Reconstruction*, 24; Gallagher, *Union War*, 151–53.

Chapter 8

1. Grant, First Inaugural Address, March 4, 1869, *PUSG*, 19:140.

2. Grant, Second Inaugural Address, March 4, 1873, *PUSG*, 24:61; M. M. Smith, "Past as a Foreign Country"; Keller, *Affairs of State*, 85–121; Summers, *Ordeal of the Reunion*, 204–27; Stockwell, *Interrupted Odyssey*, 4–8, 131–32, 179–82.

3. Grant, Second Inaugural Address, March 4, 1873, *PUSG*, 24:63.

4. Grant, Second Inaugural Address, March 4, 1873, *PUSG*, 24:62; Doyle, *Cause of All Nations*, 299–306; M. M. Smith, "Past as a Foreign Country"; Zimmerman, "Reconstruction."

5. E. Foner, *Reconstruction*, 412–59, 488–511; Hahn, *Nation under Our Feet*, 216–313; Slap, *Doom of Reconstruction*, 90–163; Calhoun, *Conceiving a New Republic*, 33–136; R. White, *Republic for Which It Stands*, 172–212.

6. Grant, Second Inaugural Address, March 4, 1873, *PUSG*, 24:64.

7. Halstead, *War Claims of the South*, 36; G. P. Downs, "Mexicanization of American Politics"; Summers, *Dangerous Stir*, 223–72; Katz, *From Appomattox to Montmartre*, 61–141.

8. Keller, *Affairs of State*, 90–91 (Banks quotation); Report of Hamilton Fish, July 14, 1870, quoted in J. D. Richardson, *Compilation of the Messages and Papers of the Presidents*, 9:4030; Grant, Annual Message, December 6, 1869, *PUSG*, 20:25; J. P. Smith, *Republican Expansionists of the Early Reconstruction Era*. This section draws heavily from Summers, *Ordeal of the Reunion*, 204–27.

9. Quotations from Seward, "Our North Pacific States," August 1869, in G. E. Baker, *Diplomatic History of the War for the Union*, 572; Sexton, "William H. Seward in the World," 398–400, 403–4, 411; Paolina, *Foundations of American Empire*, 105–9, 116–18; Chang, "Whose 'Barbarism'? Whose 'Treachery'?"

10. Seward, *Alaska: Speech of William H. Seward, at Sitka, August 12, 1869*, 16, 29; Paolina, *Foundations of American Empire*, x–xi, 2–40, 116–18; Summers, *Ordeal of the Reunion*, 208–9; Sexton, *Monroe Doctrine*, 163–64; Sexton, "William H. Seward in the World," 410–13, 418–19; LaFeber, *New Empire*, 24–31, 404, 408.

11. Grant, Annual Message, December 6, 1869, *PUSG*, 20:27 (first quotation); Nevins, *Hamilton Fish*, 196 (subsequent quotations); Ferrer, *Insurgent Cuba*, 15–69; R. J. Scott, *Degrees of Freedom*, 94–108; Sexton, "William H. Seward in the World," 413–15; Summers, *Ordeal of the Reunion*, 213–18; Schmidt-Nowara, "From Aggression to Crisis"; Childs, "Cuba, the Atlantic Crisis of the 1860s, and the Road to Abolition," 204–21; Paolina, *Foundations of American Empire*, 5.

12. "The United States and Cuba," *Harper's Weekly*, July 9, 1870, 434; Keller, *Affairs of State*, 94; Summers, *Ordeal of the Reunion*, 213–17; LaFeber, *New Empire*, 37–38; Sexton, "United States, the Cuban Rebellion, and the Multilateral Initiative of 1875."

13. Nevins, *Hamilton Fish*, 397 (quotation), 385–95, 412–23; Warner, *Idea of Continental Union*, 50, 54, 105, 117, 123, 131, 193; Cook, *Alabama Claims*, 126–27, 133; Snay, *Fenians, Freedmen, and Southern Whites*, 52–57, 65–66; LaFeber, *New Empire*, 32–34; Summers, *Ordeal of the Reunion*, 214–16; Huzzey, "Manifest Dominion," 94–98.

14. Sumner, *Alabama Claims*, 14, 32; Nevins, *Hamilton Fish*, 385–95, 412–23; Warner, *Idea of Continental Union*, 96–98, 105, 117; Cook, *Alabama Claims*, 15, 88, 107–10, 118, 141–50, 154–55, 163–66; Sexton, *Monroe Doctrine*, 166–67; Donald, *Charles Sumner and the Rights of Man*, 374–413.

15. *The Times* (London) quoted in Donald, *Charles Sumner and the Rights of Man*, 380; Frelinghuysen quoted in Keller, *Affairs of State*, 97, 96–98; Nevins, *Hamilton Fish*, 385–95, 412–23; Cook, *Alabama Claims*, 167–206; Sexton, *Monroe Doctrine*, 166–67; Myers, *Dissolving Tensions*; Huzzey, "Manifest Dominion," 99–100.

16. Such statements, framing, and questions inform the premise of Summers, *Ordeal of the Reunion*.

17. Grant, "Memorandum" (1869–70), *PUSG*, 20:76; Grant to U.S. Senate, May 31, 1870, *PUSG*, 20:154; Love, *Race over Empire*, 7, 33–35, 29–47; Eller, "Dominican Civil War, Slavery, and Spanish Annexation."

18. Grant, "Memorandum" (1869–70), *PUSG*, 20:74; Grant to U.S. Senate, May 31, 1870, *PUSG*, 20:155, 156; Love, *Race over Empire*, 45–47; M. M. Smith, "Past as a Foreign Country," 125–27; Zimmerman, "Reconstruction," 186–87.

19. Grant, "Memorandum" (1869–70), *PUSG*, 20:75, 76; Grant to U.S. Senate, May 31, 1870, *PUSG*, 20:155, 156; Sexton, *Monroe Doctrine*, 163–65; Guyatt, "America's Conservatory."

20. Douglass, "Santo Domingo: An Address in St. Louis, Missouri," January 13, 1873, in Blassingame and McKivigan, *Frederick Douglass Papers*, ser. 1, vol. 4, pp. 344, 345, 354; P. Foner, *Life and Writings of Frederick Douglass*, 4:69–70 (five final

Douglass quotations); Blight, *Frederick Douglass*, 536–45; E. Foner, *Reconstruction*, 495; Wilkins, "'They Had Heard of Emancipation and the Enfranchisement of Their Race'"; Guyatt, "America's Conservatory"; Byrd, "Black Republicans, Black Republic."

21. Schurz, "Annexation of San Domingo," January 11, 1871, in Bancroft, *Speeches, Correspondence and Political Papers of Carl Schurz*, 2:77, 75, 102; Slap, *Doom of Reconstruction*, 117–20; Love, *Race over Empire*, 53–60.

22. Schurz, "Annexation of San Domingo," 2:78, 80, 82, 99.

23. Schurz, "Annexation of San Domingo," 2:91, 90, 117, 89; Love, *Race over Empire*, 59 ("history of revolutions" quotation).

24. Summers, *Ordeal of the Reunion*, 220 (quotation); Love, *Race over Empire*, 56–70; Slap, *Doom of Reconstruction*, 119–20; E. Foner, *Reconstruction*, 495–96.

25. Keller, *Affairs of State*, 96 (*Chicago Tribune* quotation); Garnet speech printed in *Slavery in Cuba* (1872), 15–16, 18; G. P. Downs, *Second American Revolution*, 122–29; Semmes, "Exporting Reconstruction," 232–35. I thank Ryan Semmes for bringing the Garnet speech to my attention.

26. Sexton, "William H. Seward in the World," 415 (first quotations); "Mr. Seward's Speech in Salem, Oregon," in Seward, *Alaska: Speech of William H. Seward, at Sitka, August 12, 1869*, 29 (final quotation); S. L. Smith, "Beyond North and South," 567; West, *Last Indian War*, xvi–xix, 59, 101–5, 151, 292, 318–19. The states that joined the Union between 1861 and 1896 were Kansas, Nevada, Nebraska, Colorado, North Dakota, South Dakota, Montana, Washington, Idaho, Wyoming, and Utah. West Virginia was the lone nonwestern state.

27. Grant, "Annual Message," December 6, 1869, *PUSG*, 20:18, 19; Lanza, *Agrarianism and Reconstruction Politics*, 121; H. C. Richardson, *West from Appomattox*, 4–6, 113–47; Summers, *Ordeal of the Reunion*, 179–203; Dean, *Agrarian Republic*, 3, 8–9, 158–70, 170–74, 177–81.

28. Kantrowitz, "'Not Quite Constitutionalized,'" 81–89 (first quotation, p. 81); Grant, "Annual Message," December 6, 1869, Second Inaugural Address, March 4, 1873, and First Inaugural Address, March 4, 1869, all in *PUSG*, 20:38, 39, 24:63, 19:142; M. M. Smith, "Past as a Foreign Country," 136 ("both domestic and foreign" quotation); H. C. Richardson, *West from Appomattox*, 69–76; Genetin-Pilawa, *Crooked Paths to Allotment*, 62, 73–80, 89–97; Stockwell, *Interrupted Odyssey*, 4–8, 131–32, 179–82.

29. Kantrowitz, "'Not Quite Constitutionalized,'" 89 (Wisconsin Republican quotation), 75–77, 81–85, 89–91, 94; Prucha, *Great Father*, 659–715; West, "Reconstructing Race."

30. Grant, Annual Message, December 6, 1869, *PUSG*, 20:38–39; Genetin-Pilawa, *Crooked Paths to Allotment*, 64 (Parker quotation), 90–99, 104–5, 111–16, 122–30, 139, 166–67, 187–88; Genetin-Pilawa, "Ely S. Parker and the Paradox of Reconstruction Politics in Indian Country," 183–205; Kantrowitz, "'Not Quite Constitutionalized,'" 84; Wooster, *Military and United States Indian Policy*, 44–46; Priest, *Uncle Sam's Stepchildren*, 5–7, 57–164; Prucha, *Great Father*, 659–86; Stockwell, *Interrupted Odyssey*, 1–2, 47–49, 64–68, 143, 159, 179.

31. Rider on the Indian Appropriation Act, March 3, 1871, quoted in *Federal Indian Law*, 138, 211, 212; remaining quotations in Genetin-Pilawa, *Crooked Paths to Allotment*, 69, 72; Hämäläinen, "Reconstructing the Great Plains"; Saunt, "Paradox of Freedom."

32. Bellamy, *Massacres and Morality*, 86 (Sheridan quotation), 84–88; Marszalek,

Sherman, 398–99 (Sherman quotation), 377–400; Genetin-Pilawa, "Ely S. Parker and the Paradox of Reconstruction Politics in Indian Country," 193–94; Wooster, *Military and United States Indian Policy*, 41–173; Utley, *Frontier Regulars*; West, *Last Indian War*, 111–20, 140–53, 169–74, 201–13, 228–54, 307–14; Madsen, *American Exceptionalism*, 53.

33. Millett, Maslowski, and Feis, *For the Common Defense*, 221–28 (first quotation, p. 224); Grimsley, "'Rebels' and 'Redskins,'" 154–55 (subsequent quotations), 137–55; Wooster, *Military and United States Indian Policy*, 144–202; Utley, *Frontier Regulars*, 188–413; West, *Last Indian War*; Genetin-Pilawa, *Crooked Paths to Allotment*, 127–32, 140–41, 186–87; Summers, *Ordeal of the Reunion*, 186–87.

34. Prior, "Civilization, Republic, Nation," 292 (Rusling quotation); Grant, "Address at Des Moines, Iowa," September 29, 1875, *PUSG*, 26:342–44; Fluhman, *"A Peculiar People,"* 95–117, 141–42.

35. Republican Party Platform of 1872, American Presidency Project, accessed May 5, 2020, https://www.presidency.ucsb.edu/node/273303; Prior, "Civilization, Republic, Nation," 292; Fluhman, *"A Peculiar People,"* 103–6, 115–16; R. White, *Republic for Which It Stands*, 384–89; Reeve, *Religion of a Different Color*, 14–170.

36. Calhoun, *Conceiving a New Republic*, 23–24 (Stewart quotations); Paddison, "Race, Religion, and Naturalization"; S. L. Smith, *Freedom's Frontier*, 206–30; S. L. Smith, "Emancipating Peons, Excluding Coolies"; Summers, *Ordeal of the Reunion*, 198–99.

37. Republican Party Platform of 1872; S. L. Smith, "Beyond North and South"; H. C. Richardson, *West from Appomattox*, 3–4; West, "Reconstructing Race"; G. P. Downs, "World the War Made."

38. Paddison, "Race, Religion, and Naturalization," 193 (Wilson quotation); Republican Party Platform of 1872; Summers, *Ordeal of the Reunion*, 179–203; Elazar, "Civil War and the Preservation of American Federalism." Interpretations that treat the South and West as part of the same process of national reconstruction include H. C. Richardson, "North and West of Reconstruction"; West, "Reconstructing Race"; Downs and Masur, "Echoes of War"; West, *Last Indian War*, xvi–xxii, 59, 159, 292, 318–19; S. L. Smith, "Beyond North and South"; and S. L. Smith, *Freedom's Frontier*, 13–14, 175, 198–99, 205–18.

39. Jefferson Davis to Varina Davis, December 4, 1869, *PJD*, 12:411–12; Hahn, *Nation under Our Feet*, 217 (George Washington Williams quotation), 216–64; Zuczek, *State of Rebellion*, 52.

40. "Public Meeting of the Whites, from the Yorkville Enquirer, April 6, 1871," and Samuel A. Hale to Hon. H. Wilson, January 1, 1868, both in U.S. Congress, *Report of the Joint Select Committee to Inquire into the Condition of Affairs in the Late Insurrectionary States: South Carolina*, 5:1542, 1543, and *Alabama*, 10:1832, 1833.

41. Rable, *But There Was No Peace*, 8 (Shotwell quotation), 1–15; Jonathan Worth to James Rush, March 25, 1868, in J. G. Hamilton, *Correspondence of Jonathan Worth*, 2:1174; "Public Meeting of the Whites, from the Yorkville Enquirer, April 6, 1871," in U.S. Congress, *Report of the Joint Select Committee to Inquire into the Condition of Affairs in the Late Insurrectionary States: South Carolina*, 5:1542, 1543; Emberton, *Beyond Redemption*, 169–72.

42. Hogue, *Uncivil War*, 12 (quotations), 9–13; Rable, *But There Was No Peace*, 81–186; Blair, "Use of Military Force," 396–97; Grimsley, "Wars for the American South," 6–22; Guelzo, "Reconstruction as a Pure Bourgeois Revolution."

43. Pollard, *Lost Cause Regained*, 15, 211; Gallagher and Meier, "Coming to Terms with Civil War Military History," 493; Hsieh, "Total War and the American Civil War Reconsidered," 400; Summers, *Dangerous Stir*, 248–49; Egerton, *Wars of Reconstruction*, 254–59; Zuczek, *State of Rebellion*, 48–63; Emberton, *Beyond Redemption*, 180–81; Boyle, *Violence after War*, 5–7; Perman, "Counter Revolution"; Rubin, *Shattered Nation*, 163; Summers, *Ordeal of the Reunion*, 177–78; Gallagher, *Confederate War*, 157–58, 206–7n1; Kolchin, *Sphinx on the American Land*, 33–38. For an interpretation that sees the insurgency as a continuation of the Civil War, see Grimsley, "Wars for the American South."

44. Testimony of John A. Minnis, October 20, 1871, in U.S. Congress, *Report of the Joint Select Committee to Inquire into the Condition of Affairs in the Late Insurrectionary States: Alabama*, 8:570; Gillette, *Retreat from Reconstruction*, 24; Guelzo, "Reconstruction as a Pure Bourgeois Revolution."

45. Egerton, *Wars of Reconstruction*, 258 (delegation quotation); Zuczek, *State of Rebellion*, 107 (Merrill quotation); Robert K. Scott to Ulysses S. Grant, October 22, 1870, in Simpson, *Reconstruction*, 392.

46. Calhoun, *Conceiving a New Republic*, 27 (Sherman quotation); Katz, *From Appomattox to Montmartre*, 49 (Washburne quotation), 1–3, 46–58, 68; M. M. Smith, "Past as a Foreign Country," 134–36; Bernstein, "Impact of the Paris Commune in the United States," 435–45.

47. "Sympathy with France," *Harper's Weekly*, January 28, 1871, 74; "A French Republic," *Harper's Weekly*, March 4, 1871, 186; Beecher, "The Lesson from Paris," 238, 242; Katz, *From Appomattox to Montmartre*, 93, 149–51, 153–57.

48. Beecher, "The Lesson from Paris," 236; Katz, *From Appomattox to Montmartre*, 127.

49. Sefton, *United States Army and Reconstruction*, 213–25, esp. 222–23; Rable, *But There Was No Peace*, 69–74, 91–111; Zuczek, *State of Rebellion*, 55–58, 73–78, 88–97; E. Foner, *Reconstruction*, 454–59; Blair, "Use of Military Force," 396; Lang, "Union Demobilization and the Boundaries of War and Peace," 187.

50. William T. Sherman to John Sherman, January 7, 1875, in Thorndike, *Sherman Letters*, 342; Grant to U.S. Senate, January 13, 1875, *PUSG*, 26:11; Gillette, *Retreat from Reconstruction*, 88 (Terry quotation); Lang, *In the Wake of War*, 216–25.

51. Slap, *Doom of Reconstruction*, 125 (Trumbull quotation), 113 (Adams quotation), 113–18, 208–9; Blair, "Use of Military Force," 396; Gillette, *Retreat from Reconstruction*, 51–55; Summers, *Dangerous Stir*, 223–43.

52. Speech of James A. Garfield, April 4, 1871, in Simpson, *Reconstruction*, 409, 411, 410.

53. Speech of James A. Garfield, April 4, 1871, in Simpson, *Reconstruction*, 412, 414, 415.

54. "The Problem at the South," *The Nation*, March 23, 1871, 192–93; Zuczek, *State of Rebellion*, 93–99.

55. "The Problem at the South," *The Nation*, March 23, 1871, 192–93; Zuczek, *State of Rebellion*, 93–99.

56. Schurz, "Why Anti-Grant and Pro-Greeley," July 22, 1872, in Bancroft, *Speeches, Correspondence and Political Papers of Carl Schurz*, 2:398; Slap, *Doom of Reconstruction*, xv, xxiv, 8–10, 35–36, 73–77, 84–86, 94–100, 109–19, 225–28; Boyle, *Violence after War*, 5–7; Perman, "Counter Revolution"; Gallagher and Meier, "Coming to Terms with Civil War Military History," 493–94; Lang, *In the Wake of War*.

57. Grant, "Proclamation," April 20, 1871, and Second Inaugural Address, March 4, 1873, *PUSG*, 21:336–37, 24:61.

58. Motley, *Historic Progress and American Democracy*, 58–60; P. Kennedy, *Rise and Fall of the Great Powers*, 203; Sefton, *United States Army and Reconstruction*, 261; G. P. Downs, *After Appomattox*, 222–25, 251–53.

59. Speeches of Joseph H. Rainey and Robert B. Elliott, April 1, 1871, both in McFarlin, *Black Congressional Reconstruction Orators*, 199, 96–97.

60. Elliott, Speech in Congress on the Civil Rights Bill, January 1874, in Simpson, *Reconstruction*, 456, 457–58, 473, 474.

61. Schurz, "Why Anti-Grant and Pro-Greeley," July 22, 1872, and Schurz to E. L. Godkin, November 23, 1872 (final quotation), both in Bancroft, *Speeches, Correspondence and Political Papers of Carl Schurz*, 2:398, 438, 415, 448; Slap, *Doom of Reconstruction*, xvii, 114–23, 126–63; Burg, "Amnesty, Civil Rights, and the Meaning of Liberal Republicanism"; Eyal, "Charles Eliot Norton, E. L. Godkin, and the Liberal Republicans"; R. White, *Republic for Which It Stands*, 172–212.

62. Greeley, Nominating Acceptance Speech, May 20, 1872, in Simpson, *Reconstruction*, 425–27; Slap, *Doom of Reconstruction*, xiii–xvi, 181–98; Downey, "Horace Greeley and the Politicians"; E. Foner, *Reconstruction*, 499–511.

63. Schurz, "Why Anti-Grant and Pro-Greeley," July 22, 1872, in Bancroft, *Speeches, Correspondence and Political Papers of Carl Schurz*, 2:437; H. C. Richardson, *Death of Reconstruction*, 104–11, 113–21 (*Boston Evening Transcript* quotation, pp. 110–11); Slap, *Doom of Reconstruction*, 199–221; Summers, *Ordeal of the Reunion*, 335–45, 350–52; R. White, *Railroaded*, 77–87; H. C. Richardson, "North and West of Reconstruction"; R. White, *Republic for Which It Stands*, 260–73; E. Foner, *Reconstruction*, 512–63.

64. Katz, *From Appomattox to Montmartre*, 112 (*Charlottesville Weekly Chronicle* quotation); Pike, "[South Carolina] under a Negro Government," *New York Tribune*, March 29, 1873, in Simpson, *Reconstruction*, 435–39; "Socialism in South Carolina," *The Nation*, April 16, 1874, 248; H. C. Richardson, *Death of Reconstruction*, 83–121, esp. 101–7.

65. Pike, "[South Carolina] under a Negro Government," *New York Tribune*, March 29, 1873, in Simpson, *Reconstruction*, 436; Budiansky, *Bloody Shirt*, 73 (second and third quotations); Cooley, "Guarantee of Order and Republican Government in the States"; Katz, *From Appomattox to Montmartre*, 23; E. Foner, *Reconstruction*, 524–35; Gillette, *Retreat from Reconstruction*, 211–58; Calhoun, *Conceiving a New Republic*, 47–89.

66. Grimsley, "Wars for the American South," 17 (Democratic poster quotation); McPherson, *War That Forged a Nation*, 183; Hogue, *Uncivil War*, 1–13, 116–43; Rable, *But There Was No Peace*, 122–62; Emberton, *Beyond Redemption*, 180–81; Lemann, *Redemption*, 12–29; Keith, *Colfax Massacre*, 88–152.

67. Grant to U.S. Senate, January 13, 1875, *PUSG*, 26:12, 11; McPherson, *War That Forged a Nation*, 185–86; Guelzo, *Reconstruction*, 105–6; Tunnell, *Crucible of Reconstruction*, chaps. 8 and 9; Dawson, *Army Generals and Reconstruction*, 183–90; Rable, *But There Was No Peace*, 122–43.

68. Philip H. Sheridan to W. W. Belknap, January 5, 1875, in Simpson, *Reconstruction*, 525; Schurz, "Military Interference in Louisiana," January 11, 1875, in Bancroft, *Speeches, Correspondence and Political Papers of Carl Schurz*, 3:126, 123, 131, 125; McPherson, *War That Forged a Nation*, 186–88; Dawson, *Army Generals and Reconstruction*, 207–8, 219–20; Hogue, *Uncivil War*, 149–59.

69. Rable, *But There Was No Peace*, 144 (Ames quotation), 144–62; *Forest Register*, September 15, 1875, quoted in U.S. Congress, *Mississippi: Testimony as to Denial of Elective Franchise in Mississippi at the Elections of 1875 and 1876*, 1005; Emberton, *Beyond Redemption*, 180–81; Lemann, *Redemption*, 105–9, 130–39, 144–55, 179–95, 200–206.

70. Rable, *But There Was No Peace*, 153 (*Columbus Democrat* quotation), 151–61; Guelzo, *Reconstruction*, 105 (Lynch quotation); Budiansky, *Bloody Shirt*, 216 (Ames quotations); Lemann, *Redemption*, 171–73; McPherson, *War That Forged a Nation*, 189–90.

71. Grant to Edwards Pierrepont, September 13, 1875, *PUSG*, 26:312; Lemann, *Redemption*, 132 (Ames quotation); Calhoun, *Presidency of U. S. Grant*, 507–11; Calhoun, *Conceiving a New Republic*, 84–94, 101–3; Rable, *But There Was No Peace*, 156–62.

72. My interpretation of "Mexicanization" is drawn exclusively from G. P. Downs, "Mexicanization of American Politics." Morton, *Speech of Hon. O. P. Morton, Delivered in the United States Senate, January 19, 1876*; E. Foner, *Reconstruction*, 553–56; Egerton, *Wars of Reconstruction*, 311–17.

73. "What Is 'Mexicanization'?," *The Nation*, December 21, 1876, 365–66; G. P. Downs, "Mexicanization of American Politics," 387, 390–91, 393–98; Cooley, "Guarantee of Order and Republican Government in the States," 83; Zuczek, *State of Rebellion*, 197 (Balentine quotations).

74. "The Army and the States," *Harper's Weekly*, April 7, 1877, 262; Gillette, *Retreat from Reconstruction*, 187 (Hawley quotation); Calhoun, *Conceiving a New Republic*, 68 (Sherman quotation).

75. Halstead, *War Claims of the South*, 3, 9, 36; G. P. Downs, "Mexicanization of American Politics," 397–98.

76. "Political Condition of the South," *Atlantic Monthly*, February 1877, 190; "Patriotism Versus Party," *Harper's Weekly*, March 3, 1877, 162; "What Is 'Mexicanization'?," *The Nation*, December 21, 1876, 366; Guelzo, *Reconstruction*, 112–13; Rable, *But There Was No Peace*, 163–86; E. Foner, *Reconstruction*, 564–80; Zuczek, *State of Rebellion*, 188–200; Holt, *By One Vote*, 152–203.

77. Hayes, "Response to Serenade at the Home of R. C. Anderson"; Hayes, First Inaugural Address, March 5, 1877, in Mackey, *Documentary History of the American Civil War Era*, 2:395, 396; C. V. Woodward, *Reunion and Reaction*, 186–203; Gillette, *Retreat from Reconstruction*, 331–34; de Santis, "Rutherford B. Hayes and the Removal of the Troops," 417–50; E. Foner, *Reconstruction*, 575–87.

78. Hayes, First Inaugural Address, March 5, 1877, in Mackey, *Documentary History of the American Civil War Era*, 2:398–99; Blair, "Use of Military Force," 399–400.

Epilogue

1. Douglass, "West India Emancipation," August 1, 1880, in Douglass, *Life and Times of Frederick Douglass*, 608, 613.

2. Douglass, "West India Emancipation," 613, 610–11.

3. Douglass, "West India Emancipation," 609, 611, 613.

4. Tourgée, *Fool's Errand*, 338; Blum, *Reforging the White Republic*, 192–93; Christopher Hill, "Albion Winegar Tourgée," *Documenting the American South*, accessed November 5, 2019, https://docsouth.unc.edu/church/tourgee/summary.html.

5. Tourgée, *Fool's Errand*, 337, 340, 341; Blum, *Reforging the White Republic*, 192–93; G. P. Downs, "A Palace That Will Fall upon Them"; G. P. Downs, "Anarchy at the Circumference," 115–17.

6. Tourgée, *Fool's Errand*, 340, 341; Hayes, First Inaugural Address, March 5, 1877, in Mackey, *Documentary History of the American Civil War Era*, 2:396; Zuczek, *State of Rebellion*, 159 (Shand quotation).

7. Republican Party Platform of 1876, American Presidency Project, accessed May 5, 2020, https://www.presidency.ucsb.edu/node/273305; de Santis, "Rutherford B. Hayes and the Removal of the Troops," 444–45 (Hayes quotation); E. Foner, *Reconstruction*, 549–53.

8. Douglass, "West India Emancipation," 610; Speech of John Roy Lynch, February 3, 1875, in McFarlin, *Black Congressional Reconstruction Orators*, 139.

9. U. S. Grant, *Personal Memoirs*, 757; Lincoln, Gettysburg Address, November 19, 1863, accessed May 5, 2020, Avalon Project, http://avalon.law.yale.edu/19th_century /gettyb.asp. On the centrality of Union to white loyal citizens, see Hess, *Liberty, Virtue, and Progress*; Gallagher, *Union War*; and Summers, *Ordeal of the Reunion*.

10. Lincoln, Gettysburg Address, November 19, 1863, accessed May 5, 2020, Avalon Project, http://avalon.law.yale.edu/19th_century/gettyb.asp; Bancroft, "Place of Abraham Lincoln in History," *Atlantic Monthly*, June 1865, 764; U. S. Grant, *Personal Memoirs*, 762; Fredrickson, *Big Enough to Be Inconsistent*, 123–24; Gallagher, *Union War*, 6–7, 26–35, 47–49, 58–59, 62–63, 82–88, 119, 150, 161; Summers, *Ordeal of the Reunion*, 1–18.

11. Grant to Daniel H. Chamberlain, July 26, 1876, in Simpson, *Reconstruction*, 619–20 ("Government"; "privileges or protection"; "bloody revolution"); Young, *Around the World with General Grant*, 2:362–63 (remaining Grant quotations); Simpson, "Mission Impossible," 87–90, 98–100; Fairclough, "Was the Grant of Black Suffrage a Political Error?"

12. Young, *Around the World with General Grant*, 2:362–63; Simpson, "Mission Impossible," 87–90, 98–100; Fairclough, "Was the Grant of Black Suffrage a Political Error?"

13. Young, *Around the World with General Grant*, 2:362–63; Lang, "Union Demobilization and the Boundaries of War and Peace," 188–89; Simpson, "Mission Impossible," 87–90, 98–100; Fairclough, "Was the Grant of Black Suffrage a Political Error?"; G. P. Downs, *After Appomattox*, 44–51, 129–30, 176, 237–56; G. P. Downs, "Anarchy at the Circumference"; Lang, *In the Wake of War*, 233–35.

14. Simpson, "Mission Impossible," 87–90, 98–100; G. P. Downs, *After Appomattox*, 223–46, 251–53; Fairclough, "Was the Grant of Black Suffrage a Political Error?"; Fairclough, *Revolution That Failed*, 1–24; B. Thomas, "Unfinished Task of Grounding Reconstruction's Promise," 32–34; Edwards, "Reconstruction and the History of Governance"; Summers, *Ordeal of the Reunion*; Summers, *Dangerous Stir*; Guelzo, "Reconstruction as a Pure Bourgeois Revolution"; Osterhammel, *Transformation of the World*, 701; Lang, "Union Demobilization and the Boundaries of War and Peace," 189.

15. Hayes, First Inaugural Address, in Mackey, *Documentary History of the American Civil War Era*, 2:399; Summers, *Ordeal of the Reunion*, 1–6, 373–99.

16. Blight, "'What Will Peace among the Whites Bring?'"; Blight, *Race and Reunion*; Janney, *Remembering the Civil War*.

BIBLIOGRAPHY

Manuscript Collections

Library of Congress. *Abraham Lincoln Papers.* Series 1, *General Correspondence.*
    1833 to 1916: John P. Usher to Abraham Lincoln, Friday, Opinion on Fort
    Pillow Massacre. May 6, 1864. Manuscript/Mixed Material. https://www.loc
    .gov/item/mal3291800/.
Maryland Historical Society, H. Furlong Baldwin Library, Baltimore
    Harrison Collection, MS 432
    Hester Ann Wilkins Davis Manuscript Collection, MS 3203.
Massachusetts Historical Society, Boston. Adams Family Papers: An Electronic
    Archive. https://www.masshist.org/digitaladams/archive.
National Archives and Records Administration, Washington, DC. Founders Online.
    https://founders.archives.gov.
———. Founding Documents. https://archives.gov/founding-docs.
Star of the Republic Museum, Washington, Texas. Robert Emmett Bledsoe Papers.
Stratford Hall, Westmoreland County, Virginia. Lee Family Digital Archive. https://
    www.encyclopediavirginia.org.
United States Army Military Heritage Institute, Carlisle Barracks, Carlisle, PA.
    Harrisburg Civil War Roundtable Collection, James W. Denver Letter.
University of Iowa, Special Collections, University Libraries, Iowa City, IA.
    Henderson Civil War Diaries and Letters Digital Collection Online: http://
    digital.lib.uiowa.edu/cdm.
University of Michigan, Bentley Historical Library, Ann Arbor. Harrison Soule
    Papers.
University of Michigan, Clements Library, Ann Arbor. Benjamin C. Lincoln Papers,
    Schoff Civil War Collection.

Government Documents

The Statutes at Large, Treaties, and Proclamations of the United States of America.
    Vol. 12. Boston: Little, Brown, 1863.
The Statutes at Large, Treaties, and Proclamations of the United States of America.
    Vol. 13. Boston: Little, Brown, 1866.
The Statutes at Large, Treaties, and Proclamations of the United States of America.
    Vol. 14. Boston: Little, Brown, 1868.
U.S. Congress. *The Congressional Globe.* 46 vols. Washington, DC: Blair & Rives,
    1834–73.
———. *Mississippi: Testimony as to Denial of Elective Franchise in Mississippi at*
    the Elections of 1875 and 1876. Washington, DC: Government Printing Office,
    1877.
———. *Report of the Joint Committee on Reconstruction at the First Session, Thirty-*
    Ninth Congress. Washington, DC: Government Printing Office, 1866.
———. *Report of the Joint Select Committee to Inquire into the Condition of Affairs*

in the Late Insurrectionary States. 13 vols. Washington, DC: Government Printing Office, 1872.

———. *Report of the Select Committee to Inquire into the Mississippi Election of 1875, with Testimony and Documentary Evidence.* 2 vols. Washington, DC: Government Printing Office, 1876.

U.S. Department of the Interior. *Federal Indian Law.* Washington, DC: Government Printing Office, 1958.

U.S. Naval War Records Office. *Office Records of the Union and Confederate Navies in the War of the Rebellion.* 30 vols. Washington, DC: Government Printing Office, 1894–1922.

U.S. War Department. *The War of the Rebellion: A Compilation of the Official Records of the Union and Confederate Armies.* 128 vols. Washington, DC: Government Printing Office, 1880–1901.

Newspapers and Journals

Atlantic Monthly
Dallas Herald
DeBow's Review
Frank Leslie's Illustrated Newspaper
Harper's Weekly
The Liberator (Boston)

New York Times
North American Review
Richmond Enquirer
Sixth Corps
Southern Literary Messenger

Printed Primary Sources

Adams, Charles Francis, ed. *Memoirs of John Quincy Adams, Comprising Portions of His Diary from 1795 to 1848.* 12 vols. Philadelphia: J. B. Lippincott & Co., 1874–77.

Adams, John Quincy. *An Address ... Celebrating the Anniversary of Independence, at the City of Washington on the Fourth of July 1821.* Cambridge, MA: Hilliard and Metcalf, 1821.

American Presidency Project. University of California Santa Barbara. http://www.presidency.ucsb.edu.

Anderson, James H., and Nancy Anderson, eds. *Life and Letters of Judge Thomas J. Anderson and Wife.* [Columbus, Ohio]: Press of F. J. Heer, 1904.

Anderson, Martin B. "Issues of the Civil War." In *Papers and Addresses of Martin B. Anderson,* edited by William C. Morey, 130–38. Philadelphia: American Baptist Publication Society, 1895.

Andrews, Eliza Frances. *The War-Time Journal of a Georgia Girl, 1864–1865.* New York: D. Appleton, 1908.

Andrews, Sidney. *The South since the War: Fourteen Weeks of Travel and Observation in Georgia and the Carolinas.* Boston: Ticknor and Fields, 1866.

Avalon Project: Documents in Law, History, and Diplomacy. Yale Law School, Lillian Goldman Law Library. https://avalon.law.yale.edu.

Baker, George E., ed. *The Diplomatic History of the War for the Union: Being the Fifth Volume of the Works of William H. Seward.* Boston: Houghton Mifflin, 1884.

———. *The Works of William H. Seward.* 5 vols. New York: Redfield, 1853–84.

Bancroft, Frederic, ed. *Speeches, Correspondence and Political Papers of Carl Schurz.* 6 vols. New York: G. P. Putnam's Sons, 1913.

Basler, Roy P., ed. *The Collected Works of Abraham Lincoln.* 9 vols. New Brunswick, NJ: Rutgers University Press, 1953–55.

Beecher, Henry Ward. "The Lesson from Paris." In *The Sermons of Henry Ward Beecher, in Plymouth Church, Brooklyn, Sixth Series: March–September, 1871*, by Henry Ward Beecher, 235–50. New York: J. B. Ford, 1872.

———. *Universal Suffrage: An Argument, Delivered at Plymouth Church, Brooklyn ... Feb. 12, 1865*. Boston: G. C. Rand & Avery, 1865.

Bellows, Henry W. *The State and the Nation—Sacred to Christian Citizens: A Sermon Preached in All Souls' Church, New York, April 21, 1861*. New York: James Miller, 1861.

Berlin, Ira, Barbara J. Fields, Thavolia Glymph, Joseph P. Reidy, and Leslie S. Rowland, eds. *Freedom: A Documentary History of Emancipation, 1861–1867*, series 1, vol. 1: *The Destruction of Slavery*. New York: Cambridge University Press, 1985.

Berlin, Ira, Barbara Jeanne Fields, Steven F. Miller, Joseph P. Reidy, and Leslie S. Rowland, eds. *Free at Last: A Documentary History of Slavery, Freedom, and the Civil War*. New York: New Press, 1992.

Berlin, Ira, Thavolia Glymph, Steven F. Miller, Joseph P. Reidy, Leslie S. Rowland, and Julie Saville, eds. *Freedom: A Documentary History of Emancipation, 1861–1867*, series 1, vol. 3: *The Wartime Genesis of Free Labor: The Lower South*. New York: Cambridge University Press, 1985.

Berlin, Ira, Joseph P. Reidy, and Leslie S. Rowland, eds. *Freedom: A Documentary History of Emancipation, 1861–1867*, series 2: *The Black Military Experience*. New York: Cambridge University Press, 1985.

———. *Freedom's Soldiers: The Black Military Experience*. New York: Cambridge University Press, 1982.

Blassingame, John W., and John R. McKivigan, eds. *The Frederick Douglass Papers*, series 1, *Speeches, Debates, and Interviews*. 5 vols. New Haven, CT: Yale University Press, 1979–92.

Boudinot, Elias. *An Address to the Whites*. Philadelphia: William F. Geddes, 1826.

Breckinridge, John. *An Address, Delivered July 15, 1835, before the Euclean and Philomathean Societies, of the University of the City of New-York*. New York: West & Trow, 1836.

Brinton, John H. *Personal Memoirs of John H. Brinton, Civil War Surgeon, 1861–1865*. Carbondale: Southern Illinois University Press, 1996.

Brown, E. E. *The Life and Public Services of James A. Garfield*. Boston: Lothrop, 1881.

Brown, Edward. *Notes on the Origin and Necessity of Slavery*. Charleston, SC: A. E. Miller, 1826.

Brown, Norman D., ed. *One of Cleburne's Command: The Civil War Reminiscences and Diary of Captain Samuel T. Foster, Granbury's Texas Brigade, C.S.A.* Austin: University of Texas Press, 1980.

Brown, William Wells. *St. Domingo: Its Revolutions and Patriots*. Boston: Bela Marsh, 1855.

Browning, Judkin, ed. *The Southern Mind under Union Rule: The Diary of James Rumley, Beaufort, North Carolina, 1862–1865*. Gainesville: University of Florida Press, 2009.

Burlingame, Michael, ed. *Abraham Lincoln: The Observations of John G. Nicolay and John Hay*. Carbondale: Southern Illinois University Press, 2007.

Bushnell, Horace. "Our Obligations to the Dead." In *Building Eras in Religion*, by Horace Bushnell, 319–55. New York: C. Scribner's Sons, 1903.

Butler, Benjamin F. *Private and Official Correspondence of Gen. Benjamin F. Butler during the Period of the Civil War*. 5 vols. Norwood, MA: Plimpton Press, 1917.

Carter, Gari, ed. *Troubled State: Civil War Journals of Franklin Archibald Dick*. Kirksville, MO: Truman State University Press, 2008.

Channing, William Ellery. *The Works of William Ellery Channing, D.D*. 6 vols. Boston: J. Munroe and Co., 1841–43.

Clarke, James Freeman. *James Freeman Clarke: Autobiography, Diary and Correspondence*. Edited by Edward Everett Hale. Boston: Houghton, Mifflin and Co., 1899.

Clay, Henry. "Henry Clay's Advice to His Countrymen Relative to the War with Mexico," November 13, 1847. http://library.uta.edu/usmexicowar/transcription .php?content_id=224.

———. *Speech in Support of an American System for the Protection of American Industry; Delivered in the House of Representatives, on the 30th and 31st of March 1824*. Washington, DC: Columbian Office, 1824.

———. *Speech of Mr. Clay … on the Subject of Abolitionist Petitions; Delivered in the Senate of the United States, February 7, 1839*. Washington, DC: Gales and Seaton, 1839.

Cleveland, Henry. *Alexander H. Stephens, in Public and Private. With Letters and Speeches before, during, and since the War*. Philadelphia: National Publishing Company, 1866.

Clift, G. Glenn, ed. *The Private War of Lizzie Hardin: A Confederate Girl's Diary*. Frankfort: Kentucky Historical Society, 1963.

Cloud, N. B., ed. *The American Cotton Planter and the Soil of the South*. 4 vols. Montgomery, AL: N. B. Cloud, 1853–56.

Cooley, Thomas M. "The Guarantee of Order and Republican Government in the States." *International Review* 2 (1875): 57–87.

Cooper, William J., ed. *Jefferson Davis: The Essential Writings*. New York: Modern Library, 2004.

Crabtree, Beth G., and James W. Patton, eds. *"Journal of a Secesh Lady": The Diary of Catherine Ann Devereaux Edmondston, 1860–1866*. Raleigh: North Carolina Division of Archives and History, 1979.

Crist, Lynda Lasswell, et al., eds. *The Papers of Jefferson Davis*. 14 vols. Baton Rouge: Louisiana State University Press, 1971–2015.

Cutrer, Thomas W., and T. Michael Parrish, eds. *Brothers in Gray: The Civil War Letters of the Pierson Family*. Baton Rouge: Louisiana State University Press, 1997.

De Forest, John William. *A Union Officer in the Reconstruction*. New Haven, CT: Yale University Press, 1948.

Delany, Martin R. *Blake; or, the Huts of America, a Novel*. With an introduction by Floyd J. Miller. Boston: Beacon Press, 1970.

———. *The Condition, Elevation, Emigration and Destiny of the Colored People of the United States*. 1852; Baltimore, MD: Black Classic Press, 1993.

Douglass, Frederick. *The Essential Douglass: Selected Writings & Speeches*. Edited by Nicholas Buccola. Indianapolis, IN: Hackett Publishing Co., 2016.

———. *Life and Times of Frederick Douglass*. Hartford, CT: Park Publishing, 1882.

Dowdey, Clifford, and Luis H. Manarin, eds. *The Wartime Papers of R. E. Lee*. 1961; New York: Da Capo Press, 1987.

Drescher, Seymour, ed. *Tocqueville and Beaumont on Social Reform*. New York: Harper & Row, 1968.

Dumond, Dwight L., ed. *Southern Editorials on Secession*. New York: Century Co., 1931.

Duncan, Russell, ed. *Blue-Eyed Child of Fortune: The Civil War Letters of Colonel Robert Gould Shaw*. Athens: University of Georgia Press, 1992.

The 1863 Laws of War: Articles of War, General Orders No. 100, Army Regulations. Reprint, Mechanicsburg, PA: Stackpole Books, 2005.

Elliott, Stephen. *Our Cause in Harmony with the Purposes of God in Christ Jesus: A Sermon*. Savannah, GA: J. M. Cooper, 1862.

Everett, Edward. *Orations and Speeches on Various Occasions*. 4 vols. Boston: Little, Brown, 1879–83.

Faust, Drew Gilpin, ed. *The Ideology of Slavery: Proslavery Thought in the Antebellum South, 1830–1860*. Baton Rouge: Louisiana State University Press, 1981.

The Federalist Papers. Avalon Project: Documents in Law, History, and Diplomacy. Yale Law School, Lillian Goldman Law Library. https://avalon.law.yale.edu /subject_menus/fed.asp.

Findley, William. *History of the Insurrection, in Four Western Counties of Pennsylvania*. Philadelphia: Samuel Harrison Smith, 1796.

Fitzhugh, George. "The Revolutions of 1776 and 1861 Contrasted." *Southern Literary Messenger* 37, no. 12 (December 1863): 719–23.

———. *Sociology for the South, or the Failure of Free Society*. Richmond, VA: A. Morris Publisher, 1854.

Foner, Phillip S., ed. *The Life and Writings of Frederick Douglass*. 5 vols. New York: International Publishers, 1975.

Foner, Phillip S., and Yuval Taylor, eds. *Frederick Douglass: Selected Speeches and Writings*. Chicago: Lawrence Hill Books, 2000.

Ford, Jennifer W., ed. *The Hour of Our Nation's Agony: The Civil War Letters of Lt. William Cowper Nelson of Mississippi*. Knoxville: University of Tennessee Press, 2007.

Ford, Worthington Chauncey, ed. *A Cycle of Adams Letters, 1861–1865*. 2 vols. Boston: Houghton Mifflin, 1920.

Foroughi, Andrea R., ed. *Go If You Think It Your Duty: A Minnesota Couple's Civil War Letters*. St. Paul: Minnesota Historical Society, 2009.

Freidel, Frank, ed. *Union Pamphlets of the Civil War, 1861–1865*. 2 vols. Cambridge, MA: Belknap Press of Harvard University, 1967.

Gallagher, Gary W., ed. *Fighting for the Confederacy: The Personal Recollections of General Edward Porter Alexander*. Chapel Hill: University of North Carolina Press, 1989.

Geggus, David., ed. and trans. *The Haitian Revolution: A Documentary History*. Indianapolis, IN: Hackett Publishing Co., 2014.

Gienapp, William E., ed. *The Civil War and Reconstruction: A Documentary Collection*. New York: W. W. Norton, 2001.

———. *This Fiery Trial: The Speeches and Writings of Abraham Lincoln*. New York: Oxford University Press, 2001.

Gordon, Ann D., ed. *The Selected Papers of Elizabeth Cady Stanton and Susan B. Anthony*. 6 vols. New Brunswick, NJ: Rutgers University Press, 1997–2013.

Graf, LeRoy P., Ralph W. Haskins, and Paul H. Bergeron, eds. *The Papers of Andrew Johnson*. 16 vols. Knoxville: University of Tennessee Press, 1967–2000.

Grant, Ulysses S. *Personal Memoirs of Ulysses S. Grant: The Complete Annotated Edition*. Edited by John F. Marszalek. Cambridge, MA: Belknap Press of Harvard University, 2017.

Grimke, Sarah M. *Letters on the Equality of the Sexes, and the Condition of Women*. Boston: Isaac Knapp, 1838.

Halleck, Henry W. *International Law; or, Rules Regulating the Intercourse of States in Peace and War*. New York: D. Van Nostrand, 1861.

Halstead, Murat. *The War Claims of the South: The New Southern Confederacy*. Cincinnati: R. Clarke & Co., 1876.

Hamilton, J. G. de Roulhac, ed. *The Correspondence of Jonathan Worth*. 2 vols. Raleigh: Edwards & Broughton, 1909.

Hammond, James Henry. "Speech on the Justice of Receiving Petitions for the Abolition of Slavery in the District of Columbia." In *Selections from the Letters and Speeches of the Hon. James H. Hammond of South Carolina*, 15–50. New York: John F. Trow & Co., 1866.

Harwell, Richard B., ed. *Kate: The Journal of a Confederate Nurse, by Kate Cumming*. Baton Rouge: Louisiana State University Press, 1959.

Hayden, René, Anthony E. Kaye, Kate Masur, Steven F. Miller, Susan E. O'Donovan, Leslie S. Rowland, and Stephen A. West, eds. *Freedom: A Documentary History of Emancipation*, series 3, vol. 2: *Land and Labor, 1866–1867*. Chapel Hill: University of North Carolina Press, 2013.

Hayes, Rutherford B. "Response to Serenade at the Home of R. C. Anderson." December 13, 1876. https://www.rbhayes.org/clientuploads/RBHSpeeches /speech164.response_to_serenade.htm.

Heartsill, W. W. *Fourteen Hundred and 91 Days in the Confederate Army*. Wilmington, NC: Broadfoot, 1987.

Hepworth, George H. *The Whip, Hoe, and Sword; or, the Gulf-Department in '63*. Boston: Walker, Wise and Co., 1864.

Hillard, G. S. *Life and Campaigns of George B. McClellan, Major-General U.S. Army*. Boston: J. B. Lippincott, 1864.

Holloway, Carson, and Bradford P. Wilson, eds. *The Political Writings of Alexander Hamilton*. New York: Cambridge University Press, 2017.

Hubbs, G. Ward, ed. *Voices from Company D: Diaries by the Greensboro Guards, Fifth Alabama Infantry Regiment, Army of Northern Virginia*. Athens: University of Georgia Press, 2003.

Jacobs, Harriet Ann. *Incidents in the Life of a Slave Girl*. Edited by Lydia Maria Child. Boston: Published for the Author, 1861.

Jay, William. *The Life of John Jay: With Selections from His Correspondence and Miscellaneous Papers*. 2 vols. New York: J. & J. Harper, 1833.

Jefferson, Thomas. *Notes on the State of Virginia*. Edited by Frank Shuffleton. 1785; New York: Penguin Books, 1999.

Johannsen, Robert W., ed. *Democracy on Trial: A Documentary History of American Life, 1845–1877*. Urbana: University of Illinois Press, 1988.

Jones, J. B. *A Rebel War Clerk's Diary at the Confederate States Capital*. 2 vols. Philadelphia: J. B. Lippincott & Co., 1866.

Julian, George W. *The Cause and Cure of Our National Troubles*. Washington, DC: Scammell & Co., 1862.

———. *Speeches on Political Questions*. New York: Hurd and Houghton, 1872.

Kamphoefner, Walter D., and Wolfgang Helbich, eds. *Germans in the Civil War: The Letters They Wrote Home*. Chapel Hill: University of North Carolina Press, 2006.

Kellogg, Mary E., comp. *Army Life of an Illinois Soldier ... Charles W. Wills*. Carbondale: Southern Illinois University Press, 1996.

Kennedy, John Pendleton. *Border States: Their Power and Duty to the Present Disordered Condition of the Country*. Philadelphia: J. B. Lippincott & Co., 1861.

———. *Mr. Ambrose's Letters on the Rebellion*. Baltimore: Hurd & Houghton, 1865.

Kirkland, Charles P. *A Letter to Peter Cooper, on "The Treatment to Be Extended to the Rebels Individually" and "The Mode of Restoring the Rebel States to the Union."* New York: A. D. F. Randolph, 1865.

Kohl, Lawrence F., and Margaret C. Richard, eds. *Irish Green and Union Blue: The Civil War Letters of Peter Welsh*. New York: Fordham University Press, 1986.

Kuhns, Luther M. "An Army Surgeon's Letters to His Wife." *Proceedings of the Mississippi Valley Historical Association* 7 (1914): 306–20.

Lester, C. Edwards. *The Light and Dark of the Rebellion*. Philadelphia: G. W. Childs, 1863.

———. *My Consulship*. 2 vols.; New York: Cornish, Lamport & Co., 1853.

Lieber, Francis. *On Civil Liberty and Self-Government*. Philadelphia: J. B. Lippincott & Co., 1859.

———. *Guerrilla Parties Considered with Reference to the Laws and Usages of War*. New York: D. Van Nostrand, 1862.

———. *What Is Our Constitution, League, Pact, or Government?* New York: Columbia College Board of Trustees, 1861.

Lillibridge, Laurence F., ed. *Hard Marches, Hard Crackers, and Hard Beds ... the Edward Rolfe Civil War Letters and Diaries*. Prescott Valley, AZ: Lillibridge, 1993.

Livingston-Little, D. E., ed. *The Mexican War Diary of Thomas D. Tennery*. Norman: University of Oklahoma Press, 1970.

Lounsbury, Richard C., ed. *Louisa S. McCord: Political and Social Essays*. Charlottesville: University Press of Virginia, 1995.

Mackey, Thomas C., ed. *Documentary History of the American Civil War Era*. 3 vols. Knoxville: University of Tennessee Press, 2012–14.

Mattern, David B. *James Madison's "Advice to My Country."* Charlottesville: University of Virginia Press, 2013.

McFarlin, Annjennette S. *Black Congressional Reconstruction Orators and Their Orations, 1869–1879*. Metuchen, NJ: Scarecrow, 1976.

Melville, Herman. *Battle-Pieces and Aspects of the War*. New York: Harper and Brothers, 1866.

———. *White-Jacket; or, The World in a Man-of-War*. London: Richard Bentley, 1850.

Middleton, Stephen, ed. *Black Congressmen during Reconstruction: A Documentary Sourcebook*. Westport, CT: Praeger, 2002.

Miles, James Warley. *God in History: A Discourse Delivered before the Graduating Class of the College of Charleston on Sunday Evening, March 29, 1863*. Charleston, SC: Evans & Cogswell, 1863.

Mitchell, Nelson. *Oration Delivered before the Fourth of July Association on the Fourth of July, 1848*. Charleston, SC: J. S. Burges, 1849.

Moore, Frank, ed. *The Rebellion Record: A Diary of American Events*. 12 vols. New York: Putnam, 1861–63; New York: Van Nostrand, 1864–68.

Morton, Oliver P. *Speech of Gov. Oliver P. Morton at the Union State Convention ... February 23, 1864*. [Indianapolis, 1864.]

———. *Speech of Hon. O. P. Morton, Delivered in the United States Senate, January 19, 1876, on the Mississippi Election*. [Washington, DC, 1876.]

Motley, John Lothrop. *Historic Progress and American Democracy: An Address Delivered before the New-York Historical Society*. New York: Charles Scribner and Co., 1869.

Mr. Adams' Speech, on War with Great Britain and Mexico; with the Speeches of Messrs. Wise and Ingersoll, to Which It Is in Reply. Boston: Emancipator Office, 1842.

The Negro in the Military Service of the United States, 1639–1886. 5 microfilm reels. RG 94: *Records of the Adjutant General's Office, National Archives, Washington, D.C.* Washington, DC: National Archives and Records Service, 1973.

Nevins, Allan, ed. *A Diary of Battle: The Personal Journal of Colonel Charles Wainwright, 1861–1865*. 1962; New York: Da Capo Press, 1998.

Nevins, Allan, and Milton Halsey Thomas, eds. *The Diary of George Templeton Strong*. 4 vols. New York: Macmillan, 1952.

Norton, Sara, and M. A. DeWolfe Howe, eds. *Letters of Charles Eliot Norton*. 2 vols. Boston: Houghton Mifflin, 1913.

Olmsted, Frederick Law. *The Cotton Kingdom: A Traveller's Observations on Cotton and Slavery in the American Slaves States*. 2 vols. New York: Mason Brothers, 1861.

Paine, Thomas. *Collected Writings*. Edited by Eric Foner. New York: Library of America, 1995.

———. *Common Sense and Other Writings*. Edited by Gordon S. Wood. New York: Modern Library, 2003.

Perman, Michael, and Amy Murrell Taylor, eds. *Major Problems in the Civil War and Reconstruction: Documents and Essays*. Boston: Houghton Mifflin, 2011.

"Permanency of the American Union." *Niles' Weekly Register*, June 7, 1817.

Pollard, Edward A. *The Lost Cause: A New Southern History of the War of the Confederates*. New York: E. B. Treat, 1866.

———. *The Lost Cause Regained*. New York: G. W. Carleton, 1868.

Popchuck, Barry, ed. *Soldier Boy: The Civil War Letters of Charles O. Musser, 29th Iowa*. Iowa City: University of Iowa Press, 1995.

The Preservation of the Union: A National Economic Necessity. New York: W. C. Bryant & Co., 1863.

The Pro-slavery Argument, as Maintained by the Most Distinguished Writers of the Southern States. Charleston, SC: Walker, Richards, 1852.

Rankin, David, ed. *Diary of a Christian Soldier: Rufus Kingsley and the Civil War*. New York: Cambridge University Press, 2004.

Redkey, Edwin S. "Brave Black Volunteers: A Profile of the Fifty-Fourth Massachusetts Regiment." In *Hope and Glory: Essays on the Legacy of the Fifty-Fourth Massachusetts Regiment*, edited by Martin H. Blatt, Thomas J. Brown, and Donald Yacovone, 21–34. Amherst: University of Massachusetts Press, 2001.

————, ed. *A Grand Army of Black Men: Letters from African-American Soldiers in the Union Army, 1861–65*. New York: Cambridge University Press, 1992.

Republican Party Platforms. The American Presidency Project, edited by John Woolley and Gerhard Peters, University of California at Santa Barbara. https://www.presidency.ucsb.edu/people/other/republican-party-platforms.

Rhodes, Robert Hunt, ed. *All for the Union: The Diary and Letters of Elisha Hunt Rhodes*. New York: Vintage Books, 1992.

Richardson, James D., comp. *A Compilation of the Messages and Papers of the Presidents, 1789–1897*. 10 vols. Washington, DC: Government Printing Office, 1896–99.

Ripley, C. Peter, ed. *The Black Abolitionist Papers*. 5 vols. Chapel Hill: University of North Carolina Press, 1985–92.

Rollin, Frank A. [Francis]. *Life and Public Services of Martin R. Delany*. Boston: Lee and Shepard, 1883.

Rosenblatt, Emil, and Ruth Rosenblatt, eds. *Hard Marching Every Day: The Civil War Letters of Private Wilbur Fisk, 1861–1865*. Lawrence: University Press of Kansas, 1992.

Roth, Margaret B., ed. *Well Mary: Civil War Letters of a Wisconsin Volunteer*. Madison: University of Wisconsin Press, 1994.

Rowland, Dunbar, ed. *Jefferson Davis, Constitutionalist: His Letters, Papers, and Speeches*. 10 vols. Jackson: Mississippi Department of Archives and History, 1923.

Rush, Benjamin. *Essays, Literary, Moral and Philosophical*. Philadelphia: Thomas and William Bradford, 1806.

Salter, William. *The Life of James W. Grimes, Governor of Iowa, 1854–1858; a Senator of the United States, 1859–1869*. New York: D. Appleton and Company, 1876.

Schoonover, Thomas D., ed. *Mexican Lobby: Matias Romero in Washington, 1861–1867*. Lexington: University Press of Kentucky, 1986.

Schurz, Carl. "Report on the Condition of the South." *Senate Exec. Doc. 2, 39th Congress, 1st Session, December 19, 1865*. Washington, DC: General Printing Office, 1865.

Scott, Winfield. *Memoirs of Lieut.-General Scott, LL.D.* 2 vols. New York: Sheldon & Co., 1864.

Sears, Stephen W., ed. *The Civil War Papers of George B. McClellan: Selected Correspondence, 1860–1865*. New York: Ticknor & Fields, 1989.

————, ed. *The Civil War: The Second Year Told by Those Who Lived It*. New York: Library of America, 2012.

Sermons Preached in Boston on the Death of Abraham Lincoln. Boston: J. E. Tilton, 1865.

Seward, William H. *Alaska: Speech of William H. Seward, at Sitka, August 12, 1869*. Washington, DC: Philip & Solomons, 1869.

Shedd, William G. T. *The Union and the War: Sermon, Preached November 27, 1862*. New York: C. Scribner, 1863.

Sheehan-Dean, Aaron, ed. *The Civil War: The Final Year Told by Those Who Lived It*. New York: Library of America, 2014.

Sheridan, Philip H. *Personal Memoirs of P. H. Sheridan*. 2 vols. New York: Charles L. Webster, 1888.

Sherman, William T. *Memoirs of Gen. William T. Sherman*. 2 vols. New York: D. Appleton, 1891.

Silber, Nina, and Mary Beth Sievens, eds. *Yankee Correspondence: Civil War Letters between New England Soldiers and the Home Front.* Charlottesville: University Press of Virginia, 1996.

Simon, John Y., ed. *The Papers of Ulysses S. Grant.* 32 vols. Carbondale: Southern Illinois University Press, 1967–2012.

Simpson, Brooks D., ed. *The Civil War: The Third Year Told by Those Who Lived It.* New York: Library of America, 2013.

———. *Reconstruction: Voices from America's First Great Struggle for Racial Equality.* New York: Library of America, 2018.

Simpson, Brooks D., and Jean V. Berlin, eds. *Sherman's Civil War: Selected Correspondence of William T. Sherman, 1860–1865.* Chapel Hill: University of North Carolina Press, 1999.

Simpson, Brooks D., Leroy P. Graf, and John Muldowny, eds. *Advice after Appomattox: Letters to Andrew Johnson, 1865–1866.* Knoxville: University of Tennessee Press, 1987.

Simpson, Brooks D., Stephen W. Sears, and Aaron Sheehan-Dean, eds. *The Civil War: The First Year Told by Those Who Lived It.* New York: Library of America, 2011.

Slavery in Cuba: A Report of the Proceedings of the Meeting, Held at Cooper Institute, New York City, December 13, 1872, by the Cuban Anti-Slavery Committee. New York: Powers, MacGowan & Slipper, 1872.

Smith, Adam. *An Inquiry into the Nature and Causes of the Wealth of Nations.* 1776. Reprint, London: T. Nelson and Sons, 1851.

Smith, Gerrit. "Gerrit Smith on the Bailing of Jefferson Davis." [New York, 1867.]

Smith, William R. *History and Debates of the Convention of the People of Alabama ... January 1861.* Montgomery, AL: White, Pfister & Co., 1861.

Stanton, Elizabeth Cady, Susan B. Anthony, Matilda Joslyn Gage, and Ida Husted Harper, eds. *History of Woman Suffrage.* 6 vols. New York: Fowler & Wells, 1881–1922.

Stevenson, Brenda E., ed. *The Journals of Charlotte Forten Grimké.* New York: Oxford University Press, 1988.

Stillé, Charles J. *How a Free People Conduct a Long War.* Philadelphia: Collins, Printer, 1862.

———. *Northern Interests and Southern Independence: A Plea for United Action.* Philadelphia: William S. & Alfred Martien, 1863.

Stone, Kate. *Brokenburn: The Journal of Kate Stone, 1861–1868.* Edited by John Q. Anderson. Baton Rouge: Louisiana State University Press, 1955.

Story, Joseph. *A Familiar Exposition of the Constitution of the United States: Containing a Brief Commentary.* New York: Harper and Brothers, 1864.

Sumner, Charles. *The Alabama Claims: Speech of the Honourable Charles Sumner.* London: Stevens Bros., 1869.

———. *Are We a Nation? Address of Hon. Charles Sumner, before the New York Young Men's Republican Union, at the Cooper Institute,* November 19, 1867. New York: New York Young Men's Republican Union, 1867.

———. *Complete Works.* 20 vols. Boston: Lee, 1900.

———. *The Crime against Kansas, the Apologies for the Crime, the True Remedy. Speech of Hon. Charles Sumner in the Senate of the United States, 19th and 20th May, 1856.* Boston: John P. Jewett & Co., 1856.

Swisshelm, Jane Gray. *Half a Century*. 2nd ed. Chicago: Chicago Legal News Company, 1880.

Taylor, Robert J., ed. *Papers of John Adams*, 19 vols. to date. Cambridge, MA: Harvard University Press, 1977–2018.

Thorndike, Rachel Sherman, ed. *The Sherman Letters: Correspondence between General Sherman and Senator Sherman from 1837 to 1891*. New York: C. Scribner's Sons, 1894.

Thornwell, J. H. *Our Danger and Our Duty*. Columbia, SC: Southern Guardian, 1862.

Tocqueville, Alexis de. *Democracy in America*. Edited and translated by Harvey Mansfield and Delba Winthrop. Chicago: University of Chicago Press, 2002.

Tourgée, Albion W. *A Fool's Errand, by One of the Fools*. New York: Fords, Howard & Hulbert, 1879.

Vattel, Emerich de. *The Law of Nations; or, The Principles of Natural Law Applied to the Conduct and to the Affairs of Nations and of Sovereigns*. Edited and translated by Charles G. Fenwick. 1758. Reprint, Washington, DC: Carnegie Institution of Washington, 1916.

Victor, Orville James. *The History, Civil, Political and Military of the Southern Rebellion*. 2 vols. New York: James D. Torrey, 1861.

Wakelyn, Jon L., ed. *Southern Pamphlets on Secession, November 1860–April 1861*. Chapel Hill: University of North Carolina Press, 1996.

———. *Southern Unionist Pamphlets and the Civil War*. Columbia: University of Missouri Press, 1999.

Waldstreicher, David, and Matthew Mason, eds. *John Quincy Adams and the Politics of Slavery: Selections from the Diary*. New York: Oxford University Press, 2017.

Walker, David. *Walker's Appeal . . . to the Coloured Citizens of the World*. 3rd ed. Boston: David Walker, 1830.

Webster, Daniel. "The Bunker Hill Monument, June 17, 1825." *Daniel Webster: Dartmouth's Favorite Son*, accessed May 5, 2020. https://www.dartmouth.edu/~dwebster/speeches/bunker-hill.html.

———. "Second Reply to Hayne, January 26–27, 1830." *Daniel Webster: Dartmouth's Favorite Son*, accessed May 5, 2020. https://www.dartmouth.edu/~dwebster/speeches/hayne-speech.html.

Welles, Gideon. *The Diary of Gideon Welles*. 3 vols. Edited by Edgar Thaddeus Welles. Boston: Houghton Mifflin, 1911.

———. *The History of Emancipation*. New York: W. C. and F. P. Church, 1872.

White, William O. *"Our Struggle Righteous in the Sight of God": A Sermon*. Keene, NH: G. & G. H. Tilden, 1862.

Whitman, Walt. *The Complete Writings of Walt Whitman*. 10 vols. New York: Putnam, 1902.

Williams, Amelia W., and Eugene C. Barker, eds. *The Writings of Sam Houston, 1813–1863*. 8 vols. Austin: University of Texas Press, 1938–43.

Williams, James. *The Rise and Fall of the Model Republic*. London: R. Bentley, 1863.

Wilson, Clyde N., and Shirley Bright Cook, eds. *The Papers of John C. Calhoun*. 28 vols. Columbia: University of South Carolina Press, 1959–2003.

Wilson, Henry. *History of the Rise and Fall of the Slave Power in America*. 3 vols. Boston: Osgood, 1873–77.

Wilson, Joseph T. *The Black Phalanx: A History of the Negro Soldiers of the United*

States in the War of 1775–1812, 1861–'65. Hartford, CT: American Publishing Co., 1888.

Woodward, C. Vann, ed. *Mary Chesnut's Civil War.* New Haven, CT: Yale University Press, 1981.

Young, John Russell. *Around the World with General Grant.* 2 vols. New York: American News Co., 1879.

Secondary Sources

Abbott, Edith. "The Civil War and the Crime Wave of 1865–70." *Social Service Review* 1 (June 1927): 212–34.

Abbott, Richard H. *Cotton and Capital: Boston Businessmen and Antislavery Reform, 1854–1868.* Amherst: University of Massachusetts Press, 1991.

Adams, Michael C. C. *Living Hell: The Dark Side of the Civil War.* Baltimore: Johns Hopkins University Press, 2014.

Adas, Michael. *Dominance by Design: Technological Imperatives and America's Civilizing Mission.* Cambridge, MA: Harvard University Press, 2006.

Alexander, Leslie. "The Black Republic: The Influence of the Haitian Revolution on Black Political Consciousness, 1816–1862." In *African Americans and the Haitian Revolution: Selected Essays and Historical Documents*, edited by Maurice Jackson and Jacqueline Bacon, 57–80. New York: Routledge, 2009.

Alexander, Ted. "'A Regular Slave Hunt': The Army of Northern Virginia and Black Civilians in the Gettysburg Campaign." *North and South* 4 (September 2001): 82–89.

Anbinder, Tyler G. *Nativism and Slavery: The Northern Know Nothings and the Politics of the 1850s.* New York: Oxford University Press, 1992.

Anderson, Bonnie S. "The Lid Comes Off: International Radical Feminism and the Revolutions of 1848." *NWSA Journal* 10 (Summer 1998): 1–12.

Anderson, Gary Clayton. *Massacre in Minnesota: The Dakota War of 1862, the Most Violent Ethnic Conflict in American History.* Norman: University of Oklahoma Press, 2019.

Anderson, Kristen L. *Abolitionizing Missouri: German Immigrants and Racial Ideology in Nineteenth-Century America.* Baton Rouge: Louisiana State University Press, 2016.

Appelbaum, Yoni. "Impeach Donald Trump." *Atlantic Monthly*, March 2019. https://www.theatlantic.com/magazine/archive/2019/03/impeachment-trump/580468/.

Appleby, Joyce. *Inheriting the Revolution: The First Generation of Americans.* Cambridge, MA: Harvard University Press, 2000.

Arenson, Adam, and Andrew R. Graybill, eds. *Civil War Wests: Testing the Limits of the United States.* Berkeley: University of California Press, 2015.

Armitage, David. *The Declaration of Independence: A Global History.* Cambridge, MA: Harvard University Press, 2007.

Armitage, David, et al. "Interchange: Nationalism and Internationalism in the Era of the Civil War." *Journal of American History* 98 (September 2011): 455–89.

Arthur, Anthony. *General Jo Shelby's March.* Lincoln: University of Nebraska Press, 2012.

Ash, Stephen V. *A Massacre in Memphis: The Race Riot That Shook the Nation One Year after the Civil War.* New York: Hill and Wang, 2013.

————. "Poor Whites in the Occupied South, 1861–1865." *Journal of Southern History* 57 (February 1991): 39–62.

————. *When the Yankees Came: Conflict and Chaos in the Occupied South, 1861–1865.* Chapel Hill: University of North Carolina Press, 1995.

Bailyn, Bernard. *Ideological Origins of the American Revolution.* Cambridge, MA: Harvard University Press, 1967.

Baker, Jean H. "Lincoln's Narrative of American Exceptionalism." In *"We Cannot Escape History": Lincoln and the Last Best Hope of Earth*, edited by James M. McPherson, 33–44. Urbana: University of Illinois Press, 1995.

Ball, Erica L. *To Live an Antislavery Life: Personal Politics and the Antebellum Black Middle Class.* Athens: University of Georgia Press, 2012.

Banning, Lance. *The Sacred Fire of Liberty: James Madison and the Founding of the Federal Republic.* Ithaca, NY: Cornell University Press, 1995.

Barnes, L. Diane, Brian Schoen, and Frank Towers, eds. *The Old South's Modern Worlds: Slavery, Region, and Nation in the Age of Progress.* New York: Oxford University Press, 2011.

Barney, William L., ed. *A Companion to 19th-Century America.* Malden, MA: Blackwell, 2001.

————. *The Road to Secession: A New Perspective on the Old South.* New York: Praeger, 1976.

Bartek, James M. "The Rhetoric of Destruction: Racial Identity and Noncombat Immunity in the Civil War Era." PhD diss., University of Kentucky, 2010.

Bass, Patrick G. "The American Civil War and the Idea of Civil Supremacy over the Military." *Proteus* 17 (September 2000): 49–59.

Bayly, C. A. *The Birth of the Modern World, 1780–1914: Global Connections and Comparisons.* Malden, MA: Blackwell, 2004.

Beasley, Edward. *The Victorian Reinvention of Race: New Racisms and the Problem of Grouping in Human Sciences.* New York: Routledge, 2010.

Beckert, Sven. "Emancipation and Empire: Reconstructing the Worldwide Web of Cotton Production in the Age of the American Civil War." *American Historical Review* 109 (December 2004): 1405–38.

————. *Empire of Cotton: A Global History.* New York: Alfred A. Knopf, 2014.

Behrend, Justin. *Reconstructing Democracy: Grassroots Black Politics in the Deep South after the Civil War.* Athens: University of Georgia Press, 2014.

Bell, David A. *The First Total War: Napoleon's Europe and the Birth of Modern Warfare as We Know It.* New York: Houghton Mifflin, 2007.

Bellamy, Alex J. *Massacres and Morality: Mass Atrocities in an Age of Civilian Immunity.* New York: Oxford University Press, 2012.

Bender, Thomas. *A Nation among Nations: America's Place in World History.* New York: Hill and Wang, 2006.

————, ed. *Rethinking American History in a Global Age.* Berkeley: University of California Press, 2001.

Benedict, Michael Les. *A Compromise of Principle: Congressional Republicans and Reconstruction, 1863–1869.* New York: W. W. Norton, 1974.

————. "Preserving the Constitution: The Conservative Basis of Radical Reconstruction." *Journal of American History* 61 (June 1974): 65–90.

Bennett, Michael J. "The Black Flag and Confederate Soldiers: Total War from the

Bottom Up?" In *This Distracted and Anarchical People: New Answers for Old Questions about the Civil War–Era North*, edited by Andrew L. Slap and Michael Thomas Smith, 142–59. New York: Fordham University Press, 2013.

———. *Union Jacks: Yankee Sailors in the Civil War*. Chapel Hill: University of North Carolina Press, 2004.

Berg, Scott W. *38 Nooses: Lincoln, Little Crow, and the Beginning of the Frontier's End*. New York: Vintage Books, 2013.

Bergad, Laird W. *The Comparative Histories of Slavery in Brazil, Cuba, and the United States*. Cambridge and New York: Cambridge University Press, 2007.

Berkhofer, Robert F. *The White Man's Indian: Images of the American Indian from Columbus to the Present*. New York: Alfred A. Knopf, 1978.

Berkin, Carol. *A Sovereign People: The Crisis of the 1790s and the Birth of American Nationalism*. New York: Basic Books, 2017.

Berlin, Ira. *The Long Emancipation: The Demise of Slavery in the United States*. Cambridge, MA: Harvard University Press, 2015.

———. *Many Thousands Gone: The First Two Centuries of Slavery in North America*. Cambridge, MA: Harvard University Press, 1998.

Bernath, Michael T. "The Confederacy as a Moment of Possibility." *Journal of Southern History* 79 (May 2013): 299–338.

———. *Confederate Minds: The Struggle for Intellectual Independence in the Civil War South*. Chapel Hill: University of North Carolina Press, 2010.

Bernstein, Samuel. "The Impact of the Paris Commune in the United States." *Massachusetts Review* 12 (Summer 1971): 435–46.

Berry, Stephen. "The Future of Civil War Era Studies." *Journal of the Civil War Era*. https://www.journalofthecivilwarera.org/forum-the-future-of-civil-war-erastudies/.

Berthoff, Rowland. *Republic of the Dispossessed: The Exceptional Old-European Consensus in America*. Columbia: University of Missouri Press, 1997.

Beyme, Klaus von. *American as a Model: The Impact of American Democracy in the World*. London: Palgrave Macmillan, 1987.

Billias, George A. *American Constitutionalism Heard Round the World, 1776–1989: A Global Perspective*. New York: New York University Press, 2009.

Black, Jeremy. *War in the Nineteenth Century, 1800–1914*. Cambridge, MA: Polity, 2009.

Blackburn, Robin. "Lincoln and Marx." *Jacobin*, August 28, 2012. https://jacobinmag.com/2012/08/lincoln-and-marx.

———. *The Making of New World Slavery: From Baroque to the Modern, 1492–1800*. London: Verso, 2010.

———. *An Unfinished Revolution: Karl Marx and Abraham Lincoln*. London: Verso, 2011.

Blackett, R. J. M. *Building an Antislavery Wall: Black Americans in the Atlantic Abolitionist Movement, 1830–1860*. Baton Rouge: Louisiana State University Press, 1983.

———. *The Captive's Quest for Freedom: Fugitive Slaves, the 1850 Fugitive Slave Law, and the Politics of Slavery*. New York: Cambridge University Press, 2018.

———. *Divided Hearts: Britain and the American Civil War*. Baton Rouge: Louisiana State University Press, 2001.

Blackman, Rodney Jay. *Foreign Fanaticism and American Constitutional Values.* Durham, NC: Carolina Academic Press, 2010.

Blair, William A. "Finding the Ending of America's Civil War." *American Historical Review* 120 (December 2015): 1753–66.

———. "Reconciliation as a Political Strategy: The United States after Its Civil War." In *Reconciliation after Civil Wars: Global Perspectives*, edited by Paul Quigley and James Hawdon, 217–33. New York: Routledge, 2019.

———. "The Use of Military Force to Protect the Gains of Reconstruction." *Civil War History* 51 (December 2005): 388–402.

———. *With Malice toward Some: Treason and Loyalty in the Civil War Era.* Chapel Hill: University of North Carolina Press, 2014.

Bledsoe, Andrew S. *Citizen-Officers: The Union and Confederate Volunteer Junior Officer Corps in the American Civil War.* Baton Rouge: Louisiana State University Press, 2015.

Bledsoe, Andrew S., and Andrew F. Lang. "Military History and the American Civil War." In *Upon the Fields of Battle: Essays on the Military History of America's Civil War*, edited by Andrews S. Bledsoe and Andrew F. Lang, 3–19. Baton Rouge: Louisiana State University Press, 2018.

Blight, David W. *Frederick Douglass: Prophet of Freedom.* New York: Simon & Schuster, 2018.

———. *Race and Reunion: The Civil War in American Memory.* Cambridge, MA: Harvard University Press, 2001.

———. "'What Will Peace among the Whites Bring?': Reunion and Race in the Struggle over the Memory of the Civil War in American Culture." *Massachusetts Review* 34 (Autumn 1993): 393–410.

Blight, David W., and Jim Downs, eds. *Beyond Freedom: Disrupting the History of Emancipation.* Athens: University of Georgia Press, 2017.

Blum, Edward J. *Reforging the White Republic: Race, Religion, and American Nationalism, 1865–1898.* Updated ed. Baton Rouge: Louisiana State University Press, 2015.

Boles, John B. *The Great Revival: The Origins of the Southern Evangelical Mind.* Lexington: University of Press of Kentucky, 1972.

———. *Jefferson: Architect of American Liberty.* New York: Basic Books, 2017.

Bolster, W. Jeffrey. *Black Jacks: African American Seamen in the Age of Sail.* Cambridge, MA: Harvard University Press, 1997.

Bonner, Robert E. *Mastering America: Southern Slaveholders and the Crisis of American Nationhood.* New York: Cambridge University Press, 2009.

Boorstin, Daniel J. *The Genius of American Politics.* Chicago: University of Chicago Press, 1953.

Bordewich, Fergus M. *America's Great Debate: Henry Clay, Stephen A. Douglas, and the Compromise That Preserved the Union.* New York: Simon & Schuster, 2012.

Bowden, Brett. *The Empire of Civilization: The Evolution of an Imperial Idea.* Chicago: University of Chicago Press, 2014.

Bowman, Shearer Davis. *At the Precipice: Americans North and South during the Secession Crisis.* Chapel Hill: University of North Carolina Press, 2010.

Boydston, Jeanne. *Home and Work: Housework, Wages, and the Ideology of Labor in the Early Republic.* New York: Oxford University Press, 1990.

Boyle, Michael J. *Violence after War: Explaining Instability in Post-Conflict States.* Baltimore: Johns Hopkins University Press, 2014.

Bradley, Mark L. *Bluecoats and Tar Heels: Soldiers and Civilians in Reconstruction North Carolina.* Lexington: University Press of Kentucky, 2011.

Bradley, George, and Richard L. Dahlen. *From Conciliation to Conquest: The Sack of Athens and the Court-Martial of Colonel John B. Turchin.* Tuscaloosa: University of Alabama Press, 2014.

Brasher, Glenn David. *The Peninsula Campaign and the Necessity of Emancipation: African Americans and the Fight for Freedom.* Chapel Hill: University of North Carolina Press, 2012.

Breen, Patrick H. *The Land Shall Be Deluged in Blood: A New History of the Nat Turner Revolt.* New York: Oxford University Press, 2016.

Brettle, Adrian. "The Fortunes of War: Confederate Expansionist Ambitions during the American Civil War." PhD diss., University of Virginia, 2014.

———. "Struggling to Realize a Vast Future: The Civil War as a Contest over the Relative Priorities of Political Liberty and Economic Prosperity." *Journal of Policy History* 29 (April 2017): 267–88.

Bright, Charles, and Michael Geyer. "Where in the World Is America? The History of the United States in the Global Age." In *Rethinking American History in a Global Age,* edited by Thomas Bender, 63–99. Berkeley: University of California Press, 2007.

Brown, Christopher Leslie. *Moral Capital: Foundations of British Abolitionism.* Chapel Hill: University of North Carolina Press, 2006.

Bruegel, Martin. *Farm, Shop, Landing: The Rise of a Market Society in the Hudson Valley, 1780–1860.* Durham, NC: Duke University Press, 2002.

Budiansky, Stephen. *The Bloody Shirt: Terror after the Civil War.* New York: Plume, 2008.

Burg, Robert W. "Amnesty, Civil Rights, and the Meaning of Liberal Republicanism, 1862–1872." *American Nineteenth Century History* 4 (October 2003): 29–60.

Burin, Eric. *Slavery and the Peculiar Solution: A History of the American Colonization Society.* Gainesville: University Press of Florida, 2005.

Burkhardt, George S. *Confederate Rage, Yankee Wrath: No Quarter in the Civil War.* Carbondale: Southern Illinois University Press, 2007.

Burlingame, Michael. *Abraham Lincoln: A Life.* 2 vols. Baltimore: Johns Hopkins University Press, 2008.

Butler, Leslie. *Critical Americans: Victorian Intellectuals and Transatlantic Liberal Reform.* Chapel Hill: University of North Carolina Press, 2007.

Byrd, Brandon R. *The Black Republic: African Americans and the Fate of Haiti.* Philadelphia: University of Pennsylvania Press, 2019.

———. "Black Republicans, Black Republic: African-Americans, Haiti, and the Promise of Reconstruction." *Slavery and Abolition* 36 (December 2015): 545–67.

Calhoun, Charles W. *Conceiving a New Republic: The Republican Party and the Southern Question, 1869–1900.* Lawrence: University Press of Kansas, 2006.

———. *Presidency of Ulysses S. Grant.* Lawrence: University Press of Kansas, 2017.

Calhoun, Robert M. *Political Moderation in America's First Two Centuries.* New York: Cambridge University Press, 2009.

Cameron, Christopher. *To Plead Our Own Cause: African Americans in*

Massachusetts and the Making of the Antislavery Movement. Kent, OH: Kent State University Press, 2014.

Camp, Stephanie M. *Closer to Freedom: Enslaved Women and Everyday Resistance in the Plantation South.* Chapel Hill: University of North Carolina Press, 2006.

Campbell, A. E. "Excess of Isolation: Isolation and the American Civil War." *Journal of Southern History* 29 (May 1963): 161–74.

Carmichael, Peter S. *The War for the Common Soldier: How Men Thought, Fought, and Survived in Civil War Armies.* Chapel Hill: University of North Carolina Press, 2019.

Carnahan, Burrus M. *Act of Justice: Lincoln's Emancipation Proclamation and the Law of War.* Lexington: University Press of Kentucky, 2011.

———. "Lincoln, Lieber and the Laws of War: The Origins and Limits of the Principle of Military Necessity." *American Journal of International Law* 92 (April 1998): 213–31.

———. *Lincoln on Trial: Southern Civilians and the Law of War.* Lexington: University Press of Kentucky, 2010.

Carter, Dan T. "Anatomy of Fear: The Christmas Day Insurrection Scare of 1865." *Journal of Southern History* 42 (August 1976): 345–64.

———. *When the War Was Over: The Failure of Self-Reconstruction in the South, 1865–1867.* Baton Rouge: Louisiana State University Press, 1985.

Carwardine, Richard. "Lincoln's Horizons: The Nationalist as Universalist." In *The Global Lincoln*, edited by Richard Carwardine and Jay Sexton, 28–43. New York: Oxford University Press, 2011.

Castel, Albert. "The Fort Pillow Massacre: A Fresh Examination of the Evidence." *Civil War History* 4 (March 1958): 37–50.

Chang, Gordon H. "Whose 'Barbarism'? Whose 'Treachery'? Race and Civilization in the Unknown United States–Korea War of 1871." *Journal of American History* 89 (March 2003): 1331–65.

Channing, Steven A. *Crisis of Fear: Secession in South Carolina.* New York: W. W. Norton, 1970.

Chernow, Ron. *Grant.* New York: Penguin, 2017.

Childs, Matt D. "Cuba, the Atlantic Crisis of the 1860s, and the Road to Abolition." In *American Civil Wars: The United States, Latin America, Europe, and the Crisis of the 1860s*, edited by Don H. Doyle, 204–21. Chapel Hill: University of North Carolina Press, 2017.

Clark, Christopher. *The Roots of Rural Capitalism: Western Massachusetts, 1780–1860.* Ithaca, NY: Cornell University Press, 1990.

Clarke, Frances. "'Let All Nations See': Civil War Nationalism and the Memorialization of Wartime Volunteerism." *Civil War History* 52 (March 2006): 66–93.

Clavin, Matthew. "A Second Haitian Revolution: John Brown, Toussaint Louverture, and the Making of the American Civil War." *Civil War History* 54 (June 2008): 117–45.

———. *Toussaint Louverture and the American Civil War: The Promise and Peril of a Second Haitian Revolution.* Philadelphia: University of Pennsylvania Press, 2009.

Cleves, Rachel Hope. *The Reign of Terror in America: Visions of Violence from Anti-Jacobinism to Antislavery.* New York: Cambridge University Press, 2009.

Clinton, Catherine. *Harriet Tubman: The Road to Freedom*. Boston: Little, Brown, 2004.

———. *The Other Civil War: American Women in the Nineteenth Century*. New York: Hill and Wang, 1999.

Clinton, Catherine, and Nina Silber, eds. *Divided Houses: Gender and the Civil War*. New York: Oxford University Press, 1992.

Coffman, Edward M. "The Duality of the American Military Tradition: A Commentary." *Journal of Military History* 64 (October 2000): 967–80.

———. *The Old Army: A Portrait of the American Army in Peacetime, 1784–1898*. New York: Oxford University Press, 1986.

Conlin, Michael F. "Dangerous *Isms* and the Fanatical *Ists*: Antebellum Conservatives in the South and the North Confront the Modernity Conspiracy." *Journal of the Civil War Era* 4 (June 2014): 205–33.

———. *One Nation Divided by Slavery: Remembering the American Revolution While Marching toward the Civil War*. Kent, OH: Kent State University Press, 2015.

Cook, Adrian. *The Alabama Claims: American Politics and Anglo-American Relations, 1865–1872*. Ithaca, NY: Cornell University Press, 1975.

Cooper, William J., Jr. *Jefferson Davis, American*. New York: Alfred A. Knopf, 2000.

———. *Liberty and Slavery: Southern Politics to 1860*. New York: Alfred A. Knopf, 1983.

———. *The Lost Founding Father: John Quincy Adams and the Transformation of American Politics*. New York: Liveright, 2017.

———. *The South and the Politics of Slavery, 1828–1856*. Baton Rouge: Louisiana State University Press, 1992.

Cott, Nancy F. *The Bonds of Womanhood: "Woman's Sphere" in New England, 1780–1835*. New Haven, CT: Yale University Press, 1997.

Cottrol, Robert J. *The Long, Lingering Shadow: Slavery, Race, and Law in the American Hemisphere*. Athens: University of Georgia Press, 2013.

Crofts, Daniel W. *Lincoln and the Politics of Slavery: The Other Thirteenth Amendment and the Struggle to Save the Union*. Chapel Hill: University of North Carolina Press, 2016.

Crook, David Paul. *The North, the South, and the Powers, 1861–1865*. New York: Wiley, 1974.

Cumfer, Cynthia. *Separate Peoples, One Land: The Minds of Cherokees, Blacks, and Whites on the Tennessee Frontier*. Chapel Hill: University of North Carolina Press, 2007.

Cunningham, Michele. *Mexico and the Foreign Policy of Napoleon III*. New York: Palgrave, 2000.

Curti, Merle. "The Impact of the Revolutions of 1848 on American Thought." *Proceedings of the American Philosophical Society* 93 (June 1949): 209–15.

da Costa, Emilia Viotti. *Crowns of Glory, Tears of Blood: The Demerara Slave Rebellion of 1823*. New York: Oxford University Press, 1997.

Dain, Bruce R. *A Hideous Monster of the Mind: American Race Theory in the Early Republic*. Cambridge, MA: Harvard University Press, 2002.

Danielson, Joseph W. *War's Desolating Scourge: The Union's Occupation of North Alabama*. Lawrence: University Press of Kansas, 2012.

Davis, David Brion. "The Impact of the French and Haitian Revolutions." In *The*

Impact of the Haitian Revolution in the Atlantic World, edited by David Geggus, 3–9. Columbia: University of South Carolina Press, 2001.

———. *Inhuman Bondage: The Rise and Fall of Slavery in the New World*. New York: Oxford University Press, 2008.

———. *The Problem of Slavery in the Age of Emancipation*. New York: Alfred A. Knopf, 2014.

———. *The Problem of Slavery in Western Culture*. Ithaca, NY: Cornell University Press, 1966.

———. *Revolutions: Reflections on American Equality and Foreign Liberations*. Cambridge, MA: Harvard University Press, 1990.

———. *The Slave Power Conspiracy and the Paranoid Style*. Baton Rouge: Louisiana State University Press, 1982.

Davis, William C. *Rhett: The Turbulent Life and Times of a Fire-Eater*. Columbia: University of South Carolina Press, 2001.

Dawson, Joseph G., III. *Army Generals and Reconstruction: Louisiana, 1862–1877*. Baton Rouge: Louisiana State University Press, 1985.

———. "The First of the Modern Wars?" In *Themes of the American Civil War: The War between the States*, edited by Susan-Mary Grant and Brian Holden Reid, 64–80. Revised second edition; New York: Routledge, 2010.

Dean, Adam Wesley. *Agrarian Republic: Farming, Antislavery Politics, and Nature Parks in the Civil War Era*. Chapel Hill: University of North Carolina Press, 2015.

Degler, Carl N. *Neither Black nor White: Slavery and Race Relations in Brazil and the United States*. New York: Macmillan, 1971.

Deloria, Philip J. "American Master Narratives and the Problem of Indian Citizenship in the Gilded Age and Progressive Era." *Journal of the Gilded Age and Progressive Era* 14 (January 2015): 3–12.

De Santis, Vincent P. "Rutherford B. Hayes and the Removal of the Troops and the End of Reconstruction." In *Region, Race, and Reconstruction: Essays in Honor of C. Vann Woodward*, edited by J. Morton Kousser and James M. McPherson, 417–76. New York: Oxford University Press, 1982.

Dew, Charles B. *Apostles of Disunion: Southern Secession Commissioners and the Causes of the Civil War*. Charlottesville: University Press of Virginia, 2001.

Deyle, Steven. *Carry Me Back: The Domestic Slave Trade in American Life*. New York: Oxford University Press, 2005.

Dilbeck, D. H. "'The Genesis of This Little Tablet with My Name': Francis Lieber and the Wartime Origins of General Orders No. 100." *Journal of the Civil War Era* 5 (June 2015): 231–53.

———. *A More Civil War: How the Union Waged a Just War*. Chapel Hill: University of North Carolina Press, 2016.

Dobak, William A. *Freedom by the Sword: The U.S. Colored Troops, 1862–1867*. Washington, DC: Center of Military History, 2011.

Donald, David Herbert. *Charles Sumner and the Rights of Man*. New York: Alfred A. Knopf, 1970.

———. *Liberty and Union*. Boston: Little, Brown, 1978.

———. *Lincoln*. New York: Simon & Schuster, 1995.

Dorris, Jonathan T. *Pardon and Amnesty under Lincoln and Johnson: The Restoration of the Confederates to Their Rights and Privileges, 1861–1898*. Chapel Hill: University of North Carolina Press, 1953.

Downey, Matthew T. "Horace Greeley and the Politicians: The Liberal Republican Convention in 1872." *Journal of American History* 53 (March 1967): 727–50.

Downs, Gregory P. *After Appomattox: Military Occupation and the Ends of War.* Cambridge, MA: Harvard University Press, 2015.

———. "Anarchy at the Circumference: Statelessness and the Reconstruction of Authority in Emancipation North Carolina." In *After Slavery: Race, Labor, and Citizenship in the Reconstruction South*, edited by Bruce E. Baker and Brian Kelly, 98–121. Gainesville: University Press of Florida, 2013.

———. "The Mexicanization of American Politics: The United States' Transnational Path from Civil War to Stabilization." *American Historical Review* 117 (April 2012): 387–409.

———. "A Palace That Will Fall upon Them: Reconstruction as a Problem of Occupation." *Reviews in American History* 39 (March 2011): 118–26.

———. *The Second American Revolution: The Civil War-Era Struggle over Cuba and the Rebirth of the American Republic.* Chapel Hill: University of North Carolina Press, 2019.

———. "The World the War Made: The 'Disturbing Tendencies' of the Civil War and the New Map of Reconstruction." *Reviews in American History* 40 (March 2012): 88–95.

Downs, Gregory P., and Kate Masur. "Echoes of War: Rethinking Post–Civil War Governance and Politics." In *The World the Civil War Made*, edited by Gregory P. Downs and Kate Masur, 1–21. Chapel Hill: University of North Carolina Press, 2015.

———, eds. *The World the Civil War Made.* Chapel Hill: University of North Carolina Press, 2015.

Downs, Jim. *Sick from Freedom: African-American Illness and Suffering during the Civil War and Reconstruction.* New York: Oxford University Press, 2012.

Doyle, Don H., ed. *American Civil Wars: The United States, Latin America, Europe, and the Crisis of the 1860s.* Chapel Hill: University of North Carolina Press, 2017.

———. *The Cause of All Nations: An International History of the American Civil War.* New York: Basic Books, 2014.

———. "The Global Civil War." In *A Companion to the U.S. Civil War*, vol. 2, edited by Aaron Sheehan-Dean, 1103–20. Malden, MA: Wiley Blackwell, 2014.

Drescher, Seymour. "Servile Insurrection and John Brown's Body in Europe." *Journal of American History* 80 (September 1993): 499–524.

Dublin, Thomas. *Women at Work: The Transformation of Work and Community in Lowell, Massachusetts, 1826–1860.* New York: Columbia University Press, 1993.

DuBois, Ellen Carol. *Feminism and Suffrage: The Emergence of an Independent Women's Movement in America, 1848–1869.* Ithaca, NY: Cornell University Press, 1999.

Dubois, Laurent. *Avengers of the New World: The Story of the Haitian Revolution.* Cambridge, MA: Harvard University Press, 2009.

———. "Avenging America: The Politics of Violence in the Haitian Revolution." In *The World of the Haitian Revolution*, edited by David P. Geggus and Norman Fiering, 111–24. Bloomington: Indiana University Press, 2009.

Dubrulle, Hugh. *Ambivalent Nation: How Britain Imagined the American Civil War.* Baton Rouge: Louisiana State University Press, 2018.

Dun, James Alexander. "Atlantic Antislavery, American Ambition: The Problem of Slavery in United States in an Age of Disruption, 1770–1808." In *The World of the Revolutionary American Republic: Land, Labor, and Conflict for a Continent*, edited by Andrew Shankman, 218–45. New York: Routledge, 2014.

———. *Dangerous Neighbors: Making the Haitian Revolution in Early America*. Philadelphia: University of Pennsylvania Press, 2016.

DuVal, Kathleen. "Independence for Whom? Expansion and Conflict in the South and Southwest." In *The World of the Revolutionary American Republic: Land, Labor, and the Conflict for a Continent*, edited by Andrew Shankman, 97–115. New York: Routledge, 2014.

Dzelzainis, Ella, and Ruth Livesey, eds. *The American Experiment and the Idea of Democracy in British Culture, 1776–1914*. Abingdon, UK: Routledge, 2016.

Earle, Jonathan H. *Jacksonian Antislavery and the Politics of Free Soil, 1824–1854*. Chapel Hill: University of North Carolina Press, 2004.

Eaton, Clement. *The Civilization of the Old South: Writings of Clement Eaton*. Edited by Albert D. Kirwan. Lexington: University of Kentucky Press, 1968.

Edwards, Laura F. "Gender and the Changing Roles of Women." In *A Companion to 19th-Century America*, edited by William Barney, 223–37. Malden, MA: Blackwell, 2001.

———. *A Legal History of the Civil War and Reconstruction: A Nation of Rights*. New York: Cambridge University Press, 2015.

———. "Reconstruction and the History of Governance." In *The World the Civil War Made*, edited by Gregory P. Downs and Kate Masur, 22–45. Chapel Hill: University of North Carolina Press, 2015.

———. *Gendered Strife and Confusion: The Political Culture of Reconstruction*. Urbana: University of Illinois Press, 1997.

Egerton, Douglas R. *Gabriel's Rebellion: The Virginia Slave Conspiracies of 1800 and 1802*. Chapel Hill: University of North Carolina Press, 1993.

———. "Rethinking Atlantic Historiography in a Postcolonial Era: The Civil War in a Global Perspective." *Journal of the Civil War Era* 1 (March 2011): 79–95.

———. "The Slaves' Election: Frémont, Freedom, and the Slaves Conspiracies of 1856." *Civil War History* 61 (March 2015): 35–63.

———. *The Wars of Reconstruction: The Brief, Violent History of America's Most Progressive Era*. New York: Bloomsbury, 2013.

Eichhorn, Niels. *Liberty and Slavery: European Separatists, Southern Secession, and the American Civil War*. Baton Rouge: Louisiana State University Press, 2019.

Elazar, Daniel J. "The Civil War and the Preservation of American Federalism." *Publius* 1, no. 1 (1971): 39–58.

Eller, Anne. "Dominican Civil War, Slavery, and Spanish Annexation, 1844–1865." In *American Civil Wars: The United States, Latin America, Europe, and the Crisis of the 1860s*, edited by Don H. Doyle, 147–66. Chapel Hill: University of North Carolina Press, 2017.

Emberton, Carole. *Beyond Redemption: Race, Violence, and the American South after the Civil War*. Chicago: University of Chicago Press, 2013.

———. "'Only Murder Makes Men': Reconsidering the Black Military Experience." *Journal of the Civil War Era* 2 (September 2012): 369–93.

Engerman, Stanley L., and J. Matthew Gallman. "The Civil War Economy: A Modern

View." In *On the Road to Total War: The American Civil War and the German Wars of Unification, 1861–1871,* edited by Stig Förster and Jörg Nagler, 217–48. New York: Cambridge University Press, 1997.

Ernest, John. *Liberation Historiography: African American Writers and the Challenge of History, 1794–1861.* Chapel Hill: University of North Carolina Press, 2004.

Escott, Paul D. *"What Shall We Do with the Negro?": Lincoln, White Racism, and Civil War America.* Charlottesville: University of Virginia Press, 2009.

Etcheson, Nicole. *Bleeding Kansas: Contested Liberty in the Civil War Era.* Lawrence: University Press of Kansas, 2004.

Eudell, Demetrius L. *The Political Languages of Emancipation in the British Caribbean and the U.S. South.* Chapel Hill: University of North Carolina Press, 2002.

Evans, Robert John Weston, and H. Pogge Von Strandmann, eds. *The Revolutions in Europe, 1848–1849: From Reform to Reaction.* New York: Oxford University Press, 2005.

Eyal, Yonatan. "Charles Eliot Norton, E. L. Godkin, and the Liberal Republicans of 1872." *American Nineteenth Century History* 2 (March 2001): 53–74.

Fagan, Benjamin P. *The Black Newspaper and the Chosen Nation.* Athens: University of Georgia Press, 2016.

Fairclough, Adam. *The Revolution That Failed: Reconstruction in Natchitoches.* Gainesville: University Press of Florida, 2018.

———. "Was the Grant of Black Suffrage a Political Error? Reconsidering the Views of John W. Burgess, William A. Dunning, and Eric Foner on Congressional Reconstruction." *Journal of the Historical Society* 12 (June 2012): 155–88.

Fanning, Sara C. "The Roots of Early Black Nationalism: Northern African Americans' Invocations of Haiti in the Early Nineteenth Century." *Slavery and Abolition* 28 (April 2007): 61–85.

Faust, Drew Gilpin. "Altars of Sacrifice: Confederate Women and the Narratives of War." *Journal of American History* 76 (March 1990): 1200–1228.

———. *The Creation of Confederate Nationalism: Ideology and Identity in the Civil War South.* Baton Rouge: Louisiana State University Press, 1988.

———. *James Henry Hammond and the Old South: A Design for Mastery.* Baton Rouge: Louisiana State University Press, 1982.

———. *Mothers of Invention: Women of the Slaveholding South in the American Civil War.* Chapel Hill: University of North Carolina Press, 1996.

———. *This Republic of Suffering: Death and the American Civil War.* New York: Alfred A. Knopf, 2008.

Fehrenbacher, Don E. *The Slaveholding Republic: An Account of the United States Government's Relations to Slavery.* New York: Oxford University Press, 2001.

Feller, Daniel. *The Jacksonian Promise: America, 1815–1840.* Baltimore: Johns Hopkins University Press, 1995.

———. "The Market Revolution Ate My Homework." *Reviews in American History* 25 (September 1995): 408–15.

Fellman, Michael. *In the Name of God and Country: Reconsidering Terrorism in American History.* New Haven, CT: Yale University Press, 2011.

Ferrer, Ada. *Insurgent Cuba: Race, Nation, and Revolution, 1868–1898.* Chapel Hill: University of North Carolina Press, 1999.

Finkelman, Paul. "Lincoln the Lawyer, Humanitarian Concerns, and the Dakota Pardons." *William Mitchell Law Review* 39, no. 2 (2013): 405–49.

Fitz, Caitlin A. "The Hemispheric Dimensions of Early U.S. Nationalism: The War of 1812, Its Aftermath, and Spanish Independence." *Journal of American History* 102 (September 2015): 356–79.

———. *Our Sister Republics: The United States in an Age of American Revolutions*. New York: Liveright, 2016.

Fleche, Andre M. "The Civil War in the Age of Revolution." *South Central Review* 33 (Spring 2016): 5–20.

———. *The Revolution of 1861: The American Civil War in the Age of Nationalist Conflict*. Chapel Hill: University of North Carolina Press, 2012.

Floan, Howard R. *The South in Northern Eyes, 1831 to 1861*. Austin: University of Texas Press, 1958.

Fluhman, J. Spencer. *"A Peculiar People": Anti-Mormonism and the Making of Religion in Nineteenth-Century America*. Chapel Hill: University of North Carolina Press, 2012.

Foner, Eric. "American Exceptionalism, American Freedom." *Montréal Review*, January 2013. http://themontrealreview.com/2009/American-Exceptionalism -American-Freedom.php.

———. "American Freedom in a Global Age." *American Historical Review* 106 (February 2001): 1–16.

———. "Birthright Citizenship Is the Good Kind of American Exceptionalism." *The Nation*, August 25, 2015. https://www.thenation.com/article/birthright -citizenship-is-the-good-kind-of-american-exceptionalism.

———. *The Fiery Trial: Abraham Lincoln and American Slavery*. New York: W. W. Norton, 2010.

———. *Free Soil, Free Labor, Free Men: The Ideology of the Republican Party before the Civil War*. New York: Oxford University Press, 1970.

———. "The Meaning of Freedom in the Age of Emancipation." *Journal of American History* 81 (September 1994): 435–60.

———. *Nothing but Freedom: Emancipation and Its Legacy*. Baton Rouge: Louisiana State University Press, 1983.

———. *Politics and Ideology in the Age of the Civil War*. New York: Oxford University Press, 1980.

———. *Reconstruction: America's Unfinished Revolution, 1863–1877*. New York: Harper & Row, 1988.

———. *The Second Founding: How the Civil War and Reconstruction Remade the Constitution*. New York: W. W. Norton, 2019.

———. *A Short History of Reconstruction*. New York: Harper Perennial, 2015.

———. *Tom Paine and Revolutionary America*. New York: Oxford University Press, 2005.

Foos, Paul. *A Short, Offhand, Killing Affair: Soldiers and Social Conflict during the Mexican-American War*. Chapel Hill: University of North Carolina Press, 2002.

Foote, Lorien. "Civilization and Savagery in the American Civil War." *South Central Review* 33 (Spring 2016): 21–36.

Forbes, Robert Pierce. *The Missouri Compromise and Its Aftermath: Slavery and the Meaning of America*. Chapel Hill: University of North Carolina Press, 2007.

Ford, Lacy K. *Deliver Us from Evil: The Slavery Question in the Old South*. New York: Oxford University Press, 2009.

———. *The Origins of Southern Radicalism: The South Carolina Upcountry, 1801–1860*. New York: Oxford University Press, 1988.

Foreman, Amanda. *A World on Fire: An Epic History of Two Nations Divided*. London: Penguin, 2011.

Foreman, Pier Gabrielle. *Activist Sentiments: Reading Black Women in the Nineteenth Century*. Urbana: University of Illinois Press, 2010.

Förster, Stig, and Jörg Nagler, eds. *On the Road to Total War: The American Civil War and the German Wars of Unification, 1861–1871*. New York: Cambridge University Press, 1997.

Fox, Richard Wightman, and James T. Kloppenberg, eds. *A Companion to American Thought*. Malden, MA: Blackwell, 1998.

Fox-Genovese, Elizabeth. *Within the Plantation Household: Black and White Women of the Old South*. Chapel Hill: University of North Carolina Press, 1988.

Fox-Genovese, Elizabeth, and Eugene Genovese. *The Mind of the Master Class: History and Faith in the Southern Slaveholders' Worldview*. New York: Cambridge University Press, 2005.

Frazier, Donald S. *Blood and Treasure: Confederate Empire in the Southwest*. College Station: Texas A&M University Press, 1995.

Fredrickson, George M. *Big Enough to Be Inconsistent: Abraham Lincoln Confronts Slavery and Race*. Cambridge, MA: Harvard University Press, 2008.

———. *The Black Image in the White Mind: The Debate on Afro-American Character and Destiny, 1817–1914*. New York: Harper & Row, 1971.

———. "The Coming of the Lord: The Northern Protestant Clergy and the Civil War." In *Religion and the American Civil War*, edited by Randall M. Miller, Harry S. Stout, and Charles Reagan Wilson, 110–30. New York: Oxford University Press, 1998.

———. "A Man but Not a Brother: Abraham Lincoln and Racial Equality." *Journal of Southern History* 41 (February 1975): 39–58.

———. "Nineteenth-Century American History." In *Imagined Histories: Americans Interpret the Past*, edited by Anthony Molho and Gordon S. Wood, 164–84. Princeton, NJ: Princeton University Press, 1998.

———. *Why the Confederacy Did Not Fight a Guerrilla War after the Fall of Richmond: A Comparative View*. Gettysburg, PA: Gettysburg College, 1996.

Freehling, William H. *Prelude to Civil War: The Nullification Controversy in South Carolina, 1816–1836*. New York: Harper & Row, 1966.

———. *The Road to Disunion: Secessionists at Bay, 1776–1854*. New York: Oxford University Press, 1990.

———. *The Road to Disunion: Secessionists Triumphant, 1854–1861*. New York: Oxford University Press, 2007.

———. *The South vs. the South: How Anti-Confederate Southerners Shaped the Course of the Civil War*. New York: Oxford University Press, 2001.

Freehling, William H., and Craig M. Simpson. *Showdown in Virginia: The 1861 Convention and the Fate of the Union*. Charlottesville: University of Virginia Press, 2010.

Fried, Daniel. "Thomas Nast's Thanksgiving Vision of American Identity." *Atlantic*

Monthly, November 22, 2018. https://www.theatlantic.com/ideas/archive/2018 /11/uncle-sams-thanksgiving-dinner/575863.

Fry, Joseph A. *Dixie Looks Abroad: The South and U.S. Foreign Relations, 1789–1973.* Baton Rouge: Louisiana State University Press, 2002.

Gallagher, Gary W. "A Civil War Watershed: The 1862 Richmond Campaign in Perspective." In *The Richmond Campaign of 1862: The Peninsula Campaign and the Seven Days*, edited by Gary W. Gallagher, 3–27. Chapel Hill: University of North Carolina Press, 2000.

———. *The Confederate War: How Popular Will, Nationalism, and Military Strategy Could Not Stave Off Defeat.* Cambridge, MA: Harvard University Press, 1997.

———. "Fighting on Multiple Fronts: Should Campaigns against Native Americans and Confederates Be Viewed as One War or Two?" *Civil War Times* 58 (April 2019): 46–53.

———. *Lee and His Army in Confederate History.* Chapel Hill: University of North Carolina Press, 2001.

———. *The Union War.* Cambridge, MA: Harvard University Press, 2011.

Gallagher, Gary W., and Katherine Shively Meier. "Coming to Terms with Civil War Military History." *Journal of the Civil War Era* 4 (December 2014): 487–508.

Gallagher, Gary W., and Joan Waugh. *The American War: A History of the Civil War Era.* State College, PA: Flip Learning, 2019.

Gallman, J. Matthew. "Regionalism and Urbanism as Problems in Confederate Urban History." In *Confederate Cities: The Urban South during the Civil War Era*, edited by Andrew L. Slap and Frank Towers, 27–45. Chicago: University of Chicago Press, 2016.

Gamble, Richard M. *A Fiery Gospel: The Battle Hymn of the Republic and the Road to Righteous War.* Ithaca, NY: Cornell University Press, 2019.

Gatewood, Willard B., Jr. "'The Remarkable Misses Rollin': Black Women in Reconstruction South Carolina." *South Carolina Historical Magazine* 92 (July 1991): 172–88.

Geggus, David P., and Norman Fiering, eds. *The World of the Haitian Revolution.* Bloomington: Indiana University Press, 2009.

Gemme, Paola. *Domesticating Foreign Struggles: The Italian Risorgimento and Antebellum American Identity.* Athens: University of Georgia Press, 2005.

Genetin-Pilawa, C. Joseph. *Crooked Paths to Allotment: The Fight over Federal Indian Policy after the Civil War.* Chapel Hill: University of North Carolina Press, 2012.

———. "Ely S. Parker and the Paradox of Reconstruction Politics in Indian Country." In *The World the Civil War Made*, edited by Gregory P. Downs and Kate Masur, 183–205. Chapel Hill: University of North Carolina Press, 2015.

Genovese, Eugene D. *The Political Economy of Slavery: Studies in the Economy and Society of the Slave South.* New York: Vintage Books, 1967.

———. *The Slaveholders' Dilemma: Freedom and Progress in Southern Conservative Thought, 1820–1860.* Columbia: University of South Carolina Press, 1992.

———. *The World the Slaveholders Made: Two Essays in Interpretation.* New York: Pantheon Books, 1969.

Geyer, Michael, and Charles Bright. "Global Violence and Nationalizing Wars in Eurasia and America: The Geopolitics of War in the Mid-Nineteenth Century." *Comparative Studies in Society and History* 38 (October 1996): 619–57.

Gienapp, William E. *Abraham Lincoln and Civil War America: A Biography*. New York: Oxford University Press, 2002.

———. *The Origins of the Republican Party, 1852–1856*. New York: Oxford University Press, 1987.

Giesberg, Judith. *Army at Home: Women and the Civil War on the Northern Home Front*. Chapel Hill: University of North Carolina Press, 2009.

Gillette, William. *Retreat from Reconstruction, 1869–1879*. Baton Rouge: Louisiana State University Press, 1979.

Glaser, Elisabeth, and Hermann Wellenreuther, eds. *Bridging the Atlantic: The Question of American Exceptionalism in Perspective*. New York: Cambridge University Press, 2002.

Glatthaar, Joseph T. "The Civil War: A New Definition of Victory." In *Between War and Peace: How America Ends Its Wars*, edited by Matthew Moten, 107–28. New York: Free Press, 2011.

———. *Forged in Battle: The Civil War Alliance of Black Soldiers and White Officers*. New York: Free Press, 1990.

———. *The March to the Sea and Beyond: Sherman's Troops in the Savannah and Carolinas Campaigns*. New York: New York University Press, 1985.

Glaude, Eddie S. *Exodus! Religions, Race, and Nation in Early Nineteenth-Century Black America*. Chicago: University of Chicago Press, 2000.

Glickstein, Jonathan A. *American Exceptionalism, American Anxiety: Wages, Competition, and Degraded Labor in the Antebellum United States*. Charlottesville: University Press of Virginia, 2002.

Glymph, Thavolia. *Out of the House of Bondage: The Transformation of the Plantation Household*. New York: Cambridge University Press, 2008.

———. *Women's Fight: The Civil War's Battles for Home, Freedom, and Nation*. Chapel Hill: University of North Carolina Press, 2020.

Gosse, Van. "'As a Nation, the English Are Our Friends': The Emergence of African American Politics in the British Atlantic World, 1772–1861." *American Historical Review* 113 (October 2008): 1003–28.

Grant, Susan-Mary. "'How a Free People Conduct a Long War': Sustaining Opposition to Secession in the American Civil War." In *Secession as an International Phenomenon: From America's Civil War to Contemporary Separatist Movements*, edited by Don H. Doyle, 132–50. Athens: University of Georgia Press, 2010.

———. *North over South: Northern Nationalism and American Identity in the Antebellum Era*. Lawrence: University Press of Kansas, 2000.

Greenberg, Amy S. *A Wicked War: Polk, Clay, Lincoln, and the 1846 U.S. Invasion of Mexico*. New York: Alfred A. Knopf, 2012.

Greene, A. Wilson. *Civil War Petersburg: Confederate City in the Crucible of War*. Charlottesville: University of Virginia Press, 2006.

Greene, Jack P. *The Intellectual Construction of America: Exceptionalism and Identity from 1492 to 1800*. Chapel Hill: University of North Carolina Press, 1993.

Grenier, John. *The First Way of War: American War Making on the Frontier, 1607–1814*. New York: Cambridge University Press, 2005.

Griffith, Paddy. *Battle Tactics of the Civil War*. New Haven, CT: Yale University Press, 1989.

Grimsley, Mark. *The Hard Hand of War: Union Military Policy toward Southern Civilians, 1861–1865*. New York: Cambridge University Press, 1995.

———. "'Rebels' and 'Redskins': U.S. Military Conduct toward White Southerners and Native Americans in Comparative Perspective." In *Civilians in the Path of War*, edited by Mark Grimsley and Clifford J. Rogers, 137–62. Lincoln: University of Nebraska Press, 2002.

———. "Surviving Military Revolution: The U.S. Civil War." In *The Dynamics of Military Revolution, 1300–2050*, edited by MacGregor Knox, 74–91. New York: Cambridge University Press, 2001.

———. "'A Very Long Shadow': Race, Atrocity, and the American Civil War." In *Black Flag over Dixie: Racial Atrocities and Reprisals in the Civil War*, edited by Gregory J. W. Urwin, 231–44. Carbondale: Southern Illinois University Press, 2004.

———. "Wars for the American South: The First and Second Reconstructions Considered as Insurgencies." *Civil War History* 58 (March 2012): 6–36.

Guelzo, Allen C. *Abraham Lincoln as a Man of Ideas*. Carbondale: Southern Illinois University Press, 2009.

———. "Democracy and Nobility." *Weekly Standard*, January 5, 2015. http://washingtonexaminer.com/weekly-standard/democracy-and-nobility.

———. *Fateful Lightning: A New History of the Civil War and Reconstruction*. New York: Oxford University Press, 2012.

———. *Gettysburg: The Last Invasion*. New York: Alfred A. Knopf, 2013.

———. *Lincoln's Emancipation Proclamation: The End of Slavery in America*. New York: Simon & Schuster, 2004.

———. *Reconstruction: A Concise History*. New York: Oxford University Press, 2018.

———. "Reconstruction as a Pure Bourgeois Revolution." *Journal of the Abraham Lincoln Association* 39 (Winter 2018): 50–73.

———. "Statesmanship and Mr. Lincoln." *Weekly Standard*, February 9, 2018. https://www.weeklystandard.com/allen-c-guelzo/statesmanship-and-mr-lincoln.

Guterl, Matthew P. *American Mediterranean: Southern Slaveholders in the Age of Emancipation*. Cambridge, MA: Harvard University Press, 2013.

Guyatt, Nicholas. "America's Conservatory: Race, Reconstruction, and the Santo Domingo Debate." *Journal of American History* 97 (March 2011): 974–1000.

———. "'An Impossible Idea?': The Curious Career of Internal Colonization." *Journal of the Civil War Era* 4 (June 2014): 234–63.

Hacker, J. David. "A Census-Based Count of the Civil War Dead." *Civil War History* 57 (December 2011): 307–48.

Hahn, Steven. *A Nation under Our Feet: Black Political Struggles in the Rural South, from Slavery to the Great Migration*. Cambridge, MA: Belknap Press of Harvard University, 2003.

———. *A Nation without Borders: The United States and Its World in an Age of Civil Wars, 1830–1910*. New York: Penguin Books, 2017.

———. *The Political Worlds of Slavery and Freedom*. Cambridge, MA: Harvard University Press, 2009.

Hämäläinen, Pekka. "Reconstructing the Great Plains: The Long Struggle for Sovereignty and Dominance in the Heart of the Continent." *Journal of the Civil War Era* 6 (December 2016): 481–509.

Hamilton, Daniel W. *The Limits of Sovereignty: Property Confiscation in the Union and the Confederacy during the Civil War*. Chicago: University of Chicago Press, 2007.

Hanna, Alfred J., and Kathryn Hanna. *Confederate Exiles in Venezuela*. Tuscaloosa, AL: Confederate Pub. Co., 1960.

———. *Napoleon III and Mexico: American Triumph over Monarchy*. Chapel Hill: University of North Carolina Press, 1971.

Harlow, Luke E. *Religion, Race, and the Making of Confederate Kentucky, 1830–1880*. New York: Cambridge University Press, 2014.

Harris, William C. *Lincoln and the Border States: Preserving the Union*. Lawrence: University Press of Kansas, 2011.

Harrold, Stanley. *American Abolitionism: Its Direct Political Impact from Colonial Times into Reconstruction*. Charlottesville: University of Virginia Press, 2019.

Hartz, Louis. *The Liberal Tradition in America: An Interpretation of American Political Thought since the Revolution*. New York: Harcourt Brace & World, 1955.

Hattaway, Herman, and Archer Jones. *How the North Won: A Military History of the Civil War*. Urbana: University of Illinois Press, 1983.

Haynes, Carolyn A. *Divine Destiny: Gender and Race in the Nineteenth-Century Protestantism*. Jackson: University Press of Mississippi, 1998.

Henkin, David M. *The Postal Age: The Emergence of Modern Communications in Nineteenth-Century America*. Chicago: University of Chicago, 2006.

Hennessy, John J. "The Looting and Bombardment of Fredericksburg: 'Vile Spirits' or War Transformed?" In *Upon the Fields of Battle: Essays on the Military History of America's Civil War*, edited by Andrew S. Bledsoe and Andrew F. Lang, 124–64. Baton Rouge: Louisiana State University Press, 2018.

Herbert, Maeve. "Explaining the Sioux Military Commission of 1862." *Columbia Human Rights Law Review* 40 (April 2009): 743–98.

Hernández, José Angel. *Mexican American Colonization during the Nineteenth Century: A History of the U.S.-Mexico Borderlands*. New York: Cambridge University Press, 2012.

Herrera, Ricardo A. *For Liberty and the Republic: The American Citizen as Soldier, 1775–1861*. New York: New York University Press, 2015.

Herschthal, Eric. "Dreaming of Haiti." *Disunion* (blog), *New York Times*, December 21, 2012. https://opinionator.blogs.nytimes.com/2012/12/21/dreaming-of-haiti/.

Hess, Earl J. "Civil War Guerrillas in a Global, Comparative Context." In *The Guerrilla Hunters: Irregular Conflicts during the Civil War*, edited by Brian D. McKnight and Barton A. Myers, 335–53. Baton Rouge: Louisiana State University Press, 2017.

———. *Liberty, Virtue, and Progress: Northerners and Their War for the Union*. New York: Fordham University Press, 1988.

———. *The Rifle Musket in Civil War Combat: Reality and Myth*. Lawrence: University Press of Kansas, 2008.

———. *The Union Soldier in Battle: Enduring the Ordeal of Combat*. Lawrence: University Press of Kansas, 1997.

Hietala, Thomas R. *Manifest Design: American Exceptionalism and Empire*. Ithaca, NY: Cornell University Press, 2003.

Hinks, Peter P. *To Awaken My Afflicted Brethren: David Walker and the Problem of Antebellum Slave Resistance*. University Park: Pennsylvania State University Press, 1997.

Hirsch, Adam J. "The Collision of Military Cultures in Seventeenth-Century New England." *Journal of American History* 74 (March 1988): 1187–1212.

Historical Statistics of the United States, Colonial Times to 1970. Washington, DC: U.S. Department of Commerce, Bureau of the Census, 1975.

Hodgson, Godfrey. *The Myth of American Exceptionalism.* New Haven, CT: Yale University Press, 2009.

Hogue, James K. *Uncivil War: Five New Orleans Street Battles and the Rise and Fall of Radical Reconstruction.* Baton Rouge: Louisiana State University Press, 2006.

Holberton, William B. *Homeward Bound: The Demobilization of the Union and Confederate Armies, 1865–1866.* Mechanicsburg, PA: Stackpole Books, 2001.

Holcomb, Julie. "The Abolitionist Movement." *Essential Civil War Curriculum.* https://www.essentialcivilwarcurriculum.com/the-abolitionist-movement.html.

Holt, Michael F. *By One Vote: The Disputed Presidential Election of 1876.* Lawrence: University Press of Kansas, 2008.

————. *The Rise and Fall of the American Whig Party: Jacksonian Politics and the Onset of the Civil War.* New York: Oxford University Press, 1999.

Holton, Woody. *Forced Founders: Indians, Debtors, Slaves, and the Making of the American Revolution in Virginia.* Chapel Hill: University of North Carolina Press, 1999.

Honeck, Mischa. *We Are the Revolutionists: German-Speaking Immigrants and American Abolitionists after 1848.* Athens: University of Georgia Press, 2011.

Hoogenboom, Ari. "American Exceptionalism: Republicanism as Ideology." In *Bridging the Atlantic: The Question of American Exceptionalism in Perspective,* edited by Elizabeth Glaser and Hermann Wellenreuther, 43–66. New York: Cambridge University Press, 2002.

Horne, Gerald. *Deepest South: The African Slave Trade, the United States, and Brazil.* New York: New York University Press, 2006.

Horton, James Oliver. "Defending the Manhood of the Race: The Crisis of Citizenship in Black Boston at Midcentury." In *Hope and Glory: Essays on the Legacy of the 54th Massachusetts Regiment,* edited by Martin Henry Blatt, Thomas J. Brown, and Donald Yacovone, 7–20. Amherst: University of Massachusetts Press, 2001.

Horton, James Oliver, and Lois E. Horton. *In Hope of Liberty: Culture, Community, and Protest among Northern Free Blacks, 1700–1860.* New York: Oxford University Press, 1998.

Howe, Daniel Walker. *Making the American Self: Jonathan Edwards to Abraham Lincoln.* New York: Oxford University Press, 1998.

————. *The Political Culture of the American Whigs.* Chicago: University of Chicago Press, 1979.

————. *What Hath God Wrought: The Transformation of America, 1815–1848.* New York: Oxford University Press, 2007.

Hsieh, Wayne Wei-Siang. "'Go to Your Gawd Like a Soldier': Transnational Reflections on Veteranhood." *Journal of the Civil War Era* 5 (December 2015): 551–77.

————. "Total War and the American Civil War Reconsidered: The End of an Outdated 'Master Narrative.'" *Journal of the Civil War Era* 1 (September 2011): 394–408.

————. *West Pointers and the Civil War: The Old Army in War and Peace*. Chapel Hill: University of North Carolina Press, 2014.

Hunt, Alfred N. *Haiti's Influence on Antebellum America: Slumbering Volcano in the Caribbean*. Baton Rouge: Louisiana State University Press, 1988.

Hunter, Tera W. *Bound in Wedlock: Slave and Free Black Marriage in the Nineteenth Century*. Cambridge, MA: Harvard University Press, 2017.

Huntington, Samuel P. *The Soldier and the State: The Theory and Politics of Civil-Military Relations*. 1957. Reprint, Cambridge, MA: Harvard University Press, 2008.

Huston, James L. "American Revolutionaries, the Political Economy of Aristocracy, and the American Concept of the Distribution of Wealth, 1765–1900." *American Historical Review* 98 (October 1993): 1079–1105.

————. *The British Gentry, the Southern Planter, and the Northern Family Farmer: Agriculture and Sectional Antagonism in North America*. Baton Rouge: Louisiana State University Press, 2015.

————. *Calculating the Value of Union: Slavery, Property Rights, and the Economic Origins of the Civil War*. Chapel Hill: University of North Carolina Press, 2003.

————. "Theory's Failure: Malthusian Population Theory and the Projected Demise of Slavery." *Civil War History* 55 (September 2009): 354–81.

Huston, Reeve. "Land Conflict and Land Policy in the United States, 1785–1841." In *The World of the Revolutionary American Republic: Land, Labor, and the Conflict for a Continent*, edited by Andrew Shankman, 323–44. New York: Routledge, 2014.

————. "Rethinking the Origins of Partisan Democracy in the United States, 1795–1840." In *Practicing Democracy: Popular Politics in the United States from the Constitution to the Civil War*, edited by Daniel Peart and Adam I. P. Smith, 46–65. Charlottesville: University of Virginia Press, 2015.

Huzzey, Richard. "Manifest Dominion: The British Empire and the Crises of the Americas in the 1860s." In *American Civil Wars: The United States, Latin America, Europe, and the Crisis of the 1860s*, edited by Don H. Doyle, 82–106. Chapel Hill: University of North Carolina Press, 2017.

Hyman, Harold M. *A More Perfect Union: The Impact of the Civil War and Reconstruction on the Constitution*. New York: Alfred A. Knopf, 1973.

————. "Ulysses S. Grant I, Emperor of America? Some Civil-Military Continuities and Strains of the Civil War and Reconstruction." In *The United States Military under the Constitution of the United States, 1789–1989*, edited by Richard H. Kohn, 175–92. New York: New York University Press, 1991.

Icenhauer-Ramirez, Robert. *Treason on Trial: The United States v. Jefferson Davis*. Baton Rouge: Louisiana State University Press, 2019.

Israel, Jonathan I. *The Expanding Blaze: How the American Revolution Ignited the World, 1775–1848*. Princeton, NJ: Princeton University Press, 2017.

Janney, Caroline E. *Remembering the Civil War: Reunion and the Limits of Reconciliation*. Chapel Hill: University of North Carolina Press, 2013.

Jennings, Thelma. *The Nashville Convention: Southern Movement for Unity, 1848–1851*. Memphis, TN: Memphis State University Press, 1980.

Jensen, Joan M. *Loosening the Bonds: Mid-Atlantic Farm Women, 1750–1850*. New Haven, CT: Yale University Press, 1986.

Jimerson, Randall C. *The Private Civil War: Popular Thought during the Sectional Conflict*. Baton Rouge: Louisiana State University Press, 1988.

Johnson, James E. "Race, Foreign Armies and United States Colored Troops." *Disunion* (blog), *New York Times*, February 23, 2015. https://opinionator.blogs .nytimes.com/2015/02/23/race-foreign-armies-and-united-states-coloredtroops.

Johnson, James Turner. *Just War Tradition and the Restraint of War: A Moral and Historical Inquiry*. Princeton, NJ: Princeton University Press, 2016.

Johnson, Walter. "On Agency." *Journal of Social History* 37 (Autumn 2003): 113–24.

———. *River of Dark Dreams: Slavery and Empire in the Cotton Kingdom*. Cambridge, MA: Harvard University Press, 2017.

———. *Soul by Soul: Life Inside the Antebellum Slave Market*. Cambridge, MA: Harvard University Press, 2009.

Jones, Archer. *The Art of War in the Western World*. Urbana: University of Illinois Press, 2001.

Jones, Howard. *Blue and Gray Diplomacy: A History of Union and Confederate Foreign Relations*. Chapel Hill: University of North Carolina Press, 2010.

Jones, Martha S. *Birthright Citizens: A History of Race and Rights in Antebellum America*. New York: Cambridge University Press, 2018.

Jones-Rogers, Stephanie E. *They Were Her Property: White Women as Slave Owners in the American South*. New Haven, CT: Yale University Press, 2019.

Jordan, Brian Matthew. *Marching Home: Union Veterans and Their Unending Civil War*. New York: Liveright, 2014.

Jordan, Winthrop D. *White over Black: American Attitudes toward the Negro, 1550–1812*. Chapel Hill: University of North Carolina Press, 1968.

Kachun, Mitchell A. "Antebellum African Americans, Public Commemoration, and the Haitian Revolution: A Problem of Historical Mythmaking." *Journal of the Early Republic* 26 (Summer 2006): 249–73.

———. *Festivals of Freedom: Memory and Meaning in African American Emancipation Celebrations*. Amherst: University of Massachusetts Press, 2003.

Kaczorowski, Robert J. "Searching for the Intent of the Framers of the Fourteenth Amendment." *Connecticut Law Review* 5 (1972–73): 368–98.

Kammen, Michael. "The Problem of American Exceptionalism: A Reconsideration." *American Quarterly* 45 (March 1993): 1–43.

Kantrowitz, Stephen. *More Than Freedom: Fighting for Black Citizenship in a White Republic, 1829–1889*. New York: Penguin Press, 2012.

———. "'Not Quite Constitutionalized': The Meanings of 'Civilization' and the Limits of Native American Citizenship." In *The World the Civil War Made*, edited by Gregory P. Downs and Kate Masur, 75–105. Chapel Hill: University of North Carolina Press, 2015.

Karp, Matthew. "King Cotton, Emperor Slavery: Antebellum Slaveholders and the World Economy." In *The Civil War as Global Conflict: Transnational Meanings of the American Civil War*, edited by David T. Gleeson and Simon Lewis, 36–55. Columbia: University of South Carolina Press, 2014.

———. *This Vast Southern Empire: Slaveholders at the Helm of American Foreign Policy*. Cambridge, MA: Harvard University Press, 2016.

Katz, Philip M. *From Appomattox to Montmartre: Americans and the Paris Commune*. Cambridge, MA: Harvard University Press, 1998.

Kaye, Anthony E. *Joining Places: Slave Neighborhoods in the Old South*. Chapel Hill: University of North Carolina Press, 2009.

———. "The Second Slavery: Modernity in the Nineteenth-Century South and the Atlantic World." *Journal of Southern History* 75 (August 2009): 627–50.

Keith, LeeAnna. *The Colfax Massacre: The Untold Story of Black Power, White Terror, and the Death of Reconstruction*. New York: Oxford University Press, 2009.

Keller, Morton. *Affairs of State: Public Life in Late Nineteenth Century America*. Cambridge, MA: Harvard University Press, 1977.

Kelley, Mary. *Private Women, Public Stage: Literary Domesticity in Nineteenth-Century America*. New York: Oxford University Press, 1984.

Kelly, Patrick J. "European Revolutions of 1848 and the Transnational Turn in Civil War History." *Journal of the Civil War Era* 4 (September 2014): 431–43.

———. "The Lost Continent of Abraham Lincoln." *Journal of the Civil War Era* (June 2019): 223–48.

———. "The North American Crisis of the 1860s." *Journal of the Civil War Era* 2 (September 2012): 337–68.

Kelman, Ari. *A Misplaced Massacre: Struggling over the Memory of Sand Creek*. Cambridge, MA: Harvard University Press, 2013.

Kennedy, Paul. *The Rise and Fall of the Great Powers*. New York: Random House, 1988.

Kennington, Kelly. *In the Shadow of* Dred Scott*: St. Louis Freedom Suits and the Legal Culture of Slavery in Antebellum America*. Athens: University of Georgia Press, 2019.

Kent, Andrew. "The Constitution and the Laws of War during the Civil War." *Notre Dame Law Review* 85, no. 5 (2010): 1839–1930.

Kerby, Robert L. *Kirby Smith's Confederacy: The Trans-Mississippi South, 1863–1865*. New York: Columbia University Press, 1972.

Kerr-Ritchie, Jeffrey R. "Rehearsal for War: Black Militias in the Atlantic World." *Slavery and Abolition* 26 (October 2011): 1–34.

———. *Rites of August First: Emancipation in the Black Atlantic World*. Baton Rouge: Louisiana State University Press, 2007.

Klement, Frank L. *The Limits of Dissent: Clement L. Vallandigham and the Civil War*. Lexington: University Press of Kentucky, 1970.

Kolchin, Peter. *American Slavery, 1619–1877*. New York: Hill and Wang, 1993.

———. "Comparative Perspectives on Emancipation in the U.S. South: Reconstruction, Radicalism, and Russia." *Journal of the Civil War Era* 2 (June 2012): 203–32.

———. *A Sphinx on the American Land: The Nineteenth-Century South in Comparative Perspective*. Baton Rouge: Louisiana State University Press, 2003.

———. *Unfree Labor: American Slavery and Russian Serfdom*. Cambridge, MA: Harvard University Press, 1987.

Kornblith, Gary J. "Rethinking the Coming of the Civil War: A Counterfactual Exercise." *Journal of American History* 90 (June 2003): 76–105.

———. *Slavery and Sectional Strife in the Early American Republic, 1776–1821*. Plymouth, UK: Rowman & Littlefield, 2010.

Kramer, Lloyd S. "The French Revolution and the Creation of American Political Culture." In *The Global Ramifications of the French Revolution*, edited by Joseph

Klaits and Michael H. Haltzel, 26–54. Washington, DC: Woodrow Wilson Center Press, 1994.

Kreidberg, Marvin A., and Merton G. Henry. *History of Mobilization in the United States Army, 1775–1945*. Washington, DC: Department of the Army, 1955.

Kulikoff, Allan. *Abraham Lincoln and Karl Marx in Dialogue*. New York: Oxford University Press, 2017.

Kytle, Ethan J., and Blain Roberts. *Denmark Vesey's Garden: Slavery and Memory in the Cradle of the Confederacy*. New York: New Press, 2018.

LaFeber, Walter. *The New Empire: An Interpretation of American Expansion, 1860–1898*. Ithaca, NY: Cornell University Press, 1998.

Lamoreaux, Naomi R. "Rethinking the Transition to Capitalism in the Early American Northeast." *Journal of American History* 90 (September 2003): 437–61.

Lande, Jonathan. "'Lighting up the Path of Liberty and Justice': Black Abolitionist Fourth of July Celebrations and the Promise of America from the Fugitive Slave Act to the Civil War." *Journal of African American History* (forthcoming, August 2020).

———. "'Nature Marked Him for Combat': Gender and Racial Politics in Frances Rollins's Post–Civil War Biography of Martin Delany." Paper delivered at the Annual Meeting of the American Historical Association, New York, NY, January 2020.

Lang, Andrew F. "Challenging the Union Citizen-Soldier Ideal." In *The Guerrilla Hunters: Irregular Conflicts during the Civil War*, edited by Brian D. McKnight and Barton A. Myers, 305–34. Baton Rouge: Louisiana State University Press, 2017.

———. *In the Wake of War: Military Occupation, Emancipation, and Civil War America*. Baton Rouge: Louisiana State University Press, 2017.

———. "The Limits of American Exceptionalism: Military Occupation, Emancipation, and the Preservation of the Union." In *Upon the Fields of Battle: Essays on the Military History of America's Civil War*, edited by Andrew S. Bledsoe and Andrew F. Lang, 183–204. Baton Rouge: Louisiana State University Press, 2018.

———. "Republicanism, Race, and Reconstruction: The Ethos of Military Occupation in Civil War America." *Journal of the Civil War Era* 4 (December 2014): 559–89.

———. "Union Demobilization and the Boundaries of War and Peace." *Journal of the Civil War Era* 9 (June 2019): 178–95.

Lanza. Michael L. *Agrarianism and Reconstruction Politics: The Southern Homestead Act*. Baton Rouge: Louisiana State University Press, 1990.

Laurie, Bruce. *Beyond Garrison: Antislavery and Social Reform*. Cambridge: Cambridge University Press, 2005.

Lee, Wayne E. *Barbarians and Brothers: Anglo-American Warfare, 1500–1865*. New York: Oxford University Press, 2011.

———. "Mind and Matter—Cultural Analysis in American Military History: A Look at the State of the Field." *Journal of American History* 93 (March 2007): 1116–42.

Lemann, Nicholas. *Redemption: The Last Battle of the Civil War*. New York: Farrar, Straus and Giroux, 2006.

Leonard, Elizabeth D. *Lincoln's Avengers: Justice, Revenge, and Reunion after the Civil War*. New York: W. W. Norton, 2004.

Lerner, Ralph. "Commerce and Character: The Anglo-American as New-Model Man." *William and Mary Quarterly* 36 (January 1979): 3–26.

Levin, Kevin M. *Remembering the Battle of the Crater: War as Murder*. Lexington: University Press of Kentucky, 2012.

Levine, Bruce C. *Confederate Emancipation: Southern Plans to Free and Arm Slaves during the Civil War*. New York: Oxford University Press, 2008.

———. *The Spirit of 1848: German Immigrants, Labor Conflict, and the Coming of the Civil War*. Urbana: University of Illinois Press, 1992.

Lewis, James E. *The American Union and the Problem of the Neighborhood: The United States and the Collapse of the Spanish Empire, 1783–1829*. Chapel Hill: University of North Carolina Press, 1998.

Lewis, Kay Wright. *A Curse upon the Nation: Race, Freedom, and Extermination in America and the Atlantic World*. Athens: University of Georgia Press, 2019.

Limerick, Patricia Nelson. *The Legacy of Conquest: The Unbroken Past of the American West*. New York: W. W. Norton, 1987.

Lipset, Seymour Martin. *American Exceptionalism: A Double-Edged Sword*. New York: W. W. Norton, 1996.

Litke, Justin B. *Twilight of the Republic: Empire and American Exceptionalism in the American Political Tradition*. Lexington: University Press of Kentucky, 2013.

Litwack, Leon F. *Been in the Storm So Long: The Aftermath of Slavery*. New York: Alfred A. Knopf, 1979.

Love, Eric T. L. *Race over Empire: Racism and U.S. Imperialism, 1865–1900*. Chapel Hill: University of North Carolina Press, 2004.

Luker, Ralph E. "God, Man and the World of James Warley Miles, Charleston's Transcendentalist." *History of the Protestant Episcopal Church* 39 (June 1970): 101–36.

Luvaas, Jay. *The Military Legacy of the Civil War: The European Inheritance*. Lawrence: University Press of Kansas, 1988.

Lyons, Philip B. *Statesmanship and Reconstruction: Moderate versus Radical Republicans on Restoring the Union after the Civil War*. Lanham, MD: Lexington Books, 2014.

Maddox, Lucy. *Citizen Indians: Native American Intellectuals, Race, and Reform*. Ithaca, NY: Cornell University Press, 2005.

Madsen, Deborah L. *American Exceptionalism*. Jackson: University Press of Mississippi, 1998.

Magness, Phillip W. "The Île-à-Vache." *Disunion* (blog), *New York Times*, April 12, 2013. https://opinionator.blogs.nytimes.com/2013/04/12/the-le-vache-from -hope-to-disaster/.

Magness, Phillip W., and Sebastian N. Page. *Colonization after Emancipation: Lincoln and the Movement for Black Resettlement*. Columbia: University of Missouri Press, 2011.

Maizlish, Stephen E. *A Strife of Tongues: The Compromise of 1850 and the Ideological Foundations of the American Civil War*. Charlottesville: University of Virginia Press, 2018.

Majewski, John D. *Modernizing a Slave Economy: The Economic Vision of the Confederate Nation*. Chapel Hill: University of North Carolina Press, 2009.

Maltz, Earl M. *Fugitive Slave on Trial: The Anthony Burns Case and Abolitionist Outrage*. Lawrence: University Press of Kansas, 2010.

Malvasi, Mark G. "The Old Republic and the Sectional Crisis." *Modern Age* 49 (Fall 2007): 463–75.

Mancini, Matthew J. "Francis Lieber, Slavery, and the 'Genesis' of the Laws of War." *Journal of the Southern History* 77 (May 2011): 325–48.

Manning, Chandra. *What This Cruel War Was Over: Soldiers, Slavery, and the Civil War.* New York: Alfred A. Knopf, 2007.

Mansfield, Harvey C. "To the Heart of American Exceptionalism." *Wall Street Journal,* February 5, 2011. https://www.wsj.com/articles/SB10001424052748703445904576118280961147392.

Marshall, Nicholas. "The Great Exaggeration: Death and the Civil War." *Journal of the Civil War Era* 4 (March 2014): 3–27.

Marszalek, John F. *Sherman: A Soldier's Passion for Order.* New York: Free Press, 1993.

Marvel, William. *Andersonville: The Last Depot.* Chapel Hill: University of North Carolina Press, 1994.

Masich, Andrew E. *Civil War in the Southwest Borderlands, 1861–1867.* Norman: University of Oklahoma Press, 2017.

Maslowski, Peter. "The 300-Years War." In *Between War and Peace: How America Ends Its Wars,* edited by Matthew Moten, 129–54. New York: Free Press, 2011.

———. "To the Edge of Greatness: The United States, 1783–1865." In *The Making of Strategy: Rulers, States, and War,* edited by Williamson Murray, MacGregor Knox, and Alvin Bernstein, 205–41. New York: Cambridge University Press, 1994.

Mason, Matthew. *Slavery and Politics in the Early American Republic.* Chapel Hill: University of North Carolina Press, 2006.

———. "World Safe for Modernity." In *The Old South's Modern Worlds: Slavery, Region, and the Nation in the Age of Progress,* edited by L. Diane Barnes, Brian Schoen, and Frank Towers, 47–65. New York: Oxford University Press, 2011.

Masur, Kate. *An Example for All the Land: Emancipation and the Struggle over Equality in Washington, D.C.* Chapel Hill: University of North Carolina Press, 2010.

Masur, Louis P. *Lincoln's Hundred Days: The Emancipation Proclamation and the War for the Union.* Cambridge, MA: Harvard University Press, 2012.

———. *Lincoln's Last Speech: Wartime Reconstruction and the Crisis of Reunion.* New York: Oxford University Press, 2015.

Matsui, John H. *The First Republican Army: The Army of Virginia and the Radicalization of the Civil War.* Charlottesville: University of Virginia Press, 2016.

Matthews, Gelien. *Caribbean Slave Revolts and the British Abolitionist Movement.* Baton Rouge: Louisiana State University Press, 2006.

May, Robert E. *John A. Quitman: Old South Crusader.* Baton Rouge: Louisiana State University Press, 1985.

———. *Slavery, Race, and Conquest in the Tropics: Lincoln, Douglas, and the Future of Latin America.* New York: Cambridge University Press, 2013.

———. *The Southern Dream of a Caribbean Empire, 1854–1861.* Baton Rouge: Louisiana University Press, 1973.

———. "A 'Southern Strategy' for the 1850s: Northern Democrats, the Tropics, and the Expansion of the National Domain." *Louisiana Studies* 14 (Winter 1975): 333–59.

———, ed. *The Union, the Confederacy, and the Atlantic Rim*. West Lafayette, IN: Purdue University Press, 1995.

McCaffrey, James M. *Army of Manifest Destiny: The American Soldier in the Mexican War, 1846–1848*. New York: New York University Press, 1992.

McClintock, Russell. *Lincoln and the Decision for War: The Northern Response to Secession*. Chapel Hill: University of North Carolina Press, 2010.

McCurry, Stephanie. *Confederate Reckoning: Power and Politics in the Civil War South*. Cambridge, MA: Harvard University Press, 2010.

———. *Masters of Small Worlds: Yeoman Households, Gender Relations, and the Political Culture of the Antebellum South Carolina Low Country*. New York: Oxford University Press, 1995.

———. *Women's War: Fighting and Surviving the American Civil War*. Belknap Press of Harvard University.

McDaniel, W. Caleb. *The Problem of Democracy in the Age of Slavery: Garrisonian Abolitionists and Transatlantic Reform*. Baton Rouge: Louisiana State University Press, 2015.

———. *Sweet Taste of Liberty: A True Story of Slavery and Restitution in America*. New York: Oxford University Press, 2019.

McDaniel, W. Caleb, and Bethany L. Johnson. "New Approaches to Internationalizing the History of the Civil War Era: An Introduction." *Journal of the Civil War Era* 2 (June 2012): 145–50.

McGerr, Michael. "The Price of the 'New Transnational History.'" *American Historical Review* 96 (October 1991): 1056–67.

McKnight, Brian D. *Confederate Outlaw: Champ Ferguson and the Civil War in Appalachia*. Baton Rouge: Louisiana State University Press, 2011.

McPherson, James M. *Abraham Lincoln and the Second American Revolution*. New York: Oxford University Press, 1990.

———. "Antebellum Southern Exceptionalism: A New Look at an Old Question." *Civil War History* 50 (December 2004): 418–33.

———. *Battle Cry of Freedom: The Civil War Era*. New York: Oxford University Press, 1988.

———. *Drawn with the Sword: Reflections on the American Civil War*. New York: Oxford University Press, 1996.

———. "'For a Vast Future Also': Lincoln and the Millennium." In *Legacy of Disunion: The Enduring Significance of the American Civil War*, edited by Susan-Mary Grant and Peter J. Parish, 134–48. Baton Rouge: Louisiana State University Press, 2003.

———. *For Cause and Comrades: Why Men Fought in the Civil War*. New York: Oxford University Press, 1997.

———. "From Limited to Total War in America." In *On the Road to Total War: The American Civil War and the German Wars of Unification, 1861–1871*, edited by Stig Förster and Jörg Nagler, 295–310. New York: Cambridge University Press, 1997.

———. "Introduction: Last Best Hope for What?" In *"We Cannot Escape History": Lincoln and the Last Best Hope of Earth*, edited by McPherson, 1–14. Urbana: University of Illinois Press, 1995.

———. *Ordeal By Fire: The Civil War and Reconstruction*. New York: Alfred A. Knopf, 1982.

————. *The Negro's Civil War: How American Negroes Felt and Acted during the War for the Union.* New York: Ballentine Books, 1991.

————. *Tried by War: Abraham Lincoln as Commander-in-Chief.* New York: Penguin, 2008.

————. *The War That Forged a Nation: Why the Civil War Still Matters.* New York: Oxford University Press, 2015.

————. "Was It a Just War?" *New York Review of Books,* March 23, 2006, 16–19.

————. "What Caused the Civil War?" *North and South: The Official Magazine of the Civil War Society* 4 (January 2000): 12–22.

————. "Who Freed the Slaves?" *Proceedings of the American Philosophical Society* 139 (March 1995): 1–10.

————. "'The Whole Family of Man': Lincoln and the Last Best Hope Abroad." In *Drawn with the Sword: Reflections on the American Civil War,* by James M. McPherson, 208–27. New York: Oxford University Press, 1996.

Messer-Kruse, Timothy. *The Yankee International: Marxism and the American Reform Tradition, 1848–1876.* Chapel Hill: University of North Carolina Press, 1998.

Miller, Randall M., Harry S. Stout, and Charles Reagan Wilson, eds. *Religion and the American Civil War.* New York: Oxford University Press, 1998.

Millett, Allan R., Peter Maslowski, and William B. Feis. *For the Common Defense: A Military History of the United States, from 1607 to 2012.* New York: Free Press, 2012.

Mintz, Steven. "American Slavery in Comparative Perspective." *History Now,* Gilder Lehrman Institute of American History, accessed July 5, 2019. https://www .gilderlehrman.org/history-resources/teaching-resource/historical-context -american-slavery-comparative-perspective.

Mitchell, Reid. *Civil War Soldiers.* New York: Simon & Schuster, 1988.

————. *The Vacant Chair: The Northern Soldier Leaves Home.* New York: Oxford University Press, 1993.

Molho, Anthony, and Gordon S. Wood, eds. *Imagined Histories: Americans Interpret the Past.* Princeton, NJ: Princeton University Press, 1998.

Moltke-Hansen, David. "Urban Processes in the Confederacy's Development, Experience, and Consequences." In *Confederate Cities: The Urban South during the Civil War Era,* edited by Andrew L. Slap and Frank Towers, 46–73. Chicago: University of Chicago Press, 2016.

Moody, Joycelyn. *Sentimental Confessions: Spiritual Narratives of Nineteenth-Century African American Women.* Athens: University of Georgia Press, 2001.

Mora, Anthony P. *Border Dilemmas: Racial and National Uncertainties in New Mexico, 1848–1912.* Durham, NC: Duke University Press, 2011.

Morgan, Edmund S. *American Slavery, American Freedom: The Ordeal of Colonial Virginia.* New York: W. W. Norton, 1975.

————. "Slavery and Freedom: The American Paradox." *Journal of American History* 59 (June 1972): 5–29.

Morrison, Michael A. "American Reaction to European Revolutions, 1848–1852: Sectionalism, Memory, and the Revolutionary Heritage." *Civil War History* 49 (June 2003): 111–32.

————. *Slavery and the American West: The Eclipse of Manifest Destiny and the Coming of the Civil War.* Chapel Hill: University of North Carolina Press, 1999.

Moten, Matthew. *The Delafield Commission and the Military Profession*. College
 Station: Texas A&M University Press, 2000.
Murray, Williamson, and Wayne Wei-Siang Hsieh. *The Savage War: A Military
 History of the Civil War*. Princeton, NJ: Princeton University Press, 2016.
Myers, Barton A. "Partisan Ranger Petitions and the Confederacy's Authorized *Petite
 Guerre* Service." In *The Guerrilla Hunters: Irregular Conflicts during the Civil
 War*, edited by Brian D. McKnight and Barton A. Myers, 13–35. Baton Rouge:
 Louisiana State University, 2017.
Myers, Phillip E. *Dissolving Tensions: Rapprochement and Resolution in British-
 American-Canadian Relations in the Treaty of Washington Era, 1865–1914*. Kent,
 OH: Kent State University Press, 2015.
Nabors, Forrest A. *From Oligarchy to Republicanism: The Great Task of
 Reconstruction*. Columbia: University of Missouri Press, 2017.
Nagel, Paul C. *John Quincy Adams: A Public Life, a Private Life*. New York: Alfred A.
 Knopf, 1997.
———. *One Nation Indivisible: The Union in American Thought, 1776–1861*. New
 York: Oxford University Press, 1964.
Neely, Mark E., Jr. "Abraham Lincoln and Black Colonization: Benjamin Butler's
 Spurious Testimony." *Civil War History* 25 (March 1979): 77–83.
———. "'Civilized Belligerents': Abraham Lincoln and the Idea of 'Total War.'" In
 New Perspectives on the Civil War: Myths and Realities of the National Conflict,
 edited by John Y. Simon and Michael E. Stevens, 3–24. Lanham, MD: Rowman &
 Littlefield, 2002.
———. *The Civil War and the Limits of Destruction*. Cambridge, MA: Harvard
 University Press, 2007.
———. "The Civil War and the Two-Party System." In *"We Cannot Escape History":
 Lincoln and the Last Best Hope of Earth*, edited by James M. McPherson, 86–104.
 Urbana: University of Illinois Press, 1995.
———. "Colonization and the Myth That Lincoln Prepared the People for
 Emancipation." In *Lincoln's Proclamation: Emancipation Reconsidered*, edited
 by William A. Blair and Karen Fisher Younger, 45–74. Chapel Hill: University of
 North Carolina Press, 2009.
———. *The Fate of Liberty: Abraham Lincoln and Civil Liberties*. New York: Oxford
 University Press, 1991.
———. "Guerrilla Warfare, Slavery, and the Hopes of the Confederacy." *Journal of
 the Civil War Era* 6 (September 2016): 376–412.
———. *The Last Best Hope of Earth: Abraham Lincoln and the Promise of America*.
 Cambridge, MA: Harvard University Press, 1993.
———. *Lincoln and the Democrats: The Politics of Opposition in the Civil War*. New
 York: Cambridge University Press, 2017.
———. *Lincoln and the Triumph of the Nation: Constitutional Conflict in the
 American Civil War*. Chapel Hill: University of North Carolina Press, 2011.
———. "Was the Civil War a Total War?" *Civil War History* 37 (March 1991): 5–28.
Neff, Stephen C. *Justice in Blue and Gray: A Legal History of the Civil War*.
 Cambridge, MA: Harvard University Press, 2010.
———. *War and the Law of Nations: A General History*. New York: Cambridge
 University Press, 2008.

Nelson, Megan Kate. *Ruin Nation: Destruction and the American Civil War*. Athens: University of Georgia Press, 2012.

Nevins, Allan. *Hamilton Fish: The Inner Story of the Grant Administration*. New York: Dodd, Mead & Co., 1936.

Newell, Clayton R., and Charles R. Shrader. "The U.S. Army's Transition to Peace, 1865–66." *Journal of Military History* 77 (July 2013): 867–94.

Newman, Richard. "The Grammar of Emancipation: Putting Final Freedom in Context." In *Beyond Freedom: Disrupting the History of Emancipation*, edited by David W. Blight and Jim Downs, 11–25. Athens: University of Georgia Press, 2017.

———. "The Pendulum Swings: The Rise of an Anti-slavery Sentiment between the American Revolution and the Civil War." In *The World of the Revolutionary American Republic: Land, Labor, and the Conflict for a Continent*, edited by Andrew Shankman, 391–414. New York: Routledge, 2017.

———. *The Transformation of American Abolitionism: Fighting Slavery in the Early Republic*. Chapel Hill: University of North Carolina Press, 2002.

Newman, Simon. "American Political Culture and the French and Haitian Revolutions: Nathaniel Cutting and the Jefferson Republicans." In *The Impact of the Haitian Revolution in the Atlantic World*, edited by David P. Geggus, 72–91. Columbia: University of South Carolina Press, 2001.

Nichols, David A. "The Other Civil War: Lincoln and the Indians." *Minnesota History* 44 (Spring 1974): 3–15.

Nicoletti, Cynthia. *Secession on Trial: The Treason Prosecution of Jefferson Davis*. New York: Cambridge University Press, 2017.

Ninkovich, Frank A. *Global Dawn: The Cultural Foundation of American Internationalism, 1865–1890*. Cambridge, MA: Harvard University Press, 2009.

Noll, Mark A. *America's God: From Jonathan Edwards to Abraham Lincoln*. New York: Oxford University Press, 2005.

———. *The Civil War as a Theological Crisis*. Chapel Hill: University of North Carolina Press, 2006.

Nudelman, Fanny. *John Brown's Body: Slavery, Violence and the Culture of War*. Chapel Hill: University of North Carolina Press, 2004.

Nye, Russell B. "The Slave Power Conspiracy, 1830–1860." *Science and Society* 10 (Summer 1946): 262–74.

Oakes, James. *Freedom National: The Destruction of Slavery in the United States, 1861–1865*. New York: W. W. Norton, 2013.

———. *The Ruling Race: A History of American Slaveholders*. New York: Alfred A. Knopf, 1982.

———. *The Scorpion's Sting: Antislavery and the Coming of the Civil War*. New York: W. W. Norton, 2014.

———. "When Everybody Knew." In *Beyond Freedom: Disrupting the History of Emancipation*, edited by David W. Blight and Jim Downs, 104–17. Athens: University of Georgia Press, 2017.

O'Brien, Michael. *Conjectures of Order: Intellectual Life and the American South, 1810–1860*. 2 vols. Chapel Hill: University of North Carolina Press, 2004.

O'Connor, Peter. *American Sectionalism in the British Mind, 1832–1863*. Baton Rouge: Louisiana State University Press, 2017.

Ofele, Martin. *True Sons of the Republic: European Immigrants in the Union Army*. Westport, CT: Praeger, 2008.

Onuf, Peter S. "American Exceptionalism and National Identity." *American Political Thought* 1 (Spring 2012): 77–100.

———. "Antebellum Southerners and the National Idea." In *The Old South's Modern Worlds: Slavery, Region, and the Nation in the Age of Progress*, edited by L. Diane Barnes, Brian Schoen, and Frank Towers, 25–46. New York: Oxford University Press, 2011.

———. "The Empire of Liberty: Land of the Free and Home of the Slave." In *The World of the Revolutionary American Republic: Land, Labor, and Conflict for a Continent*, edited by Andrew Shankman, 195–217. New York: Routledge, 2014.

———. "'To Declare Them a Free and Independent People': Race, Slavery, and National Identity in Jefferson's Thought." *Journal of the Early Republic* 18 (Spring 1998): 1–46.

Onuf, Nicholas G., and Peter S. Onuf. *Nations, Markets, and War: Modern History and the American Civil War*. Charlottesville: University of Virginia Press, 2006.

Osterhammel, Jürgen. "In Search of a Nineteenth Century." *German Historical Institute Bulletin* 32 (Spring 2003): 9–28.

———. *The Transformation of the World: A Global History of the Nineteenth Century*. Translated by Patrick Camiller. Princeton, NJ: Princeton University Press, 2014.

Owsley, Frank L. *King Cotton Diplomacy: Foreign Relations of the Confederate States of America*. Chicago: University of Chicago Press, 1959.

Paddison, Joshua. "Race, Religion, and Naturalization: How the West Shaped Citizenship Debates in the Reconstruction Congress." In *Civil War Wests: Testing the Limits of the United States*, edited by Adam Arenson and Andrew R. Graybill, 181–201. Berkeley: University of California Press, 2015.

Pairns, James W. *Literacy and Intellectual Life in the Cherokee Nation, 1820–1906*. Norman: University of Oklahoma Press, 2013.

Paludan, Phillip Shaw. "Emancipating the Republic: Lincoln and the Means and Ends of Antislavery." In *"We Cannot Escape History": Lincoln and the Last Best Hope of Earth*, edited by James M. McPherson, 45–61. Urbana: University of Illinois Press, 1995.

———. *"A People's Contest": The Union and the Civil War, 1861–1865*. New York: Harper & Row, 1988.

———. *The Presidency of Abraham Lincoln*. Lawrence: University Press of Kansas, 1994.

———. "Religion and the American Civil War." In *Religion and the American Civil War*, edited by Randall M. Miller, Harry S. Stout, and Charles Reagan Wilson, 21–41. New York: Oxford University Press, 1998.

———. *Victims: A True Story of the Civil War*. Knoxville: University of Tennessee Press, 1981.

Paolina, Ernest N. *Foundations of American Empire: William Henry Seward and U.S. Foreign Policy*. Ithaca, NY: Cornell University Press, 1973.

Parish, Peter J. "An Exception to Most of the Rules: What Made American Nationalism Different in the Mid-Nineteenth Century?" *Prologue: Quarterly of the National Archives* 27 (Fall 1995): 218–29.

———. *The North and the Nation in the Era of the Civil War*. Edited by Adam I. P. Smith and Susan-Mary Grant. New York: Fordham University Press, 2003.

Park, Benjamin E. *American Nationalisms: Imagining Union in the Age of Revolutions, 1783–1833*. Cambridge: Cambridge University Press, 2018.

Parkinson, Robert G. *The Common Cause: Creating Race and Nation in the American Revolution*. Chapel Hill: University of North Carolina Press, 2016.

Parrish, T. Michael. "Jeff Davis Rules: General Beauregard and the Sanctity of Civilian Authority in the Confederacy." In *Jefferson Davis's Generals*, edited by Gabor S. Boritt, 46–64. New York: Oxford University Press, 1999.

Parsons, Elaine Frantz. *Ku-Klux: The Birth of the Klan during Reconstruction*. Chapel Hill: University of North Carolina Press, 2015.

Parsons, Lynn Hudson. *John Quincy Adams*. Madison, WI: Madison House, 1998.

Paulus, Carl Lawrence. *The Slaveholding Crisis: Fear of Insurrection and the Coming of the Civil War*. Baton Rouge: Louisiana State University Press, 2017.

Paulus, Sarah Bischoff. "America's Long Eulogy for Compromise: Henry Clay and American Politics." *Journal of the Civil War Era* 4 (March 2014): 28–52.

Pease, Donald E. "Anglo-American Exceptionalisms." *American Quarterly* 66 (March 2014): 197–209.

———. *The New American Exceptionalism*. Minneapolis: University of Minnesota Press, 2009.

Perdue, Theda. *The Cherokee Removal: A Brief History with Documents*. 3rd ed. Boston: Bedford–St. Martin's Press, 2016.

Perman, Michael. "Counter Revolution: The Role of Violence in Southern Redemption." In *The Facts of Reconstruction: Essays in Honor of John Hope Franklin*, edited by Eric Anderson and Alfred A. Moss Jr., 121–40. Baton Rouge: Louisiana State University Press, 1991.

———. *Reunion without Compromise: The South and Reconstruction, 1865–1868*. Cambridge: Cambridge University Press, 1973.

Persons, Stow. "The Cyclical Theory of History in Eighteenth Century America." *American Quarterly* 6 (Summer 1954): 147–63.

Pessen, Edward. "How Different from Each Other Were the Antebellum North and South?" *American Historical Review* 85 (December 1980): 1119–49.

Pfanz, Harry W. "Soldiering in the South during the Reconstruction Period, 1865–1877." PhD diss., Ohio State University, 1958.

Pfau, Michael. *The Political Style of Conspiracy: Chase, Sumner, and Lincoln*. East Lansing: Michigan State University Press, 2005.

Phillips, Christopher. "Lincoln's Grasp of War: Hard War and the Politics of Neutrality and Slavery in the Western Border States, 1861–1862." *Journal of the Civil War Era* 3 (June 2013): 184–210.

———. *The Rivers Ran Backwards: The Civil War and the Remaking of the American Middle Border*. New York: Oxford University Press, 2016.

Phillips, Gervase. "Military Morality Transformed: Weapons and Soldiers on the Nineteenth Century Battlefield." *Journal of Interdisciplinary History* 41 (Spring 2011): 565–90.

Phillips, Jason. *Diehard Rebels: The Confederate Culture of Invincibility*. Athens: University of Georgia Press, 2007.

Pocock, J. G. A. *The Machiavellian Moment: Florentine Political Thought and the Atlantic Republican Tradition*. Princeton, NJ: Princeton University Press, 1975.

Polasky, Janet. *Revolutions without Borders: The Call to Liberty in the Atlantic World*. New Haven, CT: Yale University Press, 2016.

Porter, Laura Smith. "'The Last, Best Hope of Earth': Abraham Lincoln's Perception of the Mission of America, 1834–1854." *Illinois Historical Journal* 78 (Autumn 1985): 207–16.

Post, Charles. *The American Road to Capitalism: Studies in Class-Structure, Economic Development and Political Conflict, 1620–1877.* Chicago: Haymarket Books, 2011.

Potter, David M. "The Civil War in the History of the Modern World: A Comparative View." In *The South and the Sectional Conflict*, by David M. Potter, 287–300. Baton Rouge: Louisiana State University Press, 1968.

———. "The Historian's Use of Nationalism and Vice Versa." In *The South and the Sectional Conflict*, by David M. Potter, 34–84. Baton Rouge: Louisiana State University Press, 1968.

———. *The Impending Crisis, 1848–1861.* New York: Harper & Row, 1976.

———. *People of Plenty: Economic Abundance and the American Character.* Chicago: University of Chicago Press, 1954.

Powers, Bernard E. "'Worst of All Barbarism': Racial Anxiety and the Approach of Secession in the Palmetto State." *South Carolina Historical Magazine* 112 (July–October 2011): 139–56.

Preston, Richard A., Alex Roland, and S. F. Wise, eds. *Men in Arms: A History of Warfare and Its Relationships with Western Society.* 5th ed. Fort Worth: Holt, Rinehart and Winston, 1991.

Priest, Loring Benson. *Uncle Sam's Stepchildren: The Reformation of United States Indian Policy, 1865–1887.* New Brunswick, NJ: Rutgers University Press, 1942.

Prior, David. *Between Freedom and Progress: The Lost World of Reconstruction Politics.* Baton Rouge: Louisiana State University Press, 2019.

———. "Civilization, Republic, Nation: Contested Keywords, Northern Republicans, and the Forgotten Reconstruction of Mormon Utah." *Civil War History* 56 (September 2010): 283–310.

Prucha, Francis Paul. *The Great Father: The United States Government and the American Indians.* Lincoln: University of Nebraska Press, 1984.

Pryor, Elizabeth Brown. *Reading the Man: A Portrait of Robert E. Lee.* New York: Viking, 2007.

Pryor, Elizabeth S. *Colored Travelers: Mobility and the Fight for Citizenship before the Civil War.* Chapel Hill: University of North Carolina Press, 2017.

Quigley, Paul. "Secessionists in an Age of Secession: The Slave South in Transatlantic Perspective." In *Secession as an International Phenomenon: From America's Civil War to Contemporary Separatist Movements*, edited by Don H. Doyle, 151–73. Athens: University of Georgia Press, 2010.

———. *Shifting Grounds: Nationalism and the American South, 1848–1865.* New York: Oxford University Press, 2011.

Rable, George C. *But There Was No Peace: The Role of Violence in the Politics of Reconstruction.* Athens: University of Georgia Press, 1984.

———. *The Confederate Republic: A Revolution against Politics.* Chapel Hill: University of North Carolina Press, 1994.

———. *Damn Yankees! Demoralization and Defiance in the Confederate South.* Baton Rouge: Louisiana State University Press, 2015.

———. "Fighting for Reunion: Dilemmas of Hatred and Vengeance." *Journal of the Civil War Era* 9 (September 2019): 347–77.

———. *Fredericksburg! Fredericksburg!* Chapel Hill: University of North Carolina Press, 2002.

———. *God's Almost Chosen Peoples: A Religious History of the American Civil War.* Chapel Hill: University of North Carolina Press, 2010.

———. "'Missing in Action': Women of the Confederacy." In *Divided Houses: Gender and the Civil War,* 134–46, edited by Catherine Clinton and Nina Silber. New York: Oxford University Press, 1992.

Rael, Patrick. *Black Identity and Black Protest in the Antebellum North.* Chapel Hill: University of North Carolina Press, 2002.

———. *Eighty-Eight Years: The Long Death of Slavery in the United States, 1777–1865.* Athens: University of Georgia Press, 2015.

Rakove, Jack N. *Original Meanings: Politics and Ideas in the Making of the Constitution.* New York: Alfred A. Knopf, 1996.

Ransom, Roger. "Economics of the American Civil War." *EH.Net Encyclopedia,* edited by Robert Whaples, accessed May 4, 2019. https://eh.net/encyclopedia /the-economics-of-the-civil-war.

Ray, Angela G. "Frederick Douglass on the Lyceum Circuit: Social Assimilation, Social Transformation?" *Rhetoric and Public Affairs* 5 (Winter 2002): 625–47.

Reardon, Carol. *With a Sword in One Hand and Jomini in the Other: The Problem of Military Thought in the Civil War North.* Chapel Hill: University of North Carolina Press, 2012.

Reeve, W. Paul. *Religion of a Different Color: Race and the Struggle for Whiteness.* New York: Oxford University Press, 2015.

Reidy, Joseph P. *Illusions of Emancipation: The Pursuit of Freedom and Equality in the Twilight of Slavery.* Chapel Hill: University of North Carolina Press, 2019.

Remini, Robert V. *At the Edge of the Precipice: Henry Clay and the Compromise That Saved the Union.* New York: Basic Books, 2010.

Restad, Hilde E. *American Exceptionalism: An Idea That Made a Nation and Remade the World.* New York: Routledge, 2015.

Rhodes, James Ford. "Who Burned Columbia?" *American Historical Review* 7 (April 1902): 485–93.

Richards, Leonard L. *The Life and Times of Congressman John Quincy Adams.* New York: Oxford University Press, 1986.

———. *The Slave Power: The Free North and Southern Domination, 1780–1860.* Baton Rouge: Louisiana State University Press, 2000.

Richardson, Heather Cox. *The Death of Reconstruction: Race, Labor, and Politics in the Post–Civil War North, 1865–1901.* Cambridge, MA: Harvard University Press, 2001.

———. *The Greatest Nation of the Earth: Republican Economic Policies during the Civil War.* Cambridge, MA: Harvard University Press, 1997.

———. "Largest Mass Execution in American History." *We're History,* December 26, 2014. http://werehistory.org/largest-mass-execution/.

———. "North and West of Reconstruction: Studies in Political Economy." In *Reconstructions: New Perspectives on the Postbellum United States,* edited by Thomas J. Brown, 66–90. New York: Oxford University Press, 2008.

———. *To Make Men Free: A History of the Republican Party.* New York: Basic Books, 2014.

————. *West from Appomattox: The Reconstruction of America after the Civil War.* New Haven, CT: Yale University Press, 2007.

Richter, William L. "'Outside My Profession': The Army and Civil Affairs in Reconstruction Texas." *Military History of Texas and the Southwest* 9 (1971): 5–21.

Roark, James L. *Masters without Slaves: Southern Planters in the Civil War and Reconstruction.* New York: Norton, 1977.

Roberts, Timothy M. *Distant Revolutions: 1848 and the Challenge to American Exceptionalism.* Charlottesville: University of Virginia Press, 2009.

————. "European Revolutions of 1848 and Antebellum Violence in Kansas." *Journal of the West* 44 (September 2005): 58–68.

————. "Now the Enemy Is within Our Borders: The Impact of European Revolutions on American Perceptions of Violence before the Civil War." *American Transcendental Quarterly* 17 (2003): 197–214.

————. "'Revolutions Have Become the Bloody Toy of the Multitude': European Revolutions, the South, and the Crisis of 1850." *Journal of the Early Republic* 25 (Summer 2005): 259–83.

Robertson, William S. "The Recognition of the Hispanic American Nations by the United States." *Hispanic American Historical Review* 1 (August 1918): 239–69.

Roberts-Miller, Patricia. *Fanatical Schemes: Proslavery Rhetoric and the Tragedy of Consensus.* Tuscaloosa: University of Alabama Press, 2009.

Rockman, Seth. "Slavery and Capitalism." *Journal of the Civil War Era.* https://www.journalofthecivilwarera.org/forum-the-future-of-civil-war-era-studies/the-future-of-civil-war-era-studies-slavery-and-capitalism/.

Rodgers, Daniel T. "Exceptionalism." In *Imagined Histories: Americans Interpret the Past*, edited by Anthony Molho and Gordon S. Wood, 21–40. Princeton, NJ: Princeton University Press, 1998.

————. "Republicanism: The Career of a Concept." *Journal of American History* 79 (June 1992): 11–38.

Rolle, Andrew F. *The Lost Cause: The Confederate Exodus to Mexico.* Norman: University of Oklahoma Press, 1992.

Rose, Willie Lee. *Rehearsal for Reconstruction: The Port Royal Experiment.* Indianapolis: Bobbs-Merrill, 1964.

Rosen, Hannah S. *Terror in the Heart of Freedom: Citizenship, Sexual Violence, and the Meaning of Race in the Postemancipation South.* Chapel Hill: University of North Carolina Press, 2009.

Rosenberg, John S. "Toward a New Civil War Revisionism." *American Scholar* 38 (Spring 1969): 250–72.

Ross, Dorothy. "American Exceptionalism." In *A Companion to American Thought*, edited by Richard Wightman Fox and James T. Kloppenberg, 22–23. Malden, MA: Blackwell, 1998.

————. "American Modernities, Past and Present." *American Historical Review* 116 (June 2011): 702–14.

————. "'Are We a Nation?' The Conjuncture of Nationhood and Race in the United States, 1850–1876." *Modern Intellectual History* 2 (November 2005): 327–60.

————. "Historical Consciousness in Nineteenth-Century America." *American Historical Review* 89 (October 1984): 909–28.

————. "Lincoln and the Ethics of Emancipation: Universalism, Nationalism, Exceptionalism." *Journal of American History* 96 (September 2009): 379–99.

Rothman, Adam. *Slave Country: American Expansion and the Origins of the Deep South.* Cambridge, MA: Harvard University Press, 2005.

Royster, Charles S. *The Destructive War: William Tecumseh Sherman, Stonewall Jackson, and the Americans.* New York: Alfred A. Knopf, 1993.

Rozwenc, Edwin C., ed. *The Compromise of 1850.* Boston: D. C. Heath, 1968.

Rubin, Anne Sarah. "Seventy-Six and Sixty-One: Confederates Remember the American Revolution." In *Where These Memories Grow: History, Memory, and Southern Identity*, 85–106, edited by W. Fitzhugh Brundage. Chapel Hill: University of North Carolina Press, 2000.

————. *A Shattered Nation: The Rise and Fall of the Confederacy.* Chapel Hill: University of North Carolina Press, 2005.

Rugemer, Edward B. "Jamaica's Morant Bay Rebellion and the Making of Radical Reconstruction." In *United States Reconstruction across the Americas*, edited by William A. Link, 81–112. Gainesville: University of Florida Press, 2019.

————. *The Problem of Emancipation: The Caribbean Roots of the American Civil War.* Baton Rouge: Louisiana State University Press, 2008.

————. "Why Civil War? The Politics of Slavery in Comparative Perspective: The United States, Cuba, and Brazil." In *The Civil War as Global Conflict: Transnational Meanings of the American Civil War*, edited by David T. Gleeson and Simon Lewis, 14–35. Columbia: University of South Carolina Press, 2014.

Russ, William A. "Was There Danger of a Second Civil War during Reconstruction?" *Journal of American History* 25 (June 1938): 39–58.

Samet, Elizabeth D. *Willing Obedience: Citizens, Soldiers, and the Progress of Consent in America, 1776–1898.* Stanford: Stanford University Press, 2004.

Samito, Christian G. *Becoming American under Fire: Irish Americans, African Americans, and the Politics of Citizenship during the Civil War Era.* Ithaca, NY: Cornell University Press, 2009.

————. *Lincoln and the Thirteenth Amendment.* Carbondale: Southern Illinois University Press, 2015.

Sampson, Robert D. *John L. O'Sullivan and His Times.* Kent, OH: Kent State University Press, 2004.

Saunt, Claudio. "Paradox of Freedom: Tribal Sovereignty and Emancipation during the Reconstruction of Indian Territory." *Journal of Southern History* 70 (February 2002): 63–94.

Schieffler, David G. "A 'Sickly, Pestilential, Crowded Post': The Blurred Boundary between Slavery and Freedom at Helena, Arkansas, during the Civil War." Paper presented at Eleventh Annual Conference on the Civil War, Center for Civil War Research at the University of Mississippi, Oxford, September 2017.

Schmidt, James D. *Free to Work: Labor Law, Emancipation, and Reconstruction, 1815–1880.* Athens: University of Georgia Press, 1998.

Schmidt-Nowara. "From Aggression to Crisis: The Spanish Empire in the 1860s." In *American Civil Wars: The United States, Latin America, Europe, and the Crisis of the 1860s*, edited by Don H. Doyle, 125–46. Chapel Hill: University of North Carolina Press, 2017.

Schoen, Brian. *The Fragile Fabric of Union: Cotton, Federal Politics, and the Global Origins of the Civil War.* Baltimore: Johns Hopkins University Press, 2009.

Schoonover, Thomas. *Dollars over Dominion: The Triumph of Liberalism in Mexican-United States Relations, 1861–1867*. Baton Rouge: Louisiana State University Press, 1978.

———. "Napoleon Is Coming! Maximilian Is Coming? The International History of the Civil War in the Caribbean Basin." In *The Union, the Confederacy, and the Atlantic Rim*, edited by Robert E. May, 101–30. West Lafayette, IN: Purdue University Press, 1995.

Schroeder, John H. *Mr. Polk's War: American Opposition and Dissent, 1846–1848*. Madison: University of Wisconsin Press, 1973.

Schweninger, Loren. *Appealing for Liberty: Freedom Suits in the South*. New York: Oxford University Press, 2019.

Scott, Rebecca J. *Degrees of Freedom: Louisiana and Cuba after Slavery*. Cambridge, MA: Belknap Press of Harvard University, 2005.

Sears, Stephen W. *Chancellorsville*. New York: Houghton Mifflin, 1996.

———. *George B. McClellan: The Young Napoleon*. New York: Ticknor and Fields, 1988.

Sefton, James E. *The United States Army and Reconstruction, 1865–1877*. Baton Rouge: Louisiana State University Press, 1967.

Sellers, Charles. *The Market Revolution: Jacksonian America, 1815–1846*. New York: Oxford University Press, 1991.

Semmes, Ryan Patrick. "Exporting Reconstruction: Civilization, Citizenship, and Republicanism during the Grant Administration, 1869–1877." PhD diss., Mississippi State University, 2020.

Sepinwall, Alyssa Goldstein. "The Specter of Saint-Domingue: American and French Reactions to the Haitian Revolutions." In *The World of the Haitian Revolution*, edited by David P. Geggus and Norman Fiering, 317–38. Bloomington: Indiana University Press, 2009.

Sexton, Jay. *The Monroe Doctrine: Empire and Nation in Nineteenth-Century America*. New York: Hill and Wang, 2011.

———. "Toward a Synthesis of Foreign Relations in the Civil War Era, 1848–77." *American Nineteenth Century History* 5 (Autumn 2004): 50–73.

———. "The United States, the Cuban Rebellion, and the Multilateral Initiative of 1875." *Diplomatic History* 30 (June 2006): 335–65.

———. "William H. Seward in the World." *Journal of the Civil War Era* 4 (September 2014): 398–430.

Sharp, James Roger. *American Politics in the Early Republic: The New Nation in Crisis*. New Haven, CT: Yale University Press, 1993.

Sheehan, Colleen A. *The Mind of James Madison: The Legacy of Classical Republicanism*. New York: Cambridge University Press, 2015.

Sheehan-Dean, Aaron. *The Calculus of Violence: How Americans Fought the Civil War*. Cambridge, MA: Harvard University Press, 2018.

———, ed. *A Companion to the U.S. Civil War*. 2 vols. Malden, MA: Wiley Blackwell, 2014.

———. "*Lex Talionis* in the U.S. Civil War: Retaliation and the Limits of Atrocity." In *The Civil War as Global Conflict: Transnational Meanings of the American Civil War*, edited by David T. Gleeson and Simon Lewis, 172–89. Columbia: University of South Carolina Press, 2014.

———. *Reckoning with Rebellion: War and Sovereignty in the Nineteenth Century.* Gainesville: University Press of Florida, 2020.

Shelden, Rachel A. *Washington Brotherhood: Politics, Social Life, and the Coming of the Civil War.* Chapel Hill: University of North Carolina Press, 2013.

Shulman, George. *American Prophecy: Race and Redemption in American Political Culture.* Minneapolis: University of Minnesota Press, 2008.

Sidbury, James. *Ploughshares into Swords: Race, Rebellion, and Identity in Gabriel's Virginia, 1730–1810.* New York: Cambridge University Press, 1997.

———. "Saint Domingue in Virginia: Ideology, Local Meanings, and Resistance to Slavery, 1790–1800." *Journal of Southern History* 63 (August 1997): 531–52.

Siddali, Silvana. *From Property to Person: Slavery and the Confiscation Acts, 1861–1862.* Baton Rouge: Louisiana State University Press, 2005.

Silber, Nina. *Daughters of the Union: Northern Women Fight the Civil War.* Cambridge, MA: Harvard University Press, 2005.

———. *Gender and the Sectional Conflict.* Chapel Hill: University of North Carolina Press, 2009.

Silbey, Joel H. *A Respectable Minority: The Democratic Party in the Civil War Era, 1860–1868.* New York: W. W. Norton, 1977.

———. *Storm over Texas: The Annexation Controversy and the Road to Civil War.* New York: Oxford University Press, 2005.

Silkenat, David. *Raising the White Flag: How Surrender Defined the American Civil War.* Chapel Hill: University of North Carolina Press, 2019.

Simpson, Brooks D. *Let Us Have Peace: Ulysses S. Grant and the Politics of War and Reconstruction, 1861–1868.* Chapel Hill: University of North Carolina Press, 1991.

———. "Mission Impossible: Reconstruction Policy Reconsidered." *Journal of the Civil War Era* 6 (March 2016): 85–102.

———. "Quandaries of Command: Ulysses S. Grant and Black Soldiers." In *Union and Emancipation: Essays on Politics and Race in the Civil War Era*, edited by David W. Blight and Brooks D. Simpson, 136–49. Kent, OH: Kent State University Press, 1997.

———. *Ulysses S. Grant: Triumph over Adversity, 1822–1865.* Boston: Houghton Mifflin, 2000.

Sinha, Manisha. *The Counterrevolution of Slavery: Politics and Ideology in Antebellum South Carolina.* Chapel Hill: University of North Carolina Press, 2000.

———. "Revolution or Counterrevolution? The Political Ideology of Secession in Antebellum South Carolina." *Civil War History* 46 (September 2000): 205–26.

———. *The Slave's Cause: A History of Abolition.* New Haven, CT: Yale University Press, 2016.

Skelton, William B. *An American Profession of Arms: The Army Officer Corps, 1784–1861.* Lawrence: University Press of Kansas, 1992.

Slap, Andrew L. *The Doom of Reconstruction: The Liberal Republicans in the Civil War Era.* New York: Fordham University Press, 2006.

Slap, Andrew L., and Frank Towers, eds. *Confederate Cities: The Urban South during the Civil War Era.* Chicago: University of Chicago Press, 2016.

Small, Melvin, and J. David Singer. *Resort to Arms: International and Civil Wars, 1816–1980.* Beverly Hills, CA: Sage, 1982.

Smith, Adam I. P. *The Stormy Present: Conservatism and the Problem of Slavery in Northern Politics, 1846–1865*. Chapel Hill: University of North Carolina Press, 2017.

Smith, Joe Patterson. *The Republican Expansionists of the Early Reconstruction Era*. Chicago: University of Chicago Libraries, 1933.

Smith, John David, ed. *Black Soldiers in Blue: African American Troops in the Civil War Era*. Chapel Hill: University of North Carolina Press, 2003.

Smith, Mark M. "The Past as a Foreign Country: Reconstruction Inside and Out." In *Reconstructions: New Perspectives on the Postbellum United States*, edited by Thomas J. Brown, 117–40. New York: Oxford University Press, 2008.

Smith, Michael Thomas. "Corruption European Style: The 1861 Fremont Scandal and Popular Fears in the Civil War North." *American Nineteenth Century* 10 (March 2009): 49–69.

———. *The Enemy Within: Fears of Corruption in the Civil War North*. Charlottesville: University of Virginia Press, 2011.

Smith, Stacey L. "Beyond North and South: Putting the West in the Civil War and Reconstruction." *Journal of the Civil War Era* 6 (December 2016): 566–91.

———. "Emancipating Peons, Excluding Coolies: Reconstructing Coercion in the American West." In *The World the Civil War Made*, edited by Gregory P. Downs and Kate Masur, 46–74. Chapel Hill: University of North Carolina Press, 2015.

———. *Freedom's Frontier: California and the Struggle over Unfree Labor, Emancipation, and Reconstruction*. Chapel Hill: University of North Carolina Press, 2013.

Snay, Mitchell. *Fenians, Freedmen, and Southern Whites: Race and Nationality in the Era of Reconstruction*. Baton Rouge: Louisiana State University Press, 2007.

Snyder, Christina. "The Rise and Fall and Rise of Civilizations: Indian Intellectual Culture during the Removal Era." *Journal of American History* 104 (September 2017): 386–409.

Snyder, R. Claire. *Citizen-Soldiers and Manly Warriors: Military Service and Gender in the Civic Republic Tradition*. Lanham, MD: Rowman & Littlefield, 1999.

Soodalter, Ron. "Lincoln and the Sioux." *Disunion* (blog), *New York Times*, August 20, 2012. https://opinionator.blogs.nytimes.com/2012/08/20/lincoln-and-the-sioux/.

Sperber, Jonathan. *The European Revolutions, 1848–1851*. Cambridge: Cambridge University Press, 1994.

Stanley, Amy Dru. *From Bondage to Contract: Wage Labor, Marriage, and the Market in the Age of Slave Emancipation*. New York: Cambridge University Press, 1998.

Stearns, Peter N. *The Revolutions of 1848*. London: Weidenfeld and Nicolson, 1974.

Sterling, Dorothy, ed. *We Are Your Sisters: Black Women in the Nineteenth Century*. New York: W. W. Norton, 1997.

Stern, A. E. "War Is Cruelty: The Civil War Lessons of the Dakota War in 1862." *U.S. History Scene*, November 2015. http://ushistoryscene.com/article/civil-dakota-war.

Sternhell, Yael A. "Revisionism Reinvented? The Antiwar Turn in Civil War Scholarship." *Journal of the Civil War Era* 3 (June 2013): 239–56.

———. *Routes of War: The World of Movement in the Confederate South*. Cambridge, MA: Harvard University Press, 2015.

Stewart, James Brewer. *Holy Warriors: The Abolitionists and American Slavery.* New York: Hill and Wang, 1976.

Stockwell, Mary. *Interrupted Odyssey: Ulysses S. Grant and the American Indians.* Carbondale: Southern Illinois University Press, 2018.

Stoker, Donald. *The Grand Design: Strategy and the U.S. Civil War.* New York: Oxford University Press, 2010.

Stout, Harry S. *Upon the Altar of the Nation: A Moral History of the American Civil War.* New York: Viking, 2006.

Strang, C. B. "Violence, Ethnicity, and Human Remains during the Second Seminole War." *Journal of American History* 100 (March 2014): 973–94.

Strozier, Charles B. "On the Verge of Greatness: Psychological Reflections on Lincoln at the Lyceum." *Civil War History* 36 (June 1990): 137–48.

Summers, Mark Wahlgren. *A Dangerous Stir: Fear, Paranoia, and the Making of Reconstruction.* Chapel Hill: University of North Carolina Press, 2009.

———. *The Ordeal of the Reunion: A New History of Reconstruction.* Chapel Hill: University of North Carolina Press, 2014.

Suri, Jeremi. *Liberty's Surest Guardian: American Nation-Building from the Founders to Obama.* New York: Free Press, 2014.

Sutherland, Daniel E. "Abraham Lincoln, John Pope, and the Origins of Total War." *Journal of Military History* 56 (October 1992): 567–86.

———. *American Civil War Guerrillas: Changing the Rules of Warfare.* Santa Barbara, CA: Praeger, 2013.

———. "Exiles, Emigrants, and Sojourners: The Post–Civil War Confederate Exodus in Perspective." *Civil War History* 31 (September 1985): 237–56.

———. "Guerrilla Warfare, Democracy, and the Fate of the Confederacy." *Journal of Southern History* 68 (May 2002): 259–92.

———. *A Savage Conflict: The Decisive Role of Guerrillas in the American Civil War.* Chapel Hill: University of North Carolina Press, 2009.

———. "Sideshow No Longer: A Historiographical Review of the Guerrilla War." *Civil War History* 46 (March 2000): 5–23.

———. "The Union's Counterguerrilla War, 1861–1865." In *Hybrid Warfare: Fighting Complex Opponents from the Ancient World to the Present,* edited by Williamson Murray and Peter R. Mansoor, 151–70. New York: Cambridge University Press, 2012.

Tap, Bruce. *Over Lincoln's Shoulder: The Committee on the Conduct of the War.* Lawrence: University Press of Kansas, 1998.

———. "'These Devils Are Not Fit to Live on God's Earth': War Crimes and the Committee on the Conduct of the War, 1864–1865." *Civil War History* 42 (June 1996): 116–32.

Taylor, Alan. *American Revolutions: A Continental History, 1750–1804.* New York: W. W. Norton, 2016.

Taylor, Amy Murrell. *Embattled Freedom: Journeys through the Civil War's Slave Refugee Camps.* Chapel Hill: University of North Carolina Press, 2019.

Teters, Kristopher A. *Practical Liberators: Union Officers in the Western Theater during the Civil War.* Chapel Hill: University of North Carolina Press, 2018.

Thelen, David. "Making History and Making the United States." *Journal of American Studies* 32 (December 1998): 373–97.

———. "Rethinking History and the Nation-State: Mexico and the United States." *Journal of American History* 86 (September 1999): 439–52.

Thomas, Brook. "The Unfinished Task of Grounding Reconstruction's Promise." *Journal of the Civil War Era* 7 (March 2017): 16–38.

Thomas, Emory M. "Ambivalent Visions of Victory: Davis, Lee, and Confederate Grand Strategy." In *Jefferson Davis's Generals*, edited by Gabor S. Boritt, 27–45. New York: Oxford University Press, 1999.

———. *The Confederacy as a Revolutionary Experience*. Englewood Cliffs, NJ: Prentice-Hall, 1971.

———. *The Confederate Nation, 1861–1865*. New York: Harper and Row, 1979.

———. "Jefferson Davis and the American Revolutionary Tradition." *Journal of the Illinois State Historical Society* 70 (February 1977): 2–9.

Thomas, William G., III. "Nothing Ought to Astonish Us: Confederate Civilians in the 1864 Shenandoah Valley Campaign." In *The Shenandoah Valley Campaign of 1864*, edited by Gary W. Gallagher, 222–56. Chapel Hill: University of North Carolina Press, 2006.

Thornton, J. Mills. *Politics and Power in a Slave Society: Alabama, 1800–1860*. Baton Rouge: Louisiana State University Press, 1978.

Tise, Larry E. *Proslavery: A History of the Defense of Slavery in America, 1701–1840*. Athens: University of Georgia Press, 1987.

Tocqueville, Alexis de. *Democracy in America: Historical-Critical Edition of De la démocratie en Amérique*. Edited by James T. Nolla, translated by Eduardo Schleifer, accessed September 4, 2019. https://oll.libertyfund.org/titles/2286 #Tocqueville_1532-02_EN_1229.

Torget, Andrew J. *Seeds of Empire: Cotton, Slavery, and the Transformation of the Texas Borderlands, 1800–1850*. Chapel Hill: University of North Carolina Press, 2015.

Towers, Frank J. "Partisans, New History, and Modernization: The Historiography of the Civil War's Causes, 1861–2011." *Journal of the Civil War Era* 1 (June 2011): 237–64.

Townsend, Stephen A. *The Yankee Invasion of Texas*. College Station: Texas A&M University Press, 2006.

Tucker, Ann L. *Newest Born of Nations: European Nationalist Movements and the Making of the Confederacy*. Charlottesville: University of Virginia Press, 2020.

Tunnell, Ted. *Crucible of Reconstruction: War, Radicalism, and Race in Louisiana, 1862–1877*. Baton Rouge: Louisiana State University Press, 1984.

Tuveson, Ernest Lee. *Redeemer Nation: The Idea of America's Millennial Role*. Chicago: University of Chicago Press, 1968.

Twitty, Anne. *Before* Dred Scott: *Slavery and Legal Culture in the American Confluence*. New York: Cambridge University Press, 2016.

Tyrrell, Ian R. "American Exceptionalism in an Age of International History." *American Historical Review* 96 (October 1991): 1031–55.

———. "Ian Tyrrell Responds." *American Historical Review* 96 (October 1991): 1068–72.

———. *Transnational Nation: United States History in Global Perspective since 1789*. New York: Palgrave Macmillan, 2015.

Urwin, Gregory J. W. *Black Flag over Dixie: Racial Atrocities and Reprisals in the Civil War*. Carbondale: Southern Illinois University Press, 2004.

BIBLIOGRAPHY

———. "'We Cannot Treat Negroes ... as Prisoners of War': Racial Atrocities and Reprisals in Civil War Arkansas." *Civil War History* 42 (September 1996): 193–210.

Utley, Robert M. *Frontier Regulars: The United States Army and the Indian, 1866–1891*. New York: Macmillan, 1973.

———. *Frontiersmen in Blue: The United States Army and the Indian, 1848-1865*. New York: Macmillan, 1967.

Van Cleve, George. *Slaveholders' Union: Slavery, Politics, and the Constitution in the Early American Republic*. Chicago: University of Chicago Press, 2011.

Varon, Elizabeth R. *Appomattox: Victory, Defeat, and Freedom at the End of the Civil War*. New York: Oxford University Press, 2013.

———. *Armies of Deliverance: A New History of the Civil War*. New York: Oxford University Press, 2019.

———. *Disunion! The Coming of the American Civil War, 1789-1859*. Chapel Hill: University of North Carolina Press, 2008.

Voelz, Peter Michael. *Slave and Soldier: The Military Impact of Blacks in the Colonial Americas*. New York: Garland, 1993.

Von Frank, Albert J. "John Brown, James Redpath, and the Idea of Revolution." *Civil War History* 52 (June 2006): 142–60.

Vorenberg, Michael. "Abraham Lincoln and the Politics of Black Colonization." *Journal of the Abraham Lincoln Association* 14 (Summer 1993): 22–45.

———. *Final Freedom: The Civil War, the Abolition of Slavery, and the Thirteenth Amendment*. New York: Cambridge University Press, 2001.

Waite, Kevin. "Jefferson Davis and Proslavery Visions of Empire in the Far West." *Journal of the Civil War Era* 6 (December 2016): 536–65.

———. "The Slave South in the Far West: California, the Pacific, and Proslavery Visions of Empire." PhD diss., University of Pennsylvania, 2016.

Waldstreicher, David. *In the Midst of Perpetual Fetes: The Making of American Nationalism, 1776-1820*. Chapel Hill: University of North Carolina Press, 2012.

———. *Slavery's Constitution: From Revolution to Ratification*. New York: Farrar, Straus and Giroux, 2013.

Wallace, Anthony F. C. *The Long, Bitter Trail: Andrew Jackson and the Indians*. New York: Hill and Wang, 1996.

Walters, John Bennett. "General William T. Sherman and Total War." *Journal of Southern History* 14 (November 1948): 447–80.

———. *Merchant of Terror: General Sherman and Total War*. Indianapolis: Bobbs-Merrill, 1973.

Walther, Eric H. *The Fire-Eaters*. Baton Rouge: Louisiana State University Press, 1992.

Warner, Donald F. *The Idea of Continental Union: Agitation for the Annexation of Canada to the United States, 1849-1893*. Lexington: University of Kentucky Press, 1960.

Watson, Harry L. "Conflict and Collaboration: Yeomen, Slaveholders, and Politics in the Antebellum South." *Social History* 10 (October 1985): 273–98.

———. *Liberty and Power: The Politics of Jacksonian America*. New York: Hill and Wang, 2006.

Waugh, Joan. "'I Only Knew What Was in My Mind': Ulysses S. Grant and Appomattox." *Journal of the Civil War Era* 2 (September 2012): 307–36.

———. *U. S. Grant: American Hero*. Chapel Hill: University of North Carolina Press, 2013.

Weaver, Blanche Henry Clark. "Confederate Emigration to Brazil." *Journal of Southern History* 27 (February 1961): 33–53.

Weber, Jennifer L. *Copperheads: The Rise and Fall of Lincoln's Opponents in the North*. New York: Oxford University Press, 2006.

Weigley, Russell F. "The American Military and the Principle of Civilian Control from McClellan to Powell." *Journal of Military History* 57 (October 1993): 27–58.

———. *The American Way of War: A History of United States Military Strategy and Policy*. New York: Macmillan, 1973.

Wellman, Judith. *The Road to Seneca Falls: Elizabeth Cady Stanton and the First Woman's Rights Convention*. Urbana: University of Illinois Press, 2004.

Welter, Barbara. "The Cult of True Womanhood: 1820–1860." *American Quarterly* 18 (Summer 1996): 151–74.

West, Elliott. *The Last Indian War: The Nez Perce Story*. New York: Oxford University Press, 2009.

———. "Reconstructing Race." *Western Historical Quarterly* 34 (Spring 2003): 6–26.

White, Deborah G. *Ar'n't I a Woman? Female Slaves in the Plantation South*. New York: W. W. Norton, 1999.

White, Jonathan W. *Emancipation, the Union Army, and the Reelection of Abraham Lincoln*. Baton Rouge: Louisiana State University Press, 2014.

White, Richard. *Railroaded: The Transcontinentals and the Making of Modern America*. New York: W. W. Norton & Co., 2011.

———. *The Republic for Which It Stands: The United States during Reconstruction and the Gilded Age, 1865–1896*. New York: Oxford University Press, 2017.

———. "The Winning of the West: The Expansion of the Western Sioux in the Eighteenth and Nineteenth Centuries." *Journal of American History* 65 (September 1978): 319–43.

Whitman, James Q. *The Verdict of Battle: The Law of Victory and the Making of Modern War*. Cambridge, MA: Harvard University Press, 2014.

Wiebe, Robert. "Framing U.S. History: Democracy, Nationalism, and Socialism." In *Rethinking American History in a Global Age*, edited by Thomas Bender, 236–49. Berkeley: University of California Press, 2002.

Wilentz, Sean. *Chants Democratic: New York City and the Rise of the American Working Class, 1788–1850*. New York: Oxford University Press, 1984.

———. *No Property in Man: Slavery and Antislavery at the Nation's Founding*. Cambridge, MA: Harvard University Press, 2019.

———. *The Rise of Democracy: From Jefferson to Lincoln*. New York: W. W. Norton, 2007.

Wilkins, Christopher. "'They Had Heard of Emancipation and the Enfranchisement of Their Race': The African American Colonists of Samana, Reconstruction, and the State of Santo Domingo." In *The Civil War as Global Conflict: Transnational Meanings of the American Civil War*, edited by David T. Gleeson and Simon Lewis, 211–34. Columbia: University of South Carolina Press, 2014.

Williams, Eric. *Capitalism and Slavery*. Chapel Hill: University of North Carolina Press, 1994.

Williams, Frank J., William D. Bader, and Andrew Blais. "Apple of Gold and Picture of Silver: How Abraham Lincoln Would Analyze the Fourteenth Amendment's

Equal Protection Clause." *Roger Williams University Law Review* 22 (Winter 2017): 211–46.

Williams, Kidada E. *They Left Great Marks on Me: African American Testimonies of Racial Violence from Emancipation to World War I*. New York: New York University Press, 2012.

Williams, Lorraine A. "Northern Intellectual Reaction to Military Rule during the Civil War." *Historian* 27 (May 1965): 334–49.

Williams, T. Harry. "The Military Leadership of the North and the South." In *Why the North Won the Civil War*, edited by David Herbert Donald, 38–57. Baton Rouge: Louisiana State University Press, 1960.

Wills, Brian Steel. *Inglorious Passages: Noncombat Deaths in the American Civil War*. Lawrence: University Press of Kansas, 2017.

Wilsey, John D. *American Exceptionalism and Civil Religion: Reassessing the History of an Idea*. Downers Grove, IL: InterVarsity Press, 2015.

Winik, Jay. *April 1865: The Month that Saved America*. New York: Harper Collins, 2001.

Winterer, Caroline. *American Enlightenments: Pursuing Happiness in the Age of Reason*. New Haven, CT: Yale University Press, 2016.

Witt, John Fabien. *Lincoln's Code: The Laws of War in American History*. New York: Free Press, 2012.

Wolf, Eva Sheppard. *Race and Liberty in the New Nation: Emancipation in Virginia from the Revolution to Nat Turner's Rebellion*. Baton Rouge: Louisiana State University Press, 2009.

Wood, Gordon S. *The Creation of the American Republic, 1776-1787*. Chapel Hill: University of North Carolina Press, 1969.

———. *Empire of Liberty: A History of the Early Republic, 1789-1815*. New York: Oxford University Press, 2009.

———. *The Radicalism of the American Revolution*. New York: Alfred A. Knopf, 1992.

Woods, Michael E. "The Compromise of 1850 and the Search for a Usable Past." *Journal of the Civil War Era* 9 (September 2019): 438–56.

———. *Emotional and Sectional Conflict in the Antebellum United States*. New York: Cambridge University Press, 2014.

———. "What Twenty-First-Century Historians Have Said about the Causes of Disunion: A Civil War Sesquicentennial Review of the Recent Literature." *Journal of American History* 99 (September 2012): 415–39.

Woodward, C. Vann. *The Burden of Southern History*. 1960. Reprint, Baton Rouge: Louisiana State University, 2008.

———. *Reunion and Reaction: The Compromise of 1877 and the End of Reconstruction*. Boston: Little, Brown and Co., 1951.

Woodward, Colin Edward. *Marching Masters: Slavery, Race, and the Confederate Army during the Civil War*. Charlottesville: University of Virginia Press, 2014.

Wooster, Robert. *The Military and United States Indian Policy, 1865-1903*. New Haven, CT: Yale University, 1988.

Work, David. "United States Colored Troops in Texas during Reconstruction, 1865–1867." *Southwestern Historical Quarterly* 109 (January 2006): 337–57.

Wright, Ben, and Zachary W. Dresser, eds. *Apocalypse and the Millennium in the American Civil War Era*. Baton Rouge: Louisiana State University Press, 2013.

Wright, Gavin. *Slavery and American Economic Development*. Baton Rouge: Louisiana State University Press, 2013.

Zalimas, Robert J., Jr. "Black Union Soldiers in the Postwar South, 1865–1866." MA thesis, Arizona State University, 1993.

Zimmerman, Andrew. "From the Rhine to the Mississippi: Property, Democracy, and Socialism in the American Civil War." *Journal of the Civil War Era* 5 (March 2015): 3–37.

———. "From the Second American Revolution to the First International and Back Again." In *The World the Civil War Made*, edited by Gregory P. Downs and Kate Masur, 304–36. Chapel Hill: University of North Carolina Press, 2015.

———. "Reconstruction: Transnational History." In *Reconstruction*, 171–96, edited by John David Smith. Kent, OH: Kent State University Press, 2016.

Zuczek, Richard. *State of Rebellion: Reconstruction in South Carolina*. Columbia: University of South Carolina Press, 1996.

Zvengrowski, Jeffrey. *Jefferson Davis, Napoleonic France, and the Nature of Confederate Ideology, 1815–1870*. Baton Rouge: Louisiana State University Press, 2020.

———. "They Stood Like the Old Guard of Napoleon: Jefferson Davis and the Pro-Bonaparte Democrats, 1815–1870." PhD diss., University of Virginia, 2015.

INDEX

abolitionism, 12, 17, 77–79, 83–87, 97–98, 109, 120–23, 246, 266; Confederacy as a revolution against, 18–19, 23, 131, 135, 141–48, 152, 171, 178–80, 181, 183–84, 267–68, 270, 273–76, 279–83, 291, 306–7; distinguished from antislavery, 17, 19–21, 92, 111, 113–19, 249–61, 327–29

abolitionists, 17, 19, 51, 56–62, 76–79, 81–85, 87–88, 90, 93, 97–98, 100, 105–9, 111, 116–17, 120–21, 122–24, 127, 130, 133–34, 141, 143, 146, 158, 165, 171, 181, 183, 211, 219, 225, 244–47, 253–55, 256, 258, 261–66, 267, 277, 286, 295, 316–18, 332, 339, 351–52, 368, 381, 391, 399, 401–2, 407; and colonization, 54, 249–51

Adams, Charles Francis, 99

Adams, Henry, 164, 220, 385

Adams, John, 40; on American Revolution, 31–32; on French Revolution, 38

Adams, John Quincy, 32, 45; on Central and South American revolutions, 64–66; on Missouri Crisis, 77; on Texas annexation, 88–89

African Americans, 10, 11, 14, 41, 47, 53–54, 72, 75, 84, 92, 104, 111, 162, 166, 244–81, 301, 302, 331, 333–37, 344, 365 ; and American exceptionalism, 16–17, 18, 25, 31–32, 56–62, 78–82, 106, 247–48, 261–66, 278–79, 281, 318–19, 323, 345–52, 355–56; and citizenship, 24–25, 56, 59, 114, 165–66, 262–63, 279, 296, 328–30, 340–43, 365, 399, 401–3, 404–6; enfranchisement of men, 24–25, 279, 296, 328–29, 346, 348, 355–58; and expectations for Civil War, 22–23, 158, 165–66, 169–70, 211, 230, 243, 244–49, 256–66, 278–79, 281, 318–19; and faith in concept of Union, 16–17, 18, 25, 31–32,

56–62, 79–81, 106–7, 246–48, 261–66, 278–79, 281, 318–19, 345–52, 355–56, 361–62, 371, 379–81, 382, 388–89, 391–92, 394–95, 401–3; and identification with American Revolution, 57–62, 78–81, 105–7, 246–48; and identification with Haitian Revolution, 57, 78–80, 105–6, 246, 247, 266; and political mobilization of during antebellum era, 18, 56–62, 78–82, 93–94, 105–7, 116–17, 122–23, 245–46; and political mobilization during Reconstruction, 24–25, 328–30, 335–36, 345–52, 355–56, 361–62, 371, 379–81, 382, 388–89, 391–92, 394–95, 401–7; and rejection of colonization, 16, 57–58, 253–54, 281; as Union soldiers, 22–23, 256–66, 271–81, 312–14, 323. *See also* abolitionists; emancipation; enslaved revolts and insurrections; slavery; U.S. Colored Troops (USCT)

African Civilization Society, 116

"Africanization," 11, 135, 332, 342, 353, 381

Alabama, CSS, 366–67. *See also* Geneva Arbitration

Alaska, 45, 363–65

Alexander, Edward Porter, 275, 290

Ambrose, Paul, 323–25, 472n2. *See also* Kennedy, John Pendleton

American Civil War: as a contest between belligerent nations, 185–88, 233–34, 302–5, 316–17, 340–41; as crisis of American exceptionalism, 13–15, 18–23 passim; and European intervention, 159–60, 167–69, 175–76, 249, 255–56, 442n48; global context of, 150–52, 156–62, 167–69, 175–76, 194, 199–202, 206, 257, 282–83, 299, 305–19, 399, 401; scale of death in, 201–2, 228–29, 452n66

American exceptionalism: definition and scope of, 7, 9–15, 16, 19–22, 24–26, 29–31, 32–38, 41. *See also* civilization; Union, concept of

American Party, 70. *See also* Know-Nothing Party

American Revolution, 2–4, 7–10, 12, 16–21, 29–34, 48, 51, 56–62, 64, 66, 69, 71–72, 76–77, 81–85, 100, 104, 117–19, 122, 127–28, 130, 131, 136, 140–42, 145–46, 153–54, 341–42, 348–49, 357–58, 389, 404

American System, 43. *See also* Clay, Henry

Ames, Adelbert, 350, 394–95

amnesty, 222, 237–38, 296, 331, 390. *See also* "Proclamation of Amnesty and Reconstruction"

Anderson, Martin B., 137

Anderson, Osborn Perry, 247

Andersonville prison, 285

Andrews, Eliza Frances, 307–8

Andrews, Sydney, 335

Anthony, Susan B., 166–67

antimilitarism, 26, 91, 174–75, 185, 194–95, 201–6, 208, 219–21, 297–305, 310–11, 347–48, 362, 385–90, 406. *See also* citizen-soldiers; Union/U.S. armies: demobilization of; militarism

antislavery activism, 17–18, 19–21, 26, 51, 56–62, 71–72, 76–79, 82, 84, 86–89, 93–95, 98–101, 103–7, 111–20, 123–24, 202; and colonization, 54, 83, 93, 249–54, 256–59, 260–66, 279; and relation to Reconstruction, 330, 350–51, 358, 361, 367–69, 382; role in fomenting disunion, 130–36; triumph of during Civil War, 158–66, 230–32, 244–47, 279, 297, 318–19. *See also* abolitionism

Appeal to the Coloured Citizens of the World (Walker), 79–82, 84, 86, 105, 244, 246–47, 272. *See also* Walker, David

Appomattox, 23–24, 198, 286–91, 295–96, 304, 305, 307, 309, 310, 315, 319, 338–39, 343, 353, 354, 356, 359, 381

Arapaho, 228. *See also* Sand Creek Massacre

Argentina, 175. *See also* War of the Triple Alliance

aristocrats/aristocracy, 9, 16, 30, 32–34, 38, 41–43, 63, 67, 92, 95–96, 101, 190, 195, 212, 231, 305, 308, 315, 330, 361; slaveholders defined as, 18, 24, 26, 56, 59, 71–72, 79, 97, 99–100, 113–15, 117–18, 129–30, 137–39, 152–53, 155–56, 159, 161–65, 168, 180, 209, 220–21, 226, 232, 235, 240, 262, 281, 297, 309, 329–30, 334–36, 338, 340, 345, 347, 350–51, 363–64, 375–76, 382–83, 391, 404

Arizona Territory, 149

Army of Northern Virginia, 192, 197–98, 204, 221, 256, 282, 286–90, 294–95; and Battle of the Crater, 274–75; First Corps of, 274. *See also* Confederate armies

Army of the Potomac, 196, 199, 203–5, 215, 217, 230, 255, 287, 314. *See also* Union armies

Army of Tennessee, 291, 293. *See also* Confederate armies

Army of Virginia, 217–18. *See also* Union armies

Asia, 3, 363, 372, 377

atheism, 12, 183–84, 353, 376

Athens, Alabama, 228

Atlanta, Georgia, 229, 239–40

Australia, 45

Austria, 67, 68, 151, 159, 189, 197, 236, 306–7, 309–10, 388

Bagby, George, 150

Balentine, William J., 396

Ballou, Sullivan, 190

Baltimore Sanitary Fair, 73–74, 277

Bancroft, George, 23, 404

Banks, Nathaniel P., 363

Barbados, 77, 246

barbarism: as antithesis of civilization, 11, 12, 18, 36, 41, 53, 58, 60, 86, 114–15, 120, 140, 162, 174, 187, 193, 223, 235, 241, 264, 276–78, 295, 317, 336–37,

150–51, 175, 244, 252–53, 307–8, 326, 327, 330–31, 336–37, 344, 357, 361, 365, 367–71, 399; slaveholders' desire to spread slavery into, 75–76, 108–10, 116–17, 121, 138, 148–49; slaveholding fears of enslaved insurrections in, 18, 22, 24, 52–54, 76, 78–79, 82–84, 97–98, 101–2, 108–9, 111, 120–21, 129, 271–72, 333–34. *See also* enslaved revolts and insurrections: in Caribbean; British West Indies: abolition in; French West Indies, abolition in

Catholicism, 70–71, 90–91, 118, 150, 364, 369

Central America, 63–67, 75, 86, 100–101, 109, 120–21, 129, 137, 138, 145, 153–54, 156, 163, 167, 240, 253–54, 259, 308–9, 355, 363, 370–71

Channing, William Ellery, 35–36, 40, 64

Charleston, South Carolina, 79, 83, 140, 246, 351

Charleston Mercury, 135, 150

Chase, Salmon P., 99–100

Cherokee, 46–47

Chesnut, James Sr., 86

Chesnut, Mary, 147

chevauchée, 242

Cheyenne, 228

Chicago Tribune, 276, 371

Chickasaw, 46

Child, Lydia Maria, 62–63, 154–55, 316, 317

Chile, 66

China, 133, 157, 175, 237, 363. *See also* Taiping Rebellion

Chinese, 47, 210, 377–79

Chiriqui, 252, 462n23

Chivington, John M., 228. *See also* Sand Creek Massacre

Choctaw, 46

Christmas Day massacres, 332–33. *See also* Morant Bay Rebellion

citizenship, 15, 16, 106, 165–66, 191, 192, 289, 296, 330–31, 401, 404, 405; African American quest to secure, 15–17, 22, 24–26, 54–63, 164–66, 262–66, 301, 328–29, 335–37, 339, 340–42,

350–52, 359, 365; racialized and/or gendered limits of, 41, 54–57, 59, 114–15, 147–48, 252–53, 330–32, 337–38, 373–74, 377–79, 404, 405. *See also* Civil Rights Act: of 1866; *Dred Scott v. Sanford*; Fourteenth Amendment

citizen-soldiers, 174, 188–92, 194–95, 200–201, 212, 263–66, 287–88, 290–92, 298–300, 311, 387. *See also* antimilitarism; Union/U.S. armies: demobilization of

"City on a Hill," 36, 279

civilization: antislavery/Unionist vision of, 17–20, 56–61, 76–77, 81–83, 99–100, 112–17, 119–20, 137, 140, 154–55, 162–64, 166, 182, 191–92, 214, 276–79, 284, 287–88, 295, 323–24, 342–45, 348–51, 367–69, 402–4; irreconcilable notions of, 13–15, 19, 73–75, 92–94, 96–97, 112, 124, 130, 139, 179–80, 239–40, 319, 399–407; and military conduct, 22–23, 158, 171–75, 177–78, 185–88, 194–95, 209–11, 215, 221–23, 225–32, 234, 240, 243, 267–76, 290–91, 299–300, 316–17; race and ethnicity and, 11–12, 25–26, 45–49, 54–57, 63–66, 82–86, 94–95, 105, 122, 127–28, 134–35, 210–11, 225–28, 243, 252–53, 257–60, 267–81, 306, 311–12, 314–15, 330, 331, 349–51, 352–54, 367–71, 373–80, 392, 394–95, 402; and relation to American exceptionalism, 10–12, 32, 34–38, 58–61, 63–66, 81, 89, 90, 92–94, 102–3, 105, 111, 122, 124, 130, 139, 157, 168–69, 190, 209–10, 221–23, 230–32, 241, 261–66, 276–79, 284, 287–88, 295, 299, 305, 310–12, 314–17, 329–30, 342–45, 348, 355, 357, 361–67, 371–73, 382, 388, 397, 399–407; slaveholding/Confederate vision of, 18–19, 54–56, 77–78, 83–87, 94–95, 97–98, 101–2, 107–10, 121, 127–28, 131–35, 142–45, 148, 180–84, 267–76, 279–81, 282, 291–94, 306–8, 325, 352–54, 379–80, 394–95

civil-military relations, 22, 173–74, 201–6, 295–96, 452n66

civil religion, 34–35

Civil Rights Act: of 1866, 337–41; of 1875, 395. *See also* citizenship

civil war, fear of, 14, 36–38, 325; during Reconstruction, 353–55, 362, 370–71, 378–79, 381–82, 385–87, 395–98, 406

Clark, Charles, 272

Clarke, James Freeman, 189, 297

Clarkson, Thomas, 82

Clay, Cassius M., 140

Clay, Henry, 55, 64, 96, 250; "American System" of, 43–44; and Compromise of 1850, 102–4; opposition to U.S.-Mexico War, 93–94; on Texas annexation, 89

Cleburne, Patrick, 280

Cluseret, Gustave, 190

Cobb, Howell, 281

Cobb, Thomas R. R., 110–11

Colfax Massacre, 392. *See also* Reconstruction: white southern violence/counterrevolution against

Colombia, 252

colonization: during antebellum era, 53–54, 57, 81–83, 93, 430n23; Jefferson and, 53–54, 82–83; Lincoln and, during Civil War, 249–54, 279, 462n23; rejected by African Americans, 57–58, 253–54, 261

Common Sense, 9, 34 (Paine). *See also* Paine, Thomas

communism, 108, 183

compromise: as form of political moderation, 5, 7, 12, 17, 38–40, 74–75, 78, 90, 93, 102–4, 107, 111–14, 134, 294, 327–28, 366–67, 397–99, 401, 406–7; and Republicans propose to prevent disunion, 20, 137; various oppositions to, 18–19, 59, 100–101, 115, 119, 131, 134, 137. *See also* Crisis and Compromise of 1850; Missouri Crisis and Compromise (1820); Compromise of 1877

Compromise of 1877, 397–99, 401–3, 406–7

Confederate armies, 23, 147, 171–72, 180–81, 197–98, 216–17, 355, 397; and relation to preserving slavery, 184, 191, 192, 212–14, 222, 270–76; surrender

of, 282–90, 295–96, 298, 303, 305–7, 379. *See also* Army of Northern Virginia; Army of Tennessee; citizen-soldiers

confederated governance, 134, 155–56, 337–39, 341, 348–49

Confederate States of America (Confederacy): Constitution of, 19, 144–45; and founding of, 14–15, 18–19, 127–29, 140–42; gendered aspects of, 147–48; hemispheric ambitions of, 18–19, 148–52, 305–9; as manifestation of American exceptionalism, 14–15, 18–19, 127–29, 141–52, 183–84, 266–76, 279–80, 290–92, 305–9; military culture/strategies of, 22–23, 180–82, 183–84, 191–94, 195–96, 198–99, 205–6, 215–17, 266–81, 290–93; policies toward USCT, 266–76; reject egalitarianism of American Revolution, 127–29, 146–47

confiscation (Union military policy), 162, 172–73, 187, 194, 207, 211–15, 221–24, 228–33, 236, 238, 243, 251, 270, 305. *See also* Confiscation Acts

Confiscation Acts: First, 213–14, 220; Second, 221–23, 224

Congo River, 266

conservatism, as nonideological mode of political behavior, 12–13, 14–15, 16, 19–20, 159, 415n10; disunion and Confederacy as conservative reactions against abolitionism/United States, 18–19, 127–29, 130–37, 141–52, 181, 273–76; emancipation as radical means of conservatism, 159–67, 218–32; and Republican Reconstruction policy, 325–27, 329–30, 336–43, 346–47, 349–52, 382–90, 392–98, 399, 401–7; and Union's policy toward defeated Confederates, 286–305

contingency, military and wartime, 20–22, 159–61, 212–13, 215, 217–19, 223, 235–36, 356, 399

Cooley, Thomas, 392, 396

Corinth, Mississippi, 229

Corwin, Thomas, 311–12

coups, 38, 52, 65–66, 95, 101–2, 106–7,

49, 261–63, 265, 281; opposes antebellum emigration/colonization, 57–58, 253; opposes the U.S.-Mexico War, 93–94, 96

Dowdell, James Ferguson, 145

Dred Scott v. Sanford, 59–61, 114, 118–19, 244, 264, 340. *See also* citizenship; Fourteenth Amendment

dual-army tradition, 188–89, 194–95

Dutch West Indies, 393

Early, Jubal, 307

Edmontson, Catherine, 272–73, 274, 282–85, 333

education, 33, 43–44, 62–63, 65, 68, 193; and civilization, 43–44, 47, 65, 68, 154, 163, 165–66, 361, 372–74, 376, 396; of freedpeople, 61, 154, 165–66, 330, 350, 394

Edwards, Bryan, 77

Eighth Vermont Volunteers, 231

elections, 87, 111–12, 155, 380: of 1796, 40; of 1800, 40; of 1844, 44; of 1856; of 1860, 19, 124, 127, 130–32, 134, 139, 140, 171, 244, 267, 328; of 1864, 169–70, 199, 239, 318, 330; of 1866, 339; of 1868, 355–56; of 1870; of 1872, 390; of 1874, 403; of 1876, 397–98, 402; local during Reconstruction, 380, 381, 385, 392, 393, 394–95, 397, 402; and peaceful transfers of power, 39–40, 155, 169–70, 397–98

Elliott, Robert B., 389

Elliott, Stephen, 145–46, 184

emancipation: African Americans define, 16, 25, 31, 158, 165–66, 244–49, 260–66, 277–78, 281, 313, 323, 335–36, 369, 371, 399, 401; and colonization, 53–54, 83, 93, 249–55; as condition for restoration, 237–38, 285, 289, 297, 303, 325, 327–28, 399; Confederate debate on, 279–81; Confederate opposition to, 23, 25–26, 267–77, 282–83, 291, 307–8; hemispheric, 51, 82–86, 88, 98, 107, 110, 121–23, 127–28, 130, 145–46, 148–49, 249–50, 255, 257, 267–69, 271, 324–27, 332–33, 334–35, 336–37, 349–50,

352–53, 357, 368, 370, 379; linked to cause of Union, 14–15, 20–25, 129, 157–67, 202–3, 211–12, 213–14, 217–25, 228–29, 230–32, 237–38, 255–60, 277–79, 283–84, 285, 289, 297, 302, 303, 312, 313, 316–19, 325, 335–39, 340, 358, 373, 376, 378, 392, 398, 401–4; as military necessity, 23, 89, 157–58, 173–75, 207, 211–12, 213–14, 217–25, 228–29, 230–32, 235–36, 243, 255–60, 277–79, 300–301, 399; in northern states, 17, 51; white southern hostility to during Reconstruction, 324–25, 331–35, 338, 343–44, 352–53, 379–81, 394–95, 402. *See also* Emancipation Proclamation (preliminary and final); Freedmen's Bureau; Thirteenth Amendment

Emancipation Proclamation (preliminary and final), 161, 164, 173, 224, 235–36, 257–58, 261, 271–72, 235

Emerson, Ralph Waldo, 10–11, 45–46, 89, 90, 92, 104–5, 162, 179–80, 209, 219–20

Enforcement Acts (1870–71; 1875), 384–87, 395. *See also* Reconstruction: Republican visions of

England, 32, 34, 66, 78, 79, 85, 87–88, 99, 116, 135, 145–46, 150, 159, 164–65, 187, 188, 191, 196, 197, 201, 208, 259–60, 262, 280, 283, 306–7, 313, 336, 349, 366–67, 380, 399, 401. *See also* Great Britain

English Civil War, 202

Enlightenment, 9, 22–23, 42, 52, 176–77, 222, 227, 242

Enos, R. R., 221

enslaved revolts and insurrections: Anglo-American fear of, 9–10, 19, 52–54, 75, 77–79, 81–82, 84, 87, 94, 121–22, 127, 131–35, 141, 150, 158, 184, 203, 212, 250–52, 255–57, 260–61, 279–80, 325, 331–35, 336–37; in Caribbean, 22, 82, 106–7, 123–24, 133–35, 364–65; and Confederate military policy and, 23, 267–75; as resistance to slavery, 79–82, 106–7, 123–24, 244–49, 266–67, 364–65;

294, 314–16, 340–41, 366, 393, 446n7.
See also just war doctrine; Lieber's
Code (General Orders No. 100); military necessity

Lee, Robert E., 124, 217, 275, 282, 286–
87, 306; defends slavery/opposes abolition, 55, 271; and distaste for guerrilla warfare, 216, 290–91, 292, 294;
military campaigns of, 160, 197, 198–
99, 204, 217, 256, 286–87; military
philosophy of, 181, 194–95, 198–99,
201, 216, 290–92, 294; on Reconstruction policy, 294–95, 352; on slavery,
55, 271, 294–95

Legare, Hugh S., 82

Lester, Charles Edward, 68, 161–62

Lewis, J. W., 106

liberalism, 2, 9, 24, 40, 65, 67–69, 70, 72,
92, 95, 98–99, 117–19, 150–54, 157–67,
169–70, 175–76, 190, 223, 281, 288,
301, 313, 315, 353, 357–58, 359, 363,
399, 401–2, 406

Liberal Republican Party, 362, 369, 371,
390–91

Liberator, The, 81

Liberia, 57, 250, 252, 254, 266, 336

liberty, 2–5, 7, 12–13, 16, 18, 20–21,
25–26 passim; contemporary definition of, 13, 29–31, 33, 153, 73–75, 279,
341–42, 348–50

Lieber, Francis, 47, 155, 169; and General
Orders No. 100, 22–23, 232–35, 237,
239–40, 277, 285; on the international
laws of war, 177–78, 276

Lieber's Code (General Orders No. 100),
22–23, 232–35, 237, 239–40, 277, 285.
See also laws of war; military necessity

*Life and Public Services of Martin R.
Delany* (Rollin), 351–52. *See also* Rollin, Francis

Lincoln, Abraham: and African American military service, 248, 256–59, 276,
279; on American founding, 2–5, 10,
17, 29–31, 32, 44, 71–72, 117–20, 168;
assassination of, 286, 297, 330, 354;
and colonization, 250–54, 256–58,
261; and concept of Union, 2–5, 7, 10,

12–13, 14, 17, 19–21, 26, 29–31, 32,
71–75, 117–20, 124, 128–30, 136–40,
141, 152–53, 155–57, 160–61, 168–70,
179, 182, 186, 189, 206, 211–13, 221–25,
237–38, 243, 250–54, 266, 279, 281,
286, 288–89, 325, 327–28, 331, 359,
398, 403, 404; and conservatism, 4,
10–11, 12–13, 19–20, 211–13, 403; on
disunion and secession, 5, 137–38,
152–54; and election/reelection to the
presidency, 127, 130–31, 134, 169–70,
206–7, 239, 244, 246, 267, 318, 330;
on European revolutions of 1848, 70;
and executive war powers, 157–58,
172–75, 179, 186–87, 196–97, 202–9,
211–13, 221–27, 235–36, 276, 286,
288–89; hostility toward slavery/Slave
Power, 13, 17, 71–72, 73–74, 117–20,
128–30, 138, 160–61, 163–65, 207,
217–19, 221–25, 252–53, 276, 279, 281,
404; on military necessity of emancipation, 159–60, 173, 211–13, 221–25,
235–38, 248–50, 254–58; and morality
of emancipation, 21, 128–29, 160–61,
163–65, 168, 221–25, 276, 279, 281,
318; and race, 71–72, 117–20, 250–54,
257–59, 279, 281

Lincoln, Benjamin, 214–15

Locke, John, 176

London, 164, 197, 220, 248, 256, 366

Longfellow, Henry Wadsworth, 113

Longstreet, James, 274

Louisiana Purchase, 66, 85, 111, 113

Louis XIV, 385

Louverture, Toussaint, 78, 122, 130,
135, 266. *See also* Haiti; Haitian
Revolution

Lowery, Grosvenor P., 222

Lumpkin, Joseph Henry, 107

Lynch, John Roy, 25, 394–95, 403–4

Malta, 260

Manifest Destiny, 44–47, 66, 74–75, 89,
91–94, 111, 367

Mann, Horace, 44

Marcy, William L., 210

market revolution, 2, 42–43

Marxists, 382

Maryland, military occupation of, 208–9, 214

Maximilian I (Austria), 151–52, 168, 306–10, 315–16. *See also* France: invasion and occupation of Mexico

McClellan, George B.: criticizes emancipation, 172–73, 255; as Democratic presidential candidate, 169–70; military philosophy of as general, 172–74, 196–97, 202–6, 215

McCord, Louisa, 54, 108

McCurry, Stephanie, 147

McPherson, James M., 229

Meade, George Gordon, 205

Meade, William, 136

Meagher, Thomas, 190

Melville, Herman, 34–35, 295

Memphis massacre (1866), 336, 344

Merrill, Lewis, 382

"Mexicanization," 11, 64–66, 133, 137, 240, 317, 362, 380, 381, 395–98, 403, 406

Mexican War of the Reform, 206

Mexico, 64–67, 75, 85–93, 95–98, 100, 109, 116, 118, 120, 121, 133, 137, 142, 148–49, 150–52, 163–64, 167–68, 175, 240, 260, 305–18, 336, 361, 364, 368, 369, 381, 395–98

Miles, James Warley, 184

militarism, 17, 89, 143, 171–72, 189, 195, 206, 260, 289, 297–98, 300, 304, 311–12, 314–15, 347, 361–62, 366, 385, 390, 403. *See also* antimilitarism

military necessity, 22–23, 89, 173–74, 185, 206–8, 210, 211–13, 217–24, 227, 229, 232–38, 242–43, 275–76, 280, 399 ; and Confederate policy and, 23, 275–77; emancipation as, 23, 89, 174, 211–13, 218–24, 227, 235, 280, 399; and relation to politics, 203, 236–39, 240; Union policy and, 22–23, 173–74, 185, 203, 206–7, 210–13, 217–23, 227, 229, 232–38, 242–43. *See also* laws of war; Lieber's Code (General Orders No. 100)

military occupation, 198, 208–9, 264, 292, 311; and Reconstruction policy, 24–25, 300–305, 328, 338, 345–50, 356, 384–90, 397–98, 406. *See also* antimilitarism; grasp of war; standing armies

millennialism, 182. *See also* Protestantism

Minnis, John A., 381–82

Mississippi Plan, 394–95. *See also* Reconstruction: white counterrevolution against

Mississippi River valley, 51, 66–67, 231, 257–58

Missouri Crisis and Compromise (1820), 76–79, 102, 111

Mitchell, Nelson A., 67

mob rule/violence, 3–5, 34, 39–40, 67, 112, 120, 193, 206, 343, 403

moderation, political, 4–5, 7, 13–16, 19–20, 24, 26, 36–40, 74–75, 89, 91, 93, 96, 102–4, 112–14, 119, 131, 140–41, 144–46, 153–57, 158, 163–66, 169–70, 173–74, 178–79, 188, 191, 194, 196, 206, 208, 213–14, 237–38, 240, 243, 248, 263, 276, 284–86, 288, 294–98, 314, 326–30, 335–36, 345, 355–56, 359, 363, 365–67, 371, 378, 382, 396–98, 405–6. *See also* compromise; conservatism

monarchy, 9–10, 12, 16, 30, 32–33, 37–38, 59, 62, 63–69, 71, 88, 92, 98–100, 102, 105, 112, 114, 117, 129–30, 134, 140, 143, 146, 148, 151–52, 153–57, 167–68, 179, 190–91, 239, 272, 305–16, 329–30, 344, 352, 361, 363–64, 367–68, 370, 379, 382–83, 385, 387, 388, 404

Monroe, James, 66, 85

Monroe Doctrine, 66–67, 150, 260, 308, 310, 368

Montgomery, Hugh, 306, 353

Morant Bay Rebellion, 332–33, 336–37

Mormons and Mormonism, 47, 353, 376–77, 379. *See also* Utah Territory

Morrill Land Grant Act (1862), 163, 376

Morton, Oliver P., 237, 395

Motley, John Lothrop, 12, 46, 159, 388

Pegram, William, 275
Pennington, J. W. C., 22
Perry, Benjamin, 342–43
Peru, 60, 65, 164
Petersburg, Virginia, 229, 275, 290
Phelps, John W., 230–31, 256–57
Phillips, Wendell, 258, 259, 318
Pierce, Franklin, 69, 104
Pierson, Reuben, 192
Pike, James S., 391–92
Pius IX (pope), 67
Poland, 146, 209, 380
Poland Act (1874), 377. *See also* Mormons and Mormonism
Polk, James K., 44–45, 85
Pollard, Edward, 343, 352, 381
polygamy, 376–77. *See also* Mormons and Mormonism; *Reynolds v. United States*
Pope, John, 217–18, 225, 227
popular sovereignty: as political program of Stephen A. Douglas, 111–13, 117, 119; as process of democracy, 13, 15, 139, 141–42, 145, 161, 164, 170, 301–2, 311, 378, 386, 406
populism, 5, 39, 43, 65, 203, 240
Porter, David Dixon, 286
Port Royal, South Carolina, 165–66
Portugal, 64, 79–80, 100, 260, 313
Potter, David M., 91, 95
Potts, William J., 310–11
Preston, William C., 82
Prize Cases (1863), 187
"Proclamation of Amnesty and Reconstruction" (Lincoln), 237–38
Prosser, Gabriel, 272
Protestantism, 35, 70, 366–67, 374, 379; and just war, 181–84
Puerto Rico, 368–69
Purvis, Robert, 253

Quinney, Wannuaucon, 47
Quitman, John, 110

race: and civilization, 11–12, 16–17, 25, 45–47, 54–56, 60–61, 64–66, 75, 79–81, 83, 107–8, 127–28, 132–33, 144–46, 252–53, 259–66, 267–68,

272–76, 278–81, 314–15, 331–34, 336, 341–44, 350–53, 357–58, 361–62, 364–65, 367–81, 390–92, 399–407; as source of martial restraint, 194, 227–28, 243, 375–76
rage militaire, 193
Rainey, Joseph, 389
Randolph, George Wythe, 135
Ray, Charles B., 79
reconciliation, postwar, 196, 232, 236, 238, 286, 295, 317, 330, 337, 390, 397–98, 406–7
Reconstruction: African Americans on, 24–26, 323, 335–36, 342, 344–45, 348–52, 369, 371, 388–89, 399–403, 407; contested purposes of, 23–26, 323–32, 399–407; envisioned by Lincoln as restoration, 286, 289, 327–28; fears of insurrection/second civil war in, 25–26, 332–33, 353–55; global context of, 24, 325–28, 331–33, 336–37, 349–50, 359–71, 382–84, 388; Republican visions of, 334–42, 344–52, 354–58, 359–79, 384–90, 391–98, 402–7; successes and failures of, 25–26, 357–58, 359–62, 399–407; white southern violence/counterrevolution against, 26, 336, 352–53, 379–82, 384–90, 392–98, 402–7; white southern self-reconstruction, 23–24, 327–34
Reconstruction Acts (1867), 346–49, 357, 379, 474n45
Redpath, James, 123, 247
Red Shirts, 392, 402. *See also* Reconstruction: white southern violence/counterrevolution against
"Reign of Terror," 9, 76, 112, 121, 140, 175, 236, 389. *See also* French Revolution
religion and American exceptionalism, 10, 34–35, 38, 40, 44–47, 53, 55, 59–60, 64–65, 70, 80–81, 83, 90–91, 98, 102, 117, 122, 142, 145–46, 157, 162, 172–73, 177, 181–84, 192, 194–95, 201, 209–10, 215, 247–48, 253, 263–64, 268, 278, 281, 284, 288, 297, 345, 357, 361, 373–74, 376–79, 396–97, 402, 405. *See also* Mormonism; Protestantism

Seddon, James A., 216, 270–71

Seminole, 46

Seneca Falls Convention, 63

Servosse, Comfort, 401–3. *See also* Tourgée, Albion

Seventh U.S. Cavalry, 382

Sevier, Ambrose, 87

Seward, William Henry, 39, 46; antislavery stance of, 100, 113–14, 121, 131, 363–64, 372; on civilization, 363–64, 372; as secretary of state, 156–57, 167–68, 187, 189, 203, 309–10, 312, 314

Shand, Robert Wallace, 402–3

Shaw, Robert Gould, 229–30

Shedd, William G. T., 162

Shelby, Jo, 307

Sheridan, Philip H., 242, 309, 313, 344, 375, 393

Sherman, John, 382, 396

Sherman, William T.: philosophy of just war/military force, 194, 201, 214, 228, 230, 238–43, 276, 295–97, 314, 375, 384

Shotwell, Randolph Abbott, 380

Sibley, Henry H., 226

Sickles, Daniel, 347

Siegel, Franz, 190

Singer, Charles W., 265

Sioux, 225–27, 457n118. *See also* Dakota War

slaveholders: defend Union, 10, 18–19, 31, 51, 53–56, 75, 77, 79–88, 94–95, 97–98, 101–2, 107–12, 120–21, 133, 267, 343, 381; link slavery to American exceptionalism, 10, 13, 18–19, 26, 31, 50–51, 53–56, 75, 77–78, 82–88, 90, 94–95, 97–98, 107–12, 121, 123–24, 127–30, 130–36, 141–47, 148–52, 171, 183–84, 191–92, 266–76, 279–81, 282, 306–7, 324–25, 343, 381; reject Union, 19, 123–24, 127–29, 130–36, 141–42, 144–47, 171, 180–81, 183–84, 267–68, 280–81, 282–83, 324–25

Slave Power, 17–18, 21, 23, 76, 100, 103, 106, 112–15, 117, 120, 122, 129, 140, 153–54, 161–64, 170, 178–79, 207, 219–20, 222, 224, 231, 244, 246, 264, 270, 276, 278, 288, 295, 297, 301–2, 305,

318, 323, 327–28, 336, 345, 350, 353, 355–56, 359, 361, 363, 370, 378, 382, 387, 404, 407

slavery: American compared to New World, 48–54, 325, 330, 332–33, 399, 401; as antithesis of civilization, 7, 13, 17–18, 19, 24–26, 31, 53–54, 56–62, 71–72, 73, 76–77, 79–82, 88–89, 92–94, 99–100, 104–7, 112–21, 122–24, 128–30, 152–53, 157–66, 182–83, 190–91, 218–25, 230–32, 235, 244–48, 261–66, 276–81, 283–84, 292–93, 317–19, 323–28; as basis of civilization, 10, 13, 18–19, 26, 31, 50, 53–56, 75, 77–78, 82–88, 90, 94–95, 97–98, 107–12, 121, 123–24, 127–30, 130–36, 141–47, 148–52, 183–84, 191–92, 266–76, 279–81, 282, 306–7, 324–25, 343; and capitalism, 51–52, 59, 108–9, 115, 148, 163–65, 424n43; chattel principle of, 48–52, 56, 71–72, 75, 152–53, 163–66, 218–25, 235, 266–76, 318–19; cornerstone of Confederacy, 18–19, 23, 127–30, 130–36, 141–47, 148–52, 191–92, 266–76, 279–81, 282, 306–7, 324–25; and relation to Union, 13, 14, 17, 18–22, 23, 24–26, 31–32, 48–62, 71–72, 73–124, 127–29, 130–47, 148–52, 157–66, 182–83, 190–91, 210–15, 218–25, 227–28, 230–32, 235, 244–66, 276–81, 283–84, 292–93, 296–97, 317–19, 323–28, 334–35, 364–65, 367–69, 399, 401, 404; resistance against, 16, 18, 22–23, 31–32, 51–53, 56–62, 75–77, 79–82, 105–7, 119–20, 122–23, 164–66, 179–80, 182–83, 218–25, 227–28, 230–32, 261–66, 268–69, 277–79

Simms, William Gilmore, 101

Slidell, John, 151

Smith, Adam, 42

Smith, A. P., 254

Smith, Edmund Kirby, 274

Smith, Gerrit, 316–17

socialism, 12, 18–19, 67–68, 95, 97–98, 120, 183–84, 362, 382, 387, 391–92, 446n6

Soule, Harrison, 259

South Africa, 45, 378